THE PORTABLE
Shakespeare

SEVEN PLAYS

THE SONGS

THE SONNETS

SELECTIONS
FROM THE OTHER PLAYS

THE VIKING PRESS
New York

Library of Congress Cataloging-in-Publication Data

Shakespeare, William, 1564-1616.
Shakespeare: seven plays, the songs, the sonnets,
selections from the other plays.

(The Viking portable library)
Includes index.
I. Title   II. Series.
PR2759   1986   822.3′3   86-13139
ISBN 0-517-61889-3

h g f e d c b a

Editor's Note

EVERYONE has a favorite Shakespeare in his memory: a *Lambs' Tales* that belonged to his childhood; a high-school prompt book with penciled notes in the margin; a pamphlet edition of the Sonnets treasured in a furnished room; a vellum-bound set, each play in its separate cover, that someone sent as a wedding gift; a well-thumbed encyclopedic tome, all the plays in one thick volume, that sits on the library table. There are hundreds of editions in thousands of formats. This volume makes no attempt to improve on their scholarship, their completeness, or their usefulness for study and ornament. It offers itself to the lovers of Shakespeare only for handiness and readability—its attempt to bring into small compass *most* of the things that *most* readers want to have at hand. Aside from its format, it claims novelty in only these respects: the method of choosing the plays to be included, the use of selections from the other plays, the guide to the most memorable lines and phrases from all the plays. It hopes to become, for some readers of this day, that favorite Shakespeare through which their pleasures of reading will have been enriched.

The infinite variety of Shakespeare's characters, the depths of his tragic sense, and the heights of his comedy are represented in these seven plays. His worldly wisdom and the magic of his language, which are part of our living speech and thought, are here not only in the complete plays but also in the selections. And the songs and sonnets fill out the range of his poetry.

The "public opinion poll" which guided the choice of the plays was conducted informally among one thousand readers, widely scattered geographically and in their reading tastes; not students or specialists, but known readers of general books on a fairly high literary level. Each was asked simply to vote for the seven plays he would like to have in such a volume as this. Three tragedies—*Hamlet, Macbeth,* and *Romeo and Juliet,* in that order—were far out in front of all the others. The evidence is conclusive enough to say that they are surely the favorites of American readers today. Of the other four reprinted here (*Julius Cæsar, A Midsummer Night's Dream, As You Like It, The Tempest*), it can only be said that they were chosen, with an eye to a balanced selection, from among the next nine, which ran fairly close together. The others were *Othello, The Merchant of Venice, The Taming of the Shrew, King Lear,* and *Twelfth Night.* After these, the votes dropped off rapidly. A play which all "authorities" would have placed high, with one of Shakespeare's best-loved characters in it, ranked twentieth on the list—*King Henry the Fourth, Part I.* Many will be tempted to say, with Falstaff, "Banish plump Jack, and banish all the world!" For their consolation, as well as for those who voted for the runners-up, extended space has been given to these six among the selections from the other plays that follow the seven full texts.

The text of the seven plays and of the Sonnets is that of the authoritative George Lyman Kittredge edition, used here by courtesy of Ginn and Company.

M. A. B.

Contents

THE PORTABLE
Shakespeare

Soul of the age,
The applause, delight, the wonder of our stage,
My Shakespeare, rise! . . .
Thou art a monument without a tomb,
And art alive still, while thy book doth live,
And we have wits to read, and praise to give.

He was not of an age, but for all time.

—BEN JONSON

The Tragedy of Hamlet, Prince of Denmark

NAMES OF THE ACTORS

CLAUDIUS, King of Denmark.

HAMLET, son to the former, and nephew to the present King.

POLONIUS, Lord Chamberlain.

HORATIO, friend to HAMLET.

LAERTES, son to POLONIUS.

VOLTEMAND,
CORNELIUS,
ROSENCRANTZ,
GUILDENSTERN, } courtiers.
OSRIC,
A GENTLEMAN,

A PRIEST.
MARCELLUS, } officers.
BERNARDO,
FRANCISCO, a soldier.

REYNALDO, servant to POLONIUS.

PLAYERS.

Two CLOWNS, gravediggers.

FORTINBRAS, Prince of Norway.

A NORWEGIAN CAPTAIN.

ENGLISH AMBASSADORS.

GERTRUDE, Queen of Denmark, mother to HAMLET.

OPHELIA, daughter to POLONIUS.

GHOST of HAMLET's Father.

Lords, Ladies, Officers, Soldiers, Sailors, Messengers, Attendants.

Act I: Scene I: Elsinore. A platform before the Castle.

Enter two SENTINELS—*first,* FRANCISCO, *who paces up and down at his post; then* BERNARDO, *who approaches him.*

BER. Who's there?

FRAN. Nay, answer me. Stand and unfold yourself.

BER. Long live the King!

FRAN. Bernardo?

BER. He.

FRA. You come most carefully upon your hour.

BER. 'Tis now struck twelve. Get thee to bed, Francisco.

FRAN. For this relief much thanks. 'Tis bitter cold,
And I am sick at heart.

BER. Have you had quiet guard?

FRAN.   Not a mouse stirring.

BER. Well, good night.
If you do meet Horatio and Marcellus,
The rivals of my watch, bid them make haste.

Enter HORATIO *and* MARCELLUS.

FRAN. I think I hear them. Stand, ho! Who is there?

HOR. Friends to this ground.

MAR.   And liegemen to the Dane.

FRAN. Give you good night.

MAR.   O, farewell, honest soldier.
Who hath reliev'd you?

FRAN.   Bernardo hath my place.
Give you good night.   *Exit.*

MAR.   Holla, Bernardo!

BER.   Say—
What, is Horatio there?

HOR.   A piece of him.

4

BER. Welcome, Horatio. Welcome, good Marcellus

MAR. What, has this thing appear'd again to-night?

BER. I have seen nothing.

MAR. Horatio says 'tis but our fantasy,
And will not let belief take hold of him
Touching this dreaded sight, twice seen of us.
Therefore I have entreated him along,
With us to watch the minutes of this night,
That, if again this apparition come,
He may approve our eyes and speak to it.

HOR. Tush, tush, 'twill not appear.

BER.   Sit down awhile,
And let us once again assail your ears,
That are so fortified against our story,
What we two nights have seen.

HOR.   Well, sit we down,
And let us hear Bernardo speak of this.

BER. Last night of all,
When yond same star that's westward from the pole
Had made his course t' illume that part of heaven
Where now it burns, Marcellus and myself,
The bell then beating one—

Enter GHOST.

MAR. Peace! break thee off! Look where it comes
    again!

BER. In the same figure, like the King that's dead.

MAR. Thou art a scholar; speak to it, Horatio.

BER. Looks it not like the King? Mark it, Horatio.

HOR. Most like. It harrows me with fear and wonder.

BER. It would be spoke to.

MAR.   Question it, Horatio.

HOR. What art thou that usurp'st this time of night
Together with that fair and warlike form
In which the majesty of buried Denmark

Did sometimes march? By heaven I charge thee speak!

MAR. It is offended.

BER.   See, it stalks away!

HOR. Stay! Speak, speak! I charge thee speak!

Exit GHOST.

MAR. 'Tis gone and will not answer.

BER. How now, Horatio? You tremble and look pale.
Is not this something more than fantasy?
What think you on't?

HOR. Before my God, I might not this believe
Without the sensible and true avouch
Of mine own eyes.

MAR.   Is it not like the King?

HOR. As thou art to thyself.
Such was the very armour he had on
When he th' ambitious Norway combated.
So frown'd he once when, in an angry parle,
He smote the sledded Polacks on the ice.
'Tis strange.

MAR. Thus twice before, and jump at this dead hour,
With martial stalk hath he gone by our watch.

HOR. In what particular thought to work I know not;
But, in the gross and scope of my opinion,
This bodes some strange eruption to our state.

MAR. Good now, sit down, and tell me he that knows,
Why this same strict and most observant watch
So nightly toils the subject of the land,
And why such daily cast of brazen cannon
And foreign mart for implements of war;
Why such impress of shipwrights, whose sore task
Does not divide the Sunday from the week.
What might be toward, that this sweaty haste
Doth make the night joint-labourer with the day?
Who is't that can inform me?

Hor.   That can I.
At least, the whisper goes so. Our last king,
Whose image even but now appear'd to us,
Was, as you know, by Fortinbras of Norway,
Thereto prick'd on by a most emulate pride,
Dar'd to the combat; in which our valiant Hamlet
(For so this side of our known world esteem'd him)
Did slay this Fortinbras; who, by a seal'd compact,
Well ratified by law and heraldry,
Did forfeit, with his life, all those his lands
Which he stood seiz'd of, to the conqueror;
Against the which a moiety competent
Was gaged by our king; which had return'd
To the inheritance of Fortinbras,
Had he been vanquisher, as, by the same comart
And carriage of the article design'd,
His fell to Hamlet. Now, sir, young Fortinbras,
Of unimproved mettle hot and full,
Hath in the skirts of Norway, here and there,
Shark'd up a list of lawless resolutes,
For food and diet, to some enterprise
That hath a stomach in't; which is no other,
As it doth well appear unto our state,
But to recover of us, by strong hand
And terms compulsory, those foresaid lands
So by his father lost; and this, I take it,
Is the main motive of our preparations,
The source of this our watch, and the chief head
Of this post-haste and romage in the land.
    Ber. I think it be no other but e'en so.
Well may it sort that this portentous figure
Comes armed through our watch, so like the King
That was and is the question of these wars.
    Hor. A mote it is to trouble the mind's eye.

In the most high and palmy state of Rome,
A little ere the mightiest Julius fell,
The graves stood tenantless, and the sheeted dead
Did squeak and gibber in the Roman streets;
As stars with trains of fire, and dews of blood,
Disasters in the sun; and the moist star
Upon whose influence Neptune's empire stands
Was sick almost to doomsday with eclipse.
And even the like precurse of fierce events,
As harbingers preceding still the fates
And prologue to the omen coming on,
Have heaven and earth together demonstrated
Unto our climature and countrymen.

[*Enter* GHOST *again.*]

But soft! behold! Lo, where it comes again!
I'll cross it, though it blast me.—Stay, illusion!
                                        [*Spreads his arms.*]
If thou hast any sound, or use of voice,
Speak to me.
If there be any good thing to be done,
That may to thee do ease, and grace to me,
Speak to me.
If thou art privy to thy country's fate,
Which happily foreknowing may avoid,
O, speak!
Or if thou hast uphoarded in thy life
Extorted treasure in the womb of earth
(For which, they say, you spirits oft walk in death),
                                        [*The cock crows.*]
Speak of it! Stay, and speak!—Stop it, Marcellus!
    MAR. Shall I strike at it with my partisan?
    HOR. Do, if it will not stand.
    BER.   'Tis here!
    HOR.   'Tis here!

MAR. 'Tis gone!   [*Exit* GHOST.]
We do it wrong, being so majestical,
To offer it the show of violence;
For it is as the air, invulnerable,
And our vain blows malicious mockery.

BER. It was about to speak, when the cock crew.

HOR. And then it started, like a guilty thing
Upon a fearful summons. I have heard
The cock, that is the trumpet to the morn,
Doth with his lofty and shrill-sounding throat
Awake the god of day; and at his warning,
Whether in sea or fire, in earth or air,
Th' extravagant and erring spirit hies
To his confine; and of the truth herein
This present object made probation.

MAR. It faded on the crowing of the cock.
Some say that ever, 'gainst that season comes
Wherein our Saviour's birth is celebrated,
The bird of dawning singeth all night long;
And then, they say, no spirit dare stir abroad,
The nights are wholesome, then no planets strike,
No fairy takes, nor witch hath power to charm,
So hallow'd and so gracious is the time.

HOR. So have I heard and do in part believe it.
But look, the morn, in russet mantle clad,
Walks o'er the dew of yon high eastward hill.
Break we our watch up; and by my advice
Let us impart what we have seen to-night
Unto young Hamlet; for, upon my life,
This spirit, dumb to us, will speak to him.
Do you consent we shall acquaint him with it,
As needful in our loves, fitting our duty?

MAR. Let's do't, I pray; and I this morning know
Where we shall find him most conveniently.   *Exeunt.*

Scene II: Elsinore. A room of state in the Castle.

Flourish. Enter CLAUDIUS, *King of Denmark,* GERTRUDE
the Queen, HAMLET, POLONIUS, LAERTES *and his sister*
OPHELIA, VOLTEMAND, CORNELIUS, LORDS ATTENDANT.

KING. Though yet of Hamlet our dear brother's death
The memory be green, and that it us befitted
To bear our hearts in grief, and our whole kingdom
To be contracted in one brow of woe,
Yet so far hath discretion fought with nature
That we with wisest sorrow think on him
Together with remembrance of ourselves.
Therefore our sometime sister, now our queen,
Th' imperial jointress to this warlike state,
Have we, as 'twere with a defeated joy,
With an auspicious, and a dropping eye,
With mirth in funeral, and with dirge in marriage,
In equal scale weighing delight and dole,
Taken to wife; nor have we herein barr'd
Your better wisdoms, which have freely gone
With this affair along. For all, our thanks.
Now follows, that you know, young Fortinbras,
Holding a weak supposal of our worth,
Or thinking by our late dear brother's death
Our state to be disjoint and out of frame,
Colleagued with this dream of his advantage,
He hath not fail'd to pester us with message
Importing the surrender of those lands
Lost by his father, with all bands of law,
To our most valiant brother. So much for him.
Now for ourself and for this time of meeting.
Thus much the business is: we have here writ
To Norway, uncle of young Fortinbras,
Who, impotent and bedrid, scarcely hears

Of this his nephew's purpose, to suppress
His further gait herein, in that the levies,
The lists, and full proportions are all made
Out of his subject; and we here dispatch
You, good Cornelius, and you, Voltemand,
For bearers of this greeting to old Norway,
Giving to you no further personal power
To business with the King, more than the scope
Of these dilated articles allow.   [*Gives a paper*.]
Farewell, and let your haste commend your duty.

    Cor., Volt. In that, and all things, will we show our
      duty.

    King. We doubt it nothing. Heartily farewell.

            [*Exeunt* Voltemand *and* Cornelius.]

And now, Laertes, what's the news with you?
You told us of some suit. What is't, Laertes?
You cannot speak of reason to the Dane
And lose your voice. What wouldst thou beg, Laertes,
That shall not be my offer, not thy asking?
The head is not more native to the heart,
The hand more instrumental to the mouth,
Than is the throne of Denmark to thy father.
What wouldst thou have, Laertes?

    Laer.   My dread lord,
Your leave and favour to return to France;
From whence though willingly I came to Denmark
To show my duty in your coronation,
Yet now I must confess, that duty done,
My thoughts and wishes bend again toward France
And bow them to your gracious leave and pardon.

    King. Have you your father's leave? What says Po-
      lonius?

    Pol. He hath, my lord, wrung from me my slow leave
By laboursome petition, and at last
Upon his will I seal'd my hard consent.

I do beseech you give him leave to go.

    KING. Take thy fair hour, Laertes. Time be thine,
And thy best graces spend it at thy will!
But now, my cousin Hamlet, and my son—

    HAM. [*aside*] A little more than kin, and less than
        kind!

    KING. How is it that the clouds still hang on you?

    HAM. Not so, my lord. I am too much i' th' sun.

    QUEEN. Good Hamlet, cast thy nighted colour off,
And let thine eye look like a friend on Denmark.
Do not for ever with thy vailed lids
Seek for thy noble father in the dust.
Thou know'st 'tis common. All that lives must die,
Passing through nature to eternity.

    HAM. Ay, madam, it is common.

    QUEEN.   If it be,
Why seems it so particular with thee?

    HAM. Seems, madam? Nay, it is. I know not 'seems.'
'Tis not alone my inky cloak, good mother,
Nor customary suits of solemn black,
Nor windy suspiration of forc'd breath,
No, nor the fruitful river in the eye,
Nor the dejected haviour of the visage,
Together with all forms, moods, shapes of grief,
That can denote me truly. These indeed seem,
For they are actions that a man might play;
But I have that within which passeth show—
These but the trappings and the suits of woe.

    KING. 'Tis sweet and commendable in your nature,
        Hamlet,
To give these mourning duties to your father;
But you must know, your father lost a father;
That father lost, lost his, and the survivor bound
In filial obligation for some term

To do obsequious sorrow. But to persever
In obstinate condolement is a course
Of impious stubbornness. 'Tis unmanly grief;
It shows a will most incorrect to heaven,
A heart unfortified, a mind impatient,
An understanding simple and unschool'd;
For what we know must be, and is as common
As any the most vulgar thing to sense,
Why should we in our peevish opposition
Take it to heart? Fie! 'tis a fault to heaven,
A fault against the dead, a fault to nature,
To reason most absurd, whose common theme
Is death of fathers, and who still hath cried,
From the first corse till he that died to-day,
'This must be so.' We pray you throw to earth
This unprevailing woe, and think of us
As of a father; for let the world take note
You are the most immediate to our throne,
And with no less nobility of love
Than that which dearest father bears his son
Do I impart toward you. For your intent
In going back to school in Wittenberg,
It is most retrograde to our desire;
And we beseech you, bend you to remain
Here in the cheer and comfort of our eye,
Our chiefest courtier, cousin, and our son.

    QUEEN. Let not thy mother lose her prayers, Hamlet.
I pray thee stay with us, go not to Wittenberg.

    HAM. I shall in all my best obey you, madam.

    KING. Why, 'tis a loving and a fair reply.
Be as ourself in Denmark. Madam, come.
This gentle and unforc'd accord of Hamlet
Sits smiling to my heart; in grace whereof,
No jocund health that Denmark drinks to-day

But the great cannon to the clouds shall tell,
And the King's rouse the heaven shall bruit again,
Respeaking earthly thunder. Come away.

Flourish. Exeunt all but HAMLET.

HAM. O that this too too solid flesh would melt,
Thaw, and resolve itself into a dew!
Or that the Everlasting had not fix'd
His canon 'gainst self-slaughter! O God! God!
How weary, stale, flat, and unprofitable
Seem to me all the uses of this world!
Fie on't! ah, fie! 'Tis an unweeded garden
That grows to seed; things rank and gross in nature
Possess it merely. That it should come to this!
But two months dead! Nay, not so much, not two.
So excellent a king, that was to this
Hyperion to a satyr; so loving to my mother
That he might not beteem the winds of heaven
Visit her face too roughly. Heaven and earth!
Must I remember? Why, she would hang on him
As if increase of appetite had grown
By what it fed on; and yet, within a month—
Let me not think on't! Frailty, thy name is woman!—
A little month, or ere those shoes were old
With which she followed my poor father's body
Like Niobe, all tears—why she, even she
(O God! a beast that wants discourse of reason
Would have mourn'd longer) married with my uncle;
My father's brother, but no more like my father
Than I to Hercules. Within a month,
Ere yet the salt of most unrighteous tears
Had left the flushing in her galled eyes,
She married. O, most wicked speed, to post
With such dexterity to incestuous sheets!
It is not, nor it cannot come to good.
But break my heart, for I must hold my tongue!

Enter HORATIO, MARCELLUS, *and* BERNARDO.

HOR. Hail to your lordship!

HAM.   I am glad to see you well.
Horatio!—or I do forget myself.

HOR. The same, my lord, and your poor servant ever.

HAM. Sir, my good friend—I'll change that name with
    you.
And what make you from Wittenberg, Horatio?
Marcellus?

MAR. My good lord!

HAM. I am very glad to see you.—[*To* BERNARDO]
    Good even, sir.—
But what, in faith, make you from Wittenberg?

HOR. A truant disposition, good my lord.

HAM. I would not hear your enemy say so,
Nor shall you do my ear that violence
To make it truster of your own report
Against yourself. I know you are no truant.
But what is your affair in Elsinore?
We'll teach you to drink deep ere you depart.

HOR. My lord, I came to see your father's funeral.

HAM. I prithee do not mock me, fellow student.
I think it was to see my mother's wedding.

HOR. Indeed, my lord, it followed hard upon.

HAM. Thrift, thrift, Horatio! The funeral bak'd meats
Did coldly furnish forth the marriage tables.
Would I had met my dearest foe in heaven
Or ever I had seen that day, Horatio!
My father—methinks I see my father.

HOR. O, where, my lord?

HAM.   In my mind's eye, Horatio.

HOR. I saw him once. He was a goodly king.

HAM. He was a man, take him for all in all.
I shall not look upon his like again.

HOR. My lord, I think I saw him yesternight.

HAM. Saw? who?

HOR. My lord, the King your father.

HAM.   The King my father?

HOR. Season your admiration for a while
With an attent ear, till I may deliver,
Upon the witness of these gentlemen,
This marvel to you.

HAM.   For God's love let me hear!

HOR. Two nights together had these gentlemen
(Marcellus and Bernardo) on their watch
In the dead vast and middle of the night
Been thus encount'red. A figure like your father,
Armed at point exactly, cap-a-pe,
Appears before them and with solemn march
Goes slow and stately by them. Thrice he walk'd
By their oppress'd and fear-surprised eyes,
Within his truncheon's length; whilst they distill'd
Almost to jelly with the act of fear,
Stand dumb and speak not to him. This to me
In dreadful secrecy impart they did,
And I with them the third night kept the watch;
Where, as they had deliver'd, both in time,
Form of the thing, each word made true and good,
The apparition comes. I knew your father.
These hands are not more like.

HAM.   But where was this?

MAR. My lord, upon the platform where we watch'd.

HAM. Did you not speak to it?

HOR.   My lord, I did;
But answer made it none. Yet once methought
It lifted up its head and did address
Itself to motion, like as it would speak;
But even then the morning cock crew loud,
And at the sound it shrunk in haste away
And vanish'd from our sight.

HAM.   'Tis very strange.

HOR. As I do live, my honour'd lord, 'tis true;
And we did think it writ down in our duty
To let you know of it.

HAM. Indeed, indeed, sirs. But this troubles me.
Hold you the watch to-night?

MAR., BER. We do, my lord.

HAM. Arm'd, say you?

BOTH. Arm'd, my lord.

HAM. From top to toe?

BOTH.   My lord, from head to foot.

HAM. Then saw you not his face?

HOR. O, yes, my lord! He wore his beaver up.

HAM. What, look'd he frowningly?

HOR. A countenance more in sorrow than in anger.

HAM. Pale or red?

HOR. Nay, very pale.

HAM.   And fix'd his eyes upon you?

HOR. Most constantly.

HAM.   I would I had been there.

HOR. It would have much amaz'd you.

HAM. Very like, very like. Stay'd it long?

HOR. While one with moderate haste might tell a hundred.

BOTH. Longer, longer.

HOR. Not when I saw't.

HAM. His beard was grizzled—no?

HOR. It was, as I have seen it in his life,
A sable silver'd.

HAM.   I will watch to-night.
Perchance 'twill walk again.

HOR.   I warr'nt it will.

HAM. If it assume my noble father's person,
I'll speak to it, though hell itself should gape
And bid me hold my peace. I pray you all,

If you have hitherto conceal'd this sight,
Let it be tenable in your silence still;
And whatsoever else shall hap to-night,
Give it an understanding but no tongue.
I will requite your loves. So, fare you well.
Upon the platform, 'twixt eleven and twelve,
I'll visit you.
  ALL.   Our duty to your honour.
  HAM. Your loves, as mine to you. Farewell.
         [*Exeunt all but* HAMLET.]
My father's spirit—in arms? All is not well.
I doubt some foul play. Would the night were come!
Till then sit still, my soul. Foul deeds will rise,
Though all the earth o'erwhelm them, to men's eyes.
             Exit.

Scene III: Elsinore. A room in the house of Polonius.

Enter LAERTES *and* OPHELIA.

  LAER. My necessaries are embark'd. Farewell.
And, sister, as the winds give benefit
And convoy is assistant, do not sleep,
But let me hear from you.
  OPH.   Do you doubt that?
  LAER. For Hamlet, and the trifling of his favour,
Hold it a fashion, and a toy in blood;
A violet in the youth of primy nature,
Forward, not permanent—sweet, not lasting;
The perfume and suppliance of a minute;
No more.
  OPH. No more but so?
  LAER.   Think it no more.
For nature crescent does not grow alone

In thews and bulk; but as this temple waxes,
The inward service of the mind and soul
Grows wide withal. Perhaps he loves you now,
And now no soil nor cautel doth besmirch
The virtue of his will; but you must fear,
His greatness weigh'd, his will is not his own;
For he himself is subject to his birth.
He may not, as unvalued persons do,
Carve for himself, for on his choice depends
The safety and health of this whole state,
And therefore must his choice be circumscrib'd
Unto the voice and yielding of that body
Whereof he is the head. Then if he says he loves you,
It fits your wisdom so far to believe it
As he in his particular act and place
May give his saying deed; which is no further
Than the main voice of Denmark goes withal.
Then weigh what loss your honour may sustain
If with too credent ear you list his songs,
Or lose your heart, or your chaste treasure open
To his unmast'red importunity.
Fear it, Ophelia, fear it, my dear sister,
And keep you in the rear of your affection,
Out of the shot and danger of desire.
The chariest maid is prodigal enough
If she unmask her beauty to the moon.
Virtue itself scapes not calumnious strokes.
The canker galls the infants of the spring
Too oft before their buttons be disclos'd,
And in the morn and liquid dew of youth
Contagious blastments are most imminent.
Be wary then; best safety lies in fear.
Youth to itself rebels, though none else near.

    OPH. I shall th' effect of this good lesson keep
As watchman to my heart. But, good my brother,

Do not as some ungracious pastors do,
Show me the steep and thorny way to heaven,
Whiles, like a puff'd and reckless libertine,
Himself the primrose path of dalliance treads
And recks not his own rede.

LAER.   O, fear me not!

[*Enter* POLONIUS.]

I stay too long. But here my father comes.
A double blessing is a double grace;
Occasion smiles upon a second leave.

POL. Yet here, Laertes? Aboard, aboard, for shame!
The wind sits in the shoulder of your sail,
And you are stay'd for. There—my blessing with thee!
And these few precepts in thy memory
Look thou character. Give thy thoughts no tongue,
Nor any unproportion'd thought his act.
Be thou familiar, but by no means vulgar:
Those friends thou hast, and their adoption tried,
Grapple them unto thy soul with hoops of steel;
But do not dull thy palm with entertainment
Of each new-hatch'd, unfledg'd comrade. Beware
Of entrance to a quarrel; but being in,
Bear't that th' opposed may beware of thee.
Give every man thine ear, but few thy voice;
Take each man's censure, but reserve thy judgment.
Costly thy habit as thy purse can buy,
But not express'd in fancy; rich, not gaudy;
For the apparel oft proclaims the man,
And they in France of the best rank and station
Are most select and generous, chief in that.
Neither a borrower nor a lender be;
For loan oft loses both itself and friend,
And borrowing dulls the edge of husbandry.
This above all—to thine own self be true,

And it must follow, as the night the day,
Thou canst not then be false to any man.
Farewell. My blessing season this in thee!

LAER. Most humbly do I take my leave, my lord.

POL. The time invites you. Go, your servants tend.

LAER. Farewell, Ophelia, and remember well
What I have said to you.

OPH.   'Tis in my memory lock'd,
And you yourself shall keep the key of it.

LAER. Farewell.   *Exit.*

POL. What is't, Ophelia, he hath said to you?

OPH. So please you, something touching the Lord
Hamlet.

POL. Marry, well bethought!
'Tis told me he hath very oft of late
Given private time to you, and you yourself
Have of your audience been most free and bounteous.
If it be so—as so tis put on me,
And that in way of caution—I must tell you
You do not understand yourself so clearly
As it behooves my daughter and your honour.
What is between you? Give me up the truth.

OPH. He hath, my lord, of late made many tenders
Of his affection to me.

POL. Affection? Pooh! You speak like a green girl,
Unsifted in such perilous circumstance.
Do you believe his tenders, as you call them?

OPH. I do not know, my lord, what I should think.

POL. Marry, I will teach you! Think yourself a baby
That you have ta'en these tenders for true pay,
Which are not sterling. Tender yourself more dearly,
Or (not to crack the wind of the poor phrase,
Running it thus) you'll tender me a fool.

OPH My lord, he hath importun'd me with love
In honourable fashion.

POL. Ay, fashion you may call it. Go to, go to!

OPH. And hath given countenance to his speech, my
  lord,
With almost all the holy vows of heaven.

POL. Ay, springes to catch woodcocks! I do know,
When the blood burns, how prodigal the soul
Lends the tongue vows. These blazes, daughter,
Giving more light than heat, extinct in both
Even in their promise, as it is a-making,
You must not take for fire. From this time
Be something scanter of your maiden presence.
Set your entreatments at a higher rate
Than a command to parley. For Lord Hamlet,
Believe so much in him, that he is young,
And with a larger tether may he walk
Than may be given you. In few, Ophelia,
Do not believe his vows; for they are brokers,
Not of that dye which their investments show,
But mere implorators of unholy suits,
Breathing like sanctified and pious bawds,
The better to beguile. This is for all:
I would not, in plain terms, from this time forth
Have you so slander any moment leisure
As to give words or talk with the Lord Hamlet.
Look to't, I charge you. Come your ways.

OPH. I shall obey, my lord.　　　　　　　　*Exeunt.*

Scene IV: Elsinore. The platform before the Castle.

Enter HAMLET, HORATIO, *and* MARCELLUS.

HAM. The air bites shrewdly; it is very cold.

HOR. It is a nipping and an eager air.

HAM. What hour now?

HOR.   I think it lacks of twelve.

MAR. No, it is struck.

HOR. Indeed? I heard it not. It then draws near the
    season
Wherein the spirit held his wont to walk.

       [A flourish of trumpets, and two pieces go off.]
What does this mean, my lord?

HAM. The King doth wake to-night and takes his rouse,
Keeps wassail, and the swagg'ring upspring reels,
And, as he drains his draughts of Rhenish down,
The kettledrum and trumpet thus bray out
The triumph of his pledge.

HOR.   Is it a custom?

HAM. Ay, marry, is't;
But to my mind, though I am native here
And to the manner born, it is a custom
More honour'd in the breach than the observance.
This heavy-headed revel east and west
Makes us traduc'd and tax'd of other nations;
They clip us drunkards and with swinish phrase
Soil our addition; and indeed it takes
From our achievements, though perform'd at height,
The pith and marrow of our attribute.
So oft it chances in particular men
That, for some vicious mole of nature in them,
As in their birth,—wherein they are not guilty,
Since nature cannot choose his origin,—
By the o'ergrowth of some complexion,
Oft breaking down the pales and forts of reason,
Or by some habit that too much o'erleavens
The form of plausive manners, that these men
Carrying, I say, the stamp of one defect,
Being nature's livery, or fortune's star,
Their virtues else—be they as pure as grace,
As infinite as man may undergo—

Shall in the general censure take corruption
From that particular fault. The dram of e'il
Doth all the noble substance often dout
To his own scandal.

Enter GHOST.

HOR.   Look, my lord, it comes!
HAM. Angels and ministers of grace defend us!
Be thou a spirit of health or goblin damn'd,
Bring with thee airs from heaven or blasts from hell,
Be thy intents wicked or charitable,
Thou com'st in such a questionable shape
That I will speak to thee. I'll call thee Hamlet,
King, father, royal Dane. O, answer me!
Let me not burst in ignorance, but tell
Why thy canoniz'd bones, hearsed in death,
Have burst their cerements; why the sepulchre
Wherein we saw thee quietly inurn'd,
Hath op'd his ponderous and marble jaws
To cast thee up again. What may this mean
That thou, dead corse, again in complete steel,
Revisits thus the glimpses of the moon,
Making night hideous, and we fools of nature
So horridly to shake our disposition
With thoughts beyond the reaches of our souls?
Say, why is this? wherefore? What should we do?
                     GHOST *beckons* HAMLET.
HOR. It beckons you to go away with it,
As if it some impartment did desire
To you alone.
MAR. Look with what courteous action
It waves you to a more removed ground.
But do not go with it!
HOR.   No, by no means!

HAM. It will not speak. Then will I follow it.

HOR. Do not, my lord!

HAM.   Why, what should be the fear?
I do not set my life at a pin's fee;
And for my soul, what can it do to that,
Being a thing immortal as itself?
It waves me forth again. I'll follow it.

HOR. What if it tempt you toward the flood, my lord,
Or to the dreadful summit of the cliff
That beetles o'er his base into the sea,
And there assume some other, horrible form
Which might deprive your sovereignty of reason
And draw you into madness? Think of it.
The very place puts toys of desperation,
Without more motive, into every brain
That looks so many fathoms to the sea
And hears it roar beneath.

HAM.   It waves me still.
Go on. I'll follow thee.

MAR. You shall not go, my lord.

HAM.   Hold off your hands!

HOR. Be rul'd. You shall not go.

HAM.   My fate cries out
And makes each petty artery in this body
As hardy as the Nemean lion's nerve.   [GHOST *beckons*.]
Still am I call'd. Unhand me, gentlemen.
By heaven, I'll make a ghost of him that lets me!—
I say, away!—Go on. I'll follow thee.

                     Exeunt GHOST *and* HAMLET.

HOR. He waxes desperate with imagination.

MAR. Let's follow. 'Tis not fit thus to obey him.

HOR. Have after. To what issue will this come?

MAR. Something is rotten in the state of Denmark.

HOR. Heaven will direct it.

MAR.   Nay, let's follow him.   *Exeunt*.

Scene V: Elsinore. The Castle. Another part of the fortifications.

Enter GHOST *and* HAMLET.

HAM. Whither wilt thou lead me? Speak! I'll go no
    further.

GHOST. Mark me.

HAM. I will.

GHOST. My hour is almost come,
When I to sulph'rous and tormenting flames
Must render up myself.

HAM. Alas, poor ghost!

GHOST. Pity me not, but lend thy serious hearing
To what I shall unfold.

HAM. Speak. I am bound to hear.

GHOST. So art thou to revenge, when thou shalt hear.

HAM. What?

GHOST. I am thy father's spirit,
Doom'd for a certain term to walk the night;
And for the day confin'd to fast in fires,
Till the foul crimes done in my days of nature
Are burnt and purg'd away. But that I am forbid
To tell the secrets of my prison house,
I could a tale unfold whose lightest word
Would harrow up thy soul, freeze thy young blood,
Make thy two eyes, like stars, start from their spheres,
Thy knotted and combined locks to part,
And each particular hair to stand an end
Like quills upon the fretful porpentine.
But this eternal blazon must not be
To ears of flesh and blood. List, list, O, list!
If thou didst ever thy dear father love—

HAM. O God!

GHOST. Revenge his foul and most unnatural murther.

HAM. Murther?

GHOST. Murther most foul, as in the best it is;
But this most foul, strange, and unnatural.

HAM. Haste me to know't, that I, with wings as swift
As meditation or the thoughts of love,
May sweep to my revenge.

GHOST.   I find thee apt;
And duller shouldst thou be than the fat weed
That rots itself in ease on Lethe wharf,
Wouldst thou not stir in this. Now, Hamlet, hear.
'Tis given out that, sleeping in my orchard,
A serpent stung me. So the whole ear of Denmark
Is by a forged process of my death
Rankly abus'd. But know, thou noble youth,
The serpent that did sting thy father's life
Now wears his crown.

HAM.   O my prophetic soul!
My uncle?

GHOST. Ay, that incestuous, that adulterate beast,
With witchcraft of his wit, with traitorous gifts—
O wicked wit and gifts, that have the power
So to seduce!—won to his shameful lust
The will of my most seeming-virtuous queen.
O Hamlet, what a falling-off was there,
From me, whose love was of that dignity
That it went hand in hand even with the vow
I made to her in marriage, and to decline
Upon a wretch whose natural gifts were poor
To those of mine!
But virtue, as it never will be mov'd,
Though lewdness court it in a shape of heaven,
So lust, though to a radiant angel link'd,
Will sate itself in a celestial bed
And prey on garbage.
But soft! methinks I scent the morning air.

Brief let me be. Sleeping within my orchard,
My custom always of the afternoon,
Upon my secure hour thy uncle stole,
With juice of cursed hebona in a vial,
And in the porches of my ears did pour
The leperous distilment; whose effect
Holds such an enmity with blood of man
That swift as quicksilver it courses through
The natural gates and alleys of the body,
And with a sudden vigour it doth posset
And curd, like eager droppings into milk,
The thin and wholesome blood. So did it mine;
And a most instant tetter bark'd about,
Most lazar-like, with vile and loathsome crust
All my smooth body.
Thus was I, sleeping, by a brother's hand
Of life, of crown, of queen, at once dispatch'd;
Cut off even in the blossoms of my sin,
Unhous'led, disappointed, unanel'd,
No reck'ning made, but sent to my account
With all my imperfections on my head.

    HAM. O, horrible! O, horrible! most horrible!
    GHOST. If thou hast nature in thee, bear it not.
Let not the royal bed of Denmark be
A couch for luxury and damned incest.
But, howsoever thou pursuest this act,
Taint not thy mind, nor let thy soul contrive
Against thy mother aught. Leave her to heaven,
And to those thorns that in her bosom lodge
To prick and sting her. Fare thee well at once.
The glowworm shows the matin to be near
And gins to pale his uneffectual fire.
Adieu, adieu, adieu! Remember me.   *Exit.*

    HAM. O all you host of heaven! O earth! What else?
And shall I couple hell? Hold, hold, my heart!

And you, my sinews, grow not instant old,
But bear me stiffly up. Remember thee?
Ay, thou poor ghost, while memory holds a seat
In this distracted globe. Remember thee?
Yea, from the table of my memory
I'll wipe away all trivial fond records,
All saws of books, all forms, all pressures past
That youth and observation copied there,
And thy commandment all alone shall live
Within the book and volume of my brain,
Unmix'd with baser matter. Yes, by heaven!
O most pernicious woman!
O villain, villain, smiling, damned villain!
My tables! Meet it is I set it down
That one may smile, and smile, and be a villain;
At least I am sure it may be so in Denmark.   [*Writes.*]
So, uncle, there you are. Now to my word:
It is 'Adieu, adieu! Remember me.'
I have sworn't.

    Hor. [*within*] My lord, my lord!

Enter Horatio *and* Marcellus.

Mar.   Lord Hamlet!
Hor.   Heaven secure him!
Ham. So be it!
Mar. Illo, ho, ho, my lord!
Ham. Hillo, ho, ho, boy! Come, bird, come.
Mar. How is't, my noble lord?
Hor.   What news, my lord?
Ham. O, wonderful!
Hor. Good my lord, tell it.
Ham.   No, you will reveal it.
Hor. Not I, my lord, by heaven!
Mar.   Nor I, my lord.

HAM. How say you then? Would heart of man once
     think it?
But you'll be secret?

BOTH.   Ay, by heaven, my lord.

HAM. There's ne'er a villain dwelling in all Denmark
But he's an arrant knave.

     HOR. There needs no ghost, my lord, come from the
        grave
To tell us this.

HAM.   Why, right! You are in the right!
And so, without more circumstance at all,
I hold it fit that we shake hands and part;
You, as your business and desire shall point you,
For every man hath business and desire,
Such as it is; and for my own poor part,
Look you, I'll go pray.

     HOR. These are but wild and whirling words, my lord.

HAM. I am sorry they offend you, heartily;
Yes, faith, heartily.

HOR.   There's no offence, my lord.

HAM. Yes, by Saint Patrick, but there is, Horatio,
And much offence too. Touching this vision here,
It is an honest ghost, that let me tell you.
For your desire to know what is between us,
O'ermaster't as you may. And now, good friends,
As you are friends, scholars, and soldiers,
Give me one poor request.

     HOR. What is't, my lord? We will.

HAM. Never make known what you have seen to-night.

BOTH. My lord, we will not.

HAM.   Nay, but swear't.

HOR.   In faith,
My lord, not I.

MAR.   Nor I, my lord—in faith.

HAM. Upon my sword.

MAR.   We have sworn, my lord, already.
HAM. Indeed, upon my sword, indeed.

GHOST *cries under the stage.*

GHOST. Swear.
HAM. Aha boy, say'st thou so? Art thou there, true-
    penny?
Come on! You hear this fellow in the cellarage.
Consent to swear.
HOR.   Propose the oath, my lord.
HAM. Never to speak of this that you have seen.
Swear by my sword.
GHOST. [*beneath*] Swear.
HAM. Hic et ubique? Then we'll shift our ground.
Come hither, gentlemen,
And lay your hands again upon my sword.
Never to speak of this that you have heard:
Swear by my sword.
GHOST. [*beneath*] Swear by his sword.
HAM. Well said, old mole! Canst work i' th' earth so
    fast?
A worthy pioner! Once more remove, good friends.
HOR. O day and night, but this is wondrous strange!
HAM. And therefore as a stranger give it welcome.
There are more things in heaven and earth, Horatio,
Than are dreamt of in your philosophy.
But come!
Here, as before, never, so help you mercy,
How strange or odd soe'er I bear myself
(As I perchance hereafter shall think meet
To put an antic disposition on),
That you, at such times seeing me, never shall,
With arms encumb'red thus, or this head-shake,
Or by pronouncing of some doubtful phrase,
As 'Well, well, we know,' or 'We could, an if we would,'

Or 'If we list to speak,' or 'There be, an if they might,'
Or such ambiguous giving out, to note
That you know aught of me—this not to do,
So grace and mercy at your most need help you,
Swear.

GHOST. [*beneath*] Swear.　　　　　　　*They swear.*

HAM. Rest, rest, perturbed spirit! So, gentlemen,
With all my love I do commend me to you;
And what so poor a man as Hamlet is
May do t' express his love and friending to you,
God willing, shall not lack. Let us go in together;
And still your fingers on your lips, I pray.
The time is out of joint. O cursed spite
That ever I was born to set it right!
Nay, come, let's go together.　　　　　　　*Exeunt.*

Act II: Scene I: Elsinore. A room in the house of Polonius.

Enter POLONIUS *and* REYNALDO.

POL. Give him this money and these notes, Reynaldo.

REY. I will, my lord.

POL. You shall do marvell's wisely, good Reynaldo,
Before you visit him, to make inquire
Of his behaviour.

REY.　　　　　　　My lord, I did intend it.

POL. Marry, well said, very well said. Look you, sir,
Enquire me first what Danskers are in Paris;
And how, and who, what means, and where they keep,
What company, at what expense; and finding
By this encompassment and drift of question
That they do know my son, come you more nearer
Than your particular demands will touch it.
Take you, as 'twere, some distant knowledge of him;

As thus, 'I know his father and his friends,
And in part him.' Do you mark this, Reynaldo?

    REY. Ay, very well, my lord.

    POL. 'And in part him, but,' you may say, 'not well.
But if't be he I mean, he's very wild
Addicted so and so'; and there put on him
What forgeries you please; marry, none so rank
As may dishonour him—take heed of that;
But, sir, such wanton, wild, and usual slips
As are companions noted and most known
To youth and liberty.

    REY.   As gaming, my lord?

    POL. Ay, or drinking, fencing, swearing, quarrelling,
Drabbing. You may go so far.

    REY. My lord, that would dishonour him.

    POL. Faith, no, as you may season it in the charge.
You must not put another scandal on him,
That he is open to incontinency.
That's not my meaning. But breathe his faults so quaintly
That they may seem the taints of liberty,
The flash and outbreak of a fiery mind,
A savageness in unreclaimed blood,
Of general assault.

    REY.   But, my good lord—

    POL. Wherefore should you do this?

    REY.   Ay, my lord,
I would know that.

    POL.   Marry, sir, here's my drift,
And I believe it is a fetch of warrant.
You laying these slight sullies on my son
As 'twere a thing a little soil'd i' th' working,
Mark you,
Your party in converse, him you would sound,
Having ever seen in the prenominate crimes
The youth you breathe of guilty, be assur'd

He closes with you in this consequence:
'Good sir,' or so, or 'friend,' or 'gentleman'—
According to the phrase or the addition
Of man and country—

REY.　　　　　　　　Very good, my lord.

POL. And then, sir, does 'a this—'a does—
What was I about to say? By the mass, I was about to say
something! Where did I leave?

REY. At 'closes in the consequence,' at 'friend or so,'
and 'gentleman.'

POL. At 'closes in the consequence'—Ay, marry!
He closes thus: 'I know the gentleman.
I saw him yesterday, or t'other day,
Or then, or then, with such or such; and, as you say,
There was 'a gaming; there o'ertook in's rouse;
There falling out at tennis'; or perchance,
'I saw him enter such a house of sale,'
Videlicet, a brothel, or so forth.
See you now—
Your bait of falsehood takes this carp of truth;
And thus do we of wisdom and of reach,
With windlasses and with assays of bias,
By indirections find directions out.
So, by my former lecture and advice,
Shall you my son. You have me, have you not?

REY. My lord, I have.

POL.　　　　　　　　God b' wi' ye, fare ye well!

REY. Good my lord!　　　　　　　　*Going.*

POL. Observe his inclination in yourself.

REY. I shall, my lord.

POL. And let him ply his music.

REY.　　　　　　　　Well, my lord.

POL. Farewell!　　[*Exit* REYNALDO. *Enter* OPHELIA.]
　　　　　　　How now, Ophelia? What's the matter?

OPH. O my lord, my lord, I have been so affrighted!

Pol. With what, i' th' name of God?

Oph. My lord, as I was sewing in my closet,
Lord Hamlet, with his doublet all unbrac'd,
No hat upon his head, his stockings foul'd,
Ungart'red, and down-gyved to his ankle;
Pale as his shirt, his knees knocking each other,
And with a look so piteous in purport
As if he had been loosed out of hell
To speak of horrors—he comes before me.

Pol. Mad for thy love?

Oph.   My lord, I do not know,
But truly I do fear it.

Pol.   What said he?

Oph. He took me by the wrist and held me hard;
Then goes he to the length of all his arm,
And, with his other hand thus o'er his brow,
He falls to such perusal of my face
As he would draw it. Long stay'd he so.
At last, a little shaking of mine arm,
And thrice his head thus waving up and down,
He rais'd a sigh so piteous and profound
As it did seem to shatter all his bulk
And end his being. That done, he lets me go,
And with his head over his shoulder turn'd
He seem'd to find his way without his eyes,
For out o' doors he went without their help
And to the last bended their light on me.

Pol. Come, go with me. I will go seek the King.
This is the very ecstasy of love,
Whose violent property fordoes itself
And leads the will to desperate undertakings
As oft as any passion under heaven
That does afflict our natures. I am sorry.
What, have you given him any hard words of late?

Oph. No, my good lord; but, as you did command,

I did repel his letters and denied
His access to me.

  POL.   That hath made him mad.
I am sorry that with better heed and judgment
I had not quoted him. I fear'd he did but trifle
And meant to wrack thee; but beshrew my jealousy!
By heaven, it is as proper to our age
To cast beyond ourselves in our opinions
As it is common for the younger sort
To lack discretion. Come, go we to the King.
This must be known; which, being kept close, might
  move
More grief to hide than hate to utter love.
Come   *Exeunt.*

Scene II: Elsinore. A room in the Castle.

Flourish. Enter KING *and* QUEEN, ROSENCRANTZ, *and*
    GUILDENSTERN, *cum aliis.*

 KING. Welcome, dear Rosencrantz and Guildenstern.
Moreover that we much did long to see you,
The need we have to use you did provoke
Our hasty sending. Something have you heard
Of Hamlet's transformation. So I call it,
Sith nor th' exterior nor the inward man
Resembles that it was. What it should be,
More than his father's death, that thus hath put him
So much from th' understanding of himself,
I cannot dream of. I entreat you both
That, being of so young days brought up with him,
And since so neighbour'd to his youth and haviour,
That you vouchsafe your rest here in our court
Some little time; so by your companies
To draw him on to pleasures, and to gather

So much as from occasion you may glean,
Whether aught to us unknown afflicts him thus
That, open'd, lies within our remedy.

QUEEN. Good gentlemen, he hath much talk'd of you,
And sure I am two men there are not living
To whom he more adheres. If it will please you
To show us so much gentry and good will
As to expend your time with us awhile
For the supply and profit of our hope,
Your visitation shall receive such thanks
As fits a king's remembrance.

Ros.   Both your Majesties
Might, by the sovereign power you have of us,
Put your dread pleasures more into command
Than to entreaty.

GUIL.   But we both obey,
And here give up ourselves, in the full bent,
To lay our service freely at your feet,
To be commanded.

KING. Thanks, Rosencrantz and gentle Guildenstern.

QUEEN. Thanks, Guildenstern and gentle Rosencrantz.
And I beseech you instantly to visit
My too much changed son.—Go, some of you,
And bring these gentlemen where Hamlet is.

GUIL. Heavens make our presence and our practices
Pleasant and helpful to him!

QUEEN.   Ay, amen!

      Exeunt ROSENCRANTZ *and* GUILDENSTERN, *with*
                              some ATTENDANTS.

                  Enter POLONIUS.

POL. Th' ambassadors from Norway, my good lord,
Are joyfully return'd.

KING. Thou still hast been the father of good news.

POL. Have I, my lord? Assure you, my good liege,

I hold my duty as I hold my soul,
Both to my God and to my gracious king;
And I do think—or else this brain of mine
Hunts not the trail of policy so sure
As it hath us'd to do—that I have found
The very cause of Hamlet's lunacy.

    KING. O, speak of that! That do I long to hear.

    POL. Give first admittance to th' ambassadors.
My news shall be the fruit to that great feast.

    KING. Thyself do grace to them, and bring them in.
                                     [*Exit* POLONIUS.]

He tells me, my dear Gertrude, he hath found
The head and source of all your son's distemper.

    QUEEN. I doubt it is no other but the main,
His father's death and our o'erhasty marriage.

    KING. Well, we shall sift him.

    [*Enter* POLONIUS, VOLTEMAND, *and* CORNELIUS.]
                                 Welcome, my good friends.
Say, Voltemand, what from our brother Norway?

    VOLT. Most fair return of greetings and desires.
Upon our first, he sent out to suppress
His nephew's levies; which to him appear'd
To be a preparation 'gainst the Polack,
But better look'd into, he truly found
It was against your Highness; whereat griev'd,
That so his sickness, age, and impotence
Was falsely borne in hand, sends out arrests
On Fortinbras; which he, in brief, obeys,
Receives rebuke from Norway, and, in fine,
Makes vow before his uncle never more
To give th' assay of arms against your Majesty.
Whereon old Norway, overcome with joy,
Gives him three thousand crowns in annual fee
And his commission to employ those soldiers,
So levied as before, against the Polack;

With an entreaty, herein further shown,

[*Gives a paper.*]

That it might please you to give quiet pass
Through your dominions for this enterprise,
On such regards of safety and allowance
As therein are set down.

    KING.   It likes us well;
And at our more consider'd time we'll read,
Answer, and think upon this business.
Meantime we thank you for your well-took labour.
Go to your rest; at night we'll feast together.
Most welcome home!   *Exeunt* AMBASSADORS.

    POL.   This business is well ended.
My liege, and madam, to expostulate
What majesty should be, what duty is,
Why day is day, night night, and time is time,
Were nothing but to waste night, day, and time.
Therefore, since brevity is the soul of wit,
And tediousness the limbs and outward flourishes,
I will be brief. Your noble son is mad.
Mad call I it; for, to define true madness,
What is't but to be nothing else but mad?
But let that go.

    QUEEN.   More matter, with less art.

    POL. Madam, I swear I use no art at all.
That he is mad, 'tis true: 'tis true 'tis pity;
And pity 'tis 'tis true. A foolish figure!
But farewell it, for I will use no art.
Mad let us grant him then. And now remains
That we find out the cause of this effect—
Or rather say, the cause of this defect,
For this effect defective comes by cause.
Thus it remains, and the remainder thus.
Perpend.
I have a daughter (have while she is mine),

Who in her duty and obedience, mark,
Hath given me this. Now gather, and surmise.

                [*Reads the letter:*]

'To the celestial, and my soul's idol, the most beautified
Ophelia,'—

That's an ill phrase, a vile phrase; 'beautified' is a vile
phrase. But you shall hear. Thus: [*Reads:*]

'In her excellent white bosom, these, &c.'

   QUEEN. Come this from Hamlet to her?

   POL. Good madam, stay awhile. I will be faithful.

                [*Reads:*]

      'Doubt thou the stars are fire;
        Doubt that the sun doth move;
        Doubt truth to be a liar;
        But never doubt I love.

  'O dear Ophelia, I am ill at these numbers; I have not
art to reckon my groans; but that I love thee best, O most
best, believe it. Adieu.

  'Thine evermore, most dear lady, whilst this machine
                is to him, HAMLET.'

This, in obedience, hath my daughter shown me;
And more above, hath his solicitings,
As they fell out by time, by means, and place,
All given to mine ear.

   KING.   But how hath she
Receiv'd his love?

   POL.   What do you think of me?

   KING. As of a man faithful and honourable.

   POL. I would fain prove so. But what might you think,
When I had seen this hot love on the wing
(As I perceiv'd it, I must tell you that,
Before my daughter told me), what might you,
Or my dear Majesty your queen here, think,
If I had play'd the desk or table book,
Or given my heart a winking, mute and dumb,

Or look'd upon this love with idle sight?
What might you think? No, I went round to work
And my young mistress thus I did bespeak:
'Lord Hamlet is a prince, out of thy star.
This must not be.' And then I prescripts gave her,
That she should lock herself from his resort,
Admit no messengers, receive no tokens.
Which done, she took the fruits of my advice,
And he, repulsed, a short tale to make,
Fell into a sadness, then into a fast,
Thence to a watch, thence into a weakness,
Thence to a lightness, and, by this declension,
Into the madness wherein now he raves,
And all we mourn for.

    KING.   Do you think 'tis this?

    QUEEN. It may be, very like.

    POL. Hath there been such a time—I would fain know
        that—
That I have positively said ' 'Tis so,'
When it prov'd otherwise?

    KING.   Not that I know.

    POL. [*points to his head and shoulder*] Take this from
        this, if this be otherwise.
If circumstances lead me, I will find
Where truth is hid, though it were hid indeed
Within the centre.

    KING.   How may we try it further?

    POL. You know sometimes he walks four hours to-
        gether
Here in the lobby.

    QUEEN.   So he does indeed.

    POL. At such a time I'll loose my daughter to him.
Be you and I behind an arras then.
Mark the encounter. If he love her not,
And be not from his reason fall'n thereon,

Let me be no assistant for a state,
But keep a farm and carters.

KING.   We will try it.

Enter HAMLET, *reading on a book.*

QUEEN. But look where sadly the poor wretch comes
reading.

POL. Away, I do beseech you, both away!
I'll board him presently. O, give me leave.

[*Exeunt* KING *and* QUEEN, *with* ATTENDANTS.]
How does my good Lord Hamlet?

HAM. Well, God-a-mercy.

POL. Do you know me, my lord?

HAM. Excellent well. You are a fishmonger.

POL. Not I, my lord.

HAM. Then I would you were so honest a man.

POL. Honest, my lord?

HAM. Ay, sir. To be honest, as this world goes, is to
be one man pick'd out of ten thousand.

POL. That's very true, my lord.

HAM. For if the sun breed maggots in a dead dog,
being a god kissing carrion—Have you a daughter?

POL. I have, my lord.

HAM. Let her not walk i' th' sun. Conception is a blessing, but not as your daughter may conceive. Friend, look
to't.

POL. [*aside*] How say you by that? Still harping on my
daughter. Yet he knew me not at first. He said I was a
fishmonger. He is far gone, far gone! And truly in my
youth I suff'red much extremity for love—very near this.
I'll speak to him again.—What do you read, my lord?

HAM. Words, words, words.

POL. What is the matter, my lord?

HAM. Between who?

POL. I mean, the matter that you read, my lord.

HAM. Slanders, sir; for the satirical rogue says here that old men have grey beards; that their faces are wrinkled; their eyes purging thick amber and plum-tree gum; and that they have a plentiful lack of wit, together with most weak hams. All which, sir, though I most powerfully and potently believe, yet I hold it not honesty to have it thus set down; for you yourself, sir, should be old as I am if, like a crab, you could go backward.

POL. [*aside*] Though this be madness, yet there is method in't.—Will you walk out of the air, my lord?

HAM. Into my grave?

POL. Indeed, that is out o' th' air. [*Aside*] How pregnant sometimes his replies are! a happiness that often madness hits on, which reason and sanity could not so prosperously be delivered of. I will leave him and suddenly contrive the means of meeting between him and my daughter.—My honourable lord, I will most humbly take my leave of you.

HAM. You cannot, sir, take from me anything that I will more willingly part withal—except my life, except my life, except my life.

Enter ROSENCRANTZ *and* GUILDENSTERN.

POL. Fare you well, my lord.

HAM. These tedious old fools!

POL. You go to seek the Lord Hamlet. There he is.

ROS. [*to* POLONIUS] God save you, sir!

Exit POLONIUS.

GUIL. My honour'd lord!

ROS. My most dear lord!

HAM. My excellent good friends! How dost thou, Guildenstern? Ah, Rosencrantz! Good lads, how do ye both?

ROS. As the indifferent children of the earth.

GUIL. Happy in that we are not over-happy. On Fortune's cap we are not the very button.

HAM. Nor the soles of her shoe?

ROS. Neither, my lord.

HAM. Then you live about her waist, or in the middle of her favours?

GUIL. Faith, her privates we.

HAM. In the secret parts of Fortune? O, most true! she is a strumpet. What news?

ROS. None, my lord, but that the world's grown honest.

HAM. Then is doomsday near! But your news is not true. Let me question more in particular. What have you, my good friends, deserved at the hands of Fortune that she sends you to prison hither?

GUIL. Prison, my lord?

HAM. Denmark's a prison.

ROS. Then is the world one.

HAM. A goodly one; in which there are many confines, wards, and dungeons, Denmark being one o' th' worst.

ROS. We think not so, my lord.

HAM. Why, then 'tis none to you; for there is nothing either good or bad but thinking makes it so. To me it is a prison.

ROS. Why, then your ambition makes it one. 'Tis too narrow for your mind.

HAM. O God, I could be bounded in a nutshell and count myself a king of infinite space, were it not that I have bad dreams.

GUIL. Which dreams indeed are ambition; for the very substance of the ambitious is merely the shadow of a dream.

HAM. A dream itself is but a shadow.

ROS. Truly, and I hold ambition of so airy and light a quality that it is but a shadow's shadow.

HAM. Then are our beggars bodies, and our monarchs

and outstretch'd heroes the beggars' shadows. Shall we
to th' court? for, by my fay, I cannot reason.

Both. We'll wait upon you.

Ham. No such matter! I will not sort you with the rest
of my servants; for, to speak to you like an honest man,
I am most dreadfully attended. But in the beaten way of
friendship, what make you at Elsinore?

Ros. To visit you, my lord; no other occasion.

Ham. Beggar that I am, I am even poor in thanks; but
I thank you; and sure, dear friends, my thanks are too
dear a halfpenny. Were you not sent for? Is it your own
inclining? Is it a free visitation? Come, deal justly with
me. Come, come! Nay, speak.

Guil. What should we say, my lord?

Ham. Why, anything—but to th' purpose. You were
sent for; and there is a kind of confession in your looks,
which your modesties have not craft enough to colour. I
know the good King and Queen have sent for you.

Ros. To what end, my lord?

Ham. That you must teach me. But let me conjure you
by the rights of our fellowship, by the consonancy of our
youth, by the obligation of our ever-preserved love, and
by what more dear a better proposer could charge you
withal, be even and direct with me, whether you were
sent for or no.

Ros. [*aside to* Guildenstern] What say you?

Ham. [*aside*] Nay then, I have an eye of you.—If you
love me, hold not off.

Guil. My lord, we were sent for.

Ham. I will tell you why. So shall my anticipation prevent your discovery, and your secrecy to the King and
Queen moult no feather. I have of late—but wherefore I
know not—lost all my mirth, forgone all custom of exercises; and indeed, it goes so heavily with my disposition
that this goodly frame, the earth, seems to me a sterile

promontory; this most excellent canopy, the air, look
you, this brave o'erhanging firmament, this majestical
roof fretted with golden fire—why, it appeareth no other
thing to me than a foul and pestilent congregation of
vapours. What a piece of work is a man! how noble in
reason! how infinite in faculties! in form and moving how
express and admirable! in action how like an angel! in
apprehension how like a god! the beauty of the world,
the paragon of animals! And yet to me what is this
quintessence of dust? Man delights not me—no, nor
woman neither, though by your smiling you seem to say
so.

Ros. My lord, there was no such stuff in my thoughts.

Ham. Why did you laugh then, when I said 'Man delights not me'?

Ros. To think, my lord, if you delight not in man,
what lenten entertainment the players shall receive from
you. We coted them on the way, and hither are they
coming to offer you service.

Ham. He that plays the king shall be welcome—his
Majesty shall have tribute of me; the adventurous knight
shall use his foil and target; the lover shall not sigh
gratis; the humorous man shall end his part in peace; the
clown shall make those laugh whose lungs are tickle o'
th' sere; and the lady shall say her mind freely, or the
blank verse shall halt for't. What players are they?

Ros. Even those you were wont to take such delight in,
the tragedians of the city.

Ham. How chances it they travel? Their residence,
both in reputation and profit, was better both ways.

Ros. I think their inhibition comes by the means of the
late innovation.

Ham. Do they hold the same estimation they did when
I was in the city? Are they so follow'd?

Ros. No indeed are they not.

HAM. How comes it? Do they grow rusty?

ROS. Nay, their endeavour keeps in the wonted pace; but there is, sir, an eyrie of children, little eyases, that cry out on the top of question and are most tyrannically clapp'd for't. These are now the fashion, and so berattle the common stages (so they call them) that many wearing rapiers are afraid of goose-quills and dare scarce come thither.

HAM. What, are they children? Who maintains 'em? How are they escoted? Will they pursue the quality no longer than they can sing? Will they not say afterwards, if they should grow themselves to common players (as it is most like, if their means are no better), their writers do them wrong to make them exclaim against their own succession.

ROS. Faith, there has been much to do on both sides; and the nation holds it no sin to tarre them to controversy. There was, for a while, no money bid for argument unless the poet and the player went to cuffs in the question.

HAM. Is't possible?

GUIL. O, there has been much throwing about of brains.

HAM. Do the boys carry it away?

ROS. Ay, that they do, my lord—Hercules and his load too.

HAM. It is not very strange; for my uncle is King of Denmark, and those that would make mows at him while my father lived give twenty, forty, fifty, a hundred ducats apiece for his picture in little. 'Sblood, there is something in this more than natural, if philosophy could find it out.

Flourish for the PLAYERS.

GUIL. There are the players.

HAM. Gentlemen, you are welcome to Elsinore. Your

hands, come! Th' appurtenance of welcome is fashion and ceremony. Let me comply with you in this garb, lest my extent to the players (which I tell you must show fairly outwards) should more appear like entertainment than yours. You are welcome. But my uncle-father and aunt-mother are deceiv'd.

GUIL. In what, my dear lord?

HAM. I am but mad north-north-west. When the wind is southerly I know a hawk from a handsaw.

Enter POLONIUS.

POL. Well be with you, gentlemen!

HAM. Hark you, Guildenstern—and you too—at each ear a hearer! That great baby you see there is not yet out of his swaddling clouts.

ROS. Happily he's the second time come to them; for they say an old man is twice a child.

HAM. I will prophesy he comes to tell me of the players. Mark it.—You say right, sir; a Monday morning; 'twas so indeed.

POL. My lord, I have news to tell you.

HAM. My lord, I have news to tell you. When Roscius was an actor in Rome—

POL. The actors are come hither, my lord.

HAM. Buzz, buzz!

POL. Upon my honour—

HAM. Then came each actor on his ass—

POL. The best actors in the world, either for tragedy, comedy, history, pastoral, pastoral-comical, historical-pastoral, tragical-historical, tragical-comical-historical-pastoral; scene individable, or poem unlimited. Seneca cannot be too heavy, nor Plautus too light. For the law of writ and the liberty, these are the only men.

HAM. O Jephthah, judge of Israel, what a treasure hadst thou!

POL. What treasure had he, my lord?

HAM. Why,

> 'One fair daughter, and no more,
> The which he loved passing well.'

POL. [*aside*] Still on my daughter.

HAM. Am I not i' th' right, old Jephthah?

POL. If you call me Jephthah, my lord, I have a daughter that I love passing well.

HAM. Nay, that follows not.

POL. What follows then, my lord?

HAM. Why,

> 'As by lot, God wot,'

and then, you know,

> 'It came to pass, as most like it was.'

The first row of the pious chanson will show you more; for look where my abridgement comes.

[*Enter four or five* PLAYERS.]

You are welcome, masters; welcome, all.—I am glad to see thee well.—Welcome, good friends.—O, my old friend? Why, thy face is valanc'd since I saw thee last. Com'st thou to beard me in Denmark?—What, my young lady and mistress? By'r Lady, your ladyship is nearer to heaven than when I saw you last by the altitude of a chopine. Pray God your voice, like a piece of uncurrent gold, be not crack'd within the ring.—Masters, you are all welcome. We'll e'en to't like French falconers, fly at anything we see. We'll have a speech straight. Come, give us a taste of your quality. Come, a passionate speech.

1. PLAY. What speech, my good lord?

HAM. I heard thee speak me a speech once, but it was never acted; or if it was, not above once; for the play, I remember, pleas'd not the million, 'twas caviary to the general; but it was (as I receiv'd it, and others, whose judgments in such matters cried in the top of mine) an excellent play, well digested in the scenes, set down with as much modesty as cunning. I remember one said there were no sallets in the lines to make the matter savoury, nor no matter in the phrase that might indict the author of affectation; but call'd it an honest method, as wholesome as sweet, and by very much more handsome than fine. One speech in't I chiefly lov'd. 'Twas Æneas' tale to Dido, and thereabout of it especially where he speaks of Priam's slaughter. If it live in your memory, begin at this line—let me see, let me see:

'The rugged Pyrrhus, like th' Hyrcanian beast—'
'Tis not so; it begins with Pyrrhus:

'The rugged Pyrrhus, he whose sable arms,
Black as his purpose, did the night resemble
When he lay couched in the ominous horse,
Hath now this dread and black complexion smear'd
With heraldry more dismal. Head to foot
Now is he total gules, horridly trick'd
With blood of fathers, mothers, daughters, sons,
Bak'd and impasted with the parching streets,
That lend a tyrannous and a damned light
To their lord's murther. Roasted in wrath and fire,
And thus o'ersized with coagulate gore,
With eyes like carbuncles, the hellish Pyrrhus
Old grandsire Priam seeks.'

So, proceed you.

POL. Fore God, my lord, well spoken, with good accent and good discretion.

1. PLAY. 'Anon he finds him,
Striking too short at Greeks. His antique sword,
Rebellious to his arm, lies where it falls,
Repugnant to command. Unequal match'd,
Pyrrhus at Priam drives, in rage strikes wide;
But with the whiff and wind of his fell sword

Th' unnerved father falls. Then senseless Ilium,
Seeming to feel this blow, with flaming top
Stoops to his base, and with a hideous crash
Takes prisoner Pyrrhus' ear. For lo! his sword,
Which was declining on the milky head
Of reverend Priam, seem'd i' th' air to stick.
So, as a painted tyrant, Pyrrhus stood,
And, like a neutral to his will and matter,
Did nothing.
But, as we often see, against some storm,
A silence in the heavens, the rack stand still,
The bold winds speechless, and the orb below
As hush as death—anon the dreadful thunder
Doth rend the region; so, after Pyrrhus' pause,
Aroused vengeance sets him new awork;
And never did the Cyclops' hammers fall
On Mars's armour, forg'd for proof eterne,
With less remorse than Pyrrhus' bleeding sword
Now falls on Priam.
Out, out, thou strumpet Fortune! All you gods,
In general synod take away her power;
Break all the spokes and fellies from her wheel,
And bowl the round nave down the hill of heaven,
As low as to the fiends!'

POL. This is too long.

HAM. It shall to the barber's, with your beard.—Prithee
say on. He's for a jig or a tale of bawdry, or he sleeps.
Say on; come to Hecuba.

1. PLAY. 'But who, O who, had seen the mobled
       queen—'

HAM. 'The mobled queen'?

POL. That's good! 'Mobled queen' is good.

1 PLAY. 'Run barefoot up and down, threat'ning the
       flames
With bisson rheum; a clout upon that head

Where late the diadem stood, and for a robe,
About her lank and all o'erteemed loins,
A blanket, in the alarm of fear caught up—
Who this had seen, with tongue in venom steep'd
'Gainst Fortune's state would treason have pronounc'd.
But if the gods themselves did see her then,
When she saw Pyrrhus make malicious sport
In mincing with his sword her husband's limbs,
The instant burst of clamour that she made
(Unless things mortal move them not at all)
Would have made milch the burning eyes of heaven
And passion in the gods.'

POL. Look, whe'r he has not turn'd his colour, and has tears in's eyes. Prithee no more!

HAM. 'Tis well. I'll have thee speak out the rest of this soon.—Good my lord, will you see the players well bestow'd? Do you hear? Let them be well us'd; for they are the abstract and brief chronicles of the time. After your death you were better have a bad epitaph than their ill report while you live.

POL. My lord, I will use them according to their desert.

HAM. God's bodykins, man, much better! Use every man after his desert, and who should scape whipping? Use them after your own honour and dignity. The less they deserve, the more merit is in your bounty. Take them in.

POL. Come, sirs.

HAM. Follow him, friends. We'll hear a play to-morrow.

[*Exeunt* POLONIUS *and* PLAYERS *except the* FIRST.]
Dost thou hear me, old friend? Can you play 'The Murther of Gonzago'?

1. PLAY. Ay, my lord.

HAM. We'll ha't to-morrow night. You could, for a

need, study a speech of some dozen or sixteen lines which
I would set down and insert in't, could you not?

1. PLAY. Ay, my lord.

HAM. Very well. Follow that lord—and look you mock
him not. [*Exit* FIRST PLAYER.] My good friends, I'll
leave you till night. You are welcome to Elsinore.

Ros. Good my lord!

HAM. Ay, so, God b' wi' ye!

       [*Exeunt* ROSENCRANTZ *and* GUILDENSTERN.]
                 Now I am alone.

O, what a rogue and peasant slave am I!
Is it not monstrous that this player here,
But in a fiction, in a dream of passion,
Could force his soul so to his own conceit
That, from her working, all his visage wann'd,
Tears in his eyes, distraction in's aspect,
A broken voice, and his whole function suiting
With forms to his conceit? And all for nothing!
For Hecuba!
What's Hecuba to him, or he to Hecuba,
That he should weep for her? What would he do,
Had he the motive and the cue for passion
That I have? He would drown the stage with tears
And cleave the general ear with horrid speech;
Make mad the guilty and appal the free,
Confound the ignorant, and amaze indeed
The very faculties of eyes and ears.
Yet I,
A dull and muddy-mettled rascal, peak
Like John-a-dreams, unpregnant of my cause,
And can say nothing! No, not for a king,
Upon whose property and most dear life
A damn'd defeat was made. Am I a coward?
Who calls me villain? breaks my pate across?

Plucks off my beard and blows it in my face?
Tweaks me by th' nose? gives me the lie i' th' throat
As deep as to the lungs? Who does me this, ha?
'Swounds, I should take it! for it cannot be
But I am pigeon-liver'd and lack gall
To make oppression bitter, or ere this
I should have fatted all the region kites,
With this slave's offal. Bloody, bawdy villain!
Remorseless, treacherous, lecherous, kindless villain!
O, vengeance!
Why, what an ass am I! This is most brave,
That I, the son of a dear father murther'd,
Prompted to my revenge by heaven and hell,
Must (like a whore) unpack my heart with words
And fall a-cursing like a very drab,
A scullion!
Fie upon't! foh! About, my brain! Hum, I have heard
That guilty creatures, sitting at a play,
Have by the very cunning of the scene
Been struck so to the soul that presently
They have proclaim'd their malefactions;
For murther, though it have no tongue, will speak
With most miraculous organ. I'll have these players
Play something like the murther of my father
Before mine uncle. I'll observe his looks;
I'll tent him to the quick. If he but blench,
I know my course. The spirit that I have seen
May be a devil; and the devil hath power
T' assume a pleasing shape; yea, and perhaps
Out of my weakness and my melancholy,
As he is very potent with such spirits,
Abuses me to damn me. I'll have grounds
More relative than this. The play's the thing
Wherein I'll catch the conscience of the King. *Exit.*

Act III: Scene I: Elsinore. A room in the Castle.

Enter KING, QUEEN, POLONIUS, OPHELIA, ROSENCRANTZ,
GUILDENSTERN, *and* LORDS.

KING. And can you by no drift of circumstance
Get from him why he puts on this confusion,
Grating so harshly all his days of quiet
With turbulent and dangerous lunacy?

ROS. He does confess he feels himself distracted,
But from what cause he will by no means speak.

GUIL. Nor do we find him forward to be sounded,
But with a crafty madness keeps aloof
When we would bring him on to some confession
Of his true state.

QUEEN.   Did he receive you well?

ROS. Most like a gentleman.

GUIL. But with much forcing of his disposition.

ROS. Niggard of question, but of our demands
Most free in his reply.

QUEEN.   Did you assay him
To any pastime?

ROS. Madam, it so fell out that certain players
We o'erraught on the way. Of these we told him,
And there did seem in him a kind of joy
To hear of it. They are here about the court,
And, as I think, they have already order
This night to play before him.

POL.   'Tis most true;
And he beseech'd me to entreat your Majesties
To hear and see the matter.

KING. With all my heart, and it doth much content me
To hear him so inclin'd.
Good gentlemen, give him a further edge

And drive his purpose on to these delights.

Ros. We shall, my lord.

Exeunt ROSENCRANTZ *and* GUILDENSTERN.

KING.   Sweet Gertrude, leave us too;
For we have closely sent for Hamlet hither,
That he, as 'twere by accident, may here
Affront Ophelia.
Her father and myself (lawful espials)
Will so bestow ourselves that, seeing unseen,
We may of their encounter frankly judge
And gather by him, as he is behav'd,
If't be th' affliction of his love, or no,
That thus he suffers for.

QUEEN.   I shall obey you;
And for your part, Ophelia, I do wish
That your good beauties be the happy cause
Of Hamlet's wildness. So shall I hope your virtues
Will bring him to his wonted way again,
To both your honours.

OPH.   Madam, I wish it may.

Exit QUEEN.

POL. Ophelia, walk you here.—Gracious, so please
    you,
We will bestow ourselves.—[*To* OPHELIA] Read on this
    book,
That show of such an exercise may colour
Your loneliness.—We are oft to blame in this,
'Tis too much prov'd, that with devotion's visage
And pious action we do sugar o'er
The devil himself.

KING. [*aside*] O, 'tis too true!
How smart a lash that speech doth give my conscience!
The harlot's cheek, beautied with plast'ring art,
Is not more ugly to the thing that helps it

Than is my deed to my most painted word.
O heavy burthen!

POL. I hear him coming. Let's withdraw, my lord.
                    Exeunt KING *and* POLONIUS.

Enter HAMLET.

HAM. To be, or not to be—that is the question:
Whether 'tis nobler in the mind to suffer
The slings and arrows of outrageous fortune
Or to take arms against a sea of troubles,
And by opposing end them. To die—to sleep—
No more; and by a sleep to say we end
The heartache, and the thousand natural shocks
That flesh is heir to. 'Tis a consummation
Devoutly to be wish'd. To die—to sleep.
To sleep—perchance to dream: ay, there's the rub!
For in that sleep of death what dreams may come
When we have shuffled off this mortal coil,
Must give us pause. There's the respect
That makes calamity of so long life.
For who would bear the whips and scorns of time,
Th' oppressor's wrong, the proud man's contumely,
The pangs of despis'd love, the law's delay,
The insolence of office, and the spurns
That patient merit of th' unworthy takes,
When he himself might his quietus make
With a bare bodkin? Who would these fardels bear,
To grunt and sweat under a weary life,
But that the dread of something after death—
The undiscover'd country, from whose bourn
No traveller returns—puzzles the will,
And makes us rather bear those ills we have
Than fly to others that we know not of?
Thus conscience does make cowards of us all,

And thus the native hue of resolution
Is sicklied o'er with the pale cast of thought,
And enterprises of great pith and moment
With this regard their currents turn awry
And lose the name of action.—Soft you now!
The fair Ophelia!—Nymph, in thy orisons
Be all my sins rememb'red.

OPH.   Good my lord,
How does your honour for this many a day?

HAM. I humbly thank you; well, well, well.

OPH. My lord, I have remembrances of yours
That I have longed long to re-deliver.
I pray you, now receive them.

HAM.   No, not I!
I never gave you aught.

OPH. My honour'd lord, you know right well you did,
And with them words of so sweet breath compos'd
As made the things more rich. Their perfume lost,
Take these again; for to the noble mind
Rich gifts wax poor when givers prove unkind.
There, my lord.

HAM. Ha, ha! Are you honest?

OPH. My lord?

HAM. Are you fair?

OPH. What means your lordship?

HAM. That if you be honest and fair, your honesty
should admit no discourse to your beauty.

OPH. Could beauty, my lord, have better commerce
than with honesty?

HAM. Ay, truly; for the power of beauty will sooner
transform honesty from what it is to a bawd than the
force of honesty can translate beauty into his likeness.
This was sometime a paradox, but now the time gives it
proof. I did love you once.

OPH. Indeed, my lord, you made me believe so.

HAM. You should not have believ'd me; for virtue cannot so inoculate our old stock but we shall relish of it. I loved you not.

OPH. I was the more deceived.

HAM. Get thee to a nunnery! Why wouldst thou be a breeder of sinners? I am myself indifferent honest, but yet I could accuse me of such things that it were better my mother had not borne me. I am very proud, revengeful, ambitious; with more offences at my beck than I have thoughts to put them in, imagination to give them shape, or time to act them in. What should such fellows as I do, crawling between earth and heaven? We are arrant knaves all; believe none of us. Go thy ways to a nunnery. Where's your father?

OPH. At home, my lord.

HAM. Let the doors be shut upon him, that he may play the fool nowhere but in's own house. Farewell.

OPH. O, help him, you sweet heavens!

HAM. If thou dost marry, I'll give thee this plague for thy dowry: be thou as chaste as ice, as pure as snow, thou shalt not escape calumny. Get thee to a nunnery. Go, farewell. Or if thou wilt needs marry, marry a fool; for wise men know well enough what monsters you make of them. To a nunnery, go; and quickly too. Farewell.

OPH. O heavenly powers, restore him!

HAM. I have heard of your paintings too, well enough. God hath given you one face, and you make yourselves another. You jig, you amble, and you lisp; you nickname God's creatures and make your wantonness your ignorance. Go to, I'll no more on't! it hath made me mad. I say, we will have no moe marriages. Those that are married already—all but one—shall live; the rest shall keep as they are. To a nunnery, go.   *Exit*.

OPH. O, what a noble mind is here o'er-thrown!
The courtier's, scholar's, soldier's, eye, tongue, sword,

Th' expectancy and rose of the fair state,
The glass of fashion and the mould of form,
Th' observ'd of all observers—quite, quite down!
And I, of ladies most deject and wretched,
That suck'd the honey of his music vows,
Now see that noble and most sovereign reason,
Like sweet bells jangled, out of tune and harsh;
That unmatch'd form and feature of blown youth
Blasted with ecstasy. O, woe is me
T' have seen what I have seen, see what I see!

Enter KING *and* POLONIUS.

KING. Love? his affections do not that way tend;
Nor what he spake, though it lack'd form a little,
Was not like madness. There's something in his soul
O'er which his melancholy sits on brood;
And I do doubt the hatch and the disclose
Will be some danger; which for to prevent,
I have in quick determination
Thus set it down: he shall with speed to England
For the demand of our neglected tribute.
Haply the seas, and countries different,
With variable objects, shall expel
This something-settled matter in his heart,
Whereon his brains still beating puts him thus
From fashion of himself. What think you on't?

POL. It shall do well. But yet do I believe
The origin and commencement of his grief
Sprung from neglected love.—How now, Ophelia?
You need not tell us what Lord Hamlet said.
We heard it all.—My lord, do as you please;
But if you hold it fit, after the play
Let his queen mother all alone entreat him
To show his grief. Let her be round with him;
And I'll be plac'd, so please you, in the ear

Of all their conference. If she find him not,
To England send him; or confine him where
Your wisdom best shall think.

    KING.   It shall be so.
Madness in great ones must not unwatch'd go.

Exeunt.

Scene II: Elsinore. A hall in the Castle.

Enter HAMLET *and three of the* PLAYERS.

    HAM. Speak the speech, I pray you, as I pronounc'd it to you, trippingly on the tongue. But if you mouth it, as many of our players do, I had as live the town crier spoke my lines. Nor do not saw the air too much with your hand, thus, but use all gently; for in the very torrent, tempest, and (as I may say) whirlwind of your passion, you must acquire and beget a temperance that may give it smoothness. O, it offends me to the soul to hear a robustious periwig-pated fellow tear a passion to tatters, to very rags, to split the ears of the groundlings, who (for the most part) are capable of nothing but inexplicable dumb shows and noise. I would have such a fellow whipp'd for o'erdoing Termagant. It out-herods Herod. Pray you avoid it.

    PLAYER. I warrant your honour.

    HAM. Be not too tame neither; but let your own discretion be your tutor. Suit the action to the word, the word to the action; with this special observance, that you o'erstep not the modesty of nature: for anything so overdone is from the purpose of playing, whose end, both at the first and now, was and is, to hold, as 'twere, the mirror up to nature; to show virtue her own feature, scorn her own image, and the very age and body of the time his form and pressure. Now this overdone, or come tardy off, though it make the unskilful laugh, cannot but make the judicious grieve; the censure of the which one must in your allowance o'erweigh a whole theatre of others. O, there be players that I have seen play, and heard others praise, and that highly (not to speak it profanely), that, neither having the accent of Christians, nor the gait of Christian, pagan, nor man, have so strutted and bellowed that I have thought some of Nature's journeymen had made men, and not made them well, they imitated humanity so abominably.

PLAYER. I hope we have reform'd that indifferently with us, sir.

HAM. O, reform it altogether! And let those that play your clowns speak no more than is set down for them. For there be of them that will themselves laugh, to set on some quantity of barren spectators to laugh too, though in the mean time some necessary question of the play be then to be considered. That's villanous and shows a most pitiful ambition in the fool that uses it. Go make you ready.

[*Exeunt* PLAYERS. *Enter* POLONIUS, ROSENCRANTZ, *and* GUILDENSTERN.]

How now, my lord? Will the King hear this piece of work?

POL. And the Queen too, and that presently.

HAM. Bid the players make haste [*Exit* POLONIUS.] Will you two help to hasten them?

BOTH. We will, my lord. *Exeunt they two.*

HAM. What, ho, Horatio!

Enter HORATIO.

HOR. Here, sweet lord, at your service.

HAM. Horatio, thou art e'en as just a man
As e'er my conversation cop'd withal.

Hor. O, my dear lord!

Ham.   Nay, do not think I flatter;
For what advancement may I hope from thee,
That no revenue hast but thy good spirits
To feed and clothe thee? Why should the poor be flatter'd?
No, let the candied tongue lick absurd pomp,
And crook the pregnant hinges of the knee
Where thrift may follow fawning. Dost thou hear?
Since my dear soul was mistress of her choice
And could of men distinguish, her election
Hath seal'd thee for herself. For thou hast been
As one, in suff'ring all, that suffers nothing;
A man that Fortune's buffets and rewards
Hast ta'en with equal thanks; and blest are those
Whose blood and judgment are so well commingled
That they are not a pipe for Fortune's finger
To sound what stop she please. Give me that man
That is not passion's slave, and I will wear him
In my heart's core, ay, in my heart of heart,
As I do thee. Something too much of this!
There is a play to-night before the King.
One scene of it comes near the circumstance,
Which I have told thee, of my father's death.
I prithee, when thou seest that act afoot,
Even with the very comment of thy soul
Observe my uncle. If his occulted guilt
Do not itself unkennel in one speech,
It is a damned ghost that we have seen,
And my imaginations are as foul
As Vulcan's stithy. Give him heedful note;
For I mine eyes will rivet to his face,
And after we will both our judgments join
In censure of his seeming.

Hor.　　　　　　　　Well, my lord.
If he steal aught the whilst this play is playing,
And scape detecting, I will pay the theft.
Sound a flourish. Enter Trumpets and Kettledrums.
Danish march. Enter King, Queen, Polonius, Ophelia,
Rosencrantz, Guildenstern, *and other* Lords *attend-*
　　　　　　ant, with the Guard *carrying torches.*

Ham. They are coming to the play. I must be idle.
Get you a place.

King. How fares our cousin Hamlet?

Ham. Excellent, i'faith; of the chameleon's dish. I eat
the air, promise-cramm'd. You cannot feed capons so.

King. I have nothing with this answer, Hamlet. These
words are not mine.

Ham. No, nor mine now. [*To* Polonius] My lord, you
play'd once i' th' university, you say?

Pol. That did I, my lord, and was accounted a good
actor.

Ham. What did you enact?

Pol. I did enact Julius Cæsar; I was kill'd i' th' Capitol;
Brutus kill'd me.

Ham. It was a brute part of him to kill so capital a
calf there. Be the players ready?

Ros. Ay, my lord. They stay upon your patience.

Queen. Come hither, my dear Hamlet, sit by me.

Ham. No, good mother. Here's metal more attractive.

Pol. [*to the* King] O, ho! do you mark that?

Ham. Lady, shall I lie in your lap?
　　　　　　　　　　　　Sits down at Ophelia's *feet.*

Oph. No, my lord.

Ham. I mean, my head upon your lap?

Oph. Ay, my lord.

Ham. Do you think I meant country matters?

Oph. I think nothing, my lord.

Ham. That's a fair thought to lie between maid's legs.

OPH. What is, my lord?

HAM. Nothing.

OPH. You are merry, my lord.

HAM. Who, I?

OPH. Ay, my lord.

HAM. O God, your only jig-maker! What should a man do but be merry? For look you how cheerfully my mother looks, and my father died within 's two hours.

OPH. Nay, 'tis twice two months, my lord.

HAM. So long? Nay then, let the devil wear black, for I'll have a suit of sables. O heavens! die two months ago, and not forgotten yet? Then there's hope a great man's memory may outlive his life half a year. But, by'r Lady, he must build churches then; or else shall he suffer not thinking on, with the hobby-horse, whose epitaph is 'For O, for O, the hobby-horse is forgot!'

HAUTBOYS *play. The dumb show enters. Enter a* KING *and a* QUEEN *very lovingly; the* QUEEN *embracing him, and he her. She kneels, and makes show of protestation unto him. He takes her up, and declines his head upon her neck. He lays him down upon a bank of flowers. She, seeing him asleep, leaves him. Anon comes in a fellow, takes off his crown, kisses it, pours poison in the sleeper's ears, and leaves him. The* QUEEN *returns, finds the* KING *dead, and makes passionate action. The* POISONER *with some three or four* MUTES, *come in again, seem to condole with her. The dead body is carried away. The* POISONER *woos the* QUEEN *with gifts; she seems harsh and unwilling awhile, but in the end accepts his love.*
Exeunt.

OPH. What means this, my lord?

HAM. Marry, this is miching malhecho; it means mischief.

OPH. Belike this show imports the argument of the play.

Enter PROLOGUE.

HAM. We shall know by this fellow. The players cannot keep counsel; they'll tell all.

OPH. Will he tell us what this show meant?

HAM. Ay, or any show that you'll show him. Be not you asham'd to show, he'll not shame to tell you what it means.

OPH. You are naught, you are naught! I'll mark the play.

PRO. For us, and for our tragedy,
        Here stooping to your clemency,
        We beg your hearing patiently.   *Exit.*

HAM. Is this a prologue, or the posy of a ring?

OPH. 'Tis brief, my lord.

HAM. As woman's love.

        Enter two PLAYERS *as* KING *and* QUEEN.

KING. Full thirty times hath Phœbus' cart gone round
Neptune's salt wash and Tellus' orbed ground,
And thirty dozen moons with borrowed sheen
About the world have times twelve thirties been,
Since love our hearts, and Hymen did our hands,
Unite comutual in most sacred bands.

QUEEN. So many journeys may the sun and moon
Make us again count o'er ere love be done!
But woe is me! you are so sick of late,
So far from cheer and from your former state,
That I distrust you. Yet, though I distrust,
Discomfort you, my lord, it nothing must;
For women's fear and love holds quantity,
In neither aught, or in extremity
Now what my love is, proof hath made you know;
And as my love is siz'd, my fear is so.
Where love is great, the littlest doubts are fear;
Where little fears grow great, great love grows there.

KING. Faith, I must leave thee, love, and shortly too;

My operant powers their functions leave to do.
And thou shalt live in this fair world behind,
Honour'd, belov'd, and haply one as kind
For husband shalt thou—

QUEEN.   O, confound the rest!
Such love must needs be treason in my breast.
In second husband let me be accurst!
None wed the second but who kill'd the first.

HAM. [*aside*] Wormwood, wormwood!

QUEEN. The instances that second marriage move
Are base respects of thrift, but none of love.
A second time I kill my husband dead
When second husband kisses me in bed.

KING. I do believe you think what now you speak;
But what we do determine oft we break.
Purpose is but the slave to memory,
Of violent birth, but poor validity;
Which now, like fruit unripe, sticks on the tree,
But fall unshaken when they mellow be.
Most necessary 'tis that we forget
To pay ourselves what to ourselves is debt.
What to ourselves in passion we propose,
The passion ending, doth the purpose lose.
The violence of either grief or joy
Their own enactures with themselves destroy.
Where joy most revels, grief doth most lament;
Grief joys, joy grieves, on slender accident.
This world is not for aye, nor 'tis not strange
That even our loves should with our fortunes change;
For 'tis a question left us yet to prove,
Whether love lead fortune or else fortune love.
The great man down, you mark his favourite flies,
The poor advanc'd makes friends of enemies;
And hitherto doth love on fortune tend,
For who not needs shall never lack a friend,

And who in want a hollow friend doth try,
Directly seasons him his enemy.
But, orderly to end where I begun,
Our wills and fates do so contrary run
That our devices still are overthrown;
Our thoughts are ours, their ends none of our own.
So think thou wilt no second husband wed;
But die thy thoughts when thy first lord is dead.

QUEEN. Nor earth to me give food, nor heaven light,
Sport and repose lock from me day and night,
To desperation turn my trust and hope,
An anchor's cheer in prison be my scope,
Each opposite that blanks the face of joy
Meet what I would have well, and it destroy,
Both here and hence pursue me lasting strife,
If, once a widow, ever I be wife!

HAM. If she should break it now!

KING. 'Tis deeply sworn. Sweet, leave me here awhile.
My spirits grow dull, and fain I would beguile
The tedious day with sleep.

QUEEN.   Sleep rock thy brain,

[*He sleeps.*]

And never come mischance between us twain!   *Exit.*

HAM. Madam, how like you this play?

QUEEN. The lady doth protest too much, methinks.

HAM. O, but she'll keep her word.

KING. Have you heard the argument? Is there no offence in't?

HAM. No, no! They do but jest, poison in jest; no offence i' th' world.

KING. What do you call the play?

HAM. 'The Mousetrap.' Marry, how? Tropically. This play is the image of a murther done in Vienna. Gonzago is the duke's name; his wife, Baptista. You shall see

anon. 'Tis a knavish piece of work; but what o' that? Your
Majesty, and we that have free souls, it touches us not.
Let the gall'd jade winch; our withers are unwrung.

[Enter LUCIANUS.]

This is one Lucianus, nephew to the King.

OPH. You are as good as a chorus, my lord.

HAM. I could interpret between you and your love,
if I could see the puppets dallying.

OPH. You are keen, my lord, you are keen.

HAM. It would cost you a groaning to take off my edge.

OPH. Still better, and worse.

HAM. So you must take your husbands.—Begin, murtherer. Pox, leave thy damnable faces, and begin! Come,
the croaking raven doth bellow for revenge.

LUC. Thoughts black, hands apt, drugs fit, and time
      agreeing;
Confederate season, else no creature seeing;
Thou mixture rank, of midnight weeds collected,
With Hecate's ban thrice blasted, thrice infected,
Thy natural magic and dire property
On wholesome life usurp immediately.

                Pours the poison in his ears.

HAM. He poisons him i' th' garden for's estate. His
name's Gonzago. The story is extant, and written in very
choice Italian. You shall see anon how the murtherer
gets the love of Gonzago's wife.

OPH. The King rises.

HAM. What, frighted with false fire?

QUEEN. How fares my lord?

POL. Give o'er the play.

KING. Give me some light! Away!

ALL. Lights, lights, lights!

              Exeunt all but HAMLET *and* HORATIO.

Ham. Why, let the strucken deer go weep,
>   The hart ungalled play;
>   For some must watch, while some must sleep:
>   Thus runs the world away.

Would not this, sir, and a forest of feathers—if the rest
of my fortunes turn Turk with me—with two Provincial
roses on my raz'd shoes, get me a fellowship in a cry of
players, sir?

Hor. Half a share.

Ham. A whole one I!
>   For thou dost know, O Damon dear,
>   This realm dismantled was
>   Of Jove himself; and now reigns here
>   A very, very—pajock.

Hor. You might have rhym'd.

Ham. O good Horatio, I'll take the ghost's word for
a thousand pound! Didst perceive?

Hor. Very well, my lord.

Ham. Upon the talk of the poisoning?

Hor. I did very well note him.

Ham. Aha! Come, some music! Come, the recorders!
>   For if the King like not the comedy,
>   Why then, belike he likes it not, perdy.

Come, some music!

Enter Rosencrantz *and* Guildenstern.

Guil. Good my lord, vouchsafe me a word with you.

Ham. Sir, a whole history.

Guil. The King, sir—

Ham. Ay, sir, what of him?

Guil. Is in his retirement, marvellous distemper'd.

Ham. With drink, sir?

Guil. No, my lord; rather with choler.

Ham. Your wisdom should show itself more richer to

signify this to the doctor; for for me to put him to his purgation would perhaps plunge him into far more choler.

GUIL. Good my lord, put your discourse into some frame, and start not so wildly from my affair.

HAM. I am tame, sir; pronounce.

GUIL. The Queen, your mother, in most great affliction of spirit hath sent me to you.

HAM. You are welcome.

GUIL. Nay, good my lord, this courtesy is not of the right breed. If it shall please you to make me a wholesome answer, I will do your mother's commandment; if not, your pardon and my return shall be the end of my business.

HAM. Sir, I cannot.

GUIL. What, my lord?

HAM. Make you a wholesome answer; my wit's diseas'd. But, sir, such answer as I can make, you shall command; or rather, as you say, my mother. Therefore no more, but to the matter! My mother, you say—

ROS. Then thus she says: your behaviour hath struck her into amazement and admiration.

HAM. O wonderful son, that can so stonish a mother! But is there no sequel at the heels of this mother's admiration? Impart.

ROS. She desires to speak with you in her closet ere you go to bed.

HAM. We shall obey, were she ten times our mother. Have you any further trade with us?

ROS. My lord, you once did love me.

HAM. And do still, by these pickers and stealers!

ROS. Good my lord, what is your cause of distemper? You do surely bar the door upon your own liberty, if you deny your griefs to your friend.

HAM. Sir, I lack advancement.

Ros. How can that be, when you have the voice of the King himself for your succession in Denmark?

Ham. Ay, sir, but 'while the grass grows'—the proverb is something musty.

[*Enter the* Players *with recorders.*]

O, the recorders! Let me see one. To withdraw with you —why do you go about to recover the wind of me, as if you would drive me into a toil?

Guil. O my lord, if my duty be too bold, my love is too unmannerly.

Ham. I do not well understand that. Will you play upon this pipe?

Guil. My lord, I cannot.

Ham. I pray you.

Guil. Believe me, I cannot.

Ham. I do beseech you.

Guil. I know no touch of it, my lord.

Ham. It is as easy as lying. Govern these vantages with your fingers and thumbs, give it breath with your mouth, and it will discourse most eloquent music. Look you, these are the stops.

Guil. But these cannot I command to any utt'rance of harmony. I have not the skill.

Ham. Why, look you now, how unworthy a thing you make of me! You would play upon me; you would seem to know my stops; you would pluck out the heart of my mystery; you would sound me from my lowest note to the top of my compass; and there is much music, excellent voice, in this little organ, yet cannot you make it speak. 'Sblood, do you think I am easier to be play'd on than a pipe? Call me what instrument you will, though you can fret me, you cannot play upon me.

[*Enter* Polonius.]

God bless you, sir!

POL. My lord, the Queen would speak with you and presently.

HAM. Do you see yonder cloud that's almost in shape of a camel?

POL. By th' mass, and 'tis like a camel indeed.

HAM. Methinks it is like a weasel.

POL. It is back'd like a weasel.

HAM. Or like a whale.

POL. Very like a whale.

HAM. Then will I come to my mother by-and-by.—They fool me to the top of my bent.—I will come by-and-by.

POL. I will say so.   *Exit.*

HAM. 'By-and-by' is easily said.—Leave me, friends.

Exeunt all but HAMLET.

'Tis now the very witching time of night,
When churchyards yawn, and hell itself breathes out
Contagion to this world. Now could I drink hot blood
And do such bitter business as the day
Would quake to look on. Soft! now to my mother!
O heart, lose not thy nature; let not ever
The soul of Nero enter this firm bosom.
Let me be cruel, not unnatural;
I will speak daggers to her, but use none.
My tongue and soul in this be hypocrites—
How in my words somever she be shent,
To give them seals never, my soul, consent!   *Exit.*

Scene III: A room in the Castle.

Enter KING, ROSENCRANTZ, *and* GUILDENSTERN.

KING. I like him not, nor stands it safe with us
To let his madness range. Therefore prepare you;
I your commission will forthwith dispatch,

And he to England shall along with you.
The terms of our estate may not endure
Hazard so near us as doth hourly grow
Out of his lunacies.

GUIL.   We will ourselves provide.
Most holy and religious fear it is
To keep those many many bodies safe
That live and feed upon your Majesty.

ROS. The single and peculiar life is bound
With all the strength and armour of the mind
To keep itself from noyance; but much more
That spirit upon whose weal depends and rests
The lives of many. The cesse of majesty
Dies not alone, but like a gulf doth draw
What's near it with it. It is a massy wheel,
Fix'd on the summit of the highest mount,
To whose huge spokes ten thousand lesser things
Are mortis'd and adjoin'd; which when it falls,
Each small annexment, petty consequence,
Attends the boist'rous ruin. Never alone
Did the king sigh, but with a general groan.

KING. Arm you, I pray you, to this speedy voyage;
For we will fetters put upon this fear,
Which now goes too free-footed.

BOTH.   We will haste us.

Exeunt GENTLEMEN. *Enter* POLONIUS.

POL. My lord, he's going to his mother's closet.
Behind the arras I'll convey myself
To hear the process. I'll warrant she'll tax him home;
And, as you said, and wisely was it said,
'Tis meet that some more audience than a mother,
Since nature makes them partial, should o'erhear
The speech, of vantage. Fare you well, my liege.
I'll call upon you ere you go to bed
And tell you what I know.

KING.   Thanks, dear my lord.

[*Exit* POLONIUS.]

O, my offence is rank, it smells to heaven;
It hath the primal eldest curse upon't,
A brother's murther! Pray can I not,
Though inclination be as sharp as will.
My stronger guilt defeats my strong intent,
And, like a man to double business bound,
I stand in pause where I shall first begin,
And both neglect. What if this cursed hand
Were thicker than itself with brother's blood,
Is there not rain enough in the sweet heavens
To wash it white as snow? Whereto serves mercy
But to confront the visage of offence?
And what's in prayer but this twofold force,
To be forestalled ere we come to fall,
Or pardon'd being down? Then I'll look up;
My fault is past. But, O, what form of prayer
Can serve my turn? 'Forgive me my foul murther'?
That cannot be; since I am still possess'd
Of those effects for which I did the murther—
My crown, mine own ambition, and my queen.
May one be pardon'd and retain th' offence?
In the corrupted currents of this world
Offence's gilded hand may shove by justice,
And oft 'tis seen the wicked prize itself
Buys out the law; but 'tis not so above.
There is no shuffling; there the action lies
In his true nature, and we ourselves compell'd,
Even to the teeth and forehead of our faults,
To give in evidence. What then? What rests?
Try what repentance can. What can it not?
Yet what can it when one cannot repent?
O wretched state! O bosom black as death!
O limed soul, that, struggling to be free,

Art more engag'd! Help, angels! Make assay.
Bow, stubborn knees; and heart with strings of steel,
Be soft as sinews of the new-born babe!
All may be well.　　　　　　　　　　　　　*He kneels.*

Enter HAMLET.

HAM. Now might I do it pat, now he is praying;
And now I'll do't. And so he goes to heaven,
And so am I reveng'd. That would be scann'd.
A villain kills my father; and for that,
I, his sole son, do this same villain send
To heaven.
Why, this is hire and salary, not revenge!
He took my father grossly, full of bread,
With all his crimes broad blown, as flush as May;
And how his audit stands, who knows save heaven?
But in our circumstance and course of thought,
'Tis heavy with him; and am I then reveng'd,
To take him in the purging of his soul,
When he is fit and season'd for his passage?
No.
Up, sword, and know thou a more horrid hent.
When he is drunk asleep; or in his rage;
Or in th' incestuous pleasure of his bed;
At gaming, swearing, or about some act
That has no relish of salvation in't—
Then trip him, that his heels may kick at heaven,
And that his soul may be as damn'd and black
As hell, whereto it goes. My mother stays.
This physic but prolongs thy sickly days.　　　*Exit.*
　KING. [*rises*] My words fly up, my thoughts remain
　　　below.
Words without thoughts never to heaven go.　*Exit.*

Scene IV: The Queen's closet.

Enter QUEEN *and* POLONIUS.

POL. He will come straight. Look you lay home to him.
Tell him his pranks have been too broad to bear with,
And that your Grace hath screen'd and stood between
Much heat and him. I'll silence me even here.
Pray you be round with him.

HAM. [*within*] Mother, mother, mother!

QUEEN. I'll warrant you; fear me not. Withdraw; I
hear him coming.

POLONIUS *hides behind the arras.*

Enter HAMLET.

HAM. Now, mother, what's the matter?

QUEEN. Hamlet, thou hast thy father much offended.

HAM. Mother, you have my father much offended.

QUEEN. Come, come, you answer with an idle tongue.

HAM. Go, go, you question with a wicked tongue.

QUEEN. Why, how now, Hamlet?

HAM.   What's the matter now?

QUEEN. Have you forgot me?

HAM.   No, by the rood, not so!
You are the Queen, your husband's brother's wife,
And (would it were not so!) you are my mother.

QUEEN. Nay, then I'll set those to you that can speak.

HAM. Come, come, and sit you down. You shall not
   budge!
You go not till I set you up a glass
Where you may see the inmost part of you.

QUEEN. What wilt thou do? Thou wilt not murther
   me?
Help, help, ho!

POL. [*behind*] What, ho! help, help, help!

HAM. [*draws*] How now? a rat? Dead for a ducat, dead!

   Makes a pass through the arras and kills POLONIUS.

POL. [*behind*] O, I am slain!

QUEEN.   O me, what hast thou done?

HAM. Nay, I know not. Is it the King?

QUEEN. O, what a rash and bloody deed is this!

HAM. A bloody deed—almost as bad, good mother,
As kill a king, and marry with his brother.

QUEEN. As kill a king?

HAM.   Ay, lady, it was my word.

     [*Lifts up the arras and sees* POLONIUS.]

Thou wretched, rash, intruding fool, farewell!
I took thee for thy better. Take thy fortune.
Thou find'st to be too busy is some danger.
Leave wringing of your hands. Peace! sit you down
And let me wring your heart; for so I shall
If it be made of penetrable stuff;
If damned custom have not braz'd it so
That it is proof and bulwark against sense.

QUEEN. What have I done that thou dar'st wag thy tongue
In noise so rude against me?

HAM.   Such an act
That blurs the grace and blush of modesty;
Calls virtue hypocrite; takes off the rose
From the fair forehead of an innocent love,
And sets a blister there; makes marriage vows
As false as dicers' oaths. O, such a deed
As from the body of contraction plucks
The very soul, and sweet religion makes
A rhapsody of words! Heaven's face doth glow;
Yea, this solidity and compound mass,
With tristful visage, as against the doom,
Is thought-sick at the act.

QUEEN.   Ay me, what act,
That roars so loud and thunders in the index?

HAM. Look here upon this picture, and on this,
The counterfeit presentment of two brothers.
See what a grace was seated on this brow;
Hyperion's curls; the front of Jove himself;
An eye like Mars, to threaten and command;
A station like the herald Mercury
New lighted on a heaven-kissing hill:
A combination and a form indeed
Where every god did seem to set his seal
To give the world assurance of a man.
This was your husband. Look you now what follows.
Here is your husband, like a mildew'd ear
Blasting his wholesome brother. Have you eyes?
Could you on this fair mountain leave to feed,
And batten on this moor? Ha! have you eyes?
You cannot call it love; for at your age
The heyday in the blood is tame, it's humble,
And waits upon the judgment; and what judgment
Would step from this to this? Sense sure you have,
Else could you not have motion; but sure that sense
Is apoplex'd; for madness would not err,
Nor sense to ecstasy was ne'er so thrall'd
But it reserv'd some quantity of choice
To serve in such a difference. What devil was't
That thus hath cozen'd you at hoodman-blind?
Eyes without feeling, feeling without sight,
Ears without hands or eyes, smelling sans all,
Or but a sickly part of one true sense
Could not so mope.
O shame! where is thy blush? Rebellious hell,
If thou canst mutine in a matron's bones,
To flaming youth let virtue be as wax
And melt in her own fire. Proclaim no shame

When the compulsive ardour gives the charge,
Since frost itself as actively doth burn,
And reason panders will.

QUEEN.   O Hamlet, speak no more!
Thou turn'st mine eyes into my very soul,
And there I see such black and grained spots
As will not leave their tinct.

HAM.   Nay, but to live
In the rank sweat of an enseamed bed,
Stew'd in corruption, honeying and making love
Over the nasty sty!

QUEEN.   O, speak to me no more!
These words like daggers enter in mine ears.
No more, sweet Hamlet!

HAM.   A murtherer and a villain!
A slave that is not twentieth part the tithe
Of your precedent lord; a vice of kings;
A cutpurse of the empire and the rule,
That from a shelf the precious diadem stole
And put it in his pocket!

QUEEN.   No more!

      Enter the GHOST *in his nightgown.*

HAM. A king of shreds and patches!—
Save me and hover o'er me with your wings,
You heavenly guards! What would your gracious figure?

QUEEN. Alas, he's mad!

HAM. Do you not come your tardy son to chide,
That, laps'd in time and passion, lets go by
Th' important acting of your dread command?
O, say!

GHOST. Do not forget. This visitation
Is but to whet thy almost blunted purpose.
But look, amazement on thy mother sits.
O, step between her and her fighting soul!

Conceit in weakest bodies strongest works.
Speak to her, Hamlet.

HAM.   How is it with you, lady?

QUEEN. Alas, how is't with you,
That you do bend your eye on vacancy,
And with th' incorporal air do hold discourse?
Forth at your eyes your spirits wildly peep;
And, as the sleeping soldiers in th' alarm,
Your bedded hairs, like life in excrements,
Start up and stand an end. O gentle son,
Upon the heat and flame of thy distemper
Sprinkle cool patience! Whereon do you look?

HAM. On him, on him! Look you how pale he glares!
His form and cause conjoin'd, preaching to stones,
Would make them capable.—Do not look upon me,
Lest with this piteous action you convert
My stern effects. Then what I have to do
Will want true colour—tears perchance for blood.

QUEEN. To whom do you speak this?

HAM.   Do you see nothing there?

QUEEN. Nothing at all; yet all that is I see.

HAM. Nor did you nothing hear?

QUEEN.   No, nothing but ourselves.

HAM. Why, look you there! Look how it steals away!
My father, in his habit as he liv'd!
Look where he goes even now out at the portal!

Exit GHOST.

QUEEN. This is the very coinage of your brain.
This bodiless creation ecstasy
Is very cunning in.

HAM.   Ecstasy?
My pulse as yours doth temperately keep time
And makes as healthful music. It is not madness
That I have utt'red. Bring me to the test,

And I the matter will reword; which madness
Would gambol from. Mother, for love of grace,
Lay not that flattering unction to your soul,
That not your trespass but my madness speaks.
It will but skin and film the ulcerous place,
Whiles rank corruption, mining all within,
Infects unseen. Confess yourself to heaven;
Repent what's past; avoid what is to come;
And do not spread the compost on the weeds
To make them ranker. Forgive me this my virtue;
For in the fatness of these pursy times
Virtue itself of vice must pardon beg—
Yea, curb and woo for leave to do him good.

 QUEEN. O Hamlet, thou hast cleft my heart in twain.
 HAM. O, throw away the worser part of it,
And live the purer with the other half.
Good night—but go not to my uncle's bed.
Assume a virtue, if you have it not.
That monster, custom, who all sense doth eat
Of habits evil, is angel yet in this,
That to the use of actions fair and good
He likewise gives a frock or livery,
That aptly is put on. Refrain to-night,
And that shall lend a kind of easiness
To the next abstinence; the next more easy;
For use almost can change the stamp of nature,
And either [master] the devil, or throw him out
With wondrous potency. Once more, good night;
And when you are desirous to be blest,
I'll blessing beg of you.—For this same lord,
I do repent; but heaven hath pleas'd it so,
To punish me with this, and this with me,
That I must be their scourge and minister.
I will bestow him, and will answer well

The death I gave him. So again, good night.
I must be cruel, only to be kind;
Thus bad begins, and worse remains behind.
One word more, good lady.

   QUEEN.   What shall I do?

   HAM. Not this, by no means, that I bid you do:
Let the bloat King tempt you again to bed;
Pinch wanton on your cheek; call you his mouse;
And let him, for a pair of reechy kisses,
Or paddling in your neck with his damn'd fingers,
Make you to ravel all this matter out,
That I essentially am not in madness,
But mad in craft. 'Twere good you let him know;
For who that's but a queen, fair, sober, wise,
Would from a paddock, from a bat, a gib,
Such dear concernings hide? Who would do so?
No, in despite of sense and secrecy,
Unpeg the basket on the house's top,
Let the birds fly, and like the famous ape,
To try conclusions, in the basket creep
And break your own neck down.

   QUEEN. Be thou assur'd, if words be made of breath,
And breath of life, I have no life to breathe
What thou hast said to me.

   HAM. I must to England; you know that?

   QUEEN.   Alack,
I had forgot! 'Tis so concluded on.

   HAM. There's letters seal'd; and my two schoolfellows,
Whom I will trust as I will adders fang'd,
They bear the mandate; they must sweep my way
And marshal me to knavery. Let it work;
For 'tis the sport to have the enginer
Hoist with his own petar; and 't shall go hard
But I will delve one yard below their mines

And blow them at the moon. O, 'tis most sweet
When in one line two crafts directly meet.
This man shall set me packing.
I'll lug the guts into the neighbour room.—
Mother, good night.—Indeed, this counsellor
Is now most still, most secret, and most grave,
Who was in life a foolish prating knave.
Come, sir, to draw toward an end with you.
Good night, mother.
Exit the QUEEN. *Then exit* HAMLET, *tugging in* POLONIUS.

Act IV: Scene I: Elsinore. A room in the Castle.

Enter KING *and* QUEEN, *with* ROSENCRANTZ
and GUILDENSTERN.

KING. There's matter in these sighs. These profound
      heaves
You must translate; 'tis fit we understand them.
Where is your son?
    QUEEN. Bestow this place on us a little while.
            [*Exeunt* ROSENCRANTZ *and* GUILDENSTERN.]
Ah, mine own lord, what have I seen to-night!
    KING. What, Gertrude? How does Hamlet?
    QUEEN. Mad as the sea and wind when both contend
Which is the mightier. In his lawless fit,
Behind the arras hearing something stir,
Whips out his rapier, cries 'A rat, a rat!'
And in this brainish apprehension kills
The unseen good old man.
    KING.   O heavy deed!
It had been so with us, had we been there.
His liberty is full of threats to all—
To you yourself, to us, to every one.

Alas, how shall this bloody deed be answer'd?
It will be laid to us, whose providence
Should have kept short, restrain'd, and out of haunt
This mad young man. But so much was our love
We would not understand what was most fit,
But, like the owner of a foul disease,
To keep it from divulging, let it feed
Even on the pith of life. Where is he gone?

    QUEEN. To draw apart the body he hath kill'd;
O'er whom his very madness, like some ore
Among a mineral of metals base,
Shows itself pure. He weeps for what is done.

    KING. O Gertrude, come away!
The sun no sooner shall the mountains touch
But we will ship him hence; and this vile deed
We must with all our majesty and skill
Both countenance and excuse. Ho, Guildenstern!

        [*Enter* ROSENCRANTZ *and* GUILDENSTERN.]

Friends, both, go join you with some further aid.
Hamlet in madness hath Polonius slain,
And from his mother's closet hath he dragg'd him.
Go seek him out; speak fair, and bring the body
Into the chapel. I pray you haste in this.

        [*Exeunt* ROSENCRANTZ *and* GUILDENSTERN.]
Come, Gertrude, we'll call up our wisest friends
And let them know both what we mean to do
And what's untimely done. [So haply slander—]
Whose whisper o'er the world's diameter,
As level as the cannon to his blank,
Transports his pois'ned shot—may miss our name
And hit the woundless air.—O, come away!
My soul is full of discord and dismay.

                         Exeunt.

Scene II: Elsinore. A passage in the Castle.

Enter HAMLET.

HAM. Safely stow'd.

GENTLEMEN. [*within*] Hamlet! Lord Hamlet!

HAM. But soft! What noise? Who calls on Hamlet?
O, here they come.

Enter ROSENCRANTZ *and* GUILDENSTERN.

ROS. What have you done, my lord, with the dead
　　body?

HAM. Compounded it with dust, whereto 'tis kin.

ROS. Tell us where 'tis, that we may take it thence
And bear it to the chapel.

HAM. Do not believe it.

ROS. Believe what?

HAM. That I can keep your counsel, and not mine own.
Besides, to be demanded of a sponge, what replication
should be made by the son of a king?

ROS. Take you me for a sponge, my lord?

HAM. Ay, sir; that soaks up the King's countenance,
his rewards, his authorities. But such officers do the
King best service in the end. He keeps them, like an ape,
in the corner of his jaw; first mouth'd, to be last swallowed. When he needs what you have glean'd, it is but
squeezing you and, sponge, you shall be dry again.

ROS. I understand you not, my lord.

HAM. I am glad of it. A knavish speech sleeps in a
foolish ear.

ROS. My lord, you must tell us where the body is and
go with us to the King.

HAM. The body is with the King, but the King is not
with the body. The King is a thing—

GUIL. A thing, my lord?

HAM. Of nothing. Bring me to him. Hide fox, and all
after.   *Exeunt.*

Scene III: Elsinore. A room in the Castle.

Enter KING.

KING. I have sent to seek him and to find the body.
How dangerous is it that this man goes loose!
Yet must not we put the strong law on him.
He's lov'd of the distracted multitude,
Who like not in their judgment, but their eyes;
And where 'tis so, th' offender's scourge is weigh'd,
But never the offence. To bear all smooth and even,
This sudden sending him away must seem
Deliberate pause. Diseases desperate grown
By desperate appliance are reliev'd,
Or not at all.

[*Enter* ROSENCRANTZ]

                              How now? What hath befall'n?
Ros. Where the dead body is bestow'd, my lord,
We cannot get from him.
KING.   But where is he?
Ros. Without, my lord; guarded, to know your
    pleasure.
KING. Bring him before us.
Ros. Ho, Guildenstern! Bring in my lord.
Enter HAMLET *and* GUILDENSTERN *with* ATTENDANTS.
KING. Now, Hamlet, where's Polonius?
HAM. At supper.
KING. At supper? Where?
HAM. Not where he eats, but where he is eaten. A
certain convocation of politic worms are e'en at him.
Your worm is your only emperor for diet. We fat all

creatures else to fat us, and we fat ourselves for maggots. Your fat king and your lean beggar is but variable service—two dishes, but to one table. That's the end.

KING. Alas, alas!

HAM. A man may fish with the worm that hath eat of a king, and eat of the fish that hath fed of that worm.

KING. What dost thou mean by this?

HAM. Nothing but to show you how a king may go a progress through the guts of a beggar.

KING. Where is Polonius?

HAM. In heaven. Send thither to see. If your messenger find him not there, seek him i' th' other place yourself. But indeed, if you find him not within this month, you shall nose him as you go up the stairs into the lobby.

KING. Go seek him there.   *To* ATTENDANTS.

HAM. He will stay till you come.

Exeunt ATTENDANTS.

KING. Hamlet, this deed, for thine especial safety,—
Which we do tender as we dearly grieve
For that which thou hast done,—must send thee hence
With fiery quickness. Therefore prepare thyself.
The bark is ready and the wind at help,
Th' associates tend, and everything is bent
For England.

HAM.   For England?

KING.   Ay, Hamlet.

HAM.   Good.

KING. So is it, if thou knew'st our purposes.

HAM. I see a cherub that sees them. But come, for England! Farewell, dear mother.

KING. Thy loving father, Hamlet.

HAM. My mother! Father and mother is man and wife; man and wife is one flesh; and so, my mother. Come, for England!   *Exit.*

KING. Follow him at foot; tempt him with speed
    aboard.
Delay it not; I'll have him hence to-night.
Away! for everything is seal'd and done
That else leans on th' affair. Pray you make haste.

        [Exeunt ROSENCRANTZ *and* GUILDENSTERN.]

And, England, if my love thou hold'st at aught,—
As my great power thereof may give thee sense,
Since yet thy cicatrice looks raw and red
After the Danish sword, and thy free awe
Pays homage to us,—thou mayst not coldly set
Our sovereign process, which imports at full,
By letters congruing to that effect,
The present death of Hamlet. Do it, England;
For like the hectic in my blood he rages,
And thou must cure me. Till I know 'tis done,
Howe'er my haps, my joys were ne'er begun.   *Exit.*

Scene IV: Near Elsinore.

Enter FORTINBRAS *with his* ARMY *over the stage.*

FOR. Go, Captain, from me greet the Danish king.
Tell him that by his license Fortinbras
Craves the conveyance of a promis'd march
Over his kingdom. You know the rendezvous.
If that his Majesty would aught with us,
We shall express our duty in his eye;
And let him know so.
    CAPT.   I will do't, my lord.
    FOR. Go softly on.   *Exeunt all but the* CAPTAIN.

    Enter HAMLET, ROSENCRANTZ, GUILDENSTERN,
                and others.

HAM. Good sir, whose powers are these?
CAPT. They are of Norway, sir.

HAM. How purpos'd, sir, I pray you?

CAPT. Against some part of Poland.

HAMLET. Who commands them, sir?

CAPT. The nephew to old Norway, Fortinbras.

HAM. Goes it against the main of Poland, sir,
Or for some frontier?

CAPT. Truly to speak, and with no addition,
We go to gain a little patch of ground
That hath in it no profit but the name.
To pay five ducats, five, I would not farm it;
Nor will it yield to Norway or the Pole
A ranker rate, should it be sold in fee.

HAM. Why, then the Polack never will defend it.

CAPT. Yes, it is already garrison'd.

HAM. Two thousand souls and twenty thousand ducats
Will not debate the question of this straw.
This is th' imposthume of much wealth and peace,
That inward breaks, and shows no cause without
Why the man dies.—I humbly thank you, sir.

CAPT. God b' wi' you, sir.   *Exit.*

ROS.   Will't please you go, my lord?

HAM. I'll be with you straight. Go a little before.

                         [*Exeunt all but* HAMLET.]

How all occasions do inform against me
And spur my dull revenge! What is a man,
If his chief good and market of his time
Be but to sleep and feed? A beast, no more.
Sure he that made us with such large discourse,
Looking before and after, gave us not
That capability and godlike reason
To fust in us unus'd. Now, whether it be
Bestial oblivion, or some craven scruple
Of thinking too precisely on th' event,—
A thought which, quarter'd, hath but one part wisdom
And ever three parts coward,—I do not know

Why yet I live to say 'This thing's to do,'
Sith I have cause, and will, and strength, and means
To do't. Examples gross as earth exhort me.
Witness this army of such mass and charge,
Led by a delicate and tender prince,
Whose spirit, with divine ambition puff'd,
Makes mouths at the invisible event,
Exposing what is mortal and unsure
To all that fortune, death, and danger dare,
Even for an eggshell. Rightly to be great
Is not to stir without great argument,
But greatly to find quarrel in a straw
When honour's at the stake. How stand I then,
That have a father kill'd, a mother stain'd,
Excitements of my reason and my blood,
And let all sleep, while to my shame I see
The imminent death of twenty thousand men
That for a fantasy and trick of fame
Go to their graves like beds, fight for a plot
Whereon the numbers cannot try the cause,
Which is not tomb enough and continent
To hide the slain? O, from this time forth,
My thoughts be bloody, or be nothing worth!

Exit.

Scene V: Elsinore. A room in the Castle.

Enter HORATIO, QUEEN, *and a* GENTLEMAN.

QUEEN. I will not speak with her.

GENT. She is importunate, indeed distract.
Her mood will needs be pitied.

QUEEN.   What would she have?

GENT. She speaks much of her father; says she hears
There's tricks i' th' world, and hems, and beats her heart;

Spurns enviously at straws; speaks things in doubt,
That carry but half sense. Her speech is nothing,
Yet the unshaped use of it doth move
The hearers to collection; they aim at it,
And botch the words up fit to their own thoughts;
Which, as her winks and nods and gestures yield them,
Indeed would make one think there might be thought,
Though nothing sure, yet much unhappily.

> HOR. 'Twere good she were spoken with; for she may strew

Dangerous conjectures in ill-breeding minds.

> QUEEN. Let her come in.

> > [*Exit* GENTLEMEN.]

[*Aside*] To my sick soul (as sin's true nature is)
Each toy seems prologue to some great amiss.
So full of artless jealousy is guilt
It spills itself in fearing to be spilt.

Enter OPHELIA *distracted.*

> OPH. Where is the beauteous Majesty of Denmark?
> QUEEN. How now, Ophelia?
> OPH. [*sings*] How should I your true-love know
> > From another one?
> > By his cockle hat and staff
> > And his sandal shoon.

> QUEEN. Alas, sweet lady, what imports this song?
> OPH. Say you? Nay, pray you mark.

[*Sings*] He is dead and gone, lady,
> > He is dead and gone;
> > At his head a grass-green turf,
> > At his heels a stone.

O, ho!

> QUEEN. Nay, but Ophelia—
> OPH. Pray you mark.

[*Sings*] White his shroud as the mountain snow—

Enter KING.

QUEEN. Alas, look here, my lord!

OPH. [*sings*] Larded all with sweet flowers;
> Which bewept to the grave did not go
> With true-love showers.

KING. How do you, pretty lady?

OPH. Well, God 'dild you! They say the owl was a baker's daughter. Lord, we know what we are, but know not what we may be. God be at your table!

KING. Conceit upon her father.

OPH. Pray let's have no words of this; but when they ask you what it means, say you this:

[*Sings*]   To-morrow is Saint Valentine's day,
> All in the morning betime,
> And I a maid at your window,
> To be your Valentine.
> Then up he rose and donn'd his clo'es
> And dupp'd the chamber door,
> Let in the maid, that out a maid
> Never departed more.

KING. Pretty Ophelia!

OPH. Indeed, la, without an oath, I'll make an end on't!

[*Sings*]   By Gis and by Saint Charity,
> Alack, and fie for shame!
> Young men will do't if they come to't.
> By Cock, they are to blame.
> Quoth she, 'Before you tumbled me,
> You promis'd me to wed.'

He answers:
> 'So would I 'a' done, by yonder sun,
> An thou hadst not come to my bed.'

KING. How long hath she been thus?

OPH. I hope all will be well. We must be patient; but I cannot choose but weep to think they would lay him

i' th' cold ground. My brother shall know of it; and so
I thank you for your good counsel. Come, my coach!
Good night, ladies. Good night, sweet ladies. Good
night, good night. *Exit.*

KING. Follow her close; give her good watch, I pray
you.

[*Exit Horatio.*]

O, this is the poison of deep grief; it springs
All from her father's death. O Gertrude, Gertrude,
When sorrows come, they come not single spies,
But in battalions! First, her father slain;
Next, your son gone, and he most violent author
Of his own just remove; the people muddied,
Thick and unwholesome in their thoughts and whispers
For good Polonius' death, and we have done but greenly
In hugger-mugger to inter him; poor Ophelia
Divided from herself and her fair judgment,
Without the which we are pictures or mere beasts;
Last, and as much containing as all these,
Her brother is in secret come from France;
Feeds on his wonder, keeps himself in clouds,
And wants not buzzers to infect his ear
With pestilent speeches of his father's death,
Wherein necessity, of matter beggar'd,
Will nothing stick our person to arraign
In ear and ear. O my dear Gertrude, this,
Like to a murd'ring piece, in many places
Gives me superfluous death.

A noise within.

QUEEN. Alack, what noise is this?

KING. Where are my Switzers? Let them guard the
door.

[*Enter a* MESSENGER.]

What is the matter?

MESS.   Save yourself, my lord:
The ocean, overpeering of his list,
Eats not the flats with more impetuous haste
Than young Laertes, in a riotous head,
O'erbears your officers. The rabble call him lord;
And, as the world were now but to begin,
Antiquity forgot, custom not known,
The ratifiers and props of every word,
They cry 'Choose we! Laertes shall be king!'
Caps, hands, and tongues applaud it to the clouds,
'Laertes shall be king! Laertes king!'

                          A noise within.

QUEEN. How cheerfully on the false trail they cry!
O, this is counter, you false Danish dogs!
   KING. The doors are broke.

Enter LAERTES *with others.*

   LAER. Where is this king?—Sirs, stand you all without.
   ALL. No, let's come in!
   LAER.   I pray you give me leave.
   ALL. We will, we will!
   LAER. I thank you. Keep the door. [*Exeunt his* FOL-
     LOWERS.] O thou vile king,
Give me my father!
   QUEEN.   Calmly, good Laertes.
   LAER. That drop of blood that's calm proclaims me
     bastard;
Cries cuckold to my father; brands the harlot
Even here between the chaste unsmirched brows
Of my true mother.
   KING.   What is the cause, Laertes,
That thy rebellion looks so giantlike?
Let him go, Gertrude. Do not fear our person.
There's such divinity doth hedge a king
That treason can but peep to what it would,

Acts little of his will. Tell me, Laertes,
Why thou art thus incens'd. Let him go, Gertrude.
Speak, man.

LAER. Where is my father?

KING.   Dead.

QUEEN.   But not by him!

KING. Let him demand his fill.

LAER. How came he dead? I'll not be juggled with:
To hell, allegiance! vows, to the blackest devil!
Conscience and grace, to the profoundest pit!
I dare damnation. To this point I stand,
That both the worlds I give to negligence,
Let come what comes; only I'll be reveng'd
Most throughly for my father.

KING.   Who shall stay you?

LAER. My will, not all the world!
And for my means, I'll husband them so well
They shall go far with little.

KING.   Good Laertes,
If you desire to know the certainty
Of your dear father's death, is't writ in your revenge
That swoopstake you will draw both friend and foe,
Winner and loser?

LAER. None but his enemies.

KING.   Will you know them then?

LAER. To his good friends thus wide I'll ope my arms
And, like the kind life-rend'ring pelican,
Repast them with my blood.

KING.   Why, now you speak
Like a good child and a true gentleman.
That I am guiltless of your father's death,
And am most sensibly in grief for it,
It shall as level to your judgment pierce
As day does to your eye.

A NOISE WITHIN: Let her come in.

LAER. How now? What noise is that?

[*Enter* OPHELIA.]

O heat, dry up my brains! Tears seven times salt
Burn out the sense and virtue of mine eye!
By heaven, thy madness shall be paid by weight
Till our scale turn the beam. O rose of May!
Dear maid, kind sister, sweet Ophelia!
O heavens! is't possible a young maid's wits
Should be as mortal as an old man's life?
Nature is fine in love, and where 'tis fine,
It sends some precious instance of itself
After the thing it loves.

OPH. [*sings*]
    They bore him barefac'd on the bier
        (Hey non nony, nony, hey nony)
    And in his grave rain'd many a tear.
Fare you well, my dove!

LAER. Hadst thou thy wits and didst persuade revenge,
It could not move thus.

OPH. You must sing 'A-down a-down, and you call
him a-down-a.' O, how the wheel becomes it! It is the
false steward, that stole his master's daughter.

LAER. This nothing's more than matter.

OPH. There's rosemary, that's for remembrance. Pray
you, love, remember. And there is pansies, that's for
thoughts.

LAER. A document in madness! Thoughts and remembrance fitted.

OPH. There's fennel for you, and columbines. There's
rue for you, and here's some for me. We may call it herb
of grace o'Sundays. O, you must wear your rue with a
difference! There's a daisy. I would give you some
violets, but they wither'd all when my father died. They
say he made a good end.

[Sings] For bonny sweet Robin is all my joy.

LAER. Thought and affliction, passion, hell itself,
She turns to favour and to prettiness.

OPH. *[sings]*

     And will he not come again?
     And will he not come again?
      No, no, he is dead;
      Go to thy deathbed;
     He never will come again.

     His beard was as white as snow,
     All flaxen was his poll.
      He is gone, he is gone,
      And we cast away moan.
     God 'a' mercy on his soul!

And of all Christian souls, I pray God. God b' wi' you.

LAER. Do you see this, O God?

KING. Laertes, I must commune with your grief,
Or you deny me right. Go but apart,
Make choice of whom your wisest friends you will,
And they shall hear and judge 'twixt you and me.
If by direct or by collateral hand
They find us touch'd, we will our kingdom give,
Our crown, our life, and all that we call ours,
To you in satisfaction; but if not,
Be you content to lend your patience to us,
And we shall jointly labour with your soul
To give it due content.

LAER.　　　　　Let this be so.
His means of death, his obscure funeral—
No trophy, sword, nor hatchment o'er his bones,
No noble rite nor formal ostentation,—
Cry to be heard, as 'twere from heaven to earth,
That I must call't in question.

KING.　　　　　　　　So you shall;

And where th' offence is let the great axe fall.
I pray you go with me.   *Exeunt.*

Scene VI: Elsinore. Another room in the Castle.

Enter HORATIO *with an* ATTENDANT.

HOR. What are they that would speak with me?
SERVANT. Seafaring men, sir. They say they have letters for you.
HOR. Let them come in.

[*Exit* ATTENDANT.]

I do not know from what part of the world
I should be greeted, if not from Lord Hamlet.

Enter SAILORS.

SAILOR. God bless you, sir.
HOR. Let him bless thee too.
SAILOR. 'A shall, sir, an't please him. There's a letter for you, sir,—it comes from th' ambassador that was bound for England—if your name be Horatio, as I am let to know it is.

HOR. [*reads the letter*] 'Horatio, when thou shalt have overlook'd this, give these fellows some means to the King. They have letters for him. Ere we were two days old at sea, a pirate of very warlike appointment gave us chase. Finding ourselves too slow of sail, we put on a compelled valour, and in the grapple I boarded them. On the instant they got clear of our ship; so I alone became their prisoner. They have dealt with me like thieves of mercy; but they knew what they did: I am to do a good turn for them. Let the King have the letters I have sent, and repair thou to me with as much speed as thou wouldest fly death. I have words to speak in thine ear will make thee dumb; yet are they much too light for the

bore of the matter. These good fellows will bring thee
where I am. Rosencrantz and Guildenstern hold their
course for England. Of them I have much to tell thee.
Farewell.

              'He that thou knowest thine, HAMLET.'
Come, I will give you way for these your letters,
And do't the speedier that you may direct me
To him from whom you brought them.

                               Exeunt.

Scene VII: Elsinore. Another room in the Castle.

Enter KING and LAERTES.

  KING. Now must your conscience my acquittance seal,
And you must put me in your heart for friend,
Sith you have heard, and with a knowing ear,
That he which hath your noble father slain
Pursued my life.

    LAER.   It well appears. But tell me
Why you proceeded not against these feats
So crimeful and so capital in nature,
As by your safety, wisdom, all things else,
You mainly were stirr'd up.

    KING.   O, for two special reasons,
Which may to you, perhaps, seem much unsinew'd,
But yet to me they are strong. The Queen his mother
Lives almost by his looks; and for myself,—
My virtue or my plague, be it either which,—
She's so conjunctive to my life and soul
That, as the star moves not but in his sphere,
I could not but by her. The other motive
Why to a public count I might not go
Is the great love the general gender bear him,
Who, dipping all his faults in their affection,

Would, like the spring that turneth wood to stone,
Convert his gyves to graces; so that my arrows,
Too slightly timber'd for so loud a wind,
Would have reverted to my bow again,
And not where I had aim'd them.

    LAER. And so have I a noble father lost;
A sister driven into desp'rate terms,
Whose worth, if praises may go back again,
Stood challenger on mount of all the age
For her perfections. But my revenge will come.

    KING. Break not your sleeps for that. You must not
      think
That we are made of stuff so flat and dull
That we can let our beard be shook with danger,
And think it pastime. You shortly shall hear more.
I lov'd your father, and we love ourself,
And that, I hope, will teach you to imagine—

        [*Enter a* MESSENGER *with letters.*]

How now? What news?

    MESS.   Letters, my lord, from Hamlet:
This to your Majesty; this to the Queen.

    KING. From Hamlet? Who brought them?

    MESS. Sailors, my lord, they say; I saw them not.
They were given me by Claudio; he receiv'd them
Of him that brought them.

    KING.   Laertes, you shall hear them.
Leave us.

                  [*Exit* MESSENGER.]

    [*Reads*] 'High and Mighty,—You shall know I am set
naked on your kingdom. To-morrow shall I beg leave
to see your kingly eyes; when I shall (first asking your
pardon thereunto) recount the occasion of my sudden
and more strange return.

                        'HAMLET.'

What should this mean? Are all the rest come back?
Or is it some abuse, and no such thing?

    LAER. Know you the hand?

    KING.   'Tis Hamlet's character. 'Naked!'
And in a postscript here, he says 'alone.'
Can you advise me?

    LAER. I am lost in it, my lord. But let him come!
It warms the very sickness in my heart
That I shall live and tell him to his teeth,
'Thus didest thou.'

    KING.   If it be so, Laertes
(As how should it be so? how otherwise?),
Will you be rul'd by me?

    LAER.   Ay, my lord,
So you will not o'errule me to a peace.

    KING. To thine own peace. If he be now return'd,
As checking at his voyage, and that he means
No more to undertake it, I will work him
To an exploit now ripe in my device,
Under the which he shall not choose but fall;
And for his death no wind of blame shall breathe,
But even his mother shall uncharge the practice
And call it accident.

    LAER.   My lord, I will be rul'd;
The rather, if you could devise it so
That I might be the organ.

    KING.   It falls right.
You have been talk'd of since your travel much,
And that in Hamlet's hearing, for a quality
Wherein they say you shine. Your sum of parts
Did not together pluck such envy from him
As did that one; and that, in my regard,
Of the unworthiest siege.

    LAER.   What part is that, my lord?

    KNG. A very riband in the cap of youth—

Yet needful too; for youth no less becomes
The light and careless livery that it wears
Than settled age his´sables and his weeds,
Importing health and graveness. Two months since
Here was a gentleman of Normandy.
I have seen myself, and serv'd against, the French,
And they can well on horseback; but this gallant
Had witchcraft in't. He grew unto his seat,
And to such wondrous doing brought his horse
As had he been incorps'd and demi-natur'd
With the brave beast. So far he topp'd my thought
That I, in forgery of shapes and tricks,
Come short of what he did.

  LAER.   A Norman was't?
  KING. A Norman.
  LAER. Upon my life, Lamound.
  KING.   The very same.
  LAER. I know him well. He is the brooch indeed
And gem of all the nation.

  KING. He made confession of you;
And gave you such a masterly report
For art and exercise in your defence,
And for your rapier most especially,
That he cried out 'twould be a sight indeed
If one could match you. The scrimers of their nation
He swore had neither motion, guard, nor eye,
If you oppos'd them. Sir, this report of his
Did Hamlet so envenom with his envy
That he could nothing do but wish and beg
Your sudden coming o'er to play with you.
Now, out of this—

  LAER.   What out of this, my lord?
  KING. Laertes, was your father dear to you?
Or are you like the painting of a sorrow,
A face without a heart?

LAER. Why ask you this?

KING. Not that I think you did not love your father;
But that I know love is begun by time,
And that I see, in passages of proof,
Time qualifies the spark and fire of it.
There lives within the very flame of love
A kind of wick or snuff that will abate it;
And nothing is at a like goodness still;
For goodness, growing to a plurisy,
Dies in his own too-much. That we would do,
We should do when we would; for this 'would' changes,
And hath abatements and delays as many
As there are tongues, are hands, are accidents;
And then this 'should' is like a spendthrift sigh,
That hurts by easing. But to the quick o' th' ulcer!
Hamlet comes back. What would you undertake
To show yourself your father's son in deed
More than in words?

LAER. To cut his throat i' th' church!

KING. No place indeed should murther sanctuarize;
Revenge should have no bounds. But, good Laertes,
Will you do this? Keep close within your chamber.
Hamlet return'd shall know you are come home.
We'll put on those shall praise your excellence
And set a double varnish on the fame
The Frenchman gave you; bring you in fine together
And wager on your heads. He, being remiss,
Most generous, and free from all contriving,
Will not peruse the foils; so that with ease,
Or with a little shuffling, you may choose
A sword unbated, and, in a pass of practice,
Requite him for your father.

LAER. I will do't!
And for that purpose I'll anoint my sword.
I bought an unction of a mountebank,

So mortal that, but dip a knife in it,
Where it draws blood no cataplasm so rare,
Collected from all simples that have virtue
Under the moon, can save the thing from death
This is but scratch'd withal. I'll touch my point
With this contagion, that, if I gall him slightly,
It may be death.

KING.   Let's further think of this,
Weigh what convenience both of time and means
May fit us to our shape. If this should fail,
And that our drift look through our bad performance,
'Twere better not assay'd. Therefore this project
Should have a back or second, that might hold
If this did blast in proof. Soft! let me see.
We'll make a solemn wager on your cunnings-
I ha't!
When in your motion you are hot and dry—
As make your bouts more violent to that end—
And that he calls for drink, I'll have prepar'd him
A chalice for the nonce; whereon but sipping,
If he by chance escape your venom'd stuck,
Our purpose may hold there.—But stay, what noise?

[Enter QUEEN.]

How now, sweet queen?

QUEEN. One woe doth tread upon another's heel,
So fast they follow. Your sister's drown'd, Laertes.

LAER. Drown'd! O, where?

QUEEN. There is a willow grows aslant a brook,
That shows his hoar leaves in the glassy stream.
There with fantastic garlands did she come
Of crowflowers, nettles, daisies, and long purples,
That liberal shepherds give a grosser name,
But our cold maids do dead men's fingers call them.
There on the pendent boughs her coronet weeds

Clamb'ring to hang, an envious sliver broke,
When down her weedy trophies and herself
Fell in the weeping brook. Her clothes spread wide
And, mermaid-like, awhile they bore her up;
Which time she chaunted snatches of old tunes,
As one incapable of her own distress,
Or like a creature native and indued
Unto that element; but long it could not be
Till that her garments, heavy with their drink,
Pull'd the poor wretch from her melodious lay
To muddy death.

 LAER.   Alas, then she is drown'd?
 QUEEN. Drown'd, drown'd.
 LAER. Too much of water hast thou, poor Ophelia,
And therefore I forbid my tears; but yet
It is our trick; nature her custom holds,
Let shame say what it will. When these are gone,
The woman will be out. Adieu, my lord.
I have a speech of fire, that fain would blaze
But that this folly douts it.   *Exit.*
 KING.   Let's follow, Gertrude.
How much I had to do to calm his rage!
Now fear I this will give it start again;
Therefore let's follow.   *Exeunt.*

Act V: Scene I: Elsinore. A churchyard.

Enter two CLOWNS, *with spades and pickaxes.*

 CLOWN. Is she to be buried in Christian burial when she wilfully seeks her own salvation?

 OTHER. I tell thee she is; therefore make her grave straight. The crowner hath sate on her, and finds it Christian burial.

CLOWN. How can that be, unless she drown'd herself in her own defence?

OTHER. Why, 'tis found so.

CLOWN. It must be *se offendendo;* it cannot be else. For here lies the point: if I drown myself wittingly, it argues an act; and an act hath three branches—it is to act, to do, and to perform; argal, she drown'd herself wittingly.

OTHER. Nay, but hear you, Goodman Delver!

CLOWN. Give me leave. Here lies the water; good. Here stands the man; good. If the man go to this water and drown himself, it is, will he nill he, he goes—mark you that. But if the water come to him and drown him, he drowns not himself. Argal, he that is not guilty of his own death shortens not his own life.

OTHER. But is this law?

CLOWN. Ay, marry, is't—crowner's quest law.

OTHER. Will you ha' the truth an't? If this had not been a gentlewoman, she should have been buried out o' Christian burial.

CLOWN. Why, there thou say'st! And the more pity that great folk should have count'nance in this world to drown or hang themselves more than their even-Christen. Come, my spade! There is no ancient gentlemen but gard'ners, ditchers, and grave-makers. They hold up Adam's profession.

OTHER. Was he a gentleman?

CLOWN. 'A was the first that ever bore arms.

OTHER. Why, he had none.

CLOWN. What, art a heathen? How dost thou understand the Scripture? The Scripture says Adam digg'd. Could he dig without arms? I'll put another question to thee. If thou answerest me not to the purpose, confess thyself—

OTHER. Go to!

CLOWN. What is he that builds stronger than either the mason, the shipwright, or the carpenter?

OTHER. The gallows-maker; for that frame outlives a thousand tenants.

CLOWN. I like thy wit well, in good faith. The gallows does well. But how does it well? It does well to those that do ill. Now, thou dost ill to say the gallows is built stronger than the church. Argal, the gallows may do well to thee. To't again, come!

OTHER. Who builds stronger than a mason, a shipwright, or a carpenter?

CLOWN. Ay, tell me that, and unyoke.

OTHER. Marry, now I can tell!

CLOWN. To't.

OTHER. Mass, I cannot tell.

Enter HAMLET *and* HORATIO *afar off.*

CLOWN. Cudgel thy brains no more about it, for your dull ass will not mend his pace with beating; and when you are ask'd this question next, say 'a grave-maker.' The houses he makes lasts till doomsday. Go, get thee to Yaughan; fetch me a stoup of liquor.

[*Exit* SECOND CLOWN.]
[CLOWN *digs and sings.*]
In youth when I did love, did love,
    Methought it was very sweet;
To contract—O—the time for—a—my behove,
    O, methought there—a—was nothing—a—meet.

HAM. Has this fellow no feeling of his business, that he sings at grave-making?

HOR. Custom hath made it in him a property of easiness.

HAM. 'Tis e'en so. The hand of little employment hath the daintier sense.

CLOWN. [*sings*]

> But age with his stealing steps
> Hath clawed me in his clutch,
> And hath shipped me intil the land,
> As if I had never been such.

Throws up a skull.

HAM. That skull had a tongue in it, and could sing once. How the knave jowls it to the ground, as if 'twere Cain's jawbone, that did the first murther! This might be the pate of a politician, which this ass now o'erreaches; one that would circumvent God, might it not?

HOR. It might, my lord.

HAM. Or of a courtier, which could say 'Good morrow, sweet lord! How dost thou, good lord?' This might be my Lord Such-a-one, that prais'd my Lord Such-a-one's horse when he meant to beg it—might it not?

HOR. Ay, my lord.

HAM. Why, e'en so! and now my Lady Worm's, chapless, and knock'd about the mazzard with a sexton's spade. Here's fine revolution, an we had the trick to see't. Did these bones cost no more the breeding but to play at loggets with 'em? Mine ache to think on't.

CLOWN. [*sings*]

> A pickaxe and a spade, a spade,
> For and a shrouding sheet;
> O, a pit of clay for to be made
> For such a guest is meet.

Throws up another skull.

HAM. There's another. Why may not that be the skull of a lawyer? Where be his quiddits now, his quillets, his cases, his tenures, and his tricks? Why does he suffer this rude knave now to knock him about the sconce with a dirty shovel, and will not tell him of his action of battery? Hum! This fellow might be in's time a great buyer of

land, with his statutes, his recognizances, his fines, his
double vouchers, his recoveries. Is this the fine of his
fines, and the recovery of his recoveries, to have his fine
pate full of fine dirt? Will his vouchers vouch him no
more of his purchases, and double ones too, than the
length and breadth of a pair of indentures? The very
conveyances of his lands will scarcely lie in this box; and
must th' inheritor himself have no more, ha?

Hor. Not a jot more, my lord.

Ham. Is not parchment made of sheepskins?

Hor. Ay, my lord, and of calveskins too.

Ham. They are sheep and calves which seek out assurance in that. I will speak to this fellow. Whose grave's
this, sirrah?

Clown. Mine, sir.

[*Sings*] O, a pit of clay for to be made
            For such a guest is meet.

Ham. I think it be thine indeed, for thou liest in't.

Clown. You lie out on't, sir, and therefore 'tis not
yours. For my part, I do not lie in't, yet it is mine.

Ham. Thou dost lie in't, to be in't and say it is thine.
'Tis for the dead, not for the quick; therefore thou liest.

Clown. 'Tis a quick lie, sir; 'twill away again from
me to you.

Ham. What man dost thou dig it for?

Clown. For no man, sir.

Ham. What woman then?

Clown. For none neither.

Ham. Who is to be buried in't?

Clown. One that was a woman, sir; but, rest her soul,
she's dead.

Ham. How absolute the knave is! We must speak by
the card, or equivocation will undo us. By the Lord,
Horatio, this three years I have taken note of it, the age
is grown so picked that the toe of the peasant comes so

near the heel of the courtier he galls his kibe.—How long
hast thou been a grave-maker?

CLOWN. Of all the days i' th' year, I came to't that day
that our last king Hamlet overcame Fortinbras.

HAM. How long is that since?

CLOWN. Cannot you tell that? Every fool can tell that.
It was the very day that young Hamlet was born—he that
is mad, and sent into England.

HAM. Ay, marry, why was he sent into England?

CLOWN. Why, because 'a was mad. 'A shall recover
his wits there; or, if 'a do not, 'tis no great matter there.

HAM. Why?

CLOWN. 'Twill not be seen in him there. There the
men are as mad as he.

HAM. How came he mad?

CLOWN. Very strangely, they say.

HAM. How strangely?

CLOWN. Faith, e'en with losing his wits.

HAM. Upon what ground?

CLOWN. Why, here in Denmark. I have been sexton
here, man and boy, thirty years.

HAM. How long will a man lie i' th' earth ere he rot?

CLOWN. Faith, if 'a be not rotten before 'a die (as
we have many pocky corses now-a-days that will scarce
hold the laying in), 'a will last you some eight year or
nine year. A tanner will last you nine year.

HAM. Why he more than another?

CLOWN. Why, sir, his hide is so tann'd with his trade
that 'a will keep out water a great while; and your water
is a sore decayer of your whoreson dead body. Here's a
skull now. This skull hath lien you i' th' earth three-and-
twenty years.

HAM. Whose was it?

CLOWN. A whoreson mad fellow's it was. Whose do
you think it was?

HAM. Nay, I know not.

CLOWN. A pestilence on him for a mad rogue! 'A pour'd a flagon of Rhenish on my head once. This same skull, sir, was Yorick's skull, the King's jester.

HAM. This?

CLOWN. E'en that.

HAM. Let me see. [*Takes the skull.*] Alas, poor Yorick! I knew him, Horatio. A fellow of infinite jest, of most excellent fancy. He hath borne me on his back a thousand times. And now how abhorred in my imagination it is! My gorge rises at it. Here hung those lips that I have kiss'd I know not how oft. Where be your gibes now? your gambols? your songs? your flashes of merriment that were wont to set the table on a roar? Not one now, to mock your own grinning? Quite chapfall'n? Now get you to my lady's chamber, and tell her, let her paint an inch thick, to this favour she must come. Make her laugh at that. Prithee, Horatio, tell me one thing.

HOR. What's that, my lord?

HAM. Dost thou think Alexander look'd o' this fashion i' th' earth?

HOR. E'en so.

HAM. And smelt so? Pah!   *Puts down the skull.*

HOR. E'en so, my lord.

HAM. To what base uses we may return, Horatio! Why may not imagination trace the noble dust of Alexander till he find it stopping a bunghole?

HOR. 'Twere to consider too curiously, to consider so.

HAM. No, faith, not a jot; but to follow him thither with modesty enough, and likelihood to lead it; as thus: Alexander died, Alexander was buried, Alexander returneth into dust; the dust is earth; of earth we make loam; and why of that loam (whereto he was converted) might they not stop a beer barrel?
Imperious Cæsar, dead and turn'd to clay,

Might stop a hole to keep the wind away.
O, that that earth which kept the world in awe
Should patch a wall t' expel the winter's flaw!
But soft! but soft! aside! Here comes the King—

[*Enter* PRIESTS *with a coffin in funeral procession,* KING,
QUEEN, LAERTES, *with* LORDS *attendant.*]

The Queen, the courtiers. Who is this they follow?
And with such maimed rites? This doth betoken
The corse they follow did with desp'rate hand
Fordo its own life. 'Twas of some estate.
Couch we awhile, and mark.   *Retires with* HORATIO.
    LAER. What ceremony else?
    HAM.   That is Laertes,
A very noble youth. Mark.
    LAER. What ceremony else?
    PRIEST. Her obsequies have been as far enlarg'd
As we have warranty. Her death was doubtful;
And, but that great command o'ersways the order,
She should in ground unsanctified have lodg'd
Till the last trumpet. For charitable prayers,
Shards, flints, and pebbles should be thrown on her.
Yet here she is allow'd her virgin crants,
Her maiden strewments, and the bringing home
Of bell and burial.
    LAER. Must there no more be done?
    PRIEST.   No more be done.
We should profane the service of the dead
To sing a requiem and such rest to her
As to peace-parted souls.
    LAER.   Lay her i' th' earth;
And from her fair and unpolluted flesh
May violets spring! I tell thee, churlish priest,
A minst'ring angel shall my sister be
When thou liest howling.

HAM.   What, the fair Ophelia?
QUEEN. Sweets to the sweet! Farewell.

                              [*Scatters flowers.*]

I hop'd thou shouldst have been my Hamlet's wife;
I thought thy bride-bed to have deck'd, sweet maid,
And not have strew'd thy grave.

LAER.   O, treble woe
Fall ten times treble on that cursed head
Whose wicked deed thy most ingenious sense
Depriv'd thee of! Hold off the earth awhile,
Till I have caught her once more in mine arms.

                              [*Leaps in the grave.*]

Now pile your dust upon the quick and dead
Till of this flat a mountain you have made
T' o'ertop old Pelion or the skyish head
Of blue Olympus.

HAM. [*comes forward*] What is he whose grief
Bears such an emphasis? whose phrase of sorrow
Conjures the wand'ring stars, and makes them stand
Like wonder-wounded hearers? This is I,
Hamlet the Dane.   *Leaps in after* LAERTES.

LAER.   The devil take thy soul!

                              Grapples with him.

HAM. Thou pray'st not well.
I prithee take thy fingers from my throat;
For, though I am not splenitive and rash,
Yet have I in me something dangerous,
Which let thy wisdom fear. Hold off thy hand!

KING. Pluck them asunder.

QUEEN.   Hamlet, Hamlet!

ALL. Gentlemen!

HOR.   Good my lord, be quiet.

          The ATTENDANTS *part them, and they come out of
                              the grave.*

HAM. Why, I will fight with him upon this theme
Until my eyelids will no longer wag.

QUEEN. O my son, what theme?

HAM. I lov'd Ophelia. Forty thousand brothers
Could not (with all their quantity of love)
Make up my sum. What wilt thou do for her?

KING. O, he is mad, Laertes.

QUEEN. For love of God, forbear him!

HAM. 'Swounds, show me what thou't do.
Woo't weep? woo't fight? woo't fast? woo't tear thyself?
Woo't drink up esill? eat a crocodile?
I'll do't. Dost thou come here to whine?
To outface me with leaping in her grave?
Be buried quick with her, and so will I.
And if thou prate of mountains, let them throw
Millions of acres on us, till our ground,
Singeing his pate against the burning zone,
Make Ossa like a wart! Nay, an thou'lt mouth,
I'll rant as well as thou.

QUEEN.   This is mere madness;
And thus a while the fit will work on him.
Anon, as patient as the female dove
When that her golden couplets are disclos'd,
His silence will sit drooping.

HAM.   Hear you, sir!
What is the reason that you use me thus?
I lov'd you ever. But it is no matter.
Let Hercules himself do what he may,
The cat will mew, and dog will have his day.   *Exit.*

KING. I pray thee, good Horatio, wait upon him.
                              [*Exit* HORATIO.]

[*To* LAERTES] Strengthen your patience in our last night's
          speech.
We'll put the matter to the present push.—

Good Gertrude, set some watch over your son.—
This grave shall have a living monument.
An hour of quiet shortly shall we see;
Till then in patience our proceeding be.   *Exeunt.*

Scene II: Elsinore. A hall in the Castle.

Enter HAMLET *and* HORATIO.

HAM. So much for this, sir; now shall you see the other.
You do remember all the circumstance?

HOR. Remember it, my lord!

HAM. Sir, in my heart there was a kind of fighting
That would not let me sleep. Methought I lay
Worse than the mutines in the bilboes. Rashly—
And prais'd be rashness for it; let us know,,
Our indiscretion sometime serves us well
When our deep plots do pall; and that should learn us
There's a divinity that shapes our ends,
Rough-hew them how we will—

HOR.   That is most certain.

HAM. Up from my cabin,
My sea-gown scarf'd about me, in the dark
Grop'd I to find out them; had my desire,
Finger'd their packet, and in fine withdrew
To mine own room again; making so bold
(My fears forgetting manners) to unseal
Their grand commission; where I found, Horatio
(O royal knavery!), an exact command,
Larded with many several sorts of reasons,
Importing Denmark's health, and England's too,
With, hoo! such bugs and goblins in my life—
That, on the supervise, no leisure bated,
No, not to stay the grinding of the axe,

My head should be struck off.

HOR.   Is't possible?

HAM. Here's the commission; read it at more leisure.
But wilt thou hear me how I did proceed?

HOR. I beseech you.

HAM. Being thus benetted round with villanies,
Or I could make a prologue to my brains,
They had begun the play. I sat me down;
Devis'd a new commission; wrote it fair.
I once did hold it, as our statists do,
A baseness to write fair, and labour'd much
How to forget that learning; but, sir, now
It did me yeoman's service. Wilt thou know
Th' effect of what I wrote?

HOR.   Ay, good my lord.

HAM. An earnest conjuration from the King,
As England was his faithful tributary,
As love between them like the palm might flourish,
As peace should still her wheaten garland wear
And stand a comma 'tween their amities,
And many such-like as's of great charge,
That, on the view and knowing of these contents,
Without debatement further, more or less,
He should the bearers put to sudden death,
Not shriving time allow'd.

HOR.   How was this seal'd?

HAM. Why, even in that was heaven ordinant.
I had my father's signet in my purse,
Which was the model of that Danish seal;
Folded the writ up in the form of th' other,
Subscrib'd it, gave't th' impression, plac'd it safely,
The changeling never known. Now, the next day
Was our sea-fight; and what to this was sequent
Thou know'st already.

Hor. So Guildenstern and Rosencrantz go to't.

Ham. Why, man, they did make love to this employ-
ment!
They are not near my conscience; their defeat
Does by their own insinuation grow.
'Tis dangerous when the baser nature comes
Between the pass and fell incensed points
Of mighty opposites.

Hor. 　　　　　　Why, what a king is this!

Ham. Does it not, thinks't thee, stand me now upon—
He that hath kill'd my king, and whor'd my mother;
Popp'd in between th' election and my hopes;
Thrown out his angle for my proper life,
And with such coz'nage—is't not perfect conscience
To quit him with this arm? And it's not to be damn'd
To let this canker of our nature come
In further evil?

Hor. It must be shortly known to him from England
What is the issue of the business there.

Ham. It will be short; the interim is mine,
And a man's life 's no more than to say 'one.'
But I am very sorry, good Horatio,
That to Laertes I forgot myself;
For by the image of my cause I see
The portraiture of his. I'll court his favours.
But sure the bravery of his grief did put me
Into a tow'ring passion.

Hor. 　　　　　　Peace! Who comes here?

Enter young Osric, *a courtier.*

Osr. Your lordship is right welcome back to Denmark.

Ham. I humbly thank you, sir. [*Aside to* Horatio]
Dost know this waterfly?

Hor. [*aside to* Hamlet] No, my good lord.

Ham. [*aside to* Horatio] Thy state is the more gracious; for 'tis a vice to know him. He hath much land, and fertile. Let a beast be lord of beasts, and his crib shall stand at the king's mess. 'Tis a chough; but, as I say, spacious in the possession of dirt.

Osr. Sweet lord, if your lordship were at leisure, I should impart a thing to you from his Majesty.

Ham. I will receive it, sir, with all diligence of spirit. Put your bonnet to his right use. 'Tis for the head.

Osr. I thank your lordship, it is very hot.

Ham. No, believe me, 'tis very cold; the wind is northerly.

Osr. It is indifferent cold, my lord, indeed.

Ham. But yet methinks it is very sultry and hot for my complexion.

Osr. Exceedingly, my lord; it is very sultry, as 'twere —I cannot tell how. But, my lord, his Majesty bade me signify to you that he has laid a great wager on your head. Sir, this is the matter—

Ham. I beseech you remember.

Hamlet *moves him to put on his hat.*

Osr. Nay, good my lord; for mine ease, in good faith. Sir, here is newly come to court Laertes; believe me, an absolute gentleman, full of most excellent differences, of very soft society and great showing. Indeed, to speak feelingly of him, he is the card or calendar of gentry; for you shall find in him the continent of what part a gentleman would see.

Ham. Sir, his definement suffers no perdition in you; though, I know, to divide him inventorially would dozy th' arithmetic of memory, and yet but yaw neither in respect of his quick sail. But, in the verity of extolment, I take him to be a soul of great article, and his infusion of such dearth and rareness as, to make true diction of him, his semblable is his mirror, and who else would trace him, his umbrage, nothing more.

Osr. Your lordship speaks most infallibly of him.

Ham. The concernancy, sir? Why do we wrap the gentleman in our more rawer breath?

Osr. Sir?

Hor. [*aside to* Hamlet] Is't not possible to understand in another tongue? You will do't, sir, really.

Ham. What imports the nomination of this gentleman?

Osr. Of Laertes?

Hor. [*aside*] His purse is empty already. All's golden words are spent.

Ham. Of him, sir.

Osr. I know you are not ignorant—

Ham. I would you did, sir; yet, in faith, if you did, it would not much approve me. Well, sir?

Osr. You are not ignorant of what excellence Laertes is—

Ham. I dare not confess that, lest I should compare with him in excellence; but to know a man well were to know himself.

Osr. I mean, sir, for his weapon; but in the imputation laid on him by them, in his meed he's unfellowed.

Ham. What's his weapon?

Osr. Rapier and dagger.

Ham. That's two of his weapons—but well.

Osr. The King, sir, hath wager'd with him six Barbary horses; against the which he has impon'd, as I take it, six French rapiers and poniards, with their assigns, as girdle, hangers, and so. Three of the carriages, in faith, are very dear to fancy, very responsive to the hilts, most delicate carriages, and of very liberal conceit.

Ham. What call you the carriages?

HOR. [*aside to* HAMLET] I knew you must be edified by the margent ere you had done.

OSR. The carriages, sir, are the hangers.

HAM. The phrase would be more germane to the matter if we could carry canon by our sides. I would it might be hangers till then. But on! Six Barbary horses against six French swords, their assigns, and three liberal-conceited carriages: that's the French bet against the Danish. Why is this all impon'd, as you call it?

OSR. The King, sir, hath laid that, in a dozen passes between yourself and him, he shall not exceed you three hits; he hath laid on twelve for nine, and it would come to immediate trial if your lordship would vouchsafe the answer.

HAM. How if I answer no?

OSR. I mean, my lord, the opposition of your person in trial.

HAM. Sir, I will walk here in the hall. If it please his Majesty, it is the breathing time of day with me. Let the foils be brought, the gentleman willing, and the King hold his purpose, I will win for him if I can; if not, I will gain nothing but my shame and the odd hits.

OSR. Shall I redeliver you e'en so?

HAM. To this effect, sir, after what flourish your nature will.

OSR. I commend my duty to your lordship.

HAM. Yours, yours. [*Exit* OSRIC.] He does well to commend it himself; there are no tongues else for's turn.

HOR. This lapwing runs away with the shell on his head.

HAM. He did comply with his dug before he suck'd it. Thus has he, and many more of the same bevy that I know the drossy age dotes on, only got the tune of the time and outward habit of encounter—a kind of yesty collection, which carries them through and through the most fann'd and winnowed opinions; and do but blow them to their trial—the bubbles are out.

Enter a LORD.

LORD. My lord, his Majesty commended him to you by young Osric, who brings back to him, that you attend him in the hall. He sends to know if your pleasure hold to play with Laertes, or that you will take longer time.

HAM. I am constant to my purposes; they follow the King's pleasure. If his fitness speaks, mine is ready; now or whensoever, provided I be so able as now.

LORD. The King and Queen and all are coming down.

HAM. In happy time.

LORD. The Queen desires you to use some gentle entertainment to Laertes before you fall to play.

HAM. She well instructs me.   *Exit* LORD.

HOR. You will lose this wager, my lord.

HAM. I do not think so. Since he went into France I have been in continual practice. I shall win at the odds. But thou wouldst not think how ill all's here about my heart. But it is no matter.

HOR. Nay, good my lord—

HAM. It is but foolery; but it is such a kind of gaingiving as would perhaps trouble a woman.

HOR. If your mind dislike anything, obey it. I will forestall their repair hither and say you are not fit.

HAM. Not a whit, we defy augury; there's a special providence in the fall of a sparrow. If it be now, 'tis not to come; if it be not to come, it will be now; if it be not now, yet it will come: the readiness is all. Since no man knows aught of what he leaves, what is't to leave betimes? Let be.

Enter KING, QUEEN, LAERTES, OSRIC, *and* LORDS, *with
other* ATTENDANTS *with foils and gauntlets. A Table and
flagons of wine on it.*

KING. Come, Hamlet, come, and take this hand from
   me.
        The KING *puts* LAERTES' *hand into* HAMLET'S.
HAM. Give me your pardon, sir. I have done you
   wrong;
But pardon't, as you are a gentleman.
This presence knows,
And you must needs have heard, how I am punish'd
With sore distraction. What I have done
That might your nature, honour, and exception
Roughly awake, I here proclaim was madness.
Was't Hamlet wrong'd Laertes? Never Hamlet.
If Hamlet from himself be ta'en away,
And when he's not himself does wrong Laertes,
Then Hamlet does it not, Hamlet denies it.
Who does it, then? His madness. If't be so,
Hamlet is of the faction that is wrong'd;
His madness is poor Hamlet's enemy.
Sir, in this audience,
Let my disclaiming from a purpos'd evil
Free me so far in your most generous thoughts
That I have shot my arrow o'er the house
And hurt my brother.
   LAER.   I am satisfied in nature,
Whose motive in this case should stir me most
To my revenge. But in my terms of honour
I stand aloof, and will no reconcilement
Till by some elder masters of known honour
I have a voice and precedent of peace
To keep my name ungor'd. But till that time
I do receive your offer'd love like love,
And will not wrong it.

HAM.   I embrace it freely,
And will this brother's wager frankly play.
Give us the foils. Come on.

LAER.   Come, one for me.

HAM. I'll be your foil, Laertes. In mine ignorance
Your skill shall, like a star i' th' darkest night,
Stick fiery off indeed.

LAER.   You mock me, sir.

HAM. No, by this hand.

KING. Give them the foils, young Osric.
    Cousin Hamlet,
You know the wager?

HAM.   Very well, my lord.
Your Grace has laid the odds o' th' weaker side.

KING. I do not fear it, I have seen you both;
But since he is better'd, we have therefore odds.

LAER. This is too heavy; let me see another.

HAM. This likes me well. These foils have all a length?
                                Prepare to play.

OSR. Ay, my good lord.

KING. Set me the stoups of wine upon that table.
If Hamlet give the first or second hit,
Or quit in answer of the third exchange,
Let all the battlements their ordnance fire;
The King shall drink to Hamlet's better breath,
And in the cup an union shall he throw
Richer than that which four successive kings
In Denmark's crown have worn. Give me the cups;
And let the kettle to the trumpet speak,
The trumpet to the cannoneer without,
The cannons to the heavens, the heaven to earth,
'Now the King drinks to Hamlet.' Come, begin.
And you the judges, bear a wary eye.

HAM. Come on, sir.

LAER.   Come, my lord.   *They play.*

HAM.   One.
LAER.   No.
HAM.   Judgment!
OSR. A hit, a very palpable hit.
LAER.   Well, again!
KING. Stay, give me drink. Hamlet, this pearl is thine;
Here's to thy health.

> [*Drum; trumpets sound; a piece goes off within.*]
>> Give him the cup.

HAM. I'll play this bout first; set it by awhile.
Come. [*They play.*] Another hit. What say you?
LAER. A touch, a touch; I do confess't.
KING. Our son shall win.
QUEEN.   He's fat, and scant of breath.
Here, Hamlet, take my napkin, rub thy brows.
The Queen carouses to thy fortune, Hamlet.
HAM. Good madam!
KING.   Gertrude, do not drink.
QUEEN. I will, my lord; I pray you pardon me.
KING. [*aside*] It is the poison'd cup; it is too late.
HAM. I dare not drink yet, madam; by-and-by.
QUEEN. Come, let me wipe thy face.
LAER. My lord, I'll hit him now.
KING.   I do not think't.
LAER. [*aside*] And yet it is almost against my con-
    science.
HAM. Come for the third, Laertes! You but dally.
I pray you pass with your best violence;
I am afeard you make a wanton of me.
LAER. Say you so? Come on.   *Play.*
OSR. Nothing neither way.
LAER. Have at you now!

> LAERTES *wounds* HAMLET; *then, in scuffling, they
>   change rapiers, and* HAMLET *wounds* LAERTES.

KING.   Part them! They are incens'd.

HAM. Nay come! again! *The* QUEEN *falls.*

OSR. Look to the Queen there, ho!

HOR. They bleed on both sides. How is it, my lord?

OSR. How is't, Laertes?

LAER. Why, as a woodcock to mine own springe, Osric.
I am justly kill'd with mine own treachery.

HAM. How does the Queen?

KING. She swounds to see them bleed.

QUEEN. No, no! the drink, the drink! O my dear
Hamlet!
The drink, the drink! I am poison'd. *Dies.*

HAM. O villany! Ho! let the door be lock'd.
Treachery! Seek it out. LAERTES *falls.*

LAER. It is here, Hamlet. Hamlet, thou art slain;
No med'cine in the world can do thee good.
In thee there is not half an hour of life.
The treacherous instrument is in thy hand,
Unbated and envenom'd. The foul practice
Hath turn'd itself on me. Lo, here I lie,
Never to rise again. Thy mother's poison'd.
I can no more. The King, the King's to blame.

HAM. The point envenom'd too?
Then, venom, to thy work. *Hurts the* KING.

ALL. Treason! treason!

KING. O, yet defend me, friends! I am but hurt.

HAM. Here, thou incestuous, murd'rous, damned
Dane,
Drink off this potion! Is thy union here?
Follow my mother. KING *dies.*

LAER. He is justly serv'd.
It is a poison temper'd by himself.
Exchange forgiveness with me, noble Hamlet.
Mine and my father's death come not upon thee,
Nor thine on me! *Dies.*

HAM. Heaven make thee free of it! I follow thee.
I am dead, Horatio. Wretched queen, adieu!
You that look pale and tremble at this chance,
That are but mutes or audience to this act,
Had I but time (as this fell sergeant, Death,
Is strict in his arrest) O, I could tell you—
But let it be. Horatio, I am dead;
Thou liv'st; report me and my cause aright
To the unsatisfied.

HOR.   Never believe it.
I am more an antique Roman than a Dane.
Here's yet some liquor left.

HAM.   As th'art a man,
Give me the cup. Let go! By heaven, I'll ha't.
O good Horatio, what a wounded name
(Things standing thus unknown) shall live behind me!
If thou didst ever hold me in thy heart,
Absent thee from felicity awhile,
And in this harsh world draw thy breath in pain,
To tell my story.   [*March afar off, and shot within.*]
         What warlike noise is this?

OSR. Young Fortinbras, with conquest come from
    Poland,
To the ambassadors of England gives
This warlike volley.

HAM.   O, I die, Horatio!
The potent poison quite o'ercrows my spirit.
I cannot live to hear the news from England,
But I do prophesy th' election lights
On Fortinbras. He has my dying voice.
So tell him, with th' occurrents, more and less,
Which have solicited—the rest is silence.   *Dies.*

HOR. Now cracks a noble heart. Good night, sweet
    prince,

And flights of angels sing thee to thy rest!

[*March within.*]

Why does the drum come hither?

Enter FORTINBRAS *and* ENGLISH AMBASSADORS, *with*
DRUM, COLOURS, *and* ATTENDANTS.

FORT. Where is this sight?

HOR.　　　　　　　　　What is it you would see?
If aught of woe or wonder, cease your search.

FORT. This quarry cries on havoc. O proud Death,
What feast is toward in thine eternal cell
That thou so many princes at a shot
So bloodily hast struck?

AMBASSADOR.　　　　　The sight is dismal;
And our affairs from England come too late.
The ears are senseless that should give us hearing
To tell him his commandment is fulfill'd,
That Rosencrantz and Guildenstern are dead.
Where should we have our thanks?

HOR.　　　　　　　　　Not from his mouth,
Had it th' ability of life to thank you.
He never gave commandment for their death.
But since, so jump upon this bloody question,
You from the Polack wars, and you from England,
Are here arriv'd, give order that these bodies
High on a stage be placed to the view;
And let me speak to th' yet unknowing world
How these things came about. So shall you hear
Of carnal, bloody, and unnatural acts;
Of accidental judgments, casual slaughters;
Of deaths put on by cunning and forc'd cause;
And, in this upshot, purposes mistook
Fall'n on th' inventors' heads. All this can I
Truly deliver.

FORT.　　　Let us haste to hear it,

And call the noblest to the audience.
For me, with sorrow I embrace my fortune.
I have some rights of memory in this kingdom,
Which now to claim my vantage doth invite me.

Hor. Of that I shall have also cause to speak,
And from his mouth whose voice will draw on more.
But let this same be presently perform'd,
Even while men's minds are wild, lest more mischance
On plots and errors happen.

Fort.   Let four captains
Bear Hamlet like a soldier to the stage;
For he was likely, had he been put on,
To have prov'd most royally; and for his passage
The soldiers' music and the rites of war
Speak loudly for him.
Take up the bodies. Such a sight as this
Becomes the field, but here shows much amiss.
Go, bid the soldiers shoot.

> *Exeunt marching; after the which a peal of*
> *ordinance are shot off.*

The Tragedy of Macbeth

NAMES OF THE ACTORS

DUNCAN, King of Scotland.

MALCOLM,
DONALBAIN, } his sons.

MACBETH,
BANQUO, } Generals of the Scottish Army.

MACDUFF,
LENNOX,
ROSS,
MENTEITH, } Noblemen of Scotland.
ANGUS,
CAITHNESS,

FLEANCE, son to BANQUO.

SIWARD, Earl of Northumberland, General of the English forces.

YOUNG SIWARD, his son.

SEYTON, an Officer attending on MACBETH.

BOY, son to MACDUFF.   A SERGEANT.

A PORTER.   An OLD MAN.

An ENGLISH DOCTOR.   A SCOTTISH DOCTOR.

LADY MACBETH

LADY MACDUFF.

A GENTLEWOMAN, attending on LADY MACBETH.

The WEIRD SISTERS.   HECATE.

The GHOST OF BANQUO.   Apparitions.

Lords, Gentlemen, Officers, Soldiers, Murderers, Messengers, Attendants.

Act I: Scene I: Scotland. An open place.

Thunder and lightning. Enter three WITCHES.

1. WITCH. When shall we three meet again
In thunder, lightning, or in rain?
2. WITCH. When the hurlyburly's done,
When the battle's lost and won.
3. WITCH. That will be ere the set of sun.
1. WITCH. Where the place?
2. WITCH.   Upon the heath.
3. WITCH. There to meet with Macbeth.
1. WITCH. I come, Graymalkin!
2. WITCH. Paddock calls.
3. WITCH.   Anon!
ALL. Fair is foul, and foul is fair.
Hover through the fog and filthy air.   *Exeunt.*

Scene II: A camp near Forres.

Alarum within. Enter KING DUNCAN, MALCOLM, DONAL-
BAIN, LENNOX, *with* ATTENDANTS, *meeting a bleeding*
SERGEANT.

KING. What bloody man is that? He can report,
As seemeth by his plight, of the revolt
The newest state.
MAL.   This is the sergeant
Who like a good and hardy soldier fought
'Gainst my captivity. Hail, brave friend!
Say to the King the knowledge of the broil
As thou didst leave it.
SERG.   Doubtful it stood,
As two spent swimmers that do cling together
And choke their art. The merciless Macdonwald

(Worthy to be a rebel, for to that
The multiplying villanies of nature
Do swarm upon him) from the Western Isles
Of kerns and gallowglasses is supplied;
And Fortune, on his damned quarrel smiling,
Show'd like a rebel's whore. But all's too weak;
For brave Macbeth (well he deserves that name),
Disdaining Fortune, with his brandish'd steel,
Which smok'd with bloody execution
(Like valour's minion), carv'd out his passage
Till he fac'd the slave;
Which ne'er shook hands nor bade farewell to him
Till he unseam'd him from the nave to th' chaps
And fix'd his head upon our battlements.

   KING. O valiant cousin! worthy gentleman!

   SERG. As whence the sun gins his reflection
Shipwracking storms and direful thunders break,
So from that spring whence comfort seem'd to come
Discomfort swells. Mark, King of Scotland, mark.
No sooner justice had, with valour arm'd,
Compell'd these skipping kerns to trust their heels
But the Norweyan lord, surveying vantage,
With furbish'd arms and new supplies of men,
Began a fresh assault.

   KING.   Dismay'd not this
Our captains, Macbeth and Banquo?

   SERG.   Yes,
As sparrows eagles, or the hare the lion.
If I say sooth, I must report they were
As cannons overcharg'd with double cracks, so they
Doubly redoubled strokes upon the foe.
Except they meant to bathe in reeking wounds,
Or memorize another Golgotha,
I cannot tell—
But I am faint; my gashes cry for help.

KING. So well thy words become thee as thy wounds;
They smack of honour both. Go get him surgeons.

               [Exit SERGEANT, *attended. Enter* ROSS.]

Who comes here?

   MAL.   The worthy Thane of Ross.

   LEN. What a haste looks through his eyes! So should
      he look

That seems to speak things strange.

   ROSS.   God save the King!

   KING. Whence cam'st thou, worthy thane?

   ROSS.   From Fife, great King,

Where the Norweyan banners flout the sky
And fan our people cold. Norway himself,
With terrible numbers,
Assisted by that most disloyal traitor
The Thane of Cawdor, began a dismal conflict,
Till that Bellona's bridegroom, lapp'd in proof,
Confronted him with self-comparisons,
Point against point, rebellious arm 'gainst arm,
Curbing his lavish spirit; and to conclude,
The victory fell on us.

   KING.   Great happiness!

   ROSS.   That now

Sweno, the Norways' king, craves composition;
Nor would we deign him burial of his men
Till he disbursed, at Saint Colme's Inch,
Ten thousand dollars to our general use.

   KING. No more that Thane of Cawdor shall deceive
Our bosom interest. Go pronounce his present death
And with his former title greet Macbeth.

   ROSS. I'll see it done.

   DUN. What he hath lost noble Macbeth hath won.

                            Exeunt.

Scene III: A blasted heath.

Thunder. Enter the three WITCHES.

1. WITCH. Where hast thou been, sister?
2. WITCH. Killing swine.
3. WITCH. Sister, where thou?
1. WITCH. A sailor's wife had chestnuts in her lap
And mounch'd and mounch'd and mounch'd. 'Give me,'
    quoth I.
'Aroint thee, witch!' the rump-fed ronyon cries.
Her husband's to Aleppo gone, master o' th' Tiger;
      But in a sieve I'll thither sail
      And, like a rat without a tail,
      I'll do, I'll do, and I'll do.
2. WITCH. I'll give thee a wind.
1. WITCH. Th' art kind.
3. WITCH. And I another.
1. WITCH. I myself have all the other,
      And the very ports they blow,
      All the quarters that they know
      I' th' shipman's card.
      I will drain him dry as hay.
      Sleep shall neither night nor day
      Hang upon his penthouse lid.
      He shall live a man forbid.
      Weary sev'nights, nine times nine,
      Shall he dwindle, peak, and pine.
      Though his bark cannot be lost,
      Yet it shall be tempest-tost.
      Look what I have.
2. WITCH. Show me! show me!
1. WITCH. Here I have a pilot's thumb,
      Wrack'd as homeward he did come.
                  Drum within.

3. Witch. A drum, a drum!
    Macbeth doth come.
All. The Weird Sisters, hand in hand,
    Posters of the sea and land,
    Thus do go about, about,
    Thrice to thine, and thrice to mine,
    And thrice again, to make up nine.
    Peace! The charm's wound up.

Enter Macbeth *and* Banquo.

Macb. So foul and fair a day I have not seen.
Ban. How far is't call'd to Forres? What are these,
So wither'd, and so wild in their attire,
That look not like th' inhabitants o' th' earth,
And yet are on't? Live you? or are you aught
That man may question? You seem to understand me,
By each at once her choppy finger laying
Upon her skinny lips. You should be women,
And yet your beards forbid me to interpret
That you are so.
    Macb.   Speak, if you can. What are you?
1. Witch. All hail, Macbeth! Hail to thee, Thane of
    Glamis!
2. Witch. All hail, Macbeth! Hail to thee, Thane of
    Cawdor!
3. Witch. All hail, Macbeth, that shalt be King here-
    after!
Ban. Good sir, why do you start and seem to fear
Things that do sound so fair? I' th' name of truth,
Are ye fantastical, or that indeed
Which outwardly ye show? My noble partner
You greet with present grace and great prediction
Of noble having and of royal hope,
That he seems rapt withal. To me you speak not.

If you can look into the seeds of time
And say which grain will grow and which will not,
Speak then to me, who neither beg nor fear
Your favours nor your hate.

    1. WITCH. Hail!

    2. WITCH. Hail!

    3. WITCH. Hail!

    1. WITCH. Lesser than Macbeth, and greater.

    2. WITCH. Not so happy, yet much happier.

    3. WITCH. Thou shalt get kings, though thou be none.
So all hail, Macbeth and Banquo!

    1. WITCH. Banquo and Macbeth, all hail!

    MACB. Stay, you imperfect speakers, tell me more!
By Sinel's death I know I am Thane of Glamis;
But how of Cawdor? The Thane of Cawdor lives,
A prosperous gentleman; and to be King
Stands not within the prospect of belief,
No more than to be Cawdor. Say from whence
You owe this strange intelligence, or why
Upon this blasted heath you stop our way
With such prophetic greeting. Speak, I charge you.

                                   WITCHES *vanish.*

    BAN. The earth hath bubbles, as the water has,
And these are of them. Whither are they vanish'd?

    MACB. Into the air, and what seem'd corporal melted
As breath into the wind. Would they had stay'd!

    BAN. Were such things here as we do speak about?
Or have we eaten on the insane root
That takes the reason prisoner?

    MACB. Your children shall be kings.

    BAN.   You shall be King.

    MACB. And Thane of Cawdor too. Went it not so?

    BAN. To th' selfsame tune and words. Who's here?

            Enter ROSS *and* ANGUS.

Ross. The King hath happily receiv'd, Macbeth,
The news of thy success; and when he reads
Thy personal venture in the rebels' fight,
His wonders and his praises do contend
Which should be thine or his. Silenc'd with that,
In viewing o'er the rest o' th' selfsame day,
He finds thee in the stout Norweyan ranks,
Nothing afeard of what thyself didst make,
Strange images of death. As thick as tale
Came post with post, and every one did bear
Thy praises in his kingdom's great defence
And pour'd them down before him.

Ang.   We are sent
To give thee from our royal master thanks;
Only to herald thee into his sight,
Not pay thee.

Ross. And for an earnest of a greater honour,
He bade me, from him, call thee Thane of Cawdor;
In which addition, hail, most worthy Thane!
For it is thine.

Ban.   What, can the devil speak true?

Macb. The Thane of Cawdor lives. Why do you
     dress me
In borrowed robes?

Ang.   Who was the Thane lives yet,
But under heavy judgment bears that life
Which he deserves to lose. Whether he was combin'd
With those of Norway, or did line the rebel
With hidden help and vantage, or that with both
He labour'd in his country's wrack, I know not;
But treasons capital, confess'd and prov'd,
Have overthrown him.

Macb.   [aside] Glamis, and Thane of Cawdor!
The greatest is behind.—[To Ross and Angus.] Thanks
     for your pains.

[*Aside to* BANQUO] Do you not hope your children shall
    be kings,
When those that gave the Thane of Cawdor to me
Promis'd no less to them?

    BAN. [*aside to* MACBETH] That, trusted home,
Might yet enkindle you unto the crown,
Besides the Thane of Cawdor. But 'tis strange!
And oftentimes, to win us to our harm,
The instruments of darkness tell us truths,
Win us with honest trifles, to betray 's
In deepest consequence.—
Cousins, a word, I pray you.

    MACB.   [*aside*] Two truths are told,
As happy prologues to the swelling act
Of the imperial theme.—I thank you, gentlemen.—
[*Aside*] This supernatural soliciting
Cannot be ill; cannot be good. If ill,
Why hath it given me earnest of success,
Commencing in a truth? I am Thane of Cawdor.
If good, why do I yield to that suggestion
Whose horrid image doth unfix my hair
And make my seated heart knock at my ribs
Against the use of nature? Present fears
Are less than horrible imaginings.
My thought, whose murther yet is but fantastical,
Shakes so my single state of man that function
Is smother'd in surmise and nothing is
But what is not.

    BAN.   Look how our partner's rapt.

    MACB. [*aside*] If chance will have me King, why,
    chance may crown me,
Without my stir.

    BAN.   New honours come upon him,
Like our strange garments, cleave not to their mould
But with the aid of use.

MACB.   [*aside*] Come what come may,
Time and the hour runs through the roughest day.

BAN. Worthy Macbeth, we stay upon your leisure.

MACB. Give me your favour. My dull brain was
    wrought
With things forgotten. Kind gentlemen, your pains
Are regist'red where every day I turn
The leaf to read them. Let us toward the King.
[*Aside to* BANQUO] Think upon what hath chanc'd; and,
    at more time,
The interim having weigh'd it, let us speak
Our free hearts each to other.

BAN. [*aside to* MACBETH] Very gladly.

MACB. [*aside to* BANQUO] Till then, enough.—Come,
    friends.   *Exeunt.*

Scene IV: Forres. The Palace.

Flourish. Enter KING DUNCAN, LENNOX, MALCOLM,
        DONALBAIN, *and* ATTENDANTS.

KING. Is execution done on Cawdor? Are not
Those in commission yet return'd?

MAL.   My liege,
They are not yet come back. But I have spoke
With one that saw him die; who did report
That very frankly he confess'd his treasons,
Implor'd your Highness' pardon, and set forth
A deep repentance. Nothing in his life
Became him like the leaving it. He died
As one that had been studied in his death
To throw away the dearest thing he ow'd
As 'twere a careless trifle.

KING.   There's no art

To find the mind's construction in the face.
He was a gentleman on whom I built
An absolute trust.

        [*Enter* MACBETH, BANQUO, ROSS, *and* ANGUS.]
                O worthiest cousin,
The sin of my ingratitude even now
Was heavy on me! Thou art so far before
That swiftest wing of recompense is slow
To overtake thee. Would thou hads't less deserv'd,
That the proportion both of thanks and payment
Might have been mine! Only I have left to say,
More is thy due than more than all can pay.

  MACB. The service and the loyalty I owe,
In doing it pays itself. Your Highness' part
Is to receive our duties; and our duties
Are to your throne and state children and servants,
Which do but what they should by doing everything
Safe toward your love and honour.

  KING.   Welcome hither.
I have begun to plant thee and will labour
To make thee full of growing. Noble Banquo,
That hast no less deserv'd, nor must be known
No less to have done so, let me infold thee
And hold thee to my heart.

  BAN.   There if I grow,
The harvest is your own.

  KING.   My plenteous joys,
Wanton in fulness, seek to hide themselves
In drops of sorrow. Sons, kinsmen, thanes,
And you whose places are the nearest, know
We will establish our estate upon
Our eldest, Malcolm, whom we name hereafter
The Prince of Cumberland; which honour must
Not unaccompanied invest him only,
But signs of nobleness, like stars, shall shine

On all deservers. From hence to Inverness,
And bind us further to you.

    MACB. The rest is labour, which is not us'd for you!
I'll be myself the harbinger, and make joyful
The hearing of my wife with your approach;
So, humbly take my leave.

    KING.   My worthy Cawdor!

    MACB. [*aside*] The Prince of Cumberland! That is a
        step
On which I must fall down, or else o'erleap,
For in my way it lies. Stars, hide your fires!
Let not light see my black and deep desires.
The eye wink at the hand; yet let that be,
Which the eye fears, when it is done, to see.   *Exit.*

    KING. True, worthy Banquo: he is full so valiant,
And in his commendations I am fed;
It is a banquet to me. Let's after him,
Whose care is gone before to bid us welcome.
It is a peerless kinsman.   *Flourish. Exeunt.*

Scene V: Inverness. Macbeth's Castle.

Enter MACBETH'S WIFE, *alone, with a letter.*

    LADY. [*reads*] 'They met me in the day of success;
and I have learn'd by the perfect'st report they have
more in them than mortal knowledge. When I burn'd in
desire to question them further, they made themselves
air, into which they vanish'd. Whiles I stood rapt in the
wonder of it, came missives from the King, who all-
hail'd me Thane of Cawdor, by which title, before, these
Weird Sisters saluted me, and referr'd me to the coming
on of time with "Hail, King that shalt be!" This have I
thought good to deliver thee, my dearest partner of
greatness, that thou mightst not lose the dues of re-

joicing by being ignorant of what greatness is promis'd
thee. Lay it to thy heart, and farewell.'
Glamis thou art, and Cawdor, and shalt be—
What thou art promis'd. Yet do I fear thy nature.
It is too full o' th' milk of human kindness
To catch the nearest way. Thou wouldst be great;
Art not without ambition, but without
The illness should attend it. What thou wouldst highly,
That wouldst thou holily; wouldst not play false,
And yet wouldst wrongly win. Thou'ldst have, great
    Glamis,
That which cries 'Thus thou must do,' if thou have it;
And that which rather thou dost fear to do
Than wishest should be undone. Hie thee hither,
That I may pour my spirits in thine ear
And chastise with the valour of my tongue
All that impedes thee from the golden round
Which fate and metaphysical aid doth seem
To have thee crown'd withal.

[Enter MESSENGER.]

                        What is your tidings?
MESS. The King comes here to-night.
LADY.   Thou'rt mad to say it!
Is not thy master with him? who, were't so,
Would have inform'd for preparation.
    MESS. So please you, it is true. Our Thane is coming.
One of my fellows had the speed of him,
Who, almost dead for breath, had scarcely more
Than would make up his message.
    LADY.   Give him tending;
He brings great news.

                       [Exit MESSENGER.]
           The raven himself is hoarse
That croaks the fatal entrance of Duncan

Under my battlements. Come, you spirits
That tend on mortal thoughts, unsex me here,
And fill me, from the crown to the toe, top-full
Of direst cruelty! Make thick my blood;
Stop up th' access and passage to remorse,
That no compunctious visitings of nature
Shake my fell purpose nor keep peace between
Th' effect and it! Come to my woman's breasts
And take my milk for gall, you murth'ring ministers,
Wherever in your sightless substances
You wait on nature's mischief! Come, thick night,
And pall thee in the dunnest smoke of hell,
That my keen knife see not the wound it makes,
Nor heaven peep through the blanket of the dark
To cry 'Hold, hold!'

[*Enter* MACBETH]

              Great Glamis! worthy Cawdor!
Greater than both, by the all-hail hereafter!
Thy letters have transported me beyond
This ignorant present, and I feel now
The future in the instant.

MACB.   My dearest love,
Duncan comes here to-night.

LADY.   And when goes hence?

MACB. To-morrow, as he purposes.

LADY.   O, never
Shall sun that morrow see!
Your face, my Thane, is as a book where men
May read strange matters. To beguile the time,
Look like the time; bear welcome in your eye,
Your hand, your tongue; look like the innocent flower,
But be the serpent under't. He that's coming
Must be provided for; and you shall put
This night's great business into my dispatch,

Which shall to all our nights and days to come
Give solely sovereign sway and masterdom.
    MACB. We will speak further.
    LADY.   Only look up clear.
To alter favour ever is to fear.
Leave all the rest to me.   *Exeunt.*

Scene VI: Inverness. Before Macbeth's Castle.

Hautboys and torches. Enter KING DUNCAN, MALCOLM,
DONALBAIN, BANQUO, LENNOX, MACDUFF, ROSS, ANGUS,
and ATTENDANTS.

    KING. This castle hath a pleasant seat. The air
Nimbly and sweetly recommends itself
Unto our gentle senses.
    BAN.   This guest of summer,
The temple-haunting martlet, does approve
By his lov'd mansionry that the heaven's breath
Smells wooingly here. No jutty, frieze,
Buttress, nor coign of vantage, but this bird
Hath made his pendent bed and procreant cradle.
Where they most breed and haunt, I have observ'd
The air is delicate.

Enter LADY MACBETH.

    KING.   See, see, our honour'd hostess!
The love that follows us sometime is our trouble,
Which still we thank as love. Herein I teach you
How you shall bid God 'ield us for your pains
And thank us for your trouble.
    LADY.   All our service
In every point twice done, and then done double,
Were poor and single business to contend
Against those honours deep and broad wherewith

Your Majesty loads our house. For those of old,
And the late dignities heap'd up to them,
We rest your hermits.

KING.   Where's the Thane of Cawdor?
We cours'd him at the heels and had a purpose
To be his purveyor; but he rides well,
And his great love, sharp as his spur, hath holp him
To his home before us. Fair and noble hostess,
We are your guest to-night.

LADY.   Your servants ever
Have theirs, themselves, and what is theirs, in compt,
To make their audit at your Highness' pleasure,
Still to return your own.

KING.   Give me your hand;
Conduct me to mine host. We love him highly
And shall continue our graces towards him.
By your leave, hostess.   *Exeunt.*

Scene VII: Inverness. Macbeth's Castle.

Hautboys. Torches. Enter a SEWER, *and divers* SERVANTS
with dishes and service over the stage. Then enter
MACBETH.

MACB. If it were done when 'tis done, then 'twere well
It were done quickly. If th' assassination
Could trammel up the consequence, and catch,
With his surcease, success; that but this blow
Might be the be-all and the end-all here,
But here, upon this bank and shoal of time,
We'ld jump the life to come. But in these cases
We still have judgment here, that we but teach
Bloody instructions, which, being taught, return
To plague th' inventor. This even-handed justice
Commends th' ingredience of our poison'd chalice

To our own lips. He's here in double trust:
First, as I am his kinsman and his subject—
Strong both against the deed; then, as his host,
Who should against his murtherer shut the door,
Not bear the knife myself. Besides, this Duncan
Hath borne his faculties so meek, hath been
So clear in his great office, that his virtues
Will plead like angels, trumpet-tongu'd, against
The deep damnation of his taking-off;
And pity, like a naked new-born babe,
Striding the blast, or heaven's cherubin, hors'd
Upon the sightless couriers of the air,
Shall blow the horrid deed in every eye,
That tears shall drown the wind I have no spur
To prick the sides of my intent, but only
Vaulting ambition, which o'erleaps itself
And falls on th' other side.

[*Enter* LADY MACBETH.]

                           How now? What news?
  LADY. He has almost supp'd. Why have you left the
    chamber?
  MACB. Hath he ask'd for me?
  LADY.   Know you not he has?
  MACB. We will proceed no further in this business.
He hath honour'd me of late, and I have bought
Golden opinions from all sorts of people,
Which would be worn now in their newest gloss,
Not cast aside so soon.
  LADY.   Was the hope drunk
Wherein you dress'd yourself? Hath it slept since?
And wakes it now to look so green and pale
At what it did so freely? From this time
Such I account thy love. Art thou afeard
To be the same in thine own act and valour

As thou art in desire? Wouldst thou have that
Which thou esteem'st the ornament of life,
And live a coward in thine own esteem,
Letting 'I dare not' wait upon 'I would,'
Like the poor cat i' th' adage?

MACB.   Prithee peace!
I dare do all that may become a man.
Who dares do more is none.

LADY.   What beast was't then
That made you break this enterprise to me?
When you durst do it, then you were a man;
And to be more than what you were, you would
Be so much more the man. Nor time nor place
Did then adhere, and yet you would make both.
They have made themselves, and that their fitness now
Does unmake you. I have given suck, and know
How tender 'tis to love the babe that milks me.
I would, while it was smiling in my face,
Have pluck'd my nipple from his boneless gums
And dash'd the brains out, had I so sworn as you
Have done to this.

MACB.   If we should fail?

LADY.   We fail?
But screw your courage to the sticking place,
And we'll not fail. When Duncan is asleep
(Whereto the rather shall his day's hard journey
Soundly invite him), his two chamberlains
Will I with wine and wassail so convince
That memory, the warder of the brain,
Shall be a fume, and the receipt of reason
A limbeck only. When in swinish sleep
Their drenched natures lie as in a death,
What cannot you and I perform upon
Th' unguarded Duncan? what not put upon

His spongy officers, who shall bear the guilt
Of our great quell?

MACB.   Bring forth men-children only;
For thy undaunted mettle should compose
Nothing but males. Will it not be receiv'd,
When we have mark'd with blood those sleepy two
Of his own chamber and us'd their very daggers,
That they have done't?

LADY.   Who dares receive it other,
As we shall make our griefs and clamour roar
Upon his death?

MACB.   I am settled and bend up
Each corporal agent to this terrible feat.
Away, and mock the time with fairest show;
False face must hide what the false heart doth know.

Exeunt.

Act II: Scene I: Inverness. Court of Macbeth's Castle.

Enter BANQUO, *and* FLEANCE *with a torch before him.*

BAN. How goes the night, boy?

FLE. The moon is down; I have not heard the clock.

BAN. And she goes down at twelve.

FLE.   I take't, 'tis later, sir.

BAN. Hold, take my sword. There's husbandry in
    heaven;
Their candles are all out. Take thee that too.
A heavy summons lies like lead upon me,
And yet I would not sleep. Merciful powers,
Restrain in me the cursed thoughts that nature
Gives way to in repose!

[*Enter* MACBETH, *and a* SERVANT *with a torch.*]

　　　　　　　　　　Give me my sword.

Who's there?

　MACB. A friend.

　BAN. What, sir, not yet at rest? The King's abed.
He hath been in unusual pleasure and
Sent forth great largess to your offices.
This diamond he greets your wife withal
By the name of most kind hostess, and shut up
In measureless content.

　MACB.　　　　　　　　Being unprepar'd,
Our will became the servant to defect,
Which else should free have wrought.

　BAN.　　　　　　　　　All's well
I dreamt last night of the three Weird Sisters.
To you they have show'd some truth.

　MACB.　　　　　　　　I think not of them.
Yet when we can entreat an hour to serve,
We would spend it in some words upon that business,
If you would grant the time.

　BAN.　　　　　　At your kind'st leisure.

　MACB. If you shall cleave to my consent, when 'tis,
It shall make honour for you.

　BAN.　　　　　　So I lose none
In seeking to augment it but still keep
My bosom franchis'd and allegiance clear,
I shall be counsell'd.

　MACB.　　　　Good repose the while!

　BAN. Thanks, sir. The like to you!

　　　　　　　　　Exeunt BANQUO *and* FLEANCE.

　MACB. Go bid thy mistress, when my drink is ready,
She strike upon the bell. Get thee to bed.

　　　　　　　　　　　　[*Exit* SERVANT.]

Is this a dagger which I see before me,

The handle toward my hand? Come, let me clutch thee!
I have thee not, and yet I see thee still.
Art thou not, fatal vision, sensible
To feeling as to sight? or art thou but
A dagger of the mind, a false creation,
Proceeding from the heat-oppressed brain?
I see thee yet, in form as palpable
As this which now I draw.
Thou marshall'st me the way that I was going,
And such an instrument I was to use.
Mine eyes are made the fools o' th' other senses,
Or else worth all the rest. I see thee still;
And on thy blade and dudgeon gouts of blood,
Which was not so before. There's no such thing.
It is the bloody business which informs
Thus to mine eyes. Now o'er the one half-world
Nature seems dead, and wicked dreams abuse
The curtain'd sleep. Now witchcraft celebrates
Pale Hecate's offerings; and wither'd murther,
Alarum'd by his sentinel, the wolf,
Whose howl's his watch, thus with his stealthy pace,
With Tarquin's ravishing strides, towards his design
Moves like a ghost. Thou sure and firm-set earth,
Hear not my steps which way they walk, for fear
Thy very stones prate of my whereabout
And take the present horror from the time,
Which now suits with it. Whiles I threat, he lives;
Words to the heat of deeds too cold breath gives.
                                        [*A bell rings.*]
I go, and it is done. The bell invites me.
Hear it not, Duncan, for it is a knell
That summons thee to heaven, or to hell.   *Exit.*

Scene II: Inverness. Macbeth's Castle.

Enter LADY MACBETH.

LADY. That which hath made them drunk hath made
    me bold;
What hath quench'd them hath given me fire. Hark!
    Peace!
It was the owl that shriek'd, the fatal bellman
Which gives the stern'st good-night. He is about it.
The doors are open, and the surfeited grooms
Do mock their charge with snores. I have drugg'd their
    possets,
That death and nature do contend about them
Whether they live or die.

MACB. [*within*] Who's there? What, ho?

LADY. Alack, I am afraid they have awak'd,
And 'tis not done! Th' attempt, and not the deed,
Confounds us. Hark! I laid their daggers ready;
He could not miss 'em. Had he not resembled
My father as he slept, I had done't.

[*Enter* MACBETH.]

                              My husband!

MACB. I have done the deed. Didst thou not hear a
    noise?

LADY. I heard the owl scream and the crickets cry.
Did not you speak?

MACB.   When?

LADY.   Now.

MACB.   As I descended?

LADY. Ay.

MACB. Hark!
Who lies i' th' second chamber?

LADY.   Donalbain.

MACB. This is a sorry sight.

Looks on his hands.

LADY. A foolish thought, to say a sorry sight.

MACB. There's one did laugh in's sleep, and one
cried 'Murther!'

That they did wake each other. I stood and heard them
But they did say their prayers and address'd them
Again to sleep.

LADY.   There are two lodg'd together.

MACB. One cried 'God bless us!' and 'Amen!' the
other,

As they had seen me with these hangman's hands,
List'ning their fear. I could not say 'Amen!'
When they did say 'God bless us!'

LADY.   Consider it not so deeply.

MACB. But wherefore could not I pronounce 'Amen'?
I had most need of blessing, and 'Amen'
Stuck in my throat.

LADY.   These deeds must not be thought
After these ways. So, it will make us mad.

MACB. Methought I heard a voice cry 'Sleep no more!
Macbeth does murther sleep.'—the innocent sleep,
Sleep that knits up the ravell'd sleave of care,
The death of each day's life, sore labour's bath,
Balm of hurt minds, great nature's second course,
Chief nourisher in life's feast.

LADY.   What do you mean?

MACB. Still it cried 'Sleep no more!' to all the house;
'Glamis hath murther'd sleep, and therefore Cawdor
Shall sleep no more! Macbeth shall sleep no more!'

LADY. Who was it that thus cried? Why, worthy
Thane,

You do unbend your noble strength to think
So brainsickly of things. Go get some water
And wash this filthy witness from your hand.

Why did you bring these daggers from the place?
They must lie there. Go carry them and smear
The sleepy grooms with blood.

MACB.   I'll go no more.
I am afraid to think what I have done;
Look on't again I dare not.

LADY.   Infirm of purpose!
Give me the daggers. The sleeping and the dead
Are but as pictures. 'Tis the eye of childhood
That fears a painted devil. If he do bleed,
I'll gild the faces of the grooms withal,
For it must seem their guilt.

                              Exit. Knocking within.

MACB.   Whence is that knocking?
How is't with me when every noise appals me?
What hands are here? Ha! they pluck out mine eyes!
Will all great Neptune's ocean wash this blood
Clean from my hand? No. This my hand will rather
The multitudinous seas incarnadine,
Making the green one red.

                    Enter LADY MACBETH.

LADY. My hands are of your colour, but I shame
To wear a heart so white. [*Knock.*] I hear a knocking
At the south entry. Retire we to our chamber.
A little water clears us of this deed.
How easy is it then! Your constancy
Hath left you unattended. [*Knock.*] Hark! more knock-
    ing.
Get on your nightgown, lest occasion call us
And show us to be watchers. Be not lost
So poorly in your thoughts.

MACB. To know my deed, 'twere best not know my-
    self.   [*Knock.*]
Wake Duncan with thy knocking! I would thou couldst!
                                          Exeunt.

Scene III: Inverness. Macbeth's Castle.

Enter a PORTER. *Knocking within.*

PORTER. Here's a knocking indeed! If a man were
porter of hell gate, he should have old turning the key.
[*Knock.*]Knock, knock, knock! Who's there, i' th' name
of Belzebub? Here's a farmer that hang'd himself on th'
expectation of plenty. Come in time! Have napkins enow
about you; here you'll sweat for't. [*Knock.*] Knock,
knock! Who's there, in th' other devil's name? Faith,
here's an equivocator, that could swear in both the scales
against either scale; who committed treason enough for
God's sake, yet could not equivocate to heaven. O,
come in, equivocator! [*Knock.*] Knock, knock, knock!
Who's there? Faith, here's an English tailor come hither
for stealing out of a French hose. Come in, tailor. Here
you may roast your goose. [*Knock.*] Knock, knock! Never
at quiet! What are you? But this place is too cold for
hell. I'll devil-porter it no further. I had thought to have
let in some of all professions that go the primrose way
to th' everlasting bonfire. [*Knock.*] Anon, anon! [*Opens
the gate.*] I pray you remember the porter.

Enter MACDUFF *and* LENNOX.

MACD. Was it so late, friend, ere you went to bed.
That you do lie so late?

PORT. Faith, sir, we were carousing till the second
cock; and drink, sir, is a great provoker of three things.

MACD. What three things does drink especially provoke?

PORT. Marry, sir, nose-painting, sleep, and urine.
Lechery, sir, it provokes, and unprovokes: it provokes the
desire, but it takes away the performance. Therefore
much drink may be said to be an equivocator with

lechery: it makes him, and it mars him; it sets him on, and it takes him off; it persuades him, and disheartens him; makes him stand to, and not stand to; in conclusion, equivocates him in a sleep, and, giving him the lie, leaves him.

MACD. I believe drink gave thee the lie last night.

PORT. That it did, sir, i' the very throat on me; but I requited him for his lie; and, I think, being too strong for him, though he took up my legs sometime, yet I made a shift to cast him.

MACD. Is thy master stirring?

[Enter MACBETH.]

Our knocking has awak'd him; here he comes.

LEN. Good morrow, noble sir.

MACB. 　　　　　　　　　　　Good morrow, both.

MACD. Is the King stirring, worthy Thane?

MACB. 　　　　　　　　　　　　　　　Not yet.

MACD. He did command me to call timely on him;
I have almost slipp'd the hour.

MACB. 　　　　　　　　　　I'll bring you to him.

MACD. I know this is a joyful trouble to you;
But yet 'tis one.

MACB. The labour we delight in physics pain.
This is the door.

MACD. 　　　　　I'll make so bold to call,
For 'tis my limited service. 　　　　　　　　*Exit.*

LEN. Goes the King hence to-day?

MACB. 　　　　　　　　　He does; he did appoint so.

LEN. The night has been unruly. Where we lay,
Our chimneys were blown down; and, as they say,
Lamentings heard i' th' air, strange screams of death,
And prophesying, with accents terrible,
Of dire combustion and confus'd events
New hatch'd to th' woeful time. The obscure bird

Clamour'd the livelong night. Some say the earth
Was feverous and did shake.

MACB.   'Twas a rough night.

LEN. My young remembrance cannot parallel
A fellow to it.

Enter MACDUFF.

MACD. O horror, horror, horror! Tongue nor heart
Cannot conceive nor name thee!

MACB., LEN.   What's the matter?

MACD. Confusion now hath made his masterpiece!
Most sacrilegious murther hath broke ope
The Lord's anointed temple and stole thence
The life o' th' building!

MACB.   What is't you say? the life?

LEN. Mean you his Majesty?

MACD. Approach the chamber, and destroy your sight
With a new Gorgon. Do not bid me speak.
See, and then speak yourselves.

                [*Exeunt* MACBETH *and* LENNOX.]
                   Awake, awake!

Ring the alarum bell. Murther and treason!
Banquo and Donalbain! Malcolm! awake!
Shake off this downy sleep, death's counterfeit,
And look on death itself! Up, up, and see
The great doom's image! Malcolm! Banquo!
As from your graves rise up and walk like sprites
To countenance this horror! Ring the bell!

                    Bell rings

Enter LADY MACBETH.

LADY. What's the business,
That such a hideous trumpet calls to parley
The sleepers of the house? Speak, speak!

MACD.   O gentle lady,

'Tis not for you to hear what I can speak!
The repetition in a woman's ear
Would murther as it fell.

[*Enter* BANQUO.]

                              O Banquo, Banquo,
Our royal master's murther'd!

LADY.   Woe, alas!
What, in our house?

BAN.   Too cruel anywhere.
Dear Duff, I prithee contradict thyself
And say it is not so.

Enter MACBETH, LENNOX, *and* ROSS.

MACB. Had I but died an hour before this chance,
I had liv'd a blessed time; for from this instant
There's nothing serious in mortality;
All is but toys; renown and grace is dead;
The wine of life is drawn, and the mere lees
Is left this vault to brag of.

Enter MALCOLM *and* DONALBAIN.

DON. What is amiss?

MACB.   You are, and do not know't.
The spring, the head, the fountain of your blood
Is stopp'd, the very source of it is stopp'd.

MACD. Your royal father's murther'd.

MAL.   O, by whom?

LEN. Those of his chamber, as it seem'd, had done't.
Their hands and faces were all badg'd with blood;
So were their daggers, which unwip'd we found
Upon their pillows.
They star'd and were distracted. No man's life
Was to be trusted with them.

MACB. O, yet I do repent me of my fury
That I did kill them.

   Macd.   Wherefore did you so?

   Macb. Who can be wise, amaz'd, temp'rate and furious,

Loyal and neutral, in a moment? No man.

The expedition of my violent love

Outrun the pauser, reason. Here lay Duncan,

His silver skin lac'd with his golden blood,

And his gash'd stabs look'd like a breach in nature

For ruin's wasteful entrance; there, the murtherers,

Steep'd in the colours of their trade, their daggers

Unmannerly breech'd with gore. Who could refrain

That had a heart to love and in that heart

Courage to make 's love known?

   Lady.   Help me hence, ho!

   Macd. Look to the lady.

   Mal. [*aside to* Donalbain] Why do we hold our tongues,

That most may claim this argument for ours?

   Don. [*aside to* Malcolm] What should be spoken here, where our fate,

Hid in an auger hole, may rush and seize us?

Let's away.

Our tears are not yet brew'd.

   Mal.   [*aside to* Donalbain] Nor our strong sorrow

Upon the foot of motion.

   Ban.   Look to the lady.

                  [Lady Macbeth *is carried out.*]

And when we have our naked frailties hid,

That suffer in exposure, let us meet

And question this most bloody piece of work,

To know it further. Fears and scruples shake us.

In the great hand of God I stand, and thence

Against the undivulg'd pretence I fight

Of treasonous malice.

   Macd.   And so do I.

ALL.   So all.

MACB. Let's briefly put on manly readiness
And meet i' th' hall together.

ALL.   Well contented.

Exeunt all but MALCOLM *and* DONALBAIN.

MAL. What will you do? Let's not consort with them.
To show an unfelt sorrow is an office
Which the false man does easy. I'll to England.

DON. To Ireland I. Our separated fortune
Shall keep us both the safer. Where we are,
There's daggers in men's smiles; the near in blood,
The nearer bloody.

MAL.   This murtherous shaft that's shot
Hath not yet lighted, and our safest way
Is to avoid the aim. Therefore to horse!
And let us not be dainty of leave-taking
But shift away. There's warrant in that theft
Which steals itself when there's no mercy left.

Exeunt.

Scene IV. Inverness. Without Macbeth's Castle.

Enter ROSS *with an* OLD MAN.

OLD MAN. Threescore and ten I can remember well;
Within the volume of which time I have seen
Hours dreadful and things strange; but this sore night
Hath trifled former knowings.

ROSS.   Ah, good father,
Thou seest the heavens, as troubled with man's act,
Threaten his bloody stage. By th' clock 'tis day,
And yet dark night strangles the travelling lamp.
Is't night's predominance, or the day's shame,
That darkness does the face of earth entomb
When living light should kiss it?

OLD MAN.   'Tis unnatural,
Even like the deed that's done. On Tuesday last
A falcon, tow'ring in her pride of place,
Was by a mousing owl hawk'd at and kill'd.
   Ross. And Duncan's horses (a thing most strange **and**
     certain),
Beauteous and swift, the minions of their race,
Turn'd wild in nature, broke their stalls, flung out,
Contending 'gainst obedience, as they would make
War with mankind.
   OLD MAN.   'Tis said they eat each other.
   Ross. They did so, to th' amazement of mine eyes
That look'd upon't.

               [Enter MACDUFF.*]*

             Here comes the good Macduff.
How goes the world, sir, now?
   MACD.   Why, see you not?
   Ross. Is't known who did this more than bloody deed?
   MACD. Those that Macbeth hath slain.
   Ross.   Alas, the day!
What good could they pretend?
   MACD.   They were suborn'd.
Malcolm and Donalbain, the King's two sons,
Are stol'n away and fled, which puts upon them
Suspicion of the deed.
   Ross.   'Gainst nature still!
Thriftless ambition, that wilt raven up
Thine own live's means! Then 'tis most like
The sovereignty will fall upon Macbeth.
   MACD. He is already nam'd, and gone to Scone
To be invested.
   Ross.   Where is Duncan's body?
   MACD. Carried to Colmekill,

The sacred storehouse of his predecessors
And guardian of their bones.

    Ross.   Will you to Scone?

    MACD. No, cousin, I'll to Fife.

    Ross.   Well, I will thither.

    MACD. Well, may you see things well done there.
    Adieu,
Lest our old robes sit easier than our new!

    Ross. Farewell, father.

    OLD MAN. God's benison go with you, and with those
That would make good of bad, and friends of foes!

                                   Exeunt omnes.

Act III: Scene I: Forres. The Palace.

Enter BANQUO.

    BAN. Thou hast it now—King, Cawdor, Glamis, all,
As the Weird Women promis'd; and I fear
Thou play'dst most foully for't. Yet it was said
It should not stand in thy posterity,
But that myself should be the root and father
Of many kings. If there come truth from them,
(As upon thee, Macbeth, their speeches shine),
Why, by the verities on thee made good,
May they not be my oracles as well
And set me up in hope? But, hush, no more!

Sennet sounded. Enter MACBETH, *as* KING; LADY
MACBETH, *as* QUEEN; LENNOX, ROSS, LORDS, *and*
                    ATTENDANTS.

    MACB. Here's our chief guest.

    LADY.   If he had been forgotten,
It had been as a gap in our great feast,
And all-thing unbecoming.

MACB. To-night we hold a solemn supper, sir,
And I'll request your presence.

BAN.   Let your Highness
Command upon me, to the which my duties
Are with a most indissoluble tie
For ever knit.

MACB.   Ride you this afternoon?

BAN. Ay, my good lord.

MACB. We should have else desir'd your good advice
(Which still hath been both grave and prosperous)
In this day's council; but we'll take to-morrow.
Is't far you ride?

BAN. As far, my lord, as will fill up the time
'Twixt this and supper. Go not my horse the better,
I must become a borrower of the night
For a dark hour or twain.

MACB.   Fail not our feast.

BAN. My lord, I will not.

MACB. We hear our bloody cousins are bestow'd
In England and in Ireland, not confessing
Their cruel parricide, filling their hearers
With strange invention. But of that to-morrow,
When therewithal we shall have cause of state
Craving us jointly. Hie you to horse. Adieu,
Till you return at night. Goes Fleance with you?

BAN. Ay, my good lord. Our time does call upon's.

MACB. I wish your horses swift and sure of foot,
And so I do commend you to their backs.
Farewell.   [*Exit* BANQUO.]
Let every man be master of his time
Till seven at night. To make society
The sweeter welcome, we will keep ourself
Till supper time alone. While then, God be with you!
        [*Exeunt* LORDS *and others, leaving* MACBETH *and*
                                 a SERVANT.]

Sirrah, a word with you. Attend those men
Our pleasure?
    SERV. They are, my lord, without the palace gate.
    MACB. Bring them before us.   [*Exit* SERVANT.]
                           To be thus is nothing,
But to be safely thus. Our fears in Banquo
Stick deep; and in his royalty of nature
Reigns that which would be fear'd. 'Tis much he dares,
And to that dauntless temper of his mind
He hath a wisdom that doth guide his valour
To act in safety. There is none but he
Whose being I do fear; and under him
My Genius is rebuk'd, as it is said
Mark Antony's was by Cæsar. He chid the Sisters
When first they put the name of King upon me,
And bade them speak to him. Then, prophet-like,
They hail'd him father to a line of kings.
Upon my head they plac'd a fruitless crown
And put a barren sceptre in my gripe,
Thence to be wrench'd with an unlineal hand,
No son of mine succeeding. If't be so,
For Banquo's issue have I fil'd my mind;
For them the gracious Duncan have I murther'd;
Put rancours in the vessel of my peace
Only for them, and mine eternal jewel
Given to the common enemy of man
To make them kings, the seed of Banquo kings!
Rather than so, come, Fate, into the list,
And champion me to th' utterance! Who's there?

    [*Enter* SERVANT *and two* MURTHERERS.]

Now go to the door and stay there till we call.
                         [*Exit* SERVANT.]
Was it not yesterday we spoke together?
    MURTHERERS. It was, so please your Highness.

MACB.   Well then, now
Have you consider'd of my speeches? Know
That it was he, in the times past, which held you
So under fortune, which you thought had been
Our innocent self. This I made good to you
In our last conference, pass'd in probation with you
How you were borne in hand, how cross'd; the instru-
    ments;
Who wrought with them; and all things else that might
To half a soul and to a notion craz'd
Say 'Thus did Banquo.'
    1. MUR.   You made it known to us.
    MACB. I did so; and went further, which is now
Our point of second meeting. Do you find
Your patience so predominant in your nature
That you can let this go? Are you so gospell'd
To pray for this good man and for his issue,
Whose heavy hand hath bow'd you to the grave
And beggar'd yours for ever?
    1. MUR.   We are men, my liege.
    MACB. Ay, in the catalogue ye go for men,
As hounds and greyhounds, mongrels, spaniels, curs,
Shoughs, water-rugs, and demi-wolves are clipt
All by the name of dogs. The valued file
Distinguishes the swift, the slow, the subtle,
The housekeeper, the hunter, every one
According to the gift which bounteous nature
Hath in him clos'd; whereby he does receive
Particular addition, from the bill
That writes them all alike; and so of men.
Now, if you have a station in the file,
Not i' th' worst rank of manhood, say't.
And I will put that business in your bosoms
Whose execution takes your enemy off,
Grapples you to the heart and love of us,

Who wear our health but sickly in his life,
Which in his death were perfect.

2. MUR.   I am one, my liege,
Whom the vile blows and buffets of the world
Have so incens'd that I am reckless what
I do to spite the world.

1. MUR.   And I another,
So weary with disasters, tugg'd with fortune,
That I would set my life on any chance,
To mend it or be rid on't.

MACB.   Both of you
Know Banquo was your enemy.

MURTHERERS.   True, my lord.

MACB. So is he mine; and in such bloody distance
That every minute of his being thrusts
Against my near'st of life; and though I could
With barefac'd power sweep him from my sight
And bid my will avouch it, yet I must not,
For certain friends that are both his and mine,
Whose loves I may not drop, but wail his fall
Who I myself struck down. And thence it is
That I to your assistance do make love,
Masking the business from the common eye
For sundry weighty reasons.

2. MUR.   We shall, my lord,
Perform what you command us.

1. MUR.   Though our lives—

MACB. Your spirits shine through you. Within this
    hour at most
I will advise you where to plant yourselves,
Acquaint you with the perfect spy o' th' time,
The moment on't; for't must be done to-night,
And something from the palace; always thought
That I require a clearness; and with him,
To leave no rubs nor botches in the work,

Fleance his son, that keeps him company,
Whose absence is no less material to me
Than is his father's, must embrace the fate
Of that dark hour. Resolve yourselves apart;
I'll come to you anon.

    MURTHERERS.   We are resolv'd, my lord.

    MACB. I'll call upon you straight. Abide within.

                        [*Exeunt* MURTHERERS.]

It is concluded. Banquo, thy soul's flight,
If it find heaven, must find it out to-night.

                                  Exit.

Scene II: Forres. The Palace.

Enter MACBETH'S LADY *and a* SERVANT.

    LADY. Is Banquo gone from court?

    SERV. Ay, madam, but returns again to-night.

    LADY. Say to the King I would attend his leisure
For a few words.

    SERV.   Madam, I will.   *Exit.*

    LADY.   Naught's had, all's spent,
Where our desire is got without content.
'Tis safer to be that which we destroy
Than by destruction dwell in doubtful joy.

                [*Enter* MACBETH.]

How now, my lord? Why do you keep alone,
Of sorriest fancies your companions making,
Using those thoughts which should indeed have died
With them they think on? Things without all remedy
Should be without regard. What's done is done.

    MACB. We have scotch'd the snake, not kill'd it.
She'll close, and be herself, whilst our poor malice
Remains in danger of her former tooth.

But let the frame of things disjoint, both the worlds
 suffer,
Ere we will eat our meal in fear and sleep
In the affliction of these terrible dreams
That shake us nightly. Better be with the dead,
Whom we, to gain our peace, have sent to peace,
Than on the torture of the mind to lie
In restless ecstasy. Duncan is in his grave;
After life's fitful fever he sleeps well.
Treason has done his worst. Nor steel nor poison,
Malice domestic, foreign levy, nothing,
Can touch him further.

 LADY.   Come on.
Gentle my lord, sleek o'er your rugged looks;
Be bright and jovial among your guests to-night.

 MACB. So shall I, love; and so, I pray, be you.
Let your remembrance apply to Banquo;
Present him eminence both with eye and tongue—
Unsafe the while, that we
Must lave our honours in these flattering streams
And make our faces vizards to our hearts,
Disguising what they are.

 LADY.   You must leave this.

 MACB. O, full of scorpions is my mind, dear wife!
Thou know'st that Banquo, and his Fleance, lives.

 LADY. But in them Nature's copy's not eterne.

 MACB. There's comfort yet! They are assailable.
Then be thou jocund. Ere the bat hath flown
His cloister'd flight, ere to black Hecate's summons
The shard-borne beetle with his drowsy hums
Hath rung night's yawning peal, there shall be done
A deed of dreadful note.

 LADY.   What's to be done?

 MACB. Be innocent of the knowledge, dearest chuck,
Till thou applaud the deed. Come, seeling night,

Scarf up the tender eye of pitiful day,
And with thy bloody and invisible hand
Cancel and tear to pieces that great bond
Which keeps me pale! Light thickens, and the crow
Makes wing to th' rooky wood.
Good things of day begin to droop and drowse,
Whiles night's black agents to their preys do rouse.
Thou marvell'st at my words; but hold thee still:
Things bad begun make strong themselves by ill.
So prithee go with me.   *Exeunt.*

Scene III: Forres. A park near the Palace.

Enter three MURTHERERS.

1. MUR. But who did bid thee join with us?
3. MUR.   Macbeth.
2. MUR. He needs not our mistrust, since he delivers
Our offices, and what we have to do,
To the direction just.
1. MUR.   Then stand with us.
The west yet glimmers with some streaks of day.
Now spurs the lated traveller apace
To gain the timely inn, and near approaches
The subject of our watch.
3. MUR.   Hark! I hear horses.
BAN. [*within*] Give us a light there, ho!
2. MUR.   Then 'tis he! The rest
That are within the note of expectation
Already are i' th' court.
1. MUR.   His horses go about.
3. MUR. Almost a mile; but he does usually,
So all men do, from hence to th' palace gate
Make it their walk.

Enter BANQUO, *and* FLEANCE *with a torch.*

2. MUR. A light, a light!

3. MUR. 'Tis he.

1. MUR. Stand to't.

BAN. It will be rain to-night.

1. MUR. Let it come down!

They fall upon BANQUO.

BAN. O, treachery! Fly, good Fleance, fly, fly, fly!
Thou mayst revenge. O slave!

Dies. FLEANCE *escapes.*

3. MUR. Who did strike out the light?

1. MUR. Was't not the way?

3. MUR. There's but one down; the son is fled.

2. MUR. We have lost
Best half of our affair.

1. MUR. Well, let's away, and say how much is done.

Exeunt.

Scene IV: Forres. Hall in the Palace.

Banquet prepar'd. Enter MACBETH, LADY MACBETH,
ROSS, LENNOX, LORDS, *and* ATTENDANTS.

MACB. You know your own degrees, sit down. At first
And last the hearty welcome.

LORDS. Thanks to your Majesty.

MACB. Ourself will mingle with society
And play the humble host.
Our hostess keeps her state, but in best time
We will require her welcome.

LADY. Pronounce it for me, sir, to all our friends,
For my heart speaks they are welcome.

Enter FIRST MURTHERER *to the door.*

MACB. See, they encounter thee with their hearts'
thanks.

Both sides are even. Here I'll sit i' th' midst.
Be large in mirth; anon we'll drink a measure
The table round. [*Goes to the door.*] There's blood upon
    thy face.

    MUR. 'Tis Banquo's then.

    MACB. 'Tis better thee without than he within.
Is he dispatch'd?

    MUR. My lord, his throat is cut. That I did for him.

    MACB. Thou are the best o' th' cutthroats! Yet he's
    good
That did the like for Fleance. If thou didst it,
Thou art the nonpareil.

    MUR.   Most royal sir,
Fleance is scap'd.

    MACB. [*aside*] Then comes my fit again. I had else
    been perfect;
Whole as the marble, founded as the rock,
As broad and general as the casing air.
But now I am cabin'd, cribb'd, confin'd, bound in
To saucy doubts and fears.—But Banquo's safe?

    MUR. Ay, my good lord. Safe in a ditch he bides,
With twenty trenched gashes on his head,
The least a death to nature.

    MACB.   Thanks for that!
There the grown serpent lies; the worm that's fled
Hath nature that in time will venom breed,
No teeth for th' present. Get thee gone. To-morrow
We'll hear ourselves again.

                          Exit MURDERER.

    LADY.   My royal lord,
You do not give the cheer. The feast is sold
That is not often vouch'd, while 'tis a-making,
'Tis given with welcome. To feed were best at home.
From thence, the sauce to meat is ceremony;
Meeting were bare without it.

Enter the GHOST OF BANQUO, *and sits in*
MACBETH'S *place.*

MACB. Sweet remembrancer!
Now good digestion wait on appetite,
And health on both!

LEN. May't please your Highness sit.

MACB. Here had we now our country's honour, roof'd,
Were the grac'd person of our Banquo present;
Who may I rather challenge for unkindness
Than pity for mischance!

ROSS. His absence, sir,
Lays blame upon his promise. Please't your Highness
To grace us with your royal company?

MACB. The table's full.

LEN. Here is a place reserv'd, sir.

MACB. Where?

LEN. Here, my good lord. What is't that moves your
Highness?

MACB. Which of you have done this?

LORDS. What, my good lord?

MACB. Thou canst not say I did it. Never shake
Thy gory locks at me.

ROSS. Gentlemen, rise. His Highness is not well.

LADY. Sit, worthy friends. My lord is often thus,
And hath been from his youth. Pray you keep seat.
The fit is momentary; upon a thought
He will again be well. If much you note him,
You shall offend him and extend his passion.
Feed, and regard him not.—Are you a man?

MACB. Ay, and a bold one, that dare look on that
Which might appal the devil

LADY. O proper stuff!
This is the very painting of your fear.
This is the air-drawn dagger which you said
Led you to Duncan. O, these flaws and starts

(Impostors to true fear) would well become
A woman's story at a winter's fire,
Authoriz'd by her grandam. Shame itself!
Why do you make such faces? When all's done,
You look but on a stool.

    MACB. Prithee see there! behold! look! lo! How say
       you?
Why, what care I? If thou canst nod, speak too.
If charnel houses and our graves must send
Those that we bury back, our monuments
Shall be the maws of kites.

                            Exit GHOST.
    LADY.   What, quite unmann'd in folly?
    MACB. If I stand here, I saw him.
    LADY.   Fie, for shame!
    MACB. Blood hath been shed ere now, i' th' olden
       time,
Ere humane statute purg'd the gentle weal;
Ay, and since too, murthers have been perform'd
Too terrible for the ear. The time has been
That, when the brains were out, the man would die,
And there an end! But now they rise again,
With twenty mortal murthers on their crowns,
And push us from our stools. This is more strange
Than such a murther is.
    LADY.   My worthy lord,
Your noble friends do lack you.
    MACB.   I do forget.
Do not muse at me, my most worthy friends.
I have a strange infirmity, which is nothing
To those that know me. Come, love and health to all!
Then I'll sit down. Give me some wine, fill full.

                 [*Enter* GHOST.]

I drink to th' general joy o' th' whole table,

And to our dear friend Banquo, whom we miss.
Would he were here! To all, and him, we thirst,
And all to all.

    LORDS.   Our duties, and the pledge.

    MACB. Avaunt, and quit my sight! Let the earth hide
thee!
Thy bones are marrowless, thy blood is cold;
Thou hast no speculation in those eyes
Which thou dost glare with!

    LADY.   Think of this, good peers,
But as a thing of custom. 'Tis no other.
Only it spoils the pleasure of the time.

    MACB. What man dare, I dare.
Approach thou like the rugged Russian bear,
The arm'd rhinoceros, or th' Hyrcan tiger;
Take any shape but that, and my firm nerves
Shall never tremble. Or be alive again
And dare me to the desert with thy sword.
If trembling I inhabit then, protest me
The baby of a girl. Hence, horrible shadow!
Unreal mock'ry, hence!

                            [*Exit* GHOST.]

           Why, so! Being gone,
I am a man again. Pray you sit still.

    LADY. You have displac'd the mirth, broke the good
      meeting
With most admir'd disorder.

    MACB.   Can such things be,
And overcome us like a summer's cloud
Without our special wonder? You make me strange
Even to the disposition that I owe,
When now I think you can behold such sights
And keep the natural ruby of your cheeks
When mine is blanch'd with fear.

    ROSS.   What sights, my lord?

LADY. I pray you speak not. He grows worse and
    worse;
Question enrages him. At once, good night.
Stand not upon the order of your going,
But go at once.
        LEN.   Good night, and better health
Attend his Majesty!
        LADY.   A kind góod night to all!
                Exeunt LORDS *and* ATTENDANTS.
    MACB. It will have blood, they say; blood will have
        blood.
Stones have been known to move and trees to speak;
Augures and understood relations have
By maggot-pies and choughs and rooks brought forth
The secret'st man of blood. What is the night?
    LADY. Almost at odds with morning, which is which.
    MACB. How say'st thou that Macduff denies his person
At our great bidding?
        LADY.   Did you send to him, sir?
    MACB. I hear it by the way; but I will send.
There's not a one of them but in his house
I keep a servant fee'd. I will to-morrow
(And betimes I will) unto the Weird Sisters.
More shall they speak; for now I am bent to know
By the worst means the worst. For mine own good
All causes shall give way. I am in blood
Stepp'd in so far that, should I wade no more,
Returning were as tedious as go o'er.
Strange things I have in head, that will to hand,
Which must be acted ere they may be scann'd.
    LADY. You lack the season of all natures, sleep.
    MACB. Come, we'll to sleep. My strange and self-abuse
Is the initiate fear that wants hard use.
We are yet but young in deed.

                                Exeunt.

Scene V: A heath.

Thunder. Enter the three WITCHES, *meeting* HECATE.

1. WITCH. Why, how now, Hecate? You look angerly.

HEC. Have I not reason, beldams as you are,
    Saucy and overbold? How did you dare
    To trade and traffic with Macbeth
    In riddles and affairs of death;
    And I, the mistress of your charms,
    The close contriver of all harms,
    Was never call'd to bear my part
    Or show the glory of our art?
    And, which is worse, all you have done
    Hath been but for a wayward son,
    Spiteful and wrathful, who, as others do,
    Loves for his own ends, not for you.
    But make amends now. Get you gone
    And at the pit of Acheron
    Meet me i' th' morning. Thither he
    Will come to know his destiny.
    Your vessels and your spells provide,
    Your charms and everything beside.
    I am for th' air. This night I'll spend
    Unto a dismal and a fatal end.
    Great business must be wrought ere noon.
    Upon the corner of the moon
    There hangs a vap'rous drop profound.
    I'll catch it ere it come to ground;
    And that, distill'd by magic sleights,
    Shall raise such artificial sprites
    As by the strength of their illusion
    Shall draw him on to his confusion.
    He shall spurn fate, scorn death, and bear
    His hopes 'bove wisdom, grace, and fear;

And you all know security
Is mortals' chiefest enemy.
[*Music and a song within:* 'Come away, come away,'
&c.]

Hark! I am call'd. My little spirit, see,
Sits in a foggy cloud and stays for me.

Exit.

1. WITCH. Come, let's make haste. She'll soon be
back again.

Exeunt.

Scene VI: Forres. The Palace.

Enter LENNOX *and another* LORD.

LEN. My former speeches have but hit your thoughts,
Which can interpret farther. Only I say
Things have been strangely borne. The gracious Duncan
Was pitied of Macbeth. Marry, he was dead!
And the right valiant Banquo walk'd too late;
Whom, you may say (if't please you) Fleance kill'd,
For Fleance fled. Men must not walk too late.
Who cannot want the thought how monstrous
It was for Malcolm and for Donalbain
To kill their gracious father? Damned fact!
How it did grieve Macbeth! Did he not straight,
In pious rage, the two delinquents tear,
That were the slaves of drink and thralls of sleep?
Was not that nobly done? Ay, and wisely too!
For 'twould have anger'd any heart alive
To hear the men deny't. So that I say
He has borne all things well; and I do think
That, had he Duncan's sons under his key
(As, an't please heaven, he shall not), they should find

What 'twere to kill a father. So should Fleance.
But peace! for from broad words, and 'cause he fail'd
His presence at the tyrant's feast, I hear
Macduff lives in disgrace. Sir, can you tell
Where he bestows himself?

LORD.   The son of Duncan,
From whom this tyrant holds the due of birth,
Lives in the English court, and is receiv'd
Of the most pious Edward with such grace
That the malevolence of fortune nothing
Takes from his high respect. Thither Macduff
Is gone to pray the holy King upon his aid
To wake Northumberland and warlike Siward;
That by the help of these (with Him above
To ratify the work) we may again
Give to our tables meat, sleep to our nights,
Free from our feasts and banquets bloody knives,
Do faithful homage and receive free honours—
All which we pine for now. And this report
Hath so exasperate the King that he
Prepares for some attempt of war.

LEN.   Sent he to Macduff?

LORD. He did; and with an absolute 'Sir, not I!'
The cloudy messenger turns me his back
And hums, as who should say, 'You'll rue the time
That clogs me with this answer.'

LEN.   And that well might
Advise him to a caution t'hold what distance
His wisdom can provide. Some holy angel
Fly to the court of England and unfold
His message ere he come, that a swift blessing
May soon return to this our suffering country
Under a hand accurs'd!

LORD.   I'll send my prayers with him.
                                   Exeunt.

Act IV: Scene I: A cavern. In the middle, a cauldron boiling.

Thunder. Enter the three WITCHES.

1. WITCH. Thrice the brinded cat hath mew'd.
2. WITCH. Thrice and once the hedge-pig whin'd.
3. WITCH. Harpier cries; 'tis time, 'tis time.
1. WITCH. Round about the cauldron go;
   In the poison'd entrails throw.
   Toad, that under cold stone
   Days and nights has thirty-one
   Swelt'red venom sleeping got,
   Boil thou first i' th' charmed pot.
ALL. Double, double, toil and trouble;
   Fire burn, and cauldron bubble.
2. WITCH. Fillet of a fenny snake,
   In the cauldron boil and bake;
   Eye of newt, and toe of frog,
   Wool of bat, and tongue of dog,
   Adder's fork, and blindworm's sting,
   Lizard's leg, and howlet's wing;
   For a charm of pow'rful trouble
   Like a hell-broth boil and bubble.
ALL. Double, double, toil and trouble;
   Fire burn, and cauldron bubble.
3. WITCH. Scale of dragon, tooth of wolf,
   Witch's mummy, maw and gulf
   Of the ravin'd salt-sea shark,
   Root of hemlock, digg'd i' th' dark;
   Liver of blaspheming Jew,
   Gall of goat, and slips of yew
   Sliver'd in the moon's eclipse;
   Nose of Turk and Tartar's lips;
   Finger of birth-strangled babe

Ditch-deliver'd by a drab:
Make the gruel thick and slab.
Add thereto a tiger's chaudron
For th' ingredience of our cauldron.
ALL. Double, double, toil and trouble;
Fire burn, and cauldron bubble.
2. WITCH. Cool it with a baboon's blood,
Then the charm is firm and good.
Enter HECATE *to the other three* WITCHES.
HEC. O, well done! I commend your pains,
And every one shall share i' th' gains.
And now about the cauldron sing
Like elves and fairies in a ring,
Enchanting all that you put in.
Music and a song: 'Black spirits,' &c.
Exit HECATE.
2. WITCH. By the pricking of my thumbs,
Something wicked this way comes.
Open locks,
Whoever knocks!

Enter MACBETH.

MACB. How now, you secret, black, and midnight
hags?
What is't you do?
ALL.   A deed without a name.
MACB. I conjure you by that which you profess
(Howe'er you come to know it), answer me.
Though you untie the winds and let them fight
Against the churches; though the yesty waves
Confound and swallow navigation up;
Though bladed corn be lodg'd and trees blown down;
Though castles topple on their warders' heads;
Though palaces and pyramids do slope
Their heads to their foundations; though the treasure

Of nature's germens tumble all together,
Even till destruction sicken—answer me
To what I ask you.

1. WITCH.   Speak.

2. WITCH.   Demand.

3. WITCH.   We'll answer.

1. WITCH. Say, if th' hadst rather hear it from our
  mouths

Or from our masters.

MACB.   Call 'em! Let me see 'em.

1. WITCH. Pour in sow's blood, that hath eaten
  Her nine farrow; grease that's sweaten
  From the murderer's gibbet throw
  Into the flame.

ALL.   Come, high or low;
  Thyself and office deftly show!

Thunder. FIRST APPARITION, *an Armed Head.*

MACB. Tell me, thou unknown power—

1. WITCH.   He knows thy thought.
Hear his speech, but say thou naught.

1. APPAR. Macbeth! Macbeth! Macbeth! Beware
  Macduff;

Beware the Thane of Fife. Dismiss me. Enough.

He descends.

MACB. Whate'er thou art, for thy good caution thanks!
Thou hast harp'd my fear aright. But one word more—

1. WITCH. He will not be commanded. Here's another,
More potent than the first.

Thunder. SECOND APPARITION, *a Bloody Child.*

2. APPAR. Macbeth! Macbeth! Macbeth!

MACB. Had I three ears, I'ld hear thee.

2. APPAR. Be bloody, bold, and resolute; laugh to
  scorn

The pow'r of man, for none of woman born
Shall harm Macbeth.   *Descends.*

MACB. Then live, Macduff. What need I fear of thee?
But yet I'll make assurance double sure
And take a bond of fate. Thou shalt not live!
That I may tell pale-hearted fear it lies
And sleep in spite of thunder.

[*Thunder.* THIRD APPARITION, *a Child Crowned, with
a tree in his hand.*]

                                        What is this
That rises like the issue of a king
And wears upon his baby-brow the round
And top of sovereignty?
     ALL.   Listen, but speak not to't.
     3. APPAR. Be lion-mettled, proud, and take no care
Who chafes, who frets, or where conspirers are.
Macbeth shall never vanquish'd be until
Great Birnam Wood to high Dunsinane Hill
Shall come against him.   *Descends.*
     MACB.   That will never be.
Who can impress the forest, bid the tree
Unfix his earth-bound root? Sweet bodements, good!
Rebellion's head rise never till the Wood
Of Birnam rise, and our high-plac'd Macbeth
Shall live the lease of nature, pay his breath
To time and mortal custom. Yet my heart
Throbs to know one thing. Tell me, if your art
Can tell so much—shall Banquo's issue ever
Reign in this kingdom?
     ALL.   Seek to know no more
     MACB. I will be satisfied. Deny me this,
And an eternal curse fall on you! Let me know.
Why sinks that cauldron? and what noise is this?
                                        Hautboys.

1. WITCH. Show!
2. WITCH. Show!
3. WITCH. Show!
ALL. Show his eyes, and grieve his heart!
Come like shadows, so depart!

> *A show of eight Kings, the eighth with a glass in his hand, and* BANQUO *last.*

MACB. Thou are too like the spirit of Banquo. Down!
Thy crown does sear mine eyeballs. And thy hair,
Thou other gold-bound brow, is like the first.
A third is like the former. Filthy hags!
Why do you show me this? A fourth? Start, eyes!
What, will the line stretch out to th' crack of doom?
Another yet? A seventh? I'll see no more.
And yet the eighth appears, who bears a glass
Which shows me many more; and some I see
That twofold balls and treble sceptres carry.
Horrible sight! Now I see 'tis true;
For the blood-bolter'd Banquo smiles upon me
And points at them for his. [*Apparitions vanish.*] What?
    Is this so?
1. WITCH. Ay, sir, all this is so. But why
    Stands Macbeth thus amazedly?
    Come, sisters, cheer we up his sprites
    And show the best of our delights.
    I'll charm the air to give a sound
    While you perform your antic round,
    That this great king may kindly say
    Our duties did his welcome pay.

> *Music. The* WITCHES *dance, and vanish.*

MACB Where are they? Gone? Let this pernicious hour
Stand aye accursed in the calendar!
Come in, without there!

Enter LENNOX.

LEN.   What's your Grace's will?

MACB. Saw you the Weird Sisters?

LEN.   No, my lord.

MACB. Came they not by you?

LEN.   No indeed, my lord.

MACB. Infected be the air whereon they ride,
And damn'd all those that trust them! I did hear
The galloping of horse. Who was't came by?

LEN. 'Tis two or three, my lord, that bring you word
Macduff is fled to England.

MACB.   Fled to England?

LEN. Ay, my good lord.

MACB. [*aside*]Time, thou anticipat'st my dread ex-
    ploits.
The flighty purpose never is o'ertook
Unless the deed go with it. From this moment
The very firstlings of my heart shall be
The firstlings of my hand. And even now,
To crown my thoughts with acts, be it thought and done!
The castle of Macduff I will surprise,
Seize upon Fife, give to the edge o' th' sword
His wife, his babes, and all unfortunate souls
That trace him in his line. No boasting like a fool!
This deed I'll do before this purpose cool.
But no more sights!—Where are these gentlemen?
Come, bring me where they are.   *Exeunt.*

Scene II: Fife. Macduff's Castle.

Enter MACDUFF'S WIFE, *her* SON, *and* ROSS.

WIFE. What had he done to make him fly the land?

ROSS. You must have patience, madam.

WIFE.   He had none.

His flight was madness. When our actions do not,
Our fears do make us traitors.

    Ross.   You know not
Whether it was his wisdom or his fear.

    Wife. Wisdom? To leave his wife, to leave his babes,
His mansion, and his titles, in a place
From whence himself does fly? He loves us not,
He wants the natural touch. For the poor wren,
(The most diminitive of birds) will fight,
Her young ones in her nest, against the owl.
All is the fear, and nothing is the love,
As little is the wisdom, where the flight
So runs against all reason.

    Ross.   My dearest coz,
I pray you school yourself. But for your husband,
He is noble, wise, judicious, and best knows
The fits o' th' season. I dare not speak much further;
But cruel are the times, when we are traitors
And do not know ourselves; when we hold rumour
From what we fear, yet know not what we fear,
But float upon a wild and violent sea
Each way and none. I take my leave of you.
Shall not be long but I'll be here again.
Things at the worst will cease, or else climb upward
To what they were before.—My pretty cousin,
Blessing upon you!

    Wife. Father'd he is, and yet he's fatherless.

    Ross. I am so much a fool, should I stay longer,
It would be my disgrace and your discomfort.
I take my leave at once.   *Exit.*

    Wife.   Sirrah, your father's dead;
And what will you do now? How will you live?

    Son. As birds do, mother.

    Wife.   What, with worms and flies?

    Son. With what I get, I mean; and so do they.

WIFE. Poor bird! thou'dst never fear the net nor lime,
The pitfall nor the gin.

SON. Why should I, mother? Poor birds they are not
set for.
My father is not dead, for all your saying.

WIFE. Yes, he is dead. How wilt thou do for a father?

SON. Nay, how will you do for a husband?

WIFE. Why, I can buy me twenty at any market.

SON. Then you'll buy 'em to sell again.

WIFE. Thou speak'st with all thy wit; and yet, i' faith,
With wit enough for thee.

SON. Was my father a traitor, mother?

WIFE. Ay, that he was!

SON. What is a traitor?

WIFE. Why, one that swears, and lies.

SON. And be all traitors that do so?

WIFE. Every one that does so is a traitor and must be
hang'd.

SON. And must they all be hang'd that swear and lie?

WIFE. Every one.

SON. Who must hang them?

WIFE. Why, the honest men.

SON. Then the liars and swearers are fools; for there
are liars and swearers enow to beat the honest men and
hang up them.

WIFE. Now God help thee, poor monkey!
But how wilt thou do for a father?

SON. If he were dead, you'ld weep for him. If you
would not, it were a good sign that I should quickly have
a new father.

WIFE. Poor prattler, how thou talk'st!

Enter a MESSENGER.

MESS. Bless you, fair dame! I am not to you known,
Though in your state of honour I am perfect.

I doubt some danger does approach you nearly.
If you will take a homely man's advice,
Be not found here. Hence with your little ones!
To fright you thus methinks I am too savage;
To do worse to you were fell cruelty,
Which is too nigh your person. Heaven preserve you!
I dare abide no longer.   *Exit*.
   WIFE.   Whither should I fly?
I have done no harm. But I remember now
I am in this earthly world, where to do harm
Is often laudable, to do good sometime
Accounted dangerous folly. Why then, alas,
Do I put up that womanly defence
To say I have done no harm?—What are these faces?

Enter MURTHERERS.

   MUR. Where is your husband?
   WIFE. I hope, in no place so unsanctified
Where such as thou mayst find him.
   MUR.   He's a traitor.
   SON. Thou liest, thou shag-ear'd villain!
   MUR.   What, you egg!
                              [*Stabs him.*]
Young fry of treachery!
   SON.   He has kill'd me, mother.
Run away, I pray you!   [*Dies.*]
    Exit WIFE, *crying* 'Murther!' *and pursued by the*
                              MURTHERERS.

Scene III: England. Before King Edward's Palace.

Enter MALCOLM *and* MACDUFF.

   MAL. Let us seek out some desolate shade, and there
Weep our sad bosoms empty.

MACD.   Let us rather
Hold fast the mortal sword and, like good men,
Bestride our downfall'n birthdom. Each new morn
New widows howl, new orphans cry, new sorrows
Strike heaven on the face, that it resounds
As if it felt with Scotland and yell'd out
Like syllable of dolour.
MAL.   What I believe, I'll wail;
What know, believe; and what I can redress,
As I shall find the time to friend, I will.
What you have spoke, it may be so perchance.
This tyrant, whose sole name blisters our tongues,
Was once thought honest; you have lov'd him well;
He hath not touch'd you yet. I am young; but something
You may deserve of him through me, and wisdom
To offer up a weak, poor, innocent lamb
T' appease an angry god.
    MACD. I am not treacherous.
    MAL.   But Macbeth is.
A good and virtuous nature may recoil
In an imperial charge. But I shall crave your pardon.
That which you are, my thoughts cannot transpose.
Angels are bright still, though the brightest fell.
Though all things foul would wear the brows of grace,
Yet grace must still look so.
    MACD.   I have lost my hopes.
    MAL. Perchance even there where I did find my
        doubts.
Why in that rawness left you wife and child,
Those precious motives, those strong knots of love,
Without leave-taking? I pray you,
Let not my jealousies be your dishonours,
But mine own safeties. You may be rightly just,
Whatever I shall think.
    MACD.   Bleed, bleed, poor country!

Great tyranny, lay thou thy basis sure,
For goodness dare not check thee! Wear thou thy
      wrongs;
The title is affeer'd! Fare thee well, lord.
I would not be the villain that thou think'st
For the whole space that's in the tyrant's grasp
And the rich East to boot.

MAL.   Be not offended.
I speak not as in absolute fear of you.
I think our country sinks beneath the yoke,
It weeps, it bleeds, and each new day a gash
Is added to her wounds. I think withal
There would be hands uplifted in my right;
And here from gracious England have I offer
Of goodly thousands. But, for all this,
When I shall tread upon the tyrant's head
Or wear it on my sword, yet my poor country
Shall have more vices than it had before,
More suffer and more sundry ways than ever,
By him that shall succeed.

MACD.   What should he be?

MAL. It is myself I mean; in whom I know
All the particulars of vice so grafted
That, when they shall be open'd, black Macbeth
Will seem as pure as snow, and the poor state
Esteem him as a lamb, being compar'd
With my confineless harms.

MACD.   Not in the legions
Of horrid hell can come a devil more damn'd
In evils to top Macbeth.

MAL.   I grant him bloody,
Luxurious, avaricious, false, deceitful,
Sudden, malicious, smacking of every sin
That has a name. But there's no bottom, none,
In my voluptuousness. Your wives, your daughters,

Your matrons, and your maids could not fill up
The cistern of my lust; and my desire
All continent impediments would o'erbear
That did oppose my will. Better Macbeth
Than such an one to reign.

MACD.   Boundless intemperance
In nature is a tyranny. It hath been
Th' untimely emptying of the happy throne
And fall of many kings. But fear not yet
To take upon you what is yours. You may
Convey your pleasures in a spacious plenty,
And yet seem cold—the time you may so hoodwink.
We have willing dames enough. There cannot be
That vulture in you to devour so many
As will to greatness dedicate themselves,
Finding it so inclin'd.

MAL.   With this there grows
In my most ill-compos'd affection such
A stanchless avarice that, were I King,
I should cut off the nobles for their lands,
Desire his jewels, and this other's house,
And my more-having would be as a sauce
To make me hunger more, that I should forge
Quarrels unjust against the good and loyal,
Destroying them for wealth.

MACD.   This avarice
Sticks deeper, grows with more pernicious root
Than summer-seeming lust; and it hath been
The sword of our slain kings. Yet do not fear.
Scotland hath foisons to fill up your will
Of your mere own. All these are portable,
With other graces weigh'd.

MAL. But I have none. The king-becoming graces,
As justice, verity, temp'rance, stableness,
Bounty, perseverance, mercy, lowliness,

Devotion, patience, courage, fortitude,
I have no relish of them, but abound
In the division of each several crime,
Acting it many ways. Nay, had I pow'r, I should
Pour the sweet milk of concord into hell,
Uproar the universal peace, confound
All unity on earth.

    MACD.   O Scotland, Scotland!

    MAL. If such a one be fit to govern, speak.
I am as I have spoken.

    MACD.   Fit to govern?
No, not to live. O nation miserable,
With an untitled tyrant bloody-scept'red,
When shalt thou see thy wholesome days again,
Since that the truest issue of thy throne
By his own interdiction stands accurs'd
And does blaspheme his breed? Thy royal father
Was a most sainted king; the queen that bore thee,
Oft'ner upon her knees than on her feet,
Died every day she liv'd. Fare thee well!
These evils thou repeat'st upon thyself
Have banish'd me from Scotland. O my breast,
Thy hope ends here!

    MAL.   Macduff, this noble passion,
Child of integrity, hath from my soul
Wip'd the black scruples, reconcil'd my thoughts
To thy good truth and honour. Devilish Macbeth
By many of these trains hath sought to win me
Into his power; and modest wisdom plucks me
From over-credulous haste; but God above
Deal between thee and me! for even now
I put myself to thy direction and
Unspeak mine own detraction, here abjure
The taints and blames I laid upon myself
For strangers to my nature. I am yet

Unknown to woman, never was forsworn,
Scarcely have coveted what was mine own,
At no time broke my faith, would not betray
The devil to his fellow, and delight
No less in truth than life. My first false speaking
Was this upon myself. What I am truly,
Is thine and my poor country's to command,
Whither indeed, before thy here-approach,
Old Siward with ten thousand warlike men
Already at a point was setting forth.
Now we'll together; and the chance of goodness
Be like our warranted quarrel! Why are you silent?

MACD. Such welcome and unwelcome things at once
'Tis hard to reconcile.

Enter a DOCTOR.

MAL. Well, more anon. Comes the King forth, I pray
you?

DOCT. Ay, sir. There are a crew of wretched souls
That stay his cure. Their malady convinces
The great assay of art; but at his touch,
Such sanctity hath heaven given his hand,
They presently amend.

MAL.   I thank you, doctor.

Exit DOCTOR.

MACD. What's the disease he means?

MAL.   'Tis call'd the evil:
A most miraculous work in this good king,
Which often since my here-remain in England
I have seen him do. How he solicits heaven
Himself best knows; but strangely-visited people,
All swol'n and ulcerous, pitiful to the eye,
The mere despair of surgery, he cures,
Hanging a golden stamp about their necks,
Put on with holy prayers; and 'tis spoken,

To the succeeding royalty he leaves
The healing benediction. With this strange virtue,
He hath a heavenly gift of prophecy,
And sundry blessings hang about his throne
That speak him full of grace.

Enter Ross.

MACD.   See who comes here.

MAL. My countryman; but yet I know him not.

MACD. My ever gentle cousin, welcome hither.

MAL. I know him now. Good God betimes remove
The means that makes us strangers!

Ross.   Sir, amen.

MACD. Stands Scotland where it did?

Ross.   Alas, poor country,
Almost afraid to know itself! It cannot
Be call'd our mother, but our grave; where nothing,
But who knows nothing, is once seen to smile;
Where sighs and groans, and shrieks that rent the air,
Are made, not mark'd; where violent sorrow seems
A modern ecstasy. The dead man's knell
Is there scarce ask'd for who; and good men's lives
Expire before the flowers in their caps,
Dying or ere they sicken.

MACD.   O, relation
Too nice, and yet too true!

MAL.   What's the newest grief?

Ross. That of an hour's age doth hiss the speaker;
Each minute teems a new one.

MACD.   How does my wife?

Ross. Why, well.

MACD.   And all my children?

Ross.   Well too.

MACD. The tyrant has not batter'd at their peace?

Ross. No; they were well at peace when I did leave
     'em.

MACD. Be not a niggard of your speech. How goes't?

Ross. When I came hither to transport the tidings
Which I have heavily borne, there ran a rumour
Of many worthy fellows that were out;
Which was to my belief witness'd the rather
For that I saw the tyrant's power afoot.
Now is the time of help. Your eye in Scotland
Would create soldiers, make our women fight
To doff their dire distresses.

MAL.   Be't their comfort
We are coming thither. Gracious England hath
Lent us good Siward and ten thousand men.
An older and a better soldier none
That Christendom gives out.

Ross.   Would I could answer
This comfort with the like! But I have words
That would be howl'd out in the desert air,
Where hearing should not latch them.

MACD.   What concern they?
The general cause? or is it a fee-grief
Due to some single breast?

Ross.   No mind that's honest
But in it shares some woe, though the main part
Pertains to you alone.

MACD.   If it be mine,
Keep it not from me, quickly let me have it.

Ross. Let not your ears despise my tongue for ever,
Which shall possess them with the heaviest sound
That ever yet they heard.

MACD.   Humh! I guess at it.

Ross. Your castle is surpris'd; your wife and babes
Savagely slaughter'd. To relate the manner,
Were, on the quarry of these murther'd deer,
To add the death of you.

MAL.   Merciful heaven!

What, man! Ne'er pull your hat upon your brows.
Give sorrow words. The grief that does not speak
Whispers the o'erfraught heart and bids it break.

MACD. My children too?

Ross.   Wife, children, servants, all
That could be found.

MACD.   And I must be from thence?
My wife kill'd too?

Ross.   I have said.

MAL.   Be comforted.
Let's make us med'cines of our great revenge
To cure this deadly grief.

MACD. He has no children. All my pretty ones?
Did you say all? O hell-kite! All?
What, all my pretty chickens and their dam
At one fell swoop?

MAL. Dispute it like a man.

MACD.   I shall do so;
But I must also feel it as a man.
I cannot but remember such things were
That were most precious to me. Did heaven look on
And would not take their part? Sinful Macduff,
They were all struck for thee! Naught that I am,
Not for their own demerits, but for mine,
Fell slaughter on their souls. Heaven rest them now!

MAL. Be this the whetstone of your sword. Let grief
Convert to anger; blunt not the heart, enrage it.

MACD. O, I could play the woman with mine eyes
And braggart with my tongue! But, gentle heavens,
Cut short all intermission. Front to front
Bring thou this fiend of Scotland and myself.
Within my sword's length set him. If he scape,
Heaven forgive him too!

MAL.   This tune goes manly.
Come, go we to the King. Our power is ready;

Our lack is nothing but our leave. Macbeth
Is ripe for shaking, and the pow'rs above
Put on their instruments. Receive what cheer you may.
The night is long that never finds the day.

Exeunt.

Act V: Scene I: Dunsinane. Macbeth's Castle.

Enter a DOCTOR OF PHYSIC *and a* WAITING
GENTLEWOMAN.

DOCT. I have two nights watch'd with you, but can
perceive no truth in your report. When was it she last
walk'd?

GENT. Since his Majesty went into the field I have seen
her rise from her bed, throw her nightgown upon her,
unlock her closet, take forth paper, fold it, write upon't,
read it, afterwards seal it, and again return to bed; yet
all this while in a most fast sleep.

DOCT. A great perturbation in nature, to receive at
once the benefit of sleep and do the effects of watching!
In this slumb'ry agitation, besides her walking and other
actual performances, what (at any time) have you heard
her say?

GENT. That, sir, which I will not report after her.

DOCT. You may to me, and 'tis most meet you should.

GENT. Neither to you nor any one, having no witness to
confirm my speech.

[*Enter* LADY MACBETH, *with a taper.*]

Lo you, here she comes! This is her very guise, and,
upon my life, fast asleep! Observe her; stand close.

DOCT. How came she by that light?

GENT. Why, it stood by her. She has light by her con-
tinually. 'Tis her command.

DOCT. You see her eyes are open.

GENT. Ay; but their sense is shut.

DOCT. What is it she does now? Look how she rubs her hands.

GENT. It is an accustom'd action with her, to seem thus washing her hands. I have known her continue in this a quarter of an hour.

LADY. Yet here's a spot.

DOCT. Hark, she speaks! I will set down what comes from her, to satisfy my remembrance the more strongly.

LADY. Out, damned spot! out, I say! One; two. Why then 'tis time to do't. Hell is murky. Fie, my lord, fie! a soldier, and afeard? What need we fear who knows it, when none can call our pow'r to accompt? Yet who would have thought the old man to have had so much blood in him?

DOCT. Do you mark that?

LADY. The Thane of Fife had a wife. Where is she now? What, will these hands ne'er be clean? No more o' that, my lord, no more o' that! You mar all with this starting.

DOCT. Go to, go to! You have known what you should not.

GENT. She has spoke what she should not, I am sure of that. Heaven knows what she has known.

LADY. Here's the smell of the blood still. All the perfumes of Arabia will not sweeten this little hand. Oh, oh, oh!

DOCT. What a sigh is there! The heart is sorely charg'd.

GENT. I would not have such a heart in my bosom for the dignity of the whole body.

DOCT. Well, well, well.

GENT. Pray God it be, sir.

DOCT. This disease is beyond my practice. Yet I have known those which have walk'd in their sleep who have died holily in their beds.

LADY. Wash your hands, put on your nightgown, look
not so pale! I tell you yet again, Banquo's buried. He
can not come out on's grave.

DOCT. Even so?

LADY. To bed, to bed! There's knocking at the gate.
Come, come, come, come, give me your hand! What's
done cannot be undone. To bed, to bed, to bed!   *Exit.*

DOCT. Will she go now to bed?

GENT. Directly.

DOCT. Foul whisp'rings are abroad. Unnatural deeds
Do breed unnatural troubles. Infected minds
To their deaf pillows will discharge their secrets.
More needs she the divine than the physician.
God, God forgive us all! Look after her;
Remove from her the means of all annoyance,
And still keep eyes upon her. So good night.
My mind she has mated, and amaz'd my sight.
I think, but dare not speak.

GENT.   Good night, good doctor.
                                          Exeunt.

Scene II: The country near Dunsinane.

Drum and Colours. Enter MENTEITH, CAITHNESS, ANGUS,
LENNOX, SOLDIERS.

MENT. The English pow'r is near, led on by Malcolm,
His uncle Siward, and the good Macduff.
Revenges burn in them; for their dear causes
Would to the bleeding and the grim alarm
Excite the mortified man.

ANG.   Near Birnam Wood
Shall we well meet them; that way are they coming.

CAITH. Who knows if Donalbain be with his brother?

LEN. For certain, sir, he is not. I have a file

Of all the gentry. There is Siward's son
And many unrough youths that even now
Protest their first of manhood.

MENT.   What does the tyrant?

CAITH. Great Dunsinane he strongly fortifies.
Some say he's mad; others, that lesser hate him,
Do call it valiant fury; but for certain
He cannot buckle his distemper'd cause
Within the belt of rule.

ANG.   Now does he feel
His secret murthers sticking on his hands.
Now minutely revolts upbraid his faith-breach.
Those he commands move only in command,
Nothing in love. Now does he feel his title
Hang loose about him, like a giant's robe
Upon a dwarfish thief.

MENT.   Who then shall blame
His pester'd senses to recoil and start,
When all that is within him does condemn
Itself for being there?

CAITH.   Well, march we on
To give obedience where 'tis truly ow'd.
Meet we the med'cine of the sickly weal;
And with him pour we in our country's purge
Each drop of us.

LEN.   Or so much as it needs
To dew the sovereign flower and drown the weeds.
Make we our march towards Birnam.

Exeunt, marching.

Scene III: Dunsinane. A room in the Castle.

Enter MACBETH, DOCTOR, *and* ATTENDANTS.

MACB. Bring me no more reports. Let them fly all!

Till Birnam Wood remove to Dunsinane,
I cannot taint with fear. What's the boy Malcolm?
Was he not born of woman? The spirits that know
All mortal consequences have pronounc'd me thus:
'Fear not, Macbeth. No man that's born of woman
Shall e'er have power upon thee.' Then fly, false thanes,
And mingle with the English epicures.
The mind I sway by and the heart I bear
Shall never sag with doubt nor shake with fear.

[*Enter* SERVANT.]

The devil damn thee black, thou cream-fac'd loon!
Where got'st thou that goose look?
  SERV. There is ten thousand—
  MACB.   Geese, villain?
  SERV.   Soldiers, sir.
  MACB. Go prick thy face and over-red thy fear,
Thou lily-liver'd boy. What soldiers, patch?
Death of thy soul! Those linen cheeks of thine
Are counsellors to fear. What soldiers, whey-face?
  SERV. The English force, so please you.
  MACB. Take thy face hence.

[*Exit* SERVANT.]
                Seyton!—I am sick at heart,
When I behold—Seyton, I say!—This push
Will cheer me ever, or disseat me now.
I have liv'd long enough. My way of life
Is fall'n into the sere, the yellow leaf;
And that which should accompany old age,
As honour, love, obedience, troops of friends,
I must not look to have; but, in their stead,
Curses not loud but deep, mouth-honour, breath,
Which the poor heart would fain deny, and dare not.
Seyton!

Enter SEYTON.

SEY. What's your gracious pleasure?

MACB.   What news more?

SEY. All is confirm'd, my lord, which was reported.

MACB. I'll fight, till from my bones my flesh be hack'd.
Give me my armour.

SEY.   'Tis not needed yet.

MACB. I'll put it on.
Send out moe horses, skirr the country round;
Hang those that talk of fear. Give me mine armour.
How does your patient, doctor?

DOCT.   Not so sick, my lord,
As she is troubled with thick-coming fancies
That keep her from her rest.

MACB.   Cure her of that!
Canst thou not minister to a mind diseas'd,
Pluck from the memory a rooted sorrow,
Raze out the written troubles of the brain,
And with some sweet oblivious antidote
Cleanse the stuff'd bosom of that perilous stuff
Which weighs upon the heart?

DOCT.   Therein the patient
Must minister to himself.

MACB. Throw physic to the dogs, I'll none of it!—
Come, put mine armour on. Give me my staff.—
Seyton, send out.—Doctor, the thanes fly from me.—
Come, sir, dispatch.—If thou couldst, doctor, cast
The water of my land, find her disease,
And purge it to a sound and pristine health,
I would applaud thee to the very echo,
That should applaud again.—Pull't off, I say.—
What rhubarb, senna, or what purgative drug,
Would scour these English hence? Hear'st thou of them?

DOCT. Ay, my good lord. Your royal preparation
Makes us hear something.

MACB.   Bring it after me!
I will not be afraid of death and bane
Till Birnam Forest come to Dunsinane.

*   Exeunt all but the* DOCTOR.

DOCT. Were I from Dunsinane away and clear,
Profit again should hardly draw me here.

*   Exit.*

Scene IV: Country near Birnam Wood.

Drum and Colours. Enter MALCOLM, SIWARD, MACDUFF,
SIWARD'S SON, MENTEITH, CAITHNESS, ANGUS, LENNOX,
ROSS, *and* SOLDIERS, *marching.*

MAL. Cousins, I hope the days are near at hand
That chambers will be safe.

MENT.   We doubt it nothing.

SIW. What wood is this before us?

MENT.   The Wood of Birnam.

MAL. Let every soldier hew him down a bough
And bear't before him. Thereby shall we shadow
The numbers of our host and make discovery
Err in report of us.

SOLDIERS.   It shall be done.

SIW. We learn no other but the confident tyrant
Keeps still in Dunsinane and will endure
Our setting down before't.

MAL.   'Tis his main hope;
For where there is advantage to be given,
Both more and less have given him the revolt;
And none serve with him but constrained things,
Whose hearts are absent too.

MACD.   Let our just censures
Attend the true event, and put we on
Industrious soldiership.

Siw.   The time approaches
That will with due decision make us know
What we shall say we have, and what we owe.
Thoughts speculative their unsure hopes relate,
But certain issue strokes must arbitrate;
Towards which advance the war.

Exeunt, marching.

Scene V: Dunsinane. Within the Castle.

Enter Macbeth, Seyton, *and* Soldiers, *with Drum and Colours.*

Macb. Hang out our banners on the outward walls.
The cry is still, 'They come!' Our castle's strength
Will laugh a siege to scorn. Here let them lie
Till famine and the ague eat them up.
Were they not forc'd with those that should be ours,
We might have met them dareful, beard to beard,
And beat them backward home.

[*A cry within of women.*]
                    What is that noise?

Sey. It is the cry of women, my good lord.   *Exit.*

Macb. I have almost forgot the taste of fears.
The time has been, my senses would have cool'd
To hear a night-shriek, and my fell of hair
Would at a dismal treatise rouse and stir
As life were in't. I have supp'd full with horrors.
Direness, familiar to my slaughterous thoughts,
Cannot once start me.

[*Enter* Seyton.]
                    Wherefore was that cry?

Sey. The Queen, my lord, is dead.

Macb. She should have died hereafter;

There would have been a time for such a word.
To-morrow, and to-morrow, and to-morrow
Creeps in this petty pace from day to day
To the last syllable of recorded time;
And all our yesterdays have lighted fools
The way to dusty death. Out, out, brief candle!
Life's but a walking shadow, a poor player,
That struts and frets his hour upon the stage
And then is heard no more. It is a tale
Told by an idiot, full of sound and fury,
Signifying nothing.

[*Enter a* MESSENGER.]

Thou com'st to use thy tongue. Thy story quickly!
 MESS. Gracious my lord,
I should report that which I say I saw,
But know not how to do't.
  MACB.   Well, say, sir!
 MESS. As I did stand my watch upon the hill,
I look'd toward Birnam, and anon methought
The wood began to move.
  MACB.   Liar and slave!
 MESS. Let me endure your wrath if't be not so.
Within this three mile may you see it coming;
I say, a moving grove.
  MACB.   If thou speak'st false,
Upon the next tree shalt thou hang alive,
Till famine cling thee. If thy speech be sooth,
I care not if thou dost for me as much.
I pull in resolution, and begin
To doubt th' equivocation of the fiend,
That lies like truth. 'Fear not, till Birnam wood
Do come to Dunsinane!' and now a wood
Comes toward Dunsinane. Arm, arm, and out!
If this which he avouches does appear,

There is nor flying hence nor tarrying here.
I gin to be aweary of the sun,
And wish th' estate o' th' world were now undone.
Ring the alarum bell! Blow wind, come wrack,
At least we'll die with harness on our back!

Exeunt.

Scene VI: Dunsinane. Before the Castle.

Drum and Colours. Enter MALCOLM, SIWARD, MACDUFF,
and their ARMY, *with boughs.*

MAL. Now near enough. Your leavy screens throw
down
And show like those you are. You, worthy uncle,
Shall with my cousin, your right noble son,
Lead our first battle. Worthy Macduff and we
Shall take upon's what else remains to do,
According to our order.
SIW.   Fare you well.
Do we but find the tyrant's power to-night,
Let us be beaten if we cannot fight.
MACD. Make all our trumpets speak, give them all
breath,
Those clamorous harbingers of blood and death.

Exeunt. Alarums continued.

Scene VII: Another part of the field.

Enter MACBETH.

MACB. They have tied me to a stake. I cannot fly,
But bear-like I must fight the course. What's he
That was not born of woman? Such a one
Am I to fear, or none.

Enter YOUNG SIWARD.

Y. SIW. What is thy name?

MACB.   Thou'lt be afraid to hear it.

Y. SIW. No; though thou call'st thyself a hotter name
Than any is in hell.

MACB.   My name's Macbeth.

Y. SIW. The devil himself could not pronounce a title
More hateful to mine ear.

MACB.   No, nor more fearful.

Y. SIW. Thou liest, abhorred tyrant! With my sword
I'll prove the lie thou speak'st.

                    Fight, and YOUNG SIWARD *slain.*

MACB.   Thou wast born of woman.
But swords I smile at, weapons laugh to scorn,
Brandish'd by man that's of a woman born.

                                        Exit.

Alarums. Enter MACDUFF.

MACD. That way the noise is. Tyrant, show thy face!
If thou beest slain and with no stroke of mine,
My wife and children's ghosts will haunt me still.
I cannot strike at wretched kerns, whose arms
Are hir'd to bear their staves. Either thou, Macbeth,
Or else my sword with an unbattered edge
I sheathe again undeeded. There thou shouldst be.
By this great clatter one of greatest note
Seems bruited. Let me find him, Fortune!
And more I beg not.   *Exit. Alarums.*

Enter MALCOLM *and* SIWARD.

SIW. This way, my lord. The castle's gently rend'red:
The tyrant's people on both sides do fight;
The noble thanes do bravely in the war;
The day almost itself professes yours,
And little is to do.

MAL.   We have met with foes
That strike beside us.
SIW.   Enter, sir, the castle.

                              Exeunt. Alarum.

Scene VIII: Another part of the field.

Enter MACBETH.

MACB. Why should I play the Roman fool and die
On mine own sword? Whiles I see lives, the gashes
Do better upon them.

                   Enter MACDUFF.

MACD.   Turn, hellhound, turn!
MACB. Of all men else I have avoided thee.
But get thee back! My soul is too much charg'd
With blood of thine already.
MACD.   I have no words;
My voice is in my sword, thou bloodier villain
Than terms can give thee out!

                               Fight. Alarum.
MACB.   Thou losest labour.
As easy mayst thou the intrenchant air
With thy keen sword impress as make me bleed.
Let fall thy blade on vulnerable crests.
I bear a charmed life, which must not yield
To one of woman born.
MACD.   Despair thy charm!
And let the angel whom thou still hast serv'd
Tell thee, Macduff was from his mother's womb
Untimely ripp'd.
MACB. Accursed be that tongue that tells me so,
For it hath cow'd my better part of man!
And be these juggling fiends no more believ'd,
That palter with us in a double sense,

That keep the word of promise to our ear
And break it to our hope! I'll not fight with thee!

    MACD. Then yield thee, coward,
And live to be the show and gaze o' th' time!
We'll have thee, as our rarer monsters are,
Painted upon a pole, and underwrit
'Here may you see the tyrant.'

    MACB.   I will not yield,
To kiss the ground before young Malcolm's feet
And to be baited with the rabble's curse.
Though Birnam Wood be come to Dunsinane,
And thou oppos'd, being of no woman born,
Yet I will try the last. Before my body
I throw my warlike shield. Lay on, Macduff,
And damn'd be him that first cries 'Hold, enough!'

                       Exeunt fighting. Alarums.

Retreat and flourish. Enter, with Drum and Colours,
  MALCOLM, SIWARD, ROSS, THANES, *and* SOLDIERS.

    MAL. I would the friends we miss were safe arriv'd.
    SIW. Some must go off; and yet, by these I see,
So great a day as this is cheaply bought.

    MAL. Macduff is missing, and your noble son.

    ROSS. Your son, my lord, has paid a soldier's debt.
He only liv'd but till he was a man,
The which no sooner had his prowess confirm'd
In the unshrinking station where he fought
But like a man he died.

    SIW.   Then he is dead?

    ROSS. Ay, and brought off the field. Your cause of
    sorrow
Must not be measur'd by his worth, for then
It hath no end.

    SIW.   Had he his hurts before?

    ROSS. Ay, on the front.

SIW.   Why then, God's soldier be he!
Had I as many sons as I have hairs,
I would not wish them to a fairer death.
And so his knell is knoll'd.

MAL.   He's worth more sorrow,
And that I'll spend for him.

SIW.   He's worth no more.
They say he parted well and paid his score,
And so, God be with him! Here comes newer comfort.

Enter MACDUFF, *with* MACBETH's *head.*

MACD. Hail, King! for so thou art. Behold where stands
Th' usurper's cursed head. The time is free.
I see thee compass'd with thy kingdom's pearl,
That speak my salutation in their minds;
Whose voices I desire aloud with mine—
Hail, King of Scotland!

ALL.   Hail, King of Scotland! *Flourish.*

MAL. We shall not spend a large expense of time
Before we reckon with your several loves
And make us even with you. My Thanes and kinsmen,
Henceforth be Earls, the first that ever Scotland
In such an honour nam'd. What's more to do
Which would be planted newly with the time—
As calling home our exil'd friends abroad
That fled the snares of watchful tyranny,
Producing forth the cruel ministers
Of this dead butcher and his fiendlike queen,
Who (as 'tis thought) by self and violent hands
Took off her life—this, and what needful else
That calls upon us, by the grace of Grace
We will perform in measure, time, and place.
So thanks to all at once and to each one,
Whom we invite to see us crown'd at Scone.

                    Flourish. Exeunt omnes.

The Tragedy of Romeo and Juliet

NAMES OF THE ACTORS

CHORUS.

ESCALUS, Prince of Verona.

PARIS, a young Count, kinsman to the PRINCE.

MONTAGUE,
CAPULET, } heads of two houses at variance with each other.

ROMEO, son to MONTAGUE.

MERCUTIO, kinsman to the PRINCE, and friend to ROMEO.

BENVOLIO, nephew to MONTAGUE, and friend to ROMEO.

TYBALT, nephew to LADY CAPULET.

FRIAR LAURENCE,
FRIAR JOHN, } Franciscans.

BALTHASAR, servant to ROMEO.

ABRAM, servant to MONTAGUE.

SAMPSON,
GREGORY, } servants to CAPULET.

PETER, servant to JULIET'S NURSE.   AN APOTHECARY.

THREE MUSICIANS.   AN OFFICER.

LADY MONTAGUE, wife to MONTAGUE.

LADY CAPULET, wife to CAPULET.

JULIET, daughter to CAPULET.   NURSE to JULIET.

Citizens of Verona; Gentlemen and Gentlewomen of both houses; Maskers, Torchbearers, Pages, Guards, Watchmen, Servants, and Attendants.

The Prologue

Enter CHORUS.

CHOR. Two households, both alike in dignity,
  In fair Verona, where we lay our scene,
From ancient grudge break to new mutiny,
  Where civil blood makes civil hands unclean.
From forth the fatal loins of these two foes
  A pair of star-cross'd lovers take their life;
Whose misadventur'd piteous overthrows
  Doth with their death bury their parents' strife.
The fearful passage of their death-mark'd love,
  And the continuance of their parents' rage,
Which, but their children's end, naught could remove,
  Is now the two hours' traffic of our stage;
The which if you with patient ears attend,
What here shall miss, our toil shall strive to mend.   *Exit.*

Act I: Scene I: Verona. A public place.

Enter SAMPSON *and* GREGORY (*with swords and buck-
lers*) *of the house of Capulet.*

SAMP. Gregory, on my word, we'll not carry coals.

GREG. No, for then we should be colliers.

SAMP. I mean, an we be in choler, we'll draw.

GREG. Ay, while you live, draw your neck out of collar.

SAMP. I strike quickly, being moved.

GREG. But thou art not quickly moved to strike.

SAMP. A dog of the house of Montague moves me.

GREG. To move is to stir, and to be valiant is to stand.
Therefore, if thou art moved, thou runn'st away.

SAMP. A dog of that house shall move me to stand. I
will take the wall of any man or maid of Montague's.

GREG. That shows thee a weak slave; for the weakest
goes to the wall.

SAMP. 'Tis true; and therefore women, being the weaker vessels, are ever thrust to the wall. Therefore I will push Montague's men from the wall and thrust his maids to the wall.

GREG. The quarrel is between our masters and us their men.

SAMP. 'Tis all one. I will show myself a tyrant. When I have fought with the men, I will be cruel with the maids —I will cut off their heads.

GREG. The heads of the maids?

SAMP. Ay, the heads of the maids, or their maidenheads. Take it in what sense thou wilt.

GREG. They must take it in sense that feel it.

SAMP. Me they shall feel while I am able to stand; and 'tis known I am a pretty piece of flesh.

GREG. 'Tis well thou art not fish; if thou hadst, thou hadst been poor-John. Draw thy tool! Here comes two of the house of Montagues.

Enter two other SERVINGMEN, ABRAM *and* BALTHASAR.

SAMP. My naked weapon is out. Quarrel! I will back thee.

GREG. How? turn thy back and run?

SAMP. Fear me not.

GREG. No, marry. I fear thee!

SAMP. Let us take the law of our sides; let them begin.

GREG. I will frown as I pass by, and let them take it as they list.

SAMP. Nay, as they dare. I will bite my thumb at them; which is disgrace to them, if they bear it.

ABR. Do you bite your thumb at us, sir?

SAMP. I do bite my thumb, sir.

ABR. Do you bite your thumb at us, sir?

SAMP. [*aside to* GREGORY] Is the law of our side if I say ay?

GREG. [*aside to* SAMPSON] No.

SAMP. No, sir, I do not bite my thumb at you, sir; but I bite my thumb, sir.

GREG. Do you quarrel, sir?

ABR. Quarrel, sir? No, sir.

SAMP. But if you do, sir, I am for you. I serve as good a man as you.

ABR. No better.

SAMP. Well, sir.

Enter BENVOLIO.

GREG. [*aside to* SAMPSON] Say 'better.' Here comes one of my master's kinsmen.

SAMP. Yes, better, sir.

ABR. You lie.

SAMP. Draw, if you be men. Gregory, remember thy swashing blow.   *They fight.*

BEN. Part, fools! [*Beats down their swords.*] Put up your swords. You know not what you do.

Enter TYBALT.

TYB. What, art thou drawn among these heartless hinds?
Turn thee, Benvolio! look upon thy death.

BEN. I do but keep the peace. Put up thy sword,
Or manage it to part these men with me.

TYB. What, drawn, and talk of peace? I hate the word
As I hate hell, all Montagues, and thee.
Have at thee, coward!   *They fight.*

Enter an OFFICER, *and three or four* CITIZENS *with clubs or partisans.*

OFFICER. Clubs, bills, and partisans! Strike! beat them down!

CITIZENS. Down with the Capulets! down with the Montagues!

Enter OLD CAPULET *in his gown, and his* WIFE.

CAP. What noise is this? Give me my long sword, ho!
WIFE. A crutch, a crutch! Why call you for a sword?
CAP. My sword, I say! Old Montague is come
And flourishes his blade in spite of me.

Enter OLD MONTAGUE *and his* WIFE.

MON. Thou villain Capulet!—Hold me not, let me go.
M. WIFE. Thou shalt not stir one foot to seek a foe.

Enter PRINCE ESCALUS, *with his* TRAIN.

PRINCE. Rebellious subjects, enemies to peace,
Profaners of this neighbour-stained steel—
Will they not hear? What, ho! you men, you beasts,
That quench the fire of your pernicious rage
With purple fountains issuing from your veins!
On pain of torture, from those bloody hands
Throw your mistempered weapons to the ground
And hear the sentence of your moved prince.
Three civil brawls, bred of an airy word
By thee, old Capulet, and Montague,
Have thrice disturb'd the quiet of our streets
And made Verona's ancient citizens
Cast by their grave beseeming ornaments
To wield old partisans, in hands as old,
Cank'red with peace, to part your cank'red hate.
If ever you disturb our streets again,
Your lives shall pay the forfeit of the peace.
For this time all the rest depart away.
You, Capulet, shall go along with me;
And, Montague, come you this afternoon,
To know our farther pleasure in this case,
To old Freetown, our common judgment place.
Once more, on pain of death, all men depart.
    Exeunt all but MONTAGUE, *his* WIFE, *and* BENVOLIO.

Mon. Who set this ancient quarrel new abroach?
Speak, nephew, were you by when it began?

Ben. Here were the servants of your adversary
And yours, close fighting ere I did approach.
I drew to part them. In the instant came
The fiery Tybalt, with his sword prepar'd;
Which, as he breath'd defiance to my ears,
He swung about his head and cut the winds,
Who, nothing hurt withal, hiss'd him in scorn.
While we were interchanging thrusts and blows,
Came more and more, and fought on part and part,
Till the Prince came, who parted either part.

M. Wife. O, where is Romeo? Saw you him to-day?
Right glad I am he was not at this fray.

Ben. Madam, an hour before the worshipp'd sun
Peer'd forth the golden window of the East,
A troubled mind drave me to walk abroad;
Where, underneath the grove of sycamore
That westward rooteth from the city's side,
So early walking did I see your son.
Towards him I made; but he was ware of me
And stole into the covert of the wood.
I—measuring his affections by my own,
Which then most sought where most might not be found,
Being one too many by my weary self—
Pursu'd my humour, not pursuing his,
And gladly shunn'd who gladly fled from me.

Mon. Many a morning hath he there been seen,
With tears augmenting the fresh morning's dew,
Adding to clouds more clouds with his deep sighs;
But all so soon as the all-cheering sun
Should in the farthest East begin to draw
The shady curtains from Aurora's bed,
Away from light steals home my heavy son
And private in his chamber pens himself,

Shuts up his windows, locks fair daylight out,
And makes himself an artificial night.
Black and portentous must this humour prove
Unless good counsel may the cause remove.

BEN. My noble uncle, do you know the cause?

MON. I neither know it nor can learn of him.

BEN. Have you importun'd him by any means?

MON. Both by myself and many other friends;
But he, his own affections' counsellor,
Is to himself—I will not say how true—
But to himself so secret and so close,
So far from sounding and discovery,
As is the bud bit with an envious worm
Ere he can spread his sweet leaves to the air
Or dedicate his beauty to the sun.
Could we but learn from whence his sorrows grow,
We would as willingly give cure as know.

Enter ROMEO.

BEN. See, where he comes. So please you step aside,
I'll know his grievance, or be much denied.

MON. I would thou wert so happy by thy stay
To hear true shrift. Come, madam, let's away.

Exeunt MONTAGUE *and* WIFE.

BEN. Good morrow, cousin.

ROM.   Is the day so young?

BEN. But new struck nine.

ROM.   Ay me! sad hours seem long.
Was that my father that went hence so fast?

BEN. It was. What sadness lengthens Romeo's hours?

ROM. Not having that which having makes them short.

BEN. In love?

ROM. Out—

BEN. Of love?

ROM. Out of her favour where I am in love.

BEN. Alas that love, so gentle in his view,
Should be so tyrannous and rough in proof!

ROM. Alas that love, whose view is muffled still,
Should without eyes see pathways to his will!
Where shall we dine? O me! What fray was here?
Yet tell me not, for I have heard it all.
Here's much to do with hate, but more with love.
Why then, O brawling love! O loving hate!
O anything, of nothing first create!
O heavy lightness! serious vanity!
Misshapen chaos of well-seeming forms!
Feather of lead, bright smoke, cold fire, sick health!
Still-waking sleep, that is not what it is!
This love feel I, that feel no love in this.
Dost thou not laugh?

BEN.   No, coz, I rather weep.

ROM. Good heart, at what?

BEN.   At thy good heart's oppression.

ROM. Why, such is love's transgression.
Griefs of mine own lie heavy in my breast,
Which thou wilt propagate, to have it prest
With more of thine. This love that thou hast shown
Doth add more grief to too much of mine own.
Love is a smoke rais'd with the fume of sighs;
Being purg'd, a fire sparkling in lovers' eyes;
Being vex'd, a sea nourish'd with lovers' tears.
What is it else? A madness most discreet,
A choking gall, and a preserving sweet.
Farewell, my coz.

BEN.   Soft! I will go along.
An if you leave me so, you do me wrong.

ROM. Tut! I have lost myself; I am not here:
This is not Romeo, he's some other where.

BEN. Tell me in sadness, who is that you love?

ROM. What, shall I groan and tell thee?

BEN.   Groan? Why, no;
But sadly tell me who.
 ROM. Bid a sick man in sadness make his will.
Ah, word ill urg'd to one that is so ill!
In sadness, cousin, I do love a woman.
 BEN. I aim'd so near when I suppos'd you lov'd.
 ROM. A right good markman! And she's fair I love.
 BEN. A right fair mark, fair coz, is soonest hit.
 ROM. Well, in that hit you miss. She'll not be hit
With Cupid's arrow. She hath Dian's wit,
And, in strong proof of chastity well arm'd,
From Love's weak childish bow she lives unharm'd.
She will not stay the siege of loving terms,
Nor bide th' encounter of assailing eyes,
Nor ope her lap to saint-seducing gold.
O, she is rich in beauty; only poor
That, when she dies, with beauty dies her store.
 BEN. Then she hath sworn that she will still live
  chaste?
 ROM. She hath, and in that sparing makes huge waste;
For beauty, starv'd with her severity,
Cuts beauty off from all posterity.
She is too fair, too wise, wisely too fair,
To merit bliss by making me despair.
She hath forsworn to love, and in that vow
Do I live dead that live to tell it now.
 BEN. Be rul'd by me: forget to think of her.
 ROM. O, teach me how I should forget to think!
 BEN. By giving liberty unto thine eyes.
Examine other beauties.
 ROM.   'Tis the way
To call hers (exquisite) in question more.
These happy masks that kiss fair ladies' brows,
Being black puts us in mind they hide the fair.
He that is strucken blind cannot forget

The precious treasure of his eyesight lost.
Show me a mistress that is passing fair,
What doth her beauty serve but as a note
Where I may read who pass'd that passing fair?
Farewell. Thou canst not teach me to forget.

BEN. I'll pay that doctrine, or else die in debt.

Exeunt.

Scene II: A street.

Enter CAPULET, COUNTY PARIS, *and* SERVANT—*the*
CLOWN.

CAP. But Montague is bound as well as I,
In penalty alike; and 'tis not hard, I think,
For men so old as we to keep the peace.

PAR. Of honourable reckoning are you both,
And pity 'tis you liv'd at odds so long.
But now, my lord, what say you to my suit?

CAP. But saying o'er what I have said before:
My child is yet a stranger in the world,
She hath not seen the change of fourteen years;
Let two more summers wither in their pride
Ere we may think her ripe to be a bride.

PAR. Younger than she are happy mothers made.

CAP. And too soon marr'd are those so early made.
The earth hath swallowed all my hopes but she;
She is the hopeful lady of my earth.
But woo her, gentle Paris, get her heart;
My will to her consent is but a part.
An she agree, within her scope of choice
Lies my consent and fair according voice.
This night I hold an old accustom'd feast,
Whereto I have invited many a guest,
Such as I love; and you among the store,

One more, most welcome, makes my number more.
At my poor house look to behold this night
Earth-treading stars that make dark heaven light.
Such comfort as do lusty young men feel
When well-apparell'd April on the heel
Of limping Winter treads, even such delight
Among fresh female buds shall you this night
Inherit at my house. Hear all, all see,
And like her most whose merit most shall be;
Which, on more view of many, mine, being one,
May stand in number, though in reck'ning none.
Come, go with me. [*To* SERVANT, *giving him a paper*]
                              Go, sirrah, trudge about
Through fair Verona; find those persons out
Whose names are written there, and to them say,
My house and welcome on their pleasure stay.
                              Exeunt CAPULET *and* PARIS.

SERV. Find them out whose names are written here?
It is written that the shoemaker should meddle with his
yard and the tailor with his last, the fisher with his pencil and the painter with his nets; but I am sent to find
those persons whose names are here writ, and can never
find what names the writing person hath here writ. I
must to the learned. In good time!

Enter BENVOLIO *and* ROMEO.

BEN. Tut, man, one fire burns out another's burning;
    One pain is less'ned by another's anguish;
Turn giddy, and be holp by backward turning;
    One desperate grief cures with another's languish.
Take thou some new infection to thy eye,
And the rank poison of the old will die.
    ROM. Your plantain leaf is excellent for that.
    BEN. For what, I pray thee?
    ROM.   For your broken shin.

BEN. Why, Romeo, art thou mad?

ROM. Not mad, but bound more than a madman is;
Shut up in prison, kept without my food,
Whipp'd and tormented and—God-den, good fellow.

SERV. God gi' go-den. I pray, sir, can you read?

ROM. Ay, mine own fortune in my misery.

SERV. Perhaps you have learned it without book. But
I pray, can you read anything you see?

ROM. Ay, if I know the letters and the language.

SERV. Ye say honestly. Rest you merry!

ROM. Stay, fellow; I can read.   *He reads.*
'Signior Martino and his wife and daughters;
County Anselmo and his beauteous sisters;
The lady widow of Vitruvio;
Signior Placentio and his lovely nieces;
Mercutio and his brother Valentine;
Mine uncle Capulet, his wife, and daughters;
My fair niece Rosaline and Livia;
Signior Valentio and his cousin Tybalt;
Lucio and the lively Helena.'
[*Gives back the paper.*] A fair assembly. Whither should
     they come?

SERV. Up.

ROM. Whither?

SERV. To supper, to our house.

ROM. Whose house?

SERV. My master's.

ROM. Indeed I should have ask'd you that before.

SERV. Now I'll tell you without asking. My master is
the great rich Capulet; and if you be not of the house of
Montagues, I pray come and crush a cup of wine. Rest
you merry!   *Exit.*

BEN. At this same ancient feast of Capulet's
Sups the fair Rosaline whom thou so lov'st;

With all the admired beauties of Verona.
Go thither, and with unattainted eye
Compare her face with some that I shall show,
And I will make thee think thy swan a crow.

   Rom. When the devout religion of mine eye
     Maintains such falsehood, then turn tears to fires;
And these, who, often drown'd, could never die,
     Transparent heretics, be burnt for liars!
One fairer than my love? The all-seeing sun
Ne'er saw her match since first the world begun.

   Ben. Tut! you saw her fair, none else being by,
Herself pois'd with herself in either eye;
But in that crystal scales let there be weigh'd
Your lady's love against some other maid
That I will show you shining at this feast,
And she shall scant show well that now seems best.

   Rom. I'll go along, no such sight to be shown,
But to rejoice in splendour of mine own.   *Exeunt.*

Scene III: Capulet's house.

Enter CAPULET'S WIFE, *and* NURSE.

   Wife. Nurse, where's my daughter? Call her forth to
    me.

   Nurse. Now, by my maidenhead at twelve year old,
I bade her come. What, lamb! what, ladybird!
God forbid! Where's this girl? What, Juliet!

Enter JULIET.

   Jul. How now? Who calls?
   Nurse.   Your mother.
   Jul.   Madam, I am here.
What is your will?

WIFE. This is the matter—Nurse, give leave awhile,
We must talk in secret. Nurse, come back again;
I have rememb'red me, thou 's hear our counsel.
Thou knowest my daughter's of a pretty age.

NURSE. Faith, I can tell her age unto an hour.

WIFE. She's not fourteen.

NURSE.   I'll lay fourteen of my teeth—
And yet, to my teen be it spoken, I have but four—
She is not fourteen. How long is it now
To Lammastide?

WIFE.   A fortnight and odd days.

NURSE. Even or odd, of all days in the year,
Come Lammas Eve at night shall she be fourteen.
Susan and she (God rest all Christian souls!)
Were of an age. Well, Susan is with God;
She was too good for me. But, as I said,
On Lammas Eve at night shall she be fourteen;
That shall she, marry; I remember it well.
'Tis since the earthquake now eleven years;
And she was wean'd (I never shall forget it),
Of all the days of the year, upon that day;
For I had then laid wormwood to my dug,
Sitting in the sun under the dovehouse wall.
My lord and you were then at Mantua.
Nay, I do bear a brain. But, as I said,
When it did taste the wormwood on the nipple
Of my dug and felt it bitter, pretty fool,
To see it tetchy and fall out with the dug!
Shake, quoth the dovehouse! 'Twas no need, I trow,
To bid me trudge.
And since that time it is eleven years,
For then she could stand high-lone; nay, by th' rood,
She could have run and waddled all about;
For even the day before, she broke her brow;

And then my husband (God be with his soul!
'A was a merry man) took up the child.
'Yea,' quoth he, 'dost thou fall upon thy face?
Thou wilt fall backward when thou hast more wit;
Wilt thou not, Jule?' and, by my holidam,
The pretty wretch left crying, and said 'Ay.'
To see now how a jest shall come about!
I warrant, an I should live a thousand years,
I never should forget it. 'Wilt thou not, Jule?' quoth he,
And, pretty fool, it stinted, and said 'Ay.'

WIFE. Enough of this. I pray thee hold thy peace.

NURSE. Yes, madam. Yet I cannot choose but laugh
To think it should leave crying and say 'Ay.'
And yet, I warrant, it had upon its brow
A bump as big as a young cock'rel's stone;
A perilous knock; and it cried bitterly.
'Yea,' quoth my husband, 'fall'st upon thy face?
Thou wilt fall backward when thou comest to age;
Wilt thou not, Jule?' It stinted, and said 'Ay.'

JUL. And stint thou too, I pray thee, nurse, say I.

NURSE. Peace, I have done. God mark thee to his
     grace!
Thou wast the prettiest babe that e'er I nurs'd.
An I might live to see thee married once,
I have my wish.

WIFE. Marry, that 'marry' is the very theme
I came to talk of. Tell me, daughter Juliet,
How stands your disposition to be married?

JUL. It is an honour that I dream not of.

NURSE. An honour? Were not I thine only nurse,
I would say thou hadst suck'd wisdom from thy teat.

WIFE. Well, think of marriage now. Younger than you,
Here in Verona, ladies of esteem,
Are made already mothers. By my count,

I was your mother much upon these years
That you are now a maid. Thus then in brief:
The valiant Paris seeks you for his love.

NURSE. A man, young lady! lady, such a man
As all the world—why, he's a man of wax.

WIFE. Verona's summer hath not such a flower.

NURSE. Nay, he's a flower, in faith—a very flower.

WIFE. What say you? Can you love the gentleman?
This night you shall behold him at our feast.
Read o'er the volume of young Paris' face,
And find delight writ there with beauty's pen;
Examine every married lineament,
And see how one another lends content;
And what obscur'd in this fair volume lies
Find written in the margent of his eyes.
This precious book of love, this unbound lover,
To beautify him only lacks a cover.
The fish lives in the sea, and 'tis much pride
For fair without the fair within to hide.
That book in many's eyes doth share the glory,
That in gold clasps locks in the golden story;
So shall you share all that he doth possess,
By having him making yourself no less.

NURSE. No less? Nay, bigger! Women grow by men.

WIFE. Speak briefly, can you like of Paris' love?

JUL. I'll look to like, if looking liking move;
But no more deep will I endart mine eye
Than your consent gives strength to make it fly.

Enter SERVINGMAN.

SERV. Madam, the guests are come, supper serv'd up,
you call'd, my young lady ask'd for, the nurse curs'd in
the pantry, and everything in extremity. I must hence to
wait. I beseech you follow straight.

WIFE. We follow thee. [*Exit* SERVINGMAN.] Juliet, the
County stays.

NURSE. Go, girl, seek happy nights to happy days.
Exeunt.

Scene IV: A street.

Enter ROMEO, MERCUTIO, BENVOLIO, *with five or six
other* MASKERS; TORCHBEARERS.

ROM. What, shall this speech be spoke for our excuse?
Or shall we on without apology?

BEN. The date is out of such prolixity.
We'll have no Cupid hoodwink'd with a scarf,
Bearing a Tartar's painted bow of lath,
Scaring the ladies like a crowkeeper;
Nor no without-book prologue, faintly spoke
After the prompter, for our entrance;
But, let them measure us by what they will,
We'll measure them a measure, and be gone.

ROM. Give me a torch. I am not for this ambling.
Being but heavy, I will bear the light.

MER. Nay, gentle Romeo, we must have you dance.

ROM. Not I, believe me. You have dancing shoes
With nimble soles; I have a soul of lead
So stakes me to the ground I cannot move.

MER. You are a lover. Borrow Cupid's wings
And soar with them above a common bound.

ROM. I am too sore enpierced with his shaft
To soar with his light feathers; and so bound
I cannot bound a pitch above dull woe.
Under love's heavy burthen do I sink.

MER. And, to sink in it, should you burthen love—
Too great oppression for a tender thing.

Rom. Is love a tender thing? It is too rough,
Too rude, too boist'rous, and it pricks like thorn.

Mer. If love be rough with you, be rough with love.
Prick love for pricking, and you beat love down.
Give me a case to put my visage in.
A visor for a visor! What care I
What curious eye doth quote deformities?
Here are the beetle brows shall blush for me.

Ben. Come, knock and enter; and no sooner in
But every man betake him to his legs.

Rom. A torch for me! Let wantons light of heart
Tickle the senseless rushes with their heels;
For I am proverb'd with a grandsire phrase,
I'll be a candle-holder and look on;
The game was ne'er so fair, and I am done.

Mer. Tut! dun's the mouse, the constable's own word!
If thou art Dun, we'll draw thee from the mire
Of this sir-reverence love, wherein thou stick'st
Up to the ears. Come, we burn daylight, ho!

Rom. Nay, that's not so.

Mer.   I mean, sir, in delay
We waste our lights in vain, like lamps by day.
Take our good meaning, for our judgment sits
Five times in that ere once in our five wits.

Rom. And we mean well, in going to this masque;
But 'tis no wit to go.

Mer.   Why, may one ask?

Rom. I dreamt a dream to-night.

Mer.   And so did I.

Rom. Well, what was yours?

Mer.   That dreamers often lie.

Rom. In bed asleep, while they do dream things true.

Mer. O, then I see Queen Mab hath been with you.
She is the fairies' midwife, and she comes
In shape no bigger than an agate stone

On the forefinger of an alderman,
Drawn with a team of little atomies
Athwart men's noses as they lie asleep;
Her wagon spokes made of long spinners' legs,
The cover, of the wings of grasshoppers;
Her traces, of the smallest spider's web;
Her collars, of the moonshine's wat'ry beams;
Her whip, of cricket's bone; the lash, of film;
Her wagoner, a small grey-coated gnat,
Not half so big as a round little worm
Prick'd from the lazy finger of a maid;
Her chariot is an empty hazelnut,
Made by the joiner squirrel or old grub,
Time out o' mind the fairies' coachmakers.
And in this state she gallops night by night
Through lovers' brains, and then they dream of love;
O'er courtiers' knees, that dream on curtsies straight;
O'er lawyers' fingers, who straight dream on fees;
O'er ladies' lips, who straight on kisses dream,
Which oft the angry Mab with blisters plagues,
Because their breaths with sweetmeats tainted are.
Sometime she gallops o'er a courtier's nose,
And then dreams he of smelling out a suit;
And sometime comes she with a tithe-pig's tail
Tickling a parson's nose as 'a lies asleep,
Then dreams he of another benefice.
Sometime she driveth o'er a soldier's neck,
And then dreams he of cutting foreign throats,
Of breaches, ambuscadoes, Spanish blades,
Of healths five fathom deep; and then anon
Drums in his ear, at which he starts and wakes,
And being thus frighted, swears a prayer or two
And sleeps again. This is that very Mab
That plats the manes of horses in the night
And bakes the elflocks in foul sluttish hairs,

Which once untangled much misfortune bodes.
This is the hag, when maids lie on their backs,
That presses them and learns them first to bear,
Making them women of good carriage.
This is she—
  Rom. Peace, peace, Mercutio, peace!
Thou talk'st of nothing.
  Mer.   True, I talk of dreams;
Which are the children of an idle brain,
Begot of nothing but vain fantasy;
Which is as thin of substance as the air,
And more inconstant than the wind, who woos
Even now the frozen bosom of the North
And, being anger'd, puffs away from thence,
Turning his face to the dew-dropping South.
  Ben. This wind you talk of blows us from ourselves.
Supper is done, and we shall come too late.
  Rom. I fear, too early; for my mind misgives
Some consequence, yet hanging in the stars,
Shall bitterly begin his fearful date
With this night's revels and expire the term
Of a despised life, clos'd in my breast,
By some vile forfeit of untimely death.
But he that hath the steerage of my course
Direct my sail! On, lusty gentlemen!
  Ben. Strike, drum.

                They march about the stage. Exeunt.

Scene V: Capulet's house.

SERVINGMEN *come forth with napkins.*

  1. Serv. Where's Potpan, that he helps not to take
away? He shift a trencher! he scrape a trencher!

2. SERV. When good manners shall lie all in one or two men's hands, and they unwash'd too, 'tis a foul thing.

1. SERV. Away with the join-stools, remove the court-cubbert, look to the plate. Good thou, save me a piece of marchpane and, as thou loves me, let the porter let in Susan Grindstone and Nell. Anthony, and Potpan!

2. SERV. Ay, boy, ready.

1. SERV. You are look'd for and call'd for, ask'd for and sought for, in the great chamber.

3 SERV. We cannot be here and there too. Cheerly, boys! Be brisk awhile, and the longer liver take all.

Exeunt.

Enter the MASKERS. *Enter, with* SERVANTS, CAPULET, *his* WIFE, JULIET, TYBALT, *and all the* GUESTS *and* GENTLE-WOMEN *to the* MASKERS.

CAP. Welcome, gentlemen! Ladies that have their toes
Unplagu'd with corns will have a bout with you.
Ah ha, my mistresses! which of you all
Will now deny to dance? She that makes dainty,
She I'll swear hath corns. Am I come near ye now?
Welcome, gentlemen! I have seen the day
That I have worn a visor and could tell
A whispering tale in a fair lady's ear,
Such as would please. 'Tis gone, 'tis gone, 'tis gone!
You are welcome, gentlemen! Come, musicians, play.
A hall, a hall! give room! and foot it, girls.

[*Music plays, and they dance.*]

More light, you knaves! and turn the tables up,
And quench the fire, the room is grown too hot.
Ah, sirrah, this unlook'd-for sport comes well.

Nay, sit, nay, sit, good cousin Capulet,
For you and I are past our dancing days.
How long is't now since last yourself and I
Were in a mask?

    2. CAP.   By'r Lady, thirty years.

    CAP. What, man? 'Tis not so much, 'tis not so much!
'Tis since the nuptial of Lucentio,
Come Pentecost as quickly as it will,
Some five-and-twenty years, and then we mask'd.

    2. CAP. 'Tis more, 'tis more! His son is elder, sir;
His son is thirty.

    CAP.   Will you tell me that?
His son was but a ward two years ago.

    ROM. [*to a* SERVINGMAN] What lady's that, which doth
        enrich the hand
Of yonder knight?

    SERV. I know not, sir.

    ROM. O, she doth teach the torches to burn bright!
It seems she hangs upon the cheek of night
Like a rich jewel in an Ethiop's ear—
Beauty too rich for use, for earth too dear!
So shows a snowy dove trooping with crows
As yonder lady o'er her fellows shows.
The measure done, I'll watch her place of stand
And, touching hers, make blessed my rude hand.
Did my heart love till now? Forswear it, sight!
For I ne'er saw true beauty till this night.

    TYB. This, by his voice, should be a Montague.
Fetch me my rapier, boy. What, dares the slave
Come hither, cover'd with an antic face,
To fleer and scorn at our solemnity?
Now, by the stock and honour of my kin,
To strike him dead I hold it not a sin.

    CAP. Why, how now, kinsman? Wherefore storm you
so?

Tyb. Uncle, this is a Montague, our foe;
A villain, that is hither come in spite
To scorn at our solemnity this night.

Cap. Young Romeo is it?

Tyb.   'Tis he, that villain Romeo.

Cap. Content thee, gentle coz, let him alone.
'A bears him like a portly gentleman,
And, to say truth, Verona brags of him
To be a virtuous and well-govern'd youth.
I would not for the wealth of all this town
Here in my house do him disparagement.
Therefore be patient, take no note of him.
It is my will; the which if thou respect,
Show a fair presence and put off these frowns,
An ill-beseeming semblance for a feast.

Tyb. It fits when such a villain is a guest.
I'll not endure him.

Cap.   He shall be endur'd.
What, goodman boy? I say he shall. Go to!
Am I the master here, or you? Go to!
You'll not endure him? God shall mend my soul!
You'll make a mutiny among my guests!
You will set cock-a-hoop! you'll be the man!

Tyb. Why, uncle, 'tis a shame.

Cap.   Go to, go to!
You are a saucy boy. Is't so, indeed?
This trick may chance to scathe you. I know what.
You must contrary me! Marry, 'tis time.—
Well said, my hearts!—You are a princox—go!
Be quiet, or—More light, more light!—For shame!
I'll make you quiet; what!—Cheerly, my hearts!

Tyb. Patience perforce with wilful choler meeting
Makes my flesh tremble in their different greeting.
I will withdraw; but this intrusion shall,
Now seeming sweet, convert to bitt'rest gall.   *Exit.*

Rom. If I profane with my unworthiest hand
This holy shrine, the gentle fine is this:
My lips, two blushing pilgrims, ready stand
To smooth that rough touch with a tender kiss.
Jul. Good pilgrim, you do wrong your hand too much,
Which mannerly devotion shows in this;
For saints have hands that pilgrims' hands do touch,
And palm to palm is holy palmers' kiss.
Rom. Have not saints lips, and holy palmers too?
Jul. Ay, pilgrim, lips that they must use in pray'r.
Rom. O, then, dear saint, let lips do what hands do!
They pray; grant thou, lest faith turn to despair.
Jul. Saints do not move, though grant for prayers'
    sake.
Rom. Then move not while my prayer's effect I take.
Thus from my lips, by thine my sin is purg'd.

Kisses her.

Jul. Then have my lips the sin that they have took.
Rom. Sin from my lips? O trespass sweetly urg'd!
Give me my sin again.   *Kisses her.*
Jul.   You kiss by th' book.
Nurse. Madam, your mother craves a word with you.
Rom. What is her mother?
Nurse.   Marry, bachelor,
Her mother is the lady of the house.
And a good lady, and a wise and virtuous.
I nurs'd her daughter that you talk'd withal.
I tell you, he that can lay hold of her
Shall have the chinks.
Rom.   Is she a Capulet?
O dear account! my life is my foe's debt.
Ben. Away, be gone; the sport is at the best.
Rom. Ay, so I fear; the more is my unrest.
Cap. Nay, gentlemen, prepare not to be gone;
We have a trifling foolish banquet towards.

Is it e'en so? Why then, I thank you all.
I thank you, honest gentlemen. Good night.
More torches here! [*Exeunt* MASKERS.] Come on then,
    let's to bed.
Ah, sirrah, by my fay, it waxes late;
I'll to my rest.   *Exeunt all but* JULIET *and* NURSE.

  JUL. Come hither, nurse. What is yond gentleman?
  NURSE. The son and heir of old Tiberio.
  JUL. What's he that now is going out of door?
  NURSE. Marry, that, I think, be young Petruchio.
  JUL. What's he that follows there, that would not
    dance?
  NURSE. I know not.
  JUL. Go ask his name.—If he be married,
My grave is like to be my wedding bed.
  NURSE. His name is Romeo, and a Montague,
The only son of your great enemy.
  JUL. My only love, sprung from my only hate!
Too early seen unknown, and known too late!
Prodigious birth of love it is to me
That I must love a loathed enemy.
  NURSE. What's this? what's this?
  JUL.   A rhyme I learnt even now
Of one I danc'd withal.
                    One calls within: Juliet.
  NURSE.   Anon, anon!
Come, let's away; the strangers all are gone.   *Exeunt.*

Act II.

Prologue

Enter CHORUS.

CHOR. Now old desire doth in his deathbed lie,
And young affection gapes to be his heir;

That fair for which love groan'd for and would die,
  With tender Juliet match'd, is now not fair.
Now Romeo is belov'd, and loves again,
  Alike bewitched by the charm of looks;
But to his foe suppos'd he must complain,
  And she steal love's sweet bait from fearful hooks.
Being held a foe, he may not have access
  To breathe such vows as lovers use to swear,
And she as much in love, her means much less
  To meet her new beloved anywhere;
But passion lends them power, time means, to meet,
Temp'ring extremities with extreme sweet.   *Exit.*

Scene I: A lane by the wall of Capulet's orchard.

Enter ROMEO *alone.*

ROM. Can I go forward when my heart is here?
Turn back, dull earth, and find thy centre out.
      Climbs the wall and leaps down within it.
      Enter BENVOLIO *with* MERCUTIO.
BEN. Romeo! my cousin Romeo! Romeo!
MER.   He is wise,
And, on my life, hath stol'n him home to bed.
BEN. He ran this way, and leapt this orchard wall.
Call, good Mercutio.
MER.   Nay, I'll conjure too.
Romeo! humours! madman! passion! lover!
Appear thou in the likeness of a sigh;
Speak but one rhyme, and I am satisfied!
Cry but 'Ay me!' pronounce but 'love' and 'dove';
Speak to my gossip Venus one fair word,
One nickname for her purblind son and heir,
Young Adam Cupid, he that shot so trim
When King Cophetua lov'd the beggar maid!

He heareth not, he stirreth not, he moveth not;
The ape is dead, and I must conjure him.
I conjure thee by Rosaline's bright eyes,
By her high forehead and her scarlet lip,
By her fine foot, straight leg, and quivering thigh,
And the demesnes that there adjacent lie,
That in thy likeness thou appear to us!
   BEN. An if he hear thee, thou wilt anger him.
   MER. This cannot anger him. 'Twould anger him.
To raise a spirit in his mistress' circle
Of some strange nature, letting it there stand
Till she had laid it and conjur'd it down.
That were some spite; my invocation
Is fair and honest: in his mistress' name,
I conjure only but to raise up him.
   BEN. Come, he hath hid himself among these trees
To be consorted with the humorous night.
Blind is his love and best befits the dark.
   MER. If love be blind, love cannot hit the mark.
Now will he sit under a medlar tree
And wish his mistress were that kind of fruit
As maids call medlars when they laugh alone.
O, Romeo, that she were, O that she were
An open et cetera, thou a pop'rin pear!
Romeo, good night. I'll to my truckle-bed;
This field-bed is too cold for me to sleep.
Come, shall we go?
   BEN.   Go then, for 'tis in vain
To seek him here that means not to be found. *Exeunt.*

Scene II: Capulet's orchard.

Enter ROMEO.

ROM. He jests at scars that never felt a wound.
   [*Enter* JULIET *above at a window.*]

But soft! What light through yonder window breaks?
It is the East, and Juliet is the sun!
Arise, fair sun, and kill the envious moon,
Who is already sick and pale with grief
That thou her maid art far more fair than she.
Be not her maid, since she is envious.
Her vestal livery is but sick and green,
And none but fools do wear it. Cast it off.
It is my lady; O, it is my love!
O that she knew she were!
She speaks, yet she says nothing. What of that?
Her eye discourses; I will answer it.
I am too bold; 'tis not to me she speaks.
Two of the fairest stars in all the heaven,
Having some business, do entreat her eyes
To twinkle in their spheres till they return.
What if her eyes were there, they in her head?
The brightness of her cheek would shame those stars
As daylight doth a lamp; her eyes in heaven
Would through the airy region stream so bright
That birds would sing and think it were not night.
See how she leans her cheek upon her hand!
O that I were a glove upon that hand,
That I might touch that cheek!

    Jul.   Ay me!

    Rom.   She speaks.

O, speak again, bright angel! for thou art
As glorious to this night, being o'er my head,
As is a winged messenger of heaven
Unto the white-upturned wond'ring eyes
Of mortals that fall back to gaze on him
When he bestrides the lazy-pacing clouds
And sails upon the bosom of the air.

    Jul. O Romeo, Romeo! wherefore art thou Romeo?
Deny thy father and refuse thy name!

Or, if thou wilt not, be but sworn my love,
And I'll no longer be a Capulet.

Rom. [*aside*] Shall I hear more, or shall I speak at this?

Jul. 'Tis but thy name that is my enemy.
Thou art thyself, though not a Montague.
What's Montague? It is nor hand, nor foot,
Nor arm, nor face, nor any other part
Belonging to a man. O, be some other name!
What's in a name? That which we call a rose
By any other name would smell as sweet.
So Romeo would, were he not Romeo call'd,
Retain that dear perfection which he owes
Without that title. Romeo, doff thy name;
And for that name, which is no part of thee,
Take all myself.

Rom.   I take thee at thy word.
Call me but love, and I'll be new baptiz'd;
Henceforth I never will be Romeo.

Jul. What man art thou that, thus bescreen'd in night,
So stumblest on my counsel?

Rom.   By a name
I know not how to tell thee who I am.
My name, dear saint, is hateful to myself,
Because it is an enemy to thee.
Had I it written, I would tear the word.

Jul. My ears have yet not drunk a hundred words
Of that tongue's utterance, yet I know the sound.
Art thou not Romeo, and a Montague?

Rom. Neither, fair saint, if either thee dislike.

Jul. How cam'st thou hither, tell me, and wherefore?
The orchard walls are high and hard to climb,
And the place death, considering who thou art,
If any of my kinsmen find thee here.

Rom. With love's light wings did I o'erperch these
      walls;

For stony limits cannot hold love out,
And what love can do, that dares love attempt.
Therefore thy kinsmen are no let to me.

Jul. If they do see thee, they will murther thee.

Rom. Alack, there lies more peril in thine eye
Than twenty of their swords! Look thou but sweet,
And I am proof against their enmity.

Jul. I would not for the world they saw thee here.

Rom. I have night's cloak to hide me from their sight;
And but thou love me, let them find me here.
My life were better ended by their hate
Than death prorogued, wanting of thy love.

Jul. By whose direction found'st thou out this place?

Rom. By love, that first did prompt me to enquire.
He lent me counsel, and I lent him eyes.
I am no pilot; yet, wert thou as far
As that vast shore wash'd with the farthest sea,
I would adventure for such merchandise.

Jul. Thou knowest the mask of night is on my face;
Else would a maiden blush bepaint my cheek
For that which thou hast heard me speak to-night.
Fain would I dwell on form—fain, fain deny
What I have spoke; but farewell compliment!
Dost thou love me? I know thou wilt say 'Ay';
And I will take thy word. Yet, if thou swear'st,
Thou mayst prove false. At lovers' perjuries,
They say Jove laughs. O gentle Romeo,
If thou dost love, pronounce it faithfully.
Or if thou thinkest I am too quickly won,
I'll frown, and be perverse, and say thee nay,
So thou wilt woo; but else, not for the world.
In truth, fair Montague, I am too fond,
And therefore thou mayst think my haviour light;
But trust me, gentleman, I'll prove more true
Than those that have more cunning to be strange.

I should have been more strange, I must confess,
But that thou overheard'st, ere I was ware,
My true-love passion. Therefore pardon me,
And not impute this yielding to light love,
Which the dark night hath so discovered.

Rom. Lady, by yonder blessed moon I swear,
That tips with silver all these fruit-tree tops—

Jul. O, swear not by the moon, th' inconstant moon,
That monthly changes in her circled orb,
Lest that thy love prove likewise variable.

Rom. What shall I swear by?

Jul.   Do not swear at all;
Or if thou wilt, swear by thy gracious self,
Which is the god of my idolatry,
And I'll believe thee.

Rom.   If my heart's dear love—

Jul. Well, do not swear. Although I joy in thee,
I have no joy of this contract to-night.
It is too rash, too unadvis'd, too sudden;
Too like the lightning, which doth cease to be
Ere one can say 'It lightens.' Sweet, good night!
This bud of love, by summer's ripening breath,
May prove a beauteous flow'r when next we meet.
Good night, good night! As sweet repose and rest
Come to thy heart as that within my breast!

Rom. O, wilt thou leave me so unsatisfied?

Jul. What satisfaction canst thou have to-night?

Rom. Th' exchange of thy love's faithful vow for mine.

Jul. I gave thee mine before thou didst request it;
And yet I would it were to give again.

Rom. Wouldst thou withdraw it? For what purpose,
love?

Jul. But to be frank and give it thee again.
And yet I wish but for the thing I have.
My bounty is as boundless as the sea,

My love as deep; the more I give to thee,
The more I have, for both are infinite.
I hear some noise within. Dear love, adieu!

[NURSE *calls within.*]

Anon, good nurse! Sweet Montague, be true.
Stay but a little, I will come again. *Exit.*

ROM. O blessed, blessed night! I am afeard,
Being in night, all this is but a dream,
Too flattering-sweet to be substantial.

Enter JULIET *above.*

JUL. Three words, dear Romeo, and good night indeed.
If that thy bent of love be honourable,
Thy purpose marriage, send me word to-morrow,
By one that I'll procure to come to thee,
Where and what time thou wilt perform the rite;
And all my fortunes at thy foot I'll lay
And follow thee my lord throughout the world.

NURSE. [*within*] Madam!

JUL. I come, anon.—But if thou meanest not well,
I do beseech thee—

NURSE. [*within*] Madam!

JUL. By-and-by I come.—
To cease thy suit and leave me to my grief.
To-morrow will I send.

ROM. So thrive my soul—

JUL. A thousand times good night! *Exit.*

ROM. A thousand times the worse, to want thy light!
Love goes toward love as schoolboys from their books;
But love from love, toward school with heavy looks.

Enter JULIET *again, above.*

JUL. Hist! Romeo, hist! O for a falc'ner's voice
To lure this tassel-gentle back again!
Bondage is hoarse and may not speak aloud;

Else would I tear the cave where Echo lies,
And make her airy tongue more hoarse than mine
With repetition of my Romeo's name.
Romeo!

  Rom. It is my soul that calls upon my name.
How silver-sweet sound lovers' tongues by night,
Like softest music to attending ears!

  Jul. Romeo!

  Rom.   My dear?

  Jul.   At what o'clock to-morrow
Shall I send to thee?

  Rom.   By the hour of nine.

  Jul. I will not fail. 'Tis twenty years till then.
I have forgot why I did call thee back.

  Rom. Let me stand here till thou remember it.

  Jul. I shall forget, to have thee still stand there,
Rememb'ring how I love thy company.

  Rom. And I'll still stay, to have thee still forget,
Forgetting any other home but this.

  Jul. 'Tis almost morning. I would have thee gone—
And yet no farther than a wanton's bird,
That lets it hop a little from her hand,
Like a poor prisoner in his twisted gyves,
And with a silk thread plucks it back again,
So loving-jealous of his liberty.

  Rom. I would I were thy bird.

  Jul.   Sweet, so would I.
Yet I should kill thee with much cherishing.
Good night, good night! Parting is such sweet sorrow,
That I shall say good night till it be morrow.   *Exit.*

  Rom. Sleep dwell upon thine eyes, peace in thy
     breast!
Would I were sleep and peace, so sweet to rest!
Hence will I to my ghostly father's cell,
His help to crave and my dear hap to tell.   *Exit.*

Scene III: Friar Laurence's cell.

Enter FRIAR LAURENCE *alone, with a basket.*

FRIAR. The grey-ey'd morn smiles on the frowning
    night,
Check'ring the Eastern clouds with streaks of light;
And flecked darkness like a drunkard reels
From forth day's path and Titan's fiery wheels.
Now, ere the sun advance his burning eye
The day to cheer and night's dank dew to dry,
I must up-fill this osier cage of ours
With baleful weeds and precious-juiced flowers.
The earth that's nature's mother is her tomb.
What is her burying grave, that is her womb;
And from her womb children of divers kind
We sucking on her natural bosom find;
Many for many virtues excellent,
None but for some, and yet all different.
O, mickle is the powerful grace that lies
In plants, herbs, stones, and their true qualities;
For naught so vile that on the earth doth live
But to the earth some special good doth give;
Nor aught so good but, strain'd from that fair use,
Revolts from true birth, stumbling on abuse.
Virtue itself turns vice, being misapplied,
And vice sometime's by action dignified.
Within the infant rind of this small flower
Poison hath residence, and medicine power;
For this, being smelt, with that part cheers each part;
Being tasted, slays all senses with the heart.
Two such opposed kings encamp them still
In man as well as herbs—grace and rude will;
And where the worser is predominant,
Full soon the canker death eats up that plant.

Enter ROMEO.

ROM. Good morrow, father.

FRIAR.   Benedicite!
What early tongue so sweet saluteth me?
Young son, it argues a distempered head
So soon to bid good morrow to thy bed.
Care keeps his watch in every old man's eye,
And where care lodges sleep will never lie;
But where unbruised youth with unstuff'd brain
Doth couch his limbs, there golden sleep doth reign.
Therefore thy earliness doth me assure
Thou art uprous'd with some distemp'rature;
Or if not so, then here I hit it right—
Our Romeo hath not been in bed to-night.

ROM. That last is true—the sweeter rest was mine.

FRIAR. God pardon sin! Wast thou with Rosaline?

ROM. With Rosaline, my ghostly father? No.
I have forgot that name, and that name's woe.

FRIAR. That's my good son! But where hast thou been
       then?

ROM. I'll tell thee ere thou ask it me again.
I have been feasting with mine enemy,
Where on a sudden one hath wounded me
That's by me wounded. Both our remedies
Within thy help and holy physic lies.
I bear no hatred, blessed man, for, lo,
My intercession likewise steads my foe.

FRIAR. Be plain, good son, and homely in thy drift.
Riddling confession finds but riddling shrift.

ROM. Then plainly know my heart's dear love is set
On the fair daughter of rich Capulet;
As mine on hers, so hers is set on mine,
And all combin'd, save what thou must combine
By holy marriage. When, and where, and how
We met, we woo'd, and made exchange of vow,

I'll tell thee as we pass; but this I pray,
That thou consent to marry us to-day.

    FRIAR. Holy Saint Francis! What a change is here!
Is Rosaline, that thou didst love so dear,
So soon forsaken? Young men's love then lies
Not truly in their hearts, but in their eyes.
Jesu Maria! What a deal of brine
Hath wash'd thy sallow cheeks for Rosaline!
How much salt water thrown away in waste,
To season love, that of it doth not taste!
The sun not yet thy sighs from heaven clears,
Thy old groans ring yet in mine ancient ears.
Lo, here upon thy cheek the stain doth sit
Of an old tear that is not wash'd off yet.
If e'er thou wast thyself, and these woes thine,
Thou and these woes were all for Rosaline.
And art thou chang'd? Pronounce this sentence then:
Women may fall when there's no strength in men.

    ROM. Thou chid'st me oft for loving Rosaline.

    FRIAR. For doting, not for loving, pupil mine.

    ROM. And bad'st me bury love.

    FRIAR.   Not in a grave
To lay one in, another out to have.

    ROM. I pray thee chide not. She whom I love now
Doth grace for grace and love for love allow.
The other did not so.

    FRIAR.   O, she knew well
Thy love did read by rote, that could not spell.
But come, young waverer, come go with me.
In one respect I'll thy assistant be;
For this alliance may so happy prove
To turn your households' rancour to pure love.

    ROM. O, let us hence! I stand on sudden haste.

    FRIAR. Wisely, and slow. They stumble that run fast.
                                    Exeunt.

Scene IV: A street.

Enter BENVOLIO *and* MERCUTIO.

MER. Where the devil should this Romeo be?
Came he not home to-night?

BEN. Not to his father's. I spoke with his man.

MER. Why, that same pale hard-hearted wench, that
    Rosaline,
Torments him so that he will sure run mad.

BEN. Tybalt, the kinsman to old Capulet,
Hath sent a letter to his father's house.

MER. A challenge, on my life.

BEN. Romeo will answer it.

MER. Any man that can write may answer a letter.

BEN. Nay, he will answer the letter's master, how he
dares, being dared.

MER. Alas, poor Romeo, he is already dead! stabb'd
with a white wench's black eye; shot through the ear
with a love song; the very pin of his heart cleft with the
blind bow-boy's butt-shaft; and is he a man to encounter
Tybalt?

BEN. Why, what is Tybalt?

MER. More than Prince of Cats, I can tell you. O, he's
the courageous captain of compliments. He fights as you
sing pricksong—keeps time, distance, and proportion;
rests me his minim rest, one, two, and the third in your
bosom! the very butcher of a silk button, a duellist, a
duellist! a gentleman of the very first house, of the first
and second cause. Ah, the immortal passado! the punto
reverso! the hay!

BEN. The what?

MER. The pox of such antic, lisping, affecting fantasti-
coes—these new tuners of accent! 'By Jesu, a very good
blade! a very tall man! a very good whore!' Why, is not

this a lamentable thing, grandsir, that we should be thus
afflicted with these strange flies, these fashion-mongers,
these pardona-mi's, who stand so much on the new
form that they cannot sit at ease on the old bench? O,
their bones, their bones!

Enter ROMEO.

BEN. Here comes Romeo! here comes Romeo!

MER. Without his roe, like a dried herring. O flesh,
flesh, how art thou fishified! Now is he for the numbers
that Petrarch flowed in. Laura, to his lady, was but a
kitchen wench (marry, she had a better love to berhyme
her), Dido a dowdy, Cleopatra a gypsy, Helen and Hero
hildings and harlots, Thisbe a grey eye or so, but not to
the purpose. Signior Romeo, bon jour! There's a French
salutation to your French slop. You gave us the counterfeit fairly last night.

ROM. Good morrow to you both. What counterfeit did
I give you?

MER. The slip, sir, the slip. Can you not conceive?

ROM. Pardon, good Mercutio. My business was great,
and in such a case as mine a man may strain courtesy.

MER. That's as much as to say, such a case as yours
constrains a man to bow in the hams.

ROM. Meaning, to curtsy.

MER. Thou hast most kindly hit it.

ROM. A most courteous exposition.

MER. Nay, I am the very pink of courtesy.

ROM. Pink for flower.

MER. Right.

ROM. Why, then is my pump well-flower'd.

MER. Well said! Follow me this jest now till thou hast
worn out thy pump, that, when the single sole of it is
worn, the jest may remain, after the wearing, solely singular.

Rom. O single-sol'd jest, solely singular for the single-ness!

Mer. Come between us, good Benvolio! My wits faint.

Rom. Swits and spurs, swits and spurs! or I'll cry a match.

Mer. Nay, if our wits run the wild-goose chase, I am done; for thou hast more of the wild goose in one of thy wits than, I am sure, I have in my whole five. Was I with you there for the goose?

Rom. Thou wast never with me for anything when thou wast not there for the goose.

Mer. I will bite thee by the ear for that jest.

Rom. Nay, good goose, bite not!

Mer. Thy wit is a very bitter sweeting; it is a most sharp sauce.

Rom. And is it not, then, well serv'd in to a sweet goose?

Mer. O, here's a wit of cheveril, that stretches from an inch narrow to an ell broad!

Rom. I stretch it out for that word 'broad,' which, added to the goose, proves thee far and wide a broad goose.

Mer. Why, is not this better now than groaning for love? Now art thou sociable, now art thou Romeo; now art thou what thou art, by art as well as by nature. For this drivelling love is like a great natural that runs lolling up and down to hide his bauble in a hole.

Ben. Stop there, stop there!

Mer. Thou desirest me to stop in my tale against the hair.

Ben. Thou wouldst else have made thy tale large.

Mer. O, thou art deceiv'd! I would have made it short; for I was come to the whole depth of my tale, and meant indeed to occupy the argument no longer.

Rom. Here's goodly gear!

Enter NURSE *and her man* PETER.

MER. A sail, a sail!

BEN. Two, two! a shirt and a smock.

NURSE. Peter!

PETER. Anon.

NURSE. My fan, Peter.

MER. Good Peter, to hide her face; for her fan's the fairer face of the two.

NURSE. God ye good morrow, gentlemen.

MER. God ye good-den, fair gentlewoman.

NURSE. Is it good-den?

MER. 'Tis no less, I tell ye; for the bawdy hand of the dial is now upon the prick of noon.

NURSE. Out upon you! What a man are you!

ROM. One, gentlewoman, that God hath made for himself to mar.

NURSE. By my troth, it is well said. 'For himself to mar,' quoth 'a? Gentlemen, can any of you tell me where I may find the young Romeo?

ROM. I can tell you; but young Romeo will be older when you have found him than he was when you sought him. I am the youngest of that name, for fault of a worse.

NURSE. You say well.

MER. Yea, is the worst well? Very well took, i' faith! wisely, wisely.

NURSE. If you be he, sir, I desire some confidence with you.

BEN. She will endite him to some supper.

MER. A bawd, a bawd, a bawd! So ho!

ROM. What hast thou found?

MER. No hare, sir; unless a hare, sir, in a lenten pie, that is something stale and hoar ere it be spent.

[*He walks by them and sings:*]
    An old hare hoar,
    And an old hare hoar,

Is very good meat in Lent;
But a hare that is hoar
Is too much for a score
When it hoars ere it be spent.

Romeo, will you come to your father's? We'll to dinner thither.

Rom. I will follow you.

Mer. Farewell, ancient lady. Farewell, [*sings*] lady, lady, lady.   *Exeunt* Mercutio, Benvolio.

Nurse. Marry, farewell! I pray you, sir, what saucy merchant was this that was so full of his ropery?

Rom. A gentleman, nurse, that loves to hear himself talk and will speak more in a minute than he will stand to in a month.

Nurse. An 'a speak anything against me, I'll take him down, an 'a were lustier than he is, and twenty such Jacks; and if I cannot, I'll find those that shall. Scurvy knave! I am none of his flirt-gills; I am none of his skains-mates. And thou must stand by too, and suffer every knave to use me at his pleasure!

Peter. I saw no man use you at his pleasure. If I had, my weapon should quickly have been out, I warrant you. I dare draw as soon as another man, if I see occasion in a good quarrel, and the law on my side.

Nurse. Now, afore God, I am so vex'd that every part about me quivers. Scurvy knave! Pray you, sir, a word; and, as I told you, my young lady bid me enquire you out. What she bid me say, I will keep to myself; but first let me tell ye, if ye should lead her into a fool's paradise, as they say, it were a very gross kind of behaviour, as they say; for the gentlewoman is young; and therefore, if you should deal double with her, truly it were an ill thing to be off'red to any gentlewoman, and very weak dealing.

Rom. Nurse, commend me to thy lady and mistress. I protest unto thee—

Nurse. Good heart, and i' faith I will tell her as much. Lord, Lord! she will be a joyful woman.

Rom. What wilt thou tell her, nurse? Thou dost not mark me.

Nurse. I will tell her, sir, that you do protest, which, as I take it, is a gentlemanlike offer.

Rom. Bid her devise
Some means to come to shrift this afternoon;
And there she shall at Friar Laurence' cell
Be shriv'd and married. Here is for thy pains.

Nurse. No, truly, sir; not a penny.

Rom. Go to! I say you shall.

Nurse. This afternoon, sir? Well, she shall be there.

Rom. And stay, good nurse, behind the abbey wall.
Within this hour my man shall be with thee
And bring thee cords made like a tackled stair,
Which to the high topgallant of my joy
Must be my convoy in the secret night.
Farewell. Be trusty, and I'll quit thy ·pains.
Farewell. Commend me to thy mistress.

Nurse. Now God in heaven bless thee! Hark you, sir.

Rom. What say'st thou, my dear nurse?

Nurse. Is your man secret? Did you ne'er hear say, Two may keep counsel, putting one away?

Rom. I warrant thee my man's as true as steel.

Nurse. Well, sir, my mistress is the sweetest lady. Lord, Lord! when 'twas a little prating thing—O, there is a nobleman in town, one Paris, that would fain lay knife aboard; but she, good soul, had as lieve see a toad, a very toad, as see him. I anger her sometimes, and tell her that Paris is the properer man; but I'll warrant you, when I say so, she looks as pale as any clout in the versal world. Doth not rosemary and Romeo begin both with a letter?

Rom. Ay, nurse; what of that? Both with an R.

NURSE. Ah, mocker! that's the dog's name. R is for
the—No; I know it begins with some other letter; and
she hath the prettiest sententious of it, of you and rosemary, that it would do you good to hear it.

ROM. Commend me to thy lady.

NURSE. Ay, a thousand times. [*Exit* ROMEO.] Peter!

PETER. Anon.

NURSE. Peter, take my fan, and go before, and apace.
Exeunt.

Scene V: Capulet's orchard.

Enter JULIET.

JUL. The clock struck nine when I did send the nurse;
In half an hour she promis'd to return.
Perchance she cannot meet him. That's not so.
O, she is lame! Love's heralds should be thoughts,
Which ten times faster glide than the sun's beams
Driving back shadows over low'ring hills.
Therefore do nimble-pinion'd doves draw Love,
And therefore hath the wind-swift Cupid wings.
Now is the sun upon the highmost hill
Of this day's journey, and from nine till twelve
Is three long hours; yet she is not come.
Had she affections and warm youthful blood,
She would be as swift in motion as a ball;
My words would bandy her to my sweet love,
And his to me.
But old folks, many feign as they were dead—
Unwieldy, slow, heavy and pale as lead.

[*Enter* NURSE *and* PETER.]

O God, she comes! O honey nurse, what news?
Hast thou met with him? Send thy man away.

NURSE. Peter, stay at the gate.   *Exit* PETER.

JUL. Now, good sweet nurse—O Lord, why look'st
thou sad?
Though news be sad, yet tell them merrily;
If good, thou shamest the music of sweet news
By playing it to me with so sour a face.

NURSE. I am aweary, give me leave awhile.
Fie, how my bones ache! What a jaunce have I had!

JUL. I would thou hadst my bones, and I thy news.
Nay, come, I pray thee speak. Good, good nurse, speak.

NURSE. Jesu, what haste! Can you not stay awhile?
Do you not see that I am out of breath?

JUL. How art thou out of breath when thou hast breath
To say to me that thou art out of breath?
The excuse that thou dost make in this delay
Is longer than the tale thou dost excuse.
Is thy news good or bad? Answer to that.
Say either, and I'll stay the circumstance.
Let me be satisfied, is't good or bad?

NURSE. Well, you have made a simple choice; you
know not how to choose a man. Romeo? No, not he.
Though his face be better than any man's, yet his leg
excels all men's; and for a hand and a foot, and a body,
though they be not to be talk'd on, yet they are past compare. He is not the flower of courtesy, but, I'll warrant
him, as gentle as a lamb. Go thy ways, wench; serve God.
What, have you din'd at home?

JUL. No, no. But all this did I know before. What says
he of our marriage? What of that?

NURSE. Lord, how my head aches! What a head have I!
It beats as it would fall in twenty pieces.
My back o' t' other side—ah, my back, my back!
Beshrew your heart for sending me about
To catch my death with jauncing up and down!

JUL. I' faith, I am sorry that thou art not well.
Sweet, sweet, sweet nurse, tell me, what says my love?

NURSE. Your love says, like an honest gentleman, and
a courteous, and a kind, and a handsome, and, I warrant,
a virtuous—Where is your mother?

JUL. Where is my mother? Why, she is within.
Where should she be? How oddly thou repliest!
'Your love says, like an honest gentleman,
"Where is your mother?"'

NURSE.   O God's Lady dear!
Are you so hot? Marry come up, I trow.
Is this the poultice for my aching bones?
Henceforward do your messages yourself.

JUL. Here's such a coil! Come, what says Romeo?

NURSE. Have you got leave to go to shrift to-day?

JUL. I have.

NURSE. Then hie you hence to Friar Laurence' cell;
There stays a husband to make you a wife.
Now comes the wanton blood up in your cheeks:
They'll be in scarlet straight at any news.
Hie you to church; I must another way,
To fetch a ladder, by the which your love
Must climb a bird's nest soon when it is dark.
I am the drudge, and toil in your delight;
But you shall bear the burthen soon at night.
Go; I'll to dinner; hie you to the cell.

JUL. Hie to high fortune! Honest nurse, farewell.

Exeunt.

Scene VI: Friar Laurence's cell.

Enter FRIAR LAURENCE *and* ROMEO.

FRIAR. So smile the heavens upon this holy act
That after-hours with sorrow chide us not!

ROM. Amen, amen! But come what sorrow can,
It cannot countervail the exchange of joy

That one short minute gives me in her sight.
Do thou but close our hands with holy words,
Then love-devouring death do what he dare—
It is enough I may but call her mine.

    FRIAR. These violent delights have violent ends
And in their triumph die, like fire and powder,
Which, as they kiss, consume. The sweetest honey
Is loathsome in his own deliciousness
And in the taste confounds the appetite.
Therefore love moderately: long love doth so;
Too swift arrives as tardy as too slow.

[Enter JULIET.]

Here comes the lady. O, so light a foot
Will ne'er wear out the everlasting flint.
A lover may bestride the gossamer
That idles in the wanton summer air,
And yet not fall; so light is vanity.

    JUL. Good even to my ghostly confessor.

    FRIAR. Romeo shall thank thee, daughter, for us both.

    JUL. As much to him, else is his thanks too much.

    ROM. Ah, Juliet, if the measure of thy joy
Be heap'd like mine, and that thy skill be more
To blazon it, then sweeten with thy breath
This neighbour air, and let rich music's tongue
Unfold the imagin'd happiness that both
Receive in either by this dear encounter.

    JUL. Conceit, more rich in matter than in words,
Brags of his substance, not of ornament.
They are but beggars that can count their worth;
But my true love is grown to such excess
I cannot sum up sum of half my wealth.

    FRIAR. Come, come with me, and we will make short
      work;

For, by your leaves, you shall not stay alone
Till Holy Church incorporate two in one.   *Exeunt.*

Act III: Scene I: A public place.

Enter MERCUTIO, BENVOLIO, *and* MEN.

BEN. I pray thee, good Mercutio, let's retire.
The day is hot, the Capulets abroad,
And if we meet, we shall not scape a brawl,
For now, these hot days, is the mad blood stirring.

MER. Thou art like one of these fellows that, when he
enters the confines of a tavern, claps me his sword upon
the table and says 'God send me no need of thee!' and
by the operation of the second cup draws him on the
drawer, when indeed there is no need.

BEN. Am I like such a fellow?

MER. Come, come, thou art as hot a Jack in thy mood
as any in Italy; and as soon moved to be moody, and as
soon moody to be moved.

BEN. And what to?

MER. Nay, an there were two such, we should have
none shortly, for one would kill the other. Thou! why,
thou wilt quarrel with a man that hath a hair more or a
hair less in his beard than thou hast. Thou wilt quarrel
with a man for cracking nuts, having no other reason but
because thou hast hazel eyes. What eye but such an eye
would spy out such a quarrel? Thy head is as full of
quarrels as an egg is full of meat; and yet thy head hath
been beaten as addle as an egg for quarrelling. Thou hast
quarrell'd with a man for coughing in the street, because
he hath wakened thy dog that hath lain asleep in the sun.
Didst thou not fall out with a tailor for wearing his new
doublet before Easter? with another for tying his new

shoes with old riband? And yet thou wilt tutor me from
quarrelling!

BEN. An I were so apt to quarrel as thou art, any man
should buy the fee simple of my life for an hour and a
quarter.

MER. The fee simple? O simple!

Enter TYBALT *and others.*

BEN. By my head, here come the Capulets.

MER. By my heel, I care not.

TYB. Follow me close, for I will speak to them.
Gentlemen, good den. A word with one of you.

MER. And but one word with one of us? Couple it with
something; make it a word and a blow.

TYB. You shall find me apt enough to that, sir, an you
will give me occasion.

MER. Could you not take some occasion without giving?

TYB. Mercutio, thou consortest with Romeo.

MER. Consort? What, dost thou make us minstrels?
An thou make minstrels of us, look to hear nothing but
discords. Here's my fiddlestick; here's that shall make
you dance. Zounds, consort!

BEN. We talk here in the public haunt of men.
Either withdraw unto some private place
And reason coldly of your grievances,
Or else depart. Here all eyes gaze on us.

MER. Men's eyes were made to look, and let them
    gaze.
I will not budge for no man's pleasure, I.

Enter ROMEO.

TYB. Well, peace be with you, sir. Here comes my
    man.

MER. But I'll be hang'd, sir, if he wear your livery.
Marry, go before to field, he'll be your follower!
Your worship in that sense may call him man.

TYB. Romeo, the love I bear thee can afford
No better term than this: thou art a villain.

ROM. Tybalt, the reason that I have to love thee
Doth much excuse the appertaining rage
To such a greeting. Villain am I none.
Therefore farewell. I see thou knowest me not.

TYB. Boy, this shall not excuse the injuries
That thou hast done me; therefore turn and draw.

ROM. I do protest I never injur'd thee,
But love thee better than thou canst devise
Till thou shalt know the reason of my love;
And so, good Capulet, which name I tender
As dearly as mine own, be satisfied.

MER. O calm, dishonourable, vile submission!
Alla stoccata carries it away.   [*Draws.*]
Tybalt, you ratcatcher, will you walk?

TYB. What wouldst thou have with me?

MER. Good King of Cats, nothing but one of your nine
lives. That I mean to make bold withal, and, as you shall
use me hereafter, drybeat the rest of the eight. Will you
pluck your sword out of his pilcher by the ears? Make
haste, lest mine be about your ears ere it be out.

TYB. I am for you.   *Draws.*

ROM. Gentle Mercutio, put thy rapier up.

MER. Come, sir, your passado!   *They fight.*

ROM. Draw, Benvolio; beat down their weapons.
Gentlemen, for shame! forbear this outrage!
Tybalt, Mercutio, the Prince expressly hath
Forbid this bandying in Verona streets.
Hold, Tybalt! Good Mercutio!

> TYBALT *under* ROMEO's *arm thrusts* MERCUTIO *in,*
> *and flies with his* FOLLOWERS.

MER.   I am hurt.
A plague o' both your houses! I am sped.
Is he gone and hath nothing?

BEN.   What, art thou hurt?

MER. Ay, ay, a scratch, a scratch. Marry, 'tis enough.
Where is my page? Go, villain, fetch a surgeon.

Exit PAGE.

ROM. Courage, man. The hurt cannot be much.

MER. No, 'tis not so deep as a well, nor so wide as a
church door; but 'tis enough, 'twill serve. Ask for me to-
morrow, and you shall find me a grave man. I am pep-
pered, I warrant, for this world. A plague o' both your
houses! Zounds, a dog, a rat, a mouse, a cat, to scratch a
man to death! a braggart, a rogue, a villain, that fights by
the book of arithmetic! Why the devil came you between
us? I was hurt under your arm.

ROM. I thought all for the best.

MER. Help me into some house, Benvolio,
Or I shall faint. A plague o' both your houses!
They have made worms' meat of me. I have it,
And soundly too. Your houses!

Exit, supported by BENVOLIO.

ROM. This gentleman, the Prince's near ally,
My very friend, hath got this mortal hurt
In my behalf—my reputation stain'd
With Tybalt's slander—Tybalt, that an hour
Hath been my kinsman. O sweet Juliet,
Thy beauty hath made me effeminate
And in my temper soft'ned valour's steel!

Enter BENVOLIO.

BEN. O Romeo, Romeo, brave Mercutio's dead!
That gallant spirit hath aspir'd the clouds,
Which too untimely here did scorn the earth.

Rom. This day's black fate on moe days doth depend;
This but begins the woe others must end.

Enter TYBALT.

Ben. Here comes the furious Tybalt back again.
Rom. Alive in triumph, and Mercutio slain?
Away to heaven respective lenity,
And fire-ey'd fury be my conduct now!
Now, Tybalt, take the 'villain' back again
That late thou gavest me; for Mercutio's soul
Is but a little way above our heads,
Staying for thine to keep him company.
Either thou or I, or both, must go with him.

Tyb. Thou, wretched boy, that didst consort him here,
Shalt with him hence.
Rom.   This shall determine that.
                        They fight. TYBALT *falls.*

Ben. Romeo, away, be gone!
The citizens are up, and Tybalt slain.
Stand not amaz'd. The Prince will doom thee death
If thou art taken. Hence, be gone, away!
Rom. O, I am fortune's fool!
Ben.   Why dost thou stay?
                        Exit ROMEO.

Enter CITIZENS.

Citizen. Which way ran he that kill'd Mercutio?
Tybalt, that murtherer, which way ran he?
Ben. There lies that Tybalt.
Citizen.   Up, sir, go with me.
I charge thee in the Prince's name obey.
Enter PRINCE *attended,* OLD MONTAGUE, CAPULET,
        their WIVES, *and others.*
Prince. Where are the vile beginners of this fray?

BEN. O noble Prince, I can discover all
The unlucky manage of this fatal brawl.
There lies the man, slain by young Romeo,
That slew thy kinsman, brave Mercutio.

CAP. WIFE. Tybalt, my cousin! O my brother's child!
O Prince! O husband! O, the blood is spill'd
Of my dear kinsman! Prince, as thou art true,
For blood of ours shed blood of Montague.
O cousin, cousin!

PRINCE. Benvolio, who began this bloody fray?

BEN. Tybalt, here slain, whom Romeo's hand did slay.
Romeo, that spoke him fair, bid him bethink
How nice the quarrel was, and urg'd withal
Your high displeasure. All this—uttered
With gentle breath, calm look, knees humbly bow'd—
Could not take truce with the unruly spleen
Of Tybalt deaf to peace, but that he tilts
With piercing steel at bold Mercutio's breast;
Who, all as hot, turns deadly point to point,
And, with a martial scorn, with one hand beats
Cold death aside and with the other sends
It back to Tybalt, whose dexterity
Retorts it. Romeo he cries aloud,
'Hold, friends! friends, part!' and swifter than his tongue,
His agile arm beats down their fatal points,
And 'twixt them rushes; underneath whose arm
An envious thrust from Tybalt hit the life
Of stout Mercutio, and then Tybalt fled;
But by-and-by comes back to Romeo,
Who had but newly entertain'd revenge,
And to't they go like lightning; for, ere I
Could draw to part them, was stout Tybalt slain;
And, as he fell, did Romeo turn and fly.
This is the truth, or let Benvolio die.

CAP. WIFE. He is a kinsman to the Montague;
Affection makes him false, he speaks not true.
Some twenty of them fought in this black strife,
And all those twenty could but kill one life.
I beg for justice, which thou, Prince, must give.
Romeo slew Tybalt; Romeo must not live.

PRINCE. Romeo slew him; he slew Mercutio.
Who now the price of his dear blood doth owe?

MON. Not Romeo, Prince; he was Mercutio's friend;
His fault concludes but what the law should end,
The life of Tybalt.

PRINCE. And for that offence
Immediately we do exile him hence.
I have an interest in your hate's proceeding,
My blood for your brawls doth lie ableeding;
But I'll amerce you with so strong a fine
That you shall all repent the loss of mine.
I will be deaf to pleading and excuses;
Nor tears nor prayers shall purchase out abuses.
Therefore use none. Let Romeo hence in haste,
Else, when he is found, that hour is his last.
Bear hence this body, and attend our will.
Mercy but murders, pardoning those that kill. *Exeunt*.

Scene II: Capulet's orchard.

Enter JULIET *alone*.

JUL. Gallop apace, you fiery-footed steeds,
Towards Phœbus' lodging! Such a wagoner
As Phaëton would whip you to the West
And bring in cloudy night immediately.
Spread thy close curtain, love-performing night,
That runaway eyes may wink, and Romeo

Leap to these arms untalk'd of and unseen.
Lovers can see to do their amorous rites
By their own beauties; or, if love be blind,
It best agrees with night. Come, civil night,
Thou sober-suited matron, all in black,
And learn me how to lose a winning match,
Play'd for a pair of stainless maidenhoods.
Hood my unmann'd blood, bating in my cheeks,
With thy black mantle till strange love, grown bold,
Think true love acted simple modesty.
Come, night; come, Romeo; come, thou day in night;
For thou wilt lie upon the wings of night
Whiter than new snow upon a raven's back.
Come, gentle night; come, loving, black-brow'd night;
Give me my Romeo; and, when he shall die,
Take him and cut him out in little stars,
And he will make the face of heaven so fine
That all the world will be in love with night
And pay no worship to the garish sun.
O, I have bought the mansion of a love,
But not possess'd it; and though I am sold,
Not yet enjoy'd. So tedious is this day
As is the night before some festival
To an impatient child that hath new robes
And may not wear them. O, here comes my nurse,

[*Enter* NURSE, *with cords.*]

And she brings news; and every tongue that speaks
But Romeo's name speaks heavenly eloquence.
Now, nurse, what news? What hast thou there? the cords
That Romeo bid thee fetch?

   NURSE.   Ay, ay, the cords.
                          Throws them down.

   JUL. Ay me! what news? Why dost thou wring thy
     hands?

NURSE. Ah, weraday! he's dead, he's dead, he's dead!
We are undone, lady, we are undone!
Alack the day! he's gone, he's kill'd, he's dead!

JUL. Can heaven be so envious?

NURSE.   Romeo can,
Though heaven cannot. O Romeo, Romeo!
Who ever would have thought it? Romeo!

JUL. What devil art thou that dost torment me thus?
This torture should be roar'd in dismal hell.
Hath Romeo slain himself? Say thou but 'I,'
And that bare vowel 'I' shall poison more
Than the death-darting eye of cockatrice.
I am not I, if there be such an 'I';
Or those eyes shut that make thee answer 'I.'
If he be slain, say 'I'; or if not, 'no.'
Brief sounds determine of my weal or woe.

NURSE. I saw the wound, I saw it with mine eyes,
(God save the mark!) here on his manly breast.
A piteous corse, a bloody piteous corse;
Pale, pale as ashes, all bedaub'd in blood,
All in gore-blood. I swounded at the sight.

JUL. O, break, my heart! poor bankrout, break at once!
To prison, eyes; ne'er look on liberty!
Vile earth, to earth resign; end motion here,
And thou and Romeo press one heavy bier!

NURSE. O Tybalt, Tybalt, the best friend I had!
O courteous Tybalt! honest gentleman!
That ever I should live to see thee dead!

JUL. What storm is this that blows so contrary?
Is Romeo slaught'red, and is Tybalt dead?
My dear-lov'd cousin, and my dearer lord?
Then, dreadful trumpet, sound the general doom!
For who is living, if those two are gone?

NURSE. Tybalt is gone, and Romeo banished;
Romeo that kill'd him, he is banished.

Jul. O God! Did Romeo's hand shed Tybalt's blood?

Nurse. It did, it did! alas the day, it did!

Jul. O serpent heart, hid with a flow'ring face!
Did ever dragon keep so fair a cave?
Beautiful tyrant! fiend angelical!
Dove-feather'd raven! wolvish-ravening lamb!
Despised substance of divinest show!
Just opposite to what thou justly seem'st—
A damned saint, an honourable villain!
O nature, what hadst thou to do in hell
When thou didst bower the spirit of a fiend
In mortal paradise of such sweet flesh?
Was ever book containing such vile matter
So fairly bound? O, that deceit should dwell
In such a gorgeous palace!

Nurse.   There's no trust,
No faith, no honesty in men; all perjur'd,
All forsworn, all naught, all dissemblers.
Ah, where's my man? Give me some aquavitæ.
These griefs, these woes, these sorrows make me old.
Shame come to Romeo!

Jul.   Blister'd be thy tongue
For such a wish! He was not born to shame.
Upon his brow shame is asham'd to sit;
For 'tis a throne where honour may be crown'd
Sole monarch of the universal earth.
O, what a beast was I to chide at him!

Nurse. Will you speak well of him that kill'd your
    cousin?

Jul. Shall I speak ill of him that is my husband?
Ah, poor my lord, what tongue shall smooth thy name
When I, thy three-hours wife, have mangled it?
But wherefore, villain, didst thou kill my cousin?
That villain cousin would have kill'd my husband.

Back, foolish tears, back to your native spring!
Your tributary drops belong to woe,
Which you, mistaking, offer up to joy.
My husband lives, that Tybalt would have slain;
And Tybalt's dead, that would have slain my husband.
All this is comfort; wherefore weep I then?
Some word there was, worser than Tybalt's death,
That murd'red me. I would forget it fain;
But O, it presses to my memory
Like damned guilty deeds to sinners' minds!
'Tybalt is dead, and Romeo—banished.'
That 'banished,' that one word 'banished,'
Hath slain ten thousand Tybalts. Tybalt's death
Was woe enough, if it had ended there;
Or, if sour woe delights in fellowship
And needly will be rank'd with other griefs,
Why followed not, when she said 'Tybalt's dead,'
Thy father, or thy mother, nay, or both,
Which modern lamentation might have mov'd?
But with arearward following Tybalt's death,
'Romeo is banished'—to speak that word
Is father, mother, Tybalt, Romeo, Juliet,
All slain, all dead. 'Romeo is banished'—
There is no end, no limit, measure, bound,
In that word's death; no words can that woe sound.
Where is my father and my mother, nurse?

    NURSE. Weeping and wailing over Tybalt's corse.
Will you go to them? I will bring you thither.

    JUL. Wash they his wounds with tears? Mine shall be
        spent,
When theirs are dry, for Romeo's banishment.
Take up those cords. Poor ropes, you are beguil'd,
Both you and I, for Romeo is exil'd.
He made you for a highway to my bed;

But I, a maid, die maiden-widowed.
Come, cords; come, nurse. I'll to my wedding bed;
And death, not Romeo, take my maidenhead!

    NURSE. Hie to your chamber. I'll find Romeo
To comfort you. I wot well where he is.
Hark ye, your Romeo will be here at night.
I'll to him; he is hid at Laurence' cell.

    JUL. O, find him! give this ring to my true knight
And bid him come to take his last farewell.   *Exeunt.*

Scene III: Friar Laurence's cell.

Enter FRIAR LAURENCE.

    FRIAR. Romeo, come forth; come forth, thou fearful
      man.
Affliction is enamour'd of thy parts,
And thou art wedded to calamity.

Enter ROMEO.

    ROM. Father, what news? What is the Prince's doom?
What sorrow craves acquaintance at my hand
That I yet know not?
    FRIAR.   Too familiar
Is my dear son with such sour company.
I bring thee tidings of the Prince's doom.

    ROM. What less than doomsday is the Prince's doom?

    FRIAR. A gentler judgment vanish'd from his lips—
Not body's death, but body's banishment.

    ROM. Ha, banishment? Be merciful, say 'death';
For exile hath more terror in his look,
Much more than death. Do not say 'banishment.'

    FRIAR. Hence from Verona art thou banished.
Be patient, for the world is broad and wide.

Rom. There is no world without Verona walls,
But purgatory, torture, hell itself.
Hence banished is banish'd from the world,
And world's exile is death. Then 'banishment'
Is death misterm'd. Calling death 'banishment,'
Thou cut'st my head off with a golden axe
And smilest upon the stroke that murders me.

Friar. O deadly sin! O rude unthankfulness!
Thy fault our law calls death; but the kind Prince,
Taking thy part, hath rush'd aside the law,
And turn'd that black word death to banishment.
This is dear mercy, and thou seest it not.

Rom. 'Tis torture, and not mercy. Heaven is here,
Where Juliet lives; and every cat and dog
And little mouse, every unworthy thing,
Live here in heaven and may look on her;
But Romeo may not. More validity,
More honourable state, more courtship lives
In carrion flies than Romeo. They may seize
On the white wonder of dear Juliet's hand
And steal immortal blessing from her lips,
Who, even in pure and vestal modesty,
Still blush, as thinking their own kisses sin;
But Romeo may not—he is banished.
This may flies do, when I from this must fly;
They are free men, but I am banished.
And sayest thou yet that exile is not death?
Hadst thou no poison mix'd, no sharp-ground knife,
No sudden mean of death, though ne'er so mean,
But 'banished' to kill me—'banished'?
O friar, the damned use that word in hell;
Howling attends it! How hast thou the heart,
Being a divine, a ghostly confessor,
A sin-absolver, and my friend profess'd,
To mangle me with that word 'banished'?

FRIAR. Thou fond mad man, hear me a little speak.

ROM. O, thou wilt speak again of banishment.

FRIAR. I'll give thee armour to keep off that word;
Adversity's sweet milk, philosophy,
To comfort thee, though thou art banished.

ROM. Yet 'banished'? Hang up philosophy!
Unless philosophy can make a Juliet,
Displant a town, reverse a prince's doom,
It helps not, it prevails not. Talk no more.

FRIAR. O, then I see that madmen have no ears.

ROM. How should they, when that wise men have no
eyes?

FRIAR. Let me dispute with thee of thy estate.

ROM. Thou canst not speak of that thou dost not feel.
Wert thou as young as I, Juliet thy love,
An hour but married, Tybalt murdered,
Doting like me, and like me banished,
Then mightst thou speak, then mightst thou tear thy
hair,
And fall upon the ground, as I do now,
Taking the measure of an unmade grave.

Knock within.

FRIAR. Arise; one knocks. Good Romeo, hide thyself.

ROM. Not I; unless the breath of heartsick groans,
Mist-like infold me from the search of eyes.   *Knock.*

FRIAR. Hark, how they knock! Who's there? Romeo,
arise;
Thou wilt be taken.—Stay awhile!—Stand up;   [*Knock.*]
Run to my study.—By-and-by!—God's will,
What simpleness is this!—I come, I come!   [*Knock.*]
Who knocks so hard? Whence come you? What's your
will?

NURSE. [*within*] Let me come in, and you shall know
my errand.
I come from Lady Juliet.

FRIAR.   Welcome then.

Enter NURSE.

NURSE. O holy friar, O, tell me, holy friar,
Where is my lady's lord, where's Romeo?
    FRIAR. There on the ground, with his own tears made
    drunk.
    NURSE. O, he is even in my mistress' case,
Just in her case!
    FRIAR.   O woeful sympathy!
Piteous predicament!
    NURSE.   Even so lies she,
Blubb'ring and weeping, weeping and blubbering.
Stand up, stand up! Stand, an you be a man.
For Juliet's sake, for her sake, rise and stand!
Why should you fall into so deep an O?
    ROM. [*rises*] Nurse—
    NURSE. Ah sir! ah sir! Well, death's the end of all.
    ROM. Spakest thou of Juliet? How is it with her?
Doth not she think me an old murtherer,
Now I have stain'd the childhood of our joy
With blood remov'd but little from her own?
Where is she? and how doth she? and what says
My conceal'd lady to our cancell'd love?
    NURSE. O, she says nothing, sir, but weeps and weeps;
And now falls on her bed, and then starts up,
And Tybalt calls; and then on Romeo cries,
And then down falls again.
    ROM.   As if that name,
Shot from the deadly level of a gun,
Did murther her; as that name's cursed hand
Murder'd her kinsman. O, tell me, friar, tell me,
In what vile part of this anatomy
Doth my name lodge? Tell me, that I may sack
The hateful mansion.   *Draws his dagger.*

FRIAR.   Hold thy desperate hand.
Art thou a man? Thy form cries out thou art;
Thy tears are womanish, thy wild acts denote
The unreasonable fury of a beast.
Unseemly woman in a seeming man!
Or ill-beseeming beast in seeming both!
Thou hast amaz'd me. By my holy order,
I thought thy disposition better temper'd.
Hast thou slain Tybalt? Wilt thou slay thyself?
And slay thy lady that in thy life lives,
By doing damned hate upon thyself?
Why railest thou on thy birth, the heaven, and earth?
Since birth and heaven and earth, all three do meet
In thee at once; which thou at once wouldst lose.
Fie fie, thou shamest thy shape, thy love, thy wit,
Which, like a usurer, abound'st in all,
And usest none in that true use indeed
Which should bedeck thy shape, thy love, thy wit.
Thy noble shape is but a form of wax,
Digressing from the valour of a man;
Thy dear love sworn but hollow perjury,
Killing that love which thou hast vow'd to cherish;
Thy wit, that ornament to shape and love,
Misshapen in the conduct of them both,
Like powder in a skilless soldier's flask,
Is set afire by thine own ignorance,
And thou dismemb'red with thine own defence.
What, rouse thee, man! Thy Juliet is alive,
For whose dear sake thou wast but lately dead.
There art thou happy. Tybalt would kill thee,
But thou slewest Tybalt. There art thou happy too.
The law, that threat'ned death, becomes thy friend
And turns it to exile. There art thou happy.
A pack of blessings light upon thy back;
Happiness courts thee in her best array;

But, like a misbehav'd and sullen wench,
Thou pout'st upon thy fortune and thy love.
Take heed, take heed, for such die miserable.
Go get thee to thy love, as was decreed,
Ascend her chamber, hence and comfort her.
But look thou stay not till the watch be set,
For then thou canst not pass to Mantua,
Where thou shalt live till we can find a time
To blaze your marriage, reconcile your friends,
Beg pardon of the Prince, and call thee back
With twenty hundred thousand times more joy
Than thou went'st forth in lamentation.
Go before, nurse. Commend me to thy lady,
And bid her hasten all the house to bed,
Which heavy sorrow makes them apt unto.
Romeo is coming.

    NURSE. O Lord, I could have stay'd here all the night
To hear good counsel. O, what learning is!
My lord, I'll tell my lady you will come.

    ROM. Do so, and bid my sweet prepare to chide.

    NURSE. Here is a ring she bid me give you, sir.
Hie you, make haste, for it grows very late.

    ROM. How well my comfort is reviv'd by this!

Exit.

    FRIAR. Go hence; good night; and here stands all your
        state:
Either be gone before the watch be set,
Or by the break of day disguis'd from hence.
Sojourn in Mantua. I'll find out your man,
And he shall signify from time to time
Every good hap to you that chances here.
Give me thy hand. 'Tis late. Farewell; good night.

    ROM. But that a joy past joy calls out on me,
It were a grief so brief to part with thee.
Farewell.

Exeunt.

Scene IV: Capulet's house.

Enter OLD CAPULET, *his* WIFE, *and* PARIS.

CAP. Things have fall'n out, sir, so unluckily
That we have had no time to move our daughter.
Look you, she lov'd her kinsman Tybalt dearly,
And so did I. Well, we were born to die.
'Tis very late; she'll not come down to-night.
I promise you, but for your company,
I would have been abed an hour ago.

PAR. These times of woe afford no time to woo.
Madam, good night. Commend me to your daughter.

LADY. I will, and know her mind early to-morrow;
To-night she's mew'd up to her heaviness.

CAP. Sir Paris, I will make a desperate tender
Of my child's love. I think she will be rul'd
In all respects by me; nay more, I doubt it not.
Wife, go you to her ere you go to bed;
Acquaint her here of my son Paris' love
And bid her (mark you me?) on Wednesday next—
But, soft! what day is this?

PAR.   Monday, my lord.

CAP. Monday! ha, ha! Well, Wednesday is too soon.
A Thursday let it be—a Thursday, tell her,
She shall be married to this noble earl.
Will you be ready? Do you like this haste?
We'll keep no great ado—a friend or two;
For hark you, Tybalt being slain so late,
It may be thought we held him carelessly,
Being our kinsman, if we revel much.
Therefore we'll have some half a dozen friends,
And there an end. But what say you to Thursday?

PAR. My lord, I would that Thursday were to-morrow.

Cap. Well, get you gone. A Thursday be it then.
Go you to Juliet ere you go to bed;
Prepare her, wife, against this wedding day.
Farewell, my lord.—Light to my chamber, ho!
Afore me, it is so very very late
That we may call it early by-and-by.
Good night.   *Exeunt.*

Scene V: Capulet's orchard.

Enter Romeo *and* Juliet *aloft, at the window.*

Jul. Wilt thou be gone? It is not yet near day.
It was the nightingale, and not the lark,
That pierc'd the fearful hollow of thine ear.
Nightly she sings on yond pomegranate tree.
Believe me, love, it was the nightingale.

Rom. It was the lark, the herald of the morn;
No nightingale. Look, love, what envious streaks
Do lace the severing clouds in yonder East.
Night's candles are burnt out, and jocund day
Stands tiptoe on the misty mountain tops.
I must be gone and live, or stay and die.

Jul. Yond light is not daylight; I know it, I.
It is some meteor that the sun exhales
To be to thee this night a torchbearer
And light thee on thy way to Mantua.
Therefore stay yet; thou need'st not to be gone.

Rom. Let me be ta'en, let me be put to death.
I am content, so thou wilt have it so.
I'll say yon grey is not the morning's eye,
'Tis but the pale reflex of Cynthia's brow;
Nor that is not the lark whose notes do beat
The vaulty heaven so high above our heads.

I have more care to stay than will to go.
Come, death, and welcome! Juliet wills it so.
How is't, my soul? Let's talk; it is not day.

JUL. It is, it is! Hie hence, be gone, away!
It is the lark that sings so out of tune,
Straining harsh discords and unpleasing sharps.
Some say the lark makes sweet division;
This doth not so, for she divideth us.
Some say the lark and loathed toad chang'd eyes;
O, now I would they had chang'd voices too,
Since arm from arm that voice doth us affray,
Hunting thee hence with hunt's-up to the day!
O, now be gone! More light and light it grows.

ROM. More light and light—more dark and dark our
    woes!

Enter NURSE.

NURSE. Madam!
JUL. Nurse?
NURSE. Your lady mother is coming to your chamber.
The day is broke; be wary, look about.   *Exit.*

JUL. Then, window, let day in, and let life out.
ROM. Farewell, farewell! One kiss, and I'll descend.
                              He goeth down.

JUL. Art thou gone so, my lord, my love, my friend?
I must hear from thee every day in the hour,
For in a minute there are many days.
O, by this count I shall be much in years
Ere I again behold my Romeo!

ROM. Farewell!
I will omit no opportunity
That may convey my greetings, love, to thee.

JUL. O, think'st thou we shall ever meet again?

ROM. I doubt it not; and all these woes shall serve
For sweet discourses in our time to come.

Jul. O God, I have an ill-divining soul!
Methinks I see thee, now thou art below,
As one dead in the bottom of a tomb.
Either my eyesight fails, or thou look'st pale.

Rom. And trust me, love, in my eye so do you.
Dry sorrow drinks our blood. Adieu, adieu!   *Exit.*

Jul. O Fortune, Fortune! all men call thee fickle.
If thou art fickle, what dost thou with him
That is renown'd for faith? Be fickle, Fortune,
For then I hope thou wilt not keep him long
But send him back.

Lady. [*within*] Ho, daughter! are you up?

Jul. Who is't that calls? It is my lady mother.
Is she not down so late, or up so early?
What unaccustom'd cause procures her hither?

Enter MOTHER.

Lady. Why, how now, Juliet?

Jul.   Madam, I am not well

Lady. Evermore weeping for your cousin's death?
What, wilt thou wash him from his grave with tears?
An if thou couldst, thou couldst not make him live.
Therefore have done. Some grief shows much of love;
But much of grief shows still some want of wit.

Jul. Yet let me weep for such a feeling loss.

Lady. So shall you feel the loss, but not the friend
Which you weep for.

Jul.   Feeling so the loss,
I cannot choose but ever weep the friend.

Lady. Well, girl, thou weep'st not so much for his
      death
As that the villain lives which slaughter'd him.

Jul. What villain, madam?

Lady.   That same villain Romeo.

Jul. [*aside*] Villain and he be many miles asunder.—

God pardon him! I do, with all my heart;
And yet no man like he doth grieve my heart.

LADY. That is because the traitor murderer lives.

JUL. Ay, madam, from the reach of these my hands.
Would none but I might venge my cousin's death!

LADY. We will have vengeance for it, fear thou not.
Then weep no more. I'll send to one in Mantua,
Where that same banish'd runagate doth live,
Shall give him such an unaccustom'd dram
That he shall soon keep Tybalt company;
And then I hope thou wilt be satisfied.

JUL. Indeed I never shall be satisfied
With Romeo till I behold him—dead—
Is my poor heart so for a kinsman vex'd.
Madam, if you could find out but a man
To bear a poison, I would temper it;
That Romeo should, upon receipt thereof,
Soon sleep in quiet. O, how my heart abhors
To hear him nam'd and cannot come to him,
To wreak the love I bore my cousin Tybalt
Upon his body that hath slaughter'd him!

LADY. Find thou the means, and I'll find such a man.
But now I'll tell thee joyful tidings, girl.

JUL. And joy comes well in such a needy time.
What are they, I beseech your ladyship?

LADY. Well, well, thou hast a careful father, child;
One who, to put thee from thy heaviness,
Hath sorted out a sudden day of joy
That thou expect'st not nor I look'd not for.

JUL. Madam, in happy time! What day is that?

LADY. Marry, my child, early next Thursday morn
The gallant, young, and noble gentleman,
The County Paris, at Saint Peter's Church,
Shall happily make thee there a joyful bride.

JUL. Now by Saint Peter's Church, and Peter too,

He shall not make me there a joyful bride!
I wonder at this haste, that I must wed
Ere he that should be husband comes to woo.
I pray you tell my lord and father, madam,
I will not marry yet; and when I do, I swear
It shall be Romeo, whom you know I hate,
Rather than Paris. These are news indeed!

    LADY. Here comes your father. Tell him so yourself,
And see how he will take it at your hands.

Enter CAPULET *and* NURSE.

    CAP. When the sun sets the air doth drizzle dew,
But for the sunset of my brother's son
It rains downright.
How now? a conduit, girl? What, still in tears?
Evermore show'ring? In one little body
Thou counterfeit'st a bark, a sea, a wind:
For still thy eyes, which I may call the sea,
Do ebb and flow with tears; the bark thy body is,
Sailing in this salt flood; the winds, thy sighs,
Who, raging with thy tears and they with them,
Without a sudden calm will overset
Thy tempest-tossed body. How now, wife?
Have you delivered to her our decree?

    LADY. Ay, sir; but she will none, she gives you thanks.
I would the fool were married to her grave!

    CAP. Soft! take me with you, take me with you, wife.
How? Will she none? Doth she not give us thanks?
Is she not proud? Doth she not count her blest,
Unworthy as she is, that we have wrought
So worthy a gentleman to be her bridegroom?

    JUL. Not proud you have, but thankful that you have.
Proud can I never be of what I hate,
But thankful even for hate that is meant love.

    CAP. How, how, how, how, choplogic? What is this?

'Proud'—and 'I thank you'—and 'I thank you not'—
And yet 'not proud'? Mistress minion you,
Thank me no thankings, nor proud me no prouds,
But fettle your fine joints 'gainst Thursday next
To go with Paris to Saint Peter's Church,
Or I will drag thee on a hurdle thither.
Out, you green-sickness carrion! out, you baggage!
You tallow-face!

LADY.   Fie, fie! what, are you mad?

JUL. Good father, I beseech you on my knees,
Hear me with patience but to speak a word.

CAP. Hang thee, young baggage! disobedient wretch!
I tell thee what—get thee to church a Thursday
Or never after look me in the face.
Speak not, reply not, do not answer me!
My fingers itch. Wife, we scarce thought us blest
That God had lent us but this only child;
But now I see this one is one too much,
And that we have a curse in having her.
Out on her, hilding!

NURSE.   God in heaven bless her!
You are to blame, my lord, to rate her so.

CAP. And why, my Lady Wisdom? Hold your tongue,
Good Prudence. Smatter with your gossips, go!

NURSE. I speak no treason.

CAP.   O, God-i-god-en!

NURSE. May not one speak?

CAP.   Peace, you mumbling fool!
Utter your gravity o'er a gossip's bowl,
For here we need it not.

LADY.   You are too hot.

CAP. God's bread! it makes me mad. Day, night, late,
    early,
At home, abroad, alone, in company,

Waking or sleeping, still my care hath been
To have her match'd; and having now provided
A gentleman of princely parentage,
Of fair demesnes, youthful, and nobly train'd,
Stuff'd as they say, with honourable parts,
Proportion'd as one's thought would wish a man—
And then to have a wretched puling fool,
A whining mammet, in her fortune's tender,
To answer 'I'll not wed, I cannot love;
I am too young, I pray you pardon me'!
But, an you will not wed, I'll pardon you.
Graze where you will, you shall not house with me.
Look to't, think on't; I do not use to jest.
Thursday is near; lay hand on heart, advise:
An you be mine, I'll give you to my friend;
An you be not, hang, beg, starve, die in the streets,
For, by my soul, I'll ne'er acknowledge thee,
Nor what is mine shall never do thee good.
Trust to't. Bethink you. I'll not be forsworn. *Exit.*

Jul. Is there no pity sitting in the clouds
That sees into the bottom of my grief?
O sweet my mother, cast me not away!
Delay this marriage for a month, a week;
Or if you do not, make the bridal bed
In that dim monument where Tybalt lies.

Lady. Talk not to me, for I'll not speak a word.
Do as thou wilt, for I have done with thee. *Exit.*

Jul. O God!—O nurse, how shall this be prevented?
My husband is on earth, my faith in heaven.
How shall that faith return again to earth
Unless that husband send it me from heaven
By leaving earth? Comfort me, counsel me.
Alack, alack, that heaven should practise stratagems
Upon so soft a subject as myself!

What say'st thou? Hast thou not a word of joy?
Some comfort, nurse.

    NURSE.   Faith, here it is.
Romeo is banish'd; and all the world to nothing
That he dares ne'er come back to challenge you;
Or if he do, it needs must be by stealth.
Then, since the case so stands as now it doth,
I think it best you married with the County.
O, he's a lovely gentleman!
Romeo's a dishclout to him. An eagle, madam,
Hath not so green, so quick, so fair an eye
As Paris hath. Beshrew my very heart,
I think you are happy in this second match,
For it excels your first; or if it did not,
Your first is dead—or 'twere as good he were
As living here and you no use of him.

    JUL. Speak'st thou this from thy heart?

    NURSE. And from my soul too; else beshrew them
      both.

    JUL. Amen!

    NURSE. What?

    JUL. Well, thou hast comforted me marvellous much.
Go in; and tell my lady I am gone,
Having displeas'd my father, to Laurence' cell,
To make confession and to be absolv'd.

    NURSE. Marry, I will; and this is wisely done.   *Exit.*

    JUL. Ancient damnation! O most wicked fiend!
Is it more sin to wish me thus forsworn,
Or to dispraise my lord with that same tongue
Which she hath prais'd him with above compare
So many thousand times? Go, counsellor!
Thou and my bosom henceforth shall be twain.
I'll to the friar to know his remedy.
If all else fail, myself have power to die.   *Exit.*

Act IV: Scene I: Friar Laurence's cell.

Enter FRIAR LAURENCE *and* COUNTY PARIS.

FRIAR. On Thursday, sir? The time is very short.
PAR. My father Capulet will have it so,
And I am nothing slow to slack his haste.
FRIAR. You say you do not know the lady's mind.
Uneven is the course; I like it not.
PAR. Immoderately she weeps for Tybalt's death,
And therefore have I little talk'd of love;
For Venus smiles not in a house of tears.
Now, sir, her father counts it dangerous
That she do give her sorrow so much sway,
And in his wisdom hastes our marriage
To stop the inundation of her tears,
Which, too much minded by herself alone,
May be put from her by society.
Now do you know the reason of this haste.
FRIAR. [*aside*] I would I knew not why it should be
    slow'd.—
Look, sir, here comes the lady toward my cell.

Enter JULIET.

PAR. Happily met, my lady and my wife!
JUL. That may be, sir, when I may be a wife.
PAR. That may be must be, love, on Thursday next.
JUL. What must be shall be.
FRIAR.   That's a certain text.
PAR. Come you to make confession to this father?
JUL. To answer that, I should confess to you.
PAR. Do not deny to him that you love me.
JUL. I will confess to you that I love him.

PAR. So will ye, I am sure, that you love me.

JUL. If I do so, it will be of more price,
Being spoke behind your back, than to your face.

PAR. Poor soul, thy face is much abus'd with tears.

JUL. The tears have got small victory by that,
For it was bad enough before their spite.

PAR. Thou wrong'st it more than tears with that report.

JUL. That is no slander, sir, which is a truth;
And what I spake, I spake it to my face.

PAR. Thy face is mine, and thou hast sland'red it.

JUL. It may be so, for it is not mine own.
Are you at leisure, holy father, now,
Or shall I come to you at evening mass?

FRIAR. My leisure serves me, pensive daughter, now.
My lord, we must entreat the time alone.

PAR. God shield I should disturb devotion!
Juliet, on Thursday early will I rouse ye;
Till then, adieu, and keep this holy kiss.   *Exit.*

JUL. O, shut the door! and when thou hast done so,
Come weep with me—past hope, past cure, past help!

FRIAR. Ah, Juliet, I already know thy grief;
It strains me past the compass of my wits.
I hear thou must, and nothing may prorogue it,
On Thursday next be married to this County.

JUL. Tell me not, friar, that thou hear'st of this,
Unless thou tell me how I may prevent it.
If in thy wisdom thou canst give no help,
Do thou but call my resolution wise
And with this knife I'll help it presently.
God join'd my heart and Romeo's, thou our hands;
And ere this hand, by thee to Romeo's seal'd,
Shall be the label to another deed,
Or my true heart with treacherous revolt
Turn to another, this shall slay them both.

Therefore, out of thy long-experienc'd time,
Give me some present counsel; or, behold,
'Twixt my extremes and me this bloody knife
Shall play the umpire, arbitrating that
Which the commission of thy years and art
Could to no issue of true honour bring.
Be not so long to speak. I long to die
If what thou speak'st speak not of remedy.

    FRIAR. Hold, daughter. I do spy a kind of hope,
Which craves as desperate an execution
As that is desperate which we would prevent.
If, rather than to marry County Paris,
Thou hast the strength of will to slay thyself,
Then is it likely thou wilt undertake
A thing like death to chide away this shame,
That cop'st with death himself to scape from it;
And, if thou dar'st, I'll give thee remedy.

    JUL. O, bid me leap, rather than marry Paris,
From off the battlements of yonder tower,
Or walk in thievish ways, or bid me lurk
Where serpents are; chain me with roaring bears,
Or shut me nightly in a charnel house,
O'ercover'd quite with dead men's rattling bones,
With reeky shanks and yellow chapless skulls;
Or bid me go into a new-made grave
And hide me with a dead man in his shroud—
Things that, to hear them told, have made me tremble—
And I will do it without fear or doubt,
To live an unstain'd wife to my sweet love.

    FRIAR. Hold, then. Go home, be merry, give consent
To marry Paris. Wednesday is to-morrow.
To-morrow night look that thou lie alone;
Let not the nurse lie with thee in thy chamber.
Take thou this vial, being then in bed,

And this distilled liquor drink thou off;
When presently through all thy veins shall run
A cold and drowsy humour; for no pulse
Shall keep his native progress, but surcease;
No warmth, no breath, shall testify thou livest;
The roses in thy lips and cheeks shall fade
To paly ashes, thy eyes' windows fall
Like death when he shuts up the day of life;
Each part, depriv'd of supple government,
Shall, stiff and stark and cold, appear like death;
And in this borrowed likeness of shrunk death
Thou shalt continue two-and-forty hours,
And then awake as from a pleasant sleep.
Now, when the bridegroom in the morning comes
To rouse thee from thy bed, there art thou dead.
Then, as the manner of our country is,
In thy best robes uncovered on the bier
Thou shalt be borne to that same ancient vault
Where all the kindred of the Capulets lie.
In the mean time, against thou shalt awake,
Shall Romeo by my letters know our drift;
And hither shall he come; and he and I
Will watch thy waking, and that very night
Shall Romeo bear thee hence to Mantua.
And this shall free thee from this present shame,
If no inconstant toy nor womanish fear
Abate thy valour in the acting it.

JUL. Give me, give me! O, tell not me of fear!

FRIAR. Hold! Get you gone, be strong and prosperous
In this resolve. I'll send a friar with speed
To Mantua, with my letters to thy lord.

JUL. Love give me strength! and strength shall help
afford.
Farewell, dear father. *Exeunt.*

Scene II: Capulet's house.

Enter FATHER CAPULET, MOTHER, NURSE, *and*
SERVINGMEN, *two or three.*

CAP. So many guests invite as here are writ.

[Exit a SERVINGMAN.]

Sirrah, go hire me twenty cunning cooks.

SERV. You shall have none ill, sir; for I'll try if they
can lick their fingers.

CAP. How canst thou try them so?

SERV. Marry, sir, 'tis an ill cook that cannot lick his
own fingers. Therefore he that cannot lick his fingers
goes not with me.

CAP. Go, be gone.   [*Exit* SERVINGMAN.]

We shall be much unfurnish'd for this time.

What, is my daughter gone to Friar Laurence?

NURSE. Ay, forsooth.

CAP. Well, he may chance to do some good on her.

A peevish self-will'd harlotry it is.

Enter JULIET.

NURSE. See where she comes from shrift with merry
    look.

CAP. How now, my headstrong? Where have you been
    gadding?

JUL. Where I have learnt me to repent the sin

Of disobedient opposition

To you and your behests, and am enjoin'd

By holy Laurence to fall prostrate here

To beg your pardon. Pardon, I beseech you!

Henceforward I am ever rul'd by you.

CAP. Send for the County. Go tell him of this.

I'll have this knot knit up to-morrow morning.

JUL. I met the youthful lord at Laurence' cell
And gave him what becomed love I might,
Not stepping o'er the bounds of modesty.

CAP. Why, I am glad on't. This is well. Stand up.
This is as't should be. Let me see the County.
Ay, marry, go, I say, and fetch him hither.
Now, afore God, this reverend holy friar,
All our whole city is much bound to him.

JUL. Nurse, will you go with me into my closet
To help me sort such needful ornaments
As you think fit to furnish me to-morrow?

MOTHER. No, not till Thursday. There is time enough.

CAP. Go, nurse, go with her. We'll to church to-
   morrow.   *Exeunt* JULIET *and* NURSE.

MOTHER. We shall be short in our provision.
'Tis now near night.

CAP.   Tush, I will stir about,
And all things shall be well, I warrant thee, wife.
Go thou to Juliet, help to deck up her.
I'll not to bed to-night; let me alone.
I'll play the housewife for this once. What, ho!
They are all forth; well, I will walk myself
To County Paris, to prepare him up
Against to-morrow. My heart is wondrous light,
Since this same wayward girl is so reclaim'd.   *Exeunt.*

Scene III: Juliet's chamber.

Enter JULIET *and* NURSE.

JUL. Ay, those attires are best; but, gentle nurse,
I pray thee leave me to myself to-night;
For I have need of many orisons
To move the heavens to smile upon my state,
Which, well thou knowest, is cross and full of sin.

Enter MOTHER.

MOTHER. What, are you busy, ho? Need you my help?

JUL. No, madam; we have cull'd such necessaries
As are behooffull for our state to-morrow.
So please you, let me now be left alone,
And let the nurse this night sit up with you;
For I am sure you have your hands full all
In this so sudden business.

MOTHER.   Good night.
Get thee to bed, and rest; for thou hast need.

                    Exeunt MOTHER *and* NURSE.

JUL. Farewell! God knows when we shall meet again.
I have a faint cold fear thrills through my veins
That almost freezes up the heat of life.
I'll call them back again to comfort me.
Nurse!—What should she do here?
My dismal scene I needs must act alone.
Come, vial.
What if this mixture do not work at all?
Shall I be married then to-morrow morning?
No, no! This shall forbid it. Lie thou there.

                    [*Lays down a dagger.*]

What if it be a poison which the friar
Subtilly hath minist'red to have me dead,
Lest in this marriage he should be dishonour'd
Because he married me before to Romeo?
I fear it is; and yet methinks it should not,
For he hath still been tried a holy man.
I will not entertain so bad a thought.
How if, when I am laid into the tomb,
I wake before the time that Romeo
Come to redeem me? There's a fearful point!
Shall I not then be stifled in the vault,
To whose foul mouth no healthsome air breathes in,
And there die strangled ere my Romeo comes?

Or, if I live, is it not very like
The horrible conceit of death and night,
Together with the terror of the place—
As in a vault, an ancient receptacle
Where for this many hundred years the bones
Of all my buried ancestors are pack'd;
Where bloody Tybalt, yet but green in earth,
Lies fest'ring in his shroud; where, as they say,
At some hours in the night spirits resort—
Alack, alack, is it not like that I,
So early waking—what with loathsome smells,
And shrieks like mandrakes torn out of the earth,
That living mortals, hearing them, run mad—
O, if I wake, shall I not be distraught,
Environed with all these hideous fears,
And madly play with my forefathers' joints,
And pluck the mangled Tybalt from his shroud,
And, in this rage, with some great kinsman's bone
As with a club dash out my desp'rate brains?
O, look! methinks I see my cousin's ghost
Seeking out Romeo, that did spit his body
Upon a rapier's point. Stay, Tybalt, stay!
Romeo, I come! this do I drink to thee.
She drinks and falls upon her bed within the curtains.

Scene IV: Capulet's house.

Enter LADY OF THE HOUSE *and* NURSE.

LADY. Hold, take these keys and fetch more spices,
nurse.

NURSE. They call for dates and quinces in the pastry.

Enter OLD CAPULET.

CAP. Come, stir, stir, stir! The second cock hath
crow'd,

The curfew bell hath rung, 'tis three o'clock.
Look to the bak'd meats, good Angelica;
Spare not for cost.

    NURSE.   Go, you cot-quean, go,
Get you to bed! Faith, you'll be sick to-morrow
For this night's watching.

    CAP. No, not a whit. What, I have watch'd ere now
All night for lesser cause, and ne'er been sick.

    LADY. Ay, you have been a mouse-hunt in your time;
But I will watch you from such watching now.

                      Exeunt LADY *and* NURSE.

    CAP. A jealous hood, a jealous hood!

[*Enter three or four* FELLOWS, *with spits and logs and baskets.*]

                          Now, fellow,
What is there?

    FELLOW. Things for the cook, sir; but I know not
    what.

    CAP. Make haste, make haste. [*Exit* FELLOW.] Sirrah,
    fetch drier logs.
Call Peter; he will show thee where they are.

    FELLOW. I have a head, sir, that will find out logs
And never trouble Peter for the matter.

    CAP. Mass, and well said; a merry whoreson, ha!
Thou shalt be loggerhead. [*Exit* FELLOW.] Good faith,
    'tis day.
The County will be here with music straight,
For so he said he would.   [*Play music.*]
                 I hear him near.
Nurse! Wife! What, ho! What, nurse, I say!

[*Enter* NURSE.]

Go waken Juliet; go and trim her up.
I'll go and chat with Paris. Hie, make haste,

Make haste! The Bridegroom he is come already:
Make haste, I say.   *Exeunt.*

Scene V: Juliet's chamber.

Enter NURSE.

NURSE. Mistress! what, mistress! Juliet! Fast, I war-
    rant her, she.
Why, lamb! why, lady! Fie, you slug-abed!
Why, love, I say! madam! sweetheart! Why, bride!
What, not a word? You take your pennyworths now!
Sleep for a week; for the next night, I warrant,
The County Paris hath set up his rest
That you shall rest but little. God forgive me!
Marry, and amen. How sound is she asleep!
I needs must wake her. Madam, madam, madam!
Ay, let the County take you in your bed!
He'll fright you up, i' faith. Will it not be?
                              [*Draws aside the curtains.*]
What, dress'd, and in your clothes, and down again?
I must needs wake you. Lady! lady! lady!
Alas, alas! Help, help! my lady's dead!
O weraday that ever I was born!
Some aqua-vitæ, ho! My lord! my lady!

Enter MOTHER.

MOTHER. What noise is here?
NURSE.   O lamentable day!
MOTHER. What is the matter?
NURSE.   Look, look! O heavy day!
MOTHER. O me, O me! My child, my only life!
Revive, look up, or I will die with thee!
Help, help! Call help.

Enter FATHER.

FATHER. For shame, bring Juliet forth; her lord is come.

NURSE. She's dead, deceas'd; she's dead! Alack the day!

MOTHER. Alack the day, she's dead, she's dead, she's dead!

CAP. Ha! let me see her. Out alas! she's cold,
Her blood is settled, and her joints are stiff;
Life and these lips have long been separated.
Death lies on her like an untimely frost
Upon the sweetest flower of all the field.

NURSE. O lamentable day!

MOTHER.   O woeful time!

CAP. Death, that hath ta'en her hence to make me wail,
Ties up my tongue and will not let me speak.

Enter FRIAR LAURENCE *and the* COUNTY PARIS,
with MUSICIANS.

FRIAR. Come, is the bride ready to go to church?

CAP. Ready to go, but never to return.
O son, the night before thy wedding day
Hath Death lain with thy wife. See, there she lies,
Flower as she was, deflowered by him.
Death is my son-in-law, Death is my heir;
My daughter he hath wedded. I will die
And leave him all. Life, living, all is Death's.

PAR. Have I thought long to see this morning's face,
And doth it give me such a sight as this?

MOTHER. Accurs'd, unhappy, wretched, hateful day!
Most miserable hour that e'er time saw
In lasting labour of his pilgrimage!
But one, poor one, one poor and loving child,

But one thing to rejoice and solace in,
And cruel Death hath catch'd it from my sight!

   NURSE. O woe! O woeful, woeful, woeful day!
Most lamentable day, most woeful day
That ever ever I did yet behold!
O day! O day! O day! O hateful day!
Never was seen so black a day as this.
O woeful day! O woeful day!

   PAR. Beguil'd, divorced, wronged, spited, slain!
Most detestable Death, by thee beguil'd,
By cruel cruel thee quite overthrown!
O love! O life! not life, but love in death!

   CAP. Despis'd, distressed, hated, martyr'd, kill'd!
Uncomfortable time, why cam'st thou now
To murther, murther our solemnity?
O child! O child! my soul, and not my child!
Dead art thou, dead! alack, my child is dead,
And with my child my joys are buried!

   FRIAR. Peace, ho, for shame! Confusion's cure lives
      not
In these confusions. Heaven and yourself
Had part in this fair maid; now heaven hath all,
And all the better is it for the maid.
Your part in her you could not keep from death,
But heaven keeps his part in eternal life.
The most you sought was her promotion,
For 'twas your heaven she should be advanc'd;
And weep ye now, seeing she is advanc'd
Above the clouds, as high as heaven itself?
O, in this love, you love your child so ill
That you run mad, seeing that she is well.
She's not well married that lives married long,
But she's best married that dies married young.
Dry up your tears and stick your rosemary
On this fair corse, and, as the custom is,

In all her best array bear her to church;
For though fond nature bids us all lament,
Yet nature's tears are reason's merriment.

CAP. All things that we ordained festival
Turn from their office to black funeral—
Our instruments to melancholy bells,
Our wedding cheer to a sad burial feast;
Our solemn hymns to sullen dirges change;
Our bridal flowers serve for a buried corse;
And all things change them to the contrary.

FRIAR. Sir, go you in; and, madam, go with him;
And go, Sir Paris. Every one prepare
To follow this fair corse unto her grave.
The heavens do low'r upon you for some ill;
Move them no more by crossing their high will.

       Exeunt, excepting MUSICIANS *and* NURSE.

1. MUS. Faith, we may put up our pipes and be gone.

NURSE. Honest good fellows, ah, put up, put up!
For well you know this is a pitiful case.   *Exit.*

1. MUS. Ay, by my troth, the case may be amended.

Enter PETER.

PET. Musicians, O, musicians, 'Heart's ease,' 'Heart's ease!' O, an you will have me live, play 'Heart's ease.'

1 MUS. Why 'Heart's ease'?

PET. O, musicians, because my heart itself plays 'My heart is full of woe.' O, play me some merry dump to comfort me.

1. MUS. Not a dump we! 'Tis no time to play now.

PET. You will not then?

1. MUS. No.

PET. I will then give it you soundly.

1. MUS. What will you give us?

PET. No money, on my faith, but the gleek. I will give you the minstrel.

1. Mus. Then will I give you the serving-creature.

Pet. Then will I lay the serving-creature's dagger on your pate. I will carry no crotchets. I'll re you, I'll fa you. Do you note me?

1. Mus. An you re us and fa us, you note us.

2. Mus. Pray you put up your dagger, and put out your wit.

Pet. Then have at you with my wit! I will dry-beat you with an iron wit, and put up my iron dagger. Answer me like men.

> 'When griping grief the heart doth wound,
>   And doleful dumps the mind oppress,
> Then music with her silver sound'—

Why 'silver sound'? Why 'music with her silver sound'? What say you, Simon Catling?

1. Mus. Marry, sir, because silver hath a sweet sound.

Pet. Pretty! What say you, Hugh Rebeck?

2. Mus. I say, 'silver sound' because musicians sound for silver.

Pet. Pretty too! What say you, James Soundpost?

3. Mus. Faith, I know not what to say.

Pet. O, I cry you mercy! you are the singer. I will say for you. It is 'music with her silver sound' because musicians have no gold for sounding.

> 'Then music with her silver sound
>   With speedy help doth lend redress.'   *Exit.*

1. Mus. What a pestilent knave is this same!

2. Mus. Hang him, Jack! Come, we'll in here, tarry for the mourners, and stay dinner.   *Exeunt.*

Act V: Scene I: Mantua. A street.

Enter Romeo.

Rom. If I may trust the flattering truth of sleep,
My dreams presage some joyful news at hand.

My bosom's lord sits lightly in his throne,
And all this day an unaccustom'd spirit
Lifts me above the ground with cheerful thoughts.
I dreamt my lady came and found me dead
(Strange dream that gives a dead man leave to think!)
And breath'd such life with kisses in my lips
That I reviv'd and was an emperor.
Ah me! how sweet is love itself possess'd,
When but love's shadows are so rich in joy!

[*Enter* ROMEO's *man* BALTHASAR, *booted.*]

News from Verona! How now, Balthasar?
Dost thou not bring me letters from the friar?
How doth my lady? Is my father well?
How fares my Juliet? That I ask again,
For nothing can be ill if she be well.

MAN. Then she is well, and nothing can be ill.
Her body sleeps in Capel's monument,
And her immortal part with angels lives.
I saw her laid low in her kindred's vault
And presently took post to tell it you.
O, pardon me for bringing these ill news,
Since you did leave it for my office, sir.

ROM. Is it e'en so? Then I defy you, stars!
Thou knowest my lodging. Get me ink and paper
And hire posthorses. I will hence to-night.

MAN. I do beseech you, sir, have patience.
Your looks are pale and wild and do import
Some misadventure.

ROM.　　　　　　Tush, thou art deceiv'd.
Leave me and do the thing I bid thee do.
Hast thou no letters to me from the friar?

MAN. No, my good lord.

ROM.　　　　　　　　　No matter. Get thee gone

And hire those horses. I'll be with thee straight.

[*Exit* BALTHASAR.]

Well, Juliet, I will lie with thee to-night.
Let's see for means. O mischief, thou art swift
To enter in the thoughts of desperate men!
I do remember an apothecary,
And hereabouts 'a dwells, which late I noted
In tatt'red weeds, with overwhelming brows,
Culling of simples. Meagre were his looks,
Sharp misery had worn him to the bones;
And in his needy shop a tortoise hung,
An alligator stuff'd, and other skins
Of ill-shap'd fishes; and about his shelves
A beggarly account of empty boxes,
Green earthen pots, bladders, and musty seeds,
Remnants of packthread, and old cakes of roses
Were thinly scattered, to make up a show.
Noting this penury, to myself I said,
'An if a man did need a poison now
Whose sale is present death in Mantua,
Here lives a caitiff wretch would sell it him.'
O, this same thought did but forerun my need,
And this same needy man must sell it me.
As I remember, this should be the house.
Being holiday, the beggar's shop is shut.
What, ho! apothecary!

Enter APOTHECARY.

APOTH.   Who calls so loud?
ROM. Come hither, man. I see that thou art poor.
Hold, there is forty ducats. Let me have
A dram of poison, such soon-speeding gear
As will disperse itself through all the veins
That the life-weary taker may fall dead,
And that the trunk may be discharg'd of breath

As violently as hasty powder fir'd
Doth hurry from the fatal cannon's womb.

APOTH. Such mortal drugs I have; but Mantua's law
Is death to any he that utters them.

ROM. Art thou so bare and full of wretchedness
And fearest to die? Famine is in thy cheeks,
Need and oppression starveth in thine eyes,
Contempt and beggary hangs upon thy back:
The world is not thy friend, nor the world's law;
The world affords no law to make thee rich;
Then be not poor, but break it and take this.

APOTH. My poverty but not my will consents.

ROM. I pay thy poverty and not thy will.

APOTH. Put this in any liquid thing you will
And drink it off, and if you had the strength
Of twenty men, it would dispatch you straight.

ROM. There is thy gold—worse poison to men's souls,
Doing more murther in this loathsome world,
Than these poor compounds that thou mayst
          not sell.
I sell thee poison; thou hast sold me none.
Farewell. Buy food and get thyself in flesh.
Come, cordial and not poison, go with me
To Juliet's grave; for there must I use thee.   *Exeunt.*

Scene II: Verona. Friar Laurence's cell.

Enter FRIAR JOHN *to* FRIAR LAURENCE.

JOHN. Holy Franciscan friar, brother, ho!

Enter FRIAR LAURENCE.

LAUR. This same should be the voice of Friar John.
Welcome from Mantua. What says Romeo?
Or, if his mind be writ, give me his letter.

JOHN. Going to find a barefoot brother out,
One of our order, to associate me
Here in this city visiting the sick,
And finding him, the searchers of the town,
Suspecting that we both were in a house
Where the infectious pestilence did reign,
Seal'd up the doors, and would not let us forth,
So that my speed to Mantua there was stay'd.

LAUR. Who bare my letter, then, to Romeo?

JOHN. I could not send it—here it is again—
Nor get a messenger to bring it thee,
So fearful were they of infection.

LAUR. Unhappy fortune! By my brotherhood,
The letter was not nice, but full of charge,
Of dear import; and the neglecting it
May do much danger. Friar John, go hence,
Get me an iron crow and bring it straight
Unto my cell.

JOHN.   Brother, I'll go and bring it thee.   *Exit.*

LAUR. Now must I to the monument alone.
Within this three hours will fair Juliet wake.
She will beshrew me much that Romeo
Hath had no notice of these accidents;
But I will write again to Mantua,
And keep her at my cell till Romeo come—
Poor living corse, clos'd in a dead man's tomb!   *Exit.*

Scene III: Verona. A churchyard; in it the monument of the Capulets.

Enter PARIS *and his* PAGE *with flowers and a torch.*

PAR. Give me thy torch, boy. Hence, and stand aloof.
Yet put it out, for I would not be seen.
Under yond yew tree lay thee all along,

Holding thine ear close to the hollow ground.
So shall no foot upon the churchyard tread
(Being loose, unfirm, with digging up of graves)
But thou shalt hear it. Whistle then to me,
As signal that thou hear'st something approach.
Give me those flowers. Do as I bid thee, go.

PAGE. [*aside*] I am almost afraid to stand alone
Here in the churchyard; yet I will adventure. *Retires.*

PAR. Sweet flower, with flowers thy bridal bed I strew
(O woe! thy canopy is dust and stones)
Which with sweet water nightly I will dew;
Or, wanting that, with tears distill'd by moans.
The obsequies that I for thee will keep
Nightly shall be to strew thy grave and weep
[BOY *whistles.*]
The boy gives warning something doth approach.
What cursed foot wanders this way to-night
To cross my obsequies and true love's rite?
What, with a torch? Muffle me, night, awhile. *Retires.*

Enter ROMEO, *and* BALTHASAR *with a torch, a mattock,
and a crow of iron.*

ROM. Give me that mattock and the wrenching iron.
Hold, take this letter. Early in the morning
See thou deliver it to my lord and father.
Give me the light. Upon thy life I charge thee,
Whate'er thou hearest or seest, stand all aloof
And do not interrupt me in my course.
Why I descend into this bed of death
Is partly to behold my lady's face,
But chiefly to take thence from her dead finger
A precious ring—a ring that I must use
In dear employment. Therefore hence, be gone.
But if thou, jealous, dost return to pry
In what I farther shall intend to do,

By heaven, I will tear thee joint by joint
And strew this hungry churchyard with thy limbs.
The time and my intents are savage-wild,
More fierce and more inexorable far
Than empty tigers or the roaring sea.

BAL. I will be gone, sir, and not trouble you.

ROM. So shalt thou show me friendship. Take thou that.
Live, and be prosperous; and farewell, good fellow.

BAL. [*aside*] For all this same, I'll hide me hereabout.
His looks I fear, and his intents I doubt.   *Retires.*

ROM. Thou detestable maw, thou womb of death,
Gorg'd with the dearest morsel of the earth,
Thus I enforce thy rotten jaws to open,
And in despite I'll cram thee with more food.

ROMEO *opens the tomb.*

PAR. This is that banish'd haughty Montague
That murd'red my love's cousin—with which grief
It is supposed the fair creature died—
And here is come to do some villanous shame
To the dead bodies. I will apprehend him.
Stop thy unhallowed toil, vile Montague!
Can vengeance be pursu'd further than death?
Condemned villain, I do apprehend thee.
Obey, and go with me; for thou must die.

ROM. I must indeed; and therefore came I hither.
Good gentle youth, tempt not a desp'rate man.
Fly hence and leave me. Think upon these gone;
Let them affright thee. I beseech thee, youth,
Put not another sin upon my head
By urging me to fury. O, be gone!
By heaven, I love thee better than myself,
For I come hither arm'd against myself.
Stay not, be gone. Live, and hereafter say
A madman's mercy bid thee run away.

PAR. I do defy thy conjuration
And apprehend thee for a felon here.

ROM. Wilt thou provoke me? Then have at thee, boy!
They fight.

PAGE. O Lord, they fight! I will go call the watch.
Exit. PARIS *falls.*

PAR. O, I am slain! If thou be merciful,
Open the tomb, lay me with Juliet.   *Dies.*

ROM. In faith, I will. Let me peruse this face.
Mercutio's kinsman, noble County Paris!
What said my man when my betossed soul
Did not attend him as we rode? I think
He told me Paris should have married Juliet.
Said he not so? or did I dream it so?
Or am I mad, hearing him talk of Juliet,
To think it was so? O, give me thy hand,
One writ with me in sour misfortune's book!
I'll bury thee in a triumphant grave.
A grave? O, no, a lanthorn, slaught'red youth,
For here lies Juliet, and her beauty makes
This vault a feasting presence full of light.
Death, lie thou there, by a dead man interr'd.
[Lays him in the tomb.]
How oft when men are at the point of death
Have they been merry! which their keepers call
A lightning before death. O, how may I
Call this a lightning? O my love! my wife!
Death, that hath suck'd the honey of thy breath,
Hath had no power yet upon thy beauty.
Thou art not conquer'd. Beauty's ensign yet
Is crimson in thy lips and in thy cheeks,
And death's pale flag is not advanced there.
Tybalt, liest thou there in thy bloody sheet?
O, what more favour can I do to thee
Than with that hand that cut thy youth in twain

To sunder his that was thine enemy?
Forgive me, cousin! Ah, dear Juliet,
Why art thou yet so fair? Shall I believe
That unsubstantial Death is amorous,
And that the lean abhorred monster keeps
Thee here in dark to be his paramour?
For fear of that I still will stay with thee
And never from this palace of dim night
Depart again. Here, here will I remain
With worms that are thy chambermaids. O, here
Will I set up my everlasting rest
And shake the yoke of inauspicious stars
From this world-wearied flesh. Eyes, look your last!
Arms, take your last embrace! and, lips, O you
The doors of breath, seal with a righteous kiss
A dateless bargain to engrossing death!
Come, bitter conduct; come, unsavoury guide!
Thou desperate pilot, now at once run on
The dashing rocks thy seasick weary bark!
Here's to my love! [*Drinks*.] O true apothecary!
Thy drugs are quick. Thus with a kiss I die.   *Falls*.

Enter FRIAR LAURENCE, *with lanthorn, crow, and spade.*

　　FRIAR. Saint Francis be my speed! how oft to-night
Have my old feet stumbled at graves! Who's there?
　　BAL. Here's one, a friend, and one that knows you
　　　well.
　　FRIAR. Bliss be upon you! Tell me, good my friend,
What torch is yond that vainly lends his light
To grubs and eyeless skulls? As I discern,
It burneth in the Capels' monument.
　　BAL. It doth so, holy sir; and there's my master.
One that you love.

FRIAR.   Who is it?

BAL.   Romeo.

FRAR. How long hath he been there?

BAL.   Full half an hour.

FRIAR. Go with me to the vault.

BAL.   I dare not, sir.
My master knows not but I am gone hence,
And fearfully did menace me with death
If I did stay to look on his intents.

FRIAR. Stay then; I'll go alone. Fear comes upon me.
O, much I fear some ill unthrifty thing.

BAL. As I did sleep under this yew tree here,
I dreamt my master and another fought,
And that my master slew him.

FRIAR.   Romeo!
Alack, alack, what blood is this which stains
The stony entrance of this sepulchre?
What mean these masterless and gory swords
To lie discolour'd by this place of peace?

                        [*Enters the tomb.*]

Romeo! O, pale! Who else? What, Paris too?
And steep'd in blood? Ah, what an unkind hour.
Is guilty of this lamentable chance!
The lady stirs.   JULIET *rises*

JUL. O comfortable friar! where is my lord?
I do remember well where I should be,
And there I am. Where is my Romeo?

FRIAR. I hear some noise. Lady, come from that nest
Of death, contagion, and unnatural sleep.
A greater power than we can contradict
Hath thwarted our intents. Come, come away.
Thy husband in thy bosom there lies dead;
And Paris too. Come, I'll dispose of thee
Among a sisterhood of holy nuns.

Stay not to question, for the watch is coming.
Come, go, good Juliet. I dare no longer stay.
    JUL. Go, get thee hence, for I will not away.

                                        [*Exit* FRIAR.]

What's here? A cup, clos'd in my true love's hand?
Poison, I see, hath been his timeless end.
O churl! drunk all, and left no friendly drop
To help me after? I will kiss thy lips.
Haply some poison yet doth hang on them
To make me die with a restorative.   [*Kisses him.*]
Thy lips are warm!
    CHIEF WATCH. [*within*] Lead, boy. Which way?
    JUL. Yea, noise? Then I'll be brief. O happy dagger!

                            [*Snatches* ROMEO's *dagger.*]

This is thy sheath; there rest, and let me die.

            She stabs herself and falls on ROMEO's *body.*

            Enter PARIS's BOY *and* WATCH.

    BOY. This is the place. There, where the torch doth
        burn.
    CHIEF WATCH. The ground is bloody. Search about
        the churchyard.
Go, some of you; who'er you find attach.

                        [*Exeunt some of the* WATCH.]

Pitiful sight! here lies the County slain;
And Juliet bleeding, warm, and newly dead,
Who here hath lain this two days buried.
Go, tell the Prince; run to the Capulets;
Raise up the Montagues; some others search.

                        [*Exeunt others of the* WATCH.]

We see the ground whereon these woes do lie,
But the true ground of all these piteous woes
We cannot without circumstance descry.

Enter some of the WATCH, *with* ROMEO's *man*
BALTHASAR.

2. WATCH. Here's Romeo's man. We found him in the churchyard.

CHIEF WATCH. Hold him in safety till the Prince come hither.

Enter FRIAR LAURENCE *and another* WATCHMAN.

3. WATCH. Here is a friar that trembles, sighs, and weeps.
We took this mattock and this spade from him
As he was coming from this churchyard side.

CHIEF WATCH. A great suspicion! Stay the friar too.

Enter the PRINCE *and* ATTENDANTS.

PRINCE. What misadventure is so early up,
That calls our person from our morning rest?

Enter CAPULET *and his* WIFE *with others.*

CAP. What should it be, that they so shriek abroad?

WIFE. The people in the street cry 'Romeo,'
Some 'Juliet,' and some 'Paris'; and all run,
With open outcry, toward our monument.

PRINCE. What fear is this which startles in our ears?

CHIEF WATCH. Sovereign, here lies the County Paris slain;
And Romeo dead; and Juliet, dead before,
Warm and new kill'd.

PRINCE. Search, seek, and know how this foul murder comes.

CHIEF WATCH. Here is a friar, and slaughter'd Romeo's man,
With instruments upon them fit to open
These dead men's tombs.

CAP. O heavens! O wife, look how our daughter bleeds!

This dagger hath mista'en, for, lo, his house
Is empty on the back of Montague,
And it missheathed in my daughter's bosom!

WIFE. O me! this sight of death is as a bell
That warns my old age to a sepulchre.

Enter MONTAGUE *and others.*

PRINCE. Come, Montague; for thou art early up
To see thy son and heir more early down.

MON. Alas, my liege, my wife is dead to-night!
Grief of my son's exile hath stopp'd her breath.
What further woe conspires against mine age?

PRINCE. Look, and thou shalt see.

MON. O thou untaught! what manners is in this,
To press before thy father to a grave?

PRINCE. Seal up the mouth of outrage for a while,
Till we can clear these ambiguities
And know their spring, their head, their true descent;
And then will I be general of your woes
And lead you even to death. Meantime forbear,
And let mischance be slave to patience.
Bring forth the parties of suspicion.

FRIAR. I am the greatest, able to do least,
Yet most suspected, as the time and place
Doth make against me, of this direful murther;
And here I stand, both to impeach and purge
Myself condemned and myself excus'd.

PRINCE. Then say at once what thou dost know in this.

FRIAR. I will be brief, for my short date of breath
Is not so long as is a tedious tale.
Romeo, there dead, was husband to that Juliet;
And she, there dead, that Romeo's faithful wife.
I married them; and their stol'n marriage day
Was Tybalt's doomsday, whose untimely death

Banish'd the new-made bridegroom from this city;
For whom, and not for Tybalt, Juliet pin'd.
You, to remove that siege of grief from her,
Betroth'd and would have married her perforce
To County Paris. Then comes she to me
And with wild looks bid me devise some mean
To rid her from this second marriage,
Or in my cell there would she kill herself.
Then gave I her (so tutor'd by my art)
A sleeping potion; which so took effect
As I intended, for it wrought on her
The form of death. Meantime I writ to Romeo
That he should hither come as this dire night
To help to take her from her borrowed grave,
Being the time the potion's force should cease.
But he which bore my letter, Friar John,
Was stay'd by accident, and yesternight
Return'd my letter back. Then all alone
At the prefixed hour of her waking
Came I to take her from her kindred's vault;
Meaning to keep her closely at my cell
Till I conveniently could send to Romeo.
But when I came, some minute ere the time
Of her awaking, here untimely lay
The noble Paris and true Romeo dead.
She wakes; and I entreated her come forth
And bear this work of heaven with patience;
But then a noise did scare me from the tomb,
And she, too desperate, would not go with me,
But, as it seems, did violence on herself.
All this I know, and to the marriage
Her nurse is privy; and if aught in this
Miscarried by my fault, let my old life
Be sacrific'd, some hour before his time,
Unto the rigour of severest law.

PRINCE. We still have known thee for a holy man.
Where's Romeo's man? What can he say in this?

BAL. I brought my master news of Juliet's death;
And then in post he came from Mantua
To this same place, to this same monument.
This letter he early bid me give his father,
And threat'ned me with death, going in the vault,
If I departed not and left him there.

PRINCE. Give me the letter. I will look on it.
Where is the County's page that rais'd the watch?
Sirrah, what made your master in this place?

BOY. He came with flowers to strew his lady's grave;
And bid me stand aloof, and so I did.
Anon comes one with light to ope the tomb;
And by-and-by my master drew on him;
And then I ran away to call the watch.

PRINCE. This letter doth make good the friar's words,
Their course of love, the tidings of her death;
And here he writes that he did buy a poison
Of a poor pothecary, and therewithal
Came to this vault to die, and lie with Juliet.
Where be these enemies? Capulet, Montague,
See what a scourge is laid upon your hate,
That heaven finds means to kill your joys with love!
And I, for winking at your discords too,
Have lost a brace of kinsmen. All are punish'd.

CAP. O brother Montague, give me thy hand.
This is my daughter's jointure, for no more
Can I demand.

MON.   But I can give thee more;
For I will raise her statue in pure gold,
That whiles Verona by that name is known,
There shall no figure at such rate be set
As that of true and faithful Juliet.

Cap. As rich shall Romeo's by his lady's lie—
Poor sacrifices of our enmity!

Prince. A glooming peace this morning with it brings.
The sun for sorrow will not show his head.
Go hence, to have more talk of these sad things;
Some shall be pardon'd, and some punished;
For never was a story of more woe
Than this of Juliet and her Romeo.   *Exeunt omnes.*

The Tragedy of
Julius Caesar

NAMES OF THE ACTORS

JULIUS CÆSAR.
OCTAVIUS CÆSAR,
MARCUS ANTONIUS,
M. AEMILIUS LEPIDUS,
} triumvirs after the death of JULIUS CÆSAR.

CICERO, PUBLIUS,
POPILIUS LENA,
} senators.

MARCUS BRUTUS, CASSIUS, CASCA,
TREBONIUS, LIGARIUS, CINNA,
DECIUS BRUTUS, METELLUS CIMBER,
} conspirators against JULIUS CÆSAR.

FLAVIUS and MARULLUS, tribunes of the People.
ARTEMIDORUS, a Sophist.   A SOOTHSAYER.
CINNA, a poet.   Another POET.
LUCILIUS, TITINIUS, MESSALA,
YOUNG CATO, VOLUMNIUS,
} friends to BRUTUS and CASSIUS.

CARRO, CLITUS, CLAUDIUS,
STRATO, LUCIUS, DARDANIUS,
} servants to BRUTUS.

PINDARUS, servant to CASSIUS.
A Servant to CÆSAR; to ANTONY; to OCTAVIUS.
CALPHURNIA, wife to CÆSAR.
PORTIA, wife to BRUTUS.
The GHOST OF CÆSAR.
Senators, Citizens, Guards, Attendants, &c.

Act I: Scene I: Rome. A street.

Enter FLAVIUS, MARULLUS, *and certain* COMMONERS *over the stage.*

FLAV. Hence! home, you idle creatures, get you home!
Is this a holiday? What, know you not,
Being mechanical, you ought not walk
Upon a labouring day without the sign
Of your profession? Speak, what trade art thou?

CARPENTER. Why, sir, a carpenter.

MAR. Where is thy leather apron and thy rule?
What dost thou with thy best apparel on?
You, sir, what trade are you?

COBBLER. Truly, sir, in respect of a fine workman I am
but, as you would say, a cobbler.

MAR. But what trade art thou? Answer me directly.

COB. A trade, sir, that I hope I may use with a safe
conscience, which is indeed, sir, a mender of bad soles.

MAR. What trade, thou knave? Thou naughty knave,
    what trade?

COB. Nay, I beseech you, sir, be not out with me. Yet
if you be out, sir, I can mend you.

MAR. What mean'st thou by that? Mend me, thou
    saucy fellow?

COB. Why, sir, cobble you.

FLAV. Thou art a cobbler, art thou?

COB. Truly, sir, all that I live by is with the awl. I
meddle with no tradesman's matters nor women's matters, but with all. I am indeed, sir, a surgeon to old shoes.
When they are in great danger, I recover them. As proper
men as ever trod upon neat's leather have gone upon my
handiwork.

FLAV. But wherefore art not in thy shop to-day?
Why dost thou lead these men about the streets?

COB. Truly, sir, to wear out their shoes, to get myself

into more work. But indeed, sir, we make holiday to see
Cæsar and to rejoice in his triumph.

MAR. Wherefore rejoice? What conquest brings he
home?
What tributaries follow him to Rome
To grace in captive bonds his chariot wheels?
You blocks, you stones, you worse than senseless things!
O you hard hearts, you cruel men of Rome!
Knew you not Pompey? Many a time and oft
Have you climb'd up to walls and battlements,
To tow'rs and windows, yea, to chimney tops,
Your infants in your arms, and there have sat
The livelong day, with patient expectation,
To see great Pompey pass the streets of Rome.
And when you saw his chariot but appear,
Have you not made an universal shout,
That Tiber trembled underneath her banks
To hear the replication of your sounds
Made in her concave shores?
And do you now put on your best attire?
And do you now cull out a holiday?
And do you now strew flowers in his way
That comes in triumph over Pompey's blood?
Be gone!
Run to your houses, fall upon your knees,
Pray to the gods to intermit the plague
That needs must light on this ingratitude.

FLAV. Go, go, good countrymen, and for this fault
Assemble all the poor men of your sort;
Draw them to Tiber banks, and weep your tears
Into the channel, till the lowest stream
Do kiss the most exalted shores of all.

                    [*Exeunt all the* COMMONERS.]
See, whe'r their basest metal be not mov'd.
They vanish tongue-tied in their guiltiness.

Go you down that way towards the Capitol;
This way will I. Disrobe the images
If you do find them deck'd with ceremonies.

  MAR. May we do so?
You know it is the feast of Lupercal.

  FLAV. It is no matter. Let no images
Be hung with Cæsar's trophies. I'll about
And drive away the vulgar from the streets.
So do you too, where you perceive them thick.
These growing feathers pluck'd from Cæsar's wing
Will make him fly an ordinary pitch,
Who else would soar above the view of men
And keep us all in servile fearfulness.   *Exeunt.*

Scene II: Rome. A public place.

Music. Enter CÆSAR, ANTONY *(for the course),* CAL-
PHURNIA, PORTIA, DECIUS, CICERO, BRUTUS, CASSIUS,
CASCA, *a great crowd following, among them, a* SOOTH-
SAYER; *after them,* MARULLUS *and* FLAVIUS.

  CÆS. Calphurnia.

  CASCA.   Peace, ho! Cæsar speaks.
                                          Music ceases.

  CÆS.   Calphurnia.

  CAL. Here, my lord.

  CÆS. Stand you directly in Antonius' way
When he doth run his course. Antonius.

  ANT. Cæsar, my lord?

  CÆS. Forget not in your speed, Antonius,
To touch Calphurnia; for our elders say
The barren, touched in this holy chase,
Shake off their sterile curse.

  ANT.   I shall remember.
When Cæsar says 'Do this,' it is perform'd.

CÆS. Set on, and leave no ceremony out.   *Music.*

SOOTH. Cæsar!

CÆS. Ha! Who calls?

CASCA. Bid every noise be still. Peace yet again!

                               Music ceases.

CÆS. Who is it in the press that calls on me?
I hear a tongue shriller than all the music
Cry 'Cæsar!' Speak. Cæsar is turn'd to hear.

SOOTH. Beware the ides of March.

CÆS.   What man is that?

BRU. A soothsayer bids you beware the ides of March.

CÆS. Set him before me; let me see his face.

CASS. Fellow, come from the throng; look upon Cæsar.

CÆS. What say'st thou to me now? Speak once again.

SOOTH. Beware the ides of March.

CÆS. He is a dreamer. Let us leave him. Pass.

       SENNET. *Exeunt, leaving* BRUTUS *and* CASSIUS.

CASS. Will you go see the order of the course?

BRU. Not I.

CASS. I pray you do.

BRU. I am not gamesome. I do lack some part
Of that quick spirit that is in Antony.
Let me not hinder, Cassius, your desires.
I'll leave you.

CASS. Brutus, I do observe you now of late;
I have not from your eyes that gentleness
And show of love as I was wont to have.
You bear too stubborn and too strange a hand
Over your friend that loves you.

BRU.   Cassius,
Be not deceiv'd. If I have veil'd my look,
I turn the trouble of my countenance
Merely upon myself. Vexed I am
Of late with passions of some difference,
Conceptions only proper to myself,

Which give some soil, perhaps, to my behaviours;
But let not therefore my good friends be griev'd
(Among which number, Cassius, be you one)
Nor construe any further my neglect
Than that poor Brutus, with himself at war,
Forgets the shows of love to other men.

    Cass. Then, Brutus, I have much mistook your passion;
By means whereof this breast of mine hath buried
Thoughts of great value, worthy cogitations.
Tell me, good Brutus, can you see your face?

    Bru. No, Cassius; for the eye sees not itself
But by reflection, by some other things.

    Cass. 'Tis just.
And it is very much lamented, Brutus,
That you have no such mirrors as will turn
Your hidden worthiness into your eye,
That you might see your shadow. I have heard
Where many of the best respect in Rome
(Except immortal Cæsar), speaking of Brutus
And groaning underneath this age's yoke,
Have wish'd that noble Brutus had his eyes.

    Bru. Into what dangers would you lead me, Cassius,
That you would have me seek into myself
For that which is not in me?

    Cass. Therefore, good Brutus, be prepar'd to hear;
And since you know you cannot see yourself
So well as by reflection, I, your glass,
Will modestly discover to yourself
That of yourself which you yet know not of.
And be not jealous on me, gentle Brutus.
Were I a common laugher, or did use
To stale with ordinary oaths my love
To every new protester; if you know
That I do fawn on men and hug them hard,
And after scandal them; or if you know

That I profess myself in banqueting
To all the rout, then hold me dangerous.

Flourish and shout.

Bru. What means this shouting? I do fear the people
Choose Cæsar for their king.
Cass.   Ay, do you fear it?
Then must I think you would not have it so.
Bru. I would not, Cassius; yet I love him well.
But wherefore do you hold me here so long?
What is it that you would impart to me?
If it be aught toward the general good,
Set honour in one eye and death i' th' other,
And I will look on both indifferently;
For let the gods so speed me as I love
The name of honour more than I fear death.
Cass. I know that virtue to be in you, Brutus,
As well as I do know your outward favour.
Well, honour is the subject of my story.
I cannot tell what you and other men
Think of this life; but for my single self,
I had as lief not be as live to be
In awe of such a thing as I myself.
I was born free as Cæsar; so were you.
We both have fed as well, and we can both
Endure the winter's cold as well as he.
For once, upon a raw and gusty day,
The troubled Tiber chafing with her shores,
Cæsar said to me, 'Dar'st thou, Cassius, now
Leap in with me into this angry flood
And swim to yonder point?' Upon the word,
Accoutred as I was, I plunged in
And bade him follow. So indeed he did.
The torrent roar'd, and we did buffet it
With lusty sinews, throwing it aside

And stemming it with hearts of controversy.
But ere we could arrive the point propos'd,
Cæsar cried, 'Help me, Cassius, or I sink!'
I, as Æneas, our great ancestor,
Did from the flames of Troy upon his shoulder
The old Anchises bear, so from the waves of Tiber
Did I the tired Cæsar. And this man
Is now become a god, and Cassius is
A wretched creature and must bend his body
If Cæsar carelessly but nod on him.
He had a fever when he was in Spain,
And when the fit was on him, I did mark
How he did shake. 'Tis true, this god did shake.
His coward lips did from their colour fly,
And that same eye whose bend doth awe the world
Did lose his lustre. I did hear him groan.
Ay, and that tongue of his that bade the Romans
Mark him and write his speeches in their books,
Alas, it cried, 'Give me some drink, Titinius,'
As a sick girl! Ye gods, it doth amaze me
A man of such a feeble temper should
So get the start of the majestic world
And bear the palm alone.

Shout. Flourish.

Bru. Another general shout?
I do believe that these applauses are
For some new honours that are heap'd on Cæsar.

Cass. Why, man, he doth bestride the narrow world
Like a Colossus, and we petty men
Walk under his huge legs and peep about
To find ourselves dishonourable graves.
Men at some time are masters of their fates.
The fault, dear Brutus, is not in our stars,
But in ourselves, that we are underlings.

'Brutus,' and 'Cæsar.' What should be in that 'Cæsar'?
Why should that name be sounded more than yours?
Write them together: yours is as fair a name.
Sound them: it doth become the mouth as well.
Weigh them: it is as heavy. Conjure with 'em:
'Brutus' will start a spirit as soon as 'Cæsar.'
Now in the names of all the gods at once,
Upon what meat doth this our Cæsar feed
That he is grown so great? Age, thou art sham'd!
Rome, thou hast lost the breed of noble bloods!
When went there by an age since the great Flood
But it was fam'd with more than with one man?
When could they say (till now) that talk'd of Rome
That her wide walls encompass'd but one man?
Now is it Rome indeed, and room enough,
When there is in it but one only man!
O, you and I have heard our fathers say
There was a Brutus once that would have brook'd
Th' eternal devil to keep his state in Rome
As easily as a king.
    BRU. That you do love me I am nothing jealous.
What you would work me to, I have some aim.
How I have thought of this, and of these times,
I shall recount hereafter. For this present,
I would not (so with love I might entreat you)
Be any further mov'd. What you have said
I will consider; what you have to say
I will with patience hear, and find a time
Both meet to hear and answer such high things.
Till then, my noble friend, chew upon this:
Brutus had rather be a villager
Than to repute himself a son of Rome
Under these hard conditions as this time
Is like to lay upon us.
    CASS.   I am glad

That my weak words have struck but thus much show
Of fire from Brutus.

Enter CÆSAR *and his* TRAIN.

BRU. The games are done, and Cæsar is returning.

CASS. As they pass by, pluck Casca by the sleeve,
And he will (after his sour fashion) tell you
What hath proceeded worthy note to-day.

BRU. I will do so. But look you, Cassius!
The angry spot doth glow on Cæsar's brow,
And all the rest look like a chidden train.
Calphurnia's cheek is pale, and Cicero
Looks with such ferret and such fiery eyes
As we have seen him in the Capitol,
Being cross'd in conference by some senators.

CASS. Casca will tell us what the matter is.

CÆS. Antonius.

ANT. Cæsar?

CÆS. Let me have men about me that are fat,
Sleek-headed men, and such as sleep a-nights.
Yond Cassius has a lean and hungry look.
He thinks too much. Such men are dangerous.

ANT. Fear him not, Cæsar; he's not dangerous.
He is a noble Roman, and well given.

CÆS. Would he were fatter! But I fear him not.
Yet if my name were liable to fear,
I do not know the man I should avoid
So soon as that spare Cassius. He reads much,
He is a great observer, and he looks
Quite through the deeds of men. He loves no plays
As thou dost, Antony; he hears no music.
Seldom he smiles, and smiles in such a sort
As if he mock'd himself and scorn'd his spirit
That could be mov'd to smile at anything.
Such men as he be never at heart's ease

Whiles they behold a greater than themselves,
And therefore are they very dangerous
I rather tell thee what is to be fear'd
Than what I fear; for always I am Cæsar.
Come on my right hand, for this ear is deaf,
And tell me truly what thou think'st of him.

> *Sennet. Exeunt* Cæsar *and his* Train,
> *leaving* Casca.

Casca. You pull'd me by the cloak. Would you speak
with me?

Bru. Ay, Casca. Tell us what hath chanc'd to-day
That Cæsar looks so sad.

Casca. Why, you were with him, were you not?

Bru. I should not then ask Casca what had chanc'd.

Casca. Why, there was a crown offer'd him; and being
offer'd him, he put it by with the back of his hand thus;
and then the people fell a-shouting.

Bru. What was the second noise for?

Casca. Why, for that too.

Cass. They shouted thrice. What was the last cry for?

Casca. Why, for that too.

Bru. Was the crown offer'd him thrice?

Casca. Ay, marry, was't! and he put it by thrice, every
time gentler than other; and at every putting-by mine
honest neighbours shouted.

Cass. Who offer'd him the crown?

Casca. Why, Antony.

Bru. Tell us the manner of it, gentle Casca.

Casca. I can as well be hang'd as tell the manner of it.
It was mere foolery; I did not mark it. I saw Mark Antony
offer him a crown—yet 'twas not a crown neither, 'twas
one of these coronets—and, as I told you, he put it by
once; but for all that, to my thinking, he would fain have
had it. Then he offered it to him again; then he put it by
again; but to my thinking, he was very loath to lay his

fingers off it. And then he offered it the third time. He put it the third time by; and still as he refus'd it, the rabblement hooted, and clapp'd their chopt hands, and threw up their sweaty nightcaps, and uttered such a deal of stinking breath because Cæsar refus'd the crown that it had, almost, chok'd Cæsar; for he swoonded and fell down at it. And for mine own part, I durst not laugh, for fear of opening my lips and receiving the bad air.

Cass. But soft, I pray you. What, did Cæsar swound?

Casca. He fell down in the market place and foam'd at mouth and was speechless.

Bru. 'Tis very like. He hath the falling sickness.

Cass. No, Cæsar hath it not; but you, and I, And honest Casca, we have the falling sickness.

Casca. I know not what you mean by that, but I am sure Cæsar fell down. If the tag-rag people did not clap him and hiss him, according as he pleas'd and displeas'd them, as they use to do the players in the theatre, I am no true man.

Bru. What said he when he came unto himself?

Casca. Marry, before he fell down, when he perceiv'd the common herd was glad he refus'd the crown, he pluck'd me ope his doublet and offer'd them his throat to cut. An I had been a man of any occupation, if I would not have taken him at a word I would I might go to hell among the rogues. And so he fell. When he came to himself again, he said, if he had done or said anything amiss, he desir'd their worships to think it was his infirmity. Three or four wenches where I stood cried 'Alas, good soul!' and forgave him with all their hearts. But there's no heed to be taken of them. If Cæsar had stabb'd their mothers, they would have done no less.

Bru. And after that, he came thus sad away?

Casca. Ay.

Cass. Did Cicero say anything?

CASCA. Ay, he spoke Greek.

CASS. To what effect?

CASCA. Nay, an I tell you that, I'll ne'er look you i' th' face again. But those that understood him smil'd at one another and shook their heads; but for mine own part, it was Greek to me. I could tell you more news too. Marullus and Flavius, for pulling scarfs off Cæsar's images, are put to silence. Fare you well. There was more foolery yet, if I could remember it.

CASS. Will you sup with me to-night, Casca?

CASCA. No, I am promis'd forth.

CASS. Will you dine with me to-morrow?

CASCA. Ay, if I be alive, and your mind hold, and your dinner worth the eating.

CASS. Good. I will expect you.

CASCA. Do so. Farewell both.   *Exit.*

BRU. What a blunt fellow is this grown to be!
He was quick mettle when he went to school.

CASS. So is he now in execution
Of any bold or noble enterprise,
However he puts on this tardy form.
This rudeness is a sauce to his good wit,
Which gives men stomach to disgest his words
With better appetite.

BRU. And so it is. For this time I will leave you.
To-morrow, if you please to speak with me,
I will come home to you; or if you will,
Come home to me, and I will wait for you.

CASS. I will do so. Till then, think of the world.

                             [*Exit* BRUTUS.]

Well, Brutus, thou art noble; yet I see
Thy honourable mettle may be wrought
From that it is dispos'd. Therefore it is meet
That noble minds keep ever with their likes;
For who so firm that cannot be seduc'd?

Cæsar doth bear me hard; but he loves Brutus.
If I were Brutus now and he were Cassius,
He should not humour me. I will this night,
In several hands, in at his windows throw,
As if they came from several citizens,
Writings, all tending to the great opinion
That Rome holds of his name; wherein obscurely
Cæsar's ambition shall be glanced at.
And after this let Cæsar seat him sure,
For we will shake him, or worse days endure.   *Exit.*

Scene III: Rome. A street.

Thunder and lightning. Enter, from opposite sides,
CASCA, *with his sword drawn, and* CICERO.

CIC. Good even, Casca. Brought you Cæsar home?
Why are you breathless? and why stare you so?

CASCA. Are not you mov'd when all the sway of earth
Shakes like a thing unfirm? O Cicero,
I have seen tempests when the scolding winds
Have riv'd the knotty oaks, and I have seen
Th' ambitious ocean swell and rage and foam
To be exalted with the threat'ning clouds;
But never till to-night, never till now,
Did I go through a tempest dropping fire.
Either there is a civil strife in heaven,
Or else the world, too saucy with the gods,
Incenses them to send destruction.

CIC. Why, saw you any thing more wonderful?

CASCA. A common slave (you know him well by sight)
Held up his left hand, which did flame and burn
Like twenty torches join'd; and yet his hand,
Not sensible of fire, remain'd unscorch'd.
Besides (I ha' not since put up my sword),

Against the Capitol I met a lion,
Who glar'd upon me, and went surly by
Without annoying me. And there were drawn
Upon a heap a hundred ghastly women,
Transformed with their fear, who swore they saw
Men, all in fire, walk up and down the streets.
And yesterday the bird of night did sit
Even at noonday upon the market place,
Hooting and shrieking. When these prodigies
Do so conjointly meet, let not men say
'These are their reasons—they are natural,'
For I believe they are portentous things
Unto the climate that they point upon.

   Cic. Indeed it is a strange-disposed time.
But men may construe things after their fashion,
Clean from the purpose of the things themselves.
Comes Cæsar to the Capitol to-morrow?

   Casca. He doth; for he did bid Antonius
Send word to you he would be there to-morrow.

   Cic. Good night then, Casca. This disturbed sky
Is not to walk in.

   Casca.   Farewell, Cicero.   *Exit* Cicero.

Enter Cassius.

   Cass. Who's there?

   Casca.   A Roman.

   Cass.   Casca, by your voice.

   Casca. Your ear is good. Cassius, what night is this!

   Cass. A very pleasing night to honest men.

   Casca. Who ever knew the heavens menace so?

   Cass. Those that have known the earth so full of faults.
For my part, I have walk'd about the streets,
Submitting me unto the perilous night,
And, thus unbraced, Casca, as you see,
Have bar'd my bosom to the thunder-stone;

And when the cross blue lightning seem'd to open
The breast of heaven, I did present myself
Even in the aim and very flash of it.

    CASCA. But wherefore did you so much tempt the
      heavens?
It is the part of men to fear and tremble
When the most mighty gods by tokens send
Such dreadful heralds to astonish us.

    CASS. You are dull, Casca, and those sparks of life
That should be in a Roman you do want,
Or else you use not. You look pale, and gaze,
And put on fear, and cast yourself in wonder,
To see the strange impatience of the heavens;
But if you would consider the true cause—
Why all these fires, why all these gliding ghosts,
Why birds and beasts, from quality and kind;
Why old men fool and children calculate;
Why all these things change from their ordinance,
Their natures, and preformed faculties,
To monstrous quality—why, you shall find
That heaven hath infus'd them with these spirits
To make them instruments of fear and warning
Unto some monstrous state.
Now could I, Casca, name to thee a man
Most like this dreadful night
That thunders, lightens, opens graves, and roars
As doth the lion in the Capitol;
A man no mightier than thyself or me
In personal action, yet prodigious grown
And fearful, as these strange eruptions are.

    CASCA. 'Tis Cæsar that you mean. Is it not, Cassius?

    CASS. Let it be who it is. For Romans now
Have thews and limbs like to their ancestors;
But woe the while! our fathers' minds are dead,

And we are govern'd with our mothers' spirits;
Our yoke and sufferance show us womanish.

CASCA. Indeed, they say the senators to-morrow
Mean to establish Cæsar as a king,
And he shall wear his crown by sea and land
In every place save here in Italy.

CASS. I know where I will wear this dagger then;
Cassius from bondage will deliver Cassius.
Therein, ye gods, you make the weak most strong;
Therein, ye gods, you tyrants do defeat.
Nor stony tower, nor walls of beaten brass,
Nor airless dungeon, nor strong links of iron,
Can be retentive to the strength of spirit;
But life, being weary of these worldly bars,
Never lacks power to dismiss itself.
If I know this, know all the world besides,
That part of tyranny that I do bear
I can shake off at pleasure.   *Thunder still.*

CASCA.   So can I.
So every bondman in his own hand bears
The power to cancel his captivity.

CASS. And why should Cæsar be a tyrant then?
Poor man! I know he would not be a wolf
But that he sees the Romans are but sheep;
He were no lion, were not Romans hinds.
Those that with haste will make a mighty fire
Begin it with weak straws. What trash is Rome,
What rubbish and what offal, when it serves
For the base matter to illuminate
So vile a thing as Cæsar! But, O grief,
Where hast thou led me? I, perhaps, speak this
Before a willing bondman. Then I know
My answer must be made. But I am arm'd,
And dangers are to me indifferent.

CASCA. You speak to Casca, and to such a man
That is no fleering telltale. Hold, my hand.
Be factious for redress of all these griefs,
And I will set this foot of mine as far
As who goes farthest.

CASS.   There's a bargain made.
Now know you, Casca, I have mov'd already
Some certain of the noblest-minded Romans
To undergo with me an enterprise
Of honourable-dangerous consequence;
And I do know, by this they stay for me
In Pompey's Porch; for now, this fearful night,
There is no stir or walking in the streets,
And the complexion of the element
In favour's like the work we have in hand,
Most bloody, fiery, and most terrible.

Enter CINNA.

CASCA. Stand close awhile, for here comes one in haste.
CASS. 'Tis Cinna. I do know him by his gait.
He is a friend. Cinna, where haste you so?
CIN. To find out you. Who's that? Metellus Cimber?
CASS. No, it is Casca, one incorporate
To our attempts. Am I not stay'd for, Cinna?
CIN. I am glad on't. What a fearful night is this!
There's two or three of us have seen strange sights.
CASS. Am I not stay'd for? Tell me.
CIN.   Yes, you are.
O Cassius, if you could
But win the noble Brutus to our party—
CASS. Be you content. Good Cinna, take this paper
And look you lay it in the prætor's chair,
Where Brutus may but find it. And throw this
In at his window. Set this up with wax
Upon old Brutus' statue. All this done,

Repair to Pompey's Porch, where you shall find us.
Is Decius Brutus and Trebonius there?

CIN. All but Metellus Cimber, and he's gone
To seek you at your house. Well, I will hie
And so bestow these papers as you bade me.

CASS. That done, repair to Pompey's Theatre.

[Exit CINNA.]

Come, Casca, you and I will yet ere day
See Brutus at his house. Three parts of him
Is ours already, and the man entire
Upon the next encounter yields him ours.

CASCA. O, he sits high in all the people's hearts;
And that which would appear offence in us,
His countenance, like richest alchemy,
Will change to virtue and to worthiness.

CASS. Him and his worth and our great need of him
You have right well conceited. Let us go,
For it is after midnight; and ere day
We will awake him and be sure of him.   *Exeunt.*

Act II: Scene I: Rome.

Enter BRUTUS *in his orchard.*

BRU. What, Lucius, ho!
I cannot by the progress of the stars
Give guess how near to day. Lucius, I say!
I would it were my fault to sleep so soundly.
When, Lucius, when? Awake, I say! What, Lucius!

Enter LUCIUS.

LUC. Call'd you, my lord?

BRU. Get me a taper in my study, Lucius.
When it is lighted, come and call me here.

LUC. I will, my lord.   *Exit.*

Bru. It must be by his death; and for my part,
I know no personal cause to spurn at him,
But for the general. He would be crown'd.
How that might change his nature, there's the question.
It is the bright day that brings forth the adder,
And that craves wary walking. Crown him—that!
And then I grant we put a sting in him
That at his will he may do danger with.
Th' abuse of greatness is, when it disjoins
Remorse from power. And to speak truth of Cæsar,
I have not known when his affections sway'd
More than his reason. But 'tis a common proof
That lowliness is young ambition's ladder,
Whereto the climber-upward turns his face;
But when he once attains the upmost round,
He then unto the ladder turns his back,
Looks in the clouds, scorning the base degrees
By which he did ascend. So Cæsar may.
Then lest he may, prevent. And since the quarrel
Will bear no colour for the thing he is,
Fashion it thus: that what he is, augmented,
Would run to these and these extremities;
And therefore think him as a serpent's egg,
Which, hatch'd, would as his kind grow mischievous,
And kill him in the shell.

Enter Lucius.

Luc. The taper burneth in your closet, sir.
Searching the window for a flint, I found
This paper, thus seal'd up; and I am sure
It did not lie there when I went to bed.
                          Gives him the letter.

Bru. Get you to bed again; it is not day.
Is not to-morrow, boy, the ides of March?

Luc. I know not, sir.

Bru. Look in the calendar and bring me word.

Luc. I will, sir.   *Exit.*

Bru. The exhalations, whizzing in the air,
Give so much light that I may read by them.

> *[Opens the letter and reads.]*

> 'Brutus, thou sleep'st. Awake, and see thyself!
> Shall Rome, &c. Speak, strike, redress!'

'Brutus, thou sleep'st. Awake!'
Such instigations have been often dropp'd
Where I have took them up.
'Shall Rome, &c.' Thus must I piece it out:
Shall Rome stand under one man's awe? What, Rome?
My ancestors did from the streets of Rome
The Tarquin drive when he was call'd a king.
'Speak, strike, redress!' Am I entreated
To speak and strike? O Rome, I make thee promise,
If the redress will follow, thou receivest
Thy full petition at the hand of Brutus!

Enter Lucius.

Luc. Sir, March is wasted fifteen days.

> *Knock within.*

Bru. 'Tis good. Go to the gate; somebody knocks.

> *[Exit* Lucius.*]*

Since Cassius first did whet me against Cæsar,
I have not slept.
Between the acting of a dreadful thing
And the first motion, all the interim is
Like a phantasma or a hideous dream.
The genius and the mortal instruments
Are then in council, and the state of man,
Like to a little kingdom, suffers then
The nature of an insurrection.

Enter LUCIUS.

LUC. Sir, 'tis your brother Cassius at the door,
Who doth desire to see you.

BRU.   Is he alone?

LUC. No, sir, there are moe with him.

BRU.   Do you know them?

LUC. No, sir. Their hats are pluck'd about their ears
And half their faces buried in their cloaks,
That by no means I may discover them
By any mark of favour.

BRU.   Let 'em enter. [*Exit* LUCIUS.]
They are the faction. O conspiracy,
Sham'st thou to show thy dang'rous brow by night,
When evils are most free? O, then by day
Where wilt thou find a cavern dark enough
To mask thy monstrous visage? Seek none, conspiracy.
Hide it in smiles and affability!
For if thou path, thy native semblance on,
Not Erebus itself were dim enough
To hide thee from prevention.

Enter the Conspirators, CASSIUS, CASCA, DECIUS,
CINNA, METELLUS CIMBER, *and* TREBONIUS.

CASS. I think we are too bold upon your rest.
Good morrow, Brutus. Do we trouble you?

BRU. I have been up this hour, awake all night.
Know I these men that come along with you?

CASS. Yes, every man of them; and no man here
But honours you; and every one doth wish
You had but that opinion of yourself
Which every noble Roman bears of you.
This is Trebonius.

BRU.   He is welcome hither.

CASS. This, Decius Brutus.

BRU.   He is welcome too.

CASS. This, Casca; this, Cinna; and this, Metellus
    Cimber.

BRU. They are all welcome.
What watchful cares do interpose themselves
Betwixt your eyes and night?

    CASS. Shall I entreat a word?   *They whisper.*

    DEC. Here lies the east. Doth not the day break here?

    CASCA. No.

    CIN. O, pardon, sir, it doth; and yon grey lines
That fret the clouds are messengers of day.

    CASCA. You shall confess that you are both deceiv'd.
Here, as I point my sword, the sun arises,
Which is a great way growing on the south,
Weighing the youthful season of the year.
Some two months hence, up higher toward the north
He first presents his fire; and the high east
Stands as the Capitol, directly here.

    BRU. Give me your hands all over, one by one.

    CASS. And let us swear our resolution.

    BRU. No, not an oath. If not the face of men,
The sufferance of our souls, the time's abuse—
If these be motives weak, break off betimes,
And every man hence to his idle bed.
So let high-sighted tyranny range on
Till each man drop by lottery. But if these
(As I am sure they do) bear fire enough
To kindle cowards and to steel with valour
The melting spirits of women, then, countrymen,
What need we any spur but our own cause
To prick us to redress? what other bond
Than secret Romans that have spoke the word
And will not palter? and what other oath
Than honesty to honesty engag'd
That this shall be, or we will fall for it?
Swear priests and cowards and men cautelous,

Old feeble carrions and such suffering souls
That welcome wrongs; unto bad causes swear
Such creatures as men doubt; but do not stain
The even virtue of our enterprise,
Nor th' insuppressive mettle of our spirits,
To think that or our cause or our performance
Did need an oath; when every drop of blood
That every Roman bears, and nobly bears,
Is guilty of a several bastardy
If he do break the smallest particle
Of any promise that hath pass'd from him.

    Cass. But what of Cicero? Shall we sound him.
I think he will stand very strong with us.

    Casca. Let us not leave him out.

    Cin.   No, by no means.

    Met. O, let us have him! for his silver hairs
Will purchase us a good opinion
And buy men's voices to commend our deeds.
It shall be said his judgment rul'd our hands.
Our youths and wildness shall no whit appear,
But all be buried in his gravity.

    Bru. O, name him not! Let us not break with him;
For he will never follow anything
That other men begin.

    Cass.   Then leave him out.

    Casca. Indeed he is not fit.

    Dec. Shall no man else be touch'd but only Cæsar?

    Cass. Decius, well urg'd. I think it is not meet
Mark Antony, so well belov'd of Cæsar,
Should outlive Cæsar. We shall find of him
A shrewd contriver; and you know, his means,
If he improve them, may well stretch so far
As to annoy us all; which to prevent,
Let Antony and Cæsar fall together.

    Bru. Our course will seem too bloody, Caius Cassius,

To cut the head off and then hack the limbs,
Like wrath in death and envy afterwards;
For Antony is but a limb of Cæsar.
Let us be sacrificers, but not butchers, Caius.
We all stand up against the spirit of Cæsar,
And in the spirit of men there is no blood.
O that we then could come by Cæsar's spirit
And not dismember Cæsar! But, alas,
Cæsar must bleed for it! And, gentle friends,
Let's kill him boldly, but not wrathfully;
Let's carve him as a dish fit for the gods,
Not hew him as a carcass fit for hounds.
And let our hearts, as subtle masters do,
Stir up their servants to an act of rage
And after seem to chide 'em. This shall make
Our purpose necessary, and not envious;
Which so appearing to the common eyes,
We shall be call'd purgers, not murderers.
And for Mark Antony, think not of him;
For he can do no more than Cæsar's arm
When Cæsar's head is off.

Cass.   Yet I fear him;
For in the ingrafted love he bears to Cæsar—

Bru. Alas, good Cassius, do not think of him!
If he love Cæsar, all that he can do
Is to himself—take thought, and die for Cæsar.
And that were much he should; for he is given
To sports, to wildness, and much company.

Treb. There is no fear in him. Let him not die;
For he will live, and laugh at this hereafter.

Clock strikes.

Bru. Peace! Count the clock.

Cass.   The clock hath stricken three.

Treb. 'Tis time to part.

Cass.   But it is doubtful yet

Whether Cæsar will come forth to-day or no;
For he is superstitious grown of late,
Quite from the main opinion he held once
Of fantasy, of dreams, and ceremonies.
It may be these apparent prodigies,
The unaccustom'd terror of this night,
And the persuasion of his augurers
May hold him from the Capitol to-day.

DEC. Never fear that. If he be so resolv'd,
I can o'ersway him; for he loves to hear
That unicorns may be betray'd with trees
And bears with glasses, elephants with holes,
Lions with toils, and men with flatterers;
But when I tell him he hates flatterers,
He says he does, being then most flattered.
Let me work;
For I can give his humour the true bent
And I will bring him to the Capitol.

CASS. Nay, we will all of us be there to fetch him.

BRU. By the eighth hour. Is that the uttermost?

CIN. Be that the uttermost, and fail not then.

MET. Caius Ligarius doth bear Cæsar hard,
Who rated him for speaking well of Pompey.
I wonder none of you have thought of him.

BRU. Now, good Metellus, go along by him.
He loves me well, and I have given him reasons.
Send him but hither, and I'll fashion him.

CASS. The morning comes upon's. We'll leave you,
Brutus.
And, friends, disperse yourselves; but all remember
What you have said and show yourselves true Romans.

BRU. Good gentlemen, look fresh and merrily.
Let not our looks put on our purposes,
But bear it as our Roman actors do,

With untir'd spirits and formal constancy.
And so good morrow to you every one.

                 [Exeunt, leaving BRUTUS.]

Boy! Lucius! Fast asleep? It is no matter.
Enjoy the honey-heavy dew of slumber.
Thou hast no figures nor no fantasies
Which busy care draws in the brains of men;
Therefore thou sleep'st so sound.

               Enter PORTIA.

POR.   Brutus, my lord!
   BRU. Portia! What mean you? Wherefore rise you now?
It is not for your health thus to commit
Your weak condition to the raw cold morning.
   POR. Nor for yours neither. Y' have ungently, Brutus,
Stole from my bed. And yesternight at supper
You suddenly arose and walk'd about,
Musing and sighing with your arms across;
And when I ask'd you what the matter was,
You star'd upon me with ungentle looks.
I urg'd you further; then you scratch'd your head
And too impatiently stamp'd with your foot.
Yet I insisted; yet you answer'd not,
But with an angry wafture of your hand
Gave sign for me to leave you. So I did,
Fearing to strengthen that impatience
Which seem'd too much enkindled, and withal
Hoping it was but an effect of humour,
Which sometime hath his hour with every man.
It will not let you eat nor talk nor sleep,
And could it work so much upon your shape
As it hath much prevail'd on your condition,
I should not know you Brutus. Dear my lord,
Make me acquainted with your cause of grief.

Bru. I am not well in health, and that is all.

Por. Brutus is wise and, were he not in health,
He would embrace the means to come by it.

Bru. Why, so I do. Good Portia, go to bed.

Por. Is Brutus sick, and is it physical
To walk unbraced and suck up the humours
Of the dank morning? What, is Brutus sick,
And will he steal out of his wholesome bed
To dare the vile contagion of the night,
And tempt the rheumy and unpurged air,
To add unto his sickness? No, my Brutus.
You have some sick offence within your mind,
Which by the right and virtue of my place
I ought to know of; and upon my knees
I charm you, by my once commended beauty,
By all your vows of love, and that great vow
Which did incorporate and make us one,
That you unfold to me, yourself, your half,
Why you are heavy—and what men to-night
Have had resort to you; for here have been
Some six or seven, who did hide their faces
Even from darkness.

Bru.   Kneel not, gentle Portia.

Por. I should not need if you were gentle Brutus.
Within the bond of marriage, tell me, Brutus,
Is it excepted I should know no secrets
That appertain to you? Am I yourself
But, as it were, in sort or limitation?
To keep with you at meals, comfort your bed,
And talk to you sometimes? Dwell I but in the suburbs
Of your good pleasure? If it be no more,
Portia is Brutus' harlot, not his wife.

Bru. You are my true and honourable wife,
As dear to me as are the ruddy drops
That visit my sad heart.

Por. If this were true, then should I know this secret.
I grant I am a woman; but withal
A woman that Lord Brutus took to wife.
I grant I am a woman; but withal
A woman well-reputed, Cato's daughter.
Think you I am no stronger than my sex,
Being so father'd and so husbanded?
Tell me your counsels; I will not disclose 'em.
I have made strong proof of my constancy,
Giving myself a voluntary wound
Here, in the thigh. Can I bear that with patience,
And not my husband's secrets?
    Bru.   O ye gods,
Render me worthy of this noble wife!   [Knock.]
Hark, hark! One knocks. Portia, go in awhile,
And by-and-by thy bosom shall partake
The secrets of my heart.
All my engagements I will construe to thee,
All the charactery of my sad brows.
Leave me with haste.   [Exit Portia.]
                Lucius, who's that knocks?

Enter Lucius *and* Caius Ligarius.

Luc. Here is a sick man that would speak with you.
    Bru. Caius Ligarius, that Metellus spake of.
Boy, stand aside. Caius Ligarius, how?
    Caius. Vouchsafe good-morrow from a feeble tongue.
    Bru. O, what a time have you chose out, brave Caius,
To wear a kerchief! Would you were not sick!
    Caius. I am not sick if Brutus have in hand
Any exploit worthy the name of honour.
    Bru. Such an exploit have I in hand, Ligarius,
Had you a healthful ear to hear of it.
    Caius. By all the gods that Romans bow before,

I here discard my sickness! [*Throws off his kerchief.*]
    Soul of Rome!
Brave son, deriv'd from honourable loins!
Thou like an exorcist hast conjur'd up
My mortified spirit. Now bid me run,
And I will strive with things impossible;
Yea, get the better of them. What's to do?
   BRU. A piece of work that will make sick men whole.
   CAIUS. But are not some whole that we must make
    sick?
   BRU. That must we also. What it is, my Caius,
I shall unfold to thee as we are going
To whom it must be done.
   CAIUS.   Set on your foot,
And with a heart new-fir'd I follow you,
To do I know not what; but it sufficeth
That Brutus leads me on.   *Thunder.*
   BRU.   Follow me then.   *Exeunt.*

Scene II: Rome. Cæsar's house.

Thunder and lightning. Enter JULIUS CÆSAR,
in his nightgown.

   CÆS. Nor heaven nor earth have been at peace to-
night.
Thrice hath Calphurnia in her sleep cried out
'Help, ho! They murther Cæsar!' Who's within?

Enter a SERVANT.

   SERV. My lord?
   CÆS. Go bid the priests do present sacrifice,
And bring me their opinions of success.

Serv. I will, my lord.   *Exit.*

Enter Calphurnia.

Cal. What mean you, Cæsar? Think you to walk
    forth?
You shall not stir out of your house to-day.
    Cæs. Cæsar shall forth. The things that threaten'd me
Ne'er look'd but on my back. When they shall see
The face of Cæsar, they are vanished.
    Cal. Cæsar, I never stood on ceremonies,
Yet now they fright me. There is one within,
Besides the things that we have heard and seen,
Recounts most horrid sights seen by the watch.
A lioness hath whelped in the streets,
And graves have yawn'd and yielded up their dead.
Fierce fiery warriors fought upon the clouds
In ranks and squadrons and right form of war,
Which drizzled blood upon the Capitol.
The noise of battle hurtled in the air,
Horses did neigh, and dying men did groan,
And ghosts did shriek and squeal about the streets.
O Cæsar, these things are beyond all use,
And I do fear them!
    Cæs.   What can be avoided
Whose end is purpos'd by the mighty gods?
Yet Cæsar shall go forth; for these predictions
Are to the world in general as to Cæsar.
    Cal. When beggars die there are no comets seen;
The heavens themselves blaze forth the death of princes.
    Cæs. Cowards die many times before their deaths;
The valiant never taste of death but once.
Of all the wonders that I yet have heard,
It seems to me most strange that men should fear,
Seeing that death, a necessary end,
Will come when it will come.

[Enter a SERVANT.]

What say the augurers?

SERV. They would not have you to stir forth to-day.
Plucking the entrails of an offering forth,
They could not find a heart within the beast.

CÆS. The gods do this in shame of cowardice.
Cæsar should be a beast without a heart
If he should stay at home to-day for fear.
No, Cæsar shall not. Danger knows full well
That Cæsar is more dangerous than he.
We are two lions litter'd in one day,
And I the elder and more terrible,
And Cæsar shall go forth.

CAL.   Alas, my lord!
Your wisdom is consum'd in confidence.
Do not go forth to-day. Call it my fear
That keeps you in the house and not your own.
We'll send Mark Antony to the Senate House,
And he shall say you are not well to-day.
Let me upon my knee prevail in this.

CÆS. Mark Antony shall say I am not well,
And for thy humour I will stay at home.

[Enter DECIUS.]

Here's Decius Brutus; he shall tell them so.

DEC. Cæsar, all hail! Good morrow, worthy Cæsar!
I come to fetch you to the Senate House.

CÆS. And you are come in very happy time
To bear my greeting to the senators
And tell them that I will not come to-day.
Cannot, is false; and that I dare not, falser:
I will not come to-day. Tell them so, Decius.

CAL. Say he is sick.

CÆS.   Shall Cæsar send a lie?
Have I in conquest stretch'd mine arm so far

To be afeard to tell greybeards the truth?
Decius, go tell them Cæsar will not come.

DEC. Most mighty Cæsar, let me know some cause,
Lest I be laugh'd at when I tell them so.

CÆS. The cause is in my will: I will not come.
That is enough to satisfy the Senate;
But for your private satisfaction,
Because I love you, I will let you know.
Calphurnia here, my wife, stays me at home.
She dreamt to-night she saw my statuë,
Which, like a fountain with an hundred spouts,
Did run pure blood; and many lusty Romans
Came smiling and did bathe their hands in it.
And these does she apply for warnings and portents
And evils imminent, and on her knee
Hath begg'd that I will stay at home to-day.

DEC. This dream is all amiss interpreted;
It was a vision fair and fortunate.
Your statue spouting blood in many pipes,
In which so many smiling Romans bath'd,
Signifies that from you great Rome shall suck
Reviving blood, and that great men shall press
For tinctures, stains, relics, and cognizance.
This by Calphurnia's dream is signified.

CÆS. And this way have you well expounded it.

DEC. I have, when you have heard what I can say;
And know it now. The Senate have concluded
To give this day a crown to mighty Cæsar.
If you shall send them word you will not come,
Their minds may change. Besides, it were a mock
Apt to be render'd, for some one to say
'Break up the Senate till another time,
When Cæsar's wife shall meet with better dreams.'
If Cæsar hide himself, shall they not whisper
'Lo, Cæsar is afraid'?

Pardon me, Cæsar; for my dear dear love
To your proceeding bids me tell you this,
And reason to my love is liable.

CÆS. How foolish do your fears seem now, Calphurnia!
I am ashamed I did yield to them.
Give me my robe, for I will go.

[*Enter* BRUTUS, LIGARIUS, METELLUS, CASCA,
TREBONIUS, CINNA, *and* PUBLIUS.]

And look where Publius is come to fetch me.

PUB. Good morrow, Cæsar.

CÆS.   Welcome, Publius.
What, Brutus, are you stirr'd so early too?
Good morrow, Casca. Caius Ligarius,
Cæsar was ne'er so much your enemy
As that same ague which hath made you lean.
What is't o'clock?

BRU.   Cæsar, 'tis strucken eight.

CÆS. I thank you for your pains and courtesy.

[*Enter* ANTONY.]

See! Antony, that revels long a-nights,
Is notwithstanding up. Good morrow, Antony.

ANT. So to most noble Cæsar.

CÆS.   Bid them prepare within.
I am to blame to be thus waited for.
Now, Cinna. Now, Metellus. What, Trebonius;
I have an hour's talk in store for you;
Remember that you call on me to-day;
Be near me, that I may remember you.

TREB. Cæsar, I will. [*Aside*] And so near will I be
That your best friends shall wish I had been further.

CÆS. Good friends, go in and taste some wine with me,
And we (like friends) will straightway go together.

BRU. [*aside*] That every like is not the same, O Cæsar,
The heart of Brutus erns to think upon.   *Exeunt.*

Scene III: Rome. A street near the Capitol.

Enter ARTEMIDORUS, *reading a paper.*

ART. 'Cæsar, beware of Brutus; take heed of Cassius; come
not near Casca; have an eye to Cinna; trust not Trebonius;
mark well Metellus Cimber; Decius Brutus loves thee not;
thou hast wrong'd Caius Ligarius. There is but one mind in
all these men, and it is bent against Cæsar. If thou beest not
immortal, look about you. Security gives way to conspiracy.
The mighty gods defend thee!

'Thy lover,
'ARTEMIDORUS.'

Here will I stand till Cæsar pass along
And as a suitor will I give him this.
My heart laments that virtue cannot live
Out of the teeth of emulation.
If thou read this, O Cæsar, thou mayst live;
If not, the Fates with traitors do contrive.   *Exit.*

Scene IV: Before the house of Brutus.

Enter PORTIA *and* LUCIUS.

POR. I prithee, boy, run to the Senate House.
Stay not to answer me, but get thee gone!
Why dost thou stay?
LUC.   To know my errand, madam.
POR. I would have had thee there and here again
Ere I can tell thee what thou shouldst do there.
[*Aside*] O constancy, be strong upon my side,
Set a huge mountain 'tween my heart and tongue!
I have a man's mind, but a woman's might.
How hard it is for women to keep counsel!
Art thou here yet?
LUC.   Madam, what should I do?

Run to the Capitol and nothing else?
And so return to you and nothing else?

Por. Yes, bring me word, boy, if thy lord look well,
For he went sickly forth; and take good note
What Cæsar doth, what suitors press to him.
Hark, boy! What noise is that?

Luc. I hear none, madam.

Por.   Prithee listen well.
I heard a bustling rumour like a fray,
And the wind brings it from the Capitol.

Luc. Sooth, madam, I hear nothing.

Enter the Soothsayer.

Por. Come hither, fellow. Which way hast thou been?

Sooth. At mine own house, good lady.

Por. What is't o'clock?

Sooth.   About the ninth hour, lady.

Por. Is Cæsar yet gone to the Capitol?

Sooth. Madam, not yet. I go to take my stand,
To see him pass on to the Capitol.

Por. Thou hast some suit to Cæsar, hast thou not?

Sooth. That I have, lady, if it will please Cæsar
To be so good to Cæsar as to hear me:
I shall beseech him to befriend himself.

Por. Why, know'st thou any harm's intended towards
    him?

Sooth. None that I know will be, much that I fear
    may chance.
Good morrow to you. Here the street is narrow.
The throng that follows Cæsar at the heels,
Of senators, of prætors, common suitors,
Will crowd a feeble man almost to death.
I'll get me to a place more void and there
Speak to great Cæsar as he comes along.   *Exit.*

Por. I must go in. Ay me, how weak a thing

The heart of woman is! O Brutus,
The heavens speed thee in thine enterprise!
Sure the boy heard me.—Brutus hath a suit
That Cæsar will not grant.—O, I grow faint.—
Run, Lucius, and commend me to my lord;
Say I am merry. Come to me again
And bring me word what he doth say to thee.

Exeunt severally.

Act III: Scene I: Rome. A street before the Capitol.

Flourish. Enter CÆSAR, BRUTUS, CASSIUS, CASCA, DECIUS, METELLUS, TREBONIUS, CINNA, ANTONY, LEPIDUS, ARTEMIDORUS, POPILIUS, PUBLIUS, *and the* SOOTHSAYER.

CÆS. The ides of March are come.

SOOTH. Ay, Cæsar, but not gone.

ART. Hail, Cæsar! Read this schedule.

DEC. Trebonius doth desire you to o'erread
(At your best leisure) this his humble suit.

ART. O Cæsar, read mine first; for mine's a suit
That touches Cæsar nearer. Read it, great Cæsar!

CÆS. What touches us ourself shall be last serv'd.

ART. Delay not, Cæsar! Read it instantly!

CÆS. What, is the fellow mad?

PUB.   Sirrah, give place.

CASS. What, urge you your petitions in the street?
Come to the Capitol.

CÆSAR enters the Capitol, the rest following.

POP. I wish your enterprise to-day may thrive.

CASS. What enterprise, Popilius?

POP.   Fare you well. *Advances to* CÆSAR.

BRU. What said Popilius Lena?

Cass. He wish'd to-day our enterprise might thrive.
I fear our purpose is discovered.

Bru. Look how he makes to Cæsar. Mark him.

Cass. Casca, be sudden, for we fear prevention.
Brutus, what shall be done? If this be known,
Cassius or Cæsar never shall turn back,
For I will slay myself.

Bru.   Cassius, be constant.
Popilius Lena speaks not of our purposes;
For look, he smiles, and Cæsar doth not change.

Cass. Trebonius knows his time; for look you, Brutus,
He draws Mark Antony out of the way.

                    Exeunt Antony *and* Trebonius.

Dec. Where is Metellus Cimber? Let him go
And presently prefer his suit to Cæsar.

Bru. He is address'd. Press near and second him.

Cin. Casca, you are the first that rears your hand.

Cæs. Are we all ready? What is now amiss
That Cæsar and his Senate must redress?

Met. Most high, most mighty, and most puissant
   Cæsar,
Metellus Cimber throws before thy seat
An humble heart.   *Kneels.*

Cæs.   I must prevent thee, Cimber.
These couchings and these lowly courtesies
Might fire the blood of ordinary men
And turn preordinance and first decree
Into the law of children. Be not fond
To think that Cæsar bears such rebel blood
That will be thaw'd from the true quality
With that which melteth fools—I mean, sweet words,
Low-crooked curtsies, and base spaniel fawning.
Thy brother by decree is banished.
If thou dost bend and pray and fawn for him,
I spurn thee like a cur out of my way.

Know, Cæsar doth not wrong, nor without cause
Will he be satisfied.

MET. Is there no voice more worthy than my own,
To sound more sweetly in great Cæsar's ear
For the repealing of my banish'd brother?

BRU. I kiss thy hand, but not in flattery, Cæsar,
Desiring thee that Publius Cimber may
Have an immediate freedom of repeal.

CÆS. What, Brutus?

CASS.   Pardon, Cæsar! Cæsar, pardon!
As low as to thy foot doth Cassius fall
To beg enfranchisement for Publius Cimber.

CÆS. I could be well mov'd, if I were as you;
If I could pray to move, prayers would move me:
But I am constant as the Northern Star,
Of whose true-fix'd and resting quality
There is no fellow in the firmament.
The skies are painted with unnumb'red sparks,
They are all fire, and every one doth shine;
But there's but one in all doth hold his place.
So in the world: 'Tis furnish'd well with men,
And men are flesh and blood, and apprehensive;
Yet in the number I do know but one
That unassailable holds on his rank,
Unshak'd of motion; and that I am he,
Let me a little show it, even in this—
That I was constant Cimber should be banish'd
And constant do remain to keep him so.

CIN. O Cæsar!

CÆS.   Hence! Wilt thou lift up Olympus?

DEC. Great Cæsar!

CÆS.   Doth not Brutus bootless kneel?

CASCA. Speak hands for me!

            They stab CÆSAR—CASCA first, BRUTUS last.

CÆS. Et tu, Brute?—Then fall Cæsar!   *Dies.*

CIN. Liberty! Freedom! Tyranny is dead!
Run hence, proclaim, cry it about the streets!

CASS. Some to the common pulpits and cry out
'Liberty, freedom, and enfranchisement!'

BRU. People and Senators, be not affrighted.
Fly not; stand still. Ambition's debt is paid.

CASCA. Go to the pulpit, Brutus.

DEC.   And Cassius too.

BRU. Where's Publius?

CIN. Here, quite confounded with this mutiny.

MET. Stand fast together, lest some friend of Cæsar's
Should chance—

BRU. Talk not of standing! Publius, good cheer.
There is no harm intended to your person
Nor to no Roman else. So tell them, Publius.

CASS. And leave us, Publius, lest that the people,
Rushing on us, should do your age some mischief.

BRU. Do so; and let no man abide this deed
But we the doers.

Enter TREBONIUS.

CASS.   Where is Antony?

TREB. Fled to his house amaz'd.
Men, wives, and children stare, cry out, and run,
As it were doomsday.

BRU.   Fates, we will know your pleasures.
That we shall die, we know; 'tis but the time,
And drawing days out, that men stand upon.

CASS. Why, he that cuts off twenty years of life
Cuts off so many years of fearing death.

BRU. Grant that, and then is death a benefit.
So are we Cæsar's friends, that have abridg'd
His time of fearing death. Stoop, Romans, stoop,
And let us bathe our hands in Cæsar's blood
Up to the elbows and besmear our swords.

Then walk we forth, even to the market place,
And waving our red weapons o'er our heads,
Let's all cry 'Peace, freedom, and liberty!'

CASS. Stoop then and wash. How many ages hence
Shall this our lofty scene be acted over
In states unborn and accents yet unknown!

BRU. How many times shall Cæsar bleed in sport,
That now on Pompey's basis lies along
No worthier than the dust!

CASS.   So oft as that shall be,
So often shall the knot of us be call'd
Then men that gave their country liberty.

DEC. What, shall we forth?

CASS.   Ay, every man away.
Brutus shall lead, and we will grace his heels
With the most boldest and best hearts of Rome.

Enter a SERVANT.

BRU. Soft, who comes here? A friend of Antony's.

SERV. Thus, Brutus, did my master bid me kneel;
Thus did Mark Antony bid me fall down;
And being prostrate, thus he bade me say:
Brutus is noble, wise, valiant, and honest;
Cæsar was mighty, bold, royal, and loving.
Say I love Brutus and I honour him;
Say I fear'd Cæsar, honour'd him, and lov'd him.
If Brutus will vouchsafe that Antony
May safely come to him and be resolv'd
How Cæsar hath deserv'd to lie in death,
Mark Antony shall not love Cæsar dead
So well as Brutus living; but will follow
The fortunes and affairs of noble Brutus
Thorough the hazards of this untrod state
With all true faith. So says my master Antony.

Bru. Thy master is a wise and valiant Roman.
I never thought him worse.
Tell him, so please him come unto this place,
He shall be satisfied and, by my honour,
Depart untouch'd.

    Serv.   I'll fetch him presently.   *Exit.*

    Bru. I know that we shall have him well to friend.

    Cass. I wish we may. But yet have I a mind
That fears him much; and my misgiving still
Falls shrewdly to the purpose.

Enter Antony.

    Bru. But here comes Antony. Welcome, Mark Antony.

    Ant. O mighty Cæsar! dost thou lie so low?
Are all thy conquests, glories, triumphs, spoils,
Shrunk to this little measure? Fare thee well.
I know not, gentlemen, what you intend,
Who else must be let blood, who else is rank.
If I myself, there is no hour so fit
As Cæsar's death's hour; nor no instrument
Of half that worth as those your swords, made rich
With the most noble blood of all this world.
I do beseech ye, if you bear me hard,
Now, whilst your purpled hands do reek and smoke,
Fulfil your pleasure. Live a thousand years,
I shall not find myself so apt to die;
No place will please me so, no mean of death,
As here by Cæsar, and by you cut off,
The choice and master spirits of this age.

    Bru. O Antony, beg not your death of us!
Though now we must appear bloody and cruel,
As by our hands and this our present act
You see we do, yet see you but our hands
And this the bleeding business they have done.
Our hearts you see not. They are pitiful;

And pity to the general wrong of Rome
(As fire drives out fire, so pity pity)
Hath done this deed on Cæsar. For your part,
To you our swords have leaden points, Mark Antony.
Our arms in strength of malice, and our hearts
Of brothers' temper, do receive you in
With all kind love, good thoughts, and reverence.

CASS. Your voice shall be as strong as any man's
In the disposing of new dignities.

BRU. Only be patient till we have appeas'd
The multitude, beside themselves with fear,
And then we will deliver you the cause
Why I, that did love Cæsar when I struck him,
Have thus proceeded.

ANT.   I doubt not of your wisdom.
Let each man render me his bloody hand.
First, Marcus Brutus, will I shake with you;
Next, Caius Cassius, do I take your hand;
Now, Decius Brutus, yours; now yours, Metellus;
Yours, Cinna; and, my valiant Casca, yours.
Though last, not least in love, yours, good Trebonius.
Gentlemen all—Alas, what shall I say?
My credit now stands on such slippery ground
That one of two bad ways you must conceit me,
Either a coward or a flatterer.
That I did love thee, Cæsar, O, 'tis true!
If then thy spirit look upon us now,
Shall it not grieve thee dearer than thy death
To see thy Antony making his peace,
Shaking the bloody fingers of thy foes,
Most noble! in the presence of thy corse?
Had I as many eyes as thou hast wounds,
Weeping as fast as they stream forth thy blood,
It would become me better than to close
In terms of friendship with thine enemies.

Pardon me, Julius! Here wast thou bay'd, brave hart;
Here didst thou fall; and here thy hunters stand,
Sign'd in thy spoil, and crimson'd in thy lethe.
O world, thou wast the forest to this hart;
And this indeed, O world, the heart of thee!
How like a deer, stroken by many princes,
Dost thou here lie!

CASS. Mark Antony—

ANT.   Pardon me, Caius Cassius.
The enemies of Cæsar shall say this;
Then, in a friend, it is cold modesty.

CASS. I blame you not for praising Cæsar so;
But what compact mean you to have with us?
Will you be prick'd in number of our friends,
Or shall we on, and not depend on you?

ANT. Therefore I took your hands; but was indeed
Sway'd from the point by looking down on Cæsar.
Friends am I with you all, and love you all,
Upon this hope, that you shall give me reasons
Why and wherein Cæsar was dangerous.

BRU. Or else were this a savage spectacle.
Our reasons are so full of good regard
That were you, Antony, the son of Cæsar,
You should be satisfied.

ANT.   That's all I seek;
And am moreover suitor that I may
Produce his body to the market place
And in the pulpit, as becomes a friend,
Speak in the order of his funeral.

BRU. You shall, Mark Antony.

CASS.   Brutus, a word with you.
[*Aside to* BRUTUS] You know not what you do. Do not
     consent
That Antony speak in his funeral.

Know you how much the people may be mov'd
By that which he will utter?

BRU.   [*aside to* CASSIUS] By your pardon—
I will myself into the pulpit first
And show the reason of our Cæsar's death.
What Antony shall speak, I will protest
He speaks by leave and by permission;
And that we are contented Cæsar shall
Have all true rites and lawful ceremonies.
It shall advantage more than do us wrong.

    CASS. [*aside to* BRUTUS] I know not what may fall. I
    like it not.

    BRU. Mark Antony, here, take you Cæsar's body.
You shall not in your funeral speech blame us,
But speak all good you can devise of Cæsar;
And say you do't by our permission.
Else shall you not have any hand at all
About his funeral. And you shall speak
In the same pulpit whereto I am going,
After my speech is ended.

    ANT.   Be it so.
I do desire no more.

    BRU. Prepare the body then, and follow us.

                    Exeunt, leaving ANTONY.

    ANT. O, pardon me, thou bleeding piece of earth,
That I am meek and gentle with these butchers!
Thou art the ruins of the noblest man
That ever lived in the tide of times.
Woe to the hand that shed this costly blood!
Over thy wounds now do I prophesy
(Which, like dumb mouths, do ope their ruby lips
To beg the voice and utterance of my tongue),
A curse shall light upon the limbs of men;
Domestic fury and fierce civil strife

Shall cumber all the parts of Italy;
Blood and destruction shall be so in use
And dreadful objects so familiar
That mothers shall but smile when they behold
Their infants quartered with the hands of war,
All pity chok'd with custom of fell deeds;
And Cæsar's spirit, ranging for revenge,
With Ate by his side come hot from hell,
Shall in thèse confines with a monarch's voice
Cry 'Havoc!' and let slip the dogs of war,
That this foul deed shall smell above the earth
With carrion men, groaning for burial.

[*Enter* OCTAVIUS' SERVANT.]

You serve Octavius Cæsar, do you not?
    SERV. I do, Mark Antony.
    ANT. Cæsar did write for him to come to Rome.
    SERV. He did receive his letters and is coming,
And bid me say to you by word of mouth—
O Cæsar!
    ANT. Thy heart is big. Get thee apart and weep.
Passion, I see, is catching; for mine eyes,
Seeing those beads of sorrow stand in thine,
Began to water. Is thy master coming?
    SERV. He lies to-night within seven leagues of Rome.
    ANT. Post back with speed and tell him what hath
      chanc'd.
Here is a mourning Rome, a dangerous Rome,
No Rome of safety for Octavius yet.
Hie hence and tell him so. Yet stay awhile.
Thou shalt not back till I have borne this corse
Into the market place. There shall I try
In my oration how the people take
The cruel issue of these bloody men;
According to the which thou shalt discourse

To young Octavius of the state of things.
Lend me your hand.   *Exeunt with* CÆSAR'S *body*.

Scene II: Rome. The Forum.

Enter BRUTUS *and* CASSIUS, *with the* PLEBEIANS.

PLEBEIANS. We will be satisfied! Let us be satisfied!
BRU. Then follow me and give me audience, friends.
Cassius, go you into the other street
And part the numbers.
Those that will hear me speak, let 'em stay here;
Those that will follow Cassius, go with him;
And public reasons shall be rendered
Of Cæsar's death.
1. PLEB.   I will hear Brutus speak.
2. PLEB. I will hear Cassius, and compare their reasons
When severally we hear them rendered.
          Exit CASSIUS, *with some of the* PLEBEIANS.
                    BRUTUS *goes into the pulpit*.
3. PLEB. The noble Brutus is ascended. Silence!
BRU. Be patient till the last.
Romans, countrymen, and lovers, hear me for my cause,
and be silent, that you may hear. Believe me for mine
honour, and have respect to mine honour, that you may
believe. Censure me in your wisdom, and awake your
senses, that you may the better judge. If there be any in
this assembly, any dear friend of Cæsar's, to him I say
that Brutus' love to Cæsar was no less than his. If then
that friend demand why Brutus rose against Cæsar, this
is my answer: Not that I lov'd Cæsar less, but that I
lov'd Rome more. Had you rather Cæsar were living,
and die all slaves, than that Cæsar were dead, to live all
freemen? As Cæsar lov'd me, I weep for him; as he was
fortunate, I rejoice at it; as he was valiant, I honour

him; but—as he was ambitious, I slew him. There is tears
for his love; joy for his fortune; honour for his valour;
and death for his ambition. Who is here so base that
would be a bondman? If any, speak; for him have I
offended. Who is here so rude that would not be a
Roman? If any, speak; for him have I offended. Who is
here so vile that will not love his country? If any, speak;
for him have I offended. I pause for a reply.

ALL. None, Brutus, none!

BRU. Then none have I offended. I have done no more
to Cæsar than you shall do to Brutus. The question of his
death is enroll'd in the Capitol; his glory not extenuated,
wherein he was worthy; nor his offences enforc'd, for
which he suffered death.

[*Enter* MARK ANTONY *and others, with* CÆSAR'S *body.*]

Here comes his body, mourn'd by Mark Antony, who,
though he had no hand in his death, shall receive the
benefit of his dying, a place in the commonwealth, as
which of you shall not? With this I depart, that, as I slew
my best lover for the good of Rome, I have the same dagger for myself when it shall please my country to need
my death.

ALL. Live, Brutus! live, live!

1. PLEB. Bring him with triumph home unto his house.

2. PLEB. Give him a statue with his ancestors.

3. PLEB. Let him be Cæsar.

4. PLEB.   Cæsar's better parts
Shall be crown'd in Brutus.

1. PLEB. We'll bring him to his house with shouts and
clamours.

BRU. My countrymen—

2. PLEB.   Peace! silence! Brutus speaks.

1. PLEB. Peace, ho!

BRU. Good countrymen, let me depart alone,
And, for my sake, stay here with Antony.
Do grace to Cæsar's corpse, and grace his speech
Tending to Cæsar's glories which Mark Antony,
By our permission, is allow'd to make.
I do entreat you, not a man depart,
Save I alone, till Antony have spoke.   *Exit.*

1. PLEB. Stay, ho! and let us hear Mark Antony.

3. PLEB. Let him go up into the public chair.
We'll hear him. Noble Antony, go up.

ANT. For Brutus' sake I am beholding to you.

           Goes up.

4. PLEB. What does he say of Brutus?

3. PLEB.   He says for Brutus' sake
He finds himself beholding to us all.

4. PLEB. 'Twere best he speak no harm of Brutus here!

1. PLEB. This Cæsar was a tyrant.

3. PLEB.   Nay, that's certain.
We are blest that Rome is rid of him.

2. PLEB. Peace! Let us hear what Antony can say.

ANT. You gentle Romans—

ALL.   Peace, ho! Let us hear him.

ANT. Friends, Romans, countrymen, lend me your
     ears;
I come to bury Cæsar, not to praise him.
The evil that men do lives after them;
The good is oft interred with their bones.
So let it be with Cæsar. The noble Brutus
Hath told you Cæsar was ambitious.
If it were so, it was a grievous fault,
And grievously hath Cæsar answer'd it.
Here, under leave of Brutus and the rest
(For Brutus is an honourable man;
So are they all, all honourable men),
Come I to speak in Cæsar's funeral.

He was my friend, faithful and just to me;
But Brutus says he was ambitious,
And Brutus is an honourable man.
He hath brought many captives home to Rome,
Whose ransoms did the general coffers fill.
Did this in Cæsar seem ambitious?
When that the poor have cried, Cæsar hath wept;
Ambition should be made of sterner stuff.
Yet Brutus says he was ambitious;
And Brutus is an honourable man.
You all did see that on the Lupercal
I thrice presented him a kingly crown,
Which he did thrice refuse. Was this ambition?
Yet Brutus says he was ambitious;
And sure he is an honourable man.
I speak not to disprove what Brutus spoke,
But here I am to speak what I do know.
You all did love him once, not without cause.
What cause withholds you then to mourn for him?
O judgment, thou art fled to brutish beasts,
And men have lost their reason! Bear with me.
My heart is in the coffin there with Cæsar,
And I must pause till it come back to me.

   1. PLEB. Methinks there is much reason in his sayings.
   2. PLEB. If thou consider rightly of the matter,
Cæsar has had great wrong.
   3. PLEB.   Has he not, masters?
I fear there will a worse come in his place.
   4. PLEB. Mark'd ye his words? He would not take the
     crown;
Therefore 'tis certain he was not ambitious.
   1. PLEB. If it be found so, some will dear abide it.
   2. PLEB. Poor soul! his eyes are red as fire with weep-
     ing.

3. PLEB. There's not a nobler man in Rome than
Antony.

4. PLEB. Now mark him. He begins again to speak.

ANT. But yesterday the word of Cæsar might
Have stood against the world. Now lies he there,
And none so poor to do him reverence.
O masters! If I were dispos'd to stir
Your hearts and minds to mutiny and rage,
I should do Brutus wrong, and Cassius wrong,
Who, you all know, are honourable men.
I will not do them wrong. I rather choose
To wrong the dead, to wrong myself and you,
Than I will wrong such honourable men.
But here's a parchment with the seal of Cæsar.
I found it in his closet; 'tis his will.
Let but the commons hear this testament,
Which (pardon me) I do not mean to read,
And they would go and kiss dead Cæsar's wounds
And dip their napkins in his sacred blood;
Yea, beg a hair of him for memory,
And dying, mention it within their wills,
Bequeathing it as a rich legacy
Unto their issue.

4. PLEB. We'll hear the will! Read it, Mark Antony.

ALL. The will, the will! We will hear Cæsar's will!

ANT. Have patience, gentle friends; I must not read it.
It is not meet you know how Cæsar lov'd you.
You are not wood, you are not stones, but men;
And being men, hearing the will of Cæsar,
It will inflame you, it will make you mad.
'Tis good you know not that you are his heirs;
For if you should, O, what would come of it?

4. PLEB. Read the will! We'll hear it, Antony!
You shall read us the will, Cæsar's will!

Ant. Will you be patient? Will you stay awhile?
I have o'ershot myself to tell you of it.
I fear I wrong the honourable men
Whose daggers have stabb'd Cæsar; I do fear it.

4. Pleb. They were traitors. Honourable men!

All. The will! the testament!

2. Pleb. They were villains, murderers! The will! Read
the will!

Ant. You will compel me then to read the will?
Then make a ring about the corpse of Cæsar
And let me show you him that made the will.
Shall I descend? and will you give me leave?

All. Come down.

2. Pleb. Descend.

3. Pleb. You shall have leave.   Antony *comes down.*

4. Pleb. A ring! Stand round.

1. Pleb. Stand from the hearse! Stand from the body!

2. Pleb. Room for Antony, most noble Antony!

Ant. Nay, press not so upon me. Stand far off.

All. Stand back! Room! Bear back!

Ant. If you have tears, prepare to shed them now.
You all do know this mantle. I remember
The first time ever Cæsar put it on.
'Twas on a summer's evening in his tent,
That day he overcame the Nervii.
Look, in this place ran Cassius' dagger through.
See what a rent the envious Casca made.
Through this the well-beloved Brutus stabb'd;
And as he pluck'd his cursed steel away,
Mark how the blood of Cæsar followed it,
As rushing out of doors to be resolv'd
If Brutus so unkindly knock'd or no;
For Brutus, as you know, was Cæsar's angel.
Judge, O you gods, how dearly Cæsar lov'd him!
This was the most unkindest cut of all;

For when the noble Cæsar saw him stab,
Ingratitude, more strong than traitors' arms,
Quite vanquish'd him. Then burst his mighty heart;
And in his mantle muffling up his face,
Even at the base of Pompey's statuë
(Which all the while ran blood) great Cæsar fell.
O, what a fall was there, my countrymen!
Then I, and you, and all of us fell down,
Whilst bloody treason flourish'd over us.
O, now you weep, and I perceive you feel
The dint of pity. These are gracious drops.
Kind souls, what weep you when you but behold
Our Cæsar's vesture wounded? Look you here!
Here is himself, marr'd as you see with traitors.

1. PLEB. O piteous spectacle!

2. PLEB. O noble Cæsar!

3. PLEB. O woeful day!

4. PLEB. O traitors, villains!

1. PLEB. O most bloody sight!

2. PLEB. We will be reveng'd.

ALL. Revenge! About! Seek! Burn! Fire! Kill! Slay! Let
not a traitor live!

ANT. Stay, countrymen.

1. PLEB. Peace there! Hear the noble Antony.

2. PLEB. We'll hear him, we'll follow him, we'll die
with him!

ANT. Good friends, sweet friends, let me not stir you
up
To such a sudden flood of mutiny.
They that have done this deed are honourable.
What private griefs they have, alas, I know not,
That made them do it. They are wise and honourable,
And will no doubt with reasons answer you.
I come not, friends, to steal away your hearts.
I am no orator, as Brutus is,

But (as you know me all) a plain blunt man
That love my friend; and that they know full well
That gave me public leave to speak of him.
For I have neither wit, nor words, nor worth,
Action, nor utterance, nor the power of speech
To stir men's blood. I only speak right on.
I tell you that which you yourselves do know,
Show you sweet Cæsar's wounds, poor poor dumb
    mouths,
And bid them speak for me. But were I Brutus,
And Brutus Antony, there were an Antony
Would ruffle up your spirits, and put a tongue
In every wound of Cæsar that should move
The stones of Rome to rise and mutiny.
    ALL. We'll mutiny.
    1. PLEB.   We'll burn the house of Brutus.
    3. PLEB. Away then! Come, seek the conspirators.
    ANT. Yet hear me, countrymen. Yet hear me speak.
    ALL. Peace, ho! Hear Antony, most noble Antony!
    ANT. Why, friends, you go to do you know not what.
Wherein hath Cæsar thus deserv'd your loves?
Alas, you know not! I must tell you then.
You have forgot the will I told you of.
    ALL. Most true! The will! Let's stay and hear the will.
    ANT. Here is the will, and under Cæsar's seal.
To every Roman citizen he gives,
To every several man, seventy-five drachmas.
    2. PLEB. Most noble Cæsar! We'll revenge his death!
    3. PLEB. O royal Cæsar!
    ANT. Hear me with patience.
    ALL. Peace, ho!
    ANT. Moreover, he hath left you all his walks,
His private arbours, and new-planted orchards,
On this side Tiber; he hath left them you,
And to your heirs for ever—common pleasures,

To walk abroad and recreate yourselves.
Here was a Cæsar! When comes such another?

1. PLEB. Never, never! Come, away, away!
We'll burn his body in the holy place
And with the brands fire the traitors' houses.
Take up the body.

2. PLEB. Go fetch fire!

3. PLEB. Pluck down benches!

4. PLEB. Pluck down forms, windows, anything!
                    Exeunt PLEBEIANS *with the body.*

ANT. Now let it work. Mischief, thou art afoot,
Take thou what course thou wilt.

[*Enter* SERVANT.]

                                        How now, fellow?

SERV. Sir, Octavius is already come to Rome.

ANT. Where is he?

SERV. He and Lepidus are at Cæsar's house.

ANT. And thither will I straight to visit him.
He comes upon a wish. Fortune is merry,
And in this mood will give us anything.

SERV. I heard him say Brutus and Cassius
Are rid like madmen through the gates of Rome.

ANT. Belike they had some notice of the people
How I had mov'd them. Bring me to Octavius.   *Exeunt.*

Scene III: Rome. A street.

Enter CINNA THE POET, *and after him the* PLEBEIANS.

CIN. I dreamt to-night that I did feast with Cæsar,
And things unluckily charge my fantasy.
I have no will to wander forth of doors,
Yet something leads me forth.

1. Pleb. What is your name?

2. Pleb. Whither are you going?

3. Pleb. Where do you dwell?

4. Pleb. Are you a married man or a bachelor?

2. Pleb. Answer every man directly.

1. Pleb. Ay, and briefly.

4. Pleb. Ay, and wisely.

3. Pleb. Ay, and truly, you were best.

Cin. What is my name? Whither am I going? Where do I dwell? Am I a married man or a bachelor? Then, to answer every man directly and briefly, wisely and truly: wisely I say, I am a bachelor.

2. Pleb. That's as much as to say they are fools that marry. You'll bear me a bang for that, I fear. Proceed—directly.

Cin. Directly I am going to Cæsar's funeral.

1. Pleb. As a friend or an enemy?

Cin. As a friend.

2. Pleb. That matter is answered directly.

4. Pleb. For your dwelling—briefly.

Cin. Briefly, I dwell by the Capitol.

3. Pleb. Your name, sir, truly.

Cin. Truly, my name is Cinna.

1. Pleb. Tear him to pieces! He's a conspirator.

Cin. I am Cinna the poet! I am Cinna the poet!

4. Pleb. Tear him for his bad verses! Tear him for his bad verses!

Cin. I am not Cinna the conspirator.

4. Pleb. It is no matter; his name's Cinna! Pluck but his name out of his heart, and turn him going.

3. Pleb. Tear him, tear him! Come, brands, ho! fire-brands! To Brutus', to Cassius'! Burn all! Some to Decius' house and some to Casca's; some to Ligarius'! Away, go!

Exeunt all the Plebeians *with* Cinna.

Act IV: Scene I: Rome. Antony's house.

Enter ANTONY, OCTAVIUS, *and* LEPIDUS.

ANT. These many, then, shall die; their names are
    prick'd.

OCT. Your brother too must die. Consent you, Lepi-
    dus?

LEP. I do consent—

OCT.   Prick him down, Antony.

LEP. Upon condition Publius shall not live,
Who is your sister's son, Mark Antony.

ANT. He shall not live. Look, with a spot I damn him.
But, Lepidus, go you to Cæsar's house.
Fetch the will hither, and we shall determine
How to cut off some charge in legacies.

LEP. What? shall I find you here?

OCT. Or here or at the Capitol.   *Exit* LEPIDUS.

ANT. This is a slight unmeritable man,
Meet to be sent on errands. Is it fit,
The threefold world divided, he should stand
One of the three to share it?

OCT.   So you thought him,
And took his voice who should be prick'd to die
In our black sentence and proscription.

ANT. Octavius, I have seen more days than you;
And though we lay these honours on this man
To ease ourselves of divers sland'rous loads,
He shall but bear them as the ass bears gold,
To groan and sweat under the business,
Either led or driven as we point the way;
And having brought our treasure where we will,
Then take we down his load, and turn him off
(Like to the empty ass) to shake his ears
And graze in commons.

Oct.   You may do your will;
But he's a tried and valiant soldier.

Ant. So is my horse, Octavius, and for that
I do appoint him store of provender.
It is a creature that I teach to fight,
To wind, to stop, to run directly on,
His corporal motion govern'd by my spirit.
And, in some taste, is Lepidus but so.
He must be taught, and train'd, and bid go forth:
A barren-spirited fellow; one that feeds
On objects, arts, and imitations
Which, out of use and stal'd by other men
Begin his fashion. Do not talk of him,
But as a property. And now, Octavius,
Listen great things. Brutus and Cassius
Are levying powers. We must straight make head.
Therefore let our alliance be combin'd,
Our best friends made, and our best means stretch'd out;
And let us presently go sit in council
How covert matters may be best disclos'd
And open perils surest answered.

Oct. Let us do so; for we are at the stake
And bay'd about with many enemies;
And some that smile have in their hearts, I fear,
Millions of mischiefs.   *Exeunt.*

Scene II: The camp near Sardis. Before the tent
of Brutus.

Drum. Enter Brutus, Lucilius, Lucius, *and the* Army.
Titinius *and* Pindarus *meet them.*

Bru. Stand ho!
Lucil. Give the word, ho! and stand!
Bru. What now, Lucilius? Is Cassius near?

LUCIL. He is at hand, and Pindarus is come
To do you salutation from his master.

BRU. He greets me well. Your master, Pindarus,
In his own change, or by ill officers,
Hath given me some worthy cause to wish
Things done undone; but if he be at hand,
I shall be satisfied.

PIN.   I do not doubt
But that my noble master will appear
Such as he is, full of regard and honour.

BRU. He is not doubted. A word, Lucilius,
How he receiv'd you. Let me be resolv'd.

LUCIL. With courtesy and with respect enough,
But not with such familiar instances
Nor with such free and friendly conference
As he hath us'd of old.

BRU.   Thou hast describ'd
A hot friend cooling. Ever note, Lucilius,
When love begins to sicken and decay
It useth an enforced ceremony.
There are no tricks in plain and simple faith;
But hollow men, like horses hot at hand,
Make gallant show and promise of their mettle;

                    [*Low march within.*]
But when they should endure the bloody spur,
They fall their crests, and like deceitful jades
Sink in the trial. Comes his army on?

LUCIL. They mean this night in Sardis to be quarter'd.
The greater part, the horse in general,
Are come with Cassius.

BRU.   Hark! He is arriv'd.
March gently on to meet him.

Enter CASSIUS *and his* POWERS.

CASS. Stand, ho!

BRU. Stand, ho! Speak the word along.

1. SOLD. Stand!

2. SOLD. Stand!

3. SOLD. Stand!

CASS. Most noble brother, you have done me wrong.

BRU. Judge me, you gods! wrong I mine enemies?
And if not so, how should I wrong a brother?

CASS. Brutus, this sober form of yours hides wrongs;
And when you do them—

BRU.   Cassius, be content.
Speak your griefs softly. I do know you well.
Before the eyes of both our armies here
(Which should perceive nothing but love from us)
Let us not wrangle. Bid them move away.
Then in my tent, Cassius, enlarge your griefs,
And I will give you audience.

CASS.   Pindarus,
Bid our commanders lead their charges off
A little from this ground.

BRU. Lucilius, do you the like; and let no man
Come to our tent till we have done our conference.
Let Lucius and Titinius guard our door.   *Exeunt.*

Scene III: The camp near Sardis. Within the tent
of Brutus.

Enter BRUTUS *and* CASSIUS.

CASS. That you have wrong'd me doth appear in this:
You have condemn'd and noted Lucius Pella
For taking bribes here of the Sardians;
Wherein my letters, praying on his side,
Because I knew the man, were slighted off.

BRU. You wrong'd yourself to write in such a case.

Cass. In such a time as this it is not meet
That every nice offence should bear his comment.

Bru. Let me tell you, Cassius, you yourself
Are much condemn'd to have an itching palm,
To sell and mart your offices for gold
To undeservers.

Cass.   I an itching palm?
You know that you are Brutus that speaks this,
Or, by the gods, this speech were else your last!

Bru. The name of Cassius honours this corruption,
And chastisement doth therefore hide his head.

Cass. Chastisement?

Bru. Remember March; the ides of March remember.
Did not great Julius bleed for justice sake?
What villain touch'd his body that did stab
And not for justice? What, shall one of us,
That struck the foremost man of all this world
But for supporting robbers—shall we now
Contaminate our fingers with base bribes,
And sell the mighty space of our large honours
For so much trash as may be grasped thus?
I had rather be a dog and bay the moon
Than such a Roman.

Cass.   Brutus, bait not me!
I'll not endure it. You forget yourself
To hedge me in. I am a soldier, I,
Older in practice, abler than yourself
To make conditions.

Bru.   Go to! You are not, Cassius.

Cass. I am.

Bru. I say you are not.

Cass. Urge me no more! I shall forget myself.
Have mind upon your health. Tempt me no farther.

Bru. Away, slight man!

Cass. Is't possible?

Bru. Hear me, for I will speak.
Must I give way and room to your rash choler?
Shall I be frighted when a madman stares?

Cass. O ye gods, ye gods! Must I endure all this?

Bru. All this? Ay, more! Fret till your proud heart break.
Go show your slaves how choleric you are
And make your bondmen tremble. Must I budge?
Must I observe you? Must I stand and crouch
Under your testy humour? By the gods,
You shall digest the venom of your spleen,
Though it do split you; for from this day forth
I'll use you for my mirth, yea, for my laughter,
When you are waspish.

Cass. Is it come to this?

Bru. You say you are a better soldier.
Let it appear so; make your vaunting true,
And it shall please me well. For mine own part,
I shall be glad to learn of noble men.

Cass. You wrong me every way! You wrong me, Brutus!
I said an elder soldier, not a better.
Did I say 'better'?

Bru. If you did, I care not.

Cass. When Cæsar liv'd he durst not thus have mov'd me.

Bru. Peace, peace! You durst not so have tempted him.

Cass. I durst not?

Bru. No.

Cass. What, durst not tempt him?

Bru. For your life you durst not.

Cass. Do not presume too much upon my love.
I may do that I shall be sorry for.

Bru. You have done that you should be sorry for.
There is no terror, Cassius, in your threats;

For I am arm'd so strong in honesty
That they pass by me as the idle wind,
Which I respect not. I did send to you
For certain sums of gold, which you denied me;
For I can raise no money by vile means.
By heaven, I had rather coin my heart
And drop my blood for drachmas than to wring
From the hard hands of peasants their vile trash
By any indirection. I did send
To you for gold to pay my legions,
Which you denied me. Was that done like Cassius?
Should I have answer'd Caius Cassius so?
When Marcus Brutus grows so covetous
To lock such rascal counters from his friends,
Be ready, gods, with all your thunderbolts
Dash him to pieces!

    Cass.   I denied you not.

    Bru. You did.

    Cass. I did not. He was but a fool that brought
My answer back. Brutus hath riv'd my heart.
A friend should bear his friend's infirmities,
But Brutus makes mine greater than they are.

    Bru. I do not, till you practise them on me.

    Cass. You love me not.

    Bru.   I do not like your faults.

    Cass. A friendly eye could never see such faults.

    Bru. A flatterer's would not, though they do appear
As huge as high Olympus.

    Cass. Come, Antony, and young Octavius, come!
Revenge yourselves alone on Cassius.
For Cassius is aweary of the world:
Hated by one he loves; brav'd by his brother;
Check'd like a bondman; all his faults observ'd,
Set in a notebook, learn'd and conn'd by rote
To cast into my teeth. O, I could weep

My spirit from mine eyes! There is my dagger,
And here my naked breast; within, a heart
Dearer than Pluto's mine, richer than gold.
If that thou be'st a Roman, take it forth.
I, that denied thee gold, will give my heart.
Strike as thou didst at Cæsar; for I know,
When thou didst hate him worst, thou lov'dst him better
Than ever thou lov'dst Cassius.

BRU.   Sheathe your dagger.
Be angry when you will; it shall have scope.
Do what you will; dishonour shall be humour.
O Cassius, you are yoked with a lamb
That carries anger as the flint bears fire;
Who, much enforced, shows a hasty spark,
And straight is cold again.

CASS.   Hath Cassius liv'd
To be but mirth and laughter to his Brutus
When grief and blood ill-temper'd vexeth him?

BRU. When I spoke that, I was ill-temper'd too.

CASS. Do you confess so much? Give me your hand.

BRU. And my heart too.

CASS.   O Brutus!

BRU.   What's the matter?

CASS. Have not you love enough to bear with me
When that rash humour which my mother gave me
Makes me forgetful?

BRU.   Yes, Cassius; and from henceforth,
When you are over-earnest with your Brutus,
He'll think your mother chides, and leave you so.

Enter a POET *followed by* LUCILIUS,
TITINIUS, *and* LUCIUS.

POET. Let me go in to see the generals!
There is some grudge between 'em. 'Tis not meet
They be alone.

LUCIL. You shall not come to them.

POET. Nothing but death shall stay me.

CASS. How now? What's the matter?

POET. For shame, you generals! What do you mean?
Love and be friends, as two such men should be;
For I have seen more years, I'm sure, than ye.

CASS. Ha, ha! How vilely doth this cynic rhyme!

BRU. Get you hence, sirrah! Saucy fellow, hence!

CASS. Bear with him, Brutus. 'Tis his fashion.

BRU. I'll know his humour when he knows his time.
What should the wars do with these jigging fools?
Companion, hence!

CASS.   Away, away, be gone!   *Exit* POET.

BRU. Lucilius and Titinius, bid the commanders
Prepare to lodge their companies to-night.

CASS. And come yourselves, and bring Messala with
you
Immediately to us.   *Exeunt* LUCILIUS *and* TITINIUS.

BRU.   Lucius, a bowl of wine.

                             Exit LUCIUS.

CASS. I did not think you could have been so angry.

BRU. O Cassius, I am sick of many griefs.

CASS. Of your philosophy you make no use
If you give place to accidental evils.

BRU. No man bears sorrow better. Portia is dead.

CASS. Ha! Portia?

BRU. She is dead.

CASS. How scap'd I killing when I cross'd you so?
O insupportable and touching loss!
Upon what sickness?

BRU.   Impatient of my absence,
And grief that young Octavius with Mark Antony
Have made themselves so strong; for with her death
That tidings came. With this she fell distract,
And (her attendants absent) swallow'd fire.

Cass. And died so?

Bru.   Even so.

Cass.   .   O ye immortal gods!

Enter Boy Lucius, *with wine and tapers.*

Bru. Speak no more of her. Give me a bowl of wine.
In this I bury all unkindness, Cassius.   *Drinks.*

Cass. My heart is thirsty for that noble pledge.
Fill, Lucius, till the wine o'erswell the cup.
I cannot drink too much of Brutus' love.

                        Drinks. Exit Lucius.

Enter Titinius *and* Messala.

Bru. Come in, Titinius! Welcome, good Messala.
Now sit we close about this taper here
And call in question our necessities.

Cass. Portia, art thou gone?

Bru.   No more, I pray you.
Messala, I have here received letters
That young Octavius and Mark Antony
Come down upon us with a mighty power,
Bending their expedition toward Philippi.

Mes. Myself have letters of the selfsame tenure.

Bru. With what addition?

Mes. That by proscription and bills of outlawry
Octavius, Antony, and Lepidus
Have put to death an hundred senators.

Bru. Therein our letters do not well agree.
Mine speak of seventy senators that died
By their proscriptions, Cicero being one.

Cass. Cicero one?

Mes.   Cicero is dead,
And by that order of proscription.
Had you your letters from your wife, my lord?

Bru. No, Messala.

Mes. Nor nothing in your letters writ of her?

Bru. Nothing, Messala.

Mes.   That methinks is strange.

Bru. Why ask you? Hear you·aught of her in yours?

Mes. No, my lord.

Bru. Now as you are a Roman, tell me true.

Mes. Then like a Roman bear the truth I tell;
For certain she is dead, and by strange manner.

Bru. Why, farewell, Portia. We must die, Messala.
With meditating that she must die once,
I have the patience to endure it now.

Mes. Even so great men great losses should endure.

Cass. I have as much of this in art as you,
But yet my nature could not bear it so.

Bru. Well, to our work alive. What do you think
Of marching to Philippi presently?

Cass. I do not think it good.

Bru.   Your reason?

Cass.   This it is:
'Tis better that the enemy seek us.
So shall he waste his means, weary his soldiers,
Doing himself offence, whilst we, lying still,
Are full of rest, defence, and nimbleness.

Bru. Good reasons must of force give place to better.
The people 'twixt Philippi and this ground
Do stand but in a forc'd affection;
For they have grudg'd us contribution.
The enemy, marching along by them,
By them shall make a fuller number up,
Come on refresh'd, new-added, and encourag'd;
From which advantage shall we cut him off
If at Philippi we do face him there,
These people at our back.

Cass.   Hear me, good brother.

Bru. Under your pardon. You must note beside
That we have tried the utmost of our friends,

Our legions are brimful, our cause is ripe.
The enemy increaseth every day;
We, at the height, are ready to decline.
There is a tide in the affairs of men
Which, taken at the flood, leads on to fortune;
Omitted, all the voyage of their life
Is bound in shallows and in miseries.
On such a full sea are we now afloat,
And we must take the current when it serves
Or lose our ventures.

CASS.   Then, with your will, go on.
We'll along ourselves and meet them at Philippi.

BRU. The deep of night is crept upon our talk
And nature must obey necessity,
Which we will niggard with a little rest.
There is no more to say?

CASS.   No more. Good night.
Early to-morrow will we rise and hence.

BRU. Lucius! [*Enter* LUCIUS.] My gown. [*Exit* LUCIUS.]
      Farewell, good Messala.
Good night, Titinius. Noble, noble Cassius,
Good night and good repose!

CASS.   O my dear brother,
This was an ill beginning of the night!
Never come such division 'tween our souls!
Let it not, Brutus.

Enter LUCIUS, *with the gown.*

BRU.   Everything is well.

CASS. Good night, my lord.

BRU.   Good night, good brother.

TIT., MES. Good night, Lord Brutus.

BRU.   Farewell every one.
          [*Exeunt* CASSIUS, TITINIUS, *and* MESSALA.]
Give me the gown. Where is thy instrument?

LUC. Here in the tent.

BRU.   What, thou speak'st drowsily?
Poor knave, I blame thee not; thou art o'erwatch'd.
Call Claudius and some other of my men;
I'll have them sleep on cushions in my tent.

LUC. Varro and Claudius!

Enter VARRO *and* CLAUDIUS.

VAR. Calls my lord?

BRU. I pray you, sirs, lie in my tent and sleep.
It may be I shall raise you by-and-by
On business to my brother Cassius.

VAR. So please you, we will stand and watch your
    pleasure.

BRU. I will not have it so. Lie down, good sirs.
It may be I shall otherwise bethink me.
                    [VARRO *and* CLAUDIUS *lie down.*]
Look, Lucius, here's the book I sought for so;
I put it in the pocket of my gown.

LUC. I was sure your lordship did not give it me.

BRU. Bear with me, good boy, I am much forgetful.
Canst thou hold up thy heavy eyes awhile,
And touch thy instrument a strain or two?

LUC. Ay, my lord, an't please you.

BRU.   It does, my boy.
I trouble thee too much, but thou art willing.

LUC. It is my duty, sir.

BRU. I should not urge thy duty past thy might.
I know young bloods look for a time of rest.

LUC. I have slept, my lord, already.

BRU. It was well done; and thou shalt sleep again;
I will not hold thee long. If I do live,
I will be good to thee.
                [*Music, and a song.* LUCIUS *falls asleep.*]
This is a sleepy tune. O murd'rous slumber!

Layest thou thy leaden mace upon my boy,
That plays thee music? Gentle knave, good night.
I will not do thee so much wrong to wake thee.
If thou dost nod, thou break'st thy instrument;
I'll take it from thee; and, good boy, good night.
Let me see, let me see. Is not the leaf turn'd down
Where I left reading? Here it is, I think.   [*Sits.*]

[*Enter the* GHOST OF CÆSAR.]

How ill this taper burns! Ha! who comes here?
I think it is the weakness of mine eyes
That shapes this monstrous apparition.
It comes upon me. Art thou anything?
Art thou some god, some angel, or some devil,
That mak'st my blood cold and my hair to stare?
Speak to me what thou art.

   GHOST. Thy evil spirit, Brutus.

   BRU.   Why com'st thou?

   GHOST. To tell thee thou shalt see me at Philippi.

   BRU. Well; then I shall see thee again?

   GHOST. Ay, at Philippi.

   BRU. Why, I will see thee at Philippi then.

                             [*Exit* GHOST.]

Now I have taken heart thou vanishest.
Ill spirit, I would hold more talk with thee.
Boy! Lucius! Varro! Claudius! Sirs! Awake!
Claudius!

   LUC. The strings, my lord, are false.

   BRU. He thinks he still is at his instrument.
Lucius, awake!

   LUC. My lord?

   BRU. Didst thou dream, Lucius, that thou so criedst
    out?

   LUC. My lord, I do not know that I did cry.

   BRU. Yes, that thou didst. Didst thou see anything?

Luc. Nothing, my lord.

Bru. Sleep again, Lucius. Sirrah Claudius!
[*To* Varro] Fellow thou, awake!

Var. My lord?

Clau. My lord?

Bru. Why did you so cry out, sirs, in your sleep?

Both. Did we, my lord?

Bru.   Ay. Saw you anything?

Var. No, my lord, I saw nothing.

Clau.   Nor I, my lord.

Bru. Go and commend me to my brother Cassius.
Bid him set on his pow'rs betimes before,
And we will follow.

Both.   It shall be done, my lord.   *Exeunt.*

Act V: Scene I: Near Philippi.

Enter Octavius, Antony, *and their* Army.

Oct. Now, Antony, our hopes are answered.
You said the enemy would not come down
But keep the hills and upper regions.
It proves not so. Their battles are at hand;
They mean to warn us at Philippi here,
Answering before we do demand of them.

Ant. Tut! I am in their bosoms and I know
Wherefore they do it. They could be content
To visit other places, and come down
With fearful bravery, thinking by this face
To fasten in our thoughts that they have courage.
But 'tis not so.

Enter a Messenger.

Mess.   Prepare you, generals.
The enemy comes on in gallant show;

Their bloody sign of battle is hung out,
And something to be done immediately.

ANT. Octavius, lead your battle softly on
Upon the left hand of the even field.

OCT. Upon the right hand I. Keep thou the left.

ANT. Why do you cross me in this exigent?

OCT. I do not cross you; but I will do so.   *March.*

Drum. Enter BRUTUS, CASSIUS, *and their* ARMY;
LUCILIUS, TITINIUS, MESSALA, *and others.*

BRU. They stand and would have parley.

CASS. Stand fast, Titinius. We must out and talk.

OCT. Mark Antony, shall we give sign of battle?

ANT. No, Cæsar, we will answer on their charge.
Make forth. The generals would have some words.

OCT. Stir not until the signal.

BRU. Words before blows. Is it so, countrymen?

OCT. Not that we love words better, as you do.

BRU. Good words are better than bad strokes, Octavius.

ANT. In your bad strokes, Brutus, you give good words;
Witness the hole you made in Cæsar's heart,
Crying 'Long live! Hail, Cæsar!'

CASS.   Antony,
The posture of your blows are yet unknown;
But for your words, they rob the Hybla bees,
And leave them honeyless.

ANT.   Not stingless too.

BRU. O yes, and soundless too!
For you have stol'n their buzzing, Antony,
And very wisely threat before you sting.

ANT. Villains! you did not so when your vile daggers
Hack'd one another in the sides of Cæsar.
You show'd your teeth like apes, and fawn'd like hounds,
And bow'd like bondmen, kissing Cæsar's feet;
Whilst damned Casca, like a cur, behind

Struck Cæsar on the neck. O you flatterers!

 Cass. Flatterers? Now, Brutus, thank yourself!
This tongue had not offended so to-day
If Cassius might have rul'd.

 Oct. Come, come, the cause! If arguing make us sweat,
The proof of it will turn to redder drops.
Look,
I draw a sword against conspirators.
When think you that the sword goes up again?
Never, till Cæsar's three-and-thirty wounds
Be well aveng'd, or till another Cæsar
Have added slaughter to the sword of traitors.

 Bru. Cæsar, thou canst not die by traitors' hands
Unless thou bring'st them with thee.

 Oct.   So I hope.
I was not born to die on Brutus' sword.

 Bru. O, if thou wert the noblest of thy strain,
Young man, thou couldst not die more honourable.

 Cass. A peevish schoolboy, worthless of such honour,
Join'd with a masker and a reveller!

 Ant. Old Cassius still.

 Oct.   Come, Antony. Away!
Defiance, traitors, hurl we in your teeth.
If you dare fight to-day, come to the field;
If not, when you have stomachs.

      Exeunt OCTAVIUS, ANTONY, *and* ARMY.

 Cass. Why, now blow wind, swell billow, and swim
  bark!
The storm is up, and all is on the hazard.

 Bru. Ho, Lucilius! Hark, a word with you.

        LUCILIUS *stands forth.*
Lucil.   My lord?

     BRUTUS *and* LUCILIUS *converse apart.*
Cass. Messala.   MESSALA *stands forth.*
Mes.   What says my general?

Cass.   Messala,

This is my birthday; as this very day
Was Cassius born. Give me thy hand, Messala.
Be thou my witness that against my will
(As Pompey was) am I compell'd to set
Upon one battle all our liberties.
You know that I held Epicurus strong
And his opinion. Now I change my mind
And partly credit things that do presage.
Coming from Sardis, on our former ensign
Two mighty eagles fell; and there they perch'd,
Gorging and feeding from our soldiers' hands,
Who to Philippi here consorted us.
This morning are they fled away and gone,
And in their steads do ravens, crows, and kites
Fly o'er our heads and downward look on us
As we were sickly prey. Their shadows seem
A canopy most fatal, under which
Our army lies, ready to give up the ghost.

    Mes. Believe not so.

    Cass.   I but believe it partly;
For I am fresh of spirit and resolv'd
To meet all perils very constantly.

    Bru. Even so, Lucilius.

    Cass.   Now, most noble Brutus,
The gods to-day stand friendly, that we may,
Lovers in peace, lead on our days to age!
But since the affairs of men rest still incertain,
Let's reason with the worst that may befall.
If we do lose this battle, then is this
The very last time we shall speak together.
What are you then determined to do?

    Bru. Even by the rule of that philosophy
By which I did blame Cato for the death
Which he did give himself—I know not how,

But I do find it cowardly and vile,
For fear of what might fall, so to prevent
The time of life—arming myself with patience
To stay the providence of some high powers
That govern us below.

CASS.   Then, if we lose this battle,
You are contented to be led in triumph
Thorough the streets of Rome.

BRU. No, Cassius, no. Think not, thou noble Roman,
That ever Brutus will go bound to Rome.
He bears too great a mind. But this same day
Must end that work the ides of March begun,
And whether we shall meet again I know not.
Therefore our everlasting farewell take.
For ever and for ever farewell, Cassius!
If we do meet again, why, we shall smile;
If not, why then this parting was well made.

CASS. For ever and for ever farewell, Brutus!
If we do meet again, we'll smile indeed;
If not, 'tis true this parting was well made.

BRU. Why then, lead on. O that a man might know
The end of this day's business ere it come!
But it sufficeth that the day will end,
And then the end is known. Come, ho! Away!   *Exeunt.*

Scene II: Near Philippi. The field of battle.

Alarum. Enter BRUTUS *and* MESSALA.

BRU. Ride, ride, Messala, ride, and give these bills
Unto the legions on the other side.   [*Loud alarum.*]
Let them set on at once; for I perceive
But cold demeanour in Octavius' wing,
And sudden push gives them the overthrow.
Ride, ride, Messala! Let them all come down.   *Exeunt.*

Scene III: Another part of the field.

Alarums. Enter CASSIUS *and* TITINIUS.

CASS. O, look, Titinius, look! The villains fly!
Myself have to mine own turn'd enemy.
This ensign here of mine was turning back;
I slew the coward and did take it from him.

TIT. O Cassius, Brutus gave the word too early,
Who, having some advantage on Octavius,
Took it too eagerly. His soldiers fell to spoil,
Whilst we by Antony are all enclos'd.

Enter PINDARUS.

PIN. Fly further off, my lord! fly further off!
Mark Antony is in your tents, my lord.
Fly, therefore, noble Cassius, fly far off!

CASS. This hill is far enough. Look, look, Titinius!
Are those my tents where I perceive the fire?

TIT. They are, my lord.

CASS.   Titinius, if thou lovest me,
Mount thou my horse and hide thy spurs in him
Till he have brought thee up to yonder troops
And here again, that I may rest assur'd
Whether yond troops are friend or enemy.

TIT. I will be here again even with a thought.   *Exit.*

CASS. Go, Pindarus, get higher on that hill.
My sight was ever thick. Regard Titinius,
And tell me what thou not'st about the field.

[PINDARUS *goes up.*]

This day I breathed first. Time is come round,
And where I did begin, there shall I end.
My life is run his compass. Sirrah, what news?

PIN. [*above*] O my lord!

CASS. What news?

PIN. [*above*] Titinius is enclosed round about
With horsemen that make to him on the spur.
Yet he spurs on. Now they are almost on him.
Now, Titinius!
Now some light. O, he lights too! He's ta'en.   [*Shout.*]
     And hark!
They shout for joy.
    CASS.   Come down; behold no more.
O coward that I am to live so long
To see my best friend ta'en before my face!

       [*Enter* PINDARUS *from above.*]

Come hither, sirrah.
In Parthia did I take thee prisoner;
And then I swore thee, saving of thy life,
That whatsoever I did bid thee do,
Thou shouldst attempt it. Come now, keep thine oath.
Now be a freeman, and with this good sword,
That ran through Cæsar's bowels, search this bosom.
Stand not to answer. Here, take thou the hilts;
And when my face is cover'd, as 'tis now,
Guide thou the sword. [PINDARUS *stabs him.*]—Cæsar,
     thou art reveng'd
Even with the sword that kill'd thee.   *Dies.*
    PIN. So, I am free; yet would not so have been,
Durst I have done my will. O Cassius!
Far from this country Pindarus shall run,
Where never Roman shall take note of him.   *Exit.*

      Enter TITINIUS *and* MESSALA.

    MES. It is but change, Titinius; for Octavius
Is overthrown by noble Brutus' power,
As Cassius' legions are by Antony.
    TIT. These tidings will well comfort Cassius.
    MES. Where did you leave him?

TIT.   All disconsolate,
With Pindarus his bondman, on this hill.

MES. Is not that he that lies upon the ground?

TIT. He lies not like the living. O my heart!

MES. Is not that he?

TIT.   No, this was he, Messala,
But Cassius is no more. O setting sun,
As in thy red rays thou dost sink to night,
So in his red blood Cassius' day is set!
The sun of Rome is set. Our day is gone;
Clouds, dews, and dangers come; our deeds are done!
Mistrust of my success hath done this deed.

MES. Mistrust of good success hath done this deed.
O hateful Error, Melancholy's child,
Why dost thou show to the apt thoughts of men
The things that are not? O Error, soon conceiv'd,
Thou never com'st unto a happy birth,
But kill'st the mother that engend'red thee!

TIT. What, Pindarus! Where art thou, Pindarus?

MES. Seek him, Titinius, whilst I go to meet
The noble Brutus, thrusting this report
Into his ears. I may say 'thrusting' it;
For piercing steel and darts envenomed
Shall be as welcome to the ears of Brutus
As tidings of this sight.

TIT.   Hie you, Messala,
And I will seek for Pindarus the while.   [*Exit* MESSALA.]
Why didst thou send me forth, brave Cassius?
Did I not meet thy friends, and did not they
Put on my brows this wreath of victory
And bid me give it thee? Didst thou not hear their shouts?
Alas, thou hast misconstrued everything!
But hold thee, take this garland on thy brow.
Thy Brutus bid me give it thee, and I
Will do his bidding. Brutus, come apace

And see how I regarded Caius Cassius.
By your leave, gods. This is a Roman's part.
Come, Cassius' sword, and find Titinius' heart.   *Dies.*

Alarum. Enter BRUTUS, MESSALA, YOUNG CATO, STRATO,
            VOLUMNIUS, *and* LUCILIUS.

  BRU. Where, where, Messala, doth his body lie?
  MES. Lo, yonder, and Titinius mourning it.
  BRU. Titinius' face is upward.
  CATO.   He is slain.
  BRU. O Julius Cæsar, thou art mighty yet!
Thy spirit walks abroad and turns our swords
In our own proper entrails.   *Low alarums.*
  CATO.   Brave Titinius!
Look whe'r he have not crown'd dead Cassius.
  BRU. Are yet two Romans living such as these?
The last of all the Romans, fare thee well!
It is impossible that ever Rome
Should breed thy fellow. Friends, I owe moe tears
To this dead man than you shall see me pay.
I shall find time, Cassius; I shall find time.
Come therefore, and to Thasos send his body.
His funerals shall not be in our camp,
Lest it discomfort us. Lucilius, come;
And come, young Cato. Let us to the field.
Labeo and Flavius set our battles on.
'Tis three o'clock; and, Romans, yet ere night
We shall try fortune in a second fight.   *Exeunt.*

Scene IV: Another part of the field.

Alarum. Enter BRUTUS, MESSALA, YOUNG CATO,
            LUCILIUS, *and* FLAVIUS.

  BRU. Yet, countrymen, O, yet hold up your heads!

CATO. What bastard doth not? Who will go with me?
I will proclaim my name about the field.
I am the son of Marcus Cato, ho!
A foe to tyrants, and my country's friend.
I am the son of Marcus Cato, ho!

Enter SOLDIERS *and fight.*

BRU. And I am Brutus, Marcus Brutus I!
Brutus, my country's friend! Know me for Brutus!

Exit.

YOUNG CATO *falls.*

LUCIL. O young and noble Cato, art thou down?
Why, now thou diest as bravely as Titinius,
And mayst be honour'd, being Cato's son.

1. SOLD. Yield, or thou diest.

LUCIL.   Only I yield to die.
[*Offers money.*] There is so much that thou wilt kill me
      straight.
Kill Brutus, and be honour'd in his death.

1. SOLD. We must not. A noble prisoner!

Enter ANTONY.

2. SOLD. Room ho! Tell Antony Brutus is ta'en.

1. SOLD. I'll tell the news. Here comes the general.
Brutus is ta'en! Brutus is ta'en, my lord!

ANT. Where is he?

LUCIL. Safe, Antony; Brutus is safe enough.
I dare assure thee that no enemy
Shall ever take alive the noble Brutus.
The gods defend him from so great a shame!
When you do find him, or alive or dead,
He will be found like Brutus, like himself.

ANT. This is not Brutus, friend; but, I assure you,
A prize no less in worth. Keep this man safe;
Give him all kindness. I had rather have
Such men my friends than enemies. Go on,

And see whe'r Brutus be alive or dead;
And bring us word unto Octavius' tent
How every thing is chanc'd.   *Exeunt.*

Scene V: Another part of the field.

Enter BRUTUS, DARDANIUS, CLITUS, STRATO, *and*
                    VOLUMNIUS.

BRU. Come, poor remains of friends, rest on this rock.
CLI. Statilius show'd the torchlight; but, my lord,
He came not back. He is or ta'en or slain.
BRU. Sit thee down, Clitus. Slaying is the word.
It is a deed in fashion. Hark thee, Clitus.   *Whispers.*
CLI. What, I, my lord? No, not for all the world!
BRU. Peace then. No words.
CLI.   I'll rather kill myself.
BRU. Hark thee, Dardanius.   *Whispers.*
DAR.   Shall I do such a deed?
CLI. O Dardanius!
DAR. O Clitus!
CLI. What ill request did Brutus make to thee?
DAR. To kill him, Clitus. Look, he meditates.
CLI. Now is that noble vessel full of grief,
That it runs over even at his eyes.
BRU. Come hither, good Volumnius. List a word.
VOL. What says my lord?
BRU.   Why this, Volumnius.
The ghost of Cæsar hath appear'd to me
Two several times by night—at Sardis once,
And this last night here in Philippi fields.
I know my hour is come.
VOL.   Not so, my lord.
BRU. Nay, I am sure it is, Volumnius.

Thou seest the world, Volumnius, how it goes.
Our enemies have beat us to the pit.   [*Low alarums.*]
It is more worthy to leap in ourselves
Than tarry till they push us. Good Volumnius,
Thou know'st that we two went to school together.
Even for that our love of old, I prithee
Hold thou my sword-hilts whilst I run on it.

    VOL. That's not an office for a friend, my lord.

                         Alarum still.

    CLI. Fly, fly, my lord! There is no tarrying here.

    BRU. Farewell to you; and you; and you, Volumnius.
Strato, thou hast been all this while asleep.
Farewell to thee too, Strato. Countrymen,
My heart doth joy that yet in all my life
I found no man but he was true to me.
I shall have glory by this losing day
More than Octavius and Mark Antony
By this vile conquest shall attain unto.
So fare you well at once; for Brutus' tongue
Hath almost ended his live's history.
Night hangs upon mine eyes; my bones would rest,
That have but labour'd to attain this hour.

              Alarum. Cry within: Fly, fly, fly!

    CLI. Fly, my lord, fly!

    BRU.   Hence! I will follow.

      [*Exeunt* CLITUS, DARDANIUS, *and* VOLUMNIUS.]
I prithee, Strato, stay thou by thy lord.
Thou art a fellow of a good respect;
Thy life hath had some smatch of honour in it.
Hold then my sword, and turn away thy face
While I do run upon it. Wilt thou, Strato?

    STRA. Give me your hand first. Fare you well, my lord.

    BRU. Farewell, good Strato. Cæsar, now be still.
I kill'd not thee with half so good a will.

            He runs on his sword and dies.

Alarum. Retreat. Enter OCTAVIUS, ANTONY, MESSALA,
LUCILIUS, *and the* ARMY.

OCT. What man is that?

MES. My master's man. Strato, where is thy master?

STRA. Free from the bondage you are in, Messala.
The conquerors can but make a fire of him;
For Brutus only overcame himself,
And no man else hath honour by his death.

LUCIL. So Brutus should be found. I thank thee,
Brutus,
That thou hast prov'd Lucilius' saying true.

OCT. All that serv'd Brutus, I will entertain them.
Fellow, wilt thou bestow thy time with me?

STRA. Ay, if Messala will prefer me to you.

OCT. Do so, good Messala.

MES. How died my master, Strato?

STRA. I held the sword, and he did run on it.

MES. Octavius, then take him to follow thee,
That did the latest service to my master.

ANT. This was the noblest Roman of them all.
All the conspirators save only he
Did that they did in envy of great Cæsar;
He, only in a general honest thought
And common good to all, made one of them.
His life was gentle, and the elements
So mix'd in him that Nature might stand up
And say to all the world, 'This was a man!'

OCT. According to his virtue let us use him,
With all respect and rites of burial.
Within my tent his bones to-night shall lie,
Most like a soldier, ordered honourably.
So call the field to rest, and let's away
To part the glories of this happy day.   *Exeunt omnes.*

A Midsummer Night's Dream

NAMES OF THE ACTORS

THESEUS, Duke of Athens.

EGEUS, father to HERMIA.

LYSANDER, beloved of HERMIA.

DEMETRIUS, suitor to HERMIA, approved by EGEUS.

PHILOSTRATE, Master of the Revels to THESEUS.

PETER QUINCE, a carpenter; *Prologue* in the interlude.

NICK BOTTOM, a weaver; PYRAMUS in the same.

FRANCIS FLUTE, a bellows-mender; THISBY in the same.

TOM SNOUT, a tinker; WALL in the same.

SNUG, a joiner; LION in the same.

ROBIN STARVELING, a tailor; MOONSHINE in the same.

HIPPOLYTA, Queen of the Amazons, betrothed to THESEUS.

HERMIA, daughter to EGEUS, in love with LYSANDER.

HELENA, in love with DEMETRIUS.

OBERON, King of the Fairies.

TITANIA, Queen of the Fairies.

PUCK, or ROBIN GOODFELLOW.

PEASEBLOSSOM, MOTH, COBWEB, MUSTARDSEED, } fairies.

Other Fairies attending OBERON and TITANIA. Attendants on THESEUS and HIPPOLYTA.

Act I: Scene I: Athens. The Palace of Theseus.

Enter THESEUS, HIPPOLYTA, PHILOSTRATE, *with others.*

THE. Now, fair Hippolyta, our nuptial hour
Draws on apace. Four happy days bring in
Another moon; but, O, methinks, how slow
This old moon wanes! She lingers my desires,
Like to a stepdame or a dowager,
Long withering out a young man's revenue.

HIP. Four days will quickly steep themselves in night;
Four nights will quickly dream away the time;
And then the moon, like to a silver bow
New-bent in heaven, shall behold the night
Of our solemnities.

THE.   Go, Philostrate,
Stir up the Athenian youth to merriments,
Awake the pert and nimble spirit of mirth,
Turn melancholy forth to funerals;
The pale companion is not for our pomp.

                              [*Exit* PHILOSTRATE.]

Hippolyta, I woo'd thee with my sword,
And won thy love doing thee injuries;
But I will wed thee in another key,
With pomp, with triumph, and with revelling.

Enter EGEUS *and his daughter* HERMIA, *and* LYSANDER
and DEMETRIUS.

EGE. Happy be Theseus, our renowned Duke!
THE. Thanks, good Egeus. What's the news with thee?
EGE. Full of vexation come I, with complaint
Against my child, my daughter Hermia.
Stand forth, Demetrius. My noble lord,
This man hath my consent to marry her.
Stand forth, Lysander. And, my gracious Duke,

This man hath bewitch'd the bosom of my child.
Thou, thou, Lysander, thou hast given her rhymes
And interchang'd love tokens with my child;
Thou hast by moonlight at her window sung
With feigning voice verses of feigning love,
And stol'n the impression of her fantasy
With bracelets of thy hair, rings, gauds, conceits,
Knacks, trifles, nosegays, sweetmeats—messengers
Of strong prevailment in unhardened youth.
With cunning hast thou filch'd my daughter's heart;
Turn'd her obedience, which is due to me,
To stubborn harshness. And, my gracious Duke,
Be it so she will not here before your Grace
Consent to marry with Demetrius,
I beg the ancient privilege of Athens—
As she is mine, I may dispose of her;
Which shall be either to this gentleman
Or to her death, according to our law
Immediately provided in that case.

THE. What say you, Hermia? Be advis'd, fair maid.
To you your father should be as a god;
One that compos'd your beauties; yea, and one
To whom you are but as a form in wax,
By him imprinted, and within his power
To leave the figure, or disfigure it.
Demetrius is a worthy gentleman.

HER. So is Lysander.

THE.   In himself he is;
But in this kind, wanting your father's voice,
The other must be held the worthier.

HER. I would my father look'd but with my eyes.

THE. Rather your eyes must with his judgment look.

HER. I do entreat your Grace to pardon me.
I know not by what power I am made bold,
Nor how it may concern my modesty

In such a presence here to plead my thoughts;
But I beseech your Grace that I may know
The worst that may befall me in this case
If I refuse to wed Demetrius.

THE. Either to die the death, or to abjure
For ever the society of men.
Therefore, fair Hermia, question your desires,
Know of your youth, examine well your blood,
Whether, if you yield not to your father's choice,
You can endure the livery of a nun,
For aye to be in shady cloister mew'd,
To live a barren sister all your life,
Chaunting faint hymns to the cold fruitless moon.
Thrice blessed they that master so their blood
To undergo such maiden pilgrimage;
But earthlier happy is the rose distill'd
Than that which, withering on the virgin thorn,
Grows, lives, and dies in single blessedness.

HER. So will I grow, so live, so die, my lord,
Ere I will yield my virgin patent up
Unto his lordship whose unwished yoke
My soul consents not to give sovereignty.

THE. Take time to pause; and by the next new moon—
The sealing day betwixt my love and me
For everlasting bond of fellowship—
Upon that day either prepare to die
For disobedience to your father's will,
Or else to wed Demetrius, as he would,
Or on Diana's altar to protest
For aye austerity and single life.

DEM. Relent, sweet Hermia; and, Lysander, yield
Thy crazed title to my certain right.

LYS. You have her father's love, Demetrius;
Let me have Hermia's. Do you marry him.

EGE. Scornful Lysander, true, he hath my love;

And what is mine my love shall render him;
And she is mine, and all my right of her
I do estate unto Demetrius.

Lys. I am, my lord, as well deriv'd as he,
As well possess'd; my love is more than his;
My fortunes every way as fairly rank'd
(If not with vantage) as Demetrius';
And (which is more than all these boasts can be)
I am belov'd of beauteous Hermia.
Why should not I then prosecute my right?
Demetrius, I'll avouch it to his head,
Made love to Nedar's daughter, Helena,
And won her soul; and she (sweet lady) dotes,
Devoutly dotes, dotes in idolatry,
Upon this spotted and inconstant man.

The. I must confess that I have heard so much,
And with Demetrius thought to have spoke thereof;
But, being over-full of self-affairs,
My mind did lose it. But, Demetrius, come;
And come, Egeus. You shall go with me;
I have some private schooling for you both.
For you, fair Hermia, look you arm yourself
To fit your fancies to your father's will;
Or else the law of Athens yields you up
(Which by no means we may extenuate)
To death or to a vow of single life.
Come, my Hippolyta. What cheer, my love?
Demetrius and Egeus, go along.
I must employ you in some business
Against our nuptial and confer with you
Of something nearly that concerns yourselves.

Ege. With duty and desire we follow you.

                    Exeunt, leaving Lysander *and* Hermia.

Lys. How now, my love? Why is your cheek so pale?
How chance the roses there do fade so fast?

Her. Belike for want of rain, which I could well
Beteem them from the tempest of my eyes.

Lys. Ay me! for aught that I could ever read,
Could ever hear by tale or history,
The course of true love never did run smooth;
But, either it was different in blood—

Her. O cross! too high to be enthrall'd to low!

Lys. Or else misgraffed in respect of years—

Her. O spite! too old to be engag'd to young!

Lys. Or else it stood upon the choice of friends—

Her. O hell! to choose love by another's eyes!

Lys. Or, if there were a sympathy in choice,
War, death, or sickness did lay siege to it,
Making it momentany as a sound,
Swift as a shadow, short as any dream,
Brief as the lightning in the collied night,
That, in a spleen, unfolds both heaven and earth,
And ere a man hath power to say 'Behold!'
The jaws of darkness do devour it up:
So quick bright things come to confusion.

Her. If then true lovers have been ever cross'd,
It stands as an edict in destiny.
Then let us teach our trial patience,
Because it is a customary cross,
As due to love as thoughts and dreams and sighs,
Wishes and tears, poor Fancy's followers.

Lys. A good persuasion. Therefore hear me, Hermia.
I have a widow aunt, a dowager,
Of great revenue, and she hath no child.
From Athens is her house remote seven leagues;
And she respects me as her only son.
There, gentle Hermia, may I marry thee;
And to that place the sharp Athenian law
Cannot pursue us. If thou lovest me then,
Steal forth thy father's house to-morrow night;

And in the wood, a league without the town,
Where I did meet thee once with Helena
To do observance to a morn of May,
There will I stay for thee.

HER.   My good Lysander!
I swear to thee by Cupid's strongest bow,
By his best arrow, with the golden head,
By the simplicity of Venus' doves,
By that which knitteth souls and prospers loves,
And by that fire which burn'd the Carthage queen
When the false Troyan under sail was seen,
By all the vows that ever men have broke
(In number more than ever women spoke),
In that same place thou hast appointed me
To-morrow truly will I meet with thee.

LYS. Keep promise, love. Look, here comes **Helena.**

Enter HELENA.

HER. God speed fair Helena! Whither away?
HEL. Call you me fair? That fair again unsay.
Demetrius loves your fair. O happy fair!
Your eyes are lodestars, and your tongue's sweet air
More tuneable than lark to shepherd's ear
When wheat is green, when hawthorn buds appear.
Sickness is catching. O, were favour so,
Yours would I catch, fair Hermia, ere I go!
My ear should catch your voice, my eye your eye,
My tongue should catch your tongue's sweet melody.
Were the world mine, Demetrius being bated,
The rest I'ld give to be to you translated.
O, teach me how you look, and with what art
You sway the motion of Demetrius' heart!

HER. I frown upon him; yet he loves me still.
HEL. O that your frowns would teach my smiles such
    skill!

HER. I give him curses; yet he gives me love.

HEL. O that my prayers could such affection move!

HER. The more I hate, the more he follows me.

HEL. The more I love, the more he hateth me.

HER. His folly, Helena, is no fault of mine.

HEL. None but your beauty. Would that fault were mine!

HER. Take comfort. He no more shall see my face;
Lysander and myself will fly this place.
Before the time I did Lysander see,
Seem'd Athens as a paradise to me.
O, then, what graces in my love do dwell
That he hath turn'd a heaven unto a hell!

LYS. Helen, to you our minds we will unfold.
To-morrow night, when Phœbe doth behold
Her silver visage in the wat'ry glass,
Decking with liquid pearl the bladed grass
(A time that lovers' flights doth still conceal),
Through Athens gates have we devis'd to steal.

HER. And in the wood where often you and I
Upon faint primrose beds were wont to lie,
Emptying our bosoms of their counsel sweet,
There my Lysander and myself shall meet,
And thence from Athens turn away our eyes
To seek new friends and stranger companies.
Farewell, sweet playfellow. Pray thou for us;
And good luck grant thee thy Demetrius!
Keep word, Lysander. We must starve our sight
From lovers' food till morrow deep midnight.

LYS. I will, my Hermia.   [*Exit* HERMIA.]
                    Helena, adieu.
As you on him, Demetrius dote on you!   *Exit.*

HEL. How happy some o'er other some can be!
Through Athens I am thought as fair as she.
But what of that? Demetrius thinks not so;

He will not know what all but he do know.
And as he errs, doting on Hermia's eyes,
So I, admiring of his qualities.
Things base and vile, holding no quantity,
Love can transpose to form and dignity.
Love looks not with the eyes, but with the mind;
And therefore is wing'd Cupid painted blind.
Nor hath Love's mind of any judgment taste;
Wings, and no eyes, figure unheedy haste.
And therefore is Love said to be a child,
Because in choice he is so oft beguil'd.
As waggish boys in game themselves forswear,
So the boy Love is perjur'd everywhere;
For ere Demetrius look'd on Hermia's eyne,
He hail'd down oaths that he was only mine;
And when this hail some heat from Hermia felt,
So he dissolv'd, and show'rs of oaths did melt.
I will go tell him of fair Hermia's flight.
Then to the wood will he to-morrow night
Pursue her; and for this intelligence
If I have thanks, it is a dear expense;
But herein mean I to enrich my pain,
To have his sight thither and back again.   *Exit.*

Scene II: Athens. Quince's house.

Enter QUINCE *the Carpenter, and* SNUG *the Joiner, and*
BOTTOM *the Weaver, and* FLUTE *the Bellows-mender,*
and SNOUT *the Tinker, and* STARVELING *the Tailor.*

QUINCE. Is all our company here?

BOT. You were best to call them generally, man by
man, according to the scrip.

QUINCE. Here is the scroll of every man's name which
is thought fit, through all Athens, to play in our enter-

lude before the Duke and the Duchess on his wedding
day at night.

BOT. First, good Peter Quince, say what the play
treats on; then read the names of the actors; and so grow
to a point.

QUINCE. Marry, our play is 'The most Lamentable
Comedy and most Cruel Death of Pyramus and Thisby.'

BOT. A very good piece of work, I assure you, and a
merry. Now, good Peter Quince, call forth your actors
by the scroll. Masters, spread yourselves.

QUINCE. Answer as I call you. Nick Bottom the weaver.

BOT. Ready. Name what part I am for, and proceed.

QUINCE. You, Nick Bottom, are set down for Pyramus.

BOT. What is Pyramus? a lover, or a tyrant?

QUINCE. A lover that kills himself, most gallant, for
love.

BOT. That will ask some tears in the true performing
of it. If I do it, let the audience look to their eyes! I will
move storms; I will condole in some measure. To the rest.
Yet my chief humour is for a tyrant. I could play Ercles
rarely, or a part to tear a cat in, to make all split.

> 'The raging rocks
> And shivering shocks
> Shall break the locks
>   Of prison gates;
> And Phibbus' car
> Shall shine from far
> And make and mar
>   The foolish Fates.'

This was lofty! Now name the rest of the players. This
is Ercles' vein, a tyrant's vein. A lover is more condoling.

QUINCE. Francis Flute the bellows-mender.

FLUTE. Here, Peter Quince.

QUINCE. Flute, you must take Thisby on you.

FLUTE. What is Thisby? a wand'ring knight?

QUINCE. It is the lady that Pyramus must love.

FLUTE. Nay, faith, let not me play a woman. I have a beard coming.

QUINCE. That's all one. You shall play it in a mask, and you may speak as small as you will.

BOT. An I may hide my face, let me play Thisby too. I'll speak in a monstrous little voice:—'Thisne, Thisne!' 'Ah, Pyramus, my lover dear! thy Thisby dear, and lady dear!'

QUINCE. No, no! you must play Pyramus; and, Flute, you Thisby.

BOT. Well, proceed.

QUINCE. Robin Starveling the tailor.

STARV. Here, Peter Quince.

QUINCE. Robin Starveling, you must play Thisby's mother. Tom Snout the tinker.

SNOUT. Here, Peter Quince.

QUINCE. You, Pyramus' father; myself, Thisby's father; Snug, the joiner, you the lion's part. And I hope here is a play fitted.

SNUG. Have you the lion's part written? Pray you, if it be, give it me, for I am slow of study.

QUINCE. You may do it extempore, for it is nothing but roaring.

BOT. Let me play the lion too. I will roar that I will do any man's heart good to hear me. I will roar that I will make the Duke say 'Let him roar again; let him roar again.'

QUINCE. An you should do it too terribly, you would fright the Duchess and the ladies, that they would shrike; and that were enough to hang us all.

ALL. That would hang us, every mother's son.

BOT. I grant you, friends, if you should fright the ladies out of their wits, they would have no more discretion but to hang us; but I will aggravate my voice so that I will roar you as gently as any sucking dove; I will roar you an 'twere any nightingale.

QUINCE. You can play no part but Pyramus; for Pyramus is a sweet-fac'd man; a proper man as one shall see in a summer's day; a most lovely gentlemanlike man. Therefore you must needs play Pyramus.

BOT. Well, I will undertake it. What beard were I best to play it in?

QUINCE. Why, what you will.

BOT. I will discharge it in either your straw-colour beard, your orange-tawny beard, your purple-in-grain beard, or your French-crown-colour beard, your perfit yellow.

QUINCE. Some of your French crowns have no hair at all, and then you will play barefac'd. But, masters, here are your parts; and I am to entreat you, request you, and desire you to con them by to-morrow night; and meet me in the palace wood, a mile without the town, by moon-light. There will we rehearse; for if we meet in the city, we shall be dogg'd with company, and our devices known. In the meantime I will draw a bill of properties, such as our play wants. I pray you fail me not.

BOT. We will meet; and there we may rehearse most obscenely and courageously. Take pains; be perfit. Adieu.

QUINCE. At the Duke's Oak we meet.

BOT. Enough. Hold, or cut bowstrings.　　　　*Exeunt.*

Act II: Scene I: A wood near Athens.

Enter a FAIRY *at one door, and* ROBIN GOODFELLOW *at another.*

ROB. How now, spirit? Whither wander you?

FAI. Over hill, over dale,
    Thorough bush, thorough brier,
  Over park, over pale,
    Thorough flood, thorough fire;
  I do wander everywhere,
  Swifter than the moonës sphere;
  And I serve the Fairy Queen,
  To dew her orbs upon the green.
  The cowslips tall her pensioners be;
  In their gold coats spots you see.
  Those be rubies, fairy favours;
  In those freckles live their savours.
I must go seek some dewdrops here,
And hang a pearl in every cowslip's ear.
Farewell, thou lob of spirits; I'll be gone.
Our Queen and all her elves come here anon.

ROB. The King doth keep his revels here to-night.
Take heed the Queen come not within his sight.
For Oberon is passing fell and wrath,
Because that she, as her attendant, hath
A lovely boy, stolen from an Indian king;
She never had so sweet a changeling.
And jealous Oberon would have the child
Knight of his train, to trace the forests wild;
But she perforce withholds the loved boy,
Crowns him with flowers, and makes him all her joy.
And now they never meet in grove or green,
By fountain clear or spangled starlight sheen,
But they do square, that all their elves, for fear,
Creep into acorn cups and hide them there.

FAI. Either I mistake your shape and making quite,
Or else you are that shrewd and knavish sprite
Call'd Robin Goodfellow. Are not you he
That frights the maidens of the villagery;
Skim milk, and sometimes labour in the quern,

And bootless make the breathless housewife churn;
And sometime make the drink to bear no barm;
Mislead night-wanderers, laughing at their harm?
Those that Hobgoblin call you, and sweet Puck,
You do their work, and they shall have good luck.
Are not you he?

ROB.   Thou speakest aright;
I am that merry wanderer of the night.
I jest to Oberon, and make him smile
When I a fat and bean-fed horse beguile,
Neighing in likeness of a filly foal;
And sometime lurk I in a gossip's bowl
In very likeness of a roasted crab,
And when she drinks, against her lips I bob
And on her withered dewlap pour the ale.
The wisest aunt, telling the saddest tale,
Sometime for three-foot stool mistaketh me;
Then slip I from her bum, down topples she,
And 'tailor' cries, and falls into a cough;
And then the whole quire hold their hips and loffe,
And waxen in their mirth, and neeze, and swear
A merrier hour was never wasted there.
But room, fairy! Here comes Oberon.

FAI. And here my mistress. Would that he were gone!

Enter OBERON *the* KING OF FAIRIES, *at one door, with
his Train; and the* QUEEN, TITANIA, *at another, with hers.*

OB. Ill met by moonlight, proud Titania.

QUEEN. What, jealous Oberon? Fairies, skip hence.
I have forsworn his bed and company.

OB. Tarry, rash wanton. Am not I thy lord?

QUEEN. Then I must be thy lady; but I know
When thou hast stolen away from fairyland,
And in the shape of Corin sat all day,
Playing on pipes of corn, and versing love

To amorous Phillida. Why art thou here,
Come from the farthest steep of India,
But that, forsooth, the bouncing Amazon,
Your buskin'd mistress and your warrior love,
To Theseus must be wedded, and you come
To give their bed joy and prosperity?

Ob. How canst thou thus, for shame, Titania,
Glance at my credit with Hippolyta,
Knowing I know thy love to Theseus?
Didst thou not lead him through the glimmering night
From Perigouna, whom he ravished?
And make him with fair Ægles break his faith,
With Ariadne, and Antiopa?

Queen. These are the forgeries of jealousy;
And never, since the middle summer's spring,
Met we on hill, in dale, forest, or mead,
By paved fountain or by rushy brook,
Or in the beached margent of the sea,
To dance our ringlets to the whistling wind,
But with thy brawls thou hast disturb'd our sport.
Therefore the winds, piping to us in vain,
As in revenge, have suck'd up from the sea
Contagious fogs; which falling in the land
Hath every pelting river made so proud
That they have overborne their continents.
The ox hath therefore stretch'd his yoke in vain,
The ploughman lost his sweat, and the green corn
Hath rotted ere his youth attain'd a beard;
The fold stands empty in the drowned field,
And crows are fatted with the murrion flock;
The nine men's morris is fill'd up with mud;
And the quaint mazes in the wanton green
For lack of tread are undistinguishable.
The human mortals want their winter cheer;
No night is now with hymn or carol blest.

Therefore the moon, the governess of floods,
Pale in her anger, washes all the air,
That rheumatic diseases do abound.
And thorough this distemperature we see
The seasons alter. Hoary-headed frosts
Fall in the fresh lap of the crimson rose;
And on old Hiems' thin and icy crown
An odorous chaplet of sweet summer buds
Is, as in mockery, set. The spring, the summer,
The childing autumn, angry winter change
Their wonted liveries; and the mazed world,
By their increase, now knows not which is which.
And this same progeny of evils comes
From our debate, from our dissension;
We are their parents and original.

    OB. Do you amend it then; it lies in you.
Why should Titania cross her Oberon?
I do but beg a little changeling boy
To be my henchman.

    QUEEN.   Set your heart at rest.
The fairyland buys not the child of me.
His mother was a vot'ress of my order;
And in the spiced Indian air, by night,
Full often hath she gossip'd by my side,
And sat with me on Neptune's yellow sands,
Marking th' embarked traders on the flood;
When we have laugh'd to see the sails conceive
And grow big-bellied with the wanton wind;
Which she, with pretty and with swimming gait
Following (her womb then rich with my young squire)
Would imitate, and sail upon the land
To fetch me trifles, and return again,
As from a voyage, rich with merchandise.
But she, being mortal, of that boy did die,

And for her sake do I rear up her boy;
And for her sake I will not part with him.

   Ob. How long within this wood intend you stay?

   Queen. Perchance till after Theseus' wedding day.
If you will patiently dance in our round
And see our moonlight revels, go with us.
If not, shun me, and I will spare your haunts.

   Ob. Give me that boy, and I will go with thee.

   Queen. Not for thy fairy kingdom. Fairies, away!
We shall chide downright if I longer stay.

                 Exeunt TITANIA *and her Train.*

   Ob. Well, go thy way. Thou shalt not from this grove
Till I torment thee for this injury.
My gentle Puck, come hither. Thou rememb'rest
Since once I sat upon a promontory
And heard a mermaid, on a dolphin's back,
Uttering such dulcet and harmonious breath
That the rude sea grew civil at her song,
And certain stars shot madly from their spheres
To hear the sea-maid's music.

   Puck.   I remember.

   Ob. That very time I saw (but thou couldst not)
Flying between the cold moon and the earth
Cupid, all arm'd. A certain aim he took
At a fair Vestal, throned by the West,
And loos'd his love-shaft smartly from his bow,
As it should pierce a hundred thousand hearts.
But I might see young Cupid's fiery shaft
Quench'd in the chaste beams of the wat'ry moon,
And the imperial vot'ress passed on,
In maiden meditation, fancy-free.
Yet mark'd I where the bolt of Cupid fell.
It fell upon a little Western flower,
Before milk-white, now purple with love's wound,

And maidens call it love-in-idleness.
Fetch me that flow'r; the herb I show'd thee once.
The juice of it, on sleeping eyelids laid,
Will make or man or woman madly dote
Upon the next live creature that it sees.
Fetch me this herb, and be thou here again
Ere the Leviathan can swim a league.

    Puck. I'll put a girdle round about the earth
In forty minutes.   *Exit*

    Ob.   Having once this juice,
I'll watch Titania when she is asleep
And drop the liquor of it in her eyes.
The next thing then she, waking, looks upon
(Be it on lion, bear, or wolf, or bull,
On meddling monkey, or on busy ape)
She shall pursue it with the soul of love.
And ere I take this charm from off her sight
(As I can take it with another herb)
I'll make her render up her page to me.
But who comes here? I am invisible,
And I will overhear their conference.

    Enter Demetrius, Helena *following him.*

    Dem. I love thee not; therefore pursue me not.
Where is Lysander and fair Hermia?
The one I'll slay, the other slayeth me.
Thou told'st me they were stol'n unto this wood;
And here am I, and wood within this wood
Because I cannot meet my Hermia.
Hence, get thee gone, and follow me no more!

    Hel. You draw me, you hard-hearted adamant!
But yet you draw not iron, for my heart
Is true as steel. Leave you your power to draw,
And I shall have no power to follow you.

    Dem. Do I entice you? Do I speak you fair?

Or rather do I not in plainest truth
Tell you I do not nor I cannot love you?

HEL. And even for that do I love you the more.
I am your spaniel; and, Demetrius,
The more you beat me, I will fawn on you.
Use me but as your spaniel—spurn me, strike me,
Neglect me, lose me; only give me leave
(Unworthy as I am) to follow you.
What worser place can I beg in your love
(And yet a place of high respect with me)
Than to be used as you use your dog?

DEM. Tempt not too much the hatred of my spirit;
For I am sick when I do look on thee.

HEL. And I am sick when I look not on you.

DEM. You do impeach your modesty too much
To leave the city and commit yourself
Into the hands of one that loves you not;
To trust the opportunity of night
And the ill counsel of a desert place
With the rich worth of your virginity.

HEL. Your virtue is my privilege. For that
It is not night when I do see your face,
Therefore I think I am not in the night;
Nor doth this wood lack worlds of company,
For you, in my respect, are all the world.
Then how can it be said I am alone
When all the world is here to look on me?

DEM. I'll run from thee and hide me in the brakes
And leave thee to the mercy of wild beasts.

HEL. The wildest hath not such a heart as you.
Run when you will. The story shall be chang'd:
Apollo flies, and Daphne holds the chase;
The dove pursues the griffon; the mild hind
Makes speed to catch the tiger—bootless speed,
When cowardice pursues, and valour flies!

DEM. I will not stay thy questions. Let me go!
Or if thou follow me, do not believe
But I shall do thee mischief in the wood.

HEL. Ay, in the temple, in the town, the field
You do me mischief. Fie, Demetrius!
Your wrongs do set a scandal on my sex.
We cannot fight for love, as men may do;
We should be woo'd, and were not made to woo.

[*Exit* DEMETRIUS.]

I'll follow thee, and make a heaven of hell
To die upon the hand I love so well.   *Exit.*

OB. Fare thee well, nymph. Ere he do leave this grove,
Thou shalt fly him, and he shall seek thy love.

[*Enter* PUCK.]

Hast thou the flower there? Welcome, wanderer.

PUCK. Ay, there it is.

OB.   I pray thee give it me.
I know a bank where the wild thyme blows,
Where oxlips and the nodding violet grows;
Quite over-canopied with luscious woodbine,
With sweet musk-roses, and with eglantine.
There sleeps Titania sometime of the night,
Lull'd in these flowers with dances and delight;
And there the snake throws her enamell'd skin,
Weed wide enough to wrap a fairy in;
And with the juice of this I'll streak her eyes
And make her full of hateful fantasies.
Take thou some of it and seek through this grove.
A sweet Athenian lady is in love
With a disdainful youth. Anoint his eyes;
But do it when the next thing he espies
May be the lady. Thou shalt know the man
By the Athenian garments he hath on.
Effect it with some care, that he may prove

More fond on her than she upon her love;
And look thou meet me ere the first cock crow.
    PUCK. Fear not, my lord; your servant shall do so.
                                 Exeunt.

Scene II: Another part of the wood.

Enter TITANIA, QUEEN OF FAIRIES, *with her Train.*

    QUEEN. Come, now a roundel and a fairy song;
Then, for the third part of a minute, hence—
Some to kill cankers in the musk-rose buds,
Some war with reremice for their leathren wings,
To make my small elves coats, and some keep back
The clamorous owl, that nightly hoots and wonders
At our quaint spirits. Sing me now asleep.
Then to your offices, and let me rest.

FAIRIES sing.

  1. FAI. You spotted snakes with double tongue,
        Thorny hedgehogs, be not seen;
    Newts and blindworms, do no wrong,
        Come not near our Fairy Queen.

CHORUS.

    Philomele, with melody
    Sing in our sweet lullaby;
Lulla, lulla, lullaby; lulla, lulla, lullaby:
        Never harm
        Nor spell nor charm
    Come our lovely lady nigh.
    So good night, with lullaby.

  1. FAI. Weaving spiders, come not here;
        Hence, you long-legg'd spinners, hence!
    Beetles black, approach not near;
        Worm nor snail, do no offence.

CHORUS.

    Philomele, with melody, &c.

                                  She sleeps.

2. FAI. Hence, away! Now all is well.
One aloof stand sentinel.   *Exeunt* FAIRIES.

Enter OBERON, *and squeezes the flower on*
TITANIA'S *eyelids.*

OB. What thou seest when thou dost wake,
Do it for thy true-love take;
Love and languish for his sake.
Be it ounce or cat or bear,
Pard, or boar with bristled hair
In thy eye that shall appear
When thou wak'st, it is thy dear.
Wake when some vile thing is near.   *Exit.*

Enter LYSANDER *and* HERMIA.

LYS. Fair love, you faint with wand'ring in the wood;
And to speak troth, I have forgot our way.
We'll rest us, Hermia, if you think it good,
And tarry for the comfort of the day.

HER. Be it so, Lysander. Find you out a bed;
For I upon this bank will rest my head.

LYS. One turf shall serve as pillow for us both;
One heart, one bed, two bosoms, and one troth.

HER. Nay, good Lysander. For my sake, my dear,
Lie further off yet; do not lie so near.

LYS. O, take the sense, sweet, of my innocence!
Love takes the meaning in love's conference.
I mean that my heart unto yours is knit,
So that but one heart we can make of it;
Two bosoms interchained with an oath—
So then two bosoms and a single troth.
Then by your side no bed-room me deny;
For lying so, Hermia, I do not lie.

HER. Lysander riddles very prettily.
Now much beshrew my manners and my pride
If Hermia meant to say Lysander lied!

But, gentle friend, for love and courtesy
Lie further off, in humane modesty;
Such separation as may well be said
Becomes a virtuous bachelor and a maid,
So far be distant; and good night, sweet friend.
Thy love ne'er alter till thy sweet life end!

   Lys. Amen, amen, to that fair prayer say I,
And then end life when I end loyalty!
Here is my bed. Sleep give thee all his rest!

   Her. With half that wish the wisher's eyes be press'd!

They sleep.

Enter Puck.

Puck. Through the forest have I gone,
     But Athenian found I none
     On whose eyes I might approve
     This flower's force in stirring love.
     Night and silence! Who is here?
     Weeds of Athens he doth wear.
     This is he (my master said)
     Despised the Athenian maid;
     And here the maiden, sleeping sound
     On the dank and dirty ground.
     Pretty soul! she durst not lie
     Near this lack-love, this kill-courtesy.
     Churl, upon thy eyes I throw
     All the power this charm doth owe.
     When thou wak'st, let love forbid
     Sleep his seat on thy eyelid.
     So awake when I am gone;
     For I must now to Oberon.   *Exit.*

Enter Demetrius *and* Helena, *running.*

Hel. Stay, though thou kill me, sweet Demetrius.

Dem. I charge thee, hence, and do not haunt me thus.

Hel. O, wilt thou darkling leave me? Do not so.

DEM. Stay, on thy peril! I alone will go.   *Exit.*

HEL. O, I am out of breath in this fond chase!
The more my prayer, the lesser is my grace.
Happy is Hermia, wheresoe'er she lies;
For she hath blessed and attractive eyes.
How came her eyes so bright? Not with salt tears.
If so, my eyes are oft'ner wash'd than hers.
No, no! I am as ugly as a bear;
For beasts that meet me run away for fear.
Therefore no marvel though Demetrius
Do, as a monster, fly my presence thus.
What wicked and dissembling glass of mine
Made me compare with Hermia's sphery eyne?
But who is here? Lysander! on the ground?
Dead, or asleep? I see no blood, no wound.
Lysander, if you live, good sir, awake.

LYS. [*starts up*] And run through fire I will for thy
      sweet sake.
Transparent Helena! Nature shows art,
That through thy bosom makes me see thy heart.
Where is Demetrius? O, how fit a word
Is that vile name to perish on my sword!

HEL. Do not say so, Lysander; say not so.
What though he love your Hermia? Lord! what though?
Yet Hermia still loves you. Then be content.

LYS. Content with Hermia? No! I do repent
The tedious minutes I with her have spent.
Not Hermia, but Helena I love.
Who will not change a raven for a dove?
The will of man is by his reason sway'd;
And reason says you are the worthier maid.
Things growing are not ripe until their season;
So I, being young, till now ripe not to reason;
And touching now the point of human skill,
Reason becomes the marshal to my will

And leads me to your eyes; where I o'erlook
Love's stories, written in Love's richest book.

HEL. Wherefore was I to this keen mockery born?
When at your hands did I deserve this scorn?
Is't not enough, is't not enough, young man,
That I did never, no, nor never can,
Deserve a sweet look from Demetrius' eye,
But you must flout my insufficiency?
Good troth, you do me wrong! good sooth, you do!
In such disdainful manner me to woo.
But fare you well. Perforce I must confess
I thought you lord of more true gentleness.
O, that a lady, of one man refus'd,
Should of another therefore be abus'd!   *Exit.*

LYS. She sees not Hermia. Hermia, sleep thou there,
And never mayst thou come Lysander near!
For, as a surfeit of the sweetest things
The deepest loathing to the stomach brings,
Or as the heresies that men do leave
Are hated most of those they did deceive,
So thou, my surfeit and my heresy,
Of all be hated, but the most of me!
And, all my powers, address your love and might
To honour Helen and to be her knight!   *Exit.*

HER. [*awakes*] Help me, Lysander, help me! Do thy
          best
To pluck this crawling serpent from my breast!
Ay me, for pity! What a dream was here!
Lysander, look how I do quake with fear.
Methought a serpent eat my heart away,
And you sat smiling at his cruel prey.
Lysander! What, remov'd? Lysander! lord!
What, out of hearing? gone? No sound, no word?
Alack, where are you? Speak, an if you hear.
Speak, of all loves! I swoon almost with fear.

No? Then I well perceive you are not nigh.
Either death or you I'll find immediately.   *Exit.*

Act III: Scene I: The wood. Titania lying asleep.

*Enter the Clowns—*QUINCE, SNUG, BOTTOM, FLUTE, SNOUT, *and* STARVELING.

BOT. Are we all met?

QUINCE. Pat, pat; and here's a marvail's convenient place for our rehearsal. This green plot shall be our stage, this hawthorn brake our tiring house, and we will do it in action as we will do it before the Duke.

BOT. Peter Quince!

QUINCE. What sayest thou, bully Bottom?

BOT. There are things in this Comedy of Pyramus and Thisby that will never please. First, Pyramus must draw a sword to kill himself; which the ladies cannot abide. How answer you that?

SNOUT. By'r lakin, a parlous fear!

STARV. I believe we must leave the killing out, when all is done.

BOT. Not a whit. I have a device to make all well. Write me a prologue; and let the prologue seem to say, we will do no harm with our swords, and that Pyramus is not kill'd indeed; and for the more better assurance, tell them that I Pyramus am not Pyramus, but Bottom the weaver. This will put them out of fear.

QUINCE. Well, we will have such a prologue, and it shall be written in eight and six.

BOT. No, make it two more; let it be written in eight and eight.

SNOUT. Will not the ladies be afeard of the lion?

STARV. I fear it, I promise you

Bот. Masters, you ought to consider with yourselves, to bring in (God shield us!) a lion among ladies is a most dreadful thing. For there is not a more fearful wild-fowl than your lion living; and we ought to look to't.

SNOUT. Therefore another prologue must tell he is not a lion.

Bот. Nay, you must name his name, and half his face must be seen through the lion's neck, and he himself must speak through, saying thus, or to the same defect: 'Ladies,'—or 'Fair ladies,—I would wish you'—or 'I would request you'—or 'I would entreat you—not to fear, not to tremble. My life for yours! If you think I come hither as a lion, it were pity of my life. No! I am no such thing. I am a man as other men are.' And there, indeed, let him name his name and tell them plainly he is Snug the joiner.

QUINCE. Well, it shall be so. But there is two hard things: that is, to bring the moonlight into a chamber; for, you know, Pyramus and Thisby meet by moonlight.

SNOUT. Doth the moon shine that night we play our play?

Bот. A calendar, a calendar! Look in the almanac. Find out moonshine, find out moonshine!

QUINCE. Yes, it doth shine that night.

Bот. Why, then may you leave a casement of the great chamber window, where we play, open, and the moon may shine in at the casement.

QUINCE. Ay; or else one must come in with a bush of thorns and a lantern, and say he comes to disfigure, or to present, the person of Moonshine. Then there is another thing. We must have a wall in the great chamber; for Pyramus and Thisby, says the story, did talk through the chink of a wall.

SNOUT. You can never bring in a wall. What say you, Bottom?

Bot. Some man or other must present Wall; and let him have some plaster, or some loam, or some roughcast about him, to signify wall; and let him hold his fingers thus; and through that cranny shall Pyramus and Thisby whisper.

Quince. If that may be, then all is well. Come, sit down every mother's son, and rehearse your parts. Pyramus, you begin. When you have spoken your speech, enter into that brake; and so every one according to his cue.

Enter Robin Goodfellow.

Rob. What hempen homespuns have we swagg'ring here,
So near the cradle of the Fairy Queen?
What, a play toward? I'll be an auditor;
An actor too perhaps, if I see cause.

Quince. Speak, Pyramus. Thisby, stand forth.

Pyr. Thisby, the flowers of odious savours sweet—

Quince. Odorous! odorous!

Pyr. —odours savours sweet;
So hath thy breath, my dearest Thisby dear.
But hark, a voice! Stay thou but here awhile,
And by-and-by I will to thee appear. *Exit.*

Rob. A stranger Pyramus than e'er play'd here!
Exit.

This. Must I speak now?

Quince. Ay, marry, must you; for you must understand he goes but to see a noise that he heard, and is to come again.

This. Most radiant Pyramus, most lily-white of hue,
Of colour like the red rose on triumphant brier,
Most brisky juvenal, and eke most lovely Jew,
As true as truest horse, that yet would never tire,
I'll meet thee, Pyramus, at Ninny's tomb.

QUINCE. 'Ninus' tomb,' man! Why, you must not speak that yet. That you answer to Pyramus. You speak all your part at once, cues and all. Pyramus, enter. Your cue is past; it is 'never tire.'

THIS. O—As true as truest horse, that yet would never tire.

Enter ROBIN *and* PYRAMUS *with an ass-head.*

PYR. If I were fair, Thisby, I were only thine.

QUINCE. O monstrous! O strange! We are haunted. Pray, masters! Fly, masters! Help!

Exeunt all the CLOWNS *but* BOTTOM.

ROB. I'll follow you; I'll lead you about a round,
Through bog, through bush, through brake, through brier.
Sometime a horse I'll be, sometime a hound,
A hog, a headless bear, sometime a fire;
And neigh, and bark, and grunt, and roar, and burn,
Like horse, hound, hog, bear, fire, at every turn.   *Exit.*

BOT. Why do they run away? This is a knavery of them to make me afeard.

Enter SNOUT.

SNOUT. O Bottom, thou art chang'd! What do I see on thee?

BOT. What do you see? You see an ass-head of your own, do you?   *Exit* SNOUT.

Enter QUINCE.

QUINCE. Bless thee, Bottom! bless thee! Thou art translated.   *Exit.*

BOT. I see their knavery. This is to make an ass of me; to fright me, if they could. But I will not stir from this place, do what they can. I will walk up and down here, and will sing, that they shall hear I am not afraid. [*Sings.*]

>The woosel cock so black of hue,
>　With orange-tawny bill,
>The throstle with his note so true,
>　The wren with little quill—

TITA. What angel wakes me from my flow'ry bed?
BOT. [*sings*]

>The finch, the sparrow, and the lark,
>　The plain-song cuckoo gray,
>Whose note full many a man doth mark,
>　And dares not answer nay.

For, indeed, who would set his wit to so foolish a bird?
Who would give a bird the lie, though he cry 'cuckoo'
never so?

TITA. I pray thee, gentle mortal, sing again.
Mine ear is much enamoured of thy note;
So is mine eye enthralled to thy shape;
And thy fair virtue's force (perforce) doth move me,
On the first view, to say, to swear, I love thee.

BOT. Methinks, mistress, you should have little reason
for that. And yet, to say the truth, reason and love keep
little company together now-a-days. The more the pity
that some honest neighbours will not make them friends.
Nay, I can gleek, upon occasion.

TITA. Thou art as wise as thou art beautiful.

BOT. Not so, neither; but if I had wit enough to get out
of this wood, I have enough to serve mine own turn.

TITA. Out of this wood do not desire to go.
Thou shalt remain here, whether thou wilt or no.
I am a spirit of no common rate,
The summer still doth tend upon my state;
And I do love thee. Therefore go with me.
I'll give thee fairies to attend on thee;
And they shall fetch thee jewels from the deep,
And sing while thou on pressed flowers dost sleep;
And I will purge thy mortal grossness so

That thou shalt like an airy spirit go.
Peaseblossom! Cobweb! Moth! and Mustardseed!

Enter four Fairies—PEASEBLOSSOM, COBWEB, MOTH,
and MUSTARDSEED.

PEAS. Ready.
COB. And I.
MOTH.   And I.
MUST.   And I.
ALL.   Where shall we go?
TITA. Be kind and courteous to this gentleman.
Hop in his walks and gambol in his eyes;
Feed him with apricocks and dewberries,
With purple grapes, green figs, and mulberries;
The honey-bags steal from the humblebees,
And for night tapers crop their waxen thighs,
And light them at the fiery glowworm's eyes,
To have my love to bed and to arise;
And pluck the wings from painted butterflies
To fan the moonbeams from his sleeping eyes.
Nod to him, elves, and do him courtesies.

PEAS. Hail, mortal!

COB Hail!

MOTH. Hail!

MUST. Hail!

BOT. I cry your worships mercy, heartily. I beseech
your worship's name.

COB. Cobweb.

BOT. I shall desire you of more acquaintance, good
Master Cobweb. If I cut my finger, I shall make bold
with you. Your name, honest gentleman?

PEAS. Peaseblossom.

BOT. I pray you, commend me to Mistress Squash,
your mother, and to Master Peascod, your father. Good

Master Peaseblossom, I shall desire you of more acquaintance too. Your name, I beseech you, sir?

MUST. Mustardseed.

BOT. Good Master Mustardseed, I know your patience well. That same cowardly, giantlike ox-beef hath devour'd many a gentleman of your house. I promise you your kindred hath made my eyes water ere now. I desire you of more acquaintance, good Master Mustardseed.

TITA. Come wait upon him; lead him to my bower.
The moon, methinks, looks with a wat'ry eye;
And when she weeps, weeps every little flower,
    Lamenting some enforced chastity.
Tie up my love's tongue, bring him silently.   *Exeunt*.

Scene II: Another part of the wood.

Enter OBERON, KING OF FAIRIES.

OB. I wonder if Titania be awak'd;
Then, what it was that next came in her eye,
Which she must dote on in extremity.

[*Enter* PUCK.]

Here comes my messenger. How now, mad spirit?
What night-rule now about this haunted grove?

PUCK. My mistress with a monster is in love.
Near to her close and consecrated bower,
While she was in her dull and sleeping hour,
A crew of patches, rude mechanicals,
That work for bread upon Athenian stalls,
Were met together to rehearse a play,
Intended for great Theseus' nuptial day.
The shallowest thickskin of that barren sort,
Who Pyramus presented in their sport,
Forsook his scene and ent'red in a brake.
When I did him at this advantage take,

An ass's nole I fixed on his head.
Anon his Thisby must be answered,
And forth my mimic comes. When they him spy,
As wild geese that the creeping fowler eye,
Or russet-pated choughs, many in sort,
Rising and cawing at the gun's report,
Sever themselves and madly sweep the sky;
So at his sight away his fellows fly;
And, at a stump, here o'er and o'er one falls;
He murther cries and help from Athens calls.
Their sense thus weak, lost with their fears thus strong,
Made senseless things begin to do them wrong;
For briers and thorns at their apparel snatch;
Some, sleeves—some, hats; from yielders all things catch.
I led them on in this distracted fear
And left sweet Pyramus translated there;
When in that moment (so it came to pass)
Titania wak'd, and straightway lov'd an ass.

Ob. This falls out better than I could devise.
But hast thou yet latch'd the Athenian's eyes
With the love-juice, as I did bid thee do?

Rob. I took him sleeping (that is finish'd too)
And the Athenian woman by his side,
That, when he wak'd, of force she must be ey'd.

Enter Demetrius *and* Hermia.

Ob. Stand close. This is the same Athenian.
Rob. This is the woman; but not this the man.
Dem. O, why rebuke you him that loves you so?
Lay breath so bitter on your bitter foe.
Her. Now I but chide; but I should use thee worse,
For thou, I fear, hast given me cause to curse.
If thou hast slain Lysander in his sleep,
Being o'er shoes in blood, plunge in the deep,
And kill me too.

The sun was not so true unto the day
As he to me. Would he have stolen away
From sleeping Hermia? I'll believe as soon
This whole earth may be bor'd, and that the moon
May through the centre creep, and so displease
Her brother's noontide with th' Antipodes.
It cannot be but thou hast murth'red him.
So should a murtherer look—so dead, so grim.

DEM. So should the murthered look, and so should I,
Pierc'd through the heart with your stern cruelty.
Yet you, the murtherer, look as bright, as clear,
As yonder Venus in her glimmering sphere.

HER. What's this to my Lysander? Where is he?
Ah, good Demetrius, wilt thou give him me?

DEM. I had rather give his carcass to my hounds.

HER. Out, dog! out, cur! Thou driv'st me past the bounds
Of maiden's patience. Hast thou slain him then?
Henceforth be never numb'red among men!
O, once tell true! tell true, even for my sake!
Durst thou have look'd upon him, being awake?
And hast thou kill'd him sleeping? O brave touch!
Could not a worm, an adder, do so much?
An adder did it; for with doubler tongue
Than thine (thou serpent!) never adder stung.

DEM. You spend your passion on a mispris'd mood.
I am not guilty of Lysander's blood;
Nor is he dead, for aught that I can tell.

HER. I pray thee, tell me then that he is well.

DEM. An if I could, what should I get therefore?

HER. A privilege never to see me more;
And from thy hated presence part I so.
See me no more, whether he be dead or no.   *Exit.*

DEM. There is no following her in this fierce vein.
Here therefore for a while I will remain.

So sorrow's heaviness doth heavier grow
For debt that bankrout sleep doth sorrow owe;
Which now in some slight measure it will pay,
If for his tender here I make some stay.

Lies down and sleeps.

Ob. What hast thou done? Thou hast mistaken quite
And laid the love-juice on some true-love's sight.
Of thy misprision must perforce ensue
Some true-love turn'd, and not a false turn'd true.

Rob. The fate o'errules, that, one man holding troth,
A million fail, confounding oath on oath.

Ob. About the wood! Go swifter than the wind,
And Helena of Athens look thou find.
All fancy-sick she is, and pale of cheer
With sighs of love, that costs the fresh blood dear.
By some illusion see thou bring her here.
I'll charm his eyes against she do appear.

Rob. I go, I go! Look how I go!
Swifter than arrow from the Tartar's bow.   *Exit.*

Ob.   Flower of this purple dye,
             Hit with Cupid's archery,
             Sink in apple of his eye!
             When his love he doth espy,
             Let her shine as gloriously
             As the Venus of the sky.
             When thou wak'st, if she be by,
             Beg of her for remedy.

Enter Puck.

Puck.   Captain of our fairy band,
          Helena is here at hand,
          And the youth, mistook my me,
          Pleading for a lover's fee.
          Shall we their fond pageant see?
          Lord, what fools these mortals be!

OB.   Stand aside. The noise they make
      Will cause Demetrius to awake.
PUCK. Then will two at once woo one.
      That must needs be sport alone;
      And those things do best please me
      That befall prepost'rously.

Enter LYSANDER *and* HELENA.

LYS. Why should you think that I should woo in scorn?
Scorn and derision never come in tears.
Look, when I vow, I weep; and vows so born,
  In their nativity all truth appears.
How can these things in me seem scorn to you,
Bearing the badge of faith to prove them true?
    HEL. You do advance your cunning more and more.
    When truth kills truth, O devilish-holy fray!
Those vows are Hermia's. Will you give her o'er?
    Weigh oath with oath, and you will nothing weigh.
Your vows to her and me, put in two scales,
Will even weigh; and both as light as tales.
    LYS. I had no judgment when to her I swore.
    HEL. Nor none, in my mind, now you give her o'er.
    LYS. Demetrius loves her; and he loves not you.
    DEM. [*awakes*] O Helen, goddess, nymph, perfect,
      divine!
To what, my love, shall I compare thine eyne?
Crystal is muddy. O, how ripe in show
Thy lips, those kissing cherries, tempting grow!
That pure congealed white, high Taurus' snow,
Fann'd with the eastern wind, turns to a crow
When thou hold'st up thy hand. O, let me kiss
This princess of pure white, this seal of bliss!
    HEL. O spite! O hell! I see you all are bent
To set against me for your merriment.
If you were civil and knew courtesy,

You would not do me thus much injury.
Can you not hate me, as I know you do,
But you must join in souls to mock me too?
If you were men, as men you are in show,
You would not use a gentle lady so;
To vow, and swear, and superpraise my parts,
When I am sure you hate me with your hearts.
You both are rivals, and love Hermia;
And now both rivals to mock Helena.
A trim exploit, a manly enterprise,
To conjure tears up in a poor maid's eyes
With your derision! None of noble sort
Would so offend a virgin and extort
A poor soul's patience, all to make you sport.

LYS. You are unkind, Demetrius. Be not so!
For you love Hermia. This you know I know;
And here, with all good will, with all my heart,
In Hermia's love I yield you up my part;
And yours of Helena to me bequeath,
Whom I do love, and will do to my death.

HEL. Never did mockers waste more idle breath.

DEM. Lysander, keep thy Hermia. I will none.
If e'er I lov'd her, all that love is gone.
My heart to her but as guestwise sojourn'd,
And now to Helen is it home return'd,
There to remain.

LYS.   Helen, it is not so.

DEM. Disparage not the faith thou dost not know,
Lest, to thy peril, thou aby it dear.
Look where thy love comes. Yonder is thy dear.

Enter HERMIA.

HER. Dark night, that from the eye his function takes,
The ear more quick of apprehension makes.
Wherein it doth impair the seeing sense,

It pays the hearing double recompense.
Thou art not by mine eye, Lysander, found;
Mine ear, I thank it, brought me to thy sound.
But why unkindly didst thou leave me so?

    Lys. Why should he stay whom love doth press to go?

    Her. What love could press Lysander from my side?

    Lys. Lysander's love, that would not let him bide—
Fair Helena; who more engilds the night
Than all yon fiery oes and eyes of light.
Why seek'st thou me? Could not this make thee know,
The hate I bare thee made me leave thee so?

    Her. You speak not as you think. It cannot be.

    Hel. Lo, she is one of this confederacy!
Now I perceive they have conjoin'd all three
To fashion this false sport in spite of me.
Injurious Hermia! most ungrateful maid!
Have you conspir'd, have you with these contriv'd
To bait me with this foul derision?
Is all the counsel that we two have shar'd,
The sister's vows, the hours that we have spent
When we have chid the hasty-footed time
For parting us—O, is all forgot?
All schooldays friendship, childhood innocence?
We, Hermia, like two artificial gods,
Have with our needles created both one flower,
Both on one sampler, sitting on one cushion,
Both warbling of one song, both in one key;
As if our hands, our sides, voices, and minds
Had been incorporate. So we grew together,
Like to a double cherry, seeming parted,
But yet an union in partition—
Two lovely berries moulded on one stem;
So, with two seeming bodies, but one heart;
Two of the first, like coats in heraldry,
Due but to one, and crowned with one crest.

And will you rent our ancient love asunder,
To join with men in scorning your poor friend?
It is not friendly, 'tis not maidenly!
Our sex, as well as I, may chide you for it,
Though I alone do feel the injury.

HER. I am amazed at your passionate words.
I scorn you not. It seems that you scorn me.

HEL. Have you not set Lysander, as in scorn,
To follow me and praise my eyes and face?
And made your other love, Demetrius
(Who even but now did spurn me with his foot),
To call me goddess, nymph, divine, and rare,
Precious, celestial? Wherefore speaks he this
To her he hates? And wherefore doth Lysander
Deny your love (so rich within his soul)
And tender me (forsooth) affection,
But by your setting on, by your consent?
What though I be not so in grace as you,
So hung upon with love, so fortunate;
But miserable most, to love unlov'd?
This you should pity rather than despise.

HER. I understand not what you mean by this.

HEL. Ay, do! persever, counterfeit sad looks;
Make mouths upon me when I turn my back;
Wink each at other; hold the sweet jest up.
This sport, well carried, shall be chronicled.
If you have any pity, grace, or manners,
You would not make me such an argument.
But fare ye well. 'Tis partly my own fault;
Which death or absence soon shall remedy.

LYS. Stay, gentle Helena; hear my excuse,
My love, my life, my soul, fair Helena!

HEL. O excellent!

HER.   Sweet, do not scorn her so.

DEM. If she cannot entreat, I can compel.

Lys. Thou canst compel no more than she entreat.
Thy threats have no more strength than her weak prayers.
Helen, I love thee; by my life, I do!
I swear by that which I will lose for thee
To prove him false that says I love thee not.

Dem. I say I love thee more than he can do.

Lys. If thou say so, withdraw and prove it too.

Dem. Quick, come!

Her.   Lysander, whereto tends all this?

Lys. Away, you Ethiope!

Dem.   No, no, sir! You
Seem to break loose, take on as you would follow,
But yet come not. You are a tame man, go!

Lys. Hang off, thou cat, thou burr! Vile thing, let
  loose,
Or I will shake thee from me like a serpent!

Her. Why are you grown so rude? What change is
  this,
Sweet love?

Lys.   Thy love? Out, tawny Tartar, out!
Out, loathed med'cine! O hated potion, hence!

Her. Do you not jest?

Hel.   Yes, sooth! and so do you.

Lys. Demetrius, I will keep my word with thee.

Dem. I would I had your bond; for I perceive
A weak bond holds you. I'll not trust your word.

Lys. What, should I hurt her, strike her, kill her dead?
Although I hate her, I'll not harm her so.

Her. What, can you do me greater harm than hate?
Hate me? Wherefore? O me! what news, my love?
Am not I Hermia? Are not you Lysander?
I am as fair now as I was erewhile.
Since night you lov'd me; yet since night you left me.
Why then, you left me (O, the gods forbid!)
In earnest, shall I say?

Lys.   Ay, by my life!
And never did desire to see thee more.
Therefore be out of hope, of question, doubt;
Be certain! Nothing truer. 'Tis no jest
That I do hate thee, and love Helena.

Her. O me! you juggler! you canker blossom!
You thief of love! What, have you come by night
And stol'n my love's heart from him?

Hel   Fine, i' faith!
Have you no modesty, no maiden shame,
No touch of bashfulness? What, will you tear
Impatient answers from my gentle tongue?
Fie, fie! you counterfeit, you puppet you!

Her. Puppet? Why, so! Ay, that way goes the game.
Now I perceive that she hath made compare
Between our statures; she hath urg'd her height,
And with her personage, her tall personage,
Her height (forsooth), she hath prevail'd with him.
And are you grown so high in his esteem
Because I am so dwarfish and so low?
How low am I, thou painted maypole? Speak!
How low am I? I am not yet so low
But that my nails can reach unto thine eyes.

Hel. I pray you, though you mock me, gentlemen,
Let her not hurt me. I was never curst;
I have no gift at all in shrewishness;
I am a right maid for my cowardice.
Let her not strike me. You perhaps may think,
Because she is something lower than myself,
That I can match her.

Her.   Lower? Hark again!

Hel. Good Hermia, do not be so bitter with me.
I evermore did love you, Hermia,
Did ever keep your counsels, never wrong'd you;
Save that, in love unto Demetrius,

I told him of your stealth unto this wood.
He followed you; for love I followed him;
But he hath chid me hence, and threat'ned me
To strike me, spurn me; nay, to kill me too.
And now, so you will let me quiet go,
To Athens will I bear my folly back
And follow you no further. Let me go.
You see how simple and how fond I am.

 HER. Why, get you gone! Who is't that hinders you?

 HEL. A foolish heart, that I leave here behind.

 HER. What, with Lysander?

 HEL.   With Demetrius

 LYS. Be not afraid. She shall not harm thee, Helena

 DEM. No, sir, she shall not, though you take her part.

 HEL. O, when she is angry, she is keen and shrewd!
She was a vixen when she went to school;
And though she be but little, she is fierce.

 HER. 'Little' again? nothing but 'low' and 'little'?
Why will you suffer her to flout me thus?
Let me come to her.

 LYS.   Get you gone, you dwarf!
You minimus, of hind'ring knotgrass made!
You bead, you acorn!

 DEM.   You are too officious
In her behalf that scorns your services.
Let her alone. Speak not of Helena;
Take not her part; for if thou dost intend
Never so little show of love to her,
Thou shalt aby it.

 LYS.   Now she holds me not.
Now follow, if thou dar'st, to try whose right,
Of thine or mine, is most in Helena.

 DEM. Follow? Nay, I'll go with thee, cheek by jowl.
       Exeunt LYSANDER *and* DEMETRIUS.

HER. You, mistress, all this coil is long of you.
Nay, go not back.

HEL.   I will not trust you, I,
Nor longer stay in your curst company.
Your hands than mine are quicker for a fray;
My legs are longer though, to run away.   *Exit.*

HER. I am amaz'd, and know not what to say.   *Exit.*

OB. This is thy negligence. Still thou mistak'st,
Or else committ'st thy knaveries wilfully.

PUCK. Believe me, king of shadows, I mistook.
Did not you tell me I should know the man
By the Athenian garments he had on?
And so far blameless proves my enterprise
That I have 'nointed an Athenian's eyes;
And so far am I glad it so did sort
As this their jangling I esteem a sport.

OB. Thou seest these lovers seek a place to fight.
Hie therefore, Robin, overcast the night.
The starry welkin cover thou anon
With drooping fog as black as Acheron,
And lead these testy rivals so astray
As one come not within another's way.
Like to Lysander sometime frame thy tongue,
Then stir Demetrius up with bitter wrong;
And sometime rail thou like Demetrius.
And from each other look thou lead them thus
Till o'er their brows death-counterfeiting sleep
With leaden legs and batty wings doth creep.
Then crush this herb into Lysander's eye;
Whose liquor hath this virtuous property,
To take from thence all error with his might
And make his eyeballs roll with wonted sight.
When they next wake, all this derision
Shall seem a dream and fruitless vision;

And back to Athens shall the lovers wend
With league whose date till death shall never end.
Whiles I in this affair do thee employ,
I'll to my queen and beg her Indian boy;
And then I will her charmed eye release
From monster's view, and all things shall be peace.

PUCK. My fairy lord, this must be done with haste,
For night's swift dragons cut the clouds full fast,
And yonder shines Aurora's harbinger;
At whose approach ghosts, wand'ring here and there,
Troop home to churchyards; damned spirits all,
That in crossways and floods have burial,
Already to their wormy beds are gone.
For fear lest day should look their shames upon,
They wilfully themselves exile from light,
And must for aye consort with black-brow'd night.

OB. But we are spirits of another sort.
I with the Morning's love have oft made sport;
And, like a forester, the groves may tread
Even till the eastern gate, all fiery red,
Opening on Neptune, with fair blessed beams
Turns into yellow gold his salt green streams.
But notwithstanding, haste; make no delay.
We may effect this business yet ere day.   *Exit.*

PUCK.   Up and down, up and down,
             I will lead them up and down.
             I am fear'd in field and town.
             Goblin, lead them up and down.
Here comes one.

Enter LYSANDER.

LYS. Where art thou, proud Demetrius? Speak thou
now.
ROB. Here, villain, drawn and ready. Where art thou?
LYS. I will be with thee straight.

Rob.   Follow me then
To plainer ground.   *Exit* Lysander.

Enter Demetrius.

Dem.   Lysander, speak again!
Thou runaway, thou coward, art thou fled?
Speak! In some bush? Where dost thou hide thy head?
Rob. Thou coward, art thou bragging to the stars,
Telling the bushes that thou look'st for wars,
And wilt not come? Come, recreant! come, thou child!
I'll whip thee with a rod. He is defil'd
That draws a sword on thee.
Dem.   Yea, art thou there?
Rob. Follow my voice. We'll try no manhood here.
                                    Exeunt.

Enter Lysander.

Lys. He goes before me and still dares me on;
When I come where he calls, then he is gone.
The villain is much lighter-heel'd than I.
I followed fast, but faster he did fly,
That fallen am I in dark uneven way,
And here will rest me. [*Lies down.*] Come, thou gentle
    day!
For if but once thou show me thy grey light,
I'll find Demetrius and revenge this spite.   *Sleeps.*

Enter Robin *and* Demetrius.

Rob. Ho, ho, ho! Coward, why com'st thou not?
Dem. Abide me, if thou dar'st; for well I wot
Thou run'st before me, shifting every place,
And dar'st not stand nor look me in the face.
Where art thou now?
Rob.   Come hither. I am here.
Dem. Nay then, thou mock'st me. Thou shalt buy this
    dear

If ever I thy face by daylight see.
Now, go thy way. Faintness constraineth me
To measure out my length on this cold bed.
By day's approach look to be visited.

Lies down and sleeps.

Enter HELENA.

HEL. O weary night, O long and tedious night,
  Abate thy hours! Shine comforts from the East,
That I may back to Athens by daylight
  From these that my poor company detest;
And sleep, that sometimes shuts up sorrow's eye,
Steal me awhile from mine own company. *Sleeps.*
ROB. Yet but three? Come one more.
    Two of both kinds makes up four.
    Here she comes, curst and sad.
    Cupid is a knavish lad
    Thus to make poor females mad.

Enter HERMIA.

HER. Never so weary, never so in woe;
  Bedabbled with the dew, and torn with briers;
I can no further crawl, no further go;
  My legs can keep no pace with my desires.
Here will I rest me till the break of day.
Heavens shield Lysander, if they mean a fray!

Lies down and sleeps.

ROB.   On the ground
      Sleep sound.
      I'll apply
      To your eye,
    Gentle lover, remedy.
    [*Squeezes the herb on* LYSANDER's *eyelids.*]

When thou wak'st,
Thou tak'st
True delight
In the sight
Of thy former lady's eye;
And the country proverb known,
That every man should take his own,
In your waking shall be shown:
Jack shall have Jill;
Naught shall go ill;
The man shall have his mare again, and all shall be well.

Exit.

Act IV: Scene I: The wood. Lysander, Demetrius, Helena, and Hermia, all lying asleep.

Enter TITANIA, QUEEN OF FAIRIES, *and* BOTTOM *the* CLOWN *and* FAIRIES, PEASEBLOSSOM, COBWEB, MOTH, MUSTARDSEED, *and others; and the* KING, OBERON, *behind them.*

TITA. Come, sit thee down upon this flow'ry bed,
While I thy amiable cheeks do coy,
And stick musk-roses in thy sleek smooth head,
And kiss thy fair large ears, my gentle joy.
BOT. Where's Peaseblossom?
PEAS. Ready.
BOT. Scratch my head, Peaseblossom. Where's Mounsieur Cobweb?
COB. Ready.
BOT. Mounsieur Cobweb, good mounsieur, get you your weapons in your hand, and kill me a red-hipp'd

humblebee on the top of a thistle; and, good mounsieur,
bring me the honey-bag. Do not fret yourself too much
in the action, mounsieur; and, good mounsieur, have a
care the honey-bag break not. I would be loath to have
you overflowen with a honey-bag, signior. Where's
Mounsieur Mustardseed?

Mus. Ready.

Bot. Give me your neaf, Mounsieur Mustardseed.
Pray you, leave your curtsy, good mounsieur.

Mus. What's your will?

Bot. Nothing, good mounsieur, but to help Cavalery
Peaseblossom to scratch. I must to the barber's, mounsieur; for methinks I am marvail's hairy about the face;
and I am such a tender ass, if my hair do but tickle me,
I must scratch.

Tita. What, wilt thou hear some music, my sweet love?

Bot. I have a reasonable good ear in music. Let's have
the tongs and the bones.

Tita. Or say, sweet love, what thou desirest to eat.

Bot. Truly, a peck of provender. I could munch your
good dry oats. Methinks I have a great desire to a bottle
of hay. Good hay, sweet hay, hath no fellow.

Tita. I have a venturous fairy that shall seek
The squirrel's hoard, and fetch thee thence new nuts.

Bot. I had rather have a handful or two of dried pease.
But I pray you, let none of your people stir me. I have an
exposition of sleep come upon me.

Tita. Sleep thou, and I will wind thee in my arms.
Fairies, be gone, and be all ways away.

[*Exeunt* Fairies.]

So doth the woodbine the sweet honeysuckle
Gently entwist; the female ivy so
Enrings the barky fingers of the elm.
O, how I love thee! how I dote on thee!   *They sleep.*

Enter ROBIN GOODFELLOW.

OB. [*advances*] Welcome, good Robin. Seest thou
    this sweet sight?
Her dotage now I do begin to pity;
For, meeting her of late behind the wood,
Seeking sweet favours for this hateful fool,
I did upbraid her and fall out with her.
For she his hairy temples then had rounded
With coronet of fresh and fragrant flowers;
And that same dew which sometime on the buds
Was wont to swell like round and orient pearls
Stood now within the pretty flouriets' eyes,
Like tears that did their own disgrace bewail.
When I had at my pleasure taunted her,
And she in mild terms begg'd my patience,
I then did ask of her her changeling child;
Which straight she gave me, and her fairy sent
To bear him to my bower in fairyland.
And now I have the boy, I will undo
This hateful imperfection of her eyes.
And, gentle Puck, take this transformed scalp
From off the head of this Athenian swain;
That, he awaking when the other do,
May all to Athens back again repair,
And think no more of this night's accidents
But as the fierce vexation of a dream.
But first I will release the Fairy Queen.
            Be as thou wast wont to be;
            See as thou wast wont to see.
            Dian's bud o'er Cupid's flower
            Hath such force and blessed power.
Now, my Titania! Wake you, my sweet queen.
    TITA. My Oberon, what visions have I seen!
Methought I was enamour'd of an ass.

Ob. There lies your love.

Tita.   How came these things to pass?
O, how mine eyes do loathe his visage now!

Ob. Silence awhile. Robin, take off this head.
Titania, music call; and strike more dead
Than common sleep of all these five the sense.

Tita. Music, ho, music! such as charmeth sleep!

Rob. Now, when thou wak'st, with thine own fool's
    eyes peep.

Ob. Sound, music!   [Music.]
              Come, my queen, take hands with me.
And rock the ground whereon these sleepers be.
                                        [Dance.]

Now thou and I are new in amity,
And will to-morrow midnight solemnly
Dance in Duke Theseus' house triumphantly
And bless it to all fair prosperity.
There shall the pairs of faithful lovers be
Wedded, with Theseus, all in jollity.

Rob.   Fairy King, attend and mark.
    ' I do hear the morning lark.

Ob.   Then, my queen, in silence sad
         Trip we after night's shade.
         We the globe can compass soon,
         Swifter than the wand'ring moon.

Tita.   Come, my lord, and in our flight
         Tell me how it came this night
         That I sleeping here was found
         With these mortals on the ground.   Exeunt.
              Wind horn.

Enter Theseus *and all his Train;* Hippolyta, Egeus.

The. Go, one of you, find out the forester;
For now our observation is perform'd;
And since we have the vaward of the day,

My love shall hear the music of my hounds.
Uncouple in the western valley; let them go.
Dispatch, I say, and find the forester.

[*Exit an* ATTENDANT.]

We will, fair Queen, up to the mountain's top
And mark the musical confusion
Of hounds and echo in conjunction.

HIP. I was with Hercules and Cadmus once
When in a wood of Crete they bay'd the bear
With hounds of Sparta. Never did I hear
Such gallant chiding; for, besides the groves,
The skies, the fountains, every region near
Seem'd all one mutual cry. I never heard
So musical a discord, such sweet thunder.

THE. My hounds are bred out of the Spartan kind;
So flew'd, so sanded; and their heads are hung
With ears that sweep away the morning dew;
Crook-knee'd, and dew-lapp'd like Thessalian bulls;
Slow in pursuit, but match'd in mouth like bells,
Each under each. A cry more tuneable
Was never holloa'd to nor cheer'd with horn
In Crete, in Sparta, nor in Thessaly.
Judge when you hear. But, soft! What nymphs are these?

EGE. My lord, this is my daughter here asleep;
And this, Lysander; this Demetrius is;
This Helena, old Nedar's Helena.
I wonder of their being here together.

THE. No doubt they rose up early to observe
The rite of May; and, hearing our intent,
Came here in grace of our solemnity.
But speak, Egeus. Is not this the day
That Hermia should give answer of her choice?

EGE. It is, my lord.

THE. Go, bid the huntsmen wake them with their
horns.

[Exit an ATTENDANT. *Shout within. Wind horns.*
They all start up.]

Good morrow, friends. Saint Valentine is past.
Begin these woodbirds but to couple now?

　　LYS. Pardon, my lord.　　　　　　　*They kneel.*
　　THE.　　　　　　I pray you all, stand up.
I know you two are rival enemies.
How comes this gentle concord in the world
That hatred is so far from jealousy
To sleep by hate and fear no enmity?

　　LYS. My lord, I shall reply amazedly,
Half sleep, half waking; but as yet, I swear,
I cannot truly say how I came here;
But, as I think (for truly would I speak),
And now I do bethink me, so it is—
I came with Hermia hither. Our intent
Was to be gone from Athens, where we might,
Without the peril of the Athenian law—

　　EGE. Enough, enough, my lord! you have enough.
I beg the law, the law, upon his head.
They would have stol'n away; they would, Demetrius!
Thereby to have defeated you and me—
You of your wife, and me of my consent,
Of my consent that she should be your wife.

　　DEM. My lord, fair Helen told me of their stealth,
Of this their purpose hither, to this wood;
And I in fury hither followed them,
Fair Helena in fancy following me.
But, my good lord, I wot not by what power
(But by some power it is) my love to Hermia,
Melted as the snow, seems to me now
As the remembrance of an idle gaud
Which in my childhood I did dote upon;
And all the faith, the virtue of my heart,
The object and the pleasure of mine eye,

Is only Helena. To her, my lord,
Was I betroth'd ere I saw Hermia;
But, like a sickness, did I loathe this food;
But, as in health, come to my natural taste,
Now I do wish it, love it, long for it,
And will for evermore be true to it.

THE. Fair lovers, you are fortunately met.
Of this discourse we more will hear anon.
Egeus, I will overbear your will;
For in the temple, by-and-by, with us,
These couples shall eternally be knit;
And, for the morning now is something worn,
Our purpos'd hunting shall be set aside.
Away, with us to Athens! Three and three,
We'll hold a feast in great solemnity.
Come, Hippolyta.

> *Exeunt* DUKE THESEUS, HIPPOLYTA, EGEUS, *and*
> LORDS.

DEM. These things seem small and undistinguishable,
Like far-off mountains turned into clouds.

HER. Methinks I see these things with parted eye,
When everything seems double.

HEL.   So methinks;
And I have found Demetrius like a jewel,
Mine own, and not mine own.

DEM.   Are you sure
That we are awake? It seems to me
That yet we sleep, we dream. Do not you think
The Duke was here, and bid us follow him?

HER. Yea, and my father.

HEL.   And Hippolyta.

LYS. And he did bid us follow to the temple.

DEM. Why then, we are awake. Let's follow him,
And by the way let us recount our dreams.   *Exeunt*.

BOT. [*wakes*] When my cue comes, call me, and I will

answer. My next is 'Most fair Pyramus.' Hey-ho! Peter Quince! Flute the bellows-mender! Snout the tinker! Starveling! God's my life! Stol'n hence, and left me asleep! I have had a most rare vision. I have had a dream, past the wit of man to say what dream it was. Man is but an ass if he go about to expound this dream. Methought I was—there is no man can tell what. Methought I was, and methought I had— But man is but a patch'd fool if he will offer to say what methought I had. The eye of man hath not heard, the ear of man hath not seen, man's hand is not able to taste, his tongue to conceive, nor his heart to report what my dream was. I will get Peter Quince to write a ballet of this dream. It shall be call'd 'Bottom's Dream,' because it hath no bottom; and I will sing it in the latter end of our play, before the Duke. Peradventure, to make it the more gracious, I shall sing it at her death.   *Exit.*

Scene II: Athens. Quince's house.

Enter QUINCE, FLUTE, SNOUT, *and* STARVELING.

QUINCE. Have you sent to Bottom's house? Is he come home yet?

STARV. He cannot be heard of. Out of doubt he is transported.

FLUTE. If he come not, then the play is marr'd; it goes not forward, doth it?

QUINCE. It is not possible. You have not a man in all Athens able to discharge Pyramus but he.

FLUTE. No, he hath simply the best wit of any handicraft man in Athens.

QUINCE. Yea, and the best person too, and he is a very paramour for a sweet voice.

FLUTE. You must say 'paragon.' A paramour is (God bless us!) a thing of naught.

Enter SNUG THE JOINER.

SNUG. Masters, the Duke is coming from the temple, and there is two or three lords and ladies more married. If our sport had gone forward, we had all been made men.

FLUTE. O sweet bully Bottom! Thus hath he lost sixpence a day during his life. He could not have scaped sixpence a day. An the Duke had not given him sixpence a day for playing Pyramus, I'll be hanged! He would have deserved it. Sixpence a day in Pyramus, or nothing!

Enter BOTTOM.

BOT. Where are these lads? Where are these hearts?

QUINCE. Bottom! O most courageous day! O most happy hour!

BOT. Masters, I am to discourse wonders; but ask me not what. For if I tell you, I am no true Athenian. I will tell you everything, right as it fell out.

QUINCE. Let us hear, sweet Bottom.

BOT. Not a word of me. All that I will tell you is, that the Duke hath dined. Get your apparel together, good strings to your beards, new ribbands to your pumps; meet presently at the palace; every man look o'er his part; for the short and the long is, our play is preferr'd. In any case, let Thisby have clean linen; and let not him that plays the lion pare his nails, for they shall hang out for the lion's claws. And, most dear actors, eat no onions nor garlic, for we are to utter sweet breath; and I do not doubt but to hear them say it is a sweet comedy. No more words. Away! go, away!　　　　　　　　　*Exeunt.*

Act V: Scene I: Athens. The Palace of Theseus.

Enter THESEUS, HIPPOLYTA, *and* PHILOSTRATE, *with*
LORDS *and* ATTENDANTS.

HIP. 'Tis strange, my Theseus, that these lovers speak
of.
THE. More strange than true. I never may believe
These antique fables nor these fairy toys.
Lovers and madmen have such seething brains,
Such shaping fantasies, that apprehend
More than cool reason ever comprehends.
The lunatic, the lover, and the poet
Are of imagination all compact.
One sees more devils than vast hell can hold:
That is the madman. The lover, all as frantic,
Sees Helen's beauty in a brow of Egypt.
The poet's eye, in a fine frenzy rolling,
Doth glance from heaven to earth, from earth to heaven,
And as imagination bodies forth
The forms of things unknown, the poet's pen
Turns them to shapes, and gives to airy nothing
A local habitation and a name.
Such tricks hath strong imagination
That, if it would but apprehend some joy,
It comprehends some bringer of that joy;
Or in the night, imagining some fear,
How easy is a bush suppos'd a bear!
HIP. But all the story of the night told over,
And all their minds transfigur'd so together,
More witnesseth than fancy's images
And grows to something of great constancy;
But howsoever, strange and admirable.

Enter Lovers—LYSANDER, DEMETRIUS, HERMIA, *and*
HELENA.

THE. Here come the lovers, full of joy and mirth.
Joy, gentle friends, joy and fresh days of love
Accompany your hearts!
    LYS.   More than to us
Wait in your royal walks, your board, your bed!
    THE. Come now, what masques, what dances shall we
        have,
To wear away this long age of three hours
Between our after-supper and bedtime?
Where is our usual manager of mirth?
What revels are in hands? Is there no play
To ease the anguish of a torturing hour?
Call Philostrate.
    PHIL.   Here, mighty Theseus.
    THE. Say, what abridgment have you for this evening?
What masque? what music? How shall we beguile
The lazy time, if not with some delight?
    PHIL. There is a brief how many sports are ripe.
Make choice of which your Highness will see first.
                                    Gives a paper.
    THE. 'The battle with the Centaurs, to be sung
By an Athenian eunuch to the harp.'
We'll none of that. That have I told my love
In glory of my kinsman Hercules.
'The riot of the tipsy Bacchanals,
Tearing the Thracian singer in their rage.'
That is an old device; and it was play'd
When I from Thebes came last a conqueror.
'The thrice three Muses mourning for the death
Of Learning, late deceas'd in beggary.'
That is some satire keen and critical,
Not sorting with a nuptial ceremony.

'A tedious brief scene of young Pyramus
And his love Thisby; very tragical mirth.'
Merry and tragical? tedious and brief?
That is hot ice and wondrous strange snow.
How shall we find the concord of this discord?

PHIL. A play there is, my lord, some ten words long,
Which is as brief as I have known a play;
But by ten words, my lord, it is too long,
Which makes it tedious; for in all the play
There is not one word apt, one player fitted.
And tragical, my noble lord, it is;
For Pyramus therein doth kill himself.
Which when I saw rehears'd, I must confess,
Made mine eyes water; but more merry tears
The passion of loud laughter never shed.

THE. What are they that do play it?

PHIL. Hard-handed men that work in Athens here,
Which never labour'd in their minds till now;
And now have toil'd their unbreathed memories
With this same play, against your nuptial.

THE. And we will hear it.

PHIL.   No, my noble lord;
It is not for you. I have heard it over,
And it is nothing, nothing in the world;
Unless you can find sport in their intents,
Extremely stretch'd and conn'd with cruel pain,
To do you service.

THE.   I will hear that play;
For never anything can be amiss
When simpleness and duty tender it.
Go bring them in; and take your places, ladies.

                                    Exit PHILOSTRATE.

HIP. I love not to see wretchedness o'ercharg'd,
And duty in his service perishing.

THE Why, gentle sweet, you shall see no such thing.

HIP. He says they can do nothing in this kind.

THE. The kinder we, to give them thanks for nothing.
Our sport shall be to take what they mistake;
And what poor duty cannot do, noble respect
Takes it in might, not merit.
Where I have come, great clerks have purposed
To greet me with premeditated welcomes;
Where I have seen them shiver and look pale,
Make periods in the midst of sentences,
Throttle their practis'd accent in their fears,
And, in conclusion, dumbly have broke off,
Not paying me a welcome. Trust me, sweet,
Out of this silence yet I pick'd a welcome;
And in the modesty of fearful duty
I read as much as from the rattling tongue
Of saucy and audacious eloquence.
Love, therefore, and tongue-tied simplicity
In least speak most, to my capacity.

Enter PHILOSTRATE.

PHIL. So please your Grace, the Prologue is address'd.

THE. Let him approach.

Flourish trumpets. Enter the PROLOGUE (QUINCE).

PRO. If we offend, it is with our good will.
  That you should think, we come not to offend,
But with good will. To show our simple skill,
  That is the true beginning of our end.
Consider then, we come but in despite.
  We do not come, as minding to content you,
Our true intent is. All for your delight,
  We are not here. That you should here repent you,
The actors are at hand: and, by their show,
You shall know all, that you are like to know.

THE. This fellow doth not stand upon points.

LYS. He hath rid his prologue like a rough colt; he

knows not the stop. A good moral, my lord: it is not enough to speak, but to speak true.

HIP. Indeed he hath play'd on his prologue like a child on a recorder—a sound, but not in government.

THE. His speech was like a tangled chain; nothing impaired, but all disordered. Who is next?

Enter PYRAMUS *and* THISBY, *and* WALL *and* MOONSHINE *and* LION.

PRO. Gentles, perchance you wonder at this show;
 But wonder on, till truth make all things plain.
This man is Pyramus, if you would know;
 This beauteous lady Thisby is certain.
This man, with lime and roughcast, doth present
 Wall, that vile Wall which did these lovers sunder;
And through Wall's chink, poor souls, they are content
 To whisper. At the which let no man wonder.
This man, with lantern, dog, and bush of thorn,
 Presenteth Moonshine. For, if you will know,
By moonshine did these lovers think no scorn
 To meet at Ninus' tomb, there, there to woo.
This grisly beast, which Lion hight by name,
The trusty Thisby, coming first by night,
Did scare away, or rather did affright;
 And as she fled, her mantle she did fall,
Which Lion vile with bloody mouth did stain.
Anon comes Pyramus, sweet youth and tall,
 And finds his trusty Thisby's mantle slain;
Whereat, with blade, with bloody blameful blade,
 He bravely broach'd his boiling bloody breast.
And Thisby, tarrying in mulberry shade,
 His dagger drew, and died. For all the rest,
Let Lion, Moonshine, Wall, and lovers twain
At large discourse while here they do remain.

THE. I wonder if the lion be to speak.

DEM. No wonder, my lord. One lion may, when many asses do.

   Exeunt PROLOGUE, PYRAMUS, LION, THISBY, *and*
              MOONSHINE.

WALL. In this same enterlude it doth befall
That I, one Snout by name, present a wall;
And such a wall, as I would have you think,
That had in it a crannied hole or chink;
Through which the lovers, Pyramus and Thisby,
Did whisper often, very secretly.
This loam, this roughcast, and this stone doth show
That I am that same wall. The truth is so.
And this the cranny is, right and sinister,
Through which the fearful lovers are to whisper.

THE. Would you desire lime and hair to speak better?

DEM. It is the wittiest partition that ever I heard discourse, my lord.

Enter PYRAMUS.

THE. Pyramus draws near the wall. Silence!

PYR. O grim-look'd night! O night with hue so black!
O night, which ever art when day is not!
O night, O night! alack, alack, alack,
I fear my Thisby's promise is forgot!
And thou, O wall, O sweet, O lovely wall,
That stand'st between her father's ground and mine!
Thou wall, O wall, O sweet and lovely wall,
Show me thy chink, to blink through with mine eyne!
[WALL *holds up his fingers.*]
Thanks, courteous wall. Jove shield thee well for this!
But what see I? No Thisby do I see.
O wicked wall, through whom I see no bliss,
Curs'd be thy stones for thus deceiving me!

THE. The wall, methinks, being sensible, should curse again.

PYR. No, in truth, sir, he should not. 'Deceiving me' is Thisby's cue. She is to enter now, and I am to spy her through the wall. You shall see it will fall pat as I told you. Yonder she comes.

Enter THISBY.

THIS. O Wall, full often hast thou heard my moans
For parting my fair Pyramus and me!

My cherry lips have often kiss'd thy stones,
  Thy stones with lime and hair knit up in thee.
PYR. I see a voice. Now will I to the chink,
  To spy an I can hear my Thisby's face.
Thisby!
  THIS. My love! thou art my love, I think.
  PYR. Think what thou wilt, I am thy lover's grace;
And, like Limander, am I trusty still.
  THIS. And I, like Helen, till the Fates me kill.
  PYR. Not Shafalus to Procrus was so true.
  THIS. As Shafalus to Procrus, I to you.
  PYR. O, kiss me through the hole of this vile wall!
  THIS. I kiss the wall's hole, not your lips at all.
  PYR. Wilt thou at Ninny's tomb meet me straightway?
  THIS. Tide life, tide death, I come without delay.

Exeunt PYRAMUS *and* THISBY.

WALL. Thus have I, Wall, my part discharged so;
And, being done, thus Wall away doth go.

Exit.

THE. Now is the mural down between the two neighbours.

DEM. No remedy, my lord, when walls are so wilful to hear without warning.

HIP. This is the silliest stuff that ever I heard.

THE. The best in this kind are but shadows; and the worst are no worse, if imagination amend them.

HIP. It must be your imagination then, and not theirs.

THE. If we imagine no worse of them than they of themselves, they may pass for excellent men. Here come two noble beasts in, a man and a lion.

Enter LION *and* MOONSHINE.

LION. You, ladies, you, whose gentle hearts do fear
  The smallest monstrous mouse that creeps on floor,
May now perchance both quake and tremble here,
  When lion rough in wildest rage doth roar.
Then know that I one Snug the joiner am,
A lion fell, nor else no lion's dam;
For, if I should as lion come in strife
Into this place, 'twere pity on my life.

THE. A very gentle beast, and of a good conscience.

DEM. The very best at a beast, my lord, that e'er I saw.

LYS. This lion is a very fox for his valour.

THE. True; and a goose for his discretion.

DEM. Not so, my lord; for his valour cannot carry his discretion, and the fox carries the goose.

THE. His discretion, I am sure, cannot carry his valour; for the goose carries not the fox. It is well. Leave it to his discretion, and let us listen to the moon.

MOON. This lanthorn doth the horned moon present—

DEM. He should have worn the horns on his head.

THE. He is no crescent, and his horns are invisible within the circumference.

MOON. This lanthorn doth the horned moon present.
Myself the man i' th' moon do seem to be.

THE. This is the greatest error of all the rest. The man should be put into the lanthorn. How is it else the man i' th' moon?

DEM. He dares not come there for the candle; for, you see, it is already in snuff.

HIP. I am aweary of this moon. Would he would change!

THE. It appears, by his small light of discretion, that he is in the wane; but yet, in courtesy, in all reason, we must stay the time.

LYS. Proceed, Moon.

MOON. All that I have to say is to tell you that the lanthorn is the moon; I, the man i' th' moon; this thornbush, my thornbush; and this dog, my dog.

DEM. Why, all these should be in the lanthorn; for all these are in the moon. But silence! Here comes Thisby.

Enter THISBY.

THIS. This is old Ninny's tomb. Where is my love?

LION. O!   *The* LION *roars.* THISBY *runs off.*

DEM. Well roar'd, Lion!

THE. Well run, Thisby!

HIP. Well shone, Moon! Truly, the moon shines with a good grace.

> *The* LION *tears* THISBY'S *mantle, and exit.*

THE. Well mous'd, Lion!

DEM. And then came Pyramus.

LYS. And so the lion vanish'd.

Enter PYRAMUS.

PYR. Sweet moon, I thank thee for thy sunny beams;
I thank thee, moon, for shining now so bright;
For, by thy gracious, golden, glittering gleams,
    I trust to take of truest Thisby sight.
        But stay! O spite!
        But mark, poor knight!
      What dreadful dole is here?
        Eyes, do you see?
        How can it be?
      O dainty duck! O dear!
        Thy mantle good,
        What, stain'd with blood?
      Approach, ye Furies fell!
        O Fates, come, come!
        Cut thread and thrum;
      Quail, crush, conclude, and quell!

THE. This passion, and the death of a dear friend, would go near to make a man look sad.

HIP. Beshrew my heart but I pity the man.

PYR. O, wherefore, Nature, didst thou lions frame?
Since lion vile hath here deflow'r'd my dear;
Which is—no, no!—which was the fairest dame
    That liv'd, that lov'd, that lik'd, that look'd with cheer.
        Come, tears, confound!
        Out, sword, and wound
      The pap of Pyramus!
        Ay, that left pap
        Where heart doth hop.

> [*Stabs himself.*]

Thus die I, thus, thus, thus.
   Now am I dead,
   Now am I fled;
My soul is in the sky.
   Tongue, lose thy light;
   Moon, take thy flight.

[*Exit* MOONSHINE.]

Now die, die, die, die, die!   *Dies.*

DEM. No die, but an ace, for him! for he is but one.

LYS. Less than an ace, man; for he is dead, he is
nothing.

THE. With the help of a surgeon he might yet recover,
and yet prove an ass.

HIP. How chance Moonshine is gone before Thisby
comes back and finds her lover?

Enter THISBY.

THE. She will find him by starlight. Here she comes;
and her passion ends the play.

HIP. Methinks she should not use a long one for such
a Pyramus. I hope she will be brief.

DEM. A mote will turn the balance, which Pyramus,
which Thisby, is the better; he for a man, God warr'nd
us!—she for a woman, God bless us!

LYS. She hath spied him already with those sweet eyes.

DEM. And thus she means, videlicet:

THIS.   Asleep, my love?
      What, dead, my dove?
O Pyramus, arise!
      Speak, speak! Quite dumb?
      Dead, dead? A tomb
Must cover thy sweet eyes.
      These lily lips,
      This cherry nose,
These yellow cowslip cheeks,
      Are gone, are gone.
      Lovers, make moan!

His eyes were green as leeks.
  O Sisters Three,
  Come, come to me,
With hands as pale as milk;
  Lay them in gore,
  Since you have shore
With shears his thread of silk.
  Tongue, not a word!
  Come, trusty sword;
Come, blade, my breast imbrue!
                              [*Stabs herself.*]

And farewell, friends.
Thus Thisby ends.
Adieu, adieu, adieu!
                                        Dies.

THE. Moonshine and Lion are left to bury the dead.

DEM. Ay, and Wall too.

BOT. [*starts up*] No, I assure you; the wall is down that parted their fathers. Will it please you to see the Epilogue, or to hear a Bergomask dance between two of our company?

THE. No epilogue, I pray you; for your play needs no excuse. Never excuse; for when the players are all dead, there need none to be blamed. Marry, if he that writ it had played Pyramus and hang'd himself in Thisby's garter, it would have been a fine tragedy; and so it is truly, and very notably discharg'd. But, come, your Bergomask! Let your epilogue alone.   [*A dance.*]
The iron tongue of midnight hath told twelve.
Lovers, to bed; 'tis almost fairy time.
I fear we shall outsleep the coming morn
As much as we this night have overwatch'd.
This palpable gross play hath well beguil'd
The heavy gait of night. Sweet friends, to bed.
A fortnight hold we this solemnity
In nightly revels and new jollity.   *Exeunt.*

Enter Puck, *with a broom.*

Puck. Now the hungry lion roars,
    And the wolf behowls the moon;
Whilst the heavy ploughman snores,
    All with weary task fordone.
Now the wasted brands do glow,
    Whilst the screech owl, screeching loud,
Puts the wretch that lies in woe
    In remembrance of a shroud.
Now it is the time of night
    That the graves, all gaping wide,
Every one lets forth his sprite,
    In the churchway paths to glide;
And we fairies, that do run
    By the triple Hecate's team
From the presence of the sun,
    Following darkness like a dream,
Now are frolic. Not a mouse
Shall disturb this hallowed house.
I am sent, with broom, before,
To sweep the dust behind the door.

Enter King *and* Queen of Fairies, *with all their Train.*

Ob. Through the house give glimmering light,
    By the dead and drowsy fire;
Every elf and fairy sprite
    Hop as light as bird from brier;
And this ditty, after me,
Sing, and dance it trippingly.
Tita. First rehearse your song by rote,
To each word a warbling note.
Hand in hand, with fairy grace,
Will we sing, and bless this place.

                Song and dance.

OB.   Now, until the break of day,
Through this house each fairy stray.
To the best bride-bed will we,
Which by us shall blessed be;
And the issue there create
Ever shall be fortunate.
So shall all the couples three
Ever true in loving be;
And the blots of Nature's hand
Shall not in their issue stand;
Never mole, harelip, nor scar,
Nor mark prodigious, such as are
Despised in nativity,
Shall upon their children be.
With this field-dew consecrate,
Every fairy take his gait,
And each several chamber bless,
Through this palace, with sweet peace.
And the owner of it blest
Ever shall in safety rest.
Trip away; make no stay;
Meet me all by break of day.

          Exeunt all but ROBIN GOODFELLOW.

ROB.   If we shadows have offended,
Think but this, and all is mended—
That you have but slumb'red here
While these visions did appear.
And this weak and idle theme,
No more yielding but a dream,
Gentles, do not reprehend.
If you pardon, we will mend.
And, as I am an honest Puck,
If we have unearned luck
Now to scape the serpent's tongue,

We will make amends ere long;
Else a Puck a liar call.
So, good night unto you all.
Give me your hands, if we be·friends,
And Robin shall restore amends.   *Exit.*

As You Like It

NAMES OF THE ACTORS

DUKE SENIOR, living in banishment.

DUKE FREDERICK, his brother, and usurper of his dukedom.

AMIENS,
JAQUES, } lords attending on the banished DUKE.

LE BEAU, a courtier attending on DUKE FREDERICK.

CHARLES, wrestler to DUKE FREDERICK.

OLIVER,
JAQUES DE BOYS, } sons of SIR ROWLAND DE BOYS.
ORLANDO,

ADAM,
DENNIS, } servants to OLIVER.

TOUCHSTONE, a clown.

SIR OLIVER MARTEXT, a vicar.

CORIN,
SILVIUS, } shepherds.

WILLIAM, a country fellow, in love with AUDREY.

HYMEN.

ROSALIND, daughter to the banished DUKE.

CELIA, daughter to DUKE FREDERICK.

PHEBE, a shepherdess.   AUDREY, a country wench.

Lords, Pages, and Attendants, &c.

Act I: Scene I: Oliver's orchard.

Enter ORLANDO *and* ADAM.

ORL. As I remember, Adam, it was upon this fashion: he bequeathed me by will but poor a thousand crowns, and, as thou say'st, charged my brother on his blessing to breed me well; and there begins my sadness. My brother Jaques he keeps at school, and report speaks goldenly of his profit. For my part, he keeps me rustically at home or, to speak more properly, stays me here at home unkept; for call you that keeping for a gentleman of my birth that differs not from the stalling of an ox? His horses are bred better; for, besides that they are fair with their feeding, they are taught their manage, and to that end riders dearly hir'd; but I, his brother, gain nothing under him but growth, for the which his animals on his dunghills are as much bound to him as I. Besides this nothing that he so plentifully gives me, the something that nature gave me his countenance seems to take from me. He lets me feed with his hinds, bars me the place of a brother, and, as much as in him lies, mines my gentility with my education. This is it, Adam, that grieves me; and the spirit of my father, which I think is within me, begins to mutiny against this servitude. I will no longer endure it, though yet I know no wise remedy how to avoid it.

Enter OLIVER.

ADAM. Yonder comes my master, your brother.

ORL. Go apart, Adam, and thou shalt hear how he will shake me up. ADAM *retires.*

OLI. Now, sir, what make you here?

ORL. Nothing. I am not taught to make anything.

OLI. What mar you then, sir?

ORL. Marry, sir, I am helping you to mar that which

God made, a poor unworthy brother of yours, with idleness.

OLI. Marry, sir, be better employed, and be naught awhile!

ORL. Shall I keep your hogs and eat husks with them? What prodigal portion have I spent that I should come to such penury?

OLI. Know you where you are, sir?

ORL. O, sir, very well. Here in your orchard.

OLI. Know you before whom, sir?

ORL. Ay, better than him I am before knows me. I know you are my eldest brother, and in the gentle condition of blood you should so know me. The courtesy of nations allows you my better in that you are the first born; but the same tradition takes not away my blood, were there twenty brothers betwixt us. I have as much of my father in me as you, albeit I confess your coming before me is nearer to his reverence.

OLI. What, boy!   *Strikes him.*

ORL. Come, come, elder brother, you are too young in this.   *Seizes him.*

OLI. Wilt thou lay hands on me, villain?

ORL. I am no villain. I am the youngest son of Sir Rowland de Boys; he was my father, and he is thrice a villain that says such a father begot villains. Wert thou not my brother, I would not take this hand from thy throat till this other had pull'd out thy tongue for saying so. Thou hast rail'd on thyself.

ADAM. [*comes forward*] Sweet masters, be patient! For your father's remembrance, be at accord!

OLI. Let me go, I say.

ORL. I will not till I please. You shall hear me. My father charg'd you in his will to give me good education. You have train'd me like a peasant, obscuring and hiding from me all gentlemanlike qualities. The spirit of my father grows strong in me, and I will no longer endure it. Therefore allow me such exercises as may become a gentleman, or give me the poor allottery my father left me by testament. With that I will go buy my fortunes.

Releases him.

OLI. And what wilt thou do? beg when that is spent? Well, sir, get you in. I will not long be troubled with you. You shall have some part of your will. I pray you leave me.

ORL. I will no further offend you than becomes me for my good.

OLI. Get you with him, you old dog!

ADAM. Is 'old dog' my reward? Most true, I have lost my teeth in your service. God be with my old master! he would not have spoke such a word.

Exeunt ORLANDO, ADAM.

OLI. Is it even so? Begin you to grow upon me? I will physic your rankness, and yet give no thousand crowns neither. Holla, Dennis!

Enter DENNIS.

DEN. Calls your worship?

OLI. Was not Charles the Duke's wrestler here to speak with me?

DEN. So please you, he is here at the door and importunes access to you.

OLI. Call him in. [*Exit* DENNIS.] 'Twill be a good way; and to-morrow the wrestling is.

Enter CHARLES.

CHA. Good morrow to your worship.

OLI. Good Monsieur Charles! What's the new news at the new court?

CHA. There's no news at the court, sir, but the old

news. That is, the old Duke is banished by his younger brother the new Duke, and three or four loving lords have put themselves into voluntary exile with him, whose lands and revenues enrich the new Duke; therefore he gives them good leave to wander.

OLI. Can you tell if Rosalind, the Duke's daughter, be banished with her father?

CHA. O, no! for the Duke's daughter her cousin so loves her, being ever from their cradles bred together, that she would have followed her exile, or have died to stay behind her. She is at the court, and no less beloved of her uncle than his own daughter, and never two ladies loved as they do.

OLI. Where will the old Duke live?

CHA. They say he is already in the Forest of Arden, and a many merry men with him; and there they live like the old Robin Hood of England. They say many young gentlemen flock to him every day, and fleet the time carelessly as they did in the golden world.

OLI. What, you wrestle to-morrow before the new Duke?

CHA. Marry do I, sir; and I came to acquaint you with a matter. I am given, sir, secretly to understand that your younger brother, Orlando, hath a disposition to come in disguis'd against me to try a fall. To-morrow, sir, I wrestle for my credit, and he that escapes me without some broken limb shall acquit him well. Your brother is but young and tender, and for your love I would be loath to foil him, as I must for my own honour if he come in. Therefore, out of my love to you, I came hither to acquaint you withal, that either you might stay him from his intendment, or brook such disgrace well as he shall run into, in that it is a thing of his own search and altogether against my will.

OLI. Charles, I thank thee for thy love to me, which thou shalt find I will most kindly requite. I had myself notice of my brother's purpose herein and have by underhand means laboured to dissuade him from it; but he is resolute. I'll tell thee, Charles, it is the stubbornest young fellow of France; full of ambition, an envious emulator of every man's good parts, a secret and villanous contriver against me his natural brother. Therefore use thy discretion. I had as lief thou didst break his neck as his finger. And thou wert best look to't; for if thou dost him any slight disgrace, or if he do not mightily grace himself on thee, he will practise against thee by poison, entrap thee by some treacherous device, and never leave thee till he hath ta'en thy life by some indirect means or other; for I assure thee (and almost with tears I speak it) there is not one so young and so villanous this day living. I speak but brotherly of him; but should I anatomize him to thee as he is, I must blush and weep, and thou must look pale and wonder.

CHA. I am heartily glad I came hither to you. If he come to-morrow, I'll give him his payment. If ever he go alone again, I'll never wrestle for prize more. And so God keep your worship!

OLI. Farewell, good Charles. [*Exit* CHARLES.] Now will I stir this gamester. I hope I shall see an end of him; for my soul (yet I know not why) hates nothing more than he. Yet he's gentle; never school'd and yet learned; full of noble device; of all sorts enchantingly beloved, and indeed so much in the heart of the world, and especially of my own people, who best know him, that I am altogether misprised. But it shall not be so long; this wrestler shall clear all. Nothing remains but that I kindle the boy thither, which now I'll go about.   *Exit.*

Scene II: A lawn before Duke Frederick's Palace.

Enter ROSALIND *and* CELIA.

CEL. I pray thee, Rosalind, sweet my coz, be merry.

ROS. Dear Celia, I show more mirth than I am mistress of, and would you yet I were merrier? Unless you could teach me to forget a banished father, you must not learn me how to remember any extraordinary pleasure.

CEL. Herein I see thou lov'st me not with the full weight that I love thee. If my uncle, thy banished father, had banished thy uncle, the Duke my father, so thou hadst been still with me, I could have taught my love to take thy father for mine. So wouldst thou, if the truth of thy love to me were so righteously temper'd as mine is to thee.

ROS. Well, I will forget the condition of my estate to rejoice in yours.

CEL. You know my father hath no child but I, nor none is like to have; and truly, when he dies, thou shalt be his heir; for what he hath taken away from thy father perforce, I will render thee again in affection. By mine honour, I will! and when I break that oath, let me turn monster. Therefore, my sweet Rose, my dear Rose, be merry.

ROS. From henceforth I will, coz, and devise sports. Let me see. What think you of falling in love?

CEL. Marry, I prithee do, to make sport withal! But love no man in good earnest, nor no further in sport neither than with safety of a pure blush thou mayst in honour come off again.

ROS. What shall be our sport then?

CEL. Let us sit and mock the good housewife Fortune

from her wheel, that her gifts may henceforth be bestowed equally.

Ros. I would we could do so; for her benefits are mightily misplaced, and the bountiful blind woman doth most mistake in her gifts to women.

Cel. 'Tis true; for those that she makes fair she scarce makes honest, and those that she makes honest she makes very ill-favouredly.

Ros. Nay, now thou goest from Fortune's office to Nature's. Fortune reigns in gifts of the world, not in the lineaments of Nature.

Enter Touchstone *the* Clown.

Cel. No? When Nature hath made a fair creature, may she not by Fortune fall into the fire? Though Nature hath given us wit to flout at Fortune, hath not Fortune sent in this fool to cut off the argument?

Ros. Indeed, there is Fortune too hard for Nature when Fortune makes Nature's natural the cutter-off of Nature's wit.

Cel. Peradventure this is not Fortune's work neither, but Nature's; who perceiveth our natural wits too dull to reason of such goddesses and hath sent this natural for our whetstone, for always the dulness of the fool is the whetstone of the wits. How now, wit? Whither wander you?

Touch. Mistress, you must come away to your father.

Cel. Were you made the messenger?

Touch. No, by mine honour; but I was bid to come for you.

Ros. Where learned you that oath, fool?

Touch. Of a certain knight that swore by his honour they were good pancakes, and swore by his honour the mustard was naught. Now I'll stand to it, the pancakes were naught, and the mustard was good, and yet was not the knight forsworn.

CEL. How prove you that in the great heap of your knowledge?

ROS. Ay, marry, now unmuzzle your wisdom.

TOUCH. Stand you both forth now. Stroke your chins, and swear by your beards that I am a knave.

CEL. By our beards (if we had them), thou art.

TOUCH. By my knavery (if I had it), then I were. But if you swear by that that is not, you are not forsworn. No more was this knight, swearing by his honour, for he never had any; or if he had, he had sworn it away before ever he saw those pancakes or that mustard.

CEL. Prithee, who is't that thou mean'st?

TOUCH. One that old Frederick, your father, loves.

CEL. My father's love is enough to honour him. Enough! Speak no more of him. You'll be whipp'd for taxation one of these days.

TOUCH. The more pity that fools may not speak wisely what wise men do foolishly.

CEL. By my troth, thou sayest true; for, since the little wit that fools have was silenced, the little foolery that wise men have makes a great show. Here comes Monsieur Le Beau.

Enter LE BEAU.

ROS. With his mouth full of news.

CEL. Which he will put on us as pigeons feed their young.

ROS. Then shall we be news-cramm'd.

CEL. All the better! We shall be the more marketable. —Bon jour, Monsieur Le Beau. What's the news?

LE BEAU. Fair princess, you have lost much good sport.

CEL. Sport? of what colour?

LE BEAU. What colour, madam? How shall I answer you?

ROS. As wit and fortune will.

TOUCH. Or as the Destinies decree.

CEL. Well said! That was laid on with a trowel.

TOUCH. Nay, if I keep not my rank—

ROS. Thou losest thy old smell.

LE BEAU. You amaze me, ladies. I would have told you of good wrestling, which you have lost the sight of.

ROS. Yet tell us the manner of the wrestling.

LE BEAU. I will tell you the beginning; and if it please your ladyships, you may see the end; for the best is yet to do; and here, where you are, they are coming to perform it.

CEL. Well, the beginning that is dead and buried.

LE BEAU. There comes an old man and his three sons—

CEL. I could match this beginning with an old tale.

LE BEAU. Three proper young men, of excellent growth and presence.

ROS. With bills on their necks, 'Be it known unto all men by these presents'—

LE BEAU. The eldest of the three wrestled with Charles, the Duke's wrestler; which Charles in a moment threw him and broke three of his ribs, that there is little hope of life in him. So he serv'd the second, and so the third. Yonder they lie, the poor old man, their father, making such pitiful dole over them that all the beholders take his part with weeping.

ROS. Alas!

TOUCH. But what is the sport, monsieur, that the ladies have lost?

LE BEAU. Why, this that I speak of.

TOUCH. Thus men may grow wiser every day. It *is*

the first time that ever I heard breaking of ribs was sport for ladies.

CEL. Or I, I promise thee.

ROS. But is there any else longs to see this broken music in his sides? Is there yet another dotes upon rib-breaking? Shall we see this wrestling, cousin?

LE BEAU. You must, if you stay here; for here is the place appointed for the wrestling, and they are ready to perform it.

CEL. Yonder sure they are coming. Let us now stay and see it.

Flourish. Enter DUKE FREDERICK, LORDS,
ORLANDO, CHARLES, *and* ATTENDANTS.

DUKE. Come on. Since the youth will not be entreated, his own peril on his forwardness!

ROS. Is yonder the man?

LE BEAU. Even he, madam.

CEL. Alas, he is too young! Yet he looks successfully.

DUKE. How now, daughter, and cousin! Are you crept hither to see the wrestling?

ROS. Ay, my liege, so please you give us leave.

DUKE. You will take little delight in it, I can tell you, there is such odds in the men. In pity of the challenger's youth I would fain dissuade him, but he will not be entreated. Speak to him, ladies; see if you can move him.

CEL. Call him hither, good Monsieur Le Beau.

DUKE. Do so. I'll not be by.   *Steps aside.*

LE BEAU. Monsieur the challenger the princess calls for you.

ORL. I attend them with all respect and duty.

ROS. Young man, have you challeng'd Charles the wrestler?

ORL. No, fair princess. He is the general challenger;

I come but in as others do, to try with him the strength of my youth.

CEL. Young gentleman, your spirits are too bold for your years. You have seen cruel proof of this man's strength. If you saw yourself with your eyes, or knew yourself with your judgment, the fear of your adventure would counsel you to a more equal enterprise. We pray you for your own sake to embrace your own safety and give over this attempt.

ROS. Do, young sir. Your reputation shall not therefore be misprised. We will make it our suit to the Duke that the wrestling might not go forward.

ORL. I beseech you, punish me not with your hard thoughts, wherein I confess me much guilty to deny so fair and excellent ladies anything. But let your fair eyes and gentle wishes go with me to my trial; wherein if I be foil'd, there is but one sham'd that was never gracious; if kill'd, but one dead that is willing to be so. I shall do my friends no wrong, for I have none to lament me; the world no injury, for in it I have nothing. Only in the world I fill up a place, which may be better supplied when I have made it empty.

ROS. The little strength that I have, I would it were with you.

CEL. And mine, to eke out hers.

ROS. Fare you well. Pray heaven I be deceiv'd in you!

CEL. Your heart's desires be with you!

CHA. Come, where is this young gallant that is so desirous to lie with his mother earth?

ORL. Ready, sir; but his will hath in it a more modest working.

DUKE. You shall try but one fall.

CHA. No, I warrant your Grace you shall not entreat him to a second that have so mightily persuaded him from a first.

ORL. You mean to mock me after. You should not have mock'd me before. But come your ways!

ROS. Now Hercules be thy speed, young man!

CEL. I would I were invisible, to catch the strong fellow by the leg. *Wrestle.*

ROS. O excellent young man!

CEL. If I had a thunderbolt in mine eye, I can tell who should down. CHARLES *is thrown. Shout.*

DUKE. No more, no more!

ORL. Yes, I beseech your Grace. I am not yet well breath'd.

DUKE. How dost thou, Charles?

LE BEAU. He cannot speak, my lord.

DUKE. Bear him away. [CHARLES *is borne out.*]
What is thy name, young man?

ORL. Orlando, my liege, the youngest son of Sir Rowland de Boys.

DUKE. I would thou hadst been son to some man else!
The world esteem'd thy father honourable,
But I did find him still mine enemy.
Thou shouldst have better pleas'd me with this deed,
Hadst thou descended from another house.
But fare thee well; thou art a gallant youth;
I would thou hadst told me of another father.
Exeunt DUKE, TRAIN, *and* LE BEAU.

CEL. Were I my father, coz, would I do this?

ORL. I am more proud to be Sir Rowland's son,
His youngest son, and would not change that calling
To be adopted heir to Frederick.

ROS. My father lov'd Sir Rowland as his soul,
And all the world was of my father's mind.
Had I before known this young man his son,
I should have given him tears unto entreaties
Ere he should thus have ventur'd.

CEL. Gentle cousin,

Let us go thank him and encourage him.
My father's rough and envious disposition
Sticks me at heart. Sir, you have well deserv'd.
If you do keep your promises in love
But justly as you have exceeded all promise,
Your mistress shall be happy.

Ros.   Gentleman,
                    [*Gives him a chain from her neck.*]
Wear this for me, one out of suits with fortune,
That could give more but that her hand lacks means.
Shall we go, coz?

    CEL.   Ay. Fare you well, fair gentleman.

    ORL. Can I not say 'I thank you'? My better parts
Are all thrown down, and that which here stands up
Is but a quintain, a mere liveless block.

    Ros. He calls us back. My pride fell with my fortunes;
I'll ask him what he would. Did you call, sir?
Sir, you have wrestled well, and overthrown
More than your enemies.

    CEL.   Will you go, coz?

    Ros. Have with you. Fare you well.

                            Exeunt ROSALIND *and* CELIA.

    ORL. What passion hangs these weights upon my
        tongue?
I cannot speak to her, yet she urg'd conference.

                [*Enter* LE BEAU.]

O poor Orlando, thou art overthrown!
Or Charles or something weaker masters thee.

    LE BEAU. Good sir, I do in friendship counsel you
To leave this place. Albeit you have deserv'd
High commendation, true applause, and love,
Yet such is now the Duke's condition
That he misconsters all that you have done.
The Duke is humorous. What he is, indeed,

More suits you to conceive than I to speak of.

ORL. I thank you, sir: and pray you tell me this—
Which of the two was daughter of the Duke,
That here was at the wrestling?

LE BEAU. Neither his daughter, if we judge by man-
ners;
But yet indeed the smaller is his daughter;
The other is daughter to the banish'd Duke,
And here detain'd by her usurping uncle
To keep his daughter company, whose loves
Are dearer than the natural bond of sisters.
But I can tell you that of late this Duke
Hath ta'en displeasure 'gainst his gentle niece,
Grounded upon no other argument
But that the people praise her for her virtues
And pity her for her good father's sake;
And, on my life, his malice 'gainst the lady
Will suddenly break forth. Sir, fare you well.
Hereafter, in a better world than this,
I shall desire more love and knowledge of you.

ORL. I rest much bounden to you. Fare you well.

[*Exit* LE BEAU.]

Thus must I from the smoke into the smother,
From tyrant Duke unto a tyrant brother.
But heavenly Rosalind!   *Exit.*

Scene III: A room in the Duke's Palace.

Enter CELIA *and* ROSALIND.

CEL. Why, cousin! why, Rosalind! Cupid have mercy!
not a word?

ROS. Not one to throw at a dog.

CEL. No, thy words are too precious to be cast away

upon curs; throw some of them at me. Come, lame me with reasons.

Ros. Then there were two cousins laid up, when the one should be lam'd with reasons, and the other mad without any.

Cel. But is all this for your father?

Ros. No, some of it is for my child's father. O, how full of briers is this working-day world!

Cel. They are but burrs, cousin, thrown upon thee in holiday foolery. If we walk not in the trodden paths, our very petticoats will catch them.

Ros. I could shake them off my coat. These burrs are in my heart.

Cel. Hem them away.

Ros. I would try, if I could cry 'hem!' and have him.

Cel. Come, come, wrestle with thy affections.

Ros. O, they take the part of a better wrestler than myself!

Cel. O, a good wish upon you! You will try in time, in despite of a fall. But, turning these jests out of service, let us talk in good earnest. Is it possible on such a sudden you should fall into so strong a liking with old Sir Rowland's youngest son?

Ros. The Duke my father lov'd his father dearly.

Cel. Doth it therefore ensue that you should love his son dearly? By this kind of chase, I should hate him, for my father hated his father dearly; yet I hate not Orlando.

Ros. No, faith, hate him not, for my sake!

Cel. Why should I not? Doth he not deserve well?

Enter DUKE FREDERICK, *with* LORDS.

Ros. Let me love him for that; and do you love him because I do. Look, here comes the Duke.

CEL. With his eyes full of anger.

DUKE. Mistress, dispatch you with your safest haste
And get you from our court!

ROS.   Me, uncle?

DUKE.   You, cousin.
Within these ten days if that thou beest found
So near our public court as twenty miles,
Thou diest for it.

ROS.   I do beseech your Grace
Let me the knowledge of my fault bear with me.
If with myself I hold intelligence
Or have acquaintance with mine own desires;
If that I do not dream or be not frantic,
As I do trust I am not—then, dear uncle,
Never so much as in a thought unborn
Did I offend your Highness.

DUKE.   Thus do all traitors.
If their purgation did consist in words,
They are as innocent as grace itself.
Let it suffice thee that I trust thee not.

ROS. Yet your mistrust cannot make me a traitor.
Tell me whereon the likelihood depends.

DUKE. Thou art thy father's daughter. There's enough!

ROS. So was I when your Highness took his dukedom;
So was I when your Highness banish'd him.
Treason is not inherited, my lord;
Or if we did derive it from our friends,
What's that to me? My father was no traitor.
Then, good my liege, mistake me not so much
To think my poverty is treacherous.

CEL. Dear sovereign, hear me speak.

DUKE. Ay, Celia. We stay'd her for your sake,
Else had she with her father rang'd along.

CEL. I did not then entreat to have her stay;
It was your pleasure and your own remorse.

I was too young that time to value her;
But now I know her. If she be a traitor,
Why, so am I! We still have slept together,
Rose at an instant, learn'd, play'd, eat together;
And wheresoe'er we went, like Juno's swans,
Still we went coupled and inseparable.

DUKE. She is too subtile for thee; and her smoothness,
Her very silence and her patience,
Speak to the people, and they pity her.
Thou art a fool. She robs thee of thy name,
And thou wilt show more bright and seem more virtuous
When she is gone. Then open not thy lips.
Firm and irrevocable is my doom
Which I have pass'd upon her. She is banish'd.

CEL. Pronounce that sentence then on me, my liege!
I cannot live out of her company.

DUKE. You are a fool. You, niece, provide yourself.
If you outstay the time, upon mine honour,
And in the greatness of my word, you die.

Exeunt DUKE, &c.

CEL. O my poor Rosalind! whither wilt thou go?
Wilt thou change fathers? I will give thee mine.
I charge thee be not thou more griev'd than I am.

ROS. I have more cause.

CEL.   Thou hast not, cousin.
Prithee be cheerful. Know'st thou not the Duke
Hath banish'd me, his daughter?

ROS.   That he hath not!

CEL. No? hath not? Rosalind lacks then the love
Which teacheth me that thou and I am one.
Shall we be sund'red? shall we part, sweet girl?
No! let my father seek another heir.
Therefore devise with me how we may fly,
Whither to go, and what to bear with us.
And do not seek to take your charge upon you,

To bear your griefs yourself and leave me out;
For, by this heaven, now at our sorrows pale,
Say what thou canst, I'll go along with thee!

   Ros. Why, whither shall we go?

   Cel. To seek my uncle in the Forest of Arden.

   Ros. Alas, what danger will it be to us,
Maids as we are, to travel forth so far!
Beauty provoketh thieves sooner than gold.

   Cel. I'll put myself in poor and mean attire
And with a kind of umber smirch my face;
The like do you. So shall we pass along
And never stir assailants.

   Ros.   Were it not better,
Because that I am more than common tall,
That I did suit me all points like a man?
A gallant curtleaxe upon my thigh,
A boar-spear in my hand, and—in my heart
Lie there what hidden woman's fear there will—
We'll have a swashing and a martial outside,
As many other mannish cowards have
That do outface it with their semblances.

   Cel. What shall I call thee when thou art a man?

   Ros. I'll have no worse a name than Jove's own page;
And therefore look you call me Ganymede.
But what will you be call'd?

   Cel. Something that hath a reference to my state—
No longer Celia, but Aliena.

   Ros. But, cousin, what if we assay'd to steal
The clownish fool out of your father's court?
Would he not be a comfort to our travel?

   Cel. He'll go along o'er the wide world with me.
Leave me alone to woo him. Let's away
And get our jewels and our wealth together,
Devise the fittest time and safest way
To hide us from pursuit that will be made

After my flight. Now go we in content
To liberty, and not to banishment.   *Exeunt.*

Act II: Scene I: The Forest of Arden. Before Duke Senior's cave.

Enter DUKE SENIOR, AMIENS, *and two or three*
LORDS, *like* FORESTERS.

DUKE S. Now, my co-mates and brothers in exile,
Hath not old custom made this life more sweet
Than that of painted pomp? Are not these woods
More free from peril than the envious court?
Here feel we but the penalty of Adam,
The seasons' difference; as, the icy fang
And churlish chiding of the winter's wind,
Which, when it bites and blows upon my body
Even till I shrink with cold, I smile, and say
'This is no flattery; these are counsellors
That feelingly persuade me what I am.'
Sweet are the uses of adversity,
Which, like the toad, ugly and venomous,
Wears yet a precious jewel in his head;
And this our life, exempt from public haunt,
Finds tongues in trees, books in the running brooks,
Sermons in stones, and good in everything:
I would not change it.

AMI.   Happy is your Grace
That can translate the stubbornness of fortune
Into so quiet and so sweet a style.

DUKE S. Come, shall we go and kill us venison?
And yet it irks me the poor dappled fools,
Being native burghers of this desert city,
Should, in their own confines, with forked heads
Have their round haunches gor'd.

1. LORD.   Indeed, my lord,
The melancholy Jaques grieves at that,
And in that kind swears you do more usurp
Than doth your brother that hath banish'd you.
To-day my Lord of Amiens and myself
Did steal behind him as he lay along
Under an oak, whose antique root peeps out
Upon the brook that brawls along this wood;
To the which place a poor sequest'red stag,
That from the hunter's aim had ta'en a hurt,
Did come to languish; and indeed, my lord,
The wretched animal heav'd forth such groans
That their discharge did stretch his leathern coat
Almost to bursting, and the big round tears
Cours'd one another down his innocent nose
In piteous chase; and thus the hairy fool,
Much marked of the melancholy Jaques,
Stood on th' extremest verge of the swift brook,
Augmenting it with tears.

DUKE S.   But what said Jaques?
Did he not moralize this spectacle?

1. LORD. O, yes, into a thousand similes.
First, for his weeping into the needless stream:
'Poor deer,' quoth he, 'thou mak'st a testament
As worldlings do, giving thy sum of more
To that which had too much.' Then, being alone,
Left and abandoned of his velvet friends:
' 'Tis right!' quoth he, 'thus misery doth part
The flux of company.' Anon a careless herd,
Full of the pasture, jumps along by him
And never stays to greet him: 'Ay,' quoth Jaques,
'Sweep on, you fat and greasy citizens!
'Tis just the fashion! Wherefore do you look
Upon that poor and broken bankrupt there?'
Thus most invectively he pierceth through

The body of the country, city, court;
Yea, and of this our life, swearing that we
Are mere usurpers, tyrants, and what's worse,
To fright the animals and to kill them up
In their assign'd and native dwelling place.

DUKE S. And did you leave him in this contemplation?

2. LORD. We did, my lord, weeping and commenting
Upon the sobbing deer.

DUKE S.   Show me the place.
I love to cope him in these sullen fits,
For then he's full of matter.

1. LORD. I'll bring you to him straight.   *Exeunt.*

Scene II: A room in Duke Frederick's Palace.

Enter DUKE FREDERICK, *with* LORDS.

DUKE. Can it be possible that no man saw them?
It cannot be. Some villains of my court
Are of consent and sufferance in this.

1. LORD. I cannot hear of any that did see her.
The ladies her attendants of her chamber
Saw her abed, and in the morning early
They found the bed untreasur'd of their mistress.

2. LORD. My lord, the roynish clown at whom so oft
Your Grace was wont to laugh is also missing.
Hisperia, the princess' gentlewoman,
Confesses that she secretly o'erheard
Your daughter and her cousin much commend
The parts and graces of the wrestler
That did but lately foil the sinewy Charles;
And she believes, wherever they are gone,
That youth is surely in their company.

DUKE. Send to his brother, fetch that gallant hither.
If he be absent, bring his brother to me;

I'll make him find him. Do this suddenly,
And let not search and inquisition quail
To bring again these foolish runaways.   *Exeunt.*

Scene III: Before Oliver's house.

Enter ORLANDO *and* ADAM, *meeting.*

ORL. Who's there?

ADAM. What, my young master! O my gentle master!
O my sweet master! O you memory
Of old Sir Rowland! Why, what make you here?
Why are you virtuous? Why do people love you?
And wherefore are you gentle, strong, and valiant?
Why would you be so fond to overcome
The bonny prizer of the humorous Duke?
Your praise is come too swiftly home before you.
Know you not, master, to some kind of men
Their graces serve them but as enemies?
No more do yours. Your virtues, gentle master,
Are sanctified and holy traitors to you.
O, what a world is this, when what is comely
Envenoms him that bears it!

ORL. Why, what's the matter?

ADAM.   O unhappy youth,
Come not within these doors! Within this roof
The enemy of all your graces lives.
Your brother (no, no brother! yet the son—
Yet not the son—I will not call him son
Of him I was about to call his father)
Hath heard your praises, and this night he means
To burn the lodging where you use to lie
And you within it. If he fail of that,
He will have other means to cut you off.
I overheard him and his practices.

This is no place, this house is but a butchery,
Abhor it, fear it, do not enter it!

ORL. Why, whither, Adam, wouldst thou have me go?

ADAM. No matter whither, so you come not here.

ORL. What, would'st thou have me go and beg my
food,

Or with a base and boist'rous sword enforce ˮ
A thievish living on the common road?
This I must do, or know not what to do.
Yet this I will not do, do how I can.
I rather will subject me to the malice
Of a diverted blood and bloody brother.

ADAM. But do not so. I have five hundred crowns,
The thrifty hire I sav'd under your father,
Which I did store to be my foster nurse
When service should in my old limbs lie lame
And unregarded age in corners thrown.
Take that, and he that doth the ravens feed,
Yea, providently caters for the sparrow,
Be comfort to my age! Here is the gold;
All this I give you. Let me be your servant.
Though I look old, yet I am strong and lusty;
For in my youth I never did apply
Hot and rebellious liquors in my blood,
Nor did not with unbashful forehead woo
The means of weakness and debility;
Therefore my age is as a lusty winter,
Frosty, but kindly. Let me go with you;
I'll do the service of a younger man
In all your business and necessities.

ORL. O good old man, how well in thee appears
The constant service of the antique world,
When service sweat for duty, not for meed!
Thou art not for the fashion of these times,
Where none will sweat but for promotion,

And having that, do choke their service up
Even with the having. It is not so with thee.
But, poor old man, thou prun'st a rotten tree
That cannot so much as a blossom yield
In lieu of all thy pains and husbandry.
But come thy ways! We'll go along together,
And ere we have thy youthful wages spent,
We'll light upon some settled low content.

ADAM. Master, go on, and I will follow thee
To the last gasp with truth and loyalty!
From seventeen years till now almost fourscore
Here lived I, but now live here no more.
At seventeen years many their fortunes seek,
But at fourscore it is too late a week;
Yet fortune cannot recompense me better
Than to die well and not my master's debtor.   *Exeunt.*

Scene IV: The Forest of Arden.
Near a sheepcote.

Enter ROSALIND *for* GANYMEDE, CELIA *for* ALIENA
and CLOWN, *alias* TOUCHSTONE.

ROS. O Jupiter, how weary are my spirits!

TOUCH. I care not for my spirits if my legs were not weary.

ROS. I could find in my heart to disgrace my man's apparel and to cry like a woman; but I must comfort the weaker vessel, as doublet and hose ought to show itself courageous to petticoat. Therefore, courage, good Aliena!

CEL. I pray you bear with me; I cannot go no further.

TOUCH. For my part, I had rather bear with you than bear you. Yet I should bear no cross if I did bear you, for I think you have no money in your purse.

Ros. Well, this is the Forest of Arden.

Touch. Ay, now am I in Arden, the more fool I! When I was at home, I was in a better place; but travellers must be content.

Enter Corin *and* Silvius.

Ros. Ay, be so, good Touchstone.—Look you, who
    comes here,
A young man and an old in solemn talk.

Cor. That is the way to make her scorn you still.

Sil. O Corin, that thou knew'st how I do love her!

Cor. I partly guess; for I have lov'd ere now.

Sil. No, Corin, being old, thou canst not guess,
Though in thy youth thou wast as true a lover
As ever sigh'd upon a midnight pillow.
But if thy love were ever like to mine
(As sure I think did never man love so),
How many actions most ridiculous
Hast thou been drawn to by thy fantasy!

Cor. Into a thousand that I have forgotten.

Sil. O, thou didst then never love so heartily!
If thou rememb'rest not the slightest folly
That ever love did make thee run into,
Thou hast not lov'd.
Or if thou hast not sat as I do now,
Wearing thy hearer in thy mistress' praise,
Thou hast not lov'd.
Or if thou hast not broke from company
Abruptly, as my passion now makes me,
Thou hast not lov'd. O Phebe, Phebe, Phebe!   *Exit.*

Ros. Alas, poor shepherd! Searching of thy wound,
I have by hard adventure found mine own.

Touch. And I mine. I remember, when I was in love I broke my sword upon a stone and bid him take that for coming a-night to Jane Smile; and I remember the kissing of her batlet, and the cow's dugs that her pretty chopt hands had milk'd; and I remember the wooing of a peascod instead of her, from whom I took two cods, and giving her them again, said with weeping tears, 'Wear these for my sake.' We that are true lovers run into strange capers; but as all is mortal in nature, so is all nature in love mortal in folly.

Ros. Thou speak'st wiser than thou art ware of.

Touch. Nay, I shall ne'er be ware of mine own wit till I break my shins against it.

Ros. Jove, Jove! this shepherd's passion
     Is much upon my fashion.

Touch. And mine, but it grows something stale with me.

Cel. I pray you, one of you question yond man If he for gold will give us any food.
I faint almost to death.

Touch.   Holla, you clown!

Ros. Peace, fool! he's not thy kinsman.

Cor. Who calls?

Touch.   Your betters, sir.

Cor.   Else are they very wretched.

Ros. Peace, I say!—Good even to you, friend.

Cor. And to you, gentle sir, and to you all.

Ros. I prithee, shepherd, if that love or gold Can in this desert place buy entertainment,
Bring us where we may rest ourselves and feed.
Here's a young maid with travel much oppress'd,
And faints for succour.

Cor.   Fair sir, I pity her
And wish, for her sake more than for mine own,
My fortunes were more able to relieve her;
But I am shepherd to another man
And do not shear the fleeces that I graze.
My master is of churlish disposition

And little recks to find the way to heaven
By doing deeds of hospitality.
Besides, his cote, his flocks, and bounds of feed
Are now on sale, and at our sheepcote now,
By reason of his absence, there is nothing
That you will feed on; but what is, come see,
And in my voice most welcome shall you be.

 Ros. What is he that shall buy his flock and pasture?
 Cor. That young swain that you saw here but ere-
  while,
That little cares for buying anything.

 Ros. I pray thee, if it stand with honesty,
Buy thou the cottage, pasture, and the flock,
And thou shalt have to pay for it of us.

 Cel. And we will mend thy wages. I like this place
And willingly could waste my time in it.

 Cor. Assuredly the thing is to be sold.
Go with me. If you like, upon report,
The soil, the profit, and this kind of life,
I will your very faithful feeder be
And buy it with your gold right suddenly.   *Exeunt.*

Scene V: The Forest. Before Duke Senior's cave.

Enter Amiens, Jaques, *and others.*

SONG

Ami.   Under the greenwood tree
   Who loves to lie with me,
   And turn his merry note
   Unto the sweet bird's throat,
  Come hither, come hither, come hither!
    Here shall he see
    No enemy
  But winter and rough weather.

JAQ. More, more, I prithee more!

AMI. It will make you melancholy, Monsieur Jaques.

JAQ. I thank it. More, I prithee more! I can suck melancholy out of a song as a weasel sucks eggs. More, I prithee more!

AMI. My voice is ragged. I know I cannot please you.

JAQ. I do not desire you to please me; I do desire you to sing. Come, more! another stanzo! Call you 'em stanzos?

AMI. What you will, Monsieur Jaques.

JAQ. Nay, I care not for their names; they owe me nothing. Will you sing?

AMI. More at your request than to please myself.

JAQ. Well then, if ever I thank any man, I'll thank you. But that they call compliment is like th' encounter of two dog-apes; and when a man thanks me heartily, methinks I have given him a penny, and he renders me the beggarly thanks. Come, sing! and you that will not, hold your tongues.

AMI. Well, I'll end the song. Sirs, cover the while; the Duke will drink under this tree. He hath been all this day to look you.

JAQ. And I have been all this day to avoid him. He is too disputable for my company. I think of as many matters as he; but I give heaven thanks and make no boast of them. Come, warble, come.

SONG

All together here.

Who doth ambition shun
And loves to live i' th' sun,
Seeking the food he eats,
And pleas'd with what he gets,
Come hither, come hither, come hither!
Here shall he see
No enemy
But winter and rough weather.

JAQ. I'll give you a verse to this note that I made yesterday in despite of my invention.

AMI. And I'll sing it.

JAQ. Thus it goes:

> If it do come to pass
> That any man turn ass,
> Leaving his wealth and ease
> A stubborn will to please,
> Ducdame, ducdame, ducdame!
> Here shall he see
> Gross fools as he,
> An if he will come to me.

AMI. What's that 'ducdame'?

JAQ. 'Tis a Greek invocation to call fools into a circle. I'll go sleep, if I can; if I cannot, I'll rail against all the first-born of Egypt.

AMI. And I'll go seek the Duke. His banquet is prepar'd.   *Exeunt severally.*

Scene VI: The Forest.

Enter ORLANDO *and* ADAM.

ADAM. Dear master, I can go no further. O, I die for food! Here lie I down and measure out my grave. Farewell, kind master.

ORL. Why, how now, Adam? no greater heart in thee? Live a little, comfort a little, cheer thyself a little. If this uncouth forest yield anything savage, I will either be food for it or bring it for food to thee. Thy conceit is nearer death than thy powers. For my sake be comfortable; hold death awhile at the arm's end. I will here be with thee presently; and if I bring thee not something to eat, I will give thee leave to die; but if thou diest before I come, thou art a mocker of my labour. Well said! thou

look'st cheerly, and I'll be with thee quickly. Yet thou
liest in the bleak air. Come, I will bear thee to some
shelter, and thou shalt not die for lack of a dinner if there
live anything in this desert. Cheerly, good Adam!

Exeunt.

Scene VII: The Forest. Before the Cave.

A table set out. Enter DUKE SENIOR, AMIENS, *and* LORDS,
like OUTLAWS.

DUKE S. I think he be transform'd into a beast,
For I can nowhere find him like a man.

1. LORD. My lord, he is but even now gone hence.
Here was he merry, hearing of a song.

DUKE S. If he, compact of jars, grow musical,
We shall have shortly discord in the spheres.
Go seek him; tell him I would speak with him.

Enter JAQUES.

1. LORD. He saves my labour by his own approach.

DUKE S. Why, how now, monsieur! what a life is this,
That your poor friends must woo your company!
What, you look merrily.

JAQ. A fool, a fool! I met a fool i' th' forest,
A motley fool!—a miserable world!—
As I do live by food, I met a fool,
Who laid him down and bask'd him in the sun
And rail'd on Lady Fortune in good terms,
In good set terms—and yet a motley fool.
'Good morrow, fool,' quoth I. 'No, sir,' quoth he,
'Call me not fool till heaven hath sent me fortune.'
And then he drew a dial from his poke,
And looking on it with lack-lustre eye,
Says very wisely, 'It is ten o'clock.

Thus we may see,' quoth he, 'how the world wags.
'Tis but an hour ago since it was nine,
And after one hour more 'twill be eleven;
And so, from hour to hour, we ripe and ripe,
And then, from hour to hour, we rot and rot;
And thereby hangs a tale.' When I did hear
The motley fool thus moral on the time,
My lungs began to crow like chanticleer
That fools should be so deep contemplative;
And I did laugh sans intermission
An hour by his dial. O noble fool!
A worthy fool! Motley's the only wear!

    DUKE S. What fool is this?

    JAQ. O worthy fool! One that hath been a courtier,
And says, if ladies be but young and fair,
They have the gift to know it. And in his brain,
Which is as dry as the remainder biscuit
After a voyage, he hath strange places cramm'd
With observation, the which he vents
In mangled forms. O that I were a fool!
I am ambitious for a motley coat.

    DUKE S. Thou shalt have one.

    JAQ.   It is my only suit,
Provided that you weed your better judgments
Of all opinion that grows rank in them
That I am wise. I must have liberty
Withal, as large a charter as the wind,
To blow on whom I please; for so fools have.
And they that are most galled with my folly,
They most must laugh. And why, sir, must they so?
The why is plain as way to parish church:
He that a fool doth very wisely hit
Doth very foolishly, although he smart,
Not to seem senseless of the bob. If not,
The wise man's folly is anatomiz'd

Even by the squand'ring glances of the fool.
Invest me in my motley. Give me leave
To speak my mind, and I will through and through
Cleanse the foul body of th' infected world,
If they will patiently receive my medicine.

    DUKE S. Fie on thee! I can tell what thou wouldst do.

    JAQ. What, for a counter, would I do but good?

    DUKE S. Most mischievous foul sin, in chiding sin.
For thou thyself hast been a libertine,
As sensual as the brutish sting itself;
And all th' embossed sores and headed evils
That thou with license of free foot hast caught,
Wouldst thou disgorge into the general world.

    JAQ. Why, who cries out on pride
That can therein tax any private party?
Doth it not flow as hugely as the sea
Till that the wearer's very means do ebb?
What woman in the city do I name
When that I say the city woman bears
The cost of princes on unworthy shoulders?
Who can come in and say that I mean her,
When such a one as she, such is her neighbour?
Or what is he of basest function
That says his bravery is not on my cost,
Thinking that I mean him, but therein suits
His folly to the mettle of my speech?
There then! how then? what then? Let me see wherein
My tongue hath wrong'd him. If it do him right,
Then he hath wrong'd himself. If he be free,
Why, then my taxing like a wild goose flies,
Unclaim'd of any man. But who comes here?

       Enter ORLANDO *with his sword drawn.*

    ORL. Forbear, and eat no more!

    JAQ.   Why, I have eat none yet

ORL. Nor shalt not, till necessity be serv'd.

JAQ. Of what kind should this cock come of?

DUKE S. Art thou thus bolden'd, man, by thy distress,
Or else a rude despiser of good manners,
That in civility thou seem'st so empty?

ORL. You touch'd my vein at first. The thorny point
Of bare distress hath ta'en from me the show
Of smooth civility; yet am I inland bred
And know some nurture. But forbear, I say!
He dies that touches any of this fruit
Till I and my affairs are answered.

JAQ. An you will not be answer'd with reason, I must
die.

DUKE S. What would you have? Your gentleness shall
force
More than your force move us to gentleness.

ORL. I almost die for food, and let me have it!

DUKE S. Sit down and feed, and welcome to our table.

ORL. Speak you so gently? Pardon me, I pray you.
I thought that all things had been savage here,
And therefore put I on the countenance
Of stern commandment. But whate'er you are
That in this desert inaccessible,
Under the shade of melancholy boughs,
Lose and neglect the creeping hours of time—
If ever you have look'd on better days,
If ever been where bells have knoll'd to church,
If ever sat at any good man's feast,
If ever from your eyelids wip'd a tear
And know what 'tis to pity and be pitied,
Let gentleness my strong enforcement be;
In the which hope I blush, and hide my sword.

DUKE S. True is it that we have seen better days,
And have with holy bell been knoll'd to church,
And sat at good men's feasts, and wip'd our eyes

Of drops that sacred pity hath engend'red;
And therefore sit you down in gentleness,
And take upon command what help we have
That to your wanting may be minist'red.

ORL. Then but forbear your food a little while,
Whiles, like a doe, I go to find my fawn
And give it food. There is an old poor man
Who after me hath many a weary step
Limp'd in pure love. Till he be first suffic'd,
Oppress'd with two weak evils, age and hunger,
I will not touch a bit.

DUKE S.   Go find him out,
And we will nothing waste till you return.

ORL. I thank ye, and be blest for your good comfort!
                                                    Exit.

DUKE S. Thou seest we are not all alone unhappy.
This wide and universal theatre
Presents more woeful pageants than the scene
Wherein we play in.

JAQ.   All the world's a stage,
And all the men and women merely players.
They have their exits and their entrances,
And one man in his time plays many parts,
His acts being seven ages. At first, the infant,
Mewling and puking in the nurse's arms.
Then the whining schoolboy, with his satchel
And shining morning face, creeping like snail
Unwillingly to school. And then the lover,
Sighing like furnace, with a woeful ballad
Made to his mistress' eyebrow. Then a soldier,
Full of strange oaths and bearded like the pard,
Jealous in honour, sudden and quick in quarrel,
Seeking the bubble reputation
Even in the cannon's mouth. And then the justice,
In fair round belly with good capon lin'd,

With eyes severe and beard of formal cut,
Full of wise saws and modern instances;
And so he plays his part. The sixth age shifts
Into the lean and slipper'd pantaloon,
With spectacles on nose and pouch on side;
His youthful hose, well sav'd, a world too wide
For his shrunk shank, and his big manly voice,
Turning again toward childish treble, pipes
And whistles in his sound. Last scene of all,
That ends this strange eventful history,
Is second childishness and mere oblivion,
Sans teeth, sans eyes, sans taste, sans everything.

Enter ORLANDO, *with* ADAM.

DUKE S. Welcome. Set down your venerable burthen
And let him feed.
ORL. I thank you most for him.
ADAM.   So had you need.
I scarce can speak to thank you for myself.
DUKE S. Welcome, fall to. I will not trouble you,
As yet to question you about your fortunes.
Give us some music; and, good cousin, sing.

SONG

AMI.   Blow, blow, thou winter wind,
            Thou art not so unkind
                As man's ingratitude.
            Thy tooth is not so keen,
            Because thou art not seen,
                Although thy breath be rude.
        Heigh-ho, sing heigh-ho, unto the green holly!
        Most friendship is feigning, most loving mere folly:
                Then, heigh-ho, the holly!
                This life is most jolly.
            Freeze, freeze thou bitter sky,
            That dost not bite so nigh
                As benefits forgot.

> Though thou the waters warp,
> Thy sting is not so sharp
> As friend rememb'red not.
> Heigh-ho! sing, &c.

DUKE S. If that you were the good Sir Rowland's son—
As you have whisper'd faithfully you were,
And as mine eye doth his effigies witness
Most truly limn'd and living in your face—
Be truly welcome hither. I am the Duke
That lov'd your father. The residue of your fortune,
Go to my cave and tell me. Good old man,
Thou art right welcome, as thy master is.
Support him by the arm. Give me your hand,
And let me all your fortunes understand.   *Exeunt.*

Act III: Scene I: A room in the Palace.

Enter DUKE FREDERICK, LORDS, *and* OLIVER.

DUKE. Not see him since? Sir, sir, that cannot be!
But were I not the better part made mercy,
I should not seek an absent argument
Of my revenge, thou present. But look to it!
Find out thy brother, wheresoe'er he is;
Seek him with candle; bring him dead or living
Within this twelvemonth, or turn thou no more
To seek a living in our territory.
Thy lands, and all things that thou dost call thine
Worth seizure, do we seize into our hands
Till thou canst quit thee by thy brother's mouth
Of what we think against thee.

OLI. O that your Highness knew my heart in this!
I never lov'd my brother in my life.

DUKE. More villain thou! Well, push him out of doors,
And let my officers of such a nature

Make an extent upon his house and lands.
Do this expediently and turn him going.   *Exeunt.*

Scene II: The Forest. Near the sheepcote.

Enter ORLANDO, *with a paper, which he hangs on a tree.*

ORL. Hang there, my verse, in witness of my love;
    And thou, thrice-crowned Queen of Night, survey
With thy chaste eye, from thy pale sphere above,
    Thy huntress' name that my full life doth sway.
O Rosalind! these trees shall be my books,
    And in their barks my thoughts I'll character,
That every eye which in this forest looks
    Shall see thy virtue witness'd everywhere.
Run, run, Orlando! carve on every tree
The fair, the chaste, and unexpressive she.   *Exit.*

Enter CORIN *and* TOUCHSTONE *the* CLOWN.

COR. And how like you this shepherd's life, Master Touchstone?

TOUCH. Truly, shepherd, in respect of itself, it is a good life; but in respect that it is a shepherd's life, it is naught. In respect that it is solitary, I like it very well; but in respect that it is private, it is a very vile life. Now in respect it is in the fields, it pleaseth me well; but in respect it is not in the court, it is tedious. As it is a spare life, look you, it fits my humour well; but as there is no more plenty in it, it goes much against my stomach. Hast any philosophy in thee, shepherd?

COR. No more but that I know the more one sickens, the worse at ease he is; and that he that wants money, means, and content is without three good friends; that the property of rain is to wet and fire to burn; that good pasture makes fat sheep, and that a great cause of the night is lack of the sun; that he that hath learned no wit by nature nor art may complain of good breeding, or comes of a very dull kindred.

TOUCH. Such a one is a natural philosopher. Wast ever in court, shepherd?

COR. No, truly.

TOUCH. Then thou art damn'd.

COR. Nay, I hope.

TOUCH. Truly thou art damn'd, like an ill-roasted egg, all on one side.

COR. For not being at court? Your reason.

TOUCH. Why, if thou never wast at court, thou never saw'st good manners; if thou never saw'st good manners, then thy manners must be wicked; and wickedness is sin, and sin is damnation. Thou art in a parlous state, shepherd.

COR. Not a whit, Touchstone. Those that are good manners at the court are as ridiculous in the country as the behaviour of the country is most mockable at the court. You told me you salute not at the court but you kiss your hands. That courtesy would be uncleanly if courtiers were shepherds.

TOUCH. Instance, briefly. Come, instance.

COR. Why, we are still handling our ewes, and their fells you know are greasy.

TOUCH. Why, do not your courtier's hands sweat? and is not the grease of a mutton as wholesome as the sweat of a man? Shallow, shallow! A better instance, I say. Come.

COR. Besides, our hands are hard.

TOUCH. Your lips will feel them the sooner. Shallow again! A more sounder instance, come.

COR. And they are often tarr'd over with the surgery of our sheep, and would you have us kiss tar? The courtier's hands are perfum'd with civet.

TOUCH. Most shallow man! Thou worm's meat in respect of a good piece of flesh indeed! Learn of the wise, and perpend. Civet is of a baser birth than tar—the very uncleanly flux of a cat. Mend the instance, shepherd.

COR. You have too courtly a wit for me. I'll rest.

TOUCH. Wilt thou rest damn'd? God help thee, shallow man! God make incision in thee, thou art raw!

COR. Sir, I am a true labourer; I earn that I eat, get that I wear; owe no man hate, envy no man's happiness; glad of other men's good, content with my harm; and the greatest of my pride is to see my ewes graze and my lambs suck.

TOUCH. That is another simple sin in you: to bring the ewes and the rams together and to offer to get your living by the copulation of cattle; to be bawd to a bell-wether, and to betray a she-lamb of a twelvemonth to a crooked-pated old cuckoldly ram, out of all reasonable match. If thou beest not damn'd for this, the devil himself will have no shepherds; I cannot see else how thou shouldst scape.

COR. Here comes young Master Ganymede, my new mistress's brother.

Enter ROSALIND, *reading a paper.*

ROS. 'From the east to western Inde,
No jewel is like Rosalinde.
Her worth, being mounted on the wind,
Through all the world bears Rosalinde.
All the pictures fairest lin'd
Are but black to Rosalinde.
Let no face be kept in mind
But the fair of Rosalinde.'

TOUCH. I'll rhyme you so eight years together, dinners and suppers and sleeping hours excepted. It is the right butter-women's rank to market.

ROS. Out, fool!

Touch. For a taste:

> If a hart do lack a hind,
> Let him seek out Rosalinde.
> If the cat will after kind,
> So be sure will Rosalinde.
> Winter garments must be lin'd,
> So must slender Rosalinde.
> They that reap must sheaf and bind,
> Then to cart with Rosalinde.
> Sweetest nut hath sourest rind,
> Such a nut is Rosalinde.
> He that sweetest rose will find
> Must find love's prick, and Rosalinde.

This is the very false gallop of verses! Why do you infect yourself with them?

Ros. Peace, you dull fool! I found them on a tree.

Touch. Truly the tree yields bad fruit.

Ros. I'll graff it with you, and then I shall graff it with a medlar. Then it will be the earliest fruit i' th' country; for you'll be rotten ere you be half ripe, and that's the right virtue of the medlar.

Touch. You have said; but whether wisely or no, let the forest judge.

Enter CELIA, with a writing.

Ros. Peace!

Here comes my sister reading. Stand aside.

Cel. 'Why should this a desert be,
>   For it is unpeopled? No!
> Tongues I'll hang on every tree
>   That shall civil sayings show:
> Some, how brief the life of man
>   Runs his erring pilgrimage,
> That the stretching of a span
>   Buckles in his sum of age;
> Some, of violated vows
>   'Twixt the souls of friend and friend;
> But upon the fairest boughs,
>   Or at every sentence end,

Will I "Rosalinda" write,
    Teaching all that read to know
The quintessence of every sprite
    Heaven would in little show.
Therefore heaven Nature charg'd
    That one body should be fill'd
With all graces wide-enlarg'd.
    Nature presently distill'd
Helen's cheek, but not her heart,
    Cleopatra's majesty,
Atalanta's better part,
    Sad Lucretia's modesty.
Thus Rosalinde of many parts
    By heavenly synod was devis'd,
Of many faces, eyes, and hearts,
    To have the touches dearest priz'd.
Heaven would that she these gifts should have.
And I to live and die her slave.'

Ros. O most gentle pulpiter! what tedious homily of love have you wearied your parishioners withal, and never cried, 'Have patience, good people'!

Cel. How now? Back, friends. Shepherd, go off a little. Go with him, sirrah.

Touch. Come, shepherd, let us make an honourable retreat; though not with bag and baggage, yet with scrip and scrippage.   *Exeunt* Corin *and* Touchstone.

Cel. Didst thou hear these verses?

Ros. O, yes, I heard them all, and more too; for some of them had in them more feet than the verses would bear.

Cel. That's no matter. The feet might bear the verses.

Ros. Ay, but the feet were lame, and could not bear themselves without the verse, and therefore stood lamely in the verse.

Cel. But didst thou hear without wondering how thy name should be hang'd and carved upon these trees?

Ros. I was seven of the nine days out of the wonder before you came; for look here what I found on a palm tree. I was never so berhym'd since Pythagoras' time that I was an Irish rat, which I can hardly remember.

CEL. Trow you who hath done this?

Ros. Is it a man?

CEL. And a chain that you once wore, about his neck. Change you colour?

Ros. I prithee who?

CEL. O Lord, Lord! it is a hard matter for friends to meet; but mountains may be remov'd with earthquakes, and so encounter.

Ros. Nay, but who is it?

CEL. Is it possible?

Ros. Nay, I prithee now with most petitionary vehemence, tell me who it is.

CEL. O wonderful, wonderful, and most wonderful wonderful! and yet again wonderful, and after that, out of all hooping!

Ros. Good my complexion! Dost thou think, though I am caparison'd like a man, I have a doublet and hose in my disposition? One inch of delay more is a South Sea of discovery. I prithee tell me who is it quickly, and speak apace. I would thou couldst stammer, that thou mightst pour this conceal'd man out of thy mouth as wine comes out of a narrow-mouth'd bottle—either too much at once, or none at all. I prithee take the cork out of thy mouth, that I may drink thy tidings.

CEL. So you may put a man in your belly.

Ros. Is he of God's making? What manner of man? Is his head worth a hat? or his chin worth a beard?

CEL. Nay, he hath but a little beard.

Ros. Why, God will send more, if the man will be thankful! Let me stay the growth of his beard, if thou delay me not the knowledge of his chin.

CEL. It is young Orlando, that tripp'd up the wrestler's heels and your heart both in an instant.

Ros. Nay, but the devil take mocking! Speak sad brow and true maid.

Cel. I' faith, coz, 'tis he.

Ros. Orlando?

Cel. Orlando.

Ros. Alas the day! what shall I do with my doublet and hose? What did he when thou saw'st him? What said he? How look'd he? Wherein went he? What makes he here? Did he ask for me? Where remains he? How parted he with thee? and when shalt thou see him again? Answer me in one word.

Cel. You must borrow me Gargantua's mouth first; 'tis a word too great for any mouth of this age's size. To say ay and no to these particulars is more than to answer in a catechism.

Ros. But doth he know that I am in this forest, and in man's apparel? Looks he as freshly as he did the day he wrestled?

Cel. It is as easy to count atomies as to resolve the propositions of a lover; but take a taste of my finding him, and relish it with good observance. I found him under a tree, like a dropp'd acorn.

Ros. It may well be called Jove's tree when it drops forth such fruit.

Cel. Give me audience, good madam.

Ros. Proceed.

Cel. There lay he stretch'd along like a wounded knight.

Ros. Though it be pity to see such a sight, it well becomes the ground.

Cel. Cry 'holla' to thy tongue, I prithee. It curvets unseasonably. He was furnish'd like a hunter.

Ros. O, ominous! he comes to kill my heart.

Cel. I would sing my song without a burthen. Thou bring'st me out of tune.

Ros. Do you not know I am a woman? When I think, I must speak. Sweet, say on.

Cel. You bring me out.

[*Enter* Orlando *and* Jaques.]

Soft! comes he not here?

Ros. 'Tis he! Slink by, and note him.   *They step aside.*

Jaq. I thank you for your company; but, good faith, I had as lief have been myself alone.

Orl. And so had I; but yet for fashion sake I thank you too for your society.

Jaq. God b'wi' you! Let's meet as little as we can.

Orl. I do desire we may be better strangers.

Jaq. I pray you mar no more trees with writing love songs in their barks.

Orl. I pray you mar no moe of my verses with reading them ill-favouredly.

Jaq. Rosalind is your love's name?

Orl. Yes, just.

Jaq. I do not like her name.

Orl. There was no thought of pleasing you when she was christen'd.

Jaq. What stature is she of?

Orl. Just as high as my heart.

Jaq. You are full of pretty answers. Have you not been acquainted with goldsmiths' wives, and conn'd them out of rings?

Orl. Not so; but I answer you right painted cloth, from whence you have studied your questions.

Jaq. You have a nimble wit; I think 'twas made of Atalanta's heels. Will you sit down with me? and we two will rail against our mistress the world and all our misery.

Orl. I will chide no breather in the world but myself, against whom I know most faults.

Jaq. The worst fault you have is to be in love.

ORL. 'Tis a fault I will not change for your best virtue.
I am weary of you.

JAQ. By my troth, I was seeking for a fool when I found
you.

ORL. He is drown'd in the brook. Look but in and you
shall see him.

JAQ. There I shall see mine own figure.

ORL. Which I take to be either a fool or a cipher.

JAQ. I'll tarry no longer with you. Farewell, good
Signior Love.

ORL. I am glad of your departure. Adieu, good Monsieur Melancholy.

Exit JAQUES. CELIA *and* ROSALIND *come forward.*

ROS. [*aside to* CELIA] I will speak to him like a saucy
lackey, and under that habit play the knave with him.—
Do you hear, forester?

ORL. Very well. What would you?

ROS. I pray you, what is't o'clock?

ORL. You should ask me, what time o' day. There's no
clock in the forest.

ROS. Then there is no true lover in the forest; else
sighing every minute and groaning every hour would detect the lazy foot of Time as well as a clock.

ORL. And why not the swift foot of Time? Had not
that been as proper?

ROS. By no means, sir. Time travels in divers paces
with divers persons. I'll tell you who Time ambles withal,
who Time trots withal, who Time gallops withal, and
who he stands still withal.

ORL. I prithee, who doth he trot withal?

ROS. Marry, he trots hard with a young maid between
the contract of her marriage and the day it is solemniz'd.
If the interim be but a se'nnight, Time's pace is so hard
that it seems the length of seven year.

ORL. Who ambles Time withal?

Ros. With a priest that lacks Latin and a rich man that hath not the gout; for the one sleeps easily because he cannot study, and the other lives merrily because he feels no pain; the one lacking the burthen of lean and wasteful learning, the other knowing no burthen of heavy tedious penury. These Time ambles withal.

Orl. Who doth he gallop withal?

Ros. With a thief to the gallows; for though he go as softly as foot can fall, he thinks himself too soon there.

Orl. Who stays it still withal?

Ros. With lawyers in the vacation; for they sleep between term and term, and then they perceive not how time moves.

Orl. Where dwell you, pretty youth?

Ros. With this shepherdess, my sister; here in the skirts of the forest, like fringe upon a petticoat.

Orl. Are you native of this place?

Ros. As the cony that you see dwell where she is kindled.

Orl. Your accent is something finer than you could purchase in so removed a dwelling.

Ros. I have been told so of many. But indeed an old religious uncle of mine taught me to speak, who was in his youth an inland man; one that knew courtship too well, for there he fell in love. I have heard him read many lectures against it; and I thank God I am not a woman, to be touch'd with so many giddy offences as he hath generally tax'd their whole sex withal.

Orl. Can you remember any of the principal evils that he laid to the charge of women?

Ros. There were none principal. They were all like one another as halfpence are, every one fault seeming monstrous till his fellow-fault came to match it.

Orl. I prithee recount some of them.

Ros. No, I will not cast away my physic but on those

that are sick. There is a man haunts the forest that abuses our young plants with carving 'Rosalind' on their barks; hangs odes upon hawthorns, and elegies on brambles; all, forsooth, deifying the name of Rosalind. If I could meet that fancy-monger, I would give him some good counsel, for he seems to have the quotidian of love upon him.

ORL. I am he that is so love-shak'd. I pray you tell me your remedy.

ROS. There is none of my uncle's marks upon you. He taught me how to know a man in love; in which cage of rushes I am sure you are not prisoner.

ORL. What were his marks?

ROS. A lean cheek, which you have not; a blue eye and sunken, which you have not; an unquestionable spirit, which you have not; a beard neglected, which you have not. But I pardon you for that, for simply your having in beard is a younger brother's revenue. Then your hose should be ungarter'd, your bonnet unbanded, your sleeve unbutton'd, your shoe untied, and everything about you demonstrating a careless desolation. But you are no such man: you are rather point-device in your accoustrements, as loving yourself, than seeming the lover of any other.

ORL. Fair youth, I would I could make thee believe I love.

ROS. Me believe it? You may as soon make her that you love believe it, which I warrant she is apter to do than to confess she does. That is one of the points in the which women still give the lie to their consciences. But in good sooth, are you he that hangs the verses on the trees wherein Rosalind is so admired?

ORL. I swear to thee, youth, by the white hand of Rosalind, I am that he, that unfortunate he.

ROS. But are you so much in love as your rhymes speak?

ORL. Neither rhyme nor reason can express how much.

Ros. Love is merely a madness, and, I tell you, deserves as well a dark house and a whip as madmen do; and the reason why they are not so punish'd and cured is that the lunacy is so ordinary that the whippers are in love too. Yet I profess curing it by counsel.

ORL. Did you ever cure any so?

Ros. Yes, one, and in this manner. He was to imagine me his love, his mistress; and I set him every day to woo me. At which time would I, being but a moonish youth, grieve, be effeminate, changeable, longing, and liking, proud, fantastical, apish, shallow, inconstant, full of tears, full of smiles; for every passion something and for no passion truly anything, as boys and women are for the most part cattle of this colour; would now like him, now loathe him; then entertain him, then forswear him; now weep for him, then spit at him; that I drave my suitor from his mad humour of love to a living humour of madness, which was, to forswear the full stream of the world and to live in a nook merely monastic. And thus I cur'd him; and this way will I take upon me to wash your liver as clean as a sound sheep's heart, that there shall not be one spot of love in't.

ORL. I would not be cured, youth.

Ros. I would cure you, if you would but call me Rosalind and come every day to my cote and woo me.

ORL. Now, by the faith of my love, I will! Tell me where it is.

Ros. Go with me to it, and I'll show it you; and by the way you shall tell me where in the forest you live. Will you go?

ORL. With all my heart, good youth.

Ros. Nay, you must call me Rosalind. Come, sister, will you go?   *Exeunt.*

Scene III: The Forest. Near the sheepcote.

Enter TOUCHSTONE *the* CLOWN, AUDREY, *and* JAQUES,
behind.

TOUCH. Come apace, good Audrey. I will fetch up
your goats, Audrey. And how, Audrey, am I the man yet?
Doth my simple feature content you?

AUD. Your features? Lord warrant us! What features?

TOUCH. I am here with thee and thy goats, as the most
capricious poet, honest Ovid, was among the Goths.

JAQ. [*aside*] O knowledge ill-inhabited, worse than
Jove in a thatch'd house!

TOUCH. When a man's verses cannot be understood,
nor a man's good wit seconded with the forward child,
understanding, it strikes a man more dead than a great
reckoning in a little room. Truly, I would the gods had
made thee poetical.

AUD. I do not know what poetical is. Is it honest in
deed and word? Is it a true thing?

TOUCH. No, truly; for the truest poetry is the most
feigning, and lovers are given to poetry; and what they
swear in poetry may be said, as lovers, they do feign

AUD. Do you wish then that the gods had made me
poetical?

TOUCH. I do truly. For thou swear'st to me thou art
honest. Now if thou wert a poet, I might have some hope
thou didst feign.

AUD. Would you not have me honest?

TOUCH. No, truly, unless thou wert hard-favour'd; for
honesty coupled to beauty is to have honey a sauce to
sugar.

JAQ. [*aside*] A material fool!

AUD. Well, I am not fair; and therefore I pray the gods
make me honest.

Touch. Truly, and to cast away honesty upon a foul
slut were to put good meat into an unclean dish.

Aud. I am not a slut, though I thank the gods I am foul.

Touch. Well, praised be the gods for thy foulness!
Sluttishness may come hereafter. But be it as it may be,
I will marry thee; and to that end I have been with Sir
Oliver Martext, the vicar of the next village, who hath
promis'd to meet me in this place of the forest and to
couple us.

Jaq. [*aside*] I would fain see this meeting.

Aud. Well, the gods give us joy!

Touch. Amen. A man may, if he were of a fearful
heart, stagger in this attempt; for here we have no temple
but the wood, no assembly ·but horn-beasts. But what
though? Courage! As horns are odious, they are necessary. It is said, 'Many a man knows no end of his goods.'
Right! Many a man has good horns and knows no end of
them. Well, that is the dowry of his wife; 'tis none of his
own getting. Horns? Even so. Poor men alone? No, no!
the noblest deer hath them as huge as the rascal. Is the
single man therefore blessed? No; as a wall'd town is
more worthier than a village, so is the forehead of a married man more honourable than the bare brow of a
bachelor; and by how much defence is better than no
skill, by so much is a horn more precious than to want.

[*Enter* Sir Oliver Martext.]

Here comes Sir Oliver. Sir Oliver Martext, you are well
met. Will you dispatch us here under this tree, or shall we
go with you to your chapel?

Oli. Is there none here to give the woman?

Touch. I will not take her on gift of any man.

Oli. Truly, she must be given, or the marriage is not
lawful.

Jaq. [*comes forward*] Proceed, proceed! I'll give her.

Touch. Good even, good Master What-ye-call't. How do you, sir? You are very well met. Goddild you for your last company. I am very glad to see you. Even a toy in hand here, sir. Nay, pray be cover'd.

Jaq. Will you be married, motley?

Touch. As the ox hath his bow, sir, the horse his curb, and the falcon her bells, so man hath his desires; and as pigeons bill, so wedlock would be nibbling.

Jaq. And will you, being a man of your breeding, be married under a bush like a beggar? Get you to church, and have a good priest that can tell you what marriage is. This fellow will but join you together as they join wainscot; then one of you will prove a shrunk panel, and like green timber warp, warp.

Touch. [*aside*] I am not in the mind but I were better to be married of him than of another; for he is not like to marry me well; and not being well married, it will be a good excuse for me hereafter to leave my wife.

Jaq. Go thou with me and let me counsel thee.

Touch. Come, sweet Audrey.
We must be married, or we must live in bawdry.
Farewell, good Master Oliver: not

> O sweet Oliver,
> O brave Oliver,
> Leave me not behind thee!

but

> Wind away,
> Be gone, I say!
> I will not to wedding with thee.

Exeunt JAQUES, TOUCHSTONE, *and* AUDREY.

Oli. 'Tis no matter. Ne'er a fantastical knave of them all shall flout me out of my calling.   *Exit.*

Scene IV: The Forest. Near the sheepcote.

Enter ROSALIND *and* CELIA.

Ros. Never talk to me! I will weep.

Cel. Do, I prithee; but yet have the grace to consider that tears do not become a man.

Ros. But have I not cause to weep?

Cel. As good cause as one would desire. Therefore weep.

Ros. His very hair is of the dissembling colour.

Cel. Something browner than Judas's. Marry, his kisses are Judas's own children.

Ros. I' faith, his hair is of a good colour.

Cel. An excellent colour. Your chestnut was ever the only colour.

Ros. And his kissing is as full of sanctity as the touch of holy bread.

Cel. He hath bought a pair of cast lips of Diana. A nun of winter's sisterhood kisses not more religiously; the very ice of chastity is in them.

Ros. But why did he swear he would come this morning, and comes not?

Cel. Nay, certainly there is no truth in him.

Ros. Do you think so?

Cel. Yes. I think he is not a pickpurse nor a horse-stealer; but for his verity in love, I do think him as concave as a covered goblet or a worm-eaten nut.

Ros. Not true in love?

Cel. Yes, when he is in; but I think he is not in.

Ros. You have heard him swear downright he was.

Cel. 'Was' is not 'is.' Besides, the oath of a lover is no stronger than the word of a tapster: they are both the confirmer of false reckonings. He attends here in the forest on the Duke your father.

Ros. I met the Duke yesterday and had much question with him. He ask'd me of what parentage I was. I told him, of as good as he. So he laugh'd and let me go. But what talk we of fathers when there is such a man as Orlando?

Cel. O, that's a brave man! He writes brave verses, speaks brave words, swears brave oaths, and breaks them bravely—quite traverse, athwart the heart of his lover; as a puisny tilter, that spurs his horse but on one side, breaks his staff like a noble goose. But all's brave that youth mounts and folly guides. Who comes here?

Enter Corin.

Cor. Mistress and master, you have oft enquir'd
After the shepherd that complain'd of love,
Who you saw sitting by me on the turf,
Praising the proud disdainful shepherdess
That was his mistress.

Cel.   Well, and what of him?

Cor. If you will see a pageant truly play'd
Between the pale complexion of true love
And the red glow of scorn and proud disdain,
Go hence a little, and I shall conduct you,
If you will mark it.

Ros.   O, come, let us remove!
The sight of lovers feedeth those in love.
Bring us to this sight, and you shall say
I'll prove a busy actor in their play.   *Exeunt.*

Scene V: Another part of the Forest.

Enter Silvius *and* Phebe.

Sil. Sweet Phebe, do not scorn me; do not, Phebe!
Say that you love me not, but say not so

In bitterness. The common executioner,
Whose heart th' accustom'd sight of death makes hard,
Falls not the axe upon the humbled neck
But first begs pardon. Will you sterner be
Than he that dies and lives by bloody drops?

Enter ROSALIND, CELIA, *and* CORIN, *behind.*

PHE. I would not be thy executioner.
I fly thee, for I would not injure thee.
Thou tell'st me there is murder in mine eye:
'Tis pretty, sure, and very probable
That eyes, that are the frail'st and softest things,
Who shut their coward gates on atomies,
Should be call'd tyrants, butchers, murtherers!
Now I do frown on thee with all my heart;
And if mine eyes can wound, now let them kill thee!
Now counterfeit to swound; why, now fall down;
Or if thou canst not, O, for shame, for shame,
Lie not, to say mine eyes are murtherers!
Now show the wound mine eye hath made in thee.
Scratch thee but with a pin, and there remains
Some scar of it; lean but upon a rush,
The cicatrice and capable impressure
Thy palm some moment keeps; but now mine eyes,
Which I have darted at thee, hurt thee not,
Nor I am sure there is no force in eyes
That can do hurt.
SIL.   O dear Phebe,
If ever (as that ever may be near)
You meet in some fresh cheek the power of fancy,
Then shall you know the wounds invisible
That love's keen arrows make.
PHE.   But till that time
Come not thou near me; and when that time comes,

Afflict me with thy mocks, pity me not,
As till that time I shall not pity thee.

Ros. And why, I pray you? Who might be your mother,
That you insult, exult, and all at once,
Over the wretched? What though you have no beauty—
As, by my faith, I see no more in you
Than without candle may go dark to bed!—
Must you be therefore proud and pitiless?
Why, what means this? Why do you look on me?
I see no more in you than in the ordinary
Of nature's sale-work. 'Od's my little life,
I think she means to tangle my eyes too!
No, faith, proud mistress, hope not after it.
'Tis not your inky brows, your black silk hair,
Your bugle eyeballs, nor your cheek of cream
That can entame my spirits to your worship.
You foolish shepherd, wherefore do you follow her,
Like foggy south, puffing with wind and rain?
You are a thousand times a properer man
Than she a woman. 'Tis such fools as you
That makes the world full of ill-favour'd children.
'Tis not her glass, but you, that flatters her,
And out of you she sees herself more proper
Than any of her lineaments can show her.
But, mistress, know yourself. Down on your knees,
And thank heaven, fasting, for a good man's love;
For I must tell you friendly in your ear,
Sell when you can! you are not for all markets.
Cry the man mercy, love him, take his offer.
Foul is most foul, being foul to be a scoffer.
So take her to thee, shepherd. Fare you well.

Phe. Sweet youth, I pray you chide a year together.
I had rather hear you chide than this man woo.

Ros. [to Phebe] He's fall'n in love with your foulness,
[to Silvius] and she'll fall in love with my anger. If it be

so, as fast as she answers thee with frowning looks, I'll
sauce her with bitter words.—Why look you so upon me?

PHE. For no ill will I bear you.

Ros. I pray you do not fall in love with me,
For I am falser than vows made in wine.
Besides, I like you not. If you will know my house,
'Tis at the tuft of olives, here hard by.—
Will you go, sister?—Shepherd, ply her hard.—
Come, sister.—Shepherdess, look on him better
And be not proud. Though all the world could see,
None could be so abus'd in sight as he.—
Come, to our flock.

             Exeunt ROSALIND, CELIA, *and* CORIN.

PHE. Dead shepherd, now I find thy saw of might,
'Who ever lov'd that lov'd not at first sight?'

SIL. Sweet Phebe—

PHE.   Ha! what say'st thou, Silvius?

SIL. Sweet Phebe, pity me.

PHE. Why, I am sorry for thee, gentle Silvius.

SIL. Wherever sorrow is, relief would be.
If you do sorrow at my grief in love,
By giving love your sorrow and my grief
Were both extermin'd.

PHE. Thou hast my love. Is not that neighbourly?

SIL. I would have you.

PHE.   Why, that were covetousness.
Silvius, the time was that I hated thee,
And yet it is not that I bear thee love;
But since that thou canst talk of love so well,
Thy company, which erst was irksome to me,
I will endure; and I'll employ thee too.
But do not look for further recompense
Than thine own gladness that thou art employ'd.

SIL. So holy and so perfect is my love,
And I in such a poverty of grace,

That I shall think it a most plenteous crop
To glean the broken ears after the man
That the main harvest reaps. Loose now and then
A scatt'red smile, and that I'll live upon.

    PHE. Know'st thou the youth that spoke to me ere-
        while?

    SIL. Not very well, but I have met him oft,
And he hath bought the cottage and the bounds
That the old Carlot once was master of.

    PHE. Think not I love him, though I ask for him.
'Tis but a peevish boy; yet he talks well.
But what care I for words? Yet words do well
When he that speaks them pleases those that hear.
It is a pretty youth—not very pretty—
But sure he's proud; and yet his pride becomes him.
He'll make a proper man. The best thing in him
Is his complexion; and faster than his tongue
Did make offence, his eye did heal it up.
He is not very tall; yet for his years he's tall.
His leg is but so so; and yet 'tis well.
There was a pretty redness in his lip,
A little riper and more lusty red
Than that mix'd in his cheek; 'twas just the difference
Betwixt the constant red and mingled damask.
There be some women, Silvius, had they mark'd him
In parcels as I did, would have gone near
To fall in love with him; but, for my part,
I love him not nor hate him not; and yet
I have more cause to hate him than to love him;
For what had he to do to chide at me?
He said mine eyes were black and my hair black;
And, now I am rememb'red, scorn'd at me.
I marvel why I answer'd not again.
But that's all one: omittance is no quittance.

I'll write to him a very taunting letter,
And thou shalt bear it. Wilt thou, Silvius?

SIL. Phebe, with all my heart.

PHE.   I'll write it straight;
The matter's in my head and in my heart.
I will be bitter with him and passing short.
Go with me, Silvius.   *Exeunt.*

Act IV: Scene I: The Forest. Near the sheepcote.

Enter ROSALIND *and* CELIA *and* JAQUES.

JAQ. I prithee, pretty youth, let me be better acquainted with thee.

ROS. They say you are a melancholy fellow.

JAQ. I am so. I do love it better than laughing.

ROS. Those that are in extremity of either are abominable fellows, and betray themselves to every modern censure worse than drunkards.

JAQ. Why, 'tis good to be sad and say nothing.

ROS. Why then, 'tis good to be a post.

JAQ. I have neither the scholar's melancholy, which is emulation; nor the musician's, which is fantastical; nor the courtier's, which is proud; nor the soldier's, which is ambitious; nor the lawyer's, which is politic; nor the lady's, which is nice; nor the lover's, which is all these: but it is a melancholy of mine own, compounded of many simples, extracted from many objects, and indeed the sundry contemplation of my travels, in which my often rumination wraps me in a most humorous sadness.

ROS. A traveller! By my faith, you have great reason to be sad. I fear you have sold your own lands to see other men's. Then to have seen much and to have nothing is to have rich eyes and poor hands.

JAQ. Yes, I have gain'd my experience.

Enter ORLANDO.

Ros. And your experience makes you sad. I had rather have a fool to make me merry than experience to make me sad—and to travel for it too!

ORL. Good day and happiness, dear Rosalind!

JAQ. Nay then, God b'wi' you, an you talk in blank verse!

Ros. Farewell, Monsieur Traveller. Look you lisp and wear strange suits, disable all the benefits of your own country, be out of love with your nativity and almost chide God for making you that countenance you are; or I will scarce think you have swam in a gundello. [*Exit* JAQUES.] Why, how now, Orlando? Where have you been all this while? You a lover? An you serve me such another trick, never come in my sight more.

ORL. My fair Rosalind, I come within an hour of my promise.

Ros. Break an hour's promise in love? He that will divide a minute into a thousand parts and break but a part of the thousand part of a minute in the affairs of love, it may be said of him that Cupid hath clapp'd him o' th' shoulder, but I'll warrant him heart-whole.

ORL. Pardon me, dear Rosalind.

Ros. Nay, an you be so tardy, come no more in my sight. I had as lief be woo'd of a snail.

ORL. Of a snail?

Ros. Ay, of a snail; for though he comes slowly, he carries his house on his head—a better jointure, I think, than you make a woman. Besides, he brings his destiny with him.

ORL. What's that?

Ros. Why, horns! which such as you are fain to be beholding to your wives for; but he comes armed in his fortune and prevents the slander of his wife.

Orl. Virtue is no horn-maker, and my Rosalind is virtuous.

Ros. And I am your Rosalind.

Cel. It pleases him to call you so; but he hath a Rosalind of a better leer than you.

Ros. Come, woo me, woo me! for now I am in a holiday humour and like enough to consent. What would you say to me now, an I were your very very Rosalind?

Orl. I would kiss before I spoke.

Ros. Nay, you were better speak first; and when you were gravell'd for lack of matter, you might take occasion to kiss. Very good orators, when they are out, they will spit; and for lovers, lacking (God warn us!) matter, the cleanliest shift is to kiss.

Orl. How if the kiss be denied?

Ros. Then she puts you to entreaty, and there begins new matter.

Orl. Who could be out, being before his beloved mistress?

Ros. Marry, that should you, if I were your mistress, or I should think my honesty ranker than my wit.

Orl. What, of my suit?

Ros. Not out of your apparel, and yet out of your suit. Am not I your Rosalind?

Orl. I take some joy to say you are, because I would be talking of her.

Ros. Well, in her person, I say I will not have you.

Orl. Then, in mine own person, I die.

Ros. No, faith, die by attorney. The poor world is almost six thousand years old, and in all this time there was not any man died in his own person, videlicet, in a love cause. Troilus had his brains dash'd out with a Grecian club; yet he did what he could to die before, and he is one of the patterns of love. Leander, he would have liv'd many a fair year though Hero had turn'd nun, if it had not been for a hot midsummer night; for (good youth) he went but forth to wash him in the Hellespont, and being taken with the cramp, was drown'd; and the foolish chroniclers of that age found it was 'Hero of Sestos.' But these are all lies. Men have died from time to time, and worms have eaten them, but not for love.

ORL. I would not have my right Rosalind of this mind, for I protest her frown might kill me.

ROS. By this hand, it will not kill a fly! But come, now I will be your Rosalind in a more coming-on disposition; and ask me what you will, I will grant it.

ORL. Then love me, Rosalind.

ROS. Yes, faith, will I, Fridays and Saturdays and all.

ORL. And wilt thou have me?

ROS. Ay, and twenty such.

ORL. What sayest thou?

ROS. Are you not good?

ORL. I hope so.

ROS. Why then, can one desire too much of a good thing? Come, sister, you shall be the priest and marry us. Give me your hand, Orlando. What do you say, sister?

ORL. Pray thee marry us.

CEL. I cannot say the words.

ROS. You must begin, 'Will you, Orlando'—

CEL. Go to. Will you, Orlando, have to wife this Rosalind?

ORL. I will.

ROS. Ay, but when?

ORL. Why now, as fast as she can marry us.

ROS. Then you must say, 'I take thee, Rosalind, for wife.'

ORL. I take thee, Rosalind, for wife.

ROS. I might ask you for your commission; but I do take thee, Orlando, for my husband. There's a girl goes

before the priest, and certainly a woman's thought runs
before her actions.

ORL. So do all thoughts; they are wing'd.

Ros. Now tell me how long you would have her after
you have possess'd her.

ORL. For ever and a day.

Ros. Say 'a day,' without the 'ever.' No, no, Orlando!
Men are April when they woo, December when they
wed. Maids are May when they are maids, but the sky
changes when they are wives. I will be more jealous of
thee than a Barbary cock-pigeon over his hen, more
clamorous than a parrot against rain,·more newfangled
than an ape, more giddy in my desires than a monkey.
I will weep for nothing, like Diana in the fountain, and
I will do that when you are dispos'd to be merry; I will
laugh like a hyen, and that when thou art inclin'd to
sleep.

ORL. But will my Rosalind do so?

Ros. By my life, she will do as I do.

ORL. O, but she is wise!

Ros. Or else she could not have the wit to do this. The
wiser, the waywarder. Make the doors upon a woman's
wit, and it will out at the casement; shut that, and 'twill
out at the keyhole; stop that, 'twill fly with the smoke
out at the chimney.

ORL. A man that had a wife with such a wit, he might
say, 'Wit, whither wilt?'

Ros. Nay, you might keep that check for it till you
met your wive's wit going to your neighbour's bed.

ORL. And what wit could wit have to excuse that?

Ros. Marry, to say she came to seek you there. You
shall never take her without her answer unless you take
her without her tongue. O, that woman that cannot make
her fault her husband's occasion, let her never nurse her
child herself, for she will breed it like a fool!

ORL. For these two hours, Rosalind, I will leave thee.

Ros. Alas, dear love, I cannot lack thee two hours!

ORL. I must attend the Duke at dinner. By two o'clock I will be with thee again.

Ros. Ay, go your ways, go your ways! I knew what you would prove. My friends told me as much, and I thought no less. That flattering tongue of yours won me. 'Tis but one cast away, and so, come death! Two o'clock is your hour?

ORL. Ay, sweet Rosalind.

Ros. By my troth, and in good earnest, and so God mend me, and by all pretty oaths that are not dangerous, if you break one jot of your promise or come one minute behind your hour, I will think you the most pathetical break-promise, and the most hollow lover, and the most unworthy of her you call Rosalind, that may be chosen out of the gross band of the unfaithful. Therefore beware my censure and keep your promise.

ORL. With no less religion than if thou wert indeed my Rosalind. So adieu.

Ros. Well, Time is the old justice that examines all such offenders, and let Time try. Adieu.

Exit ORLANDO.

CEL. You have simply misus'd our sex in your love-prate. We must have your doublet and hose pluck'd over your head, and show the world what the bird hath done to her own nest.

Ros. O coz, coz, coz, my pretty little coz, that thou didst know how many fathom deep I am in love! But it cannot be sounded. My affection hath an unknown bottom, like the Bay of Portugal.

CEL. Or rather, bottomless, that as fast as you pour affection in, it runs out.

Ros. No, that same wicked bastard of Venus that was

begot of thought, conceiv'd of spleen, and born of madness, that blind rascally boy that abuses every one's eyes because his own are out—let him be judge how deep I am in love. I'll tell thee, Aliena, I cannot be out of the sight of Orlando. I'll go find a shadow, and sigh till he come.

CEL. And I'll sleep.   *Exeunt.*

Scene II: The Forest. Before Duke Senior's cave.

Enter JAQUES, LORDS, *and* FORESTERS, *with a dead deer.*

JAQ. Which is he that killed the deer?

LORD. Sir, it was I.

JAQ. Let's present him to the Duke like a Roman conqueror; and it would do well to set the deer's horns upon his head for a branch of victory. Have you no song, forester, for this purpose?

LORD. Yes, sir.

JAQ. Sing it. 'Tis no matter how it be in tune, so it make noise enough.   *Music.*

SONG

> What shall he have that kill'd the deer?
> His leather skin and horns to wear.
>   Then sing him home.
>   (*The rest shall bear this burthen.*)
> Take thou no scorn to wear the horn;
> It was a crest ere thou wast born:
>   Thy father's father wore it,
>   And thy father bore it.
> The horn, the horn, the lusty horn,
> Is not a thing to laugh to scorn.

Exeunt.

Scene III: The Forest. Near the sheepcote.

Enter ROSALIND *and* CELIA.

Ros. How say you now? Is it not past two o'clock? and here much Orlando!

CEL. I warrant you, with pure love and troubled brain, he hath ta'en his bow and arrows, and is gone forth to sleep.

[*Enter* SILVIUS.]

Look who comes here.

SIL. My errand is to you, fair youth.
My gentle Phebe bid me give you this.   [*Gives a letter.*]
I know not the contents; but, as I guess
By the stern brow and waspish action
Which she did use as she was writing of it,
It bears an angry tenure. Pardon me;
I am but as a guiltless messenger.

Ros. Patience herself would startle at this letter
And play the swaggerer. Bear this, bear all!
She says I am not fair, that I lack manners;
She calls me proud, and that she could not love me,
Were man as rare as phœnix. 'Od's my will!
Her love is not the hare that I do hunt.
Why writes she so to me? Well, shepherd, well,
This is a letter of your own device.

SIL. No, I protest, I know not the contents.
Phebe did write it.

Ros.   Come, come, you are a fool,
And turn'd into the extremity of love.
I saw her hand. She has a leathern hand,
A freestone-coloured hand. I verily did think
That her old gloves were on, but 'twas her hands.
She has a housewive's hand; but that's no matter.

I say she never did invent this letter;
This is a man's invention and his hand.

    Sil. Sure it is hers.

    Ros. Why, 'tis a boisterous and a cruel style,
A style for challengers. Why, she defies me
Like Turk to Christian! Women's gentle brain
Could not drop forth such giant-rude invention,
Such Ethiop words, blacker in their effect
Than in their countenance. Will you hear the letter?

    Sil. So please you, for I never heard it yet—
Yet heard too much of Phebe's cruelty.

    Ros. She Phebes me. Mark how the tyrant writes.

[Reads.]

> 'Art thou god to shepherd turn'd,
>   That a maiden's heart hath burn'd?'

Can a woman rail thus?

    Sil. Call you this railing?

    Ros. [Reads.]

> 'Why, thy godhead laid apart,
>   Warr'st thou with a woman's heart?'

Did you ever hear such railing?

> 'Whiles the eye of man did woo me,
>   That could do no vengeance to me.'

Meaning me a beast.

> 'If the scorn of your bright eyne
>   Have power to raise such love in mine,
>   Alack, in me what strange effect
>   Would they work in mild aspect!
>   Whiles you chid me, I did love;
>   How then might your prayers move!
>   He that brings this love to thee
>   Little knows this love in me;
>   And by him seal up thy mind,
>   Whether that thy youth and kind
>   Will the faithful offer take

Of me and all that I can make,
Or else by him my love deny,
And then I'll study how to die.'

SIL. Call you this chiding?

CEL. Alas, poor shepherd!

ROS. Do you pity him? No, he deserves no pity. Wilt thou love such a woman? What, to make thee an instrument, and play false strains upon thee? Not to be endur'd! Well, go your way to her (for I see love hath made thee a tame snake) and say this to her: that if she love me, I charge her to love thee; if she will not, I will never have her unless thou entreat for her. If you be a true lover, hence, and not a word; for here comes more company.   *Exit* SILVIUS.

Enter OLIVER.

OLI. Good morrow, fair ones. Pray you, if you know,
Where in the purlieus of this forest stands
A sheepcote, fenc'd about with olive trees?

CEL. West of this place, down in the neighbour bottom..
The rank of osiers by the murmuring stream
Left on your right hand brings you to the place.
But at this hour the house doth keep itself;
There's none within.

OLI. If that an eye may profit by a tongue,
Then should I know you by description—
Such garments and such years: 'The boy is fair,
Of female favour, and bestows himself
Like a ripe sister; the woman low,
And browner than her brother.' Are not you
The owner of the house I did enquire for?

CEL. It is no boast, being ask'd, to say we are.

OLI. Orlando doth commend him to you both,

And to that youth he calls his Rosalind
He sends this bloody napkin. Are you he?

ROS. I am. What must we understand by this?

OLI. Some of my shame, if you will know of me
What man I am, and how, and why, and where
This handkercher was stain'd.

CEL.   I pray you tell it.

OLI. When last the young Orlando parted from you,
He left a promise to return again
Within an hour; and pacing through the forest,
Chewing the food of sweet and bitter fancy,
Lo, what befell! He threw his eye aside,
And mark what object did present itself.
Under an oak, whose boughs were moss'd with age
And high top bald with dry antiquity,
A wretched ragged man, o'ergrown with hair,
Lay sleeping on his back. About his neck
A green and gilded snake had wreath'd itself,
Who with her head, nimble in threats, approach'd
The opening of his mouth; but suddenly,
Seeing Orlando, it unlink'd itself
And with indented glides did slip away
Into a bush, under which bush's shade
A lioness, with udders all drawn dry,
Lay couching, head on ground, with catlike watch
When that the sleeping man should stir; for 'tis
The royal disposition of that beast
To prey on nothing that doth seem as dead.
This seen, Orlando did approach the man
And found it was his brother, his elder brother.

CEL. O, I have heard him speak of that same brother,
And he did render him the most unnatural
That liv'd amongst men.

OLI.   And well he might so do,
For well I know he was unnatural.

Ros. But, to Orlando! Did he leave him there,
Food to the suck'd and hungry lioness?

Oli. Twice did he turn his back and purpos'd so;
But kindness, nobler ever than revenge,
And nature, stronger than his just occasion,
Made him give battle to the lioness,
Who quickly fell before him; in which hurtling
From miserable slumber I awak'd.

Cel. Are you his brother?

Ros.   Was it you he rescu'd?

Cel. Was't you that did so oft contrive to kill him?

Oli. 'Twas I. But 'tis not I! I do not shame
To tell you what I was, since my conversion
So sweetly tastes, being the thing I am.

Ros. But, for the bloody napkin?

Oli.   By-and-by.
When from the first to last, betwixt us two,
Tears our recountments had most kindly bath'd,
As how I came into that desert place—
In brief, he led me to the gentle Duke,
Who gave me fresh array and entertainment,
Committing me unto my brother's love,
Who led me instantly unto his cave,
There stripp'd himself, and here upon his arm
The lioness had torn some flesh away,
Which all this while had bled; and now he fainted,
And cried, in fainting, upon Rosalind.
Brief, I recover'd him, bound up his wound;
And after some small space, being strong at heart,
He sent me hither, stranger as I am,
To tell this story, that you might excuse
His broken promise, and to give this napkin,
Dy'd in his blood, unto the shepherd youth
That he in sport doth call his Rosalind.

ROSALIND *swoons*.

CEL. Why, how now, Ganymede? sweet Ganymede!

OLI. Many will swoon when they do look on blood.

CEL. There is more in it. Cousin Ganymede!

OLI. Look, he recovers.

ROS. I would I were at home.

CEL.   We'll lead you thither.
I pray you, will you take him by the arm?

OLI. Be of good cheer, youth. You a man?
You lack a man's heart.

ROS. I do so, I confess it. Ah, sirrah, a body would
think this was well counterfeited! I pray you tell your
brother how well I counterfeited. Heigh-ho!

OLI. This was not counterfeit. There is too great testi-
mony in your complexion that it was a passion of earnest.

ROS. Counterfeit, I assure you.

OLI. Well then, take a good heart and counterfeit to
be a man.

ROS. So I do; but, i' faith, I should have been a woman
by right.

CEL. Come, you look paler and paler. Pray you draw
homewards. Good sir, go with us.

OLI. That will I; for I must bear answer back
How you excuse my brother, Rosalind.

ROS. I shall devise something. But I pray you commend
my counterfeiting to him. Will you go?   *Exeunt.*

Act V: Scene I: The Forest. Near the sheepcote.

Enter TOUCHSTONE *the* CLOWN *and* AUDREY.

TOUCH. We shall find a time, Audrey. Patience, gentle
Audrey.

AUD. Faith, the priest was good enough, for all the
old gentleman's saying.

Touch. A most wicked Sir Oliver, Audrey, a most vile Martext! But, Audrey, there is a youth here in the forest lays claim to you.

Aud. Ay, I know who 'tis. He hath no interest in me in the world. Here comes the man you mean.

Enter WILLIAM.

Touch. It is meat and drink to me to see a clown. By my troth, we that have good wits have much to answer for. We shall be flouting; we cannot hold.

Will. Good ev'n, Audrey.

Aud. God ye good ev'n, William.

Will. And good ev'n to you, sir.

Touch. Good ev'n, gentle friend. Cover thy head, cover thy head. Nay, prithee be cover'd. How old are you, friend?

Will. Five-and-twenty, sir.

Touch. A ripe age. Is thy name William?

Will. William, sir.

Touch. A fair name. Wast born i' th' forest here?

Will. Ay, sir, I thank God.

Touch. 'Thank God.' A good answer. Art rich?

Will. Faith, sir, so so.

Touch. 'So so' is good, very good, very excellent good; and yet it is not, it is but so so. Art thou wise?

Will. Ay, sir, I have a pretty wit.

Touch. Why, thou say'st well. I do now remember a saying, 'The fool doth think he is wise, but the wise man knows himself to be a fool.' The heathen philosopher, when he had a desire to eat a grape, would open his lips when he put it into his mouth, meaning thereby that grapes were made to eat and lips to open. You do love this maid?

Will. I do, sir.

Touch. Give me your hand. Art thou learned?

WILL. No, sir.

TOUCH. Then learn this of me: to have is to have; for it is a figure in rhetoric that drink, being pour'd out of a cup into a glass, by filling the one doth empty the other; for all your writers do consent that *ipse* is he. Now, you are not *ipse*, for I am he.

WILL. Which he, sir?

TOUCH. He, sir, that must marry this woman. Therefore, you clown, abandon (which is in the vulgar, leave) the society (which in the boorish is, company) of this female (which in the common is, woman); which together is, abandon the society of this female, or, clown, thou perishest; or, to thy better understanding, diest; or, to wit, I kill thee, make thee away, translate thy life into death, thy liberty into bondage. I will deal in poison with thee, or in bastinado, or in steel. I will bandy with thee in faction; I will o'errun thee with policy; I will kill thee a hundred and fifty ways. Therefore tremble and depart.

AUD. Do, good William.

WILL. God rest you merry, sir.   *Exit.*

Enter CORIN.

COR. Our master and mistress seeks you. Come away, away!

TOUCH. Trip, Audrey! trip, Audrey! I attend, I attend.
                                        Exeunt.

Scene II: The Forest. Near the sheepcote.

Enter ORLANDO *and* OLIVER.

ORL. Is't possible that on so little acquaintance you should like her? that but seeing, you should love her? and loving, woo? and wooing, she should grant? And will you persever to enjoy her?

OLI. Neither call the giddiness of it in question, the poverty of her, the small acquaintance, my sudden wooing, nor her sudden consenting; but say with me, I love Aliena; say with her that she loves me; consent with both that we may enjoy each other. It shall be to your good; for my father's house, and all the revenue that was old Sir Rowland's, will I estate upon you, and here live and die a shepherd.

Enter ROSALIND.

ORL. You have my consent. Let your wedding be tomorrow. Thither will I invite the Duke and all's contented followers. Go you and prepare Aliena; for look you, here comes my Rosalind.

Ros. God save you, brother.

OLI. And you, fair sister.   *Exit.*

Ros. O my dear Orlando, how it grieves me to see thee wear thy heart in a scarf!

ORL. It is my arm.

Ros. I thought thy heart had been wounded with the claws of a lion.

ORL. Wounded it is, but with the eyes of a lady.

Ros. Did your brother tell you how I counterfeited to sound when he show'd me your handkercher?

ORL. Ay, and greater wonders than that.

Ros. O, I know where you are! Nay, 'tis true. There was never anything so sudden but the fight of two rams and Cæsar's thrasonical brag of 'I came, saw, and overcame.' For your brother and my sister no sooner met but they look'd; no sooner look'd but they lov'd; no sooner lov'd but they sigh'd; no sooner sigh'd but they ask'd one another the reason; no sooner knew the reason but they sought the remedy: and in these degrees have they made a pair of stairs to marriage, which they will climb incontinent, or else be incontinent before marriage. They are in the very wrath of love, and they will together. Clubs cannot part them.

ORL. They shall be married to-morrow, and I will bid the Duke to the nuptial. But, O, how bitter a thing it is to look into happiness through another man's eyes! By so much the more shall I to-morrow be at the height of heart-heaviness, by how much I shall think my brother happy in having what he wishes for.

Ros. Why then, to-morrow I cannot serve your turn for Rosalind?

ORL. I can live no longer by thinking.

Ros. I will weary you then no longer with idle talking. Know of me then (for now I speak to some purpose) that I know you are a gentleman of good conceit. I speak not this that you should bear a good opinion of my knowledge, insomuch I say I know you are; neither do I labour for a greater esteem than may in some little measure draw a belief from you, to do yourself good, and not to grace me. Believe then, if you please, that I can do strange things. I have, since I was three year old, convers'd with a magician, most profound in his art and yet not damnable. If you do love Rosalind so near the heart as your gesture cries it out, when your brother marries Aliena shall you marry her. I know into what straits of fortune she is driven; and it is not impossible to me, if it appear not inconvenient to you, to set her before your eyes to-morrow human as she is, and without any danger.

ORL. Speak'st thou in sober meanings?

Ros. By my life, I do! which I tender dearly, though I say I am a magician. Therefore put you in your best array, bid your friends; for if you will be married to-morrow, you shall; and to Rosalind, if you will.

[*Enter* SILVIUS *and* PHEBE.]

Look, here comes a lover of mine and a lover of hers.

PHE. Youth, you have done me much ungentleness
To show the letter that I writ to you.

Ros. I care not if I have. It is my study
To seem despiteful and ungentle to you.
You are there followed by a faithful shepherd.
Look upon him, love him; he worships you.

PHE. Good shepherd, tell this youth what 'tis to love.

SIL. It is to be all made of sighs and tears;
And so am I for Phebe.

PHE. And I for Ganymede.

ORL. And I for Rosalind.

Ros. And I for no woman.

SIL. It is to be all made of faith and service;
And so am I for Phebe.

PHE. And I for Ganymede.

ORL. And I for Rosalind.

Ros. And I for no woman.

SIL. It is to be all made of fantasy,
All made of passion, and all made of wishes,
All adoration, duty, and observance,
All humbleness, all patience, and impatience,
All purity, all trial, all obedience;
And so am I for Phebe.

PHE. And so am I for Ganymede.

ORL. And so am I for Rosalind.

Ros. And so am I for no woman.

PHE. [to ROSALIND] If this be so, why blame you me
to love you?

SIL. [to PHEBE] If this be so, why blame you me to
love you?

ORL. If this be so, why blame you me to love you?

Ros. Who do you speak to, 'Why blame you me to
love you?'

ORL. To her that is not here, nor doth not hear.

Ros. Pray you, no more of this; 'tis like the howling of

Irish wolves against the moon. [*To* SILVIUS] I will help
you if I can.—[*To* PHEBE] I would love you if I could.—
To-morrow meet me all together.—[*To* PHEBE] I will
marry you if ever I marry woman, and I'll be married
to-morrow.—[*To* ORLANDO] I will satisfy you if ever I
satisfied man, and you shall be married to-morrow.—
[*To* SILVIUS] I will content you if what pleases you contents you, and you shall be married to-morrow.—[*To*
ORLANDO] As you love Rosalind, meet.—[*To* SILVIUS]
As you love Phebe, meet.—And as I love no woman, I'll
meet. So fare you well. I have left you commands.

SIL. I'll not fail if I live.

PHE. Nor I.

ORL. Nor I.   *Exeunt.*

Scene III: The Forest. Near the sheepcote.

Enter TOUCHSTONE *the* CLOWN *and* AUDREY.

TOUCH. To-morrow is the joyful day, Audrey; to-
morrow will we be married.

AUD. I do desire it with all my heart; and I hope it is
no dishonest desire to desire to be a woman of the world.
Here come two of the banish'd Duke's pages.

Enter two PAGES.

1. PAGE. Well met, honest gentleman.

TOUCH. By my troth, well met. Come, sit, sit, and a
song!

2. PAGE. We are for you. Sit i' th' middle.

1. PAGE. Shall we clap into't roundly, without hawk-
ing or spitting or saying we are hoarse, which are the
only prologues to a bad voice?

2. PAGE. I' faith, i' faith! and both in a tune, like two
gypsies on a horse.

SONG

It was a lover and his lass—
   With a hey, and a ho, and a hey nonino—
That o'er the green cornfield did pass
   In springtime, the only pretty ring-time,
When birds do sing, hey ding a ding, ding.
Sweet lovers love the spring.

Between the acres of the rye—
   With a hey, and a ho, and a hey nonino—
These pretty country folks would lie
   In springtime, &c.

This carol they began that hour—
   With a hey, and a ho, and a hey nonino—
How that a life was but a flower
   In springtime, &c.

And therefore take the present time—
   With a hey, and a ho, and a hey nonino—
For love is crowned with the prime
   In springtime, &c.

Touch. Truly, young gentlemen, though there was no great matter in the ditty, yet the note was very untuneable.

1. Page. You are deceiv'd, sir. We kept time, we lost not our time.

Touch. By my troth, yes! I count it but time lost to hear such a foolish song. God b'wi' you, and God mend your voices! Come, Audrey.   *Exeunt.*

Scene IV: The Forest. Near the sheepcote.

Enter Duke Senior, Amiens, Jaques, Orlando, Oliver, Celia.

Duke S. Dost thou believe, Orlando, that the boy Can do all this that he hath promised?

ORL. I sometimes do believe, and sometimes do not,
As those that fear they hope, and know they fear.

Enter ROSALIND, SILVIUS, *and* PHEBE.

ROS. Patience once more, whiles our compact is urg'd.
You say, if I bring in your Rosalind,
You will bestow her on Orlando here?
  DUKE S. That would I, had I kingdoms to give with
    her.
ROS. And you say you will have her when I bring her?
ORL. That would I, were I of all kingdoms king.
ROS. You say you'll marry me, if I be willing?
PHE. That will I, should I die the hour after.
ROS. But if you do refuse to marry me,
You'll give yourself to this most faithful shepherd?
  PHE. So is the bargain.
ROS. You say that you'll have Phebe, if she will?
  SIL. Though to have her and death were both one
    thing.
ROS. I have promis'd to make all this matter even.
Keep you your word, O Duke, to give your daughter;
You yours, Orlando, to receive his daughter;
Keep your word, Phebe, that you'll marry me,
Or else, refusing me, to wed this shepherd;
Keep your word, Silvius, that you'll marry her
If she refuse me; and from hence I go,
To make these doubts all even.

Exeunt ROSALIND *and* CELIA.

DUKE S. I do remember in this shepherd boy
Some lively touches of my daughter's favour.
  ORL. My lord, the first time that I ever saw him
Methought he was a brother to your daughter.
But, my good lord, this boy is forest-born,
And hath been tutor'd in the rudiments
Of many desperate studies by his uncle,

Whom he reports to be a great magician,
Obscured in the circle of this forest.

Enter TOUCHSTONE *the* CLOWN *and* AUDREY.

JAQ. There is, sure, another flood toward, and these
couples are coming to the ark. Here comes a pair of
very strange beasts, which in all tongues are call'd fools.

TOUCH. Salutation and greeting to you all!

JAQ. Good my lord, bid him welcome. This is the
motley-minded gentleman that I have so often met in
the forest. He hath been a courtier, he swears.

TOUCH. If any man doubt that, let him put me to my
purgation. I have trod a measure; I have flatt'red a lady;
I have been politic with my friend, smooth with mine
enemy; I have undone three tailors; I have had four
quarrels, and like to have fought one.

JAQ. And how was that ta'en up?

TOUCH. Faith, we met, and found the quarrel was
upon the seventh cause.

JAQ. How seventh cause? Good my lord, like ᵗhis
fellow.

DUKE S. I like him very well.

TOUCH. God 'ild you, sir; I desire you of the like. I
press in here, sir, amongst the rest of the country copula-
tives, to swear and to forswear, according as marriage
binds and blood breaks. A poor virgin, sir, an ill-favour'd
thing, sir, but mine own. A poor humour of mine, sir,
to take that that no man else will. Rich honesty dwells
like a miser, sir, in a poor house, as your pearl in your
foul oyster.

DUKE S. By my faith, he is very swift and sententious.

TOUCH. According to the fool's bolt, sir, and such
dulcet diseases.

Jaq. But, for the seventh cause. How did you find the quarrel on the seventh cause?

Touch. Upon a lie seven times removed (bear your body more seeming, Audrey): as thus, sir. I did dislike the cut of a certain courtier's beard. He sent me word, if I said his beard was not cut well, he was in the mind it was. This is call'd the Retort Courteous. If I sent him word again it was not well cut, he would send me word he cut it to please himself. This is call'd the Quip Modest. If again, it was not well cut, he disabled my judgment. This is call'd the Reply Churlish. If again, it was not well cut, he would answer I spake not true. This is call'd the Reproof Valiant. If again, it was not well cut, he would say I lie. This is call'd the Countercheck Quarrelsome; and so to the Lie Circumstantial and the Lie Direct.

Jaq. And how oft did you say his beard was not well cut?

Touch. I durst go no further than the Lie Circumstantial, nor he durst not give me the Lie Direct; and so we measur'd swords and parted.

Jaq. Can you nominate in order now the degrees of the lie?

Touch. O sir, we quarrel in print, by the book, as you have books for good manners. I will name you the degrees. The first, the Retort Courteous; the second, the Quip Modest; the third, the Reply Churlish; the fourth, the Reproof Valiant; the fifth, the Countercheck Quarrelsome; the sixth, the Lie with Circumstance; the seventh, the Lie Direct. All these you may avoid but the Lie Direct, and you may avoid that too, with an If. I knew when seven justices could not take up a quarrel, but when the parties were met themselves, one of them thought but of an If: as, 'If you said so, then I said so';

and they shook hands and swore brothers. Your If is
the only peacemaker. Much virtue in If.

JAQ. Is not this a rare fellow, my lord? He's as good
at anything, and yet a fool.

DUKE S. He uses his folly like a stalking horse, and
under the presentation of that he shoots his wit.

Enter HYMEN, ROSALIND, *and* CELIA. *Still music.*

HYM. Then is there mirth in heaven
  When earthly things made even
   Atone together.
  Good Duke, receive thy daughter;
  Hymen from heaven brought her,
   Yea, brought her hether,
  That thou mightst join her hand with his
  Whose heart within his bosom is.
ROS. To you I give myself, for I am yours.
           [*To* DUKE.]
To you I give myself, for I am yours. [*To* ORLANDO.]
 DUKE S. If there be truth in sight, you are my daugh-
ter.
 ORL. If there be truth in shape, you are my Rosalind.
 PHE. If sight and shape be true,
Why then, my love adieu!
 ROS. I'll have no father, if you be not he. [*To* DUKE.]
I'll have no husband, if you be not he. [*To* ORLANDO.]
Nor ne'er wed woman, if you be not she. [*To* PHEBE.]
 HYM. Peace ho! I bar confusion.
  'Tis I must make conclusion
   Of these most strange events.
  Here's eight that must take hands
  To join in Hymen's bands,
   If truth holds true contents.
  You and you no cross shall part.
       [*To* ORLANDO *and* ROSALIND.]

You and you are heart in heart.

                    [*To* OLIVER *and* CELIA.]

You to his love must accord,   [*To* PHEBE.]

Or have a woman to your lord.

You and you are sure together

                  [*To* TOUCHSTONE *and* AUDREY.]

As the winter to foul weather.

Whiles a wedlock hymn we sing,

Feed yourselves with questioning,

That reason wonder may diminish

How thus we met, and these things finish.

SONG

    Wedding is great Juno's crown—
      O blessed bond of board and bed!
    'Tis Hymen peoples every town;
      High wedlock then be honoured.
    Honour, high honour, and renown
    To Hymen, god of every town!

DUKE S. O my dear niece, welcome thou art to me,
Even daughter, welcome, in no less degree!

PHE. [*to* SILVIUS] I will not eat my word, now thou
    art mine;

Thy faith my fancy to thee doth combine.

Enter SECOND BROTHER, JAQUES DE BOYS.

2. BRO. Let me have audience for a word or two.
I am the second son of old Sir Rowland
That bring these tidings to this fair assembly.
Duke Frederick, hearing how that every day
Men of great worth resorted to this forest,
Address'd a mighty power, which were on foot
In his own conduct, purposely to take
His brother here and put him to the sword;
And to the skirts of this wild wood he came,
Where, meeting with an old religious man,

After some question with him, was converted
Both from his enterprise and from the world,
His crown bequeathing to his banish'd brother,
And all their lands restor'd to them again
That were with him exil'd. This to be true
I do engage my life.

DUKE S.　　　　Welcome, young man.
Thou offer'st fairly to thy brothers' wedding:
To one, his lands withheld; and to the other,
A land itself at large, a potent dukedom.
First, in this forest let us do those ends
That here were well begun and well begot;
And after, every of this happy number
That have endur'd shrewd days and nights with us
Shall share the good of our returned fortune,
According to the measure of their states.
Meantime forget this new-fall'n dignity
And fall into our rustic revelry.
Play, music, and you brides and bridegrooms all,
With measure heap'd in joy, to th' measures fall.

JAQ. Sir, by your patience. If I heard you rightly,
The Duke hath put on a religious life
And thrown into neglect the pompous court.

2. BRO. He hath.

JAQ. To him will I. Out of these convertites
There is much matter to be heard and learn'd.
[*To* DUKE] You to your former honour I bequeath;
Your patience and your virtue well deserves it.
[*To* ORLANDO] You to a love that your true faith doth
　　merit;
[*To* OLIVER] You to your land and love and great allies;
[*To* SILVIUS] You to a long and well-deserved bed;
[*To* TOUCHSTONE] And you to wrangling, for thy loving
　　voyage

Is but for two months victuall'd.—So, to your pleasures!
I am for other than for dancing measures.

DUKE S. Stay, Jaques, stay.

JAQ. To see no pastime I! What you would have
I'll stay to know at your abandon'd cave.   *Exit*.

DUKE S. Proceed, proceed. We will begin these rites,
As we do trust they'll end, in true delights.   *A dance*

Epilogue.

Ros. It is not the fashion to see the lady the epilogue;
but it is no more unhandsome than to see the lord the
prologue. If it be true that good wine needs no bush, 'tis
true that a good play needs no epilogue. Yet to good
wine they do use good bushes, and good plays prove
the better ·by the help of good epilogues. What a case
am I in then, that am neither a good epilogue, nor cannot insinuate with you in the behalf of a good play! I am
not furnish'd like a beggar; therefore to beg will not
become me. My way is to conjure you, and I'll begin
with the women. I charge you, O women, for the love
you bear to men, to like as much of this play as please
you; and I charge you, O men, for the love you bear to
women (as I perceive by your simp'ring none of you
hates them), that between you and the women the play
may please. If I were a woman, I would kiss as many of
you as had beards that pleas'd me, complexions that
lik'd me, and breaths that I defied not; and I am sure,
as many as have good beards, or good faces, or sweet
breaths, will, for my kind offer, when I make curtsy, bid
me farewell.   *Exeunt*.

❧❧❧❧❧❧❧❧❧❧❧❧❧❧❧❧❧❧❧❧❧❧❧❧❧❧❧❧❧❧❧

The Tempest

NAMES OF THE ACTORS

ALONSO, King of Naples.
SEBASTIAN, his brother.
PROSPERO, the right Duke of Milan.
ANTONIO, his brother, the usurping Duke of Milan.
FERDINAND, son to the King of Naples.
GONZALO, an honest old councillor.
ADRIAN and FRANCISCO, lords.
CALIBAN, a savage and deformed slave.
TRINCULO, a jester.   STEPHANO, a drunken butler.
MASTER OF A SHIP, BOATSWAIN, MARINERS.
MIRANDA, daughter to PROSPERO.
ARIEL, an airy spirit.
IRIS, CERES, JUNO,   ⎱ presented by spirits.
NYMPHS, REAPERS,   ⎰
Other Spirits attending on PROSPERO.

Act I: Scene I: On board a ship at sea.

A tempestuous noise of thunder and lightning heard.
    Enter a SHIPMASTER *and a* BOATSWAIN.

MAST. Boatswain!

BOATS. Here, master. What cheer?

MAST. Good, speak to th' mariners! Fall to't—yarely,
or we run ourselves aground! Bestir, bestir!   *Exit.*

Enter MARINERS.

BOATS. Heigh, my hearts! Cheerly, cheerly, my hearts! Yare, yare! Take in the topsail! Tend to th' master's whistle! Blow till thou burst thy wind, if room enough!

Enter ALONSO, SEBASTIAN, ANTONIO, FERDINAND, GONZALO, *and others.*

ALON. Good boatswain, have care. Where's the master? Play the men.

BOATS. I pray now, keep below.

ANT. Where is the master, bos'n?

BOATS. Do you not hear him? You mar our labour. Keep your cabins! You do assist the storm.

GON. Nay, good, be patient.

BOATS. When the sea is. Hence! What cares these roarers for the name of king? To cabin! Silence! Trouble us not!

GON. Good, yet remember whom thou hast aboard.

BOATS. None that I more love than myself. You are a Councillor. If you can command these elements to silence and work the peace of the present, we will not hand a rope more; use your authority. If you cannot, give thanks you have liv'd so long, and make yourself ready in your cabin for the mischance of the hour, if it so hap.— Cheerly, good hearts!—Out of our way, I say.   *Exit.*

GON. I have great comfort from this fellow. Methinks he hath no drowning mark upon him; his complexion is perfect gallows. Stand fast, good Fate, to his hanging! Make the rope of his destiny our cable, for our own doth little advantage. If he be not born to be hang'd, our case is miserable.   *Exeunt.*

Enter BOATSWAIN.

BOATS. Down with the topmast! Yare! Lower, lower! Bring her to try with maincourse! [*A cry within.*] A

plague upon this howling! They are louder than the
weather or our office.

[*Enter* SEBASTIAN, ANTONIO, *and* GONZALO.]

Yet again? What do you here? Shall we give o'er and
drown? Have you a mind to sink?

SEB. A pox o' your throat, you bawling, blasphemous,
incharitable dog!

BOATS. Work you then.

ANT. Hang, cur, hang, you whoreson, insolent noise-
maker! We are less afraid to be drown'd than thou art.

GON. I'll warrant him for drowning, though the ship
were no stronger than a nutshell and as leaky as an
unstanched wench.

BOATS. Lay her ahold, ahold! Set her two courses! Off
to sea again! Lay her off!

Enter MARINERS *wet.*

MARINERS. All lost! To prayers, to prayers! All lost!
　　　　　　　　　　　　　　　　　　　　Exeunt.

BOATS. What, must our mouths be cold?

GON. The King and Prince at prayers! Let's assist
　　them,
For our case is as theirs.

SEB.　　　　　　　　I am out of patience.

ANT. We are merely cheated of our lives by drunkards.
This wide-chopp'd rascal—would thou mightst lie drown-
　　ing
The washing of ten tides!

GON.　　　　　　　　He'll be hang'd yet,
Though every drop of water swear against it
And gape at wid'st to glut him.

A confused noise within: 'Mercy on us!—
We split, we split!— Farewell, my wife and children!—
Farewell, brother!—We split, we split, we split!'
　　　　　　　　　　　　　　　　　　Exit BOATSWAIN.

ANT. Let's all sink with th' King.

SEB.   Let's take leave of him.

                    Exeunt ANTONIO *and* SEBASTIAN.

GON. Now would I give a thousand furlongs of sea
for an acre of barren ground—long heath, brown furze,
anything. The wills above be done! but I would fain die
a dry death.   *Exit.*

Scene II: The island. Before Prospero's cell.

                    Enter PROSPERO *and* MIRANDA.

MIR. If by your art, my dearest father, you have
Put the wild waters in this roar, allay them.
The sky, it seems, would pour down stinking pitch
But that the sea, mounting to th' welkin's cheek,
Dashes the fire out. O, I have suffered
With those that I saw suffer! a brave vessel
(Who had no doubt some noble creature in her)
Dash'd all to pieces! O, the cry did knock
Against my very heart! Poor souls, they perish'd!
Had I been any god of power, I would
Have sunk the sea within the earth or ere
It should the good ship so have swallow'd and
The fraughting souls within her.

PROS.   Be collected.
No more amazement. Tell your piteous heart
There's no harm done.

MIR.   O, woe the day!

PROS.   No harm.
I have done nothing but in care of thee,
Of thee my dear one, thee my daughter, who
Art ignorant of what thou art, naught knowing

Of whence I am; nor that I am more better
Than Prospero, master of a full poor cell,
And thy no greater father.

MIR.   More to know
Did never meddle with my thoughts.

PROS.   'Tis time
I should inform thee farther. Lend thy hand
And pluck my magic garment from me. So,

                         [*Lays down his robe.*]

Lie there, my art. Wipe thou thine eyes; have comfort.
The direful spectacle of the wrack, which touch'd
The very virtue of compassion in thee,
I have with such provision in mine art
So safely ordered that there is no soul—
No, not so much perdition as an hair
Betid to any creature in the vessel
Which thou heard'st cry, which thou saw'st sink. Sit
        down;
For thou must now know farther.

MIR.   You have often
Begun to tell me what I am; but stopp'd
And left me to a bootless inquisition,
Concluding, 'Stay! Not yet.'

PROS.   The hour's now come;
The very minute bids thee ope thine ear.
Obey, and be attentive. Canst thou remember
A time before we came unto this cell?
I do not think thou canst, for then thou wast not
Out three years old.

MIR.   Certainly, sir, I can.

PROS. By what? By any other house or person?
Of any thing the image tell me that
Hath kept with thy remembrance.

MIR.   'Tis far off,

And rather like a dream than an assurance
That my remembrance warrants. Had I not
Four or five women once that tended me?

Pros. Thou hadst, and more, Miranda. But how is it
That this lives in thy mind? What seest thou else
In the dark backward and abysm of time?
If thou rememb'rest aught ere thou cam'st here,
How thou cam'st here thou mayst.

Mir.   But that I do not.

Pros. Twelve year since, Miranda, twelve year since,
Thy father was the Duke of Milan and
A prince of power.

Mir.   Sir, are not you my father?

Pros. Thy mother was a piece of virtue, and
She said thou wast my daughter; and thy father
Was Duke of Milan; and his only heir
A princess—no worse issued.

Mir.   O the heavens!
What foul play had we that we came from thence?
Or blessed was't we did?

Pros.   Both, both, my girl!
By foul play, as thou say'st, were we heav'd thence,
But blessedly holp hither.

Mir.   O, my heart bleeds
To think o' th' teen that I have turn'd you to,
Which is from my remembrance! Please you, farther.

Pros. My brother, and thy uncle, call'd Antonio—
I pray thee mark me—that a brother should
Be so perfidious!—he whom next thyself
Of all the world I lov'd, and to him put
The manage of my state as at that time
Through all the signories 'it was the first,
And Prospero the prime duke, being so reputed
In dignity, and for the liberal arts
Without a parallel; those being all my study,

The government I cast upon my brother
And to my state grew stranger, being transported
And rapt in secret studies—thy false uncle—
Dost thou attend me?

MIR.   Sir, most heedfully.

PROS. Being once perfected how to grant suits,
How to deny them, who t' advance, and who
To trash for over-topping, new-created
The creatures that were mine, I say, or chang'd 'em,
Or else new-form'd 'em; having both the key
Of officer and office, set all hearts i' th' state
To what tune pleas'd his ear, that now he was
The ivy which had hid my princely trunk
And suck'd my verdure out on't. Thou attend'st not!

MIR. O, good sir, I do.

PROS.   I pray thee mark me.
I thus neglecting worldly ends, all dedicated
To closeness, and the bettering of my mind
With that which, but·by being so retir'd,
O'er-priz'd all popular rate, in my false brother
Awak'd an evil nature, and my trust,
Like a good parent, did beget of him
A falsehood in its contrary as great
As my trust was, which had indeed no limit,
A confidence sans bound. He being thus lorded,
Not only with what my revenue yielded
But what my power might else exact, like one
Who having unto truth, by telling of it,
Made such a sinner of his memory
To credit his own lie, he did believe
He was indeed the Duke, out o' th' substitution
And executing th' outward face of royalty
With all prerogative. Hence his ambition growing—
Dost thou hear?

MIR.   Your tale, sir, would cure deafness.

Pros. To have no screen between this part he play'd
And him he play'd it for, he needs will be
Absolute Milan. Me (poor man) my library
Was dukedom large enough! Of temporal royalties
He thinks me now incapable; confederates
(So dry he was for sway) with th' King of Naples
To give him annual tribute, do him homage,
Subject his coronet to his crown, and bend
The dukedom yet unbow'd (alas, poor Milan!)
To most ignoble stooping.

Mir.   O the heavens!

Pros. Mark his condition, and th' event; then tell me
If this might be a brother.

Mir.   I should sin
To think but nobly of my grandmother.
Good wombs have borne bad sons.

Pros.   Now the condition.
This King of Naples, being an enemy
To me inveterate, hearkens my brother's suit;
Which was, that he, in lieu o' th' premises,
Of homage and I know not how much tribute,
Should presently extirpate me and mine
Out of the dukedom and confer fair Milan,
With all the honours, on my brother. Whereon,
A treacherous army levied, one midnight
Fated to th' purpose, did Antonio open
The gates of Milan; and, i' th' dead of darkness,
The ministers for th' purpose hurried thence
Me and thy crying self.

Mir.   Alack, for pity!
I, not rememb'ring how I cried out then,
Will cry it o'er again. It is a hint
That wrings mine eyes to't.

Pros.   Hear a little further,
And then I'll bring thee to the present business

Which now 's upon 's; without the which this story
Were most impertinent.

   MIR.   Wherefore did they not
That hour destroy us?

   PROS.   Well demanded, wench.
My tale provokes that question. Dear, they durst not,
So dear the love my people bore me; nor set
A mark so bloody on the business; but
With colours fairer painted their foul ends.
In few, they hurried us aboard a bark,
Bore us some leagues to sea; where they prepar'd
A rotten carcass of a butt, not rigg'd,
Nor tackle, sail, nor mast; the very rats
Instinctively have quit it. There they hoist us,
To cry to th' sea, that roar'd to us; to sigh
To th' winds, whose pity, sighing back again,
Did us but loving wrong.

   MIR.   Alack, what trouble
Was I then to you!

   PROS.   O, a cherubin
Thou wast that did preserve me! Thou didst smile,
Infused with a fortitude from heaven,
When I have deck'd the sea with drops full salt,
Under my burthen groan'd; which rais'd in me
An undergoing stomach, to bear up
Against what should ensue.

   MIR.   How came we ashore?

   PROS. By providence divine.
Some food we had, and some fresh water, that
A noble Neapolitan, Gonzalo,
Out of his charity, who being then appointed
Master of this design, did give us, with
Rich garments, linens, stuffs, and necessaries
Which since have steaded much. So, of his gentleness,
Knowing I lov'd my books, he furnish'd me

From mine own library with volumes that
I prize above my dukedom.

  MIR.   Would I might
But ever see that man!

  PROS.   Now I arise.
Sit still, and hear the last of our sea-sorrow.
Here in this island we arriv'd; and here
Have I, thy schoolmaster, made thee more profit
Than other princess can, that have more time
For vainer hours, and tutors not so careful.

  MIR. Heavens thank you for't! And now I pray you,
   sir,—
For still 'tis beating in my mind,—your reason
For raising this sea-storm?

  PROS.   Know thus far forth.
By accident most strange, bountiful Fortune
(Now my dear lady) hath mine enemies
Brought to this shore; and by my prescience
I find my zenith doth depend upon
A most auspicious star, whose influence
If now I court not, but omit, my fortunes
Will ever after droop. Here cease more questions.
Thou art inclin'd to sleep. 'Tis a good dulness,
And give it way. I know thou canst not choose.
            [MIRANDA *sleeps.*]
Come away, servant, come! I am ready now.
Approach, my Ariel. Come!

Enter ARIEL.

  ARI. All hail, great master! Grave sir, hail! I come
To answer thy best pleasure; be't to fly,
To swim, to dive into the fire, to ride
On the curl'd clouds. To thy strong bidding task
Ariel and all his quality.

Pros.   Hast thou, spirit,
Perform'd to point the tempest that I bade thee?
   ARI. To every article.
I boarded the King's ship. Now on the beak,
Now in the waist, the deck, in every cabin,
I flam'd amazement. Sometime I'ld divide
And burn in many places; on the topmast,
The yards, and boresprit would I flame distinctly,
Then meet and join. Jove's lightnings, the precursors
O' th' dreadful thunderclaps, more momentary
And sight-outrunning were not. The fire and cracks
Of sulphurous roaring the most mighty Neptune
Seem to besiege and make his bold waves tremble;
Yea, his dread trident shake.
   Pros.   My brave spirit!
Who was so firm, so constant, that this coil
Would not infect his reason?
   ARI.   Not a soul
But felt a fever of the mad and play'd
Some tricks of desperation. All but mariners
Plung'd in the foaming brine and quit the vessel,
Then all afire with me. The King's son Ferdinand,
With hair up-staring (then like reeds, not hair),
Was the first man that leapt; cried 'Hell is empty,
And all the devils are here!'
   Pros.   Why, that's my spirit!
But was not this nigh shore?
   ARI.   Close by, my master.
   Pros. But are they, Ariel, safe?
   ARI.   Not a hair perish'd.
On their sustaining garments not a blemish,
But fresher than before; and as thou bad'st me,
In troops I have dispers'd them 'bout the isle.
The King's son have I landed by himself,
Whom I left cooling of the air with sighs

In an odd angle of the isle, and sitting,
His arms in this sad knot.

PROS.   Of the King's ship
The mariners say how thou hast dispos'd,
And all the rest o' th' fleet.

ARI.   Safely in harbour
Is the King's ship; in the deep nook where once
Thou call'dst me up at midnight to fetch dew
From the still-vex'd Bermoothes, there she's hid;
The mariners all under hatches stow'd,
Who, with a charm join'd to their suff'red labour,
I have left asleep; and for the rest o' th' fleet,
Which I dispers'd, they all have met again,
And are upon the Mediterranean flote
Bound sadly home for Naples,
Supposing that they saw the King's ship wrack'd
And his great person perish.

PROS.   Ariel, thy charge
Exactly is perform'd; but there's more work.
What is the time o' th' day?

ARI.   Past the mid season.

PROS. At least two glasses. The time 'twixt six and now
Must by us both be spent most preciously.

ARI. Is there more toil? Since thou dost give me pains,
Let me remember thee what thou hast promis'd,
Which is not yet perform'd me.

PROS.   How now? moody?
What is't thou canst demand?

ARI.   My liberty.

PROS. Before the time be out? No more!

ARI.   I prithee,
Remember I have done thee worthy service,
Told thee no lies, made no mistakings, serv'd
Without or grudge or grumblings. Thou didst promise
To bate me a full year.

PROS.   Dost thou forget
From what a torment I did free thee?

ARI.   No.

PROS. Thou dost; and think'st it much to tread the ooze
Of the salt deep,
To run upon the sharp wind of the North,
To do me business in the veins o' th' earth
When it is bak'd with frost.

ARI.   I do not, sir.

PROS. Thou liest, malignant thing! Hast thou forgot
The foul witch Sycorax, who with age and envy
Was grown into a hoop? Hast thou forgot her?

ARI. No, sir.

PROS.   Thou hast. Where was she born? Speak!
Tell me!

ARI. Sir, in Argier.

PROS.   O, was she so? I must
Once in a month recount what thou hast been,
Which thou forget'st. This damn'd witch Sycorax,
For mischiefs manifold, and sorceries terrible
To enter human hearing, from Argier
Thou know'st was banish'd. For one thing she did
They would not take her life. Is not this true?

ARI. Ay, sir.

PROS. This blue-ey'd hag was hither brought with
child
And here was left by th' sailors. Thou, my slave,
As thou report'st thyself, wast then her servant;
And, for thou wast a spirit too delicate
To act her earthy and abhorr'd commands,
Refusing her grand hests, she did confine thee,
By help of her more potent ministers,
And in her most unmitigable rage,
Into a cloven pine; within which rift
Imprison'd thou didst painfully remain

A dozen years; within which space she died
And left thee there; where thou didst vent thy groans
As fast as millwheels strike. Then was this island
(Save for the son that she did litter here,
A freckled whelp, hag-born) not honour'd with
A human shape.

ARI.   Yes, Caliban her son.

PROS.   Dull thing, I say so! he, that Caliban
Whom now I keep in service. Thou best know'st
What torment I did find thee in. Thy groans
Did make wolves howl and penetrate the breasts
Of ever-angry bears. It was a torment
To lay upon the damn'd, which Sycorax
Could not again undo. It was mine art,
When I arriv'd and heard thee, that made gape
The pine, and let thee out.

ARI.   I thank thee, master.

PROS. If thou more murmur'st, I will rend an oak
And peg thee in his knotty entrails till
Thou hast howl'd away twelve winters.

ARI.   Pardon, master.
I will be correspondent to command
And do my spriting gently.

PROS.   Do so; and after two days
I will discharge thee.

ARI.   That's my noble master!
What shall I do? Say what! What shall I do?

PROS. Go make thyself like a nymph o' th' sea. Be
  subject
To no sight but thine and mine; invisible
To every eyeball else. Go take this shape
And hither come in't. Go! Hence with diligence!

        [*Exit* ARIEL.]

Awake, dear heart, awake! Thou hast slept well.
Awake!

Mir. The strangeness of your story put
Heaviness in me.

Pros.   Shake it off. Come on.
We'll visit Caliban, my slave, who never
Yields us kind answer.

Mir.   'Tis a villain, sir,
I do not love to look on.

Pros.   But as 'tis,
We cannot miss him. He does make our fire,
Fetch in our wood, and serves in offices
That profit us. What, ho! slave! Caliban!
Thou earth, thou! Speak!

Cal. [*within*] There's wood enough within.

Pros. Come forth, I say! There's other business for
    thee.
Come, thou tortoise! When?

[Enter Ariel *like a water nymph.]*

Fine apparition! My quaint Ariel,
Hark in thine ear.

Ari.   My lord, it shall be done.   *Exit.*

Pros. Thou poisonous slave, got by the devil himself
Upon thy wicked dam, come forth!

Enter Caliban.

Cal. As wicked dew as e'er my mother brush'd
With raven's feather from unwholesome fen
Drop on you both! A south-west blow on ye
And blister you all o'er!

Pros. For this, be sure, to-night thou shalt have
    cramps,
Side-stitches that shall pen thy breath up; urchins
Shall, for that vast of night that they may work,
All exercise on thee; thou shalt be pinch'd
As thick as honeycomb, each pinch more stinging
Than bees that made 'em.

CAL.   I must eat my dinner.
This island's mine by Sycorax my mother,
Which thou tak'st from me. When thou camest first,
Thou strok'dst me and mad'st much of me; wouldst give
      me
Water with berries in't; and teach me how
To name the bigger light, and how the less,
That burn by day, and night; and then I lov'd thee
And show'd thee all the qualities o' th' isle,
The fresh springs, brine-pits, barren place and fertile.
Cursed be I that did so! All the charms
Of Sycorax—toads, beetles, bats light on you!
For I am all the subjects that you have,
Which first was mine own king; and here you sty me
In this hard rock, whiles you do keep from me
The rest o' th' island.

PROS.   Thou most lying slave,
Whom stripes may move, not kindness! I have us'd thee,
(Filth as thou art) with humane care, and lodg'd thee
In mine own cell till thou didst seek to violate
The honour of my child.

CAL. O ho, O ho! Would 't had been done!
Thou didst prevent me; I had peopled else
This isle with Calibans.

PROS.   Abhorred slave,
Which any print of goodness wilt not take,
Being capable of all ill! I pitied thee,
Took pains to make thee speak, taught thee each hour
One thing or other. When thou didst not, savage,
Know thine own meaning, but wouldst gabble like
A thing most brutish, I endow'd thy purposes
With words that made them known. But thy vile race,
Though thou didst learn, had that in't which good
      natures
Could not abide to be with. Therefore wast thou

Deservedly confin'd into this rock, who hadst
Deserv'd more than a prison.

CAL. You taught me language, and my profit on't
Is, I know how to curse. The red plague rid you
For learning me your language!

PROS.   Hag-seed, hence!
Fetch us in fuel; and be quick, thou'rt best,
To answer other business. Shrug'st thou, malice?
If thou neglect'st or dost unwillingly
What I command, I'll rack thee with old cramps,
Fill all thy bones with achës, make thee roar
That beasts shall tremble at thy din.

CAL.   No, pray thee.
[*Aside*] I must obey. His art is of such pow'r
It would control my dam's god, Setebos,
And make a vassal of him.

PROS.   So, slave; hence! *Exit* CALIBAN.

Enter FERDINAND; *and* ARIEL (*invisible*),
playing and singing.

ARIEL'S SONG

Come unto these yellow sands,
    And then take hands.
Curtsied when you have and kiss'd,
    The wild waves whist,
Foot it featly here and there;
And, sweet sprites, the burthen bear.
    Hark, hark!
        [*Burthen, dispersedly.*] Bowgh, wawgh!
    The watchdogs bark.
        [*Burthen, dispersedly.*] Bowgh, wawgh.
    Hark, hark! I hear
    The strain of strutting chanticleer
        Cry, cock-a-diddle-dowe.

FER. Where should this music be? I' th' air, or th'
earth?

It sounds no more; and sure it waits upon
Some god o' th' island. Sitting on a bank,
Weeping again the King my father's wrack,
This music crept by me upon the waters,
Allaying both their fury and my passion
With its sweet air. Thence I have follow'd it,
Or it hath drawn me rather; but 'tis gone.
No, it begins again.

ARIEL'S SONG

Full fathom five thy father lies;
    Of his bones are coral made;
Those are pearls that were his eyes;
    Nothing of him that doth fade
But doth suffer a sea-change
Into something rich and strange.
Sea nymphs hourly ring his knell:
        [Burthen.] Ding-dong.
Hark! now I hear them—Ding-dong bell.

FER. The ditty does remember my drown'd father.
This is no mortal business, nor no sound
That the earth owes. I hear it now above me.

PROS. The fringed curtains of thine eye advance
And say what thou seest yond.

MIR.   What is't? a spirit?
Lord, how it looks about! Believe me, sir,
It carries a brave form. But 'tis a spirit.

PROS. No, wench. It eats, and sleeps, and hath such
    senses
As we have, such. This gallant which thou seest
Was in the wrack; and, but he's something stain'd
With grief (that's beauty's canker), thou mightst call
    him
A goodly person. He hath lost his fellows
And strays about to find 'em.

MIR.   I might call him

A thing divine; for nothing natural
I ever saw so noble.

PROS. [*aside*] It goes on, I see,
As my soul prompts it. Spirit, fine spirit! I'll free thee
Within two days for this.

FER. Most sure, the goddess
On whom these airs attend! Vouchsafe my pray'r
May know if you remain upon this island,
And that you will some good instruction give
How I may bear me here. My prime request,
Which I do last pronounce, is (O you wonder!)
If you be maid or no?

MIR. No wonder, sir,
But certainly a maid.

FER. My language? Heavens!
I am the best of them that speak this speech,
Were I but where 'tis spoken.

PROS. How? the best?
What wert thou if the King of Naples heard thee?

FER. A single thing, as I am now, that wonders
To hear thee speak of Naples. He does hear me;
And that he does I weep. Myself am Naples,
Who with mine eyes, never since at ebb, beheld
The King my father wrack'd.

MIR. Alack, for mercy!

FER. Yes, faith, and all his lords, the Duke of Milan
And his brave son being twain.

PROS. [*aside*] The Duke of Milan
And his more braver daughter could control thee,
If now 'twere fit to do't. At the first sight
They have chang'd eyes. Delicate Ariel,
I'll set thee free for this!—A word, good sir.
I fear you have done yourself some wrong. A word!

MIR. Why speaks my father so ungently? This
Is the third man that e'er I saw; the first

That e'er I sigh'd for. Pity move my father
To be inclin'd my way!

FER.   O, if a virgin,
And your affection not gone forth, I'll make you
The Queen of Naples.

PROS.   Soft, sir! one word more.
[*Aside*] They are both in either's pow'rs. But this swift
   business
I must uneasy make, lest too light winning
Make the prize light.—One word more! I charge thee
That thou attend me. Thou dost here usurp
The name thou ow'st not, and hast put thyself
Upon this island as a spy, to win it
From me, the lord on't.

FER.   No, as I am a man!

MIR. There's nothing ill can dwell in such a temple.
If the ill spirit have so fair a house,
Good things will strive to dwell with't.

PROS.   Follow me.—
Speak not you for him; he's a traitor.—Come!
I'll manacle thy neck and feet together;
Sea water shalt thou drink; thy food shall be
The fresh-brook mussels, wither'd roots, and husks
Wherein the acorn cradled. Follow.

FER.   No.
I will resist such entertainment till
Mine enemy has more power.

                    He draws, and is charmed from moving.

MIR   O dear father,
Make not too rash a trial of him, for
He's gentle, and not fearful.

PROS.   What, I say,
My foot my tutor?—Put thy sword up, traitor!
Who mak'st a show but dar'st not strike, thy conscience
Is so possess'd with guilt. Come, from thy ward!

For I can here disarm thee with this stick
And make thy weapon drop.

MIR.   Beseech you, father!

PROS. Hence! Hang not on my garments.

MIR.   Sir, have pity.
I'll be his surety.

PROS.   Silence! One word more
Shall make me chide thee, if not hate thee. What,
An advocate for an impostor? Hush!
Thou think'st there is no more such shapes as he,
Having seen but him and Caliban. Foolish wench!
To th' most of men this is a Caliban,
And they to him are angels.

MIR.   My affections
Are then most humble. I have no ambition
To see a goodlier man.

PROS.   Come on, obey!
Thy nerves are in their infancy again
And have no vigour in them.

FER.   So they are.
My spirits, as in a dream, are all bound up.
My father's loss, the weakness which I feel,
The wrack of all my friends, nor this man's threats
To whom I am subdu'd, are but light to me,
Might I but through my prison once a day
Behold this maid. All corners else o' th' earth
Let liberty make use of. Space enough
Have I in such a prison.

PROS. [*aside*]   It works. [*To* FERDINAND]
Come on ✓
Thou hast done well, fine Ariel! [*To* FERDINAND] Follow
    me.—
[*To* ARIEL] Hark what thou else shalt do me.

MIR.   Be of comfort.
My father's of a better nature, sir,

Than he appears by speech. This is unwonted
Which now came from him.

PROS.   Thou shalt be as free
As mountain winds; but then exactly do
All points of my command.

ARI.   To th' syllable.

PROS. Come, follow.—Speak not for him.   *Exeunt.*

Act II: Scene I: Another part of the island.

Enter ALONZO, SEBASTIAN, ANTONIO, GONZALO,
ADRIAN, FRANCISCO, *and others.*

GON. Beseech you, sir, be merry. You have cause
(So have we all) of joy; for our escape
Is much beyond our loss. Our hint of woe
Is common. Every day some sailor's wife,
The master of some merchant, and the merchant,
Have just our theme of woe; but for the miracle,
I mean our preservation, few in millions
Can speak like us. Then wisely, good sir, weigh
Our sorrow with our comfort.

ALON.   Prithee peace.

SEB. He receives comfort like cold porridge.

ANT. The visitor will not give him o'er so.

SEB. Look, he's winding up the watch of his wit; by-
and-by it will strike.

GON. Sir—

SEB. One. Tell.

GON. When every grief is entertain'd that's offer'd,
Comes to th' entertainer—

SEB. A dollar.

GON. Dolour comes to him, indeed. You have spoken
truer than you purpos'd.

SEB. You have taken it wiselier than I meant you should.

GON. Therefore, my lord—

ANT. Fie, what a spendthrift is he of his tongue!

ALON. I prithee spare.

GON. Well, I have done. But yet—

SEB. He will be talking.

ANT. Which, of he or Adrian, for a good wager, first begins to crow?

SEB. The old cock.

ANT. The cock'rel.

SEB. Done! The wager?

ANT. A laughter.

SEB. A match!

ADR. Though this island seem to be desert—

ANT. Ha, ha, ha!

SEB. So, you're paid.

ADR. Uninhabitable and almost inaccessible—

SEB. Yet—

ADR. Yet—

ANT. He could not miss't.

ADR. It must needs be of subtle, tender, and delicate temperance.

ANT. Temperance was a delicate wench.

SEB. Ay, and a subtle, as he most learnedly deliver'd.

ADR. The air breathes upon us here most sweetly.

SEB. As if it had lungs, and rotten ones.

ANT. Or as 'twere perfum'd by a fen.

GON. Here is everything advantageous to life.

ANT. True; save means to live.

SEB. Of that there's none, or little.

GON. How lush and lusty the grass looks! how green!

ANT. The ground indeed is tawny.

SEB. With an eye of green in't.

ANT. He misses not much.

SEB. No; he doth but mistake the truth totally.

GON. But the rarity of it is—which is indeed almost beyond credit—

SEB. As many vouch'd rarities are.

GON. That our garments, being, as they were, drench'd in the sea, hold, notwithstanding, their freshness and gloss, being rather new-dy'd than stain'd with salt water.

ANT. If but one of his pockets could speak, would it not say he lies?

SEB. Ay, or very falsely pocket up his report.

GON. Methinks our garments are now as fresh as when we put them on first in Afric, at the marriage of the King's fair daughter Claribel to the King of Tunis.

SEB. 'Twas a sweet marriage, and we prosper well in our return.

ADR. Tunis was never grac'd before with such a paragon to their queen.

GON. Not since widow Dido's time.

ANT. Widow? A pox o' that! How came that 'widow' in? Widow Dido!

SEB. What if he had said 'widower Æneas' too? Good Lord, how you take it!

ADR. 'Widow Dido,' said you? You make me study of that. She was of Carthage, not of Tunis.

GON. This Tunis, sir, was Carthage.

ADR. Carthage?

GON. I assure you, Carthage.

ANT. His word is more than the miraculous harp.

SEB. He hath rais'd the wall, and houses too.

ANT. What impossible matter will he make easy next?

SEB. I think he will carry this island home in his pocket and give it his son for an apple.

ANT. And, sowing the kernels of it in the sea, bring forth more islands.

GON. Ay!

Ant. Why, in good time!

Gon. Sir, we were talking that our garments seem now
as fresh as when we were at Tunis at the marriage of your
daughter, who is now Queen.

Ant. And the rarest that e'er came there.

Seb. Bate, I beseech you, widow Dido.

Ant. O, widow Dido? Ay, widow Dido!

Gon. Is not, sir, my doublet as fresh as the first day I
wore it? I mean, in a sort.

Ant. That 'sort' was well fish'd for.

Gon. When I wore it at your daughter's marriage.

Alon. You cram these words into mine ears against
The stomach of my sense. Would I had never
Married my daughter there! for, coming thence,
My son is lost; and, in my rate, she too,
Who is so far from Italy remov'd
I ne'er again shall see her. O thou mine heir
Of Naples and of Milan, what strange fish
Hath made his meal on thee?

Fran.　　　　　　　　Sir, he may live.
I saw him beat the surges under him
And ride upon their backs. He trod the water,
Whose enmity he flung aside, and breasted
The surge most swol'n that met him. His bold head
'Bove the contentious waves he kept, and oar'd
Himself with his good arms in lusty stroke
To th' shore, that o'er his wave-worn basis bow'd,
As stooping to relieve him. I not doubt
He came alive to land.

Alon.　　　　　　No, no, he's gone.

Seb. Sir, you may thank yourself for this great loss,
That would not bless our Europe with your daughter,
But rather lose her to an African,
Where she, at least, is banish'd from your eye
Who hath cause to wet the grief on't.

ALON. Prithee peace.

SEB. You were kneel'd to and importun'd otherwise
By all of us; and the fair soul herself
Weigh'd, between loathness and obedience, at
Which end o' th' beam should bow. We have lost your
    son,
I fear, for ever. Milan and Naples have
Moe widows in them of this business' making
Than we bring men to comfort them.
The fault's your own.

ALON. So is the dear'st o' th' loss.

GON. My Lord Sebastian,
The truth you speak doth lack some gentleness,
And time to speak it in. You rub the sore
When you should bring the plaster.

SEB. Very well.

ANT. And most chirurgeonly.

GON. It is foul weather in us all, good sir,
When you are cloudy.

SEB. Foul weather?

ANT. Very foul.

GON. Had I plantation of this isle, my lord—

ANT. He'd sow't with nettle seed.

SEB. Or docks, or mallows.

GON. And were the king on't, what would I do?

SEB. Scape being drunk, for want of wine.

GON. I' th' commonwealth I would by contraries
Execute all things; for no kind of traffic
Would I admit; no name of magistrate;
Letters should not be known; riches, poverty,
And use of service, none; contract, succession,
Bourn, bound of land, tilth, vineyard, none;
No use of metal, corn, or wine, or oil;
No occupation; all men idle, all;

And women too, but innocent and pure;
No sovereignty.

SEB.   Yet he would be king on't.

ANT. The latter end of his commonwealth forgets the
beginning.

GON. All things in common nature should produce
Without sweat or endeavour. Treason, felony,
Sword, pike, knife, gun, or need of any engine
Would I not have; but nature should bring forth,
Of its own kind, all foison, all abundance,
To feed my innocent people.

SEB. No marrying 'mong his subjects?

ANT. None, man! All idle—whores and knaves.

GON. I would with such perfection govern, sir,
T' excel the golden age

SEB.   Save his Majesty!

ANT. Long live Gonzalo!

GON.   And—do you mark me, sir?

ALON. Prithee no more. Thou dost talk nothing to me.

GON. I do well believe your Highness; and did it to
minister occasion to these gentlemen, who are of such
sensible and nimble lungs that they always use to laugh
at nothing.

ANT. 'Twas you we laugh'd at.

GON. Who in this kind of merry fooling am nothing to
you. So you may continue, and laugh at nothing still.

ANT. What a blow was there given!

SEB. An it had not fall'n flatlong.

GON. You are gentlemen of brave metal. You would lift
the moon out of her sphere if she would continue in it five
weeks without changing.

Enter ARIEL, *invisible, playing solemn music.*

SEB. We would so, and then go a-batfowling.

ANT. Nay, good my lord, be not angry.

GON. No, I warrant you. I will not adventure my discretion so weakly. Will you laugh me asleep, for I am very heavy?

ANT. Go sleep, and hear us.

All sleep except ALONSO, SEBASTIAN, *and* ANTONIO.

ALON. What, all so soon asleep? I wish mine eyes
Would, with themselves, shut up my thoughts. I find
They are inclin'd to do so.

SEB.   Please you, sir,
Do not omit the heavy offer of it.
It seldom visits sorrow; when it doth,
It is a comforter.

ANT.   We two, my lord,
Will guard your person while you take your rest,
And watch your safety.

ALON.   Thank you. Wondrous heavy.
                         ALONSO *sleeps. Exit* ARIEL.

SEB. What a strange drowsiness possesses them!

ANT. It is the quality o' th' climate.

SEB.   Why
Doth it not then our eyelids sink? I find not
Myself dispos'd to sleep.

ANT.   Nor I. My spirits are nimble.
They fell together all, as by consent.
They dropp'd as by a thunder-stroke. What might,
Worthy Sebastian—O, what might?—No more!
And yet methinks I see it in thy face,
What thou shouldst be. Th' occasion speaks thee, and
My strong imagination sees a crown
Dropping upon thy head.

SEB.   What? Art thou waking?

ANT. Do you not hear me speak?

SEB.   I do; and surely

It is a sleepy language, and thou speak'st
Out of thy sleep. What is it thou didst say?
This is a strange repose, to be asleep
With eyes wide open; standing, speaking, moving—
And yet so fast asleep.

ANT.   Noble Sebastian,
Thou let'st thy fortune sleep—die, rather; wink'st
Whiles thou art waking.

SEB.   Thou dost snore distinctly;
There's meaning in thy snores.

ANT. I am more serious than my custom. You
Must be so too, if heed me; which to do
Trebles thee o'er.

SEB.   Well, I am standing water.

ANT. I'll teach you how to flow.

SEB.   Do so. To ebb
Hereditary sloth instructs me.

ANT.   O,
If you but knew how you the purpose cherish
Whiles thus you mock it! how, in stripping it,
You more invest it! Ebbing men indeed
(Most often) do so near the bottom run
By their own fear or sloth.

SEB.   Prithee say on.
The setting of thine eye and cheek proclaim
A matter from thee; and a birth, indeed,
Which throes thee much to yield.

ANT.   Thus, sir:
Although this lord of weak remembrance, this
Who shall be of as little memory
When he is earth'd, hath here almost persuaded
(For he's a spirit of persuasion, only
Professes to persuade) the King his son's alive,
'Tis as impossible that he's undrown'd
As he that sleeps here swims.

SEB.   I have no hope
That he's undrown'd.

    ANT.   O, out of that no hope
What great hope have you! No hope that way is
Another way so high a hope that even
Ambition cannot pierce a wink beyond,
But doubts discovery there. Will you grant with me
That Ferdinand is drown'd?

    SEB.   He's gone.

    ANT.   Then tell me,
Who's the next heir of Naples?

    SEB.   Claribel.

    ANT. She that is Queen of Tunis; she that dwells
Ten leagues beyond man's life; she that from Naples
Can have no note, unless the sun were post—
The man i' th' moon 's too slow—till new-born chins
Be rough and razorable; she that from whom
We all were sea-swallow'd, though some cast again,
And, by that destiny, to perform an act
Whereof what's past is prologue, what to come,
In yours and my discharge.

    SEB.   What stuff is this? How say you?
'Tis true my brother's daughter 's Queen of Tunis;
So is she heir of Naples; 'twixt which regions
There is some space.

    ANT.   A space whose ev'ry cubit
Seems to cry out 'How shall that Claribel
Measure us back to Naples? Keep in Tunis,
And let Sebastian wake!' Say this were death
That now hath seiz'd them, why, they were no worse
Than now they are. There be that can rule Naples
As well as he that sleeps; lords that can prate
As amply and unnecessarily
As this Gonzalo. I myself could make
A chough of as deep chat. O, that you bore

The mind that I do! What a sleep were this
For your advancement! Do you understand me?

SEB. Methinks I do.

ANT.   And how does your content
Tender your own good fortune?

SEB.   I remember
You did supplant your brother Prospero.

ANT.   True.
And look how well my garments sit upon me,
Much feater than before! My brother's servants
Were then my fellows; now they are my men.

SEB. But, for your conscience—

ANT. Ay, sir! Where lies that? If 'twere a kibe,
'Twould put me to my slipper; but I feel not
This deity in my bosom. Twenty consciences
That stand 'twixt me and Milan, candied be they
And melt, ere they molest! Here lies your brother,
No better than the earth he lies upon
If he were that which now he's like—that's dead;
Whom I with this obedient steel (three inches of it)
Can lay to bed for ever; whiles you, doing thus,
To the perpetual wink for aye might put
This ancient morsel, this Sir Prudence, who
Should not upbraid our course. For all the rest,
They'll take suggestion as a cat laps milk;
They'll tell the clock to any business that
We say befits the hour.

SEB.   Thy case, dear friend,
Shall be my precedent. As thou got'st Milan,
I'll come by Naples. Draw thy sword. One stroke
Shall free thee from the tribute which thou payest,
And I the King shall love thee.

ANT.   Draw together;
And when I rear my hand, do you the like,
To fall it on Gonzalo.   *They draw.*

SEB.   O, but one word!

                    They converse apart.

Enter ARIEL, *invisible, with music and song.*

ARI. My master through his art foresees the danger
That you, his friend, are in, and sends me forth
(For else his project dies) to keep them living.

                  [*Sings in* GONZALO'S *ear.*]

> While you here do snoring lie,
>> Open-ey'd conspiracy
>>> His time doth take.
>> If of life you keep a care,
>> Shake off slumber and beware.
>>> Awake, Awake!

ANT. Then let us both be sudden.

GON. [*wakes*]   Now good angels
Preserve the King!
Why, how now?—[*Shakes* ALONSO.] Ho, awake!—Why
    are you drawn?
Wherefore this ghastly looking?

ALON. [*wakes*]   What's the matter?

SEB. Whiles we stood here securing your repose,
Even now, we heard a hollow burst of bellowing
Like bulls, or rather lions. Did't not wake you?
It struck mine ear most terribly.

ALON.   I heard nothing.

ANT. O, 'twas a din to fright a monster's ear,
To make an earthquake! Sure it was the roar
Of a whole herd of lions.

ALON.   Heard you this, Gonzalo?

GON. Upon mine honour, sir, I heard a humming,
And that a strange one too, which did awake me.
I shak'd you, sir, and cried. As mine eyes open'd,
I saw their weapons drawn. There was a noise;
That's verily. 'Tis best we stand upon our guard,
Or that we quit this place. Let's draw our weapons.

ALON. Lead off this ground, and let's make further
    search
For my poor son.

GON.   Heavens keep him from these beasts!
For he is sure i' th' island.

ALON.   Lead away.

ARI. Prospero my lord shall know what I have done.
So, King, go safely on to seek thy son.   *Exeunt.*

Scene II: Another part of the island.

Enter CALIBAN *with a burthen of wood.*
A noise of thunder heard.

CAL. All the infections that the sun sucks up
From bogs, fens, flats, on Prosper fall and make him
By inchmeal a disease! His spirits hear me,
And yet I needs must curse. But they'll nor pinch,
Fright me with urchin-shows, pitch me i' th' mire,
Nor lead me, like a firebrand, in the dark
Out of my way, unless he bid 'em; but
For every trifle are they set upon me;
Sometime like apes that mow and chatter at me,
And after bite me; then like hedgehogs which
Lie tumbling in my barefoot way and mount
Their pricks at my footfall; sometime am I
All wound with adders, who with cloven tongues
Do hiss me into madness.

[*Enter* TRINCULO.]

Lo, now, lo!
Here comes a spirit of his, and to torment me
For bringing wood in slowly. I'll fall flat.
Perchance he will not mind me.   *Lies down.*

TRIN. Here's neither bush nor shrub to bear off any

weather at all, and another storm brewing. I hear it sing
i' th' wind. Yond same black cloud, yond huge one, looks
like a foul bombard that would shed his liquor. If it
should thunder as it did before, I know not where to hide
my head. Yond same cloud cannot choose but fall by
pailfuls. What have we here? a man or a fish? dead or
alive? A fish: he smells like a fish; a very ancient and
fishlike smell; a kind of, not of the newest, poor-John.
A strange fish! Were I in England now, as once I was, and
had but this fish painted, not a holiday fool there but
would give a piece of silver. There would this monster
make a man. Any strange beast there makes a man. When
they will not give a doit to relieve a lame beggar, they
will lay out ten to see a dead Indian. Legg'd like a man!
and his fins like arms! Warm, o' my troth! I do now let
loose my opinion, hold it no longer: this is no fish, but
an islander, that hath lately suffered by a thunderbolt.
[*Thunder.*] Alas, the storm is come again! My best way
is to creep under his gaberdine. There is no other shelter hereabout. Misery acquaints a man with strange bed-
fellows. I will here shroud till the dregs of the storm be
past.   *Creeps under* CALIBAN's *garment.*

Enter STEPHANO, *singing; a bottle in his hand.*

STE.   I shall no more to sea, to sea;
                    Here shall I die ashore.

This is a very scurvy tune to sing at a man's funeral.
Well, here's my comfort.   [*Drinks.*]

    The master, the swabber, the boatswain, and I,
        The gunner, and his mate,
    Lov'd Mall, Meg, and Marian, and Margery,
        But none of us car'd for Kate.
        For she had a tongue with a tang,
        Would cry to a sailor 'Go hang!'
    She lov'd not the savour of tar nor of pitch;
    Yet a tailor might scratch her where'er she did itch.
        Then to sea, boys, and let her go hang!

This is a scurvy tune too; but here's my comfort. *Drinks.*

CAL. Do not torment me! O!

STE. What's the matter? Have we devils here? Do you put tricks upon 's with savages and men of Inde, ha? I have not scap'd drowning to be afeard now of your four legs; for it hath been said, 'As proper a man as ever went on four legs cannot make him give ground'; and it shall be said so again, while Stephano breathes at' nostrils.

CAL. The spirit torments me. O!

STE. This is some monster of the isle, with four legs, who hath got, as I take it, an ague. Where the devil should he learn our language? I will give him some relief, if it be but for that. If I can recover him, and keep him tame, and get to Naples with him, he's a present for any emperor that ever trod on neat's leather.

CAL. Do not torment me prithee! I'll bring my wood home faster.

STE. He's in his fit now and does not talk after the wisest. He shall taste of my bottle. If he have never drunk wine afore, it will go near to remove his fit. If I can recover him and keep him tame, I will not take too much for him; he shall pay for him that hath him, and that soundly.

CAL. Thou dost me yet but little hurt.
Thou wilt anon; I know it by thy trembling.
Now Prosper works upon thee.

STE. Come on your ways. Open your mouth. Here is that which will give language to you, cat. Open your mouth. This will shake your shaking, I can tell you, and that soundly. [*Gives* CALIBAN *drink*.] You cannot tell who's your friend. Open your chaps again.

TRIN. I should know that voice. It should be—but he is drown'd; and these are devils. O, defend me!

STE. Four legs and two voices—a most delicate monster! His forward voice now is to speak well of his friend;

his backward voice is to utter foul speeches and to detract. If all the wine in my bottle will recover him, I will help his ague. Come! [*Gives drink.*] Amen! I will pour some in thy other mouth.

TRIN. Stephano!

STE. Doth thy other mouth call me? Mercy, mercy! This is a devil, and no monster. I will leave him; I have no long spoon.

TRIN. Stephano! If thou beest Stephano, touch me and speak to me; for I am Trinculo—be not afeard—thy good friend Trinculo.

STE. If thou beest Trinculo, come forth. I'll pull thee by the lesser legs. If any be Trinculo's legs, these are they. [*Draws him out from under* CALIBAN'S *garment.*] Thou art very Trinculo indeed! How cam'st thou to be the siege of this mooncalf? Can he vent Trinculos?

TRIN. I took him to be kill'd with a thunderstroke. But art thou not drown'd, Stephano? I hope now thou art not drown'd. Is the storm overblown? I hid me under the dead mooncalf's gaberdine for fear of the storm. And art thou living, Stephano? O Stephano, two Neapolitans scap'd?

STE. Prithee do not turn me about. My stomach is not constant.

CAL. [*aside*] These be fine things an if they be not sprites.
That's a brave god and bears celestial liquor.
I will kneel to him.

STE. How didst thou scape? How cam'st thou hither? Swear by this bottle how thou cam'st hither. I escap'd upon a butt of sack which the sailors heaved o'erboard, by this bottle! which I made of the bark of a tree with mine own hands since I was cast ashore.

CAL. I'll swear upon that bottle to be thy true subject, for the liquor is not earthly.

STE. Here! Swear then how thou escap'dst.

TRIN. Swum ashore, man, like a duck. I can swim like a duck, I'll be sworn.

STE. Here, kiss the book. [*Gives him drink.*] Though thou canst swim like a duck, thou art made like a goose.

TRIN. O Stephano, hast any more of this?

STE. The whole butt, man. My cellar is in a rock by th' seaside, where my wine is hid. How now, mooncalf? How does thine ague?

CAL. Hast thou not dropp'd from heaven?

STE. Out o' th' moon, I do assure thee. I was the Man i' th' Moon when time was.

CAL. I have seen thee in her, and I do adore thee. My mistress show'd me thee, and thy dog, and thy bush.

STE. Come, swear to that; kiss the book. I will furnish it anon with new contents. Swear.   CALIBAN *drinks.*

TRIN. By this good light, this is a very shallow monster! I afeard of him? A very weak monster! The Man i' th' Moon? A most poor credulous monster! Well drawn, monster, in good sooth.

CAL. I'll show thee every fertile inch o' th' island; And I will kiss thy foot. I prithee be my god.

TRIN. By this light, a most perfidious and drunken monster! When 's god 's asleep he'll rob his bottle.

CAL. I'll kiss thy foot. I'll swear myself thy subject.

STE. Come on then. Down, and swear!

TRIN. I shall laugh myself to death at this puppy-headed monster. A most scurvy monster! I could find in my heart to beat him—

STE. Come, kiss.

TRIN. But that the poor monster's in drink. An abominable monster!

CAL. I'll show thee the best springs; I'll pluck thee berries; I'll fish for thee, and get thee wood enough.

A plague upon the tyrant that I serve!
I'll bear him no more sticks, but follow thee,
Thou wondrous man.

TRIN. A most ridiculous monster, to make a wonder
of a poor drunkard!

CAL. I prithee let me bring thee where crabs grow;
And I with my long nails will dig thee pignuts,
Show thee a jay's nest, and instruct thee how
To snare the nimble marmoset; I'll bring thee
To clust'ring filberts, and sometimes I'll get thee
Young scamels from the rock. Wilt thou go with me?

STE. I prithee now lead the way without any more talking. Trinculo, the King and all our company else being
drown'd, we will inherit here. Here, bear my bottle.
Fellow Trinculo, we'll fill him by-and-by again.

> CALIBAN *sings drunkenly.*

CAL. Farewell, master; farewell, farewell!

TRIN. A howling monster! a drunken monster!

CAL.   No more dams I'll make for fish,
              Nor fetch in firing
              At requiring,
          Nor scrape trenchering, nor wash dish.
              'Ban, 'Ban, Ca—Caliban
              Has a new master. Get a new man.

Freedom, high-day! high-day, freedom! freedom, high-
day, freedom!

STE. O brave monster! lead the way.   *Exeunt*

Act III: Scene I: Before Prospero's cell.

Enter FERDINAND, *bearing a log.*

FER. There be some sports are painful, and their
     labour
Delight in them sets off; some kinds of baseness
Are nobly undergone, and most poor matters

Point to rich ends. This my mean task
Would be as heavy to me as odious, but
The mistress which I serve quickens what's dead
And makes my labours pleasures. O, she is
Ten times more gentle than her father's crabbed;
And he's compos'd of harshness! I must remove
Some thousands of these logs and pile them up,
Upon a sore injunction. My sweet mistress
Weeps when she sees me work, and says such baseness
Had never like executor. I forget;
But these sweet thoughts do even refresh my labours
Most busiest when I do it.

   Enter Miranda; *and* Prospero *behind, unseen.*

Mir.   Alas, now pray you
Work not so hard! I would the lightning had
Burnt up those logs that you are enjoin'd to pile!
Pray set it down and rest you. When this burns,
'Twill weep for having wearied you. My father
Is hard at study. Pray now rest yourself.
He's safe for these three hours.

Fer.   O most dear mistress,
The sun will set before I shall discharge
What I must strive to do.

Mir.   If you'll sit down,
I'll bear your logs the while. Pray give me that.
I'll carry it to the pile.

Fer.   No, precious creature.
I had rather crack my sinews, break my back,
Than you should such dishonour undergo
While I sit lazy by.

Mir.   It would become me
As well as it does you; and I should do it
With much more ease; for my good will is to it,
And yours it is against.

PROS. [*aside*]　　　　Poor worm, thou art infected!
This visitation shows it.

MIR.　　　　　You look wearily.

FER. No, noble mistress. 'Tis fresh morning with me
When you are by at night. I do beseech you,
Chiefly that I might set it in my prayers,
What is your name?

MIR.　　　　Miranda. O my father,
I have broke your hest to say so!

FER.　　　　　　Admir'd Miranda!
Indeed the top of admiration, worth
What's dearest to the world! Full many a lady
I have ey'd with best regard, and many a time
Th' harmony of their tongues hath into bondage
Brought my too diligent ear; for several virtues
Have I lik'd several women; never any
With so full soul but some defect in her
Did quarrel with the noblest grace she ow'd,
And put it to the foil; but you, O you,
So perfect and so peerless, are created
Of every creature's best!

MIR.　　　　　I do not know
One of my sex; no woman's face remember,
Save, from my glass, mine own; nor have I seen
More that I may call men than you, good friend,
And my dear father. How features are abroad
I am skilless of; but, by my modesty
(The jewel in my dower), I would not wish
Any companion in the world but you;
Nor can imagination form a shape,
Besides yourself, to like of. But I prattle
Something too wildly, and my father's precepts
I therein do forget.

FER.　　　　　I am, in my condition,
A prince, Miranda; I do think, a king

(I would not so!), and would no more endure
This wooden slavery than to suffer
The fleshfly blow my mouth. Hear my soul speak!
The very instant that I saw you, did
My heart fly to your service; there resides,
To make me slave to it; and for your sake
Am I this patient log-man.

MIR.   Do you love me?

FER. O heaven, O earth, bear witness to this sound,
And crown what I profess with kind event
If I speak true! if hollowly, invert
What best is boded me to mischief! I,
Beyond all limit of what else i' th' world,
Do love, prize, honour you.

MIR.   I am a fool
To weep at what I am glad of.

PROS. [*aside*]   Fair encounter
Of two most rare affections! Heavens rain grace
On that which breeds between 'em!

FER.   Wherefore weep you?

MIR. At mine unworthiness, that dare not offer
What I desire to give, and much less take
What I shall die to want. But this is trifling;
And all the more it seeks to hide itself,
The bigger bulk it shows. Hence, bashful cunning!
And prompt me plain and holy innocence!
I am your wife, if you will marry me;
If not, I'll die your maid. To be your fellow
You may deny me; but I'll be your servant,
Whether you will or no.

FER.   My mistress, dearest!
And I thus humble ever.

MIR.   My husband then?

FER. Ay, with a heart as willing
As bondage e'er of freedom. Here's my hand.

MIR. And mine, with my heart in't; and now farewell
Till half an hour hence.

FER.   A thousand thousand!

> *Exeunt* FERDINAND *and* MIRANDA *severally.*

PROS. So glad of this as they I cannot be,
Who are surpris'd withal; but my rejoicing
At nothing can be more. I'll to my book;
For yet ere supper time must I perform
Much business appertaining.   *Exit.*

Scene II: Another part of the island.

Enter CALIBAN, STEPHANO, *and* TRINCULO.

STE. Tell not me! When the butt is out, we will drink
water; not a drop before. Therefore bear up and board
'em! Servant monster, drink to me.

TRIN. Servant monster? The folly of this island! They
say there's but five upon this isle. We are three of them.
If th' other two be brain'd like us, the state totters.

STE. Drink, servant monster, when I bid thee. Thy eyes
are almost set in thy head.

TRIN. Where should they be set else? He were a brave
monster indeed if they were set in his tail.

STE. My man-monster hath drown'd his tongue in
sack. For my part, the sea cannot drown me. I swam, ere
I could recover the shore, five-and-thirty leagues off and
on, by this light. Thou shalt be my lieutenant, monster,
or my standard.

TRIN. Your lieutenant, if you list; he's no standard.

STE. We'll not run, Monsieur Monster.

TRIN. Nor go neither; but you'll lie like dogs, and yet
say nothing neither.

STE. Mooncalf, speak once in thy life, if thou beest a
good mooncalf.

CAL. How does thy honour? Let me lick thy shoe.
I'll not serve him; he is not valiant.

TRIN. Thou liest, most ignorant monster! I am in case
to justle a constable. Why, thou debosh'd fish thou, was
there ever man a coward that hath drunk so much sack as
I to-day? Wilt thou tell a monstrous lie, being but half
a fish and half a monster?

CAL. Lo, how he mocks me! Wilt thou let him, my
lord?

TRIN. 'Lord' quoth he? That a monster should be such
a natural!

CAL. Lo, lo, again! Bite him to death I prithee.

STE. Trinculo, keep a good tongue in your head. If
you prove a mutineer—the next tree! The poor monster's
my subject, and he shall not suffer indignity.

CAL. I thank my noble lord. Wilt thou be pleas'd
To hearken once again to the suit I made to thee?

STE. Marry, will I. Kneel and repeat it; I will stand,
and so shall Trinculo.

Enter ARIEL, invisible.

CAL. As I told thee before, I am subject to a tyrant,
A sorcerer, that by his cunning hath
Cheated me of the island.

ARI. Thou liest.

CAL.   Thou liest, thou jesting monkey thou!
I would my valiant master would destroy thee.
I do not lie.

STE. Trinculo, if you trouble him any more in 's tale,
by this hand, I will supplant some of your teeth.

TRIN. Why, I said nothing.

STE. Mum then, and no more.—Proceed.

CAL. I say by sorcery he got this isle;
From me he got it. If thy greatness will

Revenge it on him—for I know thou dar'st,
But this thing dare not—

STE. That's most certain.

CAL. Thou shalt be lord of it, and I'll serve thee.

STE. How now shall this be compass'd?
Canst thou bring me to the party?

CAL. Yea, yea, my lord! I'll yield him thee asleep,
Where thou mayst knock a nail into his head.

ARI. Thou liest; thou canst not.

CAL. What a pied ninny's this! Thou scurvy patch!
I do beseech thy greatness give him blows
And take his bottle from him. When that's gone,
He shall drink naught but brine, for I'll not show him
Where the quick freshes are.

STE. Trinculo, run into no further danger. Interrupt
the monster one word further and, by this hand, I'll turn
my mercy out o' doors and make a stockfish of thee.

TRIN. Why, what did I? I did nothing. I'll go farther
off.

STE. Didst thou not say he lied?

ARI. Thou liest.

STE. Do I so? Take thou that! [*Strikes* TRINCULO.]
As you like this, give me the lie another time.

TRIN. I did not give thee the lie. Out o' your wits, and
hearing too? A pox o' your bottle! This can sack and
drinking do. A murrain on your monster, and the devil
take your fingers!

CAL. Ha, ha, ha!

STE. Now forward with your tale.—Prithee stand
further off.

CAL. Beat him enough. After a little time
I'll beat him too.

STE.   Stand farther.—Come, proceed.

CAL. Why, as I told thee, 'tis a custom with him
I' th' afternoon to sleep. There thou mayst brain him,

Having first seiz'd his books, or with a log
Batter his skull, or paunch him with a stake,
Or cut his wesand with thy knife. Remember
First to possess his books; for without them
He's but a sot, as I am, nor hath not
One spirit to command. They all do hate him
As rootedly as I. Burn but his books.
He has brave utensils (for so he calls them)
Which, when he has a house, he'll deck withal.
And that most deeply to consider is
The beauty of his daughter. He himself
Calls her a nonpareil. I never saw a woman
But only Sycorax my dam and she;
But she as far surpasseth Sycorax
As great'st does least.

STE.   Is it so brave a lass?

CAL. Ay, lord. She will become thy bed, I warrant,
And bring thee forth brave brood.

STE. Monster, I will kill this man. His daughter and
I will be king and queen, save our Graces! and Trinculo
and thyself shall be viceroys. Dost thou like the plot,
Trinculo?

TRIN. Excellent.

STE. Give me thy hand. I am sorry I beat thee; but
while thou liv'st, keep a good tongue in thy head.

CAL. Within this half hour will he be asleep.
Wilt thou destroy him then?

STE.   Ay, on mine honour.

ARI. This will I tell my master.

CAL. Thou mak'st me merry; I am full of pleasure.
Let us be jocund. Will you troll the catch
You taught me but whilere?

STE. At thy request, monster, I will do reason, any
reason. Come on, Trinculo, let us sing.   [*Sings.*]

> Flout 'em and scout 'em
> And scout 'em and flout 'em!
> Thought is free.

CAL. That's not the tune.

ARIEL *plays the tune on a tabor and pipe.*

STE. What is this same?

TRIN. This is the tune of our catch, play'd by the picture of No-body.

STE. If thou beest a man, show thyself in thy likeness. If thou beest a devil, take't as thou list.

TRIN. O, forgive me my sins!

STE. He that dies pays all debts. I defy thee. Mercy upon us!

CAL. Art thou afeard?

STE. No, monster, not I.

CAL. Be not afeard. The isle is full of noises,
Sounds and sweet airs that give delight and hurt not.
Sometimes a thousand twangling instruments
Will hum about mine ears; and sometime voices
That, if I then had wak'd after long sleep,
Will make me sleep again; and then, in dreaming,
The clouds methought would open and show riches
Ready to drop upon me, that, when I wak'd,
I cried to dream again.

STE. This will prove a brave kingdom to me, where I shall have my music for nothing.

CAL. When Prospero is destroy'd.

STE. That shall be by-and-by. I remember the story.

TRIN. The sound is going away. Let's follow it, and after do our work.

STE. Lead, monster; we'll follow. I would I could see this taborer! He lays it on. Wilt come?

TRIN. I'll follow, Stephano.   *Exeunt.*

Scene III: Another part of the island.

Enter ALONSO, SEBASTIAN, ANTONIO, GONZALO, ADRIAN,
FRANCISCO, *&c.*

GON. By'r Lakin, I can go no further, sir!
My old bones ache. Here's a maze trod indeed
Through forthrights and meanders. By your patience,
I needs must rest me.

ALON.   Old lord, I cannot blame thee,
Who am myself attach'd with weariness
To th' dulling of my spirits. Sit down and rest.
Even here I will put off my hope, and keep it
No longer for my flatterer. He is drown'd
Whom thus we stray to find; and the sea mocks
Our frustrate search on land. Well, let him go.

ANT. [*aside to* SEBASTIAN] I am right glad that he's so
  out of hope.
Do not for one repulse forgo the purpose
That you resolv'd t' effect.

SEB. [*aside to* ANTONIO] The next advantage
Will we take throughly.

ANT. [*aside to* SEBASTIAN] Let it be to-night;
For, now they are oppress'd with travel, they
Will not nor cannot use such vigilance
As when they are fresh.

SEB. [*aside to* ANTONIO] I say to-night. No more.

Solemn and strange music; and PROSPERO *on the top*
(invisible).

ALON. What harmony is this? My good friends, hark!
GON. Marvellous sweet music!

Enter several strange SHAPES, *bringing in a banquet; and*
dance about it with gentle actions of salutations; and,
inviting the KING *&c. to eat, they depart.*

ALON. Give us kind keepers, heavens! What were
    these?

SEB. A living drollery. Now I will believe
That there are unicorns; that in Arabia
There is one tree, the phœnix' throne; one phœnix
At this hour reigning there.

ANT.   I'll believe both;
And what does else want credit, come to me,
And I'll be sworn 'tis true. Travellers ne'er did lie,
Though fools at home condemn 'em.

GON.   If in Naples
I should report this now, would they believe me?
If I should say, I saw such islanders
(For certes these are people of the island),
Who, though they are of monstrous shape, yet, note,
Their manners are more gentle, kind, than of
Our human generation you shall find
Many—nay, almost any.

PROS. [aside]   Honest lord,
Thou hast said well; for some of you there present
Are worse than devils.

ALON.   I cannot too much muse
Such shapes, such gesture, and such sound, expressing
(Although they want the use of tongue) a kind
Of excellent dumb discourse.

PROS. [aside]   Praise in departing.

FRAN. They vanish'd strangely.

SEB.   No matter, since
They have left their viands behind; for we have stom-
    achs.
Will't please you taste of what is here?

ALON.   Not I.

GON. Faith, sir, you need not fear. When we were
    boys,
Who would believe that there were mountaineers

Dewlapp'd like bulls, whose throats had hanging at 'em
Wallets of flesh? or that there were such men
Whose heads stood in their breasts? which now we find
Each putter-out of five for one will bring us
Good warrant of.

    ALON.   I will stand to, and feed;
Although my last, no matter, since I feel
The best is past. Brother, my lord the Duke,
Stand to, and do as we.

Thunder and lightning. Enter ARIEL, *like a harpy; claps*
his wings upon the table; and with a quaint device the
banquet vanishes.

    ARI. You are three men of sin, whom destiny—
That hath to instrument this lower world
And what is in't—the never-surfeited sea
Hath caus'd to belch up you, and on this island,
Where man doth not inhabit—you 'mongst men
Being most unfit to live. I have made you mad;
And even with such-like valour men hang and drown
Their proper selves.

        [ALONSO, SEBASTIAN, *&c. draw their swords.*]
           You fools! I and my fellows
Are ministers of Fate. The elements,
Of whom your swords are temper'd, may as well
Wound the loud winds, or with bemock'd-at stabs
Kill the still-closing waters, as diminish
One dowle that's in my plume. My fellow ministers
Are like invulnerable. If you could hurt,
Your swords are now too massy for your strengths
And will not be uplifted. But remember
(For that's my business to you) that you three
From Milan did supplant good Prospero;
Expos'd unto the sea, which hath requit it,
Him and his innocent child; for which foul deed

The powers, delaying (not forgetting), have
Incens'd the seas and shores, yea, all the creatures,
Against your peace. Thee of thy son, Alonso,
They have bereft; and do pronounce by me
Ling'ring perdition (worse than any death
Can be at once) shall step by step attend
You and your ways; whose wraths to guard you from,
Which here, in this most desolate isle, else falls
Upon your heads, is nothing but heart's sorrow
And a clear life ensuing.

He vanishes in thunder; then, to soft music, enter the
SHAPES *again, and dance, with mocks and mows, and*
carrying out the table.

PROS. [*aside*] Bravely the figure of this harpy hast thou
Perform'd, my Ariel; a grace it had, devouring.
Of my instruction hast thou nothing bated
In what thou hadst to say. So, with good life
And observation strange, my meaner ministers
Their several kinds have done. My high charms work,
And these, mine enemies, are all knit up
In their distractions. They now are in my pow'r;
And in these fits I leave them, while I visit
Young Ferdinand, whom they suppose is drown'd,
And his and mine lov'd darling.   *Exit above.*
    GON. I' th' name of something holy, sir, why stand you
In this strange stare?
    ALON.   O, it is monstrous, monstrous!
Methought the billows spoke and told me of it;
The winds did sing it to me; and the thunder,
That deep and dreadful organ pipe, pronounc'd
The name of Prosper. It did bass my trespass.
Therefore my son i' th' ooze is bedded; and
I'll seek him deeper than e'er plummet sounded
And with him there lie mudded.   *Exit.*

SEB.   But one fiend at a time,
I'll fight their legions o'er!
ANT.   I'll be thy second.

               Exeunt SEBASTIAN *and* ANTONIO.

GON. All three of them are desperate. Their great
    guilt,
Like poison given to work a great time after,
Now gins to bite the spirits. I do beseech you,
That are of suppler joints, follow them swiftly
And hinder them from what this ecstasy
May now provoke them to.
ADR.   Follow, I pray you.

                    Exeunt omnes.

Act IV: Scene I: Before Prospero's cell.

Enter PROSPERO, FERDINAND, *and* MIRANDA.

PROS. If I have too austerely punish'd you,
Your compensation makes amends; for I
Have given you here a third of mine own life,
Or that for which I live; who once again
I tender to thy hand. All thy vexations
Were but my trials of thy love, and thou
Hast strangely stood the test. Here, afore heaven,
I ratify this my rich gift. O Ferdinand,
Do not smile at me that I boast her off,
For thou shalt find she will outstrip all praise
And make it halt behind her.
FER.   I do believe it
Against an oracle.
PROS. Then, as my gift, and thine own acquisition
Worthily purchas'd, take my daughter. But
If thou dost break her virgin-knot before
All sanctimonious ceremonies may

With full and holy rite be minist'red,
No sweet aspersion shall the heavens let fall
To make this contract grow; but barren hate,
Sour-ey'd disdain, and discord shall bestrew
The union of your bed with weeds so loathly
That you shall hate it both. Therefore take heed,
As Hymen's lamp shall light you!

FER.   As I hope
For quiet days, fair issue, and long life,
With such love as 'tis now, the murkiest den,
The most opportune place, the strong'st suggestion
Our worser genius can, shall never melt
Mine honour into lust, to take away
The edge of that day's celebration
When I shall think or Phœbus' steeds are founder'd
Or Night kept chain'd below.

PROS.   Fairly spoke.
Sit then and talk with her; she is thine own.
What, Ariel! my industrious servant, Ariel!

Enter ARIEL.

ARI. What would my potent master? Here I am.
PROS. Thou and thy meaner fellows your last service
Did worthily perform; and I must use you
In such another trick. Go bring the rabble,
O'er whom I give thee pow'r, here to this place.
Incite them to quick motion; for I must
Bestow upon the eyes of this young couple
Some vanity of mine art. It is my promise,
And they expect it from me.

ARI.   Presently?
PROS. Ay, with a twink.
ARI. Before you can say 'Come' and 'Go,'
    And breathe twice and cry, 'So, so,'
    Each one, tripping on his toe,

Will be here with mop and mow.
Do you love me, master? No?
Pros. Dearly, my delicate Ariel. Do not approach
Till thou dost hear me call.
Ari.   Well! I conceive.   *Exit.*
Pros. Look thou be true. Do not give dalliance
Too much the rein. The strongest oaths are straw
To th' fire i' th' blood. Be more abstemious,
Or else good night your vow!
Fer.   I warrant you, sir.
The white cold virgin snow upon my heart
Abates the ardour of my liver.
Pros.   Well.
Now come, my Ariel! Bring a corollary
Rather than want a spirit. Appear, and pertly!
No tongue! All eyes! Be silent.   *Soft music.*

Enter Iris.

Iris. Ceres, most bounteous lady, thy rich leas
Of wheat, rye, barley, fetches, oats, and pease;
Thy turfy mountains, where live nibbling sheep,
And flat meads thatch'd with stover, them to keep;
Thy banks with pioned and twilled brims,
Which spongy April at thy hest betrims
To make cold nymphs chaste crowns; and thy broom
          groves,
Whose shadow the dismissed bachelor loves,
Being lasslorn; thy pole-clipt vineyard;
And thy sea-marge, sterile and rocky-hard,
Where thou thyself dost air—the queen o' th' sky,
Whose wat'ry arch and messenger am I,
Bids thee leave these, and with her sovereign grace,
Here on this grass-plot, in this very place,
To come and sport. Her peacocks fly amain.
Approach, rich Ceres, her to entertain.

Enter CERES.

CER. Hail, many-coloured messenger, that ne'er
Dost disobey the wife of Jupiter,
Who, with thy saffron wings, upon my flow'rs
Diffusest honey drops, refreshing show'rs,
And with each end of thy blue bow dost crown
My bosky acres and my unshrubb'd down,
Rich scarf to my proud earth—why hath thy queen
Summon'd me hither to this short-grass'd green?

IRIS. A contract of true love to celebrate
And some donation freely to estate
On the bless'd lovers.

CER.   Tell me, heavenly bow,
If Venus or her son, as thou dost know,
Do now attend the Queen. Since they did plot
The means that dusky Dis my daughter got,
Her and her blind boy's scandal'd company
I have forsworn.

IRIS.   Of her society
Be not afraid. I met her Deity
Cutting the clouds towards Paphos, and her son
Dove-drawn with her. Here thought they to have done
Some wanton charm upon this man and maid,
Whose vows are, that no bed-right shall be paid
Till Hymen's torch be lighted; but in vain.
Mars's hot minion is return'd again;
Her waspish-headed son has broke his arrows,
Swears he will shoot no more, but play with sparrows
And be a boy right out.

Enter JUNO.

CER.   Highest queen of state,
Great Juno, comes; I know her by her gait.

JUNO. How does my bounteous sister? Go with me

To bless this twain, that they may prosperous be
And honour'd in their issue.

THEY SING

JUNO. Honour, riches, marriage blessing,
  Long continuance, and increasing,
  Hourly joys be still upon you!
  Juno sings her blessings on you.

CER. Earth's increase, foison plenty,
  Barns and garners never empty,
  Vines with clust'ring bunches growing,
  Plants with goodly burthen bowing;
  Spring come to you at the farthest
  In the very end of harvest!
  Scarcity and want shall shun you,
  Ceres' blessing so is on you.

FER. This is a most majestic vision, and
Harmonious charmingly. May I be bold
To think these spirits?
PROS.   Spirits, which by mine art
I have from their confines call'd to enact
My present fancies.
FER.   Let me live here ever!
So rare a wond'red father and a wise
Makes this place Paradise.

     JUNO *and* CERES *whisper, and send* IRIS *on*
             employment.
PROS.   Sweet now, silence!
Juno and Ceres whisper seriously.
There's something else to do. Hush and be mute,
Or else our spell is marr'd.
 IRIS. You nymphs, call'd Naiades, of the wand'ring
  brooks,
With your sedg'd crowns and ever-harmless looks,
Leave your crisp channels, and on this green land
Answer your summons. Juno does command.

Come, temperate nymphs, and help to celebrate
A contract of true love. Be not too late.

[*Enter certain* NYMPHS.]

You sunburn'd sicklemen, of August weary,
Come hither from the furrow and be merry.
Make holiday. Your rye-straw hats put on,
And these fresh nymphs encounter every one
In country footing.

Enter certain REAPERS, *properly habited. They join with
the* NYMPHS *in a graceful dance; towards the end
whereof* PROSPERO *starts suddenly and speaks; after
which, to a strange, hollow, and confused noise, they
heavily vanish.*

PROS. [*aside*] I had forgot that foul conspiracy
Of the beast Caliban and his confederates
Against my life. The minute of their plot
Is almost come.—[*To the* SPIRITS] Well done! Avoid! No
    more!

FER. This is strange. Your father's in some passion
That works him strongly.

MIR.   Never till this day
Saw I him touch'd with anger so distemper'd.

PROS. You do look, my son, in a mov'd sort,
As if you were dismay'd. Be cheerful, sir.
Our revels now are ended. These our actors,
As I foretold you, were all spirits and
Are melted into air, into thin air;
And, like the baseless fabric of this vision,
The cloud-capp'd towers, the gorgeous palaces,
The solemn temples, the great globe itself,
Yea, all which it inherit, shall dissolve,
And, like this insubstantial pageant faded,
Leave not a rack behind. We are such stuff

As dreams are made on, and our little life
Is rounded with a sleep. Sir, I am vex'd.
Bear with my weakness. My old brain is troubled.
Be not disturb'd with my infirmity.
If you be pleas'd, retire into my cell
And there repose. A turn or two I'll walk
To still my beating mind.

FER., MIR.   We wish your peace.

Exeunt.

Enter ARIEL.

PROS. Come with a thought! I thank thee, Ariel. Come.
ARI. Thy thoughts I cleave to. What's thy pleasure?
PROS.   Spirit,
We must prepare to meet with Caliban.

ARI. Ay, my commander. When I presented Ceres,
I thought to have told thee of it, but I fear'd
Lest I might anger thee.

PROS. Say again, where didst thou leave these varlets?

ARI. I told you, sir, they were redhot with drinking;
So full of valour that they smote the air
For breathing in their faces, beat the ground
For kissing of their feet; yet always bending
Towards their project. Then I beat my tabor;
At which like unback'd colts they prick'd their ears,
Advanc'd their eyelids, lifted up their noses
As they smelt music. So I charm'd their ears
That calf-like they my lowing follow'd through
Tooth'd briers, sharp furzes, pricking goss, and thorns,
Which ent'red their frail shins. At last I left them
I' th' filthy mantled pool beyond your cell,
There dancing up to th' chins, that the foul lake
O'erstunk their feet.

PROS.   This was well done, my bird.
Thy shape invisible retain thou still.

The trumpery in my house, go bring it hither
For stale to catch these thieves.

ARI.   I go, I go.   *Exit.*

PROS. A devil, a born devil, on whose nature
Nurture can never stick! on whom my pains,
Humanely taken, all, all lost, quite lost!
And as with age his body uglier grows,
So his mind cankers. I will plague them all,
Even to roaring.

[*Enter* ARIEL, *loaden with glistering apparel, etc.*]
                    Come, hang them on this line.

PROSPERO *and* ARIEL *remain, invisible. Enter* CALIBAN,
    STEPHANO, *and* TRINCULO, *all wet.*

CAL. Pray you tread softly, that the blind mole may
    not
Hear a foot fall. We now are near his cell.

STE. Monster, your fairy, which you say is a harmless
fairy, has done little better than play'd the Jack with us.

TRIN. Monster, I do smell all horse-piss, at which my
nose is in great indignation.

STE. So is mine. Do you hear, monster? If I should take
a displeasure against you, look you—

TRIN. Thou wert but a lost monster.

CAL. Good my lord, give me thy favour still.
Be patient, for the prize I'll bring thee to
Shall hoodwink this mischance. Therefore speak softly.
All's hush'd as midnight yet.

TRIN. Ay, but to lose our bottles in the pool—

STE. There is not only disgrace and dishonour in that,
monster, but an infinite loss.

TRIN. That's more to me than my wetting. Yet this is
your harmless fairy, monster.

STE. I will fetch off my bottle, though I be o'er ears for
my labour.

CAL. Prithee, my king, be quiet. Seest thou here?
This is the mouth o' th' cell. No noise, and enter.
Do that good mischief which may make this island
Thine own for ever, and I, thy Caliban,
For aye thy foot-licker.

STE. Give me thy hand. I do begin to have bloody
thoughts.

TRIN. O King Stephano! O peer! O worthy Stephano,
look what a wardrobe here is for thee!

CAL. Let it alone, thou fool! It is but trash.

TRIN. O, ho, monster! we know what belongs to a
frippery. O King Stephano!

STE. Put off that gown, Trinculo. By this hand, I'll have
that gown!

TRIN. Thy Grace shall have it.

CAL. The dropsy drown this fool! What do you mean
To dote thus on such luggage? Let't alone,
And do the murther first. If he awake,
From toe to crown he'll fill our skins with pinches,
Make us strange stuff.

STE. Be you quiet, monster. Mistress line, is not this my
jerkin? [*Takes it down.*] Now is the jerkin under the line.
Now, jerkin, you are like to lose your hair and prove a
bald jerkin.·

TRIN. Do, do! We steal by line and level, an 't like your
Grace.

STE. I thank thee for that jest. Here's a garment for't.
Wit shall not go unrewarded while I am king of this coun-
try. 'Steal by line and level' is an excellent pass of pate.
There's another garment for't.

TRIN. Monster, come put some lime upon your fingers,
and away with the rest!

CAL. I will have none on't. We shall lose our time
And all be turn'd to barnacles, or to apes
With foreheads villanous low.

STE. Monster, lay-to your fingers. Help to bear this away where my hogshead of wine is, or I'll turn you out of my kingdom. Go to, carry this.

TRIN. And this.

STE. Ay, and this.

A noise of hunters heard. Enter divers SPIRITS *in shape of dogs and hounds, hunting them about,* PROSPERO *and* ARIEL *setting them on.*

PROS. Hey, Mountain, hey!

ARI. Silver! there it goes, Silver!

PROS. Fury, Fury! There, Tyrant, there! Hark, hark!
　　　[CALIBAN, STEPHANO, *and* TRINCULO *are driven*
　　　　　　　　　　　　　　　　　　　　　　out.]

Go, charge my goblins that they grind their joints
With dry convulsions, shorten up their sinews
With aged cramps, and more pinch-spotted make them
Than pard or cat o' mountain.

ARI.　　　　　　　　　　Hark, they roar.

PROS. Let them be hunted soundly. At this hour
Lie at my mercy all mine enemies.
Shortly shall all my labours end, and thou
Shalt have the air at freedom. For a little
Follow, and do me service.　　　　　　*Exeunt.*

Act V: Scene I: Before the cell of Prospero.

Enter PROSPERO *in his magic robes, and* ARIEL.

PROS. Now does my project gather to a head.
My charms crack not, my spirits obey, and time
Goes upright with his carriage. How's the day?

ARI. On the sixth hour, at which time, my lord,
You said our work should cease.

PROS.　　　　　　　　I did say so

When first I rais'd the tempest. Say, my spirit,
How fares the King and 's followers?

ARI.   Confin'd together
In the same fashion as you gave in charge,
Just as you left them—all prisoners, sir,
In the line grove which weather-fends your cell.
They cannot budge till your release. The King,
His brother, and yours abide all three distracted,
And the remainder mourning over them,
Brimful of sorrow and dismay; but chiefly
Him that you term'd, sir, the good old Lord Gonzalo.
His tears run down his beard like winter's drops
From eaves of reeds. Your charm so strongly works 'em,
That if you now beheld them, your affections
Would become tender.

PROS.   Dost thou think so, spirit?

ARI. Mine would, sir, were I human.

PROS.   And mine shall.
Hast thou, which art but air, a touch, a feeling
Of their afflictions, and shall not myself,
One of their kind, that relish all as sharply
Passion as they, be kindlier mov'd than thou art?
Though with their high wrongs I am struck to th' quick,
Yet with my nobler reason 'gainst my fury
Do I take part. The rarer action is
In virtue than in vengeance. They being penitent,
The sole drift of my purpose doth extend
Not a frown further. Go, release them, Ariel.
My charms I'll break, their senses I'll restore,
And they shall be themselves.

ARI.   I'll fetch them, sir.   *Exit.*

PROS. [*makes a magic circle with his staff*] Ye elves of
     hills, brooks, standing lakes, and groves,
And ye that on the sands with printless foot
Do chase the ebbing Neptune, and do fly him

When he comes back; you demi-puppets that
By moonshine do the green sour ringlets make,
Whereof the ewe not bites; and you whose pastime
Is to make midnight mushrumps, that rejoice
To hear the solemn curfew; by whose aid
(Weak masters though ye be) I have bedimm'd
The noontide sun, call'd forth the mutinous winds,
And 'twixt the green sea and the azur'd vault
Set roaring war; to the dread rattling thunder
Have I given fire and rifted Jove's stout oak
With his own bolt; the strong-bas'd promontory
Have I made shake and by the spurs pluck'd up
The pine and cedar; graves at my command
Have wak'd their sleepers, op'd, and let 'em forth
By my so potent art. But this rough magic
I here abjure; and when I have requir'd
Some heavenly music (which even now I do)
To work mine end upon their senses that
This airy charm is for, I'll break my staff,
Bury it certain fathoms in the earth,
And deeper than did ever plummet sound
I'll drown my book.   [*Solemn music.*]

[*Here enters* ARIEL *before; then* ALONSO, *with a frantic
gesture, attended by* GONZALO; SEBASTIAN *and* ANTONIO
in like manner, attended by ADRIAN *and* FRANCISCO.
They all enter the circle which PROSPERO *had made, and
there stand charm'd; which* PROSPERO *observing, speaks.*]

A solemn air, and the best comforter
To an unsettled fancy, cure thy brains,
Now useless, boil'd within thy skull! There stand,
For you are spell-stopp'd.
Holy Gonzalo, honourable man,
Mine eyes, ev'n sociable to the show of thine,
Fall fellowly drops. The charm dissolves apace;

And as the morning steals upon the night,
Melting the darkness, so their rising senses
Begin to chase the ignorant fumes that mantle
Their clearer reason. O good Gonzalo,
My true preserver, and a loyal sir
To him thou follow'st! I will pay thy graces
Home both in word and deed. Most cruelly
Didst thou, Alonso, use me and my daughter.
Thy brother was a furtherer in the act.
Thou art pinch'd for't now, Sebastian. Flesh and blood,
You, brother mine, that entertain'd ambition,
Expell'd remorse and nature; who, with Sebastian
(Whose inward pinches therefore are most strong),
Would here have kill'd your king, I do forgive thee,
Unnatural though thou art. Their understanding
Begins to swell, and the approaching tide
Will shortly fill the reasonable shore,
That now lies foul and muddy. Not one of them
That yet looks on me or would know me. Ariel,
Fetch me the hat and rapier in my cell.
I will discase me, and myself present
As I was sometime Milan. Quickly, spirit!
Thou shalt ere long be free.

Exit ARIEL *and returns immediately.*

ARIEL *sings and helps to attire him.*

Where the bee sucks, there suck I;
In a cowslip's bell I lie;
There I couch when owls do cry.
On the bat's back I do fly
After summer merrily.
Merrily, merrily shall I live now
Under the blossom that hangs on the bough.

PROS. Why, that's my dainty Ariel! I shall miss thee,
But yet thou shalt have freedom. So, so, so.
To the King's ship, invisible as thou art!

There shalt thou find the mariners asleep
Under the hatches. The master and the boatswain
Being awake, enforce them to this place,
And presently, I prithee.

ARI. I drink the air before me, and return
Or ere your pulse twice beat. *Exit.*

GON. All torment, trouble, wonder, and amazement
Inhabits here. Some heavenly power guide us
Out of this fearful country!

PROS. Behold, sir King,
The wronged Duke of Milan, Prospero.
For more assurance that a living prince
Does now speak to thee, I embrace thy body,
And to thee and thy company I bid
A hearty welcome.

ALON. Whe'r thou be'st he or no,
Or some enchanted trifle to abuse me,
As late I have been, I not know. Thy pulse
Beats, as of flesh and blood; and, since I saw thee,
Th' affliction of my mind amends, with which,
I fear, a madness held me. This must crave
(An if this be at all) a most strange story.
Thy dukedom I resign and do entreat
Thou pardon me my wrongs. But how should Prospero
Be living and be here?

PROS. First, noble friend,
Let me embrace thine age, whose honour cannot
Be measur'd or confin'd.

GON. Whether this be
Or be not, I'll not swear.

PROS. You do yet taste
Some subtleties o' th' isle, that will not let you
Believe things certain. Welcome, my friends all.
[*Aside to* SEBASTIAN *and* ANTONIO] But you, my brace of
    lords, were I so minded,

I here could pluck his Highness' frown upon you,
And justify you traitors. At this time
I will tell no tales.

    SEB. [*aside*]   The devil speaks in him.

    PROS.   No.
For you, most wicked sir, whom to call brother
Would even infect my mouth, I do forgive
Thy rankest fault—all of them; and require
My dukedom of thee, which perforce I know
Thou must restore.

    ALON.   If thou beest Prospero,
Give us particulars of thy preservation;
How thou hast met us here, who three hours since
Were wrack'd upon this shore; where I have lost
(How sharp the point of this remembrance is!)
My dear son Ferdinand.

    PROS.   I am woe for't, sir.

    ALON. Irreparable is the loss, and patience
Says it is past her cure.

    PROS.   I rather think
You have not sought her help, of whose soft grace
For the like loss I have her sovereign aid
And rest myself content.

    ALON.   You the like loss?

    PROS. As great to me as late; and, supportable
To make the dear loss, have I means much weaker
Than you may call to comfort you; for I
Have lost my daughter.

    ALON.   A daughter?
O heavens, that they were living both in Naples,
The King and Queen there! That they were, I wish
Myself were mudded in that oozy bed
Where my son lies. When did you lose your daughter?

    PROS. In this last tempest. I perceive these lords
At this encounter do so much admire

That they devour their reason, and scarce think
Their eyes do offices of truth, their words
Are natural breath. But, howsoev'r you have
Been justled from your senses, know for certain
That I am Prospero, and that very duke
Which was thrust forth of Milan, who most strangely
Upon this shore, where you were wrack'd, was landed
To be the lord on't. No more yet of this;
For 'tis a chronicle of day by day,
Not a relation for a breakfast, nor
Befitting this first meeting. Welcome, sir.
This cell's my court. Here have I few attendants,
And subjects none abroad. Pray you look in.
My dukedom since you have given me again,
I will requite you with as good a thing,
At least bring forth a wonder to content ye
As much as me my dukedom.

> *Here* PROSPERO *discovers* FERDINAND *and* MIRANDA
> *playing at chess.*

MIR. Sweet lord, you play me false.

FER.   No, my dearest love,
I would not for the world.

MIR. Yes, for a score of kingdoms you should wrangle,
And I would call it fair play.

ALON.   If this prove
A vision of the island, one dear son
Shall I twice lose.

SEB.   A most high miracle!

FER. Though the seas threaten, they are merciful.
I have curs'd them without cause.   *Kneels.*

ALON.   Now all the blessings
Of a glad father compass thee about!
Arise, and say how thou cam'st here.

MIR.   O, wonder!
How many goodly creatures are there here!

How beauteous mankind is! O brave new world
That has such people in't!

PROS.   'Tis new to thee.

ALON. What is this maid with whom thou wast at play?
Your eld'st acquaintance cannot be three hours.
Is she the goddess that hath sever'd us
And brought us thus together?

FER.   Sir, she is mortal;
But by immortal providence she's mine.
I chose her when I could not ask my father
For his advice, nor thought I had one. She
Is daughter to this famous Duke of Milan,
Of whom so often I have heard renown
But never saw before; of whom I have
Receiv'd a second life; and second father
This lady makes him to me.

ALON.   I am hers.
But, O, how oddly will it sound that I
Must ask my child forgiveness!

PROS.   There, sir, stop.
Let us not burthen our remembrance with
A heaviness that's gone.

GON.   I have inly wept,
Or should have spoke ere this. Look down, you gods,
And on this couple drop a blessed crown!
For it is you that have chalk'd forth the way
Which brought us hither.

ALON.   I say amen, Gonzalo.

GON. Was Milan thrust from Milan that his issue
Should become kings of Naples? O, rejoice
Beyond a common joy, and set it down
With gold on lasting pillars. In one voyage
Did Claribel her husband find at Tunis,
And Ferdinand her brother found a wife
Where he himself was lost; Prospero his dukedom

In a poor isle; and all of us ourselves
When no man was his own.

    ALON. [*to* FERDINAND *and* MIRANDA] Give me your
        hands.
Let grief and sorrow still embrace his heart
That doth not wish you joy.

    GON.   Be it so! Amen!

    [*Enter* ARIEL, *with the* MASTER *and* BOATSWAIN
            amazedly following.]

O, look, sir; look, sir! Here is more of us!
I prophesied, if a gallows were on land,
This fellow could not drown. Now, blasphemy,
That swear'st grace o'erboard, not an oath on shore?
Hast thou no mouth by land? What is the news?

    BOATS. The best news is that we have safely found
Our king and company; the next, our ship,
Which, but three glasses since, we gave out split,
Is tight and yare and bravely rigg'd as when
We first put out to sea.

    ARI. [*aside to* PROSPERO] Sir, all this service
Have I done since I went.

    PROS. [*aside to* ARIEL] My tricksy spirit!

    ALON. These are not natural events; they strengthen
From strange to stranger. Say, how came you hither?

    BOATS. If I did think, sir, I were well awake,
I'ld strive to tell you. We were dead of sleep
And (how we know not) all clapp'd under hatches;
Where, but even now, with strange and several noises
Of roaring, shrieking, howling, jingling chains,
And moe diversity of sounds, all horrible,
We were awak'd; straightway at liberty;
Where we, in all her trim, freshly beheld
Our royal, good, and gallant ship; our master
Cap'ring to eye her. On a trice, so please you,

Even in a dream, were we divided from them
And were brought moping hither.

    ARI. [*aside to* PROSPERO] Was't well done?

    PROS. [*aside to* ARIEL] Bravely, my diligence. Thou
      shalt be free.

    ALON. This is as strange a maze as e'er men trod,
And there is in this business more than nature
Was ever conduct of. Some oracle
Must rectify our knowledge.

    PROS.   Sir, my liege,
Do not infest your mind with beating on
The strangeness of this business. At pick'd leisure,
Which shall be shortly, single I'll resolve you
(Which to you shall seem probable) of every
These happen'd accidents; till when, be cheerful
And think of each thing well. [*Aside to* ARIEL.] Come
    hither, spirit.
Set Caliban and his companions free.
Untie the spell. [*Exit* ARIEL.] How fares my gracious sir?
There are yet missing of your company
Some few odd lads that you remember not.

    Enter ARIEL, *driving in* CALIBAN, STEPHANO, *and*
      TRINCULO, *in their stol'n apparel.*

    STE. Every man shift for all the rest, and let no man
take care for himself; for all is but fortune. Coragio, bully-
monster, coragio!

    TRIN. If these be true spies which I wear in my head,
here's a goodly sight.

    CAL. O Setebos, these be brave spirits indeed!
How fine my master is! I am afraid
He will chastise me.

    SEB.   Ha, ha!
What things are these, my Lord Antonio?
Will money buy 'em?

ANT.   Very like. One of them
Is a plain fish and no doubt marketable.

PROS. Mark but the badges of these men, my lords,
Then say if they be true. This misshapen knave,
His mother was a witch, and one so strong
That could control the moon, make flows and ebbs,
And deal in her command without her power.
These three have robb'd me, and this demi-devil
(For he's a bastard one) had plotted with them
To take my life. Two of these fellows you
Must know and own; this thing of darkness I
Acknowledge mine.

CAL.   I shall be pinch'd to death.

ALON. Is not this Stephano, my drunken butler?

SEB. He is drunk now. Where had he wine?

ALON. And Trinculo is reeling ripe. Where should
      they
Find this grand liquor that hath gilded 'em?
How cam'st thou in this pickle?

TRIN. I have been in such a pickle, since I saw you last,
that I fear me will never out of my bones. I shall not fear
fly-blowing.

SEB. Why, how now, Stephano?

STE. O, touch me not! I am not Stephano, but a cramp.

PROS. You'ld be king o' the isle, sirrah?

STE. I should have been a sore one then.

ALON. This is as strange a thing as e'er I look'd on.

PROS. He is as disproportion'd in his manners
As in his shape. Go, sirrah, to my cell;
Take with you your companions. As you look
To have my pardon, trim it handsomely.

CAL. Ay, that I will! and I'll be wise hereafter,
And seek for grace. What a thrice-double ass
Was I to take this drunkard for a god
And worship this dull fool!

Pros.   Go to! Away!

Alon. Hence, and bestow your luggage where you
    found it.

Seb. Or stole it rather.

     Exeunt Caliban, Stephano, *and* Trinculo.

Pros. Sir, I invite your Highness and your train
To my poor cell, where you shall take your rest
For this one night; which, part of it, I'll waste
With such discourse as, I not doubt, shall make it
Go quick away—the story of my life,
And the particular accidents gone by
Since I came to this isle; and in the morn
I'll bring you to your ship, and so to Naples,
Where I have hope to see the nuptial
Of these our dear-belov'd solemnized;
And thence retire me to my Milan, where
Every third thought shall be my grave.

Alon.   I long
To hear the story of your life, which must
Take the ear strangely.

Pros.   I'll deliver all;
And promise you calm seas, auspicious gales,
And sail so expeditious that shall catch
Your royal fleet far off.—My Ariel, chick,
That is thy charge. Then to the elements
Be free, and fare thou well—Please you draw near.

        Exeunt omnes.

Epilogue.

Spoken by Prospero.

Now my charms are all o'erthrown,
And what strength I have's mine own,
Which is most faint. Now 'tis true

I must be here confin'd by you,
Or sent to Naples. Let me not,
Since I have my dukedom got
And pardon'd the deceiver, dwell
In this bare island by your spell;
But release me from my bands
With the help of your good hands.
Gentle breath of yours my sails
Must fill, or else my project fails,
Which was to please. Now I want
Spirits to enforce, art to enchant;
And my ending is despair
Unless I be reliev'd by prayer,
Which pierces so that it assaults
Mercy itself and frees all faults.
As you from crimes would pardon'd be,
Let your indulgence set me free.   *Exit.*

Selections

FROM THE OTHER PLAYS

From *The Merchant of Venice*

You have too much respect upon the world;
They lose it that do buy it with much care.   [*Act* I, *sc.* 1

I hold the world but as the world, Gratiano—
A stage, where every man must play a part,
And mine a sad one.   [I, 1

                           'I am Sir Oracle,
And when I ope my lips, let no dog bark!'   [I, 1

In my school days, when I had lost one shaft,
I shot his fellow of the selfsame flight
The selfsame way with more advised watch,
To find the other forth; and by adventuring both
I oft found both.   [I, 1

If to do were as easy as to know what were good to do,
chapels had been churches, and poor men's cottages
princes' palaces.   [I, 2

God made him, and therefore let him pass for a man.
                                                  [I, 2

When he is best, he is a little worse than a man; and
when he is worst, he is little better than a beast. . . .

I will do anything, Nerissa, ere I will be married to a sponge. [I, 2

BASSANIO. If it please you to dine with us.

SHYLOCK. Yes, to smell pork, to eat of the habitation which your prophet the Nazarite conjured the devil into! I will buy with you, sell with you, talk with you, walk with you, but I will not eat with you, drink with you, nor pray with you. What news on the Rialto? [I, 3

The devil can cite scripture for his purpose. [I, 3

It is a wise father that knows his own child. [II, 2

Who riseth from a feast
With that keen appetite that he sits down? [II, 6

But love is blind, and lovers cannot see
The pretty follies that themselves enjoy. [II, 6

'All that glisters is not gold.' [II, 7

SHYLOCK. I am a Jew. Hath not a Jew eyes? Hath not a Jew hands, organs, dimensions, senses, affections, passions? fed with the same food, hurt with the same weapons, subject to the same diseases, healed by the same means, warmed and cooled by the same winter and summer as a Christian is? If you prick us, do we not bleed? If you tickle us, do we not laugh? If you poison us, do we not die? And if you wrong us, shall we not revenge? If we are like you in the rest, we will resemble you in that. If a Jew wrong a Christian, what is his humility? Revenge. If a Christian wrong a Jew, what should his suffrance be by Christian example? Why, revenge. The villany you

teach me I will execute, and it shall go hard but I will
better the instruction.   [III, 1

PORTIA. The quality of mercy is not strain'd;
It droppeth as the gentle rain from heaven
Upon the place beneath. It is twice blest—
It blesseth him that gives, and him that takes.
'Tis mightiest in the mightiest. It becomes
The throned monarch better than his crown.
His sceptre shows the force of temporal power,
The attribute to awe and majesty,
Wherein doth sit the dread and fear of kings;
But mercy is above this sceptred sway;
It is enthroned in the hearts of kings,
It is an attribute to God himself;
And earthly power doth then show likest God's
When mercy seasons justice. Therefore, Jew,
Though justice be thy plea, consider this—
That, in the course of justice, none of us
Should see salvation. We do pray for mercy,
And that same prayer doth teach us all to render
The deeds of mercy. I have spoke thus much
To mitigate the justice of thy plea;
Which if thou follow, this strict court of Venice
Must needs give sentence 'gainst the merchant there.
                                                     [IV, 1

To do a great right, do a little wrong   [IV, 1

A Daniel come to judgment! yea, a Daniel!   [IV, 1

Is it so nominated in the bond?   [IV, 1

You take my house when you do take the prop
That doth sustain my house. You take my life
When you do take the means whereby I live.   [IV, 1

LORENZO. The moon shines bright. In such a night as
    this,
When the sweet wind did gently kiss the trees
And they did make no noise—in such a night
Troilus methinks mounted the Troyan walls
And sigh'd his soul toward the Grecian tents,
Where Cressid lay that night.
JESSICA.   In such a night
Did Thisbe fearfully o'ertrip the dew,
And saw the lion's shadow ere himself,
And ran dismay'd away.
LOR.   In such a night
Stood Dido with a willow in her hand
Upon the wild sea-banks, and waft her love
To come again to Carthage.
JES.   In such a night
Medea gathered the enchanted herbs
That did renew old Æson.
LOR.   In such a night
Did Jessica steal from the wealthy Jew,
And with an unthrift love did run from Venice
As far as Belmont.
JES.   In such a night
Did young Lorenzo swear he lov'd her well,
Stealing her soul with many vows of faith,
And ne'er a true one.
LOR.   In such a night
Did pretty Jessica (like a little shrow)
Slander her love, and he forgave it her.
JES. I would out-night you, did no body come;
But, hark, I hear the footing of a man. . . .

Lor. How sweet the moonlight sleeps upon this bank!
Here will we sit and let the sounds of music
Creep in our ears. Soft stillness and the night
Become the touches of sweet harmony.
Sit, Jessica. Look how the floor of heaven
Is thick inlaid with patines of bright gold.
There's not the smallest orb which thou behold'st
But in his motion like an angel sings,
Still quiring to the young-ey'd cherubins;
Such harmony is in immortal souls;
But whilst this muddy vesture of decay
Doth grossly close it in, we cannot hear it.

[*Enter* Musicians.]

Come, ho, and wake Diana with a hymn!
With sweetest touches pierce your mistress' ear
And draw her home with music.   *Play music.*
   Jes. I am never merry when I hear sweet music.
   Lor. The reason is, your spirits are attentive.
For do but note a wild and wanton herd,
Or race of youthful and unhandled colts,
Fetching mad bounds, bellowing and neighing loud,
Which is the hot condition of their blood:
If they but hear perchance a trumpet sound,
Or any air of music touch their ears,
You shall perceive them make a mutual stand,
Their savage eyes turn'd to a modest gaze
By the sweet power of music. Therefore the poet
Did feign that Orpheus drew trees, stones, and floods,
Since naught so stockish, hard, and full of rage
But music for the time doth change his nature.
The man that hath no music in himself,
Nor is not mov'd with concord of sweet sounds,
Is fit for treasons, stratagems, and spoils;
The motions of his spirit are dull as night,

And his affections dark as Erebus.
Let no such man be trusted. Mark the music.

Enter PORTIA *and* NERISSA.

POR. That light we see is burning in my hall.
How far that little candle throws his beams!
So shines a good deed in a naughty world.
    NER. When the moon shone, we did not see the candle.
    POR. So doth the greater glory dim the less.
A substitute shines brightly as a king
Until a king be by; and then his state
Empties itself, as doth an inland brook
Into the main of waters. Music! hark!
    NER. It is your music, madam, of the house.
    POR. Nothing is good, I see, without respect.
Methinks it sounds much sweeter than by day.
    NER. Silence bestows that virtue on it, madam.
    POR. The crow doth sing as sweetly as the lark
When neither is attended; and I think
The nightingale, if she should sing by day
When every goose is cackling, would be thought
No better a musician than the wren.
How many things by season seasoned are
To their right praise and true perfection!
Peace, ho! The moon sleeps with Endymion,
And would not be awak'd.   *Music ceases.*   [V, 1

From *Othello*

IAGO.   I will wear my heart upon my sleeve
For daws to peck at. I am not what I am.   *Act* I, *sc.* 1

OTHELLO. Most potent, grave, and reverend signiors,
My very noble, and approv'd good masters,

That I have ta'en away this old man's daughter,
It is most true; true I have married her.
The very head and front of my offending
Hath this extent, no more. Rude am I in my speech,
And little bless'd with the soft phrase of peace;
For since these arms of mine had seven years' pith
Till now some nine moons wasted, they have us'd
Their dearest action in the tented field;
And little of this great world can I speak
More than pertains to feats of broil and battle;
And therefore little shall I grace my cause
In speaking for myself. Yet, by your gracious patience,
I will a round unvarnish'd tale deliver
Of my whole course of love—what drugs, what charms,
What conjuration, and what mighty magic
(For such proceeding am I charg'd withal)
I won his daughter. . . .
Her father lov'd me, oft invited me;
Still question'd me the story of my life
From year to year—the battles, sieges, fortunes
That I have pass'd.
I ran it through, even from my boyish days
To th' very moment that he bade me tell it.
Wherein I spake of most disastrous chances,
Of moving accidents by flood and field;
Of hairbreadth scapes i' th' imminent deadly breach;
Of being taken by the insolent foe
And sold to slavery; of my redemption thence
And portance in my travel's history,
Wherein of anters vast and deserts idle,
Rough quarries, rocks, and hills. whose heads touch
    heaven,
It was my hint to speak—such was the process;
And of the Cannibals that each other eat,
The Anthropophagi, and men whose heads

Do grow beneath their shoulders. This to hear
Would Desdemona seriously incline;
But still the house affairs would draw her thence;
Which ever as she could with haste dispatch,
She'ld come again, and with a greedy ear
Devour up my discourse. Which I observing,
Took once a pliant hour, and found good means
To draw from her a prayer of earnest heart
That I would all my pilgrimage dilate,
Whereof by parcels she had something heard,
But not intentively. I did consent,
And often did beguile her of her tears
When I did speak of some distressful stroke
That my youth suffer'd. My story being done,
She gave me for my pains a world of sighs.
She swore, in faith, 'twas strange, 'twas passing strange;
'Twas pitiful, 'twas wondrous pitiful.
She wish'd she had not heard it; yet she wish'd
That heaven had made her such a man. She thank'd me;
And bade me, if I had a friend that lov'd her,
I should but teach him how to tell my story,
And that would woo her. Upon this hint I spake.
She lov'd me for the dangers I had pass'd,
And I lov'd her that she did pity them.
This only is the witchcraft I have us'd.   [I, 3

IAGO. Virtue? a fig! 'Tis in ourselves that we are thus
or thus. . . .

It is merely a lust of the blood and a permission of the
will. Come, be a man! Drown thyself? Drown cats and
blind puppies! I have professed me thy friend, and I confess me knit to thy deserving with cables of perdurable
toughness. I could never better stead thee than now. Put
money in thy purse. Follow these wars; defeat thy favour
with an usurped beard. I say, put money in thy purse. It

cannot be that Desdemona should long continue her love
to the Moor—put money in thy purse—nor he his to her.
It was a violent commencement, and thou shalt see an
answerable sequestration. Put but money in thy purse.
These Moors are changeable in their wills. Fill thy purse
with money. The food that to him now is as luscious as
locusts shall be to him shortly as bitter as coloquintida.
She must change for youth. When she is sated with his
body, she will find the error of her choice. She must have
change, she must. Therefore put money in thy purse. If
thou wilt needs damn thyself, do it a more delicate way
than drowning. Make all the money thou canst. If sancti-
mony and a frail vow betwixt an erring barbarian and a
supersubtle Venetian be not too hard for my wits and
all the tribe of hell, thou shalt enjoy her. Therefore make
money. A pox of drowning thyself! It is clean out of the
way. Seek thou rather to be hanged in compassing thy
joy than to be drowned and go without her.   [I, 3

She that was ever fair, and never proud;
Had tongue at will, and yet was never loud; . . .
She that could think, and ne'er disclose her mind;
See suitors following, and not look behind:
She was a wight (if ever such wight were)—
To suckle fools and chronicle small beer.   [II, 1

Cassio. Reputation, reputation, reputation! O, I have
lost my reputation! I have lost the immortal part of myself, and what remains is bestial. . . .

Iago. Reputation is an idle and most false imposition;
oft got without merit and lost without deserving. . . .

Cas. O God! that men should put an enemy in their
mouths to steal away their brains! . . .

Iago. Come, come, good wine is a good familiar creature if it be well used. Exclaim no more against it. [II, 3

Dull not device by coldness and delay. [II, 3

OTH. Excellent wretch! Perdition catch my soul
But I do love thee! and when I love thee not,
Chaos is come again. . . .
                              What dost thou say, Iago?
IAGO. Good name in man and woman, dear my lord,
Is the immediate jewel of their souls.
Who steals my purse steals trash; 'tis something, nothing;
'Twas mine, 'tis his, and has been slave to thousands;
But he that filches from me my good name
Robs me of that which not enriches him
And makes me poor indeed.
    OTH. By heaven, I'll know thy thoughts! . . .
    IAGO. O, beware, my lord, of jealousy!
It is the green-ey'd monster, which doth mock
The meat it feeds on. . . .
    OTH. . . . If I do prove her haggard,
Though that her jesses were my dear heartstrings,
I'ld whistle her off and let her down the wind
To prey at fortune. Haply, for I am black
And have not those soft parts of conversation
That chamberers have, or for I am declin'd
Into the vale of years (yet that's not much),
She's gone. I am abus'd, and my relief
Must be to loathe her. O curse of marriage,
That we can call these delicate creatures ours,
And not their appetites! I had rather be a toad
And live upon the vapour of a dungeon
Than keep a corner in the thing I love
For others' uses. [III, 3

    IAGO.   Trifles light as air
Are to the jealous confirmations strong
As proofs of holy writ. This may do something.
The Moor already changes to my poison. . . .

Look where he comes! Not poppy nor mandragora,
Nor all the drowsy syrups of the world,
Shall ever medicine thee to that sweet sleep
Which thou ow'dst yesterday. . . .

    OTH. I swear 'tis better to be much abus'd
Than but to know't a little. . . .
He that is robb'd, not wanting what is stol'n,
Let him not know't, and he's not robb'd at all. . . .

               . . . O, now for ever
Farewell the tranquil mind! farewell content!
Farewell the plumed troop, and the big wars
That make ambition virtue! O, farewell!
Farewell the neighing steed and the shrill trump,
The spirit-stirring drum, th' ear-piercing fife,
The royal banner, and all quality,
Pride, pomp, and circumstance of glorious war!
And O ye mortal engines whose rude throats
Th' immortal Jove's dread clamours counterfeit,
Farewell! Othello's occupation's gone!   [III, 3

    OTH. It is the cause, it is the cause, my soul.
Let me not name it to you, you chaste stars!
It is the cause. Yet I'll not shed her blood,
Nor scar that whiter skin of hers than snow,
And smooth as monumental alabaster.
Yet she must die, else she'll betray more men.
Put out the light, and then put out the light.
If I quench thee, thou flaming minister,
I can again thy former light restore,
Should I repent me; but once put out thy light,
Thou cunning'st pattern of excelling nature,
I know not where is that Promethean heat
That can thy light relume. When I have pluck'd the rose,
I cannot give it vital growth again;
It needs must wither. I'll smell it on the tree.   [V, 2

OTH. Soft you! a word or two before you go.
I have done the state some service, and they know't—
No more of that. I pray you, in your letters,
When you shall these unlucky deeds relate,
Speak of me as I am. Nothing extenuate,
Nor set down aught in malice. Then must you speak
Of one that lov'd not wisely, but too well;
Of one not easily jealous, but, being wrought,
Perplex'd in the extreme; of one whose hand
(Like the base Indian) threw a pearl away
Richer than all his tribe; of one whose subdu'd eyes,
Albeit unused to the melting mood,
Drop tears as fast as the Arabian trees
Their medicinal gum. Set you down this;
And say besides that in Aleppo once,
Where a malignant and a turban'd Turk
Beat a Venetian and traduc'd the state,
I took by th' throat the circumcised dog
And smote him—thus.   *He stabs himself.*   [V, 2

From *Twelfth Night*

DUKE. If music be the food of love, play on,
Give me excess of it, that, surfeiting,
The appetite may sicken, and so die.
That strain again! It had a dying fall;
O, it came o'er my ear like the sweet sound
That breathes upon a bank of violets,
Stealing and giving odour! Enough, no more!
'Tis not so sweet now as it was before.
O spirit of love, how quick and fresh art thou!
That, notwithstanding thy capacity
Receiveth as the sea, naught enters there,

Of what validity and pitch soe'er,
But falls into abatement and low price
Even in a minute! So full of shapes is fancy
That it alone is high fantastical.   [*Act* I, *sc.* 1

When my tongue blabs, then let mine eyes not see.
                                               [I, 2

'Tis beauty truly blent, whose red and white
Nature's own sweet and cunning hand laid on.
Lady, you are the cruell'st she alive
If you will lead these graces to the grave,
And leave the world no copy.   [I, 5

Halloa your name to the reverberate hills
And make the babbling gossip of the air
Cry out 'Olivia!'   [I, 5

DUKE. Too old, by heaven! Let still the woman take
An elder than herself: so wears she to him,
So sways she level in her husband's heart;
For, boy, however we do praise ourselves,
Our fancies are more giddy and unfirm,
More longing,. wavering, sooner lost and won,
Than women's are.
  VIOLA.   I think it well, my lord.
  DUKE. Then let thy love be younger than thyself,
Or thy affection cannot hold the bent;
For women are as roses, whose fair flow'r,
Being once display'd, doth fall that very hour.
  VIO. And so they are; alas, that they are so!
To die, even when they to perfection grow!

              Enter CURIO *and* CLOWN.

  DUKE. O, fellow, come, the song we had last night.
Mark it, Cesario; it is old and plain.

The spinsters and the knitters in the sun,
And the free maids that weave their thread with bones,
Do use to chant it. It is silly sooth,
And dallies with the innocence of love
Like the old age.   [II, 4

Vio. My father had a daughter lov'd a man
As it might be perhaps, were I a woman,
I should your lordship.
    Duke.   And what's her history?
    Vio. A blank, my lord. She never told her love,
But let concealment, like a worm i' th' bud,
Feed on her damask cheek. She pin'd in thought;
And, with a green and yellow melancholy,
She sat like Patience on a monument,
Smiling at grief. Was not this love indeed?
We men may say more, swear more; but indeed
Our shows are more than will; for still we prove
Much in our vows but little in our love.   [II, 4

Malvolio. [reads] 'If this fall into thy hand, revolve.
In my stars I am above thee; but be not afraid of greatness. Some are born great, some achieve greatness, and
some have greatness thrust upon 'em. Thy Fates open
their hands; let thy blood and spirit embrace them; and
to inure thyself to what thou art like to be, cast thy
humble slough and appear fresh. Be opposite with a kinsman, surly with servants. Let thy tongue tang arguments
of state; put thyself into the trick of singularity. She thus
advises thee that sighs for thee. Remember who commended thy yellow stockings and wished to see thee ever
cross-gartered. I say, remember. Go to, thou art made, if
thou desirest to be so. If not, let me see thee a steward
still, the fellow of servants, and not worthy to touch For-

tune's fingers. Farewell. She that would alter services
with thee,   THE FORTUNATE UNHAPPY.'

[II, 5

Foolery, sir, does walk about the orb like the sun; it
shines everywhere.   [III, 1

OLIVIA. O, what a deal of scorn looks beautiful
In the contempt and anger of his lip!
A murd'rous guilt shows not itself more soon
Than love that would seem hid: love's night is noon.
Cesario, by the roses of the spring,
By maidhood, honour, truth, and everything,
I love thee so that, maugre all thy pride,
Nor wit nor reason can my passion hide.
Do not extort thy reasons from this clause,
For that I woo, thou therefore hast no cause;
But rather reason thus with reason fetter:
Love sought is good, but given unsought is better [III, 1

This is very midsummer madness.   [III, 4

If this were played upon a stage now, I could condemn
it as an improbable fiction.   [III, 4

Still you keep o' th' windy side of the law.   [III, 4

I have heard of some kind of men that put quarrels
purposely on others to taste their valour.   [III, 4

Out of my lean and low ability
I'll lend you something.   [III, 4

I hate ingratitude more in a man
Than lying, vainness, babbling, drunkenness,

Or any taint of vice whose strong corruption
Inhabits our frail blood. [III, 4

And thus the whirligig of time brings in his revenges.
[V, 1

From *The Taming of the Shrew*

Come, madam wife, sit by my side and let the world
slip. We shall ne'er be younger. [*Induction, sc.* 2

I have Pisa left
And am to Padua come as he that leaves
A shallow plash to plunge him in the deep,
And with satiety seeks to quench his thirst.
[*Act* I, *sc.* 1

No profit grows where is no pleasure ta'en;
In brief, sir, study what you most affect. [I, 1

There's small choice in rotten apples. [I, 1

HORTENSIO. What happy gale
Blows you to Padua here from old Verona?
PETRUCHIO. Such wind as scatters young men through
the world
To seek their fortunes further than at home,
Where small experience grows. [I, 2

PET. Think you a little din can daunt mine ears?
Have I not in my time heard lions roar?
Have I not heard the sea, puff'd up with winds,
Rage like an angry boar chafed with sweat?
Have I not heard great ordnance in the field,

And heaven's artillery thunder in the skies?
Have I not in a pitched battle heard
Loud 'larums, neighing steeds, and trumpets' clang?
And do you tell me of a woman's tongue,
That gives not half so great a blow to th' ear
As will a chestnut in a farmer's fire?
Tush, tush! Fear boys with bugs! [I, 2

And do as adversaries do in law—
Strive mightily, but eat and drink as friends. [I, 2

A cold world, Curtis, in every office but thine; and
therefore fire! [IV, 1

PET. My falcon now is sharp, and passing empty,
And till she stoop she must not be full-gorg'd,
For then she never looks upon her lure.
Another way I have to man my haggard,
To make her come, and know her keeper's call:
That is, to watch her, as we watch these kites
That bate and beat and will not be obedient.
She eat no meat to-day, nor none shall eat;
Last night she slept not, nor to-night she shall not.
As with the meat, some undeserved fault
I'll find about the making of the bed;
And here I'll fling the pillow, there the bolster,
This way the coverlet, another way the sheets.
Ay, and amid this hurly I intend
That all is done in reverend care of her;
And in conclusion, she shall watch all night;
And if she chance to nod, I'll rail and brawl
And with the clamour keep her still awake.
This is a way to kill a wife with kindness,
And thus I'll curb her mad and headstrong humour.
He that knows better how to tame a shrew,
Now let him speak: 'tis charity to shew. [IV, 1

Kindness in women, not their beauteous looks,
Shall win my love.   [IV, 2

   KATHERINA. The more my wrong, the more his spite
      appears.
What, did he marry me to famish me?
Beggars that come unto my father's door
Upon entreaty have a present alms;
If not, elsewhere they meet with charity;
But I, who never knew how to entreat,
Nor never needed that I should entreat,
Am starv'd for meat, giddy for lack of sleep;
With oaths kept waking, and with brawling fed.
And that which spites me more than all these wants—
He does it under name of perfect love;
As who should say, if I should sleep or eat,
'Twere deadly sickness or else present death.   [IV, 3

Our purses shall be proud, our garments poor;
For 'tis the mind that makes the body rich;
And as the sun breaks through the darkest clouds,
So honour peereth in the meanest habit.   [IV, 3

He that is giddy thinks the world turns round.   [V, 2

   KATH. A woman mov'd is like a fountain troubled,
Muddy, ill-seeming, thick, bereft of beauty;
And while it is so, none so dry or thirsty
Will deign to sip or touch one drop of it.
Thy husband is thy lord, thy life, thy keeper,
Thy head, thy sovereign; one that cares for thee
And for thy maintenance; commits his body
To painful labour both by sea and land,
To watch the night in storms, the day in cold,
Whilst thou li'st warm at home, secure and safe,

And craves no other tribute at thy hands
But love, fair looks, and true obedience—
Too little payment for so great a debt.
Such duty as the subject owes the prince,
Even such a woman oweth to her husband;
And when she is froward, peevish, sullen, sour,
And not obedient to his honest will,
What is she but a foul contending rebel
And graceless traitor to her loving lord?
I am asham'd that women are so simple
To offer war where they should kneel for peace;
Or seek for rule, supremacy, and sway
When they are bound to serve, love, and obey.
Why are our bodies soft and weak and smooth,
Unapt to toil and trouble in the world,
But that our soft conditions and our hearts
Should well agree with our external parts?
Come, come, you froward and unable worms!
My mind hath been as big as one of yours,
My heart as great, my reason haply more,
To bandy word for word and frown for frown;
But now I see our lances are but straws,
Our strength as weak, our weakness past compare,
That seeming to be most which we indeed least are.

                                          [V, 2

From *King Lear*

CORDELIA. Unhappy that I am, I cannot heave
My heart into my mouth. I love your Majesty
According to my bond; no more nor less.
    LEAR. How, how, Cordelia? Mend your speech a
        little,
Lest it may mar your fortunes.

Cor.   Good my lord,
You have begot me, bred me, lov'd me; I
Return those duties back as are right fit,
Obey you, love you, and most honour you.
Why have my sisters husbands, if they say
They love you all? Haply, when I shall wed,
That lord whose hand must take my plight shall carry
Half my love with him, half my care and duty.
Sure I shall never marry like my sisters,
To love my father all.
    Lear. But goes thy heart with this?
    Cor.   Ay, good my lord.
    Lear. So young, and so untender?
    Cor. So young, my lord, and true.
    Lear. Let it be so! thy truth then be thy dower!
For, by the sacred radiance of the sun,
The mysteries of Hecate and the night;
By all the operation of the orbs
From whom we do exist and cease to be;
Here I disclaim all my paternal care,
Propinquity and property of blood,
And as a stranger to my heart and me
Hold thee from this for ever.   [*Act* I, *sc.* 1

Edmund. This is the excellent foppery of the world,
that, when we are sick in fortune, often the surfeit of our
own behaviour, we make guilty of our disasters the sun,
the moon, and the stars; as if we were villains on necessity; fools by heavenly compulsion; knaves, thieves, and
treachers by spherical predominance; drunkards, liars,
and adulterers by an enforced obedience of planetary influence; and all that we are evil in, by a divine thrusting
on. An admirable evasion of whoremaster man, to lay
his goatish disposition to the charge of a star!   [I, 2

How sharper than a serpent's tooth it is
To have a thankless child!   [I, 4

LEAR. O, reason not the need! Our basest beggars
Are in the poorest thing superfluous.
Allow not nature more than nature needs,
Man's life is cheap as beast's. Thou art a lady:
If only to go warm were gorgeous,
Why, nature needs not what thou gorgeous wear'st,
Which scarcely keeps thee warm. But, for true need—
You heavens, give me that patience, patience I need!
You see me here, you gods, a poor old man,
As full of grief as age; wretched in both.
If it be you that stirs these daughters' hearts
Against their father, fool me not so much
To bear it tamely; touch me with noble anger,
And let not women's weapons, water drops,
Stain my man's cheeks! No, you unnatural hags!
I will have such revenges on you both
That all the world shall—I will do such things—
What they are yet, I know not; but they shall be
The terrors of the earth! You think I'll weep.
No, I'll not weep.
I have full cause of weeping, but this heart
Shall break into a hundred thousand flaws
Or ere I'll weep. O fool, I shall go mad!   [II, 4

LEAR. Blow, winds, and crack your cheeks! rage! blow!
You cataracts and hurricanoes, spout
Till you have drench'd our steeples, drown'd the cocks!
You sulph'rous and thought-executing fires,
Vaunt-couriers to oak-cleaving thunderbolts,
Singe my white head! And thou, all-shaking thunder,
Strike flat the thick rotundity o' th' world,

Crack Nature's moulds, all germains spill at once,
That make ingrateful man! . . .
Rumble thy bellyful! Spit, fire! spout, rain!
Nor rain, wind, thunder, fire are my daughters.
I tax not you, you elements, with unkindness.
I never gave you kingdom, call'd you children,
You owe me no subscription. Then let fall
Your horrible pleasure. Here I stand your slave,
A poor, infirm, weak, and despis'd old man.
But yet I call you servile ministers,
That will with two pernicious daughters join
Your high-engender'd battles 'gainst a head
So old and white as this! O! O! 'tis foul! [III, 2

There was never yet fair woman but she made mouths in
  a glass. [III, 2

   I am a man
More sinn'd against than sinning. [III, 2

O, that way madness lies; let me shun that! [III, 4

 LEAR. Poor naked wretches, wheresoe'er you are,
That bide the pelting of this pitiless storm,
How shall your houseless heads and unfed sides,
Your loop'd and window'd raggedness, defend you
From seasons such as these? O, I have ta'en
Too little care of this! Take physic, pomp;
Expose thyself to feel what wretches feel,
That thou mayest shake the superflux to them
And show the heavens more just. [III, 4

 EDGAR. This is the foul fiend Flibbertigibbet. He begins at curfew, and walks till the first cock. He gives the
web and the pin, squints the eye, and makes the harelip;

mildews the white wheat, and hurts the poor creature of
earth.   [III, 4

As flies to wanton boys are we to th' gods.
They kill us for their sport.   [IV, 1

LEAR. Ay, every inch a king! . . . Give me an ounce
of civet, good apothecary, to sweeten my imagination.
                                                [IV, 6

                        Men must endure
Their going hence, even as their coming hither;
Ripeness is all.   [V, 2

The gods are just, and of our pleasant vices
Make instruments to scourge us.   [V, 3

                        Her voice was ever soft,
Gentle, and low—an excellent thing in woman.   [V, 3

Vex not his ghost. O, let him pass! He hates him
That would upon the rack of this tough world
Stretch him out longer.   [V, 3

From *The Two Gentlemen of Verona*

I have no other but a woman's reason:
I think him so because I think him so.   [*Act.* I, *sc.* 2

They do not love that do not show their love.   [I, 2

O, they love least that let men know their love. [I, 2

O, how this spring of love resembleth
   The uncertain glory of an April day,
Which now shows all the beauty of the sun,
   And by-and-by a cloud takes all away!   [I, 3

   VALENTINE. Win her with gifts, if she respect not
     words.
Dumb jewels often in their silent kind
More than quick words do move a woman's mind.
   DUKE. But she did scorn a present that I sent her.
   VAL. A woman sometime scorns what best contents
     her.
Send her another! Never give her o'er,
For scorn at first makes after-love the more.
If she do frown, 'tis not in hate of you,
But rather to beget more love in you.
If she do chide, 'tis not to have you gone,
For why, the fools are mad if left alone.
Take no repulse, whatever she doth say;
For 'Get you gone!' she doth not mean 'Away!'
Flatter and praise, commend, extol their graces;
Though ne'er so black, say they have angels' faces.
That man that hath a tongue, I say is no man
If with his tongue he cannot win a woman.   [III, 1

To make a virtue of necessity.   [IV, 1

How use doth breed a habit in a man!   [V, 4

From *Measure for Measure*

      Our doubts are traitors
And make us lose the good we oft might win
By fearing to attempt.   [*Act.* I, *sc.* 4

'Tis one thing to be tempted, Escalus,
Another thing to fall. I not deny
The jury, passing on the prisoner's life,
May in the sworn twelve have a thief or two
Guiltier than him they try.   [II, 1

Well, heaven forgive him, and forgive us all!
Some rise by sin, and some by virtue fall.   [II, 1

Condemn the fault, and not the actor of it?   [II, 2

ISABELLA.   O, it is excellent
To have a giant's strength; but it is tyrannous
To use it like a giant. . . .
                    Could great men thunder
As Jove himself does, Jove would ne'er be quiet,
For every pelting petty officer
Would use his heaven for thunder—nothing but thunder!
Merciful heaven,
Thou rather with thy sharp and sulphurous bolt
Split'st the unwedgeable and gnarled oak
Than the soft myrtle. But man, proud man,
Drest in a little brief authority,
Most ignorant of what he's most assur'd
(His glassy essence), like an angry ape,
Plays such fantastic tricks before high heaven
As make the angels weep; who, with our spleens,
Would all themselves laugh mortal. . . .
Great men may jest with saints. 'Tis wit in them,
But in the less, foul profanation. . . .
That in the captain 's but a choleric word
Which in the soldier is flat blasphemy.   [II, 2

The miserable have no other medicine
But only hope.   [III, 1

The sense of death is most in apprehension,
And the poor beetle that we tread upon,
In corporal sufferance finds a pang as great
As when a giant dies.   [III, 1

              If I must die
I will encounter darkness as a bride
And hug it in mine arms.   [III, 1

    CLAUDIO. Ay, but to die, and go we know not where;
To lie in cold obstruction and to rot;
This sensible warm motion to become
A kneaded clod; and the delighted spirit
To bathe in fiery floods, or to reside
In thrilling region of thick-ribbed ice,
To be imprison'd in the viewless winds
And blown with restless violence round about
The pendent world; or to be worse than worst
Of those that lawless and incertain thought
Imagines howling! 'Tis too horrible!
The weariest and most loathed worldly life
That age, ache, penury, and imprisonment
Can lay on nature is a paradise
To what we fear of death.   [III, 1

            Truth is truth
To the end of reckoning.   [V, 1

From *Much Ado About Nothing*

    He wears his faith but as the fashion of his hat; it ever
changes with the next block   [*Act* I, *sc.* 1

Speak low if you speak love.   [II, 1

Lord, I could not endure a husband with a beard on
his face. I had rather lie in the woollen!   [II, 1

Friendship is constant in all other things
Save in the office and affairs of love.
Therefore all hearts in love use their own tongues;
Let every eye negotiate for itself
And trust no agent.   [II, 1

He hath a heart as sound as a bell; and his tongue is
the clapper, for what his heart thinks, his tongue speaks.
                                                      [III, 2

Every one can master a grief but he that has it.   [III, 2

                       For it so falls out
That what we have we prize not to the worth
Whiles we enjoy it, but being lack'd and lost,
Why, then we rack the value, then we find
The virtue that possession would not show us
Whiles it was ours.   [IV, 1

LEONATO.   I pray thee cease thy counsel,
Which falls into mine ears as profitless
As water in a sieve. Give not me counsel,
Nor let no comforter delight mine ear
But such a one whose wrongs do suit with mine. . . .
If such a one will smile and stroke his beard,
Bid sorrow wag, cry 'hem' when he should groan,
Patch grief with proverbs, make misfortune drunk
With candle-wasters—bring him yet to me,
And I of him will gather patience.
But there is no such man; for, brother, men
Can counsel and speak comfort to that grief
Which they themselves not feel; but, tasting it,

Their counsel turns to passion, which before
Would give preceptial medicine to rage,
Fetter strong madness in a silken thread,
Charm ache with air and agony with words.
No, no! 'Tis all men's office to speak patience
To those that wring under the load of sorrow,
But no man's virtue nor sufficiency
To be so moral when he shall endure
The like himself. Therefore give me no counsel.
My griefs cry louder than advertisement. . . .
I pray thee peace. I will be flesh and blood;
For there was never yet philosopher
That could endure the toothache patiently,
However they have writ the style of gods
And made a push at chance and sufferance.   [V, 1

From *Love's Labour's Lost*

At Christmas I no more desire a rose
Than wish a snow in May's newfangled shows,
But like of each thing that in season grows.   [*Act* I, *sc.* 1

A child of our grandmother Eve, a female, or, for thy
more sweet understanding, a woman.   [I, 1

Remuneration—O, that's the Latin word for three
farthings.   [III, 1

Sir, he hath never fed of the dainties that are bred in
a book. He hath not eat paper, as it were; he hath not

drunk ink. His intellect is not replenished; he is only an
animal, only sensible to the duller parts.   [IV, 2

BEROWNE. A lover's eyes will gaze an eagle blind.
A lover's ear will hear the lowest sound
When the suspicious head of theft is stopp'd.
Love's feeling is more soft and sensible
Than are the tender horns of cockled snails.
Love's tongue proves dainty Bacchus gross in taste.
For valour, is not Love a Hercules,
Still climbing trees in the Hesperides?
Subtle as Sphinx; as sweet and musical
As bright Apollo's lute, strung with his hair.
And when Love speaks, the voice of all the gods
Make heaven drowsy with the harmony.
Never durst poet touch a pen to write
Until his ink were temp'red with Love's sighs.
O, then his lines would ravish savage ears
And plant in tyrants mild humility.
From women's eyes this doctrine I derive.
They sparkle still the right Promethean fire;
They are the books, the arts, the academes,
That show, contain, and nourish all the world.
Else none at all in aught proves excellent.   [IV, 3

He draweth out the thread of his verbosity finer than
the staple of his argument.   [V, 1

They have been at a great feast of languages and
stolen the scraps.   [V, 1

A jest's prosperity lies in the ear
Of him that hears it, never in the tongue
Of him that makes it.   [V, 2

From *All's Well That Ends Well*

> Love all, trust a few,
> Do wrong to none. Be able for thine enemy
> Rather in power than use, and keep thy friend
> Under thy own life's key. Be check'd for silence
> But never tax'd for speech.   [*Act* I, *sc.* 1

HELENA.   'Twere all one
That I should love a bright particular star
And think to wed it, he is so above me.
In his bright radiance and collateral light
Must I be comforted, not in his sphere.
Th' ambition in my love thus plagues itself.
The hind that would be mated by the lion
Must die for love. . . .
Our remedies oft in ourselves do lie,
Which we ascribe to heaven. The fated sky
Gives us free scope; only doth backward pull
Our slow designs when we ourselves are dull.
What power is it which mounts my love so high?
That makes me see, and cannot feed mine eye?
The mightiest space in fortune nature brings
To join like likes and kiss like native things.
Impossible be strange attempts to those
That weigh their pains in sense, and do suppose
What hath been cannot be. Who ever strove
To show her merit that did miss her love?   [I, 1

I am driven on by the flesh; and he must needs go that
the devil drives.   [I, 3

Oft expectation fails, and most oft there
Where most it promises; and oft it hits
Where hope is coldest and despair most fits.   [II, 1

A young man married is a man that's marr'd.   [II, 3

To make the coming hour o'erflow with joy
And pleasure drown the brim.   [II, 4

I am a man whom Fortune hath cruelly scratch'd.   [V, 2

           Praising what is lost
Makes the remembrance dear.   [V, 3

For we are old, and on our quick'st decrees
Th' inaudible and noiseless foot of time
Steals, ere we can effect them.   [V, 3

           Love that comes too late,
Like a remorseful pardon slowly carried,
To the great sender turns a sour offence.   [V, 3

From *The Winter's Tale*

           One good deed dying tongueless
Slaughters a thousand waiting upon that.   [*Act.* I, *sc.* 2

A sad tale's best for winter.   [II, 1

           There's some ill planet reigns
I must be patient till the heavens look
With an aspect more favourable.   [II, 1

I am a feather for each wind that blows [II, 3

A snapper-up of unconsidered trifles. [IV, 3

PERDITA. Reverend sirs,
For you there's rosemary and rue; these keep
Seeming and savour all the winter long.
. . . Here's flow'rs for you:
Hot lavender, mints, savory, marjoram;
The marigold, that goes to bed wi' th' sun
And with him rises weeping. These are flowers
Of middle summer, and I think they are given
To men of middle age.
. . . Now, my fair'st friend,
I would I had some flow'rs o' th' spring that might
Become your time of day. . . .
. . . Daffodils
That come before the swallow dares and take
The winds of March with beauty; violets—dim,
But sweeter than the lids of Juno's eyes
Or Cytherea's breath; pale primeroses,
That die unmarried ere they can behold
Bright Phœbus in his strength (a malady
Most incident to maids); bold oxlips and
The crown imperial; lilies of all kinds,
The flow'r-de-luce being one! [IV, 4

From *King John*

Heaven lay not my transgression to my charge!
[*Act* I, *sc.* 1

Courage mounteth with occasion. [II, 1

I will instruct my sorrows to be proud,
For grief is proud, and makes his owner stoop. [III, 1

I had a thing to say,
But I will fit it with some better time. [III, 3

CONSTANCE. Grief fills the room up of my absent child:
Lies in his bed, walks up and down with me,
Puts on his pretty looks, repeats his words,
Remembers me of all his gracious parts,
Stuffs out his vacant garments with his form.
Then have I reason to be fond of grief?
Fare you well. Had you such a loss as I,
I could give better comfort than you do. [III, 4

Life is as tedious as a twice-told tale
Vexing the dull ear of a drowsy man. [III, 4

To guard a title that was rich before,
To gild refined gold, to paint the lily,
To throw a perfume on the violet,
To smooth the ice, or add another hue
Unto the rainbow, or with taper light
To seek the beauteous eye of heaven to garnish,
Is wasteful and ridiculous excess. [IV, 2

And oftentimes excusing of a fault
Doth make the fault the worse by the excuse. [IV, 2

How oft the sight of means to do ill deeds
Make deeds ill done! [IV, 2

The day shall not be up so soon as I
To try the fair adventure of to-morrow. [V, 5

This England never did, nor never shall,
Lie at the proud foot of a conqueror
But when it first did help to wound itself.
Now these her princes are come home again,
Come the three corners of the world in arms,
And we shall shock them. Naught shall make us rue
If England to itself do rest but true.   [V, 7

From *Richard the Second*

MOWBRAY. The purest treasure mortal times afford
Is spotless reputation. That away,
Men are but gilded loam or painted clay.
A jewel in a ten times barr'd-up chest
Is a bold spirit in a loyal breast.
Mine honour is my life. Both grow in one;
Take honour from me, and my life is done.   [*Act* I, *sc.* 1

JOHN OF GAUNT. All places that the eye of heaven
        visits
Are to a wise man ports and happy havens.
Teach thy necessity to reason thus:
There is no virtue like necessity. . . .
    BOLINGBROKE. O, who can hold a fire in his hand
By thinking on the frosty Caucasus?
Or cloy the hungry edge of appetite
By bare imagination of a feast?
Or wallow naked in December snow
By thinking on fantastic summer's heat?
O, no! The apprehension of the good
Gives but the greater feeling to the worse.
Fell sorrow's tooth doth never rankle more
Than when he bites, but lanceth not the sore.   [I, 4

JOHN OF GAUNT. Methinks I am a prophet new inspir'd
And thus, expiring, do foretell of him:
His rash fierce blaze of riot cannot last,
For violent fires soon burn out themselves;
Small show'rs last long, but sudden storms are short;
He tires betimes that spurs too fast betimes;
With eager feeding food doth choke the feeder;
Light vanity, insatiate cormorant,
Consuming means, soon preys upon itself.
This royal throne of kings, this scept'red isle,
This earth of majesty, this seat of Mars,
This other Eden, demi-paradise,
This fortress built by Nature for herself
Against infection and the hand of war,
This happy breed of men, this little world,
This precious stone set in the silver sea,
Which serves it in the office of a wall,
Or as a moat defensive to a house,
Against the envy of less happier lands;
This blessed plot, this earth, this realm, this England,
This nurse, this teeming womb of royal kings,
Fear'd by their breed and famous by their birth,
Renowned for their deeds as far from home,
For Christian service and true chivalry,
As is the sepulchre in stubborn Jewry
Of the world's ransom, blessed Mary's son;
This land of such dear souls, this dear dear land,
Dear for her reputation through the world,
Is now leas'd out (I die pronouncing it)
Like to a tenement or pelting farm.
England, bound in with the triumphant sea,
Whose rocky shore beats back the envious siege
Of wat'ry Neptune, is now bound in with shame,
With inky blots and rotten parchment bonds.
That England that was wont to conquer others

Hath made a shameful conquest of itself.
Ah, would the scandal vanish with my life,
How happy then were my ensuing death!   [II, 1

The caterpillars of the commonwealth,
Which I have sworn to weed and pluck away.   [II, 3

SALISBURY. Ah, Richard! with the eyes of heavy mind,
I see thy glory, like a shooting star,
Fall to the base earth from the firmament.
Thy sun sets weeping in the lowly West,
Witnessing storms to come, woe, and unrest;
Thy friends are fled to wait upon thy foes,
And crossly to thy good all fortune goes.   [II, 4

Eating the bitter bread of banishment.   [III, 1

Not all the water in the rough rude sea
Can wash the balm off from an anointed king.   [III, 2

O, call back yesterday, bid time return.   [III, 2

KING RICHARD.   Of comfort no man speak!
Let's talk of graves, of worms, and epitaphs,
Make dust our paper, and with rainy eyes
Write sorrow on the bosom of the earth.
Let's choose executors and talk of wills.
And yet not so—for what can we bequeath,
Save our deposed bodies to the ground?
Our lands, our lives, and all are Bolingbroke's,
And nothing can we call our own but death
And that small model of the barren earth
Which serves as paste and cover to our bones.
For God's sake let us sit upon the ground
And tell sad stories of the death of kings!

How some have been depos'd, some slain in war,
Some haunted by the ghosts they have depos'd,
Some poisoned by their wives, some sleeping kill'd—
All murdered; for within the hollow crown
That rounds the mortal temples of a king
Keeps Death his court; and there the antic sits,
Scoffing his state and grinning at his pomp;
Allowing him a breath, a little scene,
To monarchize, be fear'd, and kill with looks;
Infusing him with self and vain conceit,
As if this flesh which walls about our life
Were brass impregnable; and humour'd thus,
Comes at the last, and with a little pin
Bores through his castle wall, and farewell king!
Cover your heads, and mock not flesh and blood
With solemn reverence. Throw away respect,
Tradition, form, and ceremonious duty;
For you have but mistook me all this while.
I live with bread like you, feel want, taste grief,
Need friends. Subjected thus,
How can you say to me I am a king?   [III, 2

KING RICHARD.   I'll read enough
When I do see the very book indeed
Where all my sins are writ, and that's myself.

[Enter one with a glass.]

Give me the glass, and therein will I read.
No deeper wrinkles yet? Hath sorrow struck
So many blows upon this face of mine
And made no deeper wounds? O flattering glass,
Like to my followers in prosperity,
Thou dost beguile me! Was this face the face
That every day under his household roof
Did keep ten thousand men? Was this the face

That like the sun did make beholders wink?
Was this the face that fac'd so many follies
And was at last outfac'd by Bolingbroke?
A brittle glory shineth in this face.
As brittle as the glory is the face,

                [Dashes the glass to the floor.]
For there it is, crack'd in a hundred shivers.
Mark, silent king, the moral of this sport—
How soon my sorrow hath destroy'd my face.   [IV, 1

As in a theatre the eyes of men,
After a well-grac'd actor leaves the stage,
Are idly bent on him that enters next,
Thinking his prattle to be tedious,
Even so, or with much more contempt, men's eyes
Did scowl on gentle Richard.   [V, 2

From *The Merry Wives of Windsor*

Here will be an old abusing of God's patience and the
king's English.   *Act* I, *sc.* 4

Why, then the world's mine oyster,
Which I with sword will open   [II, 2

O, what a world of vile ill-favour'd faults
Looks handsome in three hundred pounds a year! [III, 4

A kind heart he hath. A woman would run through fire
and water for such a kind heart.   [III, 4

FALSTAFF. Go fetch me a quart of sack; put a toast in't. Have I liv'd to be carried in a basket like a barrow of butcher's offal? and to be thrown in the Thames? Well, if I be serv'd such another trick, I'll have my brains ta'en out and butter'd, and give them to a dog for a new-year's gift. 'Sblood! The rogues slighted me into the river with as little remorse as they would have drown'd a blind bitch's puppies, fifteen i' th' litter. And you may know by my size that I have a kind of alacrity in sinking. If the bottom were as deep as hell, I should down. I had been drown'd but that the shore was shelvy and shallow—a death that I abhor; for the water swells a man, and what a thing should I have been when I had been swell'd! I should have been a mountain of mummy.   [III, 5

They say there is divinity in odd numbers, either in nativity, chance, or death.   [V, 1

From *Henry the Fourth*

PART ONE

KING. So shaken as we are, so wan with care,
Find we a time for frighted peace to pant
And breathe short-winded accents of new broils
To be commenc'd in stronds afar remote.
No more the thirsty entrance of this soil
Shall daub her lips with her own children's blood.
No more shall trenching war channel her fields,
Nor bruise her flow'rets with the armed hoofs
Of hostile paces Those opposed eyes
Which, like the meteors of a troubled heaven,
All of one nature, of one substance bred,
Did lately meet in the intestine shock
And furious close of civil butchery,

Shall now in mutual well-beseeming ranks
March all one way and be no more oppos'd
Against acquaintance, kindred, and allies.
The edge of war, like an ill-sheathed knife,
No more shall cut his master. Therefore, friends,
As far as to the sepulchre of Christ—
Whose soldier now, under whose blessed cross
We are impressed and engag'd to fight—
Forthwith a power of English shall we levy,
Whose arms were moulded in their mother's womb
To chase these pagans in those holy fields
Over whose acres walk'd those blessed feet
Which fourteen hundred years ago were nail'd
For our advantage on the bitter cross.   [*Act* I, *sc.* 1

FALSTAFF. Now, Hal, what time of day is it, lad?

PRINCE OF WALES. Thou art so fat with drinking of old
sack, and unbuttoning thee after supper, and sleeping
upon benches after noon, that thou hast forgotten to demand that truly which thou wouldest truly know. What
a devil hast thou to do with the time of the day? Unless
hours were cups of sack, and minutes capons, and clocks
the tongues of bawds, and dials the signs of leaping
houses, and the blessed sun himself a fair hot wench in
flame-coloured taffeta, I see no reason why thou shouldst
be so superfluous to demand the time of the day.

FAL. Indeed you come near me now, Hal; for we that
take purses go by the moon and the seven stars, and not
by Phœbus, he, that wandering knight so fair. And I
prithee, sweet wag, when thou art king, as, God save thy
Grace—Majesty I should say for grace thou wilt have
none—

PRINCE. What, none?

FAL. No, by my troth; not so much as will serve to be
prologue to an egg and butter.

PRINCE. Well, how then? Come, roundly, roundly.

FAL. Marry, then, sweet wag, when thou art king, let not us that are squires of the night's body be called thieves of the day's beauty. Let us be Diana's Foresters, Gentlemen of the Shade, Minions of the Moon; and let men say we be men of good government, being governed as the sea is, by our noble and chaste mistress the moon, under whose countenance we steal. . . . 'Sblood, I am as melancholy as a gib-cat or a lugged bear.

PRINCE. Or an old lion, or a lover's lute.

FAL. Yea, or the drone of a Lincolnshire bagpipe.

PRINCE. What sayest thou to a hare, or the melancholy of Moor Ditch?

FAL. Thou hast the most unsavoury similes, and art indeed the most comparative, rascalliest, sweet young prince. But, Hal, I prithee trouble me no more with vanity. I would to God thou and I knew where a commodity of good names were to be bought. An old lord of the Council rated me the other day in the street about you, sir, but I marked him not; and yet he talked very wisely, but I regarded him not; and yet he talked wisely, and in the street too.

PRINCE. Thou didst well; for wisdom cries out in the streets, and no man regards it

FAL. O, thou hast damnable iteration, and art indeed able to corrupt a saint. Thou hast done much harm upon me, Hal—God forgive thee for it! Before I knew thee, Hal, I knew nothing; and now am I, if a man should speak truly, little better than one of the wicked. I must give over this life, and I will give it over! By the Lord, an I do not, I am a villain! I'll be damned for never a king's son in Christendom.   [I, 2

If all the year were playing holidays,
To sport would be as tedious as to work.   [I, 2

You tread upon my patience. [I, 3

HOTSPUR. My liege, I did deny no prisoners.
But I remember, when the fight was done,
When I was dry with rage and extreme toil,
Breathless and faint, leaning upon my sword,
Came there a certain lord, neat and trimly dress'd,
Fresh as a bridegroom; and his chin new reap'd
Show'd like a stubble land at harvest home.
He was perfumed like a milliner,
And 'twixt his finger and his thumb he held
A pouncet box, which ever and anon
He gave his nose, and took't away again;
Who therewith angry, when it next came there,
Took it in snuff; and still he smil'd and talk'd;
And as the soldiers bore dead bodies by,
He call'd them untaught knaves, unmannerly,
To bring a slovenly unhandsome corse
Betwixt the wind and his nobility.
With many holiday and lady terms
He questioned me, amongst the rest demanded
My prisoners in your Majesty's behalf.
I then, all smarting with my wounds being cold,
To be so pest'red with a popingay,
Out of my grief and my impatience
Answer'd neglectingly, I know not what—
He should, or he should not; for he made me mad
To see him shine so brisk, and smell so sweet,
And talk so like a waiting gentlewoman
Of guns and drums and wounds—God save the mark!—
And telling me the sovereignest thing on earth
Was parmaceti for an inward bruise;
And that it was great pity, so it was,
This villanous saltpetre should be digg'd
Out of the bowels of the harmless earth,

Which many a good tall fellow had destroy'd
So cowardly; and but for these vile guns,
He would himself have been a soldier.
This bald unjointed chat of his, my lord,
I answered indirectly, as I said,
And I beseech you, let not his report
Come current for an accusation
Betwixt my love and your high majesty.   [I, 3

    HOTSPUR. By heaven, methinks it were an easy leap
To pluck bright honour from the pale-fac'd moon,
Or dive into the bottom of the deep,
Where fathom line could never touch the ground,
And pluck up drowned honour by the locks,
So he that doth redeem her thence might wear
Without corrival all her dignities;
But out upon this half-fac'd fellowship!   [I, 3

               Falstaff sweats to death,
And lards the lean earth as he walks along.   [II, 2

Out of this nettle, danger, we pluck this flower, safety.
                                   [II, 3

A plague of all cowards, I say.   [II, 4

    There lives not three good men unhang'd in England;
and one of them is fat, and grows old.   [II, 4

Banish plump Jack, and banish all the world.   [II, 4

    GLENDOWER. I can call spirits from the vasty deep.
    HOTSPUR. Why, so can I, or so can any man;
But will they come when you do call for them?   [III, 1

Tell truth and shame the devil.   [III, 1

HOTSPUR. I had rather be a kitten and cry mew
Than one of these same metre ballet-mongers.
I had rather hear a brazen canstick turn'd
Or a dry wheel grate on the axletree,
And that would set my teeth nothing on edge,
Nothing so much as mincing poetry.
'Tis like the forc'd gait of a shuffling nag.   [III, 1

FALSTAFF. Bardolph, am I not fallen away vilely since
this last action? Do I not bate? Do I not dwindle? Why,
my skin hangs about me like an old lady's loose gown! I
am withered like an old apple John. Well, I'll repent,
and that suddenly, while I am in some liking. I shall be
out of heart shortly, and then I shall have no strength to
repent. An I have not forgotten what the inside of a
church is made of, I am a peppercorn, a brewer's horse.
The inside of a church! Company, villanous company,
hath been the spoil of me.   [III, 3

Zounds! how has he the leisure to be sick
In such a justling time? . . .
                              This sickness doth infect
The very lifeblood of our enterprise.   [IV, 1

          I could be well content
To entertain the lag-end of my life
With quiet hours.   [V, 1

PRINCE. Why, thou owest God a death.   *Exit.*
FALSTAFF. 'Tis not due yet. I would be loath to pay
him before his day. What need I be so forward with him
that calls not on me? Well, 'tis no matter; honour pricks
me on. Yea, but how if honour prick me off when I come
on? How then? Can honour set to a leg? No. Or an arm?
No. Or take away the grief of a wound? No. Honour

hath no skill in surgery then? No. What is honour? A word. What is that word honour? Air. A trim reckoning! Who hath it? He that died a Wednesday. Doth he feel it? No. Doth he hear it? No. 'Tis insensible then? Yea, to the dead. But will it not live with the living? No. Why? Detraction will not suffer it. Therefore I'll none of it. Honour is a mere scutcheon—and so ends my catechism.   [V, 1

The time of life is short!
To spend that shortness basely were too long
If life did ride upon a dial's point,
Still ending at the arrival of an hour.   [V, 2

Adieu, and take thy praise with thee to heaven!
Thy ignominy sleep with thee in the grave,
But not rememb'red in thy epitaph!   [V, 2

PRINCE. What, old acquaintance? Could not all this flesh
Keep in a little life? Poor Jack, farewell!
I could have better spared a better man.   *Exit.*
FALSTAFF. . . . The better part of valour is discretion.   [V, 2

From *Henry the Fourth*

PART TWO

KING. How many thousand of my poorest subjects
Are at this hour asleep! O sleep, O gentle sleep!
Nature's soft nurse, how have I frighted thee,
That thou no more wilt weigh my eyelids down
And steep my senses in forgetfulness?

Why rather, sleep, liest thou in smoky cribs,
Upon uneasy pallets stretching thee,
And hush'd with buzzing night-flies to thy slumber,
Than in the perfum'd chambers of the great,
Under the canopies of costly state,
And lull'd with sound of sweetest melody?
O thou dull god, why liest thou with the vile
In loathsome beds, and leav'st the kingly couch
A watchcase or a common 'larum-bell?
Wilt thou upon the high and giddy mast
Seel up the shipboy's eyes, and rock his brains
In cradle of the rude imperious surge,
And in the visitation of the winds,
Who take the ruffian billows by the top,
Curling their monstrous heads, and hanging them
With deaf'ning clamour in the slippery clouds,
That with the hurly death itself awakes?
Canst thou, O partial sleep, give thy repose
To the wet seaboy in an hour so rude,
And in the calmest and most stillest night,
With all appliances and means to boot,
Deny it to a king? Then, happy low, lie down!
Uneasy lies the head that wears a crown.　　[*Act* III, *sc.* 1

A man can die but once; we owe God a death.　　[III, 2

KING. And wherefore should these good news make
　　me sick?
Will Fortune never come with both hands full,
But write her fair words still in foulest letters?
She either gives a stomach, and no food
(Such are the poor, in health), or else a feast,
And takes away the stomach—such are the rich
That have abundance and enjoy it not.　　[IV, 4

A foutra for the world and worldlings base!
I speak of Africa and golden joys.   [V, 3

Under which king, Besonian? Speak, or die!   [V, 3

How ill white hairs become a fool and jester!   [V, 5

From *Henry the Fifth*

HOSTESS. [*of Falstaff*] Nay sure, he's not in hell! He's
in Arthur's bosom, if ever man went to Arthur's bosom.
'A made a finer end, and went away an it had been any
christom child. 'A parted ev'n just between twelve and
one, ev'n at the turning o' th' tide. For after I saw him
fumble with the sheets, and play with flowers, and smile
upon his fingers' ends, I knew there was but one way; for
his nose was as sharp as a pen, and 'a babbled of green
fields. 'How now, Sir John?' quoth I. 'What, man? be o'
good cheer.' So 'a cried out 'God, God, God!' three or
four times. Now I, to comfort him, bid him 'a should not
think of God; I hop'd there was no need to trouble himself with any such thoughts yet. So 'a bade me lay more
clothes on his feet. I put my hand into the bed and felt
them, and they were as cold as any stone. Then I felt to
his knees, and so upward and upward, and all was as cold
as any stone.

NYM. They say he cried out of sack.

HOSTESS. Ay, that 'a did.

BARDOLPH. And of women.

HOSTESS. Nay, that 'a did not.

BOY. Yes, that 'a did, and said they were devils incar-
nate.

HOSTESS. 'A could never abide carnation; 'twas a colour
he never liked.   [*Act* II, *sc.* 3

KING. Once more unto the breach, dear friends, once
    more;
Or close the wall up with our English dead!
In peace there's nothing so becomes a man
As modest stillness and humility;
But when the blast of war blows in our ears,
Then imitate the action of the tiger:
Stiffen the sinews, summon up the blood,
Disguise fair nature with hard-favour'd rage;
Then lend the eye a terrible aspect;
Let it pry through the portage of the head
Like the brass cannon; let the brow o'erwhelm it
As fearfully as doth a galled rock
O'erhang and jutty his confounded base,
Swill'd with the wild and wasteful ocean.
Now set the teeth and stretch the nostril wide,
Hold hard the breath and bend up every spirit
To his full height! On, on, you noble English,
Whose blood is fet from fathers of war-proof!
Fathers that like so many Alexanders
Have in these parts from morn till even fought,
And sheath'd their swords for lack of argument.
Dishonour not your mothers; now attest
That those whom you call'd fathers did beget you!
Be copy now to men of grosser blood
And teach them how to war! And you, good yeomen,
Whose limbs were made in England, show us here
The mettle of your pasture. Let us swear
That you are worth your breeding; which I doubt not,
For there is none of you so mean and base
That hath not noble lustre in your eyes.
I see you stand like greyhounds in the slips,
Straining upon the start. The game's afoot!
Follow your spirit; and upon this charge
Cry 'God for Harry! England and Saint George!'   [III, 1

From *Henry the Sixth*

PART ONE

Glory is like a circle in the water,
Which never ceaseth to enlarge itself
Till by broad spreading it disperse to naught. [*Act* I, *sc.* 2

WARWICK. Between two hawks, which flies the higher
   pitch—
Between two dogs, which hath the deeper mouth—
Between two blades, which bears the better temper—
Between two horses, which doth bear him best—
Between two girls, which hath the merriest eye—
I have perhaps some shallow spirit of judgment;
But in these nice sharp quillets of the law,
Good faith, I am no wiser than a daw.   [II, 4

She's beautiful, and therefore to be woo'd;
She is a woman, therefore to be won.   [V, 3

From *Henry the Sixth*

PART TWO

KING. What stronger breastplate than a heart un-
   tainted?
Thrice is he arm'd that hath his quarrel just,
And he but naked, though lock'd up in steel,
Whose conscience with injustice is corrupted.   [III, 2

DICK BUTCHER. The first thing we do, let's kill all the
lawyers.

JACK CADE Nay, that I mean to do. Is not this a
lamentable thing, that of the skin of an innocent lamb

should be made parchment? that parchment, being
scribbled o'er, should undo a man? Some say the bee
stings; but I say 'tis the bee's wax; for I did but seal once
to a thing, and I was never mine own man since.   [IV, 2

JACK CADE. What canst thou answer to my Majesty for
giving up of Normandy unto Mounsieur Basimecu, the
Dauphin of France? Be it known unto thee by these presence, even the presence of Lord Mortimer, that I am the
besom that must sweep the court clean of such filth as
thou art. Thou hast most traitorously corrupted the youth
of the realm in erecting a grammar school; and whereas,
before, our forefathers had no other books but the score
and the tally, thou hast caused printing to be used, and,
contrary to the King, his crown and dignity, thou hast
built a paper mill. It will be proved to thy face that thou
hast men about thee that usually talk of a noun and a
verb and such abominable words as no Christian ear can
endure to hear. Thou hast appointed justices of peace, to
call poor men before them about matters they were not
able to answer. Moreover, thou hast put them in prison,
and because they could not read, thou hast hanged them,
when, indeed, only for that cause they have been most
worthy to live.   [IV, 7

From *Henry the Sixth*

PART THREE

But Hercules himself must yield to odds;
And many strokes, though with a little axe,
Hews down and fells the hardest-timber'd oak.   [II, 1

The smallest worm will turn, being trodden on.   [II, 2

RICHARD. Why, then I do but dream on sovereignty,
Like one that stands upon a promontory
And spies a far-off shore where he would tread,
Wishing his foot were equal with his eye,
And chides the sea that sunders him from thence,
Saying he'll lade it dry to have his way:
So do I wish the crown, being so far off;
And so I chide the means that keeps me from it,
And so, I say, I'll cut the causes off,
Flattering me with impossibilities.
My eye's too quick, my heart o'erweens too much,
Unless my hand and strength could equal them. . . .
Why, I can smile, and murder whiles I smile,
And cry 'Content!' to that which grieves my heart,
And wet my cheeks with artificial tears,
And frame my face to all occasions.
I'll drown more sailors than the mermaid shall;
I'll slay more gazers than the basilisk;
I'll play the orator as well as Nestor,
Deceive more slily than Ulysses could,
And, like a Sinon, take another Troy.
I can add colours to the chameleon,
Change shapes with Proteus for advantages,
And set the murderous Machiavel to school.
Can I do this, and cannot get a crown?
Tut, were it farther off, I'll pluck it down.   [III, 2

From *Richard the Third*

RICHARD. Now is the winter of our discontent
Made glorious summer by this sun of York,
And all the clouds that low'rd upon our house

In the deep bosom of the ocean buried.
Now are our brows bound with victorious wreaths,
Our bruised arms hung up for monuments,
Our stern alarums chang'd to merry meetings,
Our dreadful marches to delightful measures.
Grim-visag'd War hath smooth'd his wrinkled front,
And now, instead of mounting barbed steeds
To fright the souls of fearful adversaries,
He capers nimbly in a lady's chamber
To the lascivious pleasing of a lute.
But I, that am not shap'd for sportive tricks
Nor made to court an amorous looking glass;
I, that am rudely stamp'd, and want love's majesty
To strut before a wanton ambling nymph;
I, that am curtail'd of this fair proportion,
Cheated of feature by dissembling Nature,
Deform'd, unfinish'd, sent before my time
Into this breathing world, scarce half made up,
And that so lamely and unfashionable
That dogs bark at me as I halt by them—
Why, I, in this weak piping time of peace,
Have no delight to pass away the time,
Unless to see my shadow in the sun
And descant on mine own deformity.
And therefore, since I cannot prove a lover
To entertain these fair well-spoken days,
I am determined to prove a villain
And hate the idle pleasures of these days.   [*Act* I, *sc.* 1

His better doth not breathe upon the earth.   [I, 2

Look how my ring encompasseth thy finger,
Even so thy breast encloseth my poor heart.
Wear both of them, for both of them are thine.   [I, 2

Was ever woman in this humour woo'd?
Was ever woman in this humour won? [I, 2

A sweeter and a lovelier gentleman—
Fram'd in the prodigality of nature,
Young, valiant, wise, and (no doubt) right royal—
The spacious world cannot again afford. [I, 2

And thus I clothe my naked villany
With odd old ends stol'n forth of holy writ,
And seem a saint when most I play the devil. [I, 3

Thou art a widow; yet thou art a mother
And hast the comfort of thy children left. [II, 2

The tyrannous and bloody act is done,
The most arch deed of piteous massacre
That ever yet this land was guilty of. . . .
Their lips were four red roses on a stalk,
And in their summer beauty kiss'd each other. [IV, 3

True hope is swift and flies with swallow's wings;
Kings it makes gods, and meaner creatures kings. [V, 2

RICHARD. Give me another horse! Bind up my wounds!
Have mercy, Jesu! Soft! I did but dream.
O coward conscience, how dost thou afflict me!
The lights burn blue. It is now dead midnight.
Cold fearful drops stand on my trembling flesh.
What do I fear? Myself? There's none else by.
Richard loves Richard: that is, I am I.
Is there a murderer here? No. Yes, I am.
Then fly. What, from myself? Great reason why—
Lest I revenge myself upon myself?

Alack, I love myself. Wherefore? For any good
That I myself have done unto myself?
O no! Alas, I rather hate myself
For hateful deeds committed by myself.
I am a villain. Yet I lie, I am not.
Fool, of thyself speak well. Fool, do not flatter.
My conscience hath a thousand several tongues,
And every tongue brings in a several tale,
And every tale condemns me for a villain.
Perjury, perjury, in the high'st degree,
Murder, stern murder, in the dir'st degree,
All several sins, all us'd in each degree,
Throng to the bar, crying all 'Guilty! guilty!'
I shall despair. There is no creature loves me;
And if I die, no soul shall pity me.
Nay, wherefore should they, since that I myself
Find in myself no pity to myself?　　　　　　　[V, 3

A horse! a horse! my kingdom for a horse!　　　[V, 6

From *Henry the Eighth*

Heat not a furnace for your foe so hot
That it do singe yourself.　　　　　　　[*Act* I, *sc.* 1

WOLSEY. Farewell, a long farewell, to all my greatness!
This is the state of man: to-day he puts forth
The tender leaves of hopes; to-morrow blossoms
And bears his blushing honours thick upon him;
The third day comes a frost, a killing frost,
And when he thinks, good easy man, full surely
His greatness is a-ripening, nips his root,

And then he falls, as I do. I have ventur'd,
Like little wanton boys that swim on bladders,
This many summers in a sea of glory;
But far beyond my depth. My high-blown pride
At length broke under me, and now has left me,
Weary and old with service, to the mercy
Of a rude stream that must for ever hide me.
Vain pomp and glory of this world, I hate ye!
I feel my heart new open'd. O, how wretched
Is that poor man that hangs on princes' favours!
There is betwixt that smile we would aspire to,
That sweet aspect of princes, and their ruin
More pangs and fears than wars or women have;
And when he falls, he falls like Lucifer,
Never to hope again. . . .

I know myself now, and I feel within me
A peace above all earthly dignities,
A still and quiet conscience. . . .

Had I but serv'd my God with half the zeal
I serv'd my king, he would not in mine age
Have left me naked to mine enemies.

[III, 2

From *Troilus and Cressida*

CRESSIDA. But you are wise,
Or else you love not; for to be wise and love
Exceeds man's might: that dwells with gods above.
    TROILUS. . . . I am as true as truth's simplicity
And simpler than the infancy of truth.
    CRES. In that I'll war with you.
    TRO. O virtuous fight,
When right with right wars who shall be most right!

True swains in love shall in the world to come
Approve their truth by Troilus. When their rhymes,
Full of protest, of oath, and big compare,
Want similes, truth tir'd with iteration—
'As true as steel, as plantage to the moon,
As sun to day, as turtle to her mate,
As iron to adamant, as earth to th' centre'—
Yet, after all comparisons of truth,
As truth's authentic author to be cited,
'As true as Troilus' shall crown up the verse
And sanctify the numbers.

CRES.   Prophet may you be!
If I be false, or swerve a hair from truth,
When time is old and hath forgot itself,
When water drops have worn the stones of Troy,
And blind oblivion swallow'd cities up,
And mighty states characterless are grated
To dusty nothing—yet let memory,
From false to false, among false maids in love,
Upbraid my falsehood! When th' have said 'as false
As air, as water, wind, or sandy earth,
As fox to lamb, or wolf to heifer's calf,
Pard to the hind, or stepdame to her son'—
'Yea,' let them say, to stick the heart of falsehood,
'As false as Cressid.'   [*Act* III, *sc.* 2

ULYSSES. Time hath, my lord, a wallet at his back,
Wherein he puts alms for oblivion. . . .
For Time is like a fashionable host,
That slightly shakes his parting guest by th' hand,
And with his arms outstretch'd as he would fly
Grasps in the comer. The welcome ever smiles,
And farewell goes out sighing. Let not virtue seek
Remuneration for the thing it was!
For beauty, wit,

High birth, vigour of bone, desert in service,
Love, friendship, charity, are subjects all
To envious and calumniating Time.
One touch of nature makes the whole world kin,
That all with one consent praise new-born gauds,
Though they are made and moulded of things past,
And give to dust that is a little gilt
More laud than gilt o'erdusted.   [III, 3

My mind is troubled like a fountain stirr'd,
And I myself see not the bottom of it.   [III, 3

From *Coriolanus*

VOLUMNIA. I pray you, daughter, sing, or express yourself in a more comfortable sort. If my son were my husband, I should freelier rejoice in that absence wherein he
won honour than in the embracements of his bed where
he would show most love. When yet he was but tender-
bodied and the only son of my womb, when youth with
comeliness plucked all gaze his way, when for a day of
kings' entreaties a mother should not sell him an hour
from her beholding, I (considering how honour would
become such a person; that it was no better than picture-
like to hang by the wall, if renown made it not stir) was
pleased to let him seek danger where he was like to find
fame. To a cruel war I sent him, from whence he returned, his brows bound with oak. I tell thee, daughter, I
sprang not more in joy at first hearing he was a man-child
than now in first seeing he had proved himself a man.

VIRGILIA. But had he died in the business, madam,
how then?

VOL. Then his good report should have been my son;

I therein would have found issue. Hear me profess sincerely, had I a dozen sons, each in my love alike, and none less dear than thine and my good Marcius, I had rather had eleven die nobly for their country than one voluptuously surfeit out of action. [*Act* I, *sc.* 3

From *Antony and Cleopatra*

CLEOPATRA.   . . . Did I, Charmian,
Ever love Cæsar so?
CHARMIAN.   O that brave Cæsar!
CLEO. Be chok'd with such another emphasis!
Say 'the brave Antony.'
CHAR.   The valiant Cæsar!
CLEO. By Isis, I will give thee bloody teeth
If thou with Cæsar paragon again
My man of men!
CHAR.   By your most gracious pardon,
I sing but after you.
CLEO.   My salad days,
When I was green in judgment, cold in blood,
To say as I said then.   [*Act* I, *sc.* 5

ENOBARBUS. The barge she sat in, like a burnish'd
    throne,
Burn'd on the water. The poop was beaten gold;
Purple the sails, and so perfumed that
The winds were lovesick with them; the oars were silver,
Which to the tune of flutes kept stroke, and made
The water which they beat to follow faster,
As amorous of their strokes. For her own person,
It beggar'd all description. She did lie

In her pavilion, cloth-of-gold of tissue,
O'erpicturing that Venus where we see
The fancy outwork nature. On each side her
Stood pretty dimpled boys, like smiling Cupids,
With divers-colour'd fans, whose wind did seem
To glow the delicate cheeks which they did cool,
And what they undid did. . . .
Her gentlewomen, like the Nereides,
So many mermaids, tended her i' th' eyes,
And made their bends adornings. At the helm
A seeming mermaid steers. The silken tackle
Swell with the touches of those flower-soft hands
That yarely frame the office. From the barge
A strange invisible perfume hits the sense
Of the adjacent wharfs. The city cast
Her people out upon her; and Antony,
Enthron'd i' th' market place, did sit alone,
Whistling to th' air; which, but for vacancy,
Had gone to gaze on Cleopatra too,
And made a gap in nature. . . .
Age cannot wither her nor custom stale
Her infinite variety. Other women cloy
The appetites they feed, but she makes hungry
Where most she satisfies.   [II, 2

ANTONY. To business that we love we rise betime
And go to't with delight. . . .
This morning, like the spirit of a youth
That means to be of note, begins betimes.   [IV, 4

ANTONY. Sometime we see a cloud that's dragonish;
A vapour sometime like a bear or lion,
A tower'd citadel, a pendent rock,
A forked mountain, or blue promontory
With trees upon't that nod unto the world

And mock our eyes with air. Thou hast seen these signs;
They are black Vesper's pageants.

EROS.   Ay, my lord.

ANT. That which is now a horse, even with a thought
The rack dislimns, and makes it indistinct
As water is in water.

EROS.   It does, my lord.

ANT. My good knave Eros, now thy captain is
Even such a body. Here I am Antony;
Yet cannot hold this visible shape, my knave.   [IV, 14

ANTONY. I am dying, Egypt, dying; only
I here importune death awhile, until
Of many thousand kisses the poor last
I lay upon thy lips. . . .

CLEOPATRA. The crown o' th' earth doth melt. My lord!
O, wither'd is the garland of the war,
The soldier's pole is fall'n! Young boys and girls
Are level now with men. The odds is gone,
And there is nothing left remarkable
Beneath the visiting moon.   [IV, 15

CLEOPATRA. Give me my robe, put on my crown. I
    have
Immortal longings in me. Now no more
The juice of Egypt's grape shall moist this lip.
Yare, yare, good Iras; quick. Methinks I hear
Antony call. I see him rouse himself
To praise my noble act. I hear him mock
The luck of Cæsar, which the gods give men
To excuse their after wrath. Husband, I come!
Now to that name my courage prove my title!
I am fire and air; my other elements
I give to baser life. So, have you done?
Come then and take the last warmth of my lips.

Farewell, kind Charmian. Iras, long farewell.

                [*Kisses them.* Iras *falls and dies.*]

Have I the aspic in my lips? Dost fall?
If thou and nature can so gently part,
The stroke of death is as a lover's pinch,
Which hurts, and is desir'd. Dost thou lie still?
If thus thou vanishest, thou tell'st the world
It is not worth leave-taking.

    CHARMIAN. Dissolve, thick cloud, and rain, that I may
        say
The gods themselves do weep!

    CLEO.   This proves me base.
If she first meet the curled Antony, ˙
He'll make demand of her, and spend that kiss
Which is my heaven to have. Come, thou mortal wretch,

          [*To an asp, which she applies to her breast.*]

With thy sharp teeth this knot intrinsicate
Of life at once untie. Poor venomous fool,
Be angry, and dispatch. O, couldst thou speak,
That I might hear thee call great Cæsar ass
Unpolicied!

    CHAR.   O Eastern star!

    CLEO.   Peace, peace!
Dost thou not see my baby at my breast,
That sucks the nurse asleep?

    CHAR.   O, break! O, break!

    CLEO. As sweet as balm, as soft as air, as gentle—
O Antony! Nay, I will take thee too:

          [*Applies another asp to her arm.*]

What should I stay—   *Dies.*

    CHAR. In this wild world? So fare thee well.   [V, 2

Songs from the Plays

Who is Silvia? What is she,
   That all our swains commend her?
Holy, fair, and wise is she:
   The heaven such grace did lend her,
That she might admired be.

Is she kind as she is fair?
   For beauty lives with kindness.
Love doth to her eyes repair
   To help him of his blindness,
And being help'd, inhabits there.

Then to Silvia let us sing
   That Silvia is excelling;
She excels each mortal thing
   Upon the dull earth dwelling.
To her let us garlands bring.
         —*The Two Gentlemen of Verona*

Fie on sinful fantasy!
Fie on lust and luxury!
Lust is but a bloody fire,
Kindled with unchaste desire,
Fed in heart, whose flames aspire
As thoughts do blow them higher and higher.

Pinch him, fairies, mutually;
    Pinch him for his villany;
Pinch him and burn him and turn him about
Till candles and starlight and moonshine be out.
                    —*The Merry Wives of Windsor*

Take, O, take those lips away
    That so sweetly were forsworn;
And those eyes, the break of day,
    Lights that do mislead the morn;
But my kisses bring again, bring again;
Seals of love, but seal'd in vain, seal'd in vain.
                    —*Measure for Measure*

Sigh no more, ladies, sigh no more!
    Men were deceivers ever,
One foot in sea, and one on shore;
    To one thing constant never.
        Then sigh not so,
        But let them go,
    And be you blithe and bonny,
Converting all your sounds of woe
    Into Hey nonny, nonny.

Sing no more ditties, sing no moe
    Of dumps so dull and heavy!
The fraud of men was ever so,
    Since summer first was leavy.
        Then sigh not so
        But let them go,
    And be you blithe and bonny,
Converting all your sounds of woe
    Into Hey nonny, nonny.
                    —*Much Ado About Nothing*

Pardon, goddess of the night,
Those that slew thy virgin knight;
For the which, with songs of woe,
Round about her tomb they go.
　　Midnight, assist our moan,
　　Help us to sigh and groan.
　　　　Heavily, heavily.
　　Graves, yawn and yield your dead,
　　Till death be uttered
　　　　Heavily, heavily.
　　　　　　　—*Much Ado About Nothing*

If she be made of white and red,
　　Her faults will ne'er be known;
For blushing cheeks by faults are bred
　　And fears by pale white shown.
Then if she fear, or be to blame,
　　By this you shall not know;
For still her cheeks possess the same
　　Which native she doth owe.
　　　　　　　—*Love's Labour's Lost*

On a day—alack the day!—
Love, whose month is ever May,
Spied a blossom passing fair
Playing in the wanton air.
Through the velvet leaves the wind,
All unseen, can passage find;
That the lover, sick to death,
Wish'd himself the heaven's breath.
'Air,' quoth he, 'thy cheeks may blow.
Air, would I might triumph so!

But, alack, my head is sworn
Ne'er to pluck thee from thy thorn:
Vow, alack, for youth unmeet,
Youth so apt to pluck a sweet!
Do not call it sin in me
That I am forsworn for thee;
Thou for whom Jove would swear
Juno but an Æthiop were,
And deny himself for Jove,
Turning mortal for thy love.'

—Love's Labour's Lost

When daisies pied and violets blue
  And lady-smocks all silver-white
And cuckoo-buds of yellow hue
  Do paint the meadows with delight,
The cuckoo then on every tree,
Mocks married men; for thus sings he,
                'Cuckoo!
Cuckoo, cuckoo!' O word of fear,
Unpleasing to a married ear!

When shepherds pipe on oaten straws,
  And merry larks are ploughmen's clocks;
When turtles tread and rooks and daws,
  And maidens bleach their summer smocks,
The cuckoo then on every tree,
Mocks married men; for thus sings he:
                'Cuckoo!
Cuckoo, cuckoo!' O word of fear,
Unpleasing to a married ear!

When icicles hang by the wall,
   And Dick the shepherd blows his nail,
And Tom bears logs into the hall,
   And milk comes frozen home in pail,
When blood is nipp'd, and ways be foul,
Then nightly sings the staring owl:
                'Tu-who!
Tu-whit, tu-who!' a merry note,
While greasy Joan doth keel the pot.

When all aloud the wind doth blow,
   And coughing drowns the parson's saw,
And birds sit brooding in the snow,
   And Marian's nose looks red and raw;
When roasted crabs hiss in the bowl,
Then nightly sings the staring owl:
                'Tu-who!
Tu-whit, tu-who!' a merry note,
While greasy Joan doth keel the pot.
                —Love's Labour's Lost

Tell me, where is fancy bred,
Or in the heart, or in the head?
How begot, how nourished?
   Reply, reply.
It is engend'red in the eyes,
With gazing fed; and fancy dies
In the cradle where it lies;
   Let us ring fancy's knell.
   I'll begin it—Ding, dong, bell.
   Ding, dong, bell.
                —The Merchant of Venice

O mistress mine, where are you roaming?
O, stay and hear! your true-love's coming,
   That can sing both high and low.
Trip no further, pretty sweeting;
Journeys end in lovers meeting,
   Every wise man's son, doth know.

What is love? 'Tis not hereafter;
Present mirth hath present laughter;
   What's to come is still unsure:
In delay there lies no plenty;
Then come kiss me, sweet and twenty!
   Youth's a stuff will not endure.
                          —Twelfth Night

Come away, come away, death,
   And in sad cypress let me be laid.
Fly away, fly away, breath;
   I am slain by a fair cruel maid.
My shroud of white, stuck all with yew,
   O, prepare it!
My part of death, no one so true
   Did share it.

Not a flower, not a flower sweet,
   On my black coffin let there be strown;
Not a friend, not a friend greet
   My poor corpse, where my bones shall be thrown.
A thousand thousand sighs to save,
   Lay me, O, where
Sad true lover never find my grave,
   To weep there!
                          —Twelfth Night

When that I was and a little tiny boy,
  With hey, ho, the wind and the rain,
A foolish thing was but a toy,
  For the rain it raineth every day.

But when I came to man's estate,
  With hey, ho, the wind and the rain,
'Gainst knaves and thieves men shut their gate,
  For the rain it raineth every day.

But when I came, alas! to wive,
  With hey, ho, the wind and the rain,
By swaggering could I never thrive,
  For the rain it raineth every day.

But when I came unto my beds,
  With hey, ho, the wind and the rain,
With tosspots still had drunken heads,
  For the rain it raineth every day.

A great while ago the world begun,
  With hey, ho, the wind and the rain;
But that's all one, our play is done,
  And we'll strive to please you every day.
                              —*Twelfth Night*

When daffodils begin to peer,
  With heigh! the doxy over the dale—
Why, then comes in the sweet o' the year,
  For the red blood reigns in the winter's pale.

The white sheet bleaching on the hedge—
  With heigh! the sweet birds, O, how they sing!
Doth set my pugging tooth on edge,
  For a quart of ale, is a dish for a king.

The lark, that tirra-lyra chants,—
  With heigh! with heigh! the thrush and the jay—
Are summer songs for me and my aunts,
  While we lie tumbling in the hay.

—The Winter's Tale

But shall I go mourn for that, my dear?
  The pale moon shines by night;
And when I wander here and there,
  I then do most go right.

If tinkers may have leave to live
  And bear the sow-skin budget,
Then my account I well may give,
  And in the stocks avouch it.

—The Winter's Tale

Lawn as white as driven snow;
Cypress black as e'er was crow;
Gloves as sweet as damask roses;
Masks for faces and for noses;
Bugle bracelet, necklace amber,
Perfume for a lady's chamber;
Golden quoifs and stomachers
For my lads to give their dears;
Pins, and poking sticks of steel:
What maids lack from head to heel.
Come buy of me, come! come buy, come buy!
Buy, lads, or else your lasses cry. Come buy!

—The Winter's Tale

Will you buy any tape,
Or lace for your cape,
My dainty duck, my dear-a?
　　Any silk, any thread,
　　Any toys for your head
Of the new'st and fin'st, fin'st wear-a?
　　Come to the pedlar.
　　Money's a meddler
That doth utter all men's wear-a.
　　　　　　—The Winter's Tale

Orpheus with his lute made trees
And the mountain tops that freeze
　　Bow themselves when he did sing.
To his music plants and flowers
Ever sprung, as sun and showers
　　There had made a lasting spring.

Everything that heard him play,
Even the billows of the sea,
　　Hung their heads, and then lay by.
In sweet music is such art
Killing care and grief of heart
　　Fall asleep, or hearing, die.
　　　　　　—Henry the Eighth

Hark hark! the lark at heaven's gate sings,
　　And Phœbus gins arise,
His steeds to water at those springs
　　On chalic'd flowers that lies;
And winking Mary-buds begin
　　To ope their golden eyes.
With every thing that pretty is,
　　My lady sweet, arise;
　　　　Arise, arise!
　　　　　　—Cymbeline

Fear no more the heat o' th' sun
   Nor the furious winter's rages;
Thou thy worldly task hast done,
   Home art gone, and ta'en thy wages.
Golden lads and girls all must,
As chimney-sweepers, come to dust.

Fear no more the frown o' th' great;
   Thou art past the tyrant's stroke.
Care no more to clothe and eat;
   To thee the reed is as the oak.
The sceptre, learning, physic, must
All follow this and come to dust.

Fear no more the lightning flash—
   Nor th' all-dreaded thunder stone;
Fear not slander, censure rash;
   Thou hast finish'd joy and moan.
All lovers young, all lovers must
Consign to thee and come to dust.

No exorciser harm thee!
Nor no witchcraft charm thee!
Ghost unlaid forbear thee!
Nothing ill come near thee!
Quiet consummation have,
And renowned be thy grave!

—Cymbeline

Note

Songs in the plays printed in full can be found on the following pages:

Sonnets

TO. THE. ONLIE. BEGETTER. OF.

THESE. INSUING. SONNETS.

MR. W. H. ALL. HAPPINESSE.

AND. THAT. ETERNITIE.

PROMISED.

BY.

OUR. EVER-LIVING. POET.

WISHETH.

THE. WELL-WISHING.

ADVENTURER. IN.

SETTING.

FORTH.

T. T.

I

From fairest creatures we desire increase,
That thereby beauty's rose might never die,
But as the riper should by time decease,
His tender heir might bear his memory;
But thou, contracted to thine own bright eyes,
Feed'st thy light's flame with self-substantial fuel,
Making a famine where abundance lies,
Thyself thy foe, to thy sweet self too cruel.
Thou that art now the world's fresh ornament
And only herald to the gaudy spring,
Within thine own bud buriest thy content
And, tender churl, mak'st waste in niggarding.
    Pity the world, or else this glutton be,
    To eat the world's due, by the grave and thee.

II

When forty winters shall besiege thy brow
And dig deep trenches in thy beauty's field,
Thy youth's proud livery, so gaz'd on now,
Will be a tatter'd weed of small worth held.
Then being ask'd where all thy beauty lies,
Where all the treasure of thy lusty days,
To say, within thine own deep-sunken eyes
Were an all-eating shame and thriftless praise.
How much more praise deserv'd thy beauty's use
If thou couldst answer, 'This fair child of mine
Shall sum my count and make my old excuse,'
Proving his beauty by succession thine!
    This were to be new made when thou art old
    And see thy blood warm when thou feel'st it cold.

III

Look in thy glass and tell the face thou viewest
Now is the time that face should form another,
Whose fresh repair if now thou not renewest,
Thou dost beguile the world, unbless some mother.
For where is she so fair whose unear'd womb
Disdains the tillage of thy husbandry?
Or who is he so fond will be the tomb
Of his self-love, to stop posterity?
Thou art thy mother's glass, and she in thee
Calls back the lovely April of her prime.
So thou through windows of thine age shalt see,
Despite of wrinkles, this thy golden time.
    But if thou live remem'bred not to be,
    Die single, and thine image dies with thee.

IV

Unthrifty loveliness, why dost thou spend
Upon thyself thy beauty's legacy?
Nature's bequest gives nothing, but doth lend,
And, being frank, she lends to those are free.
Then, beauteous niggard, why dost thou abuse
The bounteous largess given thee to give?
Profitless usurer, why dost thou use
So great a sum of sums, yet canst not live?
For, having traffic with thyself alone,
Thou of thyself thy sweet self dost deceive.
Then how, when nature calls thee to be gone,
What acceptable audit canst thou leave?
 Thy unus'd beauty must be tomb'd with thee,
 Which, used, lives th' executor to be.

V

Those hours that with gentle work did frame
The lovely gaze where every eye doth dwell,
Will play the tyrants to the very same
And that unfair which fairly doth excel;
For never-resting time leads summer on
To hideous winter and confounds him there,
Sap check'd with frost and lusty leaves quite gone,
Beauty o'ersnow'd and bareness everywhere.
Then, were not summer's distillation left
A liquid prisoner pent in walls of glass,
Beauty's effect with beauty were bereft—
Nor it, nor no remembrance what it was;
 But flowers distill'd, though they with winter meet,
 Leese but their show—their substance still lives sweet.

VI

Then let not winter's ragged hand deface
In thee thy summer ere thou be distill'd.
Make sweet some vial; treasure thou some place
With beauty's treasure ere it be self-kill'd.
That use is not forbidden usury
Which happies those that pay the willing loan:
That's for thyself to breed another thee,
Or ten times happier, be it ten for one.
Ten times thyself were happier than thou art,
If ten of thine ten times refigur'd thee.
Then what could death do if thou shouldst depart,
Leaving thee living in posterity?
   Be not self-will'd, for thou art much too fair
   To be death's conquest and make worms thine heir.

VII

Lo, in the Orient when the gracious light
Lifts up his burning head, each under eye
Doth homage to his new-appearing sight,
Serving with looks his sacred majesty;
And having climb'd the steep-up heavenly hill,
Resembling strong youth in his middle age,
Yet mortal looks adore his beauty still,
Attending on his golden pilgrimage;
But when from highmost pitch, with weary car,
Like feeble age he reeleth from the day,
The eyes (fore duteous) now converted are
From his low tract and look another way.
   So thou, thyself outgoing in thy noon,
   Unlook'd on diest unless thou get a son.

VIII

Music to hear, why hear'st thou music sadly?
Sweets with sweets war not, joy delights in joy.
Why lov'st thou that which thou receiv'st not gladly,
Or else receiv'st with pleasure thine annoy?
If the true concord of well-tuned sounds,
By unions married, do offend thine ear,
They do but sweetly chide thee, who confounds
In singleness the parts that thou shouldst bear.
Mark how one string, sweet husband to another,
Strikes each in each by mutual ordering;
Resembling sire and child and happy mother,
Who, all in one, one pleasing note do sing;
    Whose speechless song, being many, seeming one,
    Sings this to thee: 'Thou single wilt prove none.'

IX

Is it for fear to wet a widow's eye
That thou consum'st thyself in single life?
Ah! if thou issueless shalt hap to die,
The world will wail thee like a makeless wife;
The world will be thy widow, and still weep
That thou no form of thee hast left behind
When every private widow well may keep,
By children's eyes, her husband's shape in mind.
Look, what an unthrift in the world doth spend
Shifts but his place, for still the world enjoys it;
But beauty's waste hath in the world an end,
And kept unus'd, the user so destroys it.
    No love toward others in that bosom sits
    That on himself such murd'rous shame commits.

X

For shame! Deny that thou bear'st love to any,
Who for thyself art so unprovident.
Grant, if thou wilt, thou art belov'd of many,
But that thou none lov'st is most evident;
For thou art so possess'd with murd'rous hate
That 'gainst thyself thou stick'st not to conspire,
Seeking that beauteous roof to ruinate
Which to repair should be thy chief desire.
O, change thy thought, that I may change my mind!
Shall hate be fairer lodg'd than gentle love?
Be as thy presence is, gracious and kind,
Or to thyself at least kind-hearted prove.
　　Make thee another self for love of me,
　　That beauty still may live in thine or thee.

XI

As fast as thou shalt wane, so fast thou grow'st
In one of thine, from that which thou departest;
And that fresh blood which youngly thou bestow'st
Thou mayst call thine when thou from youth convertest.
Herein lives wisdom, beauty, and increase;
Without this, folly, age, and cold decay.
If all were minded so, the times should cease,
And threescore year would make the world away.
Let those whom Nature hath not made for store,
Harsh, featureless, and rude, barrenly perish.
Look, whom she best endow'd she gave the more,
Which bounteous gift thou shouldst in bounty cherish.
　　She carv'd thee for her seal, and meant thereby
　　Thou shouldst print more, not let that copy die.

XII

When I do count the clock that tells the time
And see the brave day sunk in hideous night,
When I behold the violet past prime
And sable curls all silver'd o'er with white,
When lofty trees I see barren of leaves,
Which erst from heat did canopy the herd,
And summer's green all girded up in sheaves
Borne on the bier with white and bristly beard—
Then of thy beauty do I question make
That thou among the wastes of time must go,
Since sweets and beauties do themselves forsake
And die as fast as they see others grow,
    And nothing 'gainst Time's scythe can make defence
    Save breed, to brave him when he takes thee hence.

XIII

O, that you were yourself! but, love, you are
No longer yours than you yourself here live.
Against this coming end you should prepare
And your sweet semblance to some other give.
So should that beauty which you hold in lease
Find no determination; then you were
Yourself again after yourself's decease
When your sweet issue your sweet form should bear.
Who lets so fair a house fall to decay,
Which husbandry in honour might uphold
Against the stormy gusts of winter's day
And barren rage of death's eternal cold?
    O, none but unthrifts! Dear my love, you know
    You had a father—let your son say so.

XIV

Not from the stars do I my judgment pluck,
And yet methinks I have astronomy;
But not to tell of good or evil luck,
Of plagues, of dearths, or seasons' quality;
Nor can I fortune to brief minutes tell,
Pointing to each his thunder, rain, and wind,
Or say with princes if it shall go well
By oft predict that I in heaven find;
But from thine eyes my knowledge I derive,
And, constant stars, in them I read such art
As truth and beauty shall together thrive
If from thyself to store thou wouldst convert;
    Or else of thee this I prognosticate:
    Thy end is truth's and beauty's doom and date.

XV

When I consider every thing that grows
Holds in perfection but a little moment,
That this huge stage presenteth naught but shows
Whereon the stars in secret influence comment;
When I perceive that men as plants increase,
Cheered and check'd even by the selfsame sky,
Vaunt in their youthful sap, at height decrease,
And wear their brave state out of memory:
Then the conceit of this inconstant stay
Sets you most rich in youth·before my sight,
Where wasteful Time debateth with Decay
To change your day of youth to sullied night
    And, all in war with Time for love of you,
    As he takes from you, I ingraft you new.

XVI

But wherefore do not you a mightier way
Make war upon this bloody tyrant, Time?
And fortify yourself in your decay
With means more blessed than my barren rhyme?
Now stand you on the top of happy hours;
And many maiden gardens, yet unset,
With virtuous wish would bear your living flowers,
Much liker than your painted counterfeit.
So should the lines of life that life repair
Which this time's pencil, or my pupil pen,
Neither in inward worth nor outward fair
Can make you live yourself in eyes of men.
    To give away yourself keeps yourself still,
      And you must live, drawn by your own sweet skill.

XVII

Who will believe my verse in time to come
If it were fill'd with your most high deserts?
Though yet, heaven knows, it is but as a tomb
Which hides your life and shows not half your parts.
If I could write the beauty of your eyes
And in fresh numbers number all your graces,
The age to come would say, 'This poet lies!
Such heavenly touches ne'er touch'd earthly faces.'
So should my papers (yellowed with their age)
Be scorn'd, like old men of less truth than tongue,
And your true rights be term'd a poet's rage
And stretched metre of an antique song.
    But were some child of yours alive that time,
      You should live twice—in it, and in my rhyme.

XVIII

Shall I compare thee to a summer's day?
Thou art more lovely and more temperate.
Rough winds do shake the darling buds of May,
And summer's lease hath all too short a date.
Sometime too hot the eye of heaven shines,
And often is his gold complexion dimm'd;
And every fair from fair sometime declines,
By chance, or nature's changing course, untrimm'd;
But thy eternal summer shall not fade
Nor lose possession of that fair thou ow'st,
Nor shall Death brag thou wand'rest in his shade
When in eternal lines to time thou grow'st.
   So long as men can breathe or eyes can see,
    So long lives this, and this gives life to thee.

XIX

Devouring Time, blunt thou the lion's paws
And make the earth devour her own sweet brood;
Pluck the keen teeth from the fierce tiger's jaws
And burn the long-liv'd phœnix in her blood;
Make glad and sorry seasons as thou fleets,
And do whate'er thou wilt, swift-footed Time,
To the wide world and all her fading sweets;
But I forbid thee one most heinous crime:
O, carve not with thy hours my love's fair brow,
Nor draw no lines there with thine antique pen!
Him in thy course untainted do allow
For beauty's pattern to succeeding men.
   Yet do thy worst, old Time! Despite thy wrong,
    My love shall in my verse ever live young.

XX

A woman's face, with Nature's own hand painted,
Hast thou, the master mistress of my passion;
A woman's gentle heart, but not acquainted
With shifting change, as is false women's fashion;
An eye more bright than theirs, less false in rolling,
Gilding the object whereupon it gazeth;
A man in hue all hues in his controlling,
Which steals men's eyes and women's souls amazeth.
And for a woman wert thou first created,
Till Nature as she wrought thee fell a-doting
And by addition me of thee defeated
By adding one thing to my purpose nothing.
    But since she prick'd thee out for women's pleasure,
    Mine be thy love, and thy love's use their treasure.

XXI

So is it not with me as with that Muse
Stirr'd by a painted beauty to his verse,
Who heaven itself for ornament doth use
And every fair with his fair doth rehearse;
Making a couplement of proud compare
With sun and moon, with earth and sea's rich gems,
With April's first-born flowers, and all things rare
That heaven's air in this huge rondure hems.
O, let me, true in love, but truly write,
And then believe me, my love is as fair
As any mother's child, though not so bright
As those gold candles fix'd in heaven's air.
    Let them say more that like of hearsay well;
    I will not praise that purpose not to sell.

XXII

My glass shall not persuade me I am old
So long as youth and thou are of one date;
But when in thee time's furrows I behold,
Then look I death my days should expiate.
For all that beauty that doth cover thee
Is but the seemly raiment of my heart,
Which in thy breast doth live, as thine in me.
How can I then be elder than thou art?
O, therefore, love, be of thyself so wary
As I, not for myself, but for thee will,
Bearing thy heart, which I will keep so chary
As tender nurse her babe from faring ill.
 Presume not on thy heart when mine is slain:
 Thou gav'st me thine, not to give back again.

XXIII

As an unperfect actor on the stage
Who with his fear is put besides his part,
Or some fierce thing replete with too much rage,
Whose strength's abundance weakens his own heart;
So I, for fear of trust, forget to say
The perfect ceremony of love's rite,
And in mine own love's strength seem to decay,
O'ercharg'd with burthen of mine own love's might.
O, let my looks be then the eloquence
And dumb presagers of my speaking breast,
Who plead for love, and look for recompense,
More than that tongue that more hath more express'd.
 O, learn to read what silent love hath writ!
 To hear with eyes belongs to love's fine wit.

XXIV

Mine eye hath play'd the painter and hath stell'd
Thy beauty's form in table of my heart;
My body is the frame wherein 'tis held,
And perspective it is best painter's art.
For through the painter must you see his skill
To find where your true image pictur'd lies,
Which in my bosom's shop is hanging still,
That hath his windows glazed with thine eyes.
Now see what good turns eyes for eyes have done:
Mine eyes have drawn thy shape, and thine for me
Are windows to my breast, wherethrough the sun
Delights to peep, to gaze therein on thee.
    Yet eyes this cunning want to grace their art—
    They draw but what they see, know not the heart.

XXV

Let those who are in favour with their stars
Of public honour and proud titles boast,
Whilst I, whom fortune of such triumph bars,
Unlook'd for joy in that I honour most.
Great princes' favourites their fair leaves spread
But as the marigold at the sun's eye;
And in themselves their pride lies buried,
For at a frown they in their glory die.
The painful warrior famoused for fight,
After a thousand victories once foil'd,
Is from the book of honour rased quite,
And all the rest forgot for which he toil'd.
    Then happy I, that love and am beloved
    Where I may not remove nor be removed.

XXVI

Lord of my love, to whom in vassalage
Thy merit hath my duty strongly knit,
To thee I send this written embassage,
To witness duty, not to show my wit:
Duty so great, which wit so poor as mine
May make seem bare, in wanting words to show it,
But that I hope some good conceit of thine
In thy soul's thought (all naked) will bestow it;
Till whatsoever star that guides my moving
Points on me graciously with fair aspect,
And puts apparel on my tattered loving
To show me worthy of thy sweet respect.
    Then may I dare to boast how I do love thee;
    Till then not show my head where thou mayst prove
      me.

XXVII

Weary with toil, I haste me to my bed,
The dear repose for limbs with travel tired;
But then begins a journey in my head
To work my mind when body's work's expired.
For then my thoughts, from far where I abide,
Intend a zealous pilgrimage to thee,
And keep my drooping eyelids open wide,
Looking on darkness which the blind do see;
Save that my soul's imaginary sight
Presents thy shadow to my sightless view,
Which, like a jewel hung in ghastly night,
Makes black night beauteous and her old face new.
    Lo, thus, by day my limbs, by night my mind,
    For thee, and for myself, no quiet find.

XXVIII

How can I then return in happy plight
That am debarr'd the benefit of rest,
When day's oppression is not eas'd by night,
But day by night and night by day oppress'd,
And each, though enemies to either's reign,
Do in consent shake hands to torture me,
The one by toil, the other to complain
How far I toil, still farther off from thee?
I tell the day, to please him, thou art bright
And dost him grace when clouds do blot the heaven;
So flatter I the swart-complexion'd night,
When sparkling stars twire not, thou gild'st the even.
   But day doth daily draw my sorrows longer,
     And night doth nightly make grief's strength seem
      stronger.

XXIX

When, in disgrace with Fortune and men's eyes,
I all alone beweep my outcast state,
And trouble deaf heaven with my bootless cries,
And look upon myself and curse my fate,
Wishing me like to one more rich in hope,
Featur'd like him, like him with friends possess'd,
Desiring this man's art, and that man's scope,
With what I most enjoy contented least;
Yet in these thoughts myself almost despising,
Haply I think on thee, and then my state,
Like to the lark at break of day arising
From sullen earth, sings hymns at heaven's gate;
   For thy sweet love rememb'red such wealth brings
    That then I scorn to change my state with kings.

XXX

When to the sessions of sweet silent thought
I summon up remembrance of things past,
I sigh the lack of many a thing I sought
And with old woes new wail my dear time's waste.
Then can I drown an eye (unus'd to flow)
For precious friends hid in death's dateless night,
And weep afresh love's long since cancell'd woe,
And moan th' expense of many a vanish'd sight.
Then can I grieve at grievances foregone,
And heavily from woe to woe tell o'er
The sad account of fore-bemoaned moan,
Which I new pay as if not paid before.
    But if the while I think on thee, dear friend,
    All losses are restor'd and sorrows end.

XXXI

Thy bosom is endeared with all hearts
Which I by lacking have supposed dead;
And there reigns love, and all love's loving parts,
And all those friends which I thought buried.
How many a holy and obsequious tear
Hath dear religious love stol'n from mine eye,
As interest of the dead, which now appear
But things remov'd that hidden in thee lie!
Thou art the grave where buried love doth live,
Hung with the trophies of my lovers gone,
Who all their parts of me to thee did give:
That due of many now is thine alone.
    Their images I lov'd I view in thee,
    And thou (all they) hast all the all of me.

XXXII

If thou survive my well-contented day
When that churl Death my bones with dust shall cover,
And shalt by fortune once more resurvey
These poor rude lines of thy deceased lover,
Compare them with the bett'ring of the time,
And though they be outstripp'd by every pen,
Reserve them for my love not for their rhyme,
Exceeded by the height of happier men.
O, then vouchsafe me but this loving thought:
'Had my friend's Muse grown with this growing age,
A dearer birth than this his love had brought,
To march in ranks of better equipage;
 But since he died, and poets better prove,
 Theirs for their style I'll read, his for his love.'

XXXIII

Full many a glorious morning have I seen
Flatter the mountain tops with sovereign eye,
Kissing with golden face the meadows green,
Gilding pale streams with heavenly alchemy;
Anon permit the basest clouds to ride
With ugly rack on his celestial face
And from the forlorn world his visage hide,
Stealing unseen to West with this disgrace.
Even so my sun one early morn did shine
With all triumphant splendour on my brow;
But, out alack! he was but one hour mine,
The region cloud hath mask'd him from me now.
 Yet him for this my love no whit disdaineth;
 Suns of the world may stain when heaven's sun
  staineth.

XXXIV

Why didst thou promise such a beauteous day
And make me travel forth without my cloak,
To let base clouds o'ertake me in my way,
Hiding thy brav'ry in their rotten smoke?
'Tis not enough that through the cloud thou break
To dry the rain on my storm-beaten face,
For no man well of such a salve can speak
That heals the wound, and cures not the disgrace:
Nor can thy shame give physic to my grief;
Though thou repent, yet I have still the loss.
Th' offender's sorrow lends but weak relief
To him that bears the strong offence's cross.
    Ah, but those tears are pearl which thy love sheeds,
    And they are rich and ransom all ill deeds.

XXXV

No more be griev'd at that which thou hast done:
Roses have thorns, and silver fountains mud;
Clouds and eclipses stain both moon and sun,
And loathsome canker lives in sweetest bud.
All men make faults, and even I in this,
Authorizing thy trespass with compare,
Myself corrupting, salving thy amiss,
Excusing thy sins more than thy sins are;
For to thy sensual fault I bring in sense—
Thy adverse party is thy advocate—
And 'gainst myself a lawful plea commence.
Such civil war is in my love and hate
    That I an accessary needs must be
    To that sweet thief which sourly robs from me.

XXXVI

Let me confess that we two must be twain,
Although our undivided loves are one.
So shall those blots that do with me remain,
Without thy help by me be borne alone.
In our two loves there is but one respect,
Though in our lives a separable spite,
Which though it alter not love's sole effect,
Yet doth it steal sweet hours from love's delight.
I may not evermore acknowledge thee,
Lest my bewailed guilt should do thee shame;
Nor thou with public kindness honour me,
Unless thou take that honour from thy name.
    But do not so. I love thee in such sort
    As, thou being mine, mine is thy good report.

XXXVII

As a decrepit father takes delight
To see his active child do deeds of youth,
So I, made lame by Fortune's dearest spite,
Take all my comfort of thy worth and truth;
For whether beauty, birth, or wealth, or wit,
Or any of these all, or all, or more,
Entitled in thy parts do crowned sit,
I make my love engrafted to this store.
So then I am not lame, poor, nor despis'd
Whilst that this shadow doth such substance give
That I in thy abundance am suffic'd
And by a part of all thy glory live.
    Look what is best—that best I wish in thee.
    This wish I have; then ten times happy me!

XXXVIII

How can my Muse want subject to invent
While thou dost breathe, that pour'st into my verse
Thine own sweet argument, too excellent
For every vulgar paper to rehearse?
O, give thyself the thanks if aught in me
Worthy perusal stand against thy sight;
For who's so dumb that cannot write to thee,
When thou thyself dost give invention light?
Be thou the tenth Muse, ten times more in worth
Than those old nine which rhymers invocate;
And he that calls on thee, let him bring forth
Eternal numbers to outlive long date.
    If my slight Muse do please these curious days,
    The pain be mine, but thine shall be the praise.

XXXIX

O, how thy worth with manners may I sing
When thou art all the better part of me?
What can mine own praise to mine own self bring?
And what is't but mine own when I praise thee?
Even for this let us divided live
And our dear love lose name of single one,
That by this separation I may give
That due to thee which thou deserv'st alone.
O absence, what a torment wouldst thou prove,
Were it not thy sour leisure gave sweet leave
To entertain the time with thoughts of love,
Which time and thoughts so sweetly doth deceive,
    And that thou teachest how to make one twain—
    By praising him here who doth hence remain!

XL

Take all my loves, my love, yea, take them all!
What hast thou then more than thou hadst before?
No love, my love, that thou mayst true love call;
All mine was thine before thou hadst this more.
Then, if for my love thou my love receivest,
I cannot blame thee for my love thou usest;
But yet be blam'd if thou thyself deceivest
By wilful taste of what thyself refusest.
I do forgive thy robb'ry, gentle thief,
Although thou steal thee all my poverty;
And yet love knows it is a greater grief
To bear love's wrong than hate's known injury.
  Lascivious grace, in whom all ill well shows,
  Kill me with spites; yet we must not be foes.

XLI

Those pretty wrongs that liberty commits
When I am sometime absent from thy heart,
Thy beauty and thy years full well befits,
For still temptation follows where thou art.
Gentle thou art, and therefore to be won;
Beauteous thou art, therefore to be assailed;
And when a woman woos, what woman's son
Will sourly leave her till she have prevailed?
Ay me! but yet thou mightst my seat forbear,
And chide thy beauty and thy straying youth,
Who lead thee in their riot even there
Where thou art forc'd to break a twofold truth—
  Hers, by thy beauty tempting her to thee,
  Thine, by thy beauty being false to me.

XLII

That thou hast her, it is not all my grief,
And yet it may be said I lov'd her dearly;
That she hath thee is of my wailing chief,
A loss in love that touches me more nearly.
Loving offenders, thus I will excuse ye:
Thou dost love her because thou know'st I love her,
And for my sake even so doth she abuse me,
Suff'ring my friend for my sake to approve her.
If I lose thee, my loss is my love's gain,
And losing her, my friend hath found that loss:
Both find each other, and I lose both twain,
And both for my sake lay on me this cross.
    But here's the joy—my friend and I are one.
    Sweet flattery! then she loves but me alone.

XLIII

When most I wink, then do mine eyes best see,
For all the day they view things unrespected,
But when I sleep, in dreams they look on thee
And, darkly bright, are bright in dark directed.
Then thou, whose shadow shadows doth make bright,
How would thy shadow's form form happy show
To the clear day with thy much clearer light
When to unseeing eyes thy shade shines so!
How would, I say, mine eyes be blessed made
By looking on thee in the living day,
When in dead night thy fair imperfect shade
Through heavy sleep on sightless eyes doth stay!
    All days are nights to see till I see thee,
    And nights bright days when dreams do show thee me.

XLIV

If the dull substance of my flesh were thought,
Injurious distance should not stop my way;
For then, despite of space, I would be brought,
From limits far remote, where thou dost stay.
No matter then although my foot did stand
Upon the farthest earth remov'd from thee;
For nimble thought can jump both sea and land
As soon as think the place where he would be.
But, ah, thought kills me that I am not thought,
To leap large lengths of miles when thou art gone,
But that, so much of earth and water wrought,
I must attend time's leisure with my moan,
    Receiving naught by elements so slow
    But heavy tears, badges of either's woe.

XLV

The other two, slight air and purging fire,
Are both with thee, wherever I abide;
The first my thought, the other my desire,
These present-absent with swift motion slide.
For when these quicker elements are gone
In tender embassy of love to thee,
My life, being made of four, with two alone
Sinks down to death, oppress'd with melancholy;
Until live's composition be recured
By those swift messengers return'd from thee,
Who even but now come back again, assured
Of thy fair health, recounting it to me.
    This told, I joy; but then no longer glad,
    I send them back again and straight grow sad.

XLVI

Mine eye and heart are at a mortal war
How to divide the conquest of thy sight;
Mine eye my heart thy picture's sight would bar,
My heart mine eye the freedom of that right.
My heart doth plead that thou in him dost lie
(A closet never pierc'd with crystal eyes);
But the defendant doth that plea deny
And says in him thy fair appearance lies.
To 'cide this title is impanneled
A quest of thoughts, all tenants to the heart,
And by their verdict is determined
The clear eye's moiety and the dear heart's part:
    As thus—mine eye's due is thy outward part,
    And my heart's right thy inward love of heart.

XLVII

Betwixt mine eye and heart a league is took,
And each doth good turns now unto the other.
When that mine eye is famish'd for a look,
Or heart in love with sighs himself doth smother,
With my love's picture then my eye doth feast
And to the painted banquet bids my heart.
Another time mine eye is my heart's guest
And in his thoughts of love doth share a part.
So, either by thy picture or my love,
Thyself away art present still with me;
For thou not farther than my thoughts canst move,
And I am still with them, and they with thee;
    Or, if they sleep, thy picture in my sight
    Awakes my heart to heart's and eye's delight.

XLVIII

How careful was I, when I took my way,
Each trifle under truest bars to thrust,
That to my use it might unused stay
From hands of falsehood, in sure wards of trust!
But thou, to whom my jewels trifles are,
Most worthy comfort, now my greatest grief,
Thou, best of dearest, and mine only care,
Art left the prey of every vulgar thief.
Thee have I not lock'd up in any chest,
Save where thou art not, though I feel thou art,
Within the gentle closure of my breast,
From whence at pleasure thou mayst come and part;
   And even thence thou wilt be stol'n, I fear,
   For truth proves thievish for a prize so dear.

XLIX

Against that time (if ever that time come)
When I shall see thee frown on my defects,
When as thy love hath cast his utmost sum,
Call'd to that audit by advis'd respects;
Against that time when thou shalt strangely pass
And scarcely greet me with that sun, thine eye,
When love, converted from the thing it was,
Shall reasons find of settled gravity—
Against that time do I ensconce me here
Within the knowledge of mine own desart,
And this my hand against myself uprear,
To guard the lawful reasons on thy part.
   To leave poor me thou hast the strength of laws,
   Since why to love I can allege no cause.

L

How heavy do I journey on the way
When what I seek (my weary travel's end)
Doth teach that ease and that repose to say,
'Thus far the miles are measur'd from thy friend!'
The beast that bears me, tired with my woe,
Plods dully on, to bear that weight in me,
As if by some instinct the wretch did know
His rider lov'd not speed, being made from thee.
The bloody spur cannot provoke him on
That sometimes anger thrusts into his hide;
Which heavily he answers with a groan,
More sharp to me than spurring to his side;
    For that same groan doth put this in my mind—
    My grief lies onward and my joy behind.

LI

Thus can my love excuse the slow offence
Of my dull bearer when from thee I speed:
From where thou art, why should I haste me thence?
Till I return, of posting is no need.
O, what excuse will my poor beast then find
When swift extremity can seem but slow?
Then should I spur, though mounted on the wind,
In winged speed no motion shall I know.
Then can no horse with my desire keep pace;
Therefore desire, of perfect'st love being made,
Shall neigh (no dull flesh) in his fiery race;
But love, for love, thus shall excuse my jade—
    Since from thee going he went wilful slow,
    Towards thee I'll run and give him leave to go.

LII

So am I as the rich whose blessed key
Can bring him to his sweet up-locked treasure,
The which he will not ev'ry hour survey,
For blunting the fine point of seldom pleasure.
Therefore are feasts so solemn and so rare,
Since, seldom coming, in the long year set,
Like stones of worth they thinly placed are,
Or captain jewels in the carcanet.
So is the time that keeps you as my chest,
Or as the wardrobe which the robe doth hide,
To make some special instant special blest
By new unfolding his imprison'd pride.
    Blessed are you, whose worthiness gives scope,
    Being had, to triumph, being lack'd, to hope.

LIII

What is your substance, whereof are you made,
That millions of strange shadows on you tend?
Since every one hath, every one, one shade,
And you, but one, can every shadow lend.
Describe Adonis, and the counterfeit
Is poorly imitated after you.
On Helen's cheek all art of beauty set,
And you in Grecian tires are painted new.
Speak of the spring, and foison of the year:
The one doth shadow of your beauty show,
The other as your bounty doth appear,
And you in every blessed shape we know.
    In all external grace you have some part,
    But you like none, none you, for constant heart.

LIV

O, how much more doth beauty beauteous seem
By that sweet ornament which truth doth give!
The rose looks fair, but fairer we it deem
For that sweet odour which doth in it live.
The canker blooms have full as deep a dye
As the perfumed tincture of the roses,
Hang on such thorns, and play as wantonly
When summer's breath their masked buds discloses;
But, for their virtue only is their show,
They live unwoo'd and unrespected fade,
Die to themselves. Sweet roses do not so:
Of their sweet deaths are sweetest odours made.
   And so of you, beauteous and lovely youth,
    When that shall vade, by verse distills your truth.

LV

Not marble nor the gilded monuments
Of princes shall outlive this pow'rful rhyme;
But you shall shine more bright in these contents
Than unswept stone, besmear'd with sluttish time.
When wasteful war shall statues overturn,
And broils root out the work of masonry,
Nor Mars his sword nor war's quick fire shall burn
The living record of your memory.
'Gainst death and all-oblivious enmity
Shall you pace forth; your praise shall still find room
Even in the eyes of all posterity
That wear this world out to the ending doom
   So, till the judgment that yourself arise,
    You live in this, and dwell in lovers' eyes.

LVI

Sweet love, renew thy force; be it not said
Thy edge should blunter be than appetite,
Which but to-day by feeding is allay'd,
To-morrow sharp'ned in his former might.
So, love, be thou: although to-day thou fill
Thy hungry eyes even till they wink with fulness,
To-morrow see again, and do not kill
The spirit of love with a perpetual dulness.
Let this sad int'rim like the ocean be
Which parts the shore where two contracted new
Come daily to the banks, that, when they see
Return of love, more blest may be the view;
 Or call it winter, which, being full of care,
  Makes summer's welcome thrice more wish'd, more
  rare.

LVII

Being your slave, what should I do but tend
Upon the hours and times of your desire?
I have no precious time at all to spend,
Nor services to do, till you require.
Nor dare I chide the world-without-end hour
Whilst I, my sovereign, watch the clock for you,
Nor think the bitterness of absence sour
When you have bid your servant once adieu.
Nor dare I question with my jealous thought
Where you may be, or your affairs suppose,
But, like a sad slave, stay and think of nought
Save where you are how happy you make those.
 So true a fool is love that in your will,
  Though you do anything, he thinks no ill.

LVIII

That god forbid that made me first your slave
I should in thought control your times of pleasure,
Or at your hand th' account of hours to crave,
Being your vassal bound to stay your leisure!
O, let me suffer (being at your beck)
Th' imprison'd absence of your liberty;
And patience, tame to sufferance, bide each check
Without accusing you of injury.
Be where you list; your charter is so strong
That you yourself may privilege your time
To what you will; to you it doth belong
Yourself to pardon of self-doing crime.
    I am to wait, though waiting so be hell;
    Not blame your pleasure, be it ill or well.

LIX

If there be nothing new, but that which is
Hath been before, how are our brains beguil'd,
Which, labouring for invention, bear amiss
The second burthen of a former child!
O that record could with a backward look,
Even of five hundreth courses of the sun,
Show me your image in some antique book,
Since mind at first in character was done!
That I might see what the old world could say
To this composed wonder of your frame;
Whether we are mended, or whe'r better they,
Or whether revolution be the same.
    O, sure I am the wits of former days
    To subjects worse have given admiring praise.

LX

Like as the waves make towards the pebbled shore,
So do our minutes hasten to their end;
Each changing place with that which goes before,
In sequent toil all forwards do contend.
Nativity, once in the main of light,
Crawls to maturity, wherewith being crown'd,
Crooked eclipses 'gainst his glory fight,
And Time that gave doth now his gift confound.
Time doth transfix the flourish set on youth
And delves the parallels in beauty's brow,
Feeds on the rarities of nature's truth,
And nothing stands but for his scythe to mow;
    And yet to times in hope my verse shall stand,
    Praising thy worth, despite his cruel hand.

LXI

Is it thy will thy image should keep open
My heavy eyelids to the weary night?
Dost thou desire my slumbers should be broken
While shadows like to thee do mock my sight?
Is it thy spirit that thou send'st from thee
So far from home into my deeds to pry,
To find out shames and idle hours in me,
The scope and tenure of thy jealousy?
O, no! thy love, though much, is not so great.
It is my love that keeps mine eye awake;
Mine own true love that doth my rest defeat,
To play the watchman ever for thy sake.
    For thee watch I whilst thou dost wake elsewhere,
    From me far off, with others all too near.

LXII

Sin of self-love possesseth all mine eye
And all my soul and all my every part;
And for this sin there is no remedy,
It is so grounded inward in my heart.
Methinks no face so gracious is as mine,
No shape so true, no truth of such account,
And for myself mine own worth do define
As I all other in all worths surmount.
But when my glass shows me myself indeed,
Beated and chopt with tann'd antiquity,
Mine own self-love quite contrary I read;
Self so self-loving were iniquity.
   'Tis thee (myself) that for myself I praise,
    Painting my age with beauty of thy days.

LXIII

Against my love shall be as I am now,
With Time's injurious hand crush'd and o'erworn;
When hours have drain'd his blood, and fill'd his brow
With lines and wrinkles; when his youthful morn
Hath travell'd on to age's steepy night,
And all those beauties whereof now he's king
Are vanishing, or vanish'd out of sight,
Stealing away the treasure of his spring—
For such a time do I now fortify
Against confounding age's cruel knife,
That he shall never cut from memory
My sweet love's beauty, though my lover's life.
   His beauty shall in these black lines be seen,
    And they shall live, and he in them still green.

LXIV

When I have seen by Time's fell hand defaced
The rich proud cost of outworn buried age;
When sometime lofty towers I see down rased,
And brass eternal slave to mortal rage;
When I have seen the hungry ocean gain
Advantage on the kingdom of the shore,
And the firm soil win of the wat'ry main,
Increasing store with loss, and loss with store;
When I have seen such interchange of state,
Or state itself confounded, to decay;
Ruin hath taught me thus to ruminate,
That Time will come and take my love away.
   This thought is as a death, which cannot choose
   But weep to have that which it fears to lose.

LXV

Since brass, nor stone, nor earth, nor boundless sea,
But sad mortality o'ersways their power,
How with this rage shall beauty hold a plea,
Whose action is no stronger than a flower?
O, how shall summer's honey breath hold out
Against the wrackful siege of batt'ring days,
When rocks impregnable are not so stout,
Nor gates of steel so strong, but Time decays?
O fearful meditation! Where, alack,
Shall Time's best jewel from Time's chest lie hid?
Or what strong hand can hold his swift foot back?
Or who his spoil of beauty can forbid?
   O, none! unless this miracle have might,
   That in black ink my love may still shine bright.

LXVI

Tir'd with all these, for restful death I cry:
As, to behold desert a beggar born,
And needy nothing trimm'd in jollity,
And purest faith unhappily forsworn,
And gilded honour shamefully misplac'd,
And maiden virtue rudely strumpeted,
And right perfection wrongfully disgrac'd,
And strength by limping sway disabled,
And art made tongue-tied by authority,
And folly (doctor-like) controlling skill,
And simple truth miscall'd simplicity,
And captive good attending captain ill.
 Tir'd with all these, from these would I be gone,
 Save that, to die, I leave my love alone.

LXVII

Ah, wherefore with infection should he live
And with his presence grace impiety,
That sin by him advantage should achieve
And lace itself with his society?
Why should false painting imitate his cheek
And steal dead seeing of his living hue?
Why should poor beauty indirectly seek
Roses of shadow, since his rose is true?
Why should he live, now Nature bankrout is,
Beggar'd of blood to blush through lively veins?
For she hath no exchequer now but his,
And, proud of many, lives upon his gains.
 O, him she stores, to show what wealth she had
 In days long since, before these last so bad.

LXVIII

Thus is his cheek the map of days outworn,
When beauty liv'd and died as flowers do now,
Before these bastard signs of fair were born
Or durst inhabit on a living brow;
Before the golden tresses of the dead,
The right of sepulchres, were shorn away
To live a second life on second head;
Ere beauty's dead fleece made another gay.
In him those holy antique hours are seen,
Without all ornament, itself and true,
Making no summer of another's green,
Robbing no old to dress his beauty new;
    And him as for a map doth Nature store,
    To show false Art what beauty was of yore.

LXIX

Those parts of thee that the world's eye doth view
Want nothing that the thought of hearts can mend.
All tongues (the voice of souls) give thee that due,
Utt'ring bare truth, even so as foes commend.
Thy outward thus with outward praise is crown'd;
But those same tongues that give thee so thine own
In other accents do this praise confound
By seeing farther than the eye hath shown.
They look into the beauty of thy mind,
And that in guess they measure by thy deeds;
Then, churls, their thoughts (although their eyes were
    kind)
To thy fair flower add the rank smell of weeds;
    But why thy odour matcheth not thy show,
    The soil is this—that thou dost common grow.

LXX

That thou art blam'd shall not be thy defect,
For slander's mark was ever yet the fair;
The ornament of beauty is suspect,
A crow that flies in heaven's sweetest air.
So thou be good, slander doth but approve
Thy worth the greater, being woo'd of time;
For canker vice the sweetest buds doth love,
And thou present'st a pure unstained prime.
Thou hast pass'd by the ambush of young days,
Either not assail'd, or victor being charg'd;
Yet this thy praise cannot be so thy praise
To tie up envy, evermore enlarg'd.
　　If some suspect of ill mask'd not thy show,
　　Then thou alone kingdoms of hearts shouldst owe.

LXXI

No longer mourn for me when I am dead
Than you shall hear the surly sullen bell
Give warning to the world that I am fled
From this vile world, with vilest worms to dwell.
Nay, if you read this line, remember not
The hand that writ it; for I love you so
That I in your sweet thoughts would be forgot
If thinking on me then should make you woe.
O, if, I say, you look upon this verse
When I, perhaps, compounded am with clay,
Do not so much as my poor name rehearse,
But let your love even with my life decay,
　　Lest the wise world should look into your moan
　　And mock you with me after I am gone.

LXXII

O, lest the world should task you to recite
What merit liv'd in me, that you should love
After my death, dear love, forget me quite,
For you in me can nothing worthy prove;
Unless you would devise some virtuous lie,
To do more for me than mine own desert
And hang more praise upon deceased I
Than niggard truth would willingly impart.
O, lest your true love may seem false in this,
That you for love speak well of me untrue,
My name be buried where my body is,
And live no more to shame nor me nor you!
    For I am sham'd by that which I bring forth,
    And so should you, to love things nothing worth.

LXXIII

That time of year thou mayst in me behold
When yellow leaves, or none, or few, do hang
Upon those boughs which shake against the cold,
Bare ruin'd choirs where late the sweet birds sang.
In me thou see'st the twilight of such day
As after sunset fadeth in the West,
Which by-and-by black night doth take away,
Death's second self, that seals up all in rest.
In me thou see'st the glowing of such fire
That on the ashes of his youth doth lie,
As the deathbed whereon it must expire,
Consum'd with that which it was nourish'd by.
    This thou perceiv'st, which makes thy love more
        strong,
    To love that well which thou must leave ere long.

LXXIV

But be contented. When that fell arrest
Without all bail shall carry me away,
My life hath in this line some interest,
Which for memorial still with thee shall stay.
When thou reviewest this, thou dost review
The very part was consecrate to thee.
The earth can have but earth, which is his due;
My spirit is thine, the better part of me.
So then thou hast but lost the dregs of life,
The prey of worms, my body being dead—
The coward conquest of a wretch's knife,
Too base of thee to be remembered.
    The worth of that is that which it contains,
    And that is this, and this with thee remains.

LXXV

So are you to my thoughts as food to life,
Or as sweet-season'd showers are to the ground;
And for the peace of you I hold such strife
As 'twixt a miser and his wealth is found:
Now proud as an enjoyer, and anon
Doubting the filching age will steal his treasure;
Now counting best to be with you alone,
Then better'd that the world may see my pleasure;
Sometime all full with feasting on your sight,
And by-and-by clean starved for a look;
Possessing or pursuing no delight
Save what is had or must from you be took.
    Thus do I pine and surfeit day by day,
    Or gluttoning on all, or all away.

LXXVI

Why is my verse so barren of new pride?
So far from variation or quick change?
Why, with the time, do I not glance aside
To new-found methods and to compounds strange?
Why write I still all one, ever the same,
And keep invention in a noted weed,
That every word doth almost tell my name,
Showing their birth, and where they did proceed?
O, know, sweet love, I always write of you,
And you and love are still my argument:
So all my best is dressing old words new,
Spending again what is already spent;
 For as the sun is daily new and old,
 So is my love still telling what is told.

LXXVII

Thy glass will show thee how thy beauties wear,
Thy dial how thy precious minutes waste.
The vacant leaves thy mind's imprint will bear,
And of this book this learning mayst thou taste.
The wrinkles which thy glass will truly show,
Of mouthed graves will give thee memory.
Thou by thy dial's shady stealth mayst know
Time's thievish progress to eternity.
Look, what thy memory cannot contain,
Commit to these waste blanks, and thou shalt find
Those children nurs'd, deliver'd from thy brain,
To take a new acquaintance of thy mind.
 These offices, so oft as thou wilt look,
 Shall profit thee and much enrich thy book.

LXXVIII

So oft have I invok'd thee for my Muse
And found such fair assistance in my verse
As every alien pen hath got my use
And under thee their poesy disperse.
Thine eyes, that taught the dumb on high to sing
And heavy ignorance aloft to fly,
Have added feathers to the learned's wing
And given grace a double majesty.
Yet be most proud of that which I compile,
Whose influence is thine, and born of thee.
In others' works thou dost but mend the style,
And arts with thy sweet graces graced be;
    But thou art all my art and dost advance
    As high as learning my rude ignorance.

LXXIX

Whilst I alone did call upon thy aid,
My verse alone had all thy gentle grace;
But now my gracious numbers are decay'd,
And my sick Muse doth give another place.
I grant, sweet love, thy lovely argument
Deserves the travail of a worthier pen;
Yet what of thee thy poet doth invent
He robs thee of, and pays it thee again.
He lends thee virtue, and he stole that word
From thy behaviour. Beauty doth he give,
And found it in thy cheek. He can afford
No praise to thee but what in thee doth live.
    Then thank him not for that which he doth say,
    Since what he owes thee thou thyself dost pay.

LXXX

O, how I faint when I of you do write,
Knowing a better spirit doth use your name
And in the praise thereof spends all his might
To make me tongue-tied, speaking of your fame!
But since your worth, wide as the ocean is,
The humble as the proudest sail doth bear,
My saucy bark, inferior far to his,
·On your broad main doth wilfully appear.
Your shallowest help will hold me up afloat
Whilst he upon your soundless deep doth ride;
Or, being wrack'd, I am a worthless boat,
He of tall building and of goodly pride.
    Then if he thrive, and I be cast away,
    The worst was this: my love was my decay.

LXXXI

Or I shall live your epitaph to make,
Or you survive when I in earth am rotten.
From hence your memory death cannot take,
Although in me each part will be forgotten.
Your name from hence immortal life shall have,
Though I, once gone, to all the world must die.
The earth can yield me but a common grave
When you entombed in men's eyes shall lie.
Your monument shall be my gentle verse,
Which eyes not yet created shall o'erread;
And tongues to be your being shall rehearse
When all the breathers of this world are dead.
    You still shall live (such virtue hath my pen)
    Where breath most breathes, even in the mouths of
    men.

LXXXII

I grant thou wert not married to my Muse
And therefore mayst without attaint o'erlook
The dedicated words which writers use
Of their fair subject, blessing every book.
Thou art as fair in knowledge as in hue,
Finding thy worth a limit past my praise;
And therefore art enforc'd to seek anew
Some fresher stamp of the time-bettering days.
And do so, love; yet when they have devis'd
What strained touches rhetoric can lend,
Thou, truly fair, wert truly sympathiz'd
In true plain words by thy true-telling friend;
    And their gross painting might be better us'd
    Where cheeks need blood; in thee it is abus'd.

LXXXIII

I never saw that you did painting need,
And therefore to your fair no painting set;
I found (or thought I found) you did exceed
The barren tender of a poet's debt;
And therefore have I slept in your report,
That you yourself, being extant, well might show
How far a modern quill doth come too short,
Speaking of worth, what worth in you doth grow.
This silence for my sin you did impute,
Which shall be most my glory, being dumb;
For I impair not beauty, being mute,
When others would give life, and bring a tomb.
    There lives more life in one of your fair eyes
    Than both your poets can in praise devise.

LXXXIV

Who is it that says most which can say more
Than this rich praise—that you alone are you?
In whose confine immured is the store
Which should example where your equal grew.
Lean penury within that pen doth dwell
That to his subject lends not some small glory;
But he that writes of you, if he can tell
That you are you, so dignifies his story.
Let him but copy what in you is writ,
Not making worse what nature made so clear,
And such a counterpart shall fame his wit,
Making his style admired everywhere.
    You to your beauteous blessings add a curse,
      Being fond on praise, which makes your praises worse.

LXXXV

My tongue-tied Muse in manners holds her still
While comments of your praise, richly compil'd,
Reserve their character with golden quill
And precious phrase by all the Muses fil'd.
I think good thoughts whilst other write good words,
And, like unlettered clerk, still cry 'Amen'
To every hymn that able spirit affords
In polish'd form of well-refined pen.
Hearing you prais'd, I say ' 'Tis so, 'tis true!'
And to the most of praise add something more;
But that is in my thought, whose love to you,
Though words come hindmost, holds his rank before.
    Then others for the breath of words respect;
      Me for my dumb thoughts, speaking in effect.

LXXXVI

Was it the proud full sail of his great verse,
Bound for the prize of all-too-precious you,
That did my ripe thoughts in my brain inhearse,
Making their tomb the womb wherein they grew?
Was it his spirit, by spirits taught to write
Above a mortal pitch, that struck me dead?
No, neither he, nor his compeers by night
Giving him aid, my verse astonished.
He, nor that affable familiar ghost
Which nightly gulls him with intelligence,
As victors, of my silence cannot boast—
I was not sick of any fear from thence;
    But when your countenance fill'd up his line,
    Then lack'd I matter; that enfeebled mine.

LXXXVII

Farewell! thou art too dear for my possessing,
And like enough thou know'st thy estimate.
The charter of thy worth gives thee releasing;
My bonds in thee are all determinate.
For how do I hold thee but by thy granting,
And for that riches where is my deserving?
The cause of this fair gift in me is wanting,
And so my patent back again is swerving.
Thyself thou gav'st, thy own worth then not knowing,
Or me, to whom thou gav'st it, else mistaking:
So thy great gift, upon misprision growing,
Comes home again, on better judgment making.
    Thus have I had thee as a dream doth flatter—
    In sleep a king, but waking no such matter.

LXXXVIII

When thou shalt be dispos'd to set me light
And place my merit in the eye of scorn,
Upon thy side against myself I'll fight
And prove thee virtuous, though thou art forsworn.
With mine own weakness being best acquainted,
Upon thy part I can set down a story
Of faults conceal'd wherein I am attainted,
That thou, in losing me, shalt win much glory.
And I by this will be a gainer too;
For, bending all my loving thoughts on thee,
The injuries that to myself I do,
Doing thee vantage, double vantage me.
 Such is my love, to thee I so belong,
 That for thy right myself will bear all wrong.

LXXXIX

Say that thou didst forsake me for some fault,
And I will comment upon that offence.
Speak of my lameness, and I straight will halt,
Against thy reasons making no defence.
Thou canst not, love, disgrace me half so ill,
To set a form upon desired change,
As I'll myself disgrace, knowing thy will.
I will acquaintance strangle and look strange,
Be absent from thy walks, and in my tongue
Thy sweet beloved name no more shall dwell,
Lest I (too much profane) should do it wrong
And haply of our old acquaintance tell.
 For thee, against myself I'll vow debate,
 For I must ne'er love him whom thou dost hate.

XC

Then hate me when thou wilt! if ever, now!
Now, while the world is bent my deeds to cross,
Join with the spite of fortune, make me bow,
And do not drop in for an after-loss.
Ah, do not, when my heart hath scap'd this sorrow,
Come in the rearward of a conquer'd woe;
Give not a windy night a rainy morrow,
To linger out a purpos'd overthrow.
If thou wilt leave me, do not leave me last,
When other petty griefs have done their spite,
But in the onset come. So shall I taste
At first the very worst of fortune's might;
 And other strains of woe, which now seem woe,
 Compar'd with loss of thee will not seem so.

XCI

Some glory in their birth, some in their skill,
Some in their wealth, some in their body's force;
Some in their garments, though newfangled ill;
Some in their hawks and hounds, some in their horse;
And every humour hath his adjunct pleasure,
Wherein it finds a joy above the rest;
But these particulars are not my measure:
All these I better in one general best.
Thy love is better than high birth to me,
Richer than wealth, prouder than garments' cost,
Of more delight than hawks or horses be,
And having thee, of all men's pride I boast—
 Wretched in this alone, that thou mayst take
 All this away and me most wretched make.

XCII

But do thy worst to steal thyself away,
For term of life thou art assured mine;
And life no longer than thy love will stay,
For it depends upon that love of thine.
Then need I not to fear the worst of wrongs
When in the least of them my life hath end.
I see a better state to me belongs
Than that which on thy humour doth depend.
Thou canst not vex me with inconstant mind,
Since that my life on thy revolt doth lie.
O, what a happy title do I find,
Happy to have thy love, happy to die!
　　But what's so blessed-fair that fears no blot?
　　Thou mayst be false, and yet I know it not.

XCIII

So shall I live, supposing thou art true,
Like a deceived husband; so love's face
May still seem love to me, though alter'd new—
Thy looks with me, thy heart in other place.
For there can live no hatred in thine eye;
Therefore in that I cannot know thy change.
In many's looks the false heart's history
Is writ in moods and frowns and wrinkles strange;
But heaven in thy creation did decree
That in thy face sweet love should ever dwell;
Whate'er thy thoughts or thy heart's workings be,
Thy looks should nothing thence but sweetness tell.
　　How like Eve's apple doth thy beauty grow
　　If thy sweet virtue answer not thy show!

XCIV

They that have pow'r to hurt and will do none,
That do not do the thing they most do show,
Who, moving others, are themselves as stone,
Unmoved, cold, and to temptation slow—
They rightly do inherit heaven's graces
And husband nature's riches from expense;
They are the lords and owners of their faces,
Others but stewards of their excellence.
The summer's flow'r is to the summer sweet,
Though to itself it only live and die;
But if that flow'r with base infection meet,
The basest weed outbraves his dignity:
    For sweetest things turn sourest by their deeds;
    Lilies that fester smell far worse than weeds.

XCV

How sweet and lovely dost thou make the shame
Which, like a canker in the fragrant rose,
Doth spot the beauty of thy budding name!
O, in what sweets dost thou thy sins enclose!
That tongue that tells the story of thy days
(Making lascivious comments on thy sport)
Cannot dispraise but in a kind of praise:
Naming thy name blesses an ill report.
O, what a mansion have those vices got
Which for their habitation chose out thee,
Where beauty's veil doth cover every blot
And all things turns to fair that eyes can see!
    Take heed, dear heart, of this large privilege.
    The hardest knife ill us'd doth lose his edge.

XCVI

Some say thy fault is youth, some wantonness;
Some say thy grace is youth and gentle sport.
Both grace and faults are lov'd of more and less;
Thou mak'st faults graces that to thee resort.
As on the finger of a throned queen
The basest jewel will be well esteem'd,
So are those errors that in thee are seen
To truths translated and for true things deem'd.
How many lambs might the stern wolf betray
If like a lamb he could his looks translate!
How many gazers mightst thou lead away
If thou wouldst use the strength of all thy state!
    But do not so. I love thee in such sort
    As, thou being mine, mine is thy good report.

XCVII

How like a winter hath my absence been
From thee, the pleasure of the fleeting year!
What freezings have I felt, what dark days seen!
What old December's bareness everywhere!
And yet this time remov'd was summer's time,
The teeming autumn, big with rich increase,
Bearing the wanton burthen of the prime,
Like widowed wombs after their lords' decease;
Yet this abundant issue seem'd to me
But hope of orphans and unfathered fruit;
For summer and his pleasures wait on thee,
And, thou away, the very birds are mute;
    Or, if they sing, 'tis with so dull a cheer
    That leaves look pale, dreading the winter's near.

XCVIII

From you have I been absent in the spring,
When proud-pied April, dress'd in all his trim,
Hath put a spirit of youth in everything,
That heavy Saturn laugh'd and leapt with him,
Yet nor the lays of birds, nor the sweet smell
Of different flowers in odour and in hue,
Could make me any summer's story tell,
Or from their proud lap pluck them where they grew;
Nor did I wonder at the lily's white,
Nor praise the deep vermilion in the rose:
They were but sweet, but figures of delight,
Drawn after you, you pattern of all those.
    Yet seem'd it winter still, and, you away,
    As with your shadow I with these did play.

XCIX

The forward violet thus did I chide:
Sweet thief, whence didst thou steal thy sweet that
    smells,
If not from my love's breath? The purple pride
Which on thy soft cheek for complexion dwells
In my love's veins thou hast too grossly dy'd.
The lily I condemned for thy hand;
And buds of marjoram had stol'n thy hair.
The roses fearfully on thorns did stand,
One blushing shame, another white despair;
A third, nor red nor white, had stol'n of both,
And to his robb'ry had annex'd thy breath;
But, for his theft, in pride of all his growth
A vengeful canker eat him up to death.
    More flowers I noted, yet I none could see
    But sweet or colour it had stol'n from thee.

C

Where art thou, Muse, that thou forget'st so long
To speak of that which gives thee all thy might?
Spend'st thou thy fury on some worthless song,
Dark'ning thy pow'r to lend base subjects light?
Return, forgetful Muse, and straight redeem
In gentle numbers time so idly spent.
Sing to the ear that doth thy lays esteem
And gives thy pen both skill and argument.
Rise, resty Muse, my love's sweet face survey,
If Time have any wrinkle graven there.
If any, be a satire to decay
And make Time's spoils despised everywhere.
    Give my love fame faster than Time wastes life:
    So thou prevent'st his scythe and crooked knife.

CI

O truant Muse, what shall be thy amends
For thy neglect of truth in beauty dy'd?
Both truth and beauty on my love depends;
So dost thou too, and therein dignified.
Make answer, Muse. Wilt thou not haply say,
'Truth needs no colour, with his colour fix'd;
Beauty no pencil, beauty's truth to lay;
But best is best, if never intermix'd'?
Because he needs no praise, wilt thou be dumb?
Excuse not silence so; for't lies in thee
To make him much outlive a gilded tomb
And to be prais'd of ages yet to be.
    Then do thy office, Muse. I teach thee how
    To make him seem, long hence, as he shows now.

CII

My love is strength'ned, though more weak in seeming;
I love not less, though less the show appear.
That love is merchandiz'd whose rich esteeming
The owner's tongue doth publish everywhere.
Our love was new, and then but in the spring,
When I was wont to greet it with my lays.
As Philomel in summer's front doth sing
And stops her pipe in growth of riper days;
Not that the summer is less pleasant now
Than when her mournful hymns did hush the night,
But that wild music burthens every bough,
And sweets grown common lose their dear delight.
    Therefore, like her, I sometime hold my tongue,
    Because I would not dull you with my song.

CIII

Alack, what poverty my Muse brings forth,
That, having such a scope to show her pride,
The argument all bare is of more worth
Than when it hath my added praise beside!
O, blame me not if I no more can write!
Look in your glass, and there appears a face
That overgoes my blunt invention quite,
Dulling my lines and doing me disgrace.
Were it not sinful then, striving to mend,
To mar the subject that before was well?
For to no other pass my verses tend
Than of your graces and your gifts to tell;
    And more, much more, than in my verse can sit
    Your own glass shows you when you look in it.

CIV

To me, fair friend, you never can be old,
For as you were when first your eye I ey'd,
Such seems your beauty still. Three winters cold
Have from the forests shook three summers' pride,
Three beauteous springs to yellow autumn turn'd
In process of the seasons have I seen,
Three April perfumes in three hot Junes burn'd,
Since first I saw you fresh, which yet are green.
Ah, yet doth beauty, like a dial hand,
Steal from his figure, and no pace perceiv'd!
So your sweet hue, which methinks still doth stand,
Hath motion, and mine eye may be deceiv'd;
    For fear of which, hear this, thou age unbred:
    Ere you were born was beauty's summer dead.

CV

Let not my love be call'd idolatry
Nor my beloved as an idol show,
Since all alike my songs and praises be
To one, of one, still such, and ever so.
Kind is my love to-day, to-morrow kind,
Still constant in a wondrous excellence;
Therefore my verse, to constancy confin'd,
One thing expressing, leaves out difference.
'Fair, kind, and true,' is all my argument,
'Fair, kind, and true,' varying to other words;
And in this change is my invention spent,
Three themes in one, which wondrous scope affords.
    Fair, kind, and true have often liv'd alone,
    Which three till now never kept seat in one.

CVI

When in the chronicle of wasted time
I see descriptions of the fairest wights,
And beauty making beautiful old rhyme
In praise of ladies dead and lovely knights,
Then, in the blazon of sweet beauty's best,
Of hand, of foot, of lip, of eye, of brow,
I see their antique pen would have express'd
Even such a beauty as you master now.
So all their praises are but prophecies
Of this our time, all you prefiguring;
And, for they look'd but with divining eyes,
They had not skill enough your worth to sing;
    For we, which now behold these present days,
    Have eyes to wonder, but lack tongues to praise.

CVII

Not mine own fears, nor the prophetic soul
Of the wide world, dreaming on things to come,
Can yet the lease of my true love control,
Suppos'd as forfeit to a confin'd doom.
The mortal moon hath her eclipse endur'd,
And the sad augurs mock their own presage;
Incertainties now crown themselves assur'd,
And peace proclaims olives of endless age.
Now with the drops of this most balmy time
My love looks fresh, and Death to me subscribes,
Since, spite of him, I'll live in this poor rhyme
While he insults o'er dull and speechless tribes;
    And thou in this shalt find thy monument
    When tyrants' crests and tombs of brass are spent.

CVIII

What's in the brain that ink may character
Which hath not figur'd to thee my true spirit?
What's new to speak, what new to register,
That may express my love or thy dear merit?
Nothing, sweet boy; but yet, like prayers divine,
I must each day say o'er the very same;
Counting no old thing old, thou mine, I thine,
Even as when first I hallowed thy fair name.
So that eternal love in love's fresh case
Weighs not the dust and injury of age,
Nor gives to necessary wrinkles place,
But makes antiquity for aye his page,
    Finding the first conceit of love there bred
    Where time and outward form would show it dead.

CIX

O, never say that I was false of heart,
Though absence seem'd my flame to qualify!
As easy might I from myself depart
As from my soul, which in thy breast doth lie.
That is my home of love. If I have rang'd,
Like him that travels I return again,
Just to the time, not with the time exchang'd,
So that myself bring water for my stain.
Never believe, though in my nature reign'd
All frailties that besiege all kinds of blood,
That it could so preposterously be stain'd
To leave for nothing all thy sum of good;
    For nothing this wide universe I call
    Save thou, my rose; in it thou art my all.

CX

Alas, 'tis true I have gone here and there
And made myself a motley to the view,
Gor'd mine own thoughts, sold cheap what is most dear,
Made old offences of affections new.
Most true it is that I have look'd on truth
Askance and strangely; but, by all above,
These blenches gave my heart another youth,
And worse essays prov'd thee my best of love.
Now all is done, have what shall have no end!
Mine appetite I never more will grind
On newer proof, to try an older friend,
A god in love, to whom I am confin'd.
    Then give me welcome, next my heaven the best,
    Even to thy pure and most most loving breast.

CXI

O, for my sake do you with Fortune chide,
The guilty goddess of my harmful deeds,
That did not better for my life provide
Than public means which public manners breeds.
Thence comes it that my name receives a brand;
And almost thence my nature is subdu'd
To what it works in, like the dyer's hand.
Pity me then, and wish I were renew'd,
Whilst, like a willing patient, I will drink
Potions of eysell 'gainst my strong infection;
No bitterness that I will bitter think,
Nor double penance, to correct correction.
    Pity me, then, dear friend, and I assure ye
    Even that your pity is enough to cure me.

CXII

Your love and pity doth th' impression fill
Which vulgar scandal stamp'd upon my brow;
For what care I who calls me well or ill,
So you o'er-green my bad, my good allow?
You are my all the world, and I must strive
To know my shames and praises from your tongue—
None else to me, nor I to none alive,
That my steel'd sense or changes right or wrong.
In so profound abysm I throw all care
Of others' voices that my adder's sense
To critic and to flatterer stopped are.
Mark how with my neglect I do dispense:
   You are so strongly in my purpose bred
   That all the world besides methinks are dead.

CXIII

Since I left you, mine eye is in my mind;
And that which governs me to go about
Doth part his function and is partly blind,
Seems seeing, but effectually is out;
For it no form delivers to the heart
Of bird, of flow'r, or shape which it doth latch;
Of his quick objects hath the mind no part,
Nor his own vision holds what it doth catch;
For if it see the rud'st or gentlest sight,
The most sweet favour or deformed'st creature,
The mountain or the sea, the day or night,
The crow or dove, it shapes them to your feature.
   Incapable of more, replete with you,
   My most true mind thus mak'th mine eye untrue.

CXIV

Or whether doth my mind, being crown'd with you,
Drink up the monarch's plague, this flattery?
Or whether shall I say mine eye saith true,
And that your love taught it this alchemy,
To make of monsters and things indigest
Such cherubins as your sweet self resemble,
Creating every bad a perfect best
As fast as objects to his beams assemble?
O, 'tis the first! 'Tis flatt'ry in my seeing,
And my great mind most kingly drinks it up.
Mine eye well knows what with his gust is greeing,
And to his palate doth prepare the cup.
  If it be poison'd, 'tis the lesser sin
    That mine eye loves it and doth first begin.

CXV

Those lines that I before have writ do lie,
Even those that said I could not love you dearer.
Yet then my judgment knew no reason why
My most full flame should afterwards burn clearer.
But reckoning Time, whose million'd accidents
Creep in 'twixt vows and change decrees of kings,
Tan sacred beauty, blunt the sharp'st intents,
Divert strong minds to th' course of alt'ring things—
Alas, why, fearing of Time's tyranny,
Might I not then say 'Now I love you best'
When I was certain o'er incertainty,
Crowning the present, doubting of the rest?
  Love is a babe. Then might I not say so,
    To give full growth to that which still doth grow.

CXVI

Let me not to the marriage of true minds
Admit impediments. Love is not love
Which alters when it alteration finds
Or bends with the remover to remove.
O, no! it is an ever-fixed mark
That looks on tempests and is never shaken;
It is the star to every wand'ring bark,
Whose worth's unknown, although his highth be taken.
Love's not Time's fool, though rosy lips and cheeks
Within his bending sickle's compass come.
Love alters not with his brief hours and weeks,
But bears it out even to the edge of doom.
 If this be error, and upon me proved,
 I never writ, nor no man ever loved.

CXVII

Accuse me thus: that I have scanted all
Wherein I should your great deserts repay;
Forgot upon your dearest love to call,
Whereto all bonds do tie me day by day;
That I have frequent been with unknown minds
And given to time your own dear-purchas'd right;
That I have hoisted sail to all the winds
Which should transport me farthest from your sight.
Book both my wilfulness and errors down,
And on just proof surmise accumulate;
Bring me within the level of your frown,
But shoot not at me in your wakened hate;
 Since my appeal says I did strive to prove
 The constancy and virtue of your love.

CXVIII

Like as, to make our appetites more keen,
With eager compounds we our palate urge;
As, to prevent our maladies unseen,
We sicken to shun sickness when we purge:
Even so, being full of your ne'er-cloying sweetness,
To bitter sauces did I frame my feeding;
And, sick of welfare, found a kind of meetness
To be diseas'd ere that there was true needing.
Thus policy in love, t' anticipate
The ills that were not, grew to faults assured,
And brought to medicine a healthful state,
Which, rank of goodness, would by ill be cured.
  But thence I learn, and find the lesson true,
  Drugs poison him that so fell sick of you.

CXIX

What potions have I drunk of Siren tears,
Distill'd from limbecks foul as hell within,
Applying fears to hopes and hopes to fears,
Still losing when I saw myself to win!
What wretched errors hath my heart committed
Whilst it hath thought itself so blessed never!
How have mine eyes out of their spheres been fitted
In the distraction of this madding fever!
O benefit of ill! Now I find true
That better is by evil still made better;
And ruin'd love, when it is built anew,
Grows fairer than at first, more strong, far greater.
  So I return rebuk'd to my content,
  And gain by ills thrice more than I have spent.

CXX

That you were once unkind befriends me now,
And for that sorrow which I then did feel
Needs must I under my transgression bow,
Unless my nerves were brass or hammered steel.
For if you were by my unkindness shaken,
As I by yours, y'have pass'd a hell of time,
And I, a tyrant, have no leisure taken
To weigh how once I suffered in your crime.
O that our night of woe might have rememb'red
My deepest sense how hard true sorrow hits,
And soon to you, as you to me then, tend'red
The humble salve which wounded bosoms fits!
    But that your trespass now becomes a fee;
    Mine ransoms yours, and yours must ransom me.

CXXI

'Tis better to be vile than vile esteemed
When not to be receives reproach of being,
And the just pleasure lost, which is so deemed
Not by our feeling but by others' seeing.
For why should others' false adulterate eyes
Give salutation to my sportive blood?
Or on my frailties why are frailer spies,
Which in their wills count bad what I think good?
No, I am that I am; and they that level
At my abuses reckon up their own.
I may be straight though they themselves be bevel;
By their rank thoughts my deeds must not be shown,
    Unless this general evil they maintain—
    All men are bad and in their badness reign.

CXXII

Thy gift, thy tables, are within my brain
Full character'd with lasting memory,
Which shall above that idle rank remain
Beyond all date, even to eternity;
Or, at the least, so long as brain and heart
Have faculty by nature to subsist,
Till each to raz'd oblivion yield his part
Of thee, thy record never can be miss'd.
That poor retention could not so much hold,
Nor need I tallies thy dear love to score.
Therefore to give them from me was I bold,
To trust those tables that receive thee more.
  To keep an adjunct to remember thee
  Were to import forgetfulness in me.

CXXIII

No, Time, thou shalt not boast that I do change!
Thy pyramids built up with newer might
To me are nothing novel, nothing strange;
They are but dressings of a former sight.
Our dates are brief, and therefore we admire
What thou dost foist upon us that is old,
And rather make them born to our desire
Than think that we before have heard them told.
Thy registers and thee I both defy,
Not wond'ring at the present nor the past;
For thy records and what we see doth lie,
Made more or less by thy continual haste.
  This I do vow, and this shall ever be—
  I will be true, despite thy scythe and thee.

CXXIV

If my dear love were but the child of state,
It might for Fortune's bastard be unfather'd,
As subject to Time's love or to Time's hate,
Weeds among weeds, or flowers with flowers gather'd.
No, it was builded far from accident;
It suffers not in smiling pomp, nor falls
Under the blow of thralled discontent,
Whereto th' inviting time our fashion calls.
It fears not Policy, that heretic
Which works on leases of short-numb'red hours,
But all alone stands hugely politic,
That it nor grows with heat nor drowns with show'rs.
    To this I witness call the fools of time,
      Which die for goodness, who have liv'd for crime.

CXXV

Were't aught to me I bore the canopy,
With my extern the outward honouring,
Or laid great bases for eternity,
Which prove more short than waste or ruining?
Have I not seen dwellers on form and favour
Lose all, and more, by paying too much rent,
For compound sweet forgoing simple savour—
Pitiful thrivers, in their gazing spent?
No, let me be obsequious in thy heart,
And take thou my oblation, poor but free,
Which is not mix'd with seconds, knows no art
But mutual render, only me for thee.
    Hence, thou suborn'd informer! A true soul
      When most impeach'd stands least in thy control.

CXXVI

O thou, my lovely boy, who in thy power
Dost hold Time's fickle glass, his sickle hour;
Who hast by waning grown, and therein show'st
Thy lovers withering as thy sweet self grow'st—
If Nature (sovereign mistress over wrack),
As thou goest onwards, still will pluck thee back,
She keeps thee to this purpose, that her skill
May time disgrace, and wretched minutes kill.
Yet fear her, O thou minion of her pleasure!
She may detain, but not still keep, her treasure;
  Her audit, though delay'd, answer'd must be,
  And her quietus is to render thee.

CXXVII

In the old age black was not counted fair,
Or if it were, it bore not beauty's name;
But now is black beauty's successive heir,
And beauty slander'd with a bastard shame;
For since each hand hath put on nature's power,
Fairing the foul with art's false borrow'd face,
Sweet beauty hath no name, no holy bower,
But is profan'd, if not lives in disgrace.
Therefore my mistress' brows are raven black,
Her eyes so suited, and they mourners seem
At such who, not born fair, no beauty lack,
Sland'ring creation with a false esteem.
  Yet so they mourn, becoming of their woe,
  That every tongue says beauty should look so.

CXXVIII

How oft, when thou, my music, music play'st
Upon that blessed wood whose motion sounds
With thy sweet fingers when thou gently sway'st
The wiry concord that mine ear confounds,
Do I envy those jacks that nimble leap
To kiss the tender inward of thy hand,
Whilst my poor lips, which should that harvest reap,
At the wood's boldness by thee blushing stand!
To be so tickled, they would change their state
And situation with those dancing chips
O'er whom thy fingers walk with gentle gait,
Making dead wood more blest than living lips.
　　Since saucy jacks so happy are in this,
　　Give them thy fingers, me thy lips to kiss.

CXXIX

Th' expense of spirit in a waste of shame
Is lust in action; and till action, lust
Is perjur'd, murd'rous, bloody, full of blame,
Savage, extreme, rude, cruel, not to trust;
Enjoy'd no sooner but despised straight;
Past reason hunted, and no sooner had,
Past reason hated, as a swallowed bait
On purpose laid to make the taker mad;
Mad in pursuit, and in possession so;
Had, having, and in quest to have, extreme;
A bliss in proof—and prov'd, a very woe;
Before, a joy propos'd; behind, a dream.
　　All this the world well knows; yet none knows well
　　To shun the heaven that leads men to this hell.

CXXX

My mistress' eyes are nothing like the sun;
Coral is far more red than her lips' red;
If snow be white, why then her breasts are dun;
If hairs be wires, black wires grow on her head.
I have seen roses damask'd, red and white,
But no such roses see I in her cheeks;
And in some perfumes is there more delight
Than in the breath that from my mistress reeks.
I love to hear her speak; yet well I know
That music hath a far more pleasing sound.
I grant I never saw a goddess go:
My mistress, when she walks, treads on the ground.
  And yet, by heaven, I think my love as rare
  As any she belied with false compare.

CXXXI

Thou art as tyrannous, so as thou art,
As those whose beauties proudly make them cruel;
For well thou know'st to my dear-doting heart
Thou art the fairest and most precious jewel.
Yet, in good faith, some say that thee behold,
Thy face hath not the power to make love groan.
To say they err I dare not be so bold,
Although I swear it to myself alone.
And, to be sure that is not false I swear,
A thousand groans, but thinking on thy face,
One on another's neck, do witness bear
Thy black is fairest in my judgment's place.
  In nothing art thou black save in thy deeds,
  And thence this slander, as I think, proceeds.

CXXXII

Thine eyes I love, and they, as pitying me,
Knowing thy heart torments me with disdain,
Have put on black and loving mourners be,
Looking with pretty ruth upon my pain.
And truly not the morning sun of heaven
Better becomes the grey cheeks of the East,
Nor that full star that ushers in the even
Doth half that glory to the sober West,
As those two mourning eyes become thy face.
O, let it then as well beseem thy heart
To mourn for me, since mourning doth thee grace,
And suit thy pity like in every part.
    Then will I swear beauty herself is black
    And all they foul that thy complexion lack.

CXXXIII

Beshrew that heart that makes my heart to groan
For that deep wound it gives my friend and me!
Is't not enough to tortune me alone
But slave to slavery my sweet'st friend must be?
Me from myself thy cruel eye hath taken,
And my next self thou harder hast engrossed.
Of him, myself, and thee I am forsaken—
A torment thrice threefold thus to be crossed.
Prison my heart in thy steel bosom's ward;
But then my friend's heart let my poor heart bail;
Whoe'er keeps me, let my heart be his guard:
Thou canst not then use rigour in my jail.
    And yet thou wilt; for I, being pent in thee,
    Perforce am thine, and all that is in me.

CXXXIV

So, now I have confess'd that he is thine
And I myself am mortgag'd to thy will,
Myself I'll forfeit, so that other mine
Thou wilt restore to be my comfort still.
But thou wilt not, nor he will not be free,
For thou art covetous, and he is kind;
He learn'd but surety-like to write for me
Under that bond that him as fast doth bind.
The statute of thy beauty thou wilt take,
Thou usurer that put'st forth all to use,
And sue a friend came debtor for my sake:
So him I lose through my unkind abuse.
　　Him have I lost, thou hast both him and me;
　　He pays the whole, and yet am I not free.

CXXXV

Whoever hath her wish, thou hast thy Will,
And Will to boot, and Will in overplus.
More than enough am I that vex thee still,
To thy sweet will making addition thus.
Wilt thou, whose will is large and spacious,
Not once vouchsafe to hide my will in thine?
Shall will in others seem right gracious
And in my will no fair acceptance shine?
The sea, all water, yet receives rain still
And in abundance addeth to his store;
So thou, being rich in Will, add to thy Will
One will of mine to make thy large Will more.
　　Let no unkind no fair beseechers kill;
　　Think all but one, and me in that one Will.

CXXXVI

If thy soul check thee that I come so near,
Swear to thy blind soul that I was thy Will,
And will, thy soul knows, is admitted there:
Thus far for love my love-suit, sweet, fulfil.
Will will fulfil the treasure of thy love,
Ay, fill it full with wills, and my will one.
In things of great receipt with ease we prove
Among a number one is reckon'd none.
Then in the number let me pass untold,
Though in thy store's account I one must be;.
For nothing hold me, so it please thee hold
That nothing me, a something, sweet, to thee.
    Make but my name thy love, and love that still,
    And then thou lovest me, for my name is Will.

CXXXVII

Thou blind fool, Love, what dost thou to mine eyes
That they behold, and see not what they see?
They know what beauty is, see where it lies,
Yet what the best is take the worst to be.
If eyes, corrupt by over-partial looks,
Be anchor'd in the bay where all men ride,
Why of eyes' falsehood hast thou forged hooks,
Whereto the judgment of my heart is tied?
Why should my heart think that a several plot
Which my heart knows the wide world's common place?
Or mine eyes seeing this, say this is not,
To put fair truth upon so foul a face?
    In things right true my heart and eyes have erred,
    And to this false plague are they now transferred.

CXXXVIII

When my love swears that she is made of truth
I do believe her, though I know she lies,
That she might think me some untutor'd youth,
Unlearned in the world's false subtilties.
Thus vainly thinking that she thinks me young,
Although she knows my days are past the best,
Simply I credit her false-speaking tongue:
On both sides thus is simple truth suppress'd.
But wherefore says she not she is unjust?
And wherefore say not I that I am old?
O, love's best habit is in seeming trust,
And age in love loves not to have years told.
　　Therefore I lie with her and she with me,
　　And in our faults by lies we flattered be.

CXXXIX

O, call not me to justify the wrong
That thy unkindness lays upon my heart!
Wound me not with thine eye, but with thy tongue;
Use power with power, and slay me not by art!
Tell me thou lov'st elsewhere; but in my sight,
Dear heart, forbear to glance thine eye aside.
What need'st thou wound with cunning when thy might
Is more than my o'erpress'd defence can bide?
Let me excuse thee:—Ah, my love well knows
Her pretty looks have been mine enemies;
And therefore from my face she turns my foes,
That they elsewhere might dart their injuries.
　　Yet do not so; but since I am near slain,
　　Kill me outright with looks and rid my pain.

CXL

Be wise as thou art cruel; do not press
My tongue-tied patience with too much disdain;
Lest sorrow lend me words, and words express
The manner of my pity-wanting pain.
If I might teach thee wit, better it were,
Though not to love, yet, love, to tell me so;
As testy sick men, when their deaths be near,
No news but health from their physicians know.
For if I should despair, I should grow mad,
And in my madness might speak ill of thee.
Now this ill-wresting world is grown so bad
Mad slanderers by mad ears believed be.
  That I may not be so, nor thou belied,
  Bear thine eyes straight, though thy proud heart go
    wide.

CXLI

In faith, I do not love thee with mine eyes,
For they in thee a thousand errors note;
But 'tis my heart that loves what they despise,
Who in despite of view is pleas'd to dote.
Nor are mine ears with thy tongue's tune delighted;
Nor tender feeling to base touches prone,
Nor taste, nor smell, desire to be invited
To any sensual feast with thee alone;
But my five wits nor my five senses can
Dissuade one foolish heart from serving thee,
Who leaves unsway'd the likeness of a man,
Thy proud heart's slave and vassal wretch to be.
  Only my plague thus far I count my gain,
  That she that makes me sin awards me pain.

CXLII

Love is my sin, and thy dear virtue hate,
Hate of my sin, grounded on sinful loving.
O, but with mine compare thou thine own state,
And thou shalt find it merits not reproving!
Or if it do, not from those lips of thine,
That have profan'd their scarlet ornaments
And seal'd false bonds of love as oft as mine,
Robb'd others' beds' revenues of their rents.
Be it lawful I love thee as thou lov'st those
Whom thine eyes woo as mine importune thee.
Root pity in thy heart, that, when it grows,
Thy pity may deserve to pitied be.
    If thou dost seek to have what thou dost hide,
    By self-example mayst thou be denied!

CXLIII

Lo, as a careful housewife runs to catch
One of her feathered creatures broke away,
Sets down her babe, and makes all swift dispatch
In pursuit of the thing she would have stay;
Whilst her neglected child holds her in chase,
Cries to catch her whose busy care is bent
To follow that which flies before her face,
Not prizing her poor infant's discontent—
So runn'st thou after that which flies from thee,
Whilst I thy babe chase thee afar behind;
But if thou catch thy hope, turn back to me
And play the mother's part, kiss me, be kind.
    So will I pray that thou mayst have thy Will,
    If thou turn back and my loud crying still.

CXLIV

Two loves I have, of comfort and despair,
Which like two spirits do suggest me still.
The better angel is a man right fair,
The worser spirit a woman colour'd ill.
To win me soon to hell, my female evil
Tempteth my better angel from my side,
And would corrupt my saint to be a devil,
Wooing his purity with her foul pride.
And whether that my angel be turn'd fiend
Suspect I may, yet not directly tell;
But being both from me, both to each friend,
I guess one angel in another's hell.
   Yet this shall I ne'er know, but live in doubt,
   Till my bad angel fire my good one out.

CXLV

Those lips that Love's own hand did make
Breath'd forth the sound that said 'I hate'
To me that languish'd for her sake;
But when she saw my woeful state,
Straight in her heart did mercy come,
Chiding that tongue that ever sweet
Was us'd in giving gentle doom,
And taught it thus anew to greet:
'I hate' she alter'd with an end
That follow'd it as gentle day
Doth follow night, who, like a fiend,
From heaven to hell is flown away.
   'I hate' from hate away she threw,
   And sav'd my life, saying 'not you.'

CXLVI

Poor soul, the centre of my sinful earth,
. . . these rebel pow'rs that thee array,
Why dost thou pine within and suffer dearth,
Painting thy outward walls so costly gay?
Why so large cost, having so short a lease,
Dost thou upon thy fading mansion spend?
Shall worms, inheritors of this excess,
Eat up thy charge? Is this thy body's end?
Then, soul, live thou upon thy servant's loss,
And let that pine to aggravate thy store;
Buy terms divine in selling hours of dross;
Within be fed, without be rich no more.
   So shalt thou feed on Death, that feeds on men,
   And Death once dead, there's no more dying then.

CXLVII

My love is as a fever, longing still
For that which longer nurseth the disease;
Feeding on that which doth preserve the ill,
Th' uncertain sickly appetite to please.
My Reason, the physician to my Love,
Angry that his prescriptions are not kept,
Hath left me, and I desperate now approve
Desire is death, which physic did except.
Past cure I am, now reason is past care,
And frantic-mad with evermore unrest;
My thoughts and my discourse as madmen's are,
At random from the truth vainly express'd;
   For I have sworn thee fair, and thought thee bright,
   Who art as black as hell, as dark as night.

CXLVIII

O me, what eyes hath Love put in my head,
Which have no correspondence with true sight!
Or, if they have, where is my judgment fled,
That censures falsely what they see aright?
If that be fair whereon my false eyes dote,
What means the world to say it is not so?
If it be not, then love doth well denote
Love's eye is not so true as all men's no.
How can it? O, how can Love's eye be true,
That is so vex'd with watching and with tears?
No marvel then though I mistake my view:
The sun itself sees not till heaven clears.
    O cunning Love! with tears thou keep'st me blind,
    Lest eyes well-seeing thy foul faults should find.

CXLIX

Canst thou, O cruel! say I love thee not
When I against myself with thee partake?
Do I not think on thee when I forgot
Am of myself, all tyrant for thy sake?
Who hateth thee that I do call my friend?
On whom frown'st thou that I do fawn upon?
Nay, if thou low'r'st on me, do I not spend
Revenge upon myself with present moan?
What merit do I in myself respect
That is so proud thy service to despise,
When all my best doth worship thy defect,
Commanded by the motion of thine eyes?
    But, love, hate on, for now I know thy mind:
    Those that can see thou lov'st, and I am blind.

CL

O, from what pow'r hast thou this pow'rful might
With insufficiency my heart to sway?
To make me give the lie to my true sight
And swear that brightness doth not grace the day?
Whence hast thou this becoming of things ill,
That in the very refuse of thy deeds
There is such strength and warrantise of skill
That in my mind thy worst all best exceeds?
Who taught thee how to make me love thee more,
The more I hear and see just cause of hate?
O, though I love what others do abhor,
With others thou shouldst not abhor my state!
 If thy unworthiness rais'd love in me,
 More worthy I to be belov'd of thee.

CLI

Love is too young to know what conscience is;
Yet who knows not conscience is born of love?
Then, gentle cheater, urge not my amiss,
Lest guilty of my faults thy sweet self prove.
For, thou betraying me, I do betray
My nobler part to my gross body's treason;
My soul doth tell my body that he may
Triumph in love; flesh stays no farther reason,
But, rising at thy name, doth point out thee
As his triumphant prize. Proud of this pride,
He is contented thy poor drudge to be,
To stand in thy affairs, fall by thy side.
 No want of conscience hold it that I call
 Her 'love' for whose dear love I rise and fall.

CLII

In loving thee thou know'st I am forsworn,
But thou art twice forsworn, to me love swearing;
In act thy bed-vow broke, and new faith torn
In vowing new hate after new love bearing.
But why of two oaths' breach do I accuse thee
When I break twenty? I am perjur'd most;
For all my vows are oaths but to misuse thee,
And all my honest faith in thee is lost;
For I have sworn deep oaths of thy deep kindness,
Oaths of thy love, thy truth, thy constancy;
And, to enlighten thee, gave eyes to blindness,
Or made them swear against the thing they see;
   For I have sworn thee fair—more perjur'd I,
   To swear against the truth so foul a lie!   ,

CLIII

Cupid laid by his brand and fell asleep.
A maid of Dian's this advantage found
And his love-kindling fire did quickly steep
In a cold valley-fountain of that ground;
Which borrow'd from this holy fire of Love
A dateless lively heat, still to endure,
And grew a seething bath, which yet men prove
Against strange maladies a sovereign cure.
But at my mistress' eye Love's brand new fired,
The boy for trial needs would touch my breast.
I, sick withal, the help of bath desired
And thither hied, a sad distemper'd guest,
   But found no cure. The bath for my help lies
   Where Cupid got new fire—my mistress' eyes.

CLIV

The little Love-god, lying once asleep,
Laid by his side his heart-inflaming brand,
Whilst many nymphs that vow'd chaste life to keep
Came tripping by; but in her maiden hand
The fairest votary took up that fire
Which many legions of true hearts had warm'd;
And so the general of hot desire
Was sleeping by a virgin hand disarm'd.
This brand she quenched in a cool well by,
Which from Love's fire took heat perpetual,
Growing a bath and healthful remedy
For men diseas'd; but I, my mistress' thrall,
 Came there for cure, and this by that I prove—
 Love's fire heats water, water cools not love.

Key-Word Index

TO ALL THE PLAYS

This index is simply a memory aid to help the reader find familiar quotations or favorite passages of which he may recall only words or phrases, and to identify the source or context of Shakespeare quotations encountered elsewhere.

Each reference has been listed under one or more prominent key words, usually nouns or verbs: thus "The quality of mercy is not strain'd" will be found under "MERCY: quality." A few complete phrases are also entered under the word with which they normally begin, even if it is not a key word: "Such stuff as dreams are made on"; "This was a man." If you fail to find what you want under the first word that occurs to you, try another. The identifying words or phrases following the key words are not necessarily those that come next in the quotation.

The numbers refer to page and line in this volume: 128, *17* is page 128, line 17. This index covers the seven complete plays and also the selections from the other plays.

FOOL: (*Cont.*)
  now in Arden, 492, *2*
  whining mammet, 281, *8*
  white hairs, 671, *4*
FOOLERY: shines everywhere, 639, *4*
Fool's paradise, 251, *29*
FOOLS: speak wisely, 475, *19*
FOPPERY: of the world, 644, *24*
For this relief much thanks, 4, *9*
FORGIVE: us all, 649, *6*
FORTRESS: built by Nature, 659, *13*
FORTUNE: both hands full, 670, *27*
  buffets and rewards, 63, *14*
  crossly, 660, *12*
  cruelly scratch'd, 655, *7*
  fickle, 277, *7*
  out of suits with, 480, *8*
  outrageous, 57, *6*
  rebel's whore, 133, *6*
Foul deeds will rise, 18, *12*
Foul play, 18, *11*
FOUNTAIN: pure blood, 345, *12*
Frailty, thy name is woman, 14, *21*
FREE: mountain winds, 574, *4*
Fresh as a bridegroom, 666, *7*
FRIENDS: grapple with hoops of steel, 20, *18*
  Romans, countrymen, 361, *22*
  three good, 504, *26*
FRIENDSHIP: affairs of love, 651, *4*
Full of sound and fury, 204, *10*
FUNERAL: bak'd meats, 15, *24*
  speak in the order, 356, *29*
FURNACE: for your foe, 678, *19*

GARLAND: wither'd, 684, *16*
GASP: follow to the last, 491, *10*
Gentle as a lamb, 254, *25*
GENTLEMAN: sweeter and lovelier, 677, *3*
Gentlemen of the Shade, 665, *5*
Get thee to a nunnery, 59, *5*
GHOST: him that lets me, 25, *27*
GHOSTS: shriek and squeal, 343, *19*
GIDDY: world turns round, 642, *21*
GIFTS: wax poor, 58, *20*
GIRDLE: round the earth, 414, *8*

Give sorrow words, 195, *2*
GLASS: beguile me, 661, *30*
  of fashion, 60, *2*
  therein read, 661, *25*
GLORY: brittle, 662, *5*
  circle in the water, 673, *1*
  greater dim the less, 630, *7*
  shooting star, 660, *7*
GLOVE: touch cheek, 238, *24*
GOD: serv'd with half the zeal, 679, *19*
GODDESS: airs attend, 571, *7*
GODS: kill for sport, 647, *4*
  make instruments, 647, *11*
GOLD: saint-seducing, 219, *15*
  worse poison, 299, *17*
GOLGOTHA: memorize another, 133, *33*
Good night, sweet prince, 127, *33*
Good wine needs no bush, 551, *10*
GOOD: dangerous folly, 187, *12*
  interred with bones, 361, *26*
  thinking makes, 44, *22*
GRACE: my cause, 631, *11*
  plants, herbs, stones, 244, *17*
  seated on this brow, 79, *5*
GRACES: justice, verity, etc., 190, *34*
  serve as enemies, 489, *14*
GRAVE: every third thought, 623, *16*
GRAVE-MAKER: Adam's profession, 107, *26*
  house lasts, 108, *20*
GRAVES: tenantless, 8, *3*
  worms, epitaphs, 660, *18*
  yawn'd, 343, *13*
GREATNESS: thrust upon 'em, 638, *22*
Greek to me, 325, *6*
Green girl, 21, *25*
Green-ey'd monster, 634, *15*
GREYHOUNDS: in the slips, 672, *32*
GRIEF: absent child, 657, *5*
  beauty's canker, 570, *30*
  does not speak, 195, *2*
  full as age, 645, *12*
  master, 651, *10*
  shows much love, 277, *21*
GRIEFS: advertisement, 652, *10*
GROUNDLINGS: split the ears, 61, *15*
GUILT: artless jealousy, 92, *15*